Sustainable Development in EU Foreign Investment Law

Nijhoff International Investment Law Series

Series Editors

Prof. Eric De Brabandere (*Leiden University*)
Prof. Tarcisio Gazzini (*University of East Anglia*)
Prof. Stephan W. Schill (*University of Amsterdam*)
Prof. Attila Tanzi (*University of Bologna*)

Editorial Board

Andrea K. Bjorklund (McGill University) – Juan Pablo Bohoslavsky (UNCTAD and Universidad Nacional de Rio Negro, Argentina) – Chester Brown (University of Sydney) – Patrick Dumberry (University of Ottawa) – Michael Ewing-Chow (National University of Singapore) – Susan D. Franck (American University) – Ursula Kriebaum (University of Vienna) – Makane Mbengue (University of Geneva) – Catherine A. Rogers (Penn State Law) – Christian Tams (University of Glasgow) – Andreas Ziegler (University of Glasgow)

VOLUME 19

The titles published in this series are listed at *brill.com/iils*

Sustainable Development in EU Foreign Investment Law

By

Stefanie Schacherer

BRILL
NIJHOFF

LEIDEN | BOSTON

Cover illustration: "Waldandacht", an image created by Silvia Binninger, Germany, 2021.

Library of Congress Cataloging-in-Publication Data

Names: Schacherer, Stefanie, 1988- author.
Title: Sustainable development in EU foreign investment law / by Stefanie Schacherer.
Description: Leiden ; Boston : Brill Nijhoff, [2021] | Series: Nijhoff international investment law series, 2351-9542 ; volume 19 | Based on author's thesis (doctoral - Universität Wien and Université de Genève, 2019) issued under title: Sustainable development in the post-Lisbon international investment law-making of the European Union. | Includes bibliographical references and index. | Summary: "In Sustainable Development in EU Foreign Investment Law, Stefanie Schacherer offers an account of the legal effects of sustainable development within the EU's international investment policy and global investment governance. The author provides a clear assessment of how the EU contributes to the ongoing debate on sustainable development integration in international investment agreements. By analysing the EU's post-Lisbon treaty practice, the author critically assesses to what extent the EU managed to operationalise a sustainable-development-driven foreign investment policy.
Identifiers: LCCN 2021026860 (print) | LCCN 2021026861 (ebook) | ISBN 9789004465879 (hardback) | ISBN 9789004465886 (ebook)
Subjects: LCSH: Investments, Foreign–Law and legislation–European Union countries. | Sustainable development–Law and legislation–European Union countries.
Classification: LCC KJE6433 .S33 2021 (print) | LCC KJE6433 (ebook) | DDC 346.24/092–dc23
LC record available at https://lccn.loc.gov/2021026860
LC ebook record available at https://lccn.loc.gov/2021026861

Typeface for the Latin, Greek, and Cyrillic scripts: "Brill". See and download: brill.com/brill-typeface.

ISSN 2351-9542
ISBN 978-90-04-46587-9 (hardback)
ISBN 978-90-04-46588-6 (e-book)

Copyright 2021 by Koninklijke Brill NV, Leiden, The Netherlands.
Koninklijke Brill NV incorporates the imprints Brill, Brill Nijhoff, Brill Hotei, Brill Schöningh, Brill Fink, Brill mentis, Vandenhoeck & Ruprecht, Böhlau Verlag and V&R Unipress
All rights reserved. No part of this publication may be reproduced, translated, stored in a retrieval system, or transmitted in any form or by any means, electronic, mechanical, photocopying, recording or otherwise, without prior written permission from the publisher. Requests for re-use and/or translations must be addressed to Koninklijke Brill NV via brill.com or copyright.com.

This book is printed on acid-free paper and produced in a sustainable manner.

Contents

List of Abbreviations XIII
Preface XVI

1 Introduction 1
  1.1 The Distinctiveness of the EU as a Global Actor 5
  1.2 Assumptions Regarding Investment Treaties 6
  1.3 Outline of the Argument 13

PART 1
Conceptual and Normative Framework of SD Integration in International Law and EU Law

2 Sustainable Development in the International Legal Order 19
  2.1 Historical Developments 20
    2.1.1 *The Rio Conference and Its Follow-Up Process* 21
    2.1.2 *Legal Effects of SD in International Treaties* 25
  2.2 SD and the Dichotomy of Goals and Means 27
    2.2.1 *The Importance of the Principle of Integration* 27
    2.2.2 *Other SD Principles* 31
      2.2.2.1 Inter-Generational Equity 31
      2.2.2.2 Intra-Generational Equity 32
      2.2.2.3 Other Principles of International Environmental Law 33
      2.2.2.4 Human Rights and Fundamental Labour Principles 34
      2.2.2.5 The Principle of Participation 35
      2.2.2.6 The Principle of Good Governance 36
    2.2.3 *The Legal Nature of SD* 36
      2.2.3.1 Is SD Part of Customary International Law? 37
      2.2.3.2 SD and Discretion 39
      2.2.3.3 Connecting the Dots 40
  2.3 The Integration of SD in International Investment Agreements (IIAS) 41
  2.4 IIAS and SD-Advancing Investment 44
    2.4.1 *Not Subsidising Unsustainable Investment: The Definition of Investment* 45

		2.4.1.1	Foreign Direct Investments versus Financial Investments 46
		2.4.1.2	The Contribution to the Host State's Development 48
		2.4.1.3	The Legality Requirement 53
		2.4.1.4	Registration and Approval Requirements 56
	2.4.2	*Provisions on Investment Liberalisation: Boon or Bane for SD?* 58	
2.5	IIAS and Domestic Regulation on SD 62		
	2.5.1	*More Precise Provisions* 64	
	2.5.2	*Flexibility Clauses* 68	
		2.5.2.1	Police Powers Exception 70
		2.5.2.2	General Exceptions 73
		2.5.2.3	Other Flexibility Clauses 76
	2.5.3	*SD and Investor-State Dispute Settlement* 77	
		2.5.3.1	Debates about Whether ISDS Undermines SD 78
		2.5.3.2	Is It Possible to Design an ISDS System Consistent with SD? 81
	2.5.4	*Ensuring Interpretation in Light of SD* 82	
2.6	IIAS and International Cooperation on SD 83		
	2.6.1	*Avoiding a Race to the Bottom and Enhancing SD Standards* 84	
	2.6.2	*Addressing SD-Investment Issues of Global Concern* 86	
	2.6.3	*Responsible Investment and the Balancing of Rights and Obligations of Investors* 89	
	2.6.4	*Measuring the SD Impacts of IIAS* 93	
2.7	Concluding Remarks 95		

3 Sustainable Development in the EU Legal Order 100

3.1	The Reception of SD as a Union Objective 101		
	3.1.1	*SD in EU Primary Law* 104	
	3.1.2	*Legal and Political Impacts of SD* 108	
3.2	SD—A Union Objective Unlike Any Other? 111		
	3.2.1	*The Changing Position of Objectives in the EU Legal Order* 112	
		3.2.1.1	SD as a General and Horizontal Objective 116
		3.2.1.2	SD and the Values of the EU 118
	3.2.2	*The Legal Effects of SD and Its Limits* 119	
		3.2.2.1	Discretionary Powers of the EU Institutions 122
		3.2.2.2	The Choice of the Appropriate Legal Basis 125

3.3 Legal Means of EU Law Supportive of SD   128
    3.3.1 *Social and Environmental Integration*   129
    3.3.2 *The Requirement of Policy Coherence*   133
3.4 Contours of the Substantive Scope of SD under EU Law   136
    3.4.1 *Articulation of SD within EU Internal Policies*   138
        3.4.1.1 Key Internal Policy Areas with SD Components   138
        3.4.1.2 The Concept of "Sustainable Growth"   141
    3.4.2 *Articulation of SD within EU External Action*   143
        3.4.2.1 Key External Policy Areas with SD Components   143
        3.4.2.2 The "Eradication of Poverty"   144
3.5 Concluding Remarks   146

4 **Sustainable Development—An Integral Part of EU Investment Law-Making**   148
   4.1 The Evolution of International Investment Law-Making of the EU   149
       4.1.1 *Pre-Lisbon EU Investment Law-Making*   150
       4.1.2 *Post-Lisbon: Building an Autonomous EU Investment Policy*   156
   4.2 EU Competence over Foreign Investment and SD   161
       4.2.1 *Exclusive Competence over Foreign Direct Investment*   163
       4.2.2 *Shared Implied External Competence over Non-Direct Investment*   164
       4.2.3 *Forms of Investment Regulation Falling under EU Competence*   167
       4.2.4 *Investor-State Dispute Settlement*   169
       4.2.5 *SD—Stretching the Scope of the CCP*   171
   4.3 SD and the Re-Orientation of the Common Commercial Policy   177
       4.3.1 *Managing the Interplay of Multiple Objectives within the CCP*   178
           4.3.1.1 SD among Other General Objectives   178
           4.3.1.2 SD and the Specific CCP Objectives   180
       4.3.2 *Horizontal Coherence: The CCP and Other EU Policies*   183
       4.3.3 *Turning the SD Objective into Investment Strategies*   185
   4.4 EU International Investment Agreements   191
       4.4.1 *The Decision-Making Procedure for the Conclusion of EU IIAs*   191
       4.4.2 *EU IIAs as Mixed Agreements*   193

- 4.4.3 Content and Scope of EU IIAS 195
  - 4.4.3.1 The Market Integration Model 196
  - 4.4.3.2 The Investment Liberalisation and Protection Model 199
- 4.5 SD and the Autonomy of the EU Legal Order 201
  - 4.5.1 In Compliance with the Autonomy of the EU Legal Order: The Investment Court System (ICS) 202
    - 4.5.1.1 The Principle 202
    - 4.5.1.2 The Court's Monopoly of Final Interpretation 205
  - 4.5.2 Safeguarding Regulatory Autonomy 209
    - 4.5.2.1 The Court's Assumption-Based Risk Assessment 213
    - 4.5.2.2 The Court's Instructions on How to Implement EU IIAS 214
  - 4.5.3 Implications for the EU as a Global Actor 215
- 4.6 Concluding Remarks 219

PART 2
Legal Effects of SD and the Emerging Transformation of International Investment Law and Governance

5 The Integration of Sustainable Development through Regulatory Linkages between Investment, Labour Standards and Environmental Protection under EU IIAS 225
- 5.1 Establishing a Level Playing Field for Investment in the Context of SD 227
  - 5.1.1 Non-Lowering of Standards Clauses 228
  - 5.1.2 Implementation of International Standards 232
    - 5.1.2.1 International Labour Standards 233
    - 5.1.2.2 Multilateral Environmental Agreements (MEAS) 235
  - 5.1.3 Promoting High Levels of Protection 238
- 5.2 Institutional and Procedural Arrangements 241
  - 5.2.1 Institutional Set-Up 242
  - 5.2.2 Enforcement of the Commitments on Labour and the Environment 245
    - 5.2.2.1 A Two-Stage Framework for Dispute Resolution 245
    - 5.2.2.2 Soft Enforcement and Sanction-Based Enforcement 247

        5.2.3   *Transparency and Public Information*   252
        5.2.4   Ex post *SD Review of IIA Implementation*   255
   5.3 Additional Fields of Cooperation on SD-Investment Linkages   257
        5.3.1   *Climate Change Mitigation and Renewable Energy Sources*   258
        5.3.2   *Human Rights*   261
        5.3.3   *Development Cooperation*   265
        5.3.4   *Anti-Corruption*   267
   5.4 Fostering the Responsibility of Foreign Investors   270
        5.4.1   *Direct versus Indirect Investor Obligations*   271
                5.4.1.1   CSR Commitments Addressed to States/the EU   272
                5.4.1.2   CSR Commitments Directly Addressed to Foreign Investors   274
        5.4.2   *Issues of Enforcing Investor Obligations*   276
   5.5 SD Integration during the Negotiation Phase of EU IIAS   279
        5.5.1   *The Procedure of Sustainability Impact Assessments*   281
        5.5.2   *The Methodology of Sustainability Impact Assessments*   282
        5.5.3   *Sustainability Impact Assessment in Practice*   284
                5.5.3.1   The SIA Process Relating to the CETA   285
                5.5.3.2   The SIA Process Relating to the EU-Japan FTA   286
                5.5.3.3   The SIA Process Relating to the China-EU CAI   287
        5.5.4   *Benefits and Limits of Sustainability Impact Assessments*   288
   5.6 Concluding Remarks   292

6 **Sustainable Development Integration in the Realm of Investment Liberalisation and Protection under EU IIAS**   296
   6.1 Re-Balancing Investment Protection with SD Interests under EU IIA   298
        6.1.1   *Fair and Equitable Treatment*   298
        6.1.2   *Indirect Expropriation*   305
                6.1.2.1   Clarifying the Meaning of Indirect Expropriation   306
                6.1.2.2   Permitted Regulation   308
        6.1.3   *A Specific Provision on the Right to Regulate*   311
                6.1.3.1   Reaffirming the Right to Regulate   312
                6.1.3.2   Regulations on State Subsidies   315
        6.1.4   *The Post-Establishment Obligation of Non-Discrimination*   318
        6.1.5   *General Exception Clauses for SD Regulatory Flexibility under EU IIAS*   322

		6.1.5.1	Permissible Objectives 325

              6.1.5.2   The Nexus Requirement "necessary for" 328

6.2 The Lack of SD Integration in the Regulation of Investment Liberalisation under EU IIAS 328
    6.2.1 *Pre-Establishment Rights* 329
    6.2.2 *Prohibitions of Market Access Restrictions* 332
    6.2.3 *Prohibitions of Performance Requirements* 334

6.3 The Notion of Investment: Limited SD Integration under EU IIAS 336
    6.3.1 *Narrowing Down the Scope of the Definition* 337
    6.3.2 *Enumerating Certain Criteria* 340
    6.3.3 *In Accordance with Host State Law* 344

6.4 Procedural Aspects of Investor-State Dispute Resolution Relevant for SD 348
    6.4.1 *Transparency and amicus curiae Participation* 349
    6.4.2 *Exclusions from the Scope of Investor-State Dispute Resolution* 352

6.5 Concluding Remarks 353

7 Sustainable Development Integration in the Interpretation of EU IIAS 357

7.1 SD as the Objective of EU IIAS 358
    7.1.1 *Preambles and Objectives Provisions* 358
    7.1.2 *Embedding EU IIAs in the Global SD Agenda* 362

7.2 The Relationship between Provisions on Investment and TSD Chapters 363
    7.2.1 *Mutual Reinforcement and Coherence* 364
    7.2.2 *The Right to Regulate—A Crosscutting Issue* 366
    7.2.3 *Mutual Exclusion Concerning Dispute Settlement* 367

7.3 General Interpretative Techniques 369
    7.3.1 *Object and Purpose* 369
    7.3.2 *Contextual Interpretation* 371
    7.3.3 *Evolutionary Interpretation* 374

7.4 Methods for the Balancing between Competing Interests 376
    7.4.1 *Integration* 376
    7.4.2 *Proportionality Analysis* 380
    7.4.3 *Standard of Review and Deference* 382

7.5 Concluding Remarks 384

8 **Conclusion**   386
   8.1   On the EU as a Global Actor   387
   8.2   On the EU's Discretion to Integrate SD   391
   8.3   Outlook: IIAs and Other Instruments   394

Bibliography   399
Table of Cases   427
Table of Treaties, Legislation and Other Documents   437
   Index   453

Abbreviations

ACP	African, Caribbean and Pacific States
AETR	European Agreement concerning the Work of Crews of Vehicles Engaged in International Road Transport
AG	Advocate General
ASEAN	Association of East Asian Nations
BIT	Bilateral investment treaty
CAFTA-DR	Central America Free Trade Area-Dominican Republic
CARIFORUM	Caribbean Forum
CBDR	Common but differentiated responsibility
CSD	Commission on Sustainable Development
CCP	Common commercial policy
CETA	Comprehensive Economic and Trade Agreement
CFI	Court of First Instance
CFREU	Charter of Fundamental Rights of the European Union
CIFA	Cooperation and Investment Facilitation Agreement
CITES	Convention on International Trade in Endangered Species of Wild Fauna and Flora
CJEU	Court of Justice of the European Union
CML Rev	Common Market Law Review
COMESA	Common Market for Eastern and Southern Africa
CPTPP	Comprehensive and Progressive Trans-Pacific Partnership
CSR	Corporate social responsibility
DAG	Domestic Advisory Group
DG	Directorate-General
ECJ	European Court of Justice
ECOWAS	Economic Community of West African States
ECT	Energy Charter Treaty
EDF	European Development Fund
EIA	Environmental impact assessment
EMA	Euro-Mediterranean Agreement
EPA	Economic Partnership Agreement
EU	European Union
EUCCAI	European Union-China Comprehensive Agreement on Investment
EUJFTA	European Union-Japan Free Trade Agreement
EUKFTA	European Union-Korea Free Trade Agreement
EUMERFTA	European Union-MERCOSUR Free Trade Agreement
EUMFTA	European Union-Mexico Free Trade Agreement

EuR	Europarecht
EURATOM	European Atomic Energy Community
EUSFTA	European Union-Singapore Free Trade Agreement
EUSIPA	European Union-Singapore Investment Protection Agreement
EUVFTA	European Union-Vietnam Free Trade Agreement
EUVIPA	European Union-Vietnam Investment Protection Agreement
FDI	Foreign direct investment
FET	Fair and equitable treatment
FTA	Free trade agreement
GATT	General Agreement on Tariffs and Trade
GATS	General Agreement on Trade in Services
GC	General Court
GSP	Generalised tariff preferences
G20	Group of Twenty
ICJ	International Court of Justice
ICS	Investment Court System
ICSID	International Centre for the Settlement of Investment Disputes
IIA	International investment agreement
IISD	International Institute for Sustainable Development
ILC	International Law Commission
ILO	International Labour Organization
IPA	Investment protection agreement
IPFSD	Investment Policy Framework for Sustainable Development
ISDS	Investor-State dispute settlement
ITLOS	International Tribunal for the Law of the Sea
MEA	Multilateral environmental agreement
MERCOSUR	Mercado Común del Sur
MFN	Most-favoured nation
MNE	Multinational enterprise
NAAEC	North American Agreement on Environmental Cooperation
NAALC	North American Agreement on Labor Cooperation
NAFTA	Nord American Free Trade Agreement
NCP	National Contact Point
NDC	Nationally Determined Contribution
OECD	Organization for Economic Cooperation and Development
OJ	Official Journal of the European Union
PACER	Pacific Agreement on Closer Economic Relations
PAIC	Pan-African Investment Code
PCA	Permanent Court of Arbitration
PCA	Partnership and Association Agreement

SAA	Stabilisation and Association Agreement
SADC	South African Development Community
SD	Sustainable development
SDG	Sustainable Development Goal
SIA	Sustainability Impact Assessment
TEC	Treaty Establishing the European Community
TEU	Treaty on European Union
TFEU	Treaty on the Functioning of the European Union
TRIMS	Trade-Related Investment Measures
TSD	Trade and Sustainable Development
TTIP	Transatlantic Trade and Investment Partnership
UAE	United Arab Emirates
UN	United Nations
UNCAC	United Nations Convention against Corruption
UNCITRAL	United National Commission on International Trade Law
UNCTAD	United Nations Conference for Trade and Development
UNEA	United Nations Environment Assembly
UNEP	United Nations Environmental Programme
UNFCCC	United Nations Framework Convention on Climate Change
UNGP	United Nations Guiding Principle on Business and Human Rights
USA	United States of America
USMCA	United States-Mexico-Canada Agreement
VCTL	Vienna Convention on the Law of Treaties
WTO	World Trade Organization
YEL	Yearbook of European Law

Preface

The idea for this book was born when the concept of sustainable development was given new impetus by the adoption of the Sustainable Development Goals (SDGS) in 2015. Simultaneously, the concept's affirmed purposes for international economic law, including the drafting and design of international investment agreements (IIAS), were widely discussed. The question I wanted to further pursue was whether the integration of sustainable development in international investment law is a purely political undertaking, or whether such integration is required by law. The case of the EU appeared to be a particularly good object of study, for two reasons. First, sustainable development is among the binding Union objectives, which the EU must pursue in all its policies. Second, the EU thrives on shaping and contributing to the development of international law, which includes aligning international economic law with sustainable development.

EU foreign investment law is a fast-moving topic, and so it happened that the present book's analysis and research were finalised before the EU concluded the critical Comprehensive Agreement on Investment with China. The book's finalisation, in November 2020, also preceded the outcomes of the first expert panel report under a Trade and Sustainable Development Chapter under the EU-Korea Free Trade Agreement. In January 2021, the experts concluded that Korea was in breach of the agreement's labour commitments. I hope the reader can understand that both developments are only covered to a limited extent in this book.

Indeed, the present book must be read and understood within the fast-changing legal environment of EU and international investment law. The EU IIAS constantly evolve regarding their investment disciplines and provisions that are relevant for sustainable development. Moreover, many significant processes are ongoing, such as the negotiations on a modernised Energy Charter Treaty, the discussions on investment facilitation for development at the World Trade Organization, and the EU's numerous ongoing bilateral negotiations with key investment partners.

Despite the challenges in capturing a moving target, the present book offers a comprehensive account of the normative framework of sustainable development and its functions under international and EU law. It explains how the EU's constitutional order shapes the latter as a global actor, and how it contributes to the international community's endeavour to align international investment law with sustainable development.

With this book, I hope that sustainable development receives more serious attention from lawyers and policy-makers. The concept should no longer merely be used as a slogan for political purposes to justify the conclusion of IIAs. Many of the provisions under EU IIAs highlight that the legal concretisation of sustainable development within international investment law has become rich and manifold.

>Geneva, Switzerland
>February 2021

CHAPTER 1

Introduction

The legal effects of sustainable development (SD) within international investment law are emerging, building a more comprehensive regulatory framework for foreign investment. One aspect that is sometimes overlooked in the debate is the dynamic of international investment law's current structure of governance. This includes questions of the role played by certain actors in contributing to the alignment of international investment law with SD and the existing normative requirements to integrate SD more concretely. The present book seeks to fill this gap and examines the debate on SD and international investment law from a governance perspective. Its focus is on one key global actor, the European Union (EU).[1] Unpacking the normative SD requirements applicable to the EU reveals the concept's strong legal embedment in the EU legal order. As one of the Union objectives, SD must be integrated in EU foreign investment law and policy.

With the competence shift provoked through the entry into force of the Lisbon Treaty in 2009, the EU has become an international actor within international investment law.[2] According to the EU treaties, the international investment policy of the EU is subject to a number of general objectives that are to be pursued at the international level.[3] One of these key objectives is the concept of SD. The Court of Justice of the European Union (CJEU), which has in the past fostered the characteristic of the EU as a value-oriented global actor,[4] held that SD "henceforth forms an integral part" of the investment law-making

---

1   The EU has become the most important player in the context of international investment before the United States of America. The EU's share of outward investment per year is one-third of the total global stock, and the EU's share of inward investment is one-quarter of the total global stock. See Eurostat, 'World stocks of foreign direct investment, 2017 (% of total)', available at <http://ec.europa.eu/eurostat/statistics-explained/index.php/World_direct_investment_patterns>.
2   TFEU, Art 207(1) in combination with Art 3(1)(e). See also, ECJ, Opinion 2/15, *Free Trade Agreement with Singapore*, EU:C:2017:376, paras 33–37 and 109.
3   TEU, Art 21(1) and (2). Among such objectives can be found the promotion of human rights, democracy, peace, the rule of law, the eradication of poverty and SD.
4   Eg ECJ, Joined Cases C-584/10 P, C-593/10 P *Commission, UK and Council v Kadi* (Kadi II), EU:C:2013:518, para 131: "[...] the maintenance of international peace and security and the protection of the fundamental rights and freedoms of the person concerned [...] those being shared values of the UN and the European Union".

of the EU.⁵ Moreover, the Court set out that EU primary law "includes new aspects of contemporary international trade policy".⁶ In other words, SD guides the EU as a global actor in this field, making clear that not only purely economic objectives such as liberalisation and market access should be the focus of its investment law-making. The EU institutions, mainly the European Commission, are in charge of turning the objective of SD and the integration thereof into a more concrete EU investment strategy by using their political discretion to concretise the general and more abstract EU primary law setting. According to statements of the European Commission, EU investment law-making shall be "responsible".⁷ In the eyes of the Commission, this endeavour requires that EU IIAS are to be consistent with core labour standards, environmental protection and the aim of including developing countries into the world economy thereby pointing to the heart of SD.⁸ The SD objective of the EU is *a priori* perfectly aligned with the current reform endeavours of international investment law seeking to integrate SD. Hence, the hypothesis can be made that the EU has the potential to be an important actor in transforming international investment law in light of SD.⁹

Against this background, the central question that the book examines is *whether and to what extent the post-Lisbon international investment law-making of the EU integrates SD?* Put differently, this book is on how the EU acts, reacts and contributes to the debate on the articulation between international investment law and SD. Is the EU a normative power that is proactive or reactive with respect to integrating SD? Is it proposing new norms or sticking to state-of-the-art investment law-making? Thus, the question is not how the international debate ought to look like or what the reform outcomes should be. The question is what the EU does and what the EU ought to do to integrate SD into international investment law.

---

5   See Opinion 2/15, above note 2, para 147: "It follows that the objective of sustainable development henceforth forms an integral part of the common commercial policy". The EU's investment law-making is part of the common commercial policy under TFEU, Art 207.
6   Ibid, para 141. See TEU, Arts 3(5) and 21.
7   European Commission Communication, 'Trade for All - Towards a more responsible trade and investment policy', COM (2015) 497 final.
8   Cremona M, 'Distinguished Essay: A Quiet Revolution—The Changing Nature of the EU's Common Commercial Policy' in: Bungenberg M et al (eds), *European Yearbook of International Economic Law 2017*, vol 8 (Springer International Publishing 2017) 6. See also, European Commission, above note 7.
9   European Commission, above note 7, 21. The Commission considers that the EU has a "special responsibility to lead the reform of the global investment regime, as its founder and main actor".

The purpose of the present book is to provide an account of the conceptual and normative framework applicable to the EU to integrate SD into IIAS by analysing the legal tools and instruments through which the EU engages with the controversial relationship between SD and international investment law. The book employs a double benchmark analysis of the EU's investment law-making. The first benchmark derives from the international normative framework of SD. International legal principles, soft law and current developments concerning SD create legal obligations and expectations[10] that the EU cannot ignore.[11] In particular, the vast a growing practice of States, international organisations and non-governmental organisations seeking to formulate concrete treaty terms and standards on the articulation of the SD-investment nexus form a conceptual and normative framework against which the EU investment law-making can be assessed. The second benchmark arises from the EU's constitutional framework. The focus here is whether the EU lives up to its own "self-imposed" obligations and expectations based on EU primary law and policy strategies adopted by EU institutions. Testing the impact of SD, which is stated as a principle and objective under the EU treaties, provides insights on the normative impacts of SD and whether it can effectively be operationalised in EU external action, including the EU's international investment law-making.[12] Due to the double benchmark approach, the book covers both, international law and EU law. Thereby, it seeks to be accessible for EU external relations law and international investment law experts.

Lastly, it is important to indicate from the outset the limits of the scope of the enquiry. While the book touches upon many controversial aspects of the discussion on the SD-investment nexus, such controversies could only be treated with the degree of depth necessary to inform the appraisal of the EU as a global actor. Moreover, this book confines itself to a legal assessment of the degree and manner in which SD has been integrated into IIAS. In this respect, the study cannot purport to evaluate actual SD impacts within the EU and its partner countries as a consequence of SD integration in international investment law-making.[13]

---

10 The term "legal expectations" describes those SD obligations for which the legal status is unclear or of soft law status.
11 TEU, Art 3(5) states that the EU "shall contribute to [...] the strict observance and the development of international law [...]."
12 Eeckhout P, 'A Normative Basis for EU External Relations? Protecting Internal Values Beyond the Single Market', in: Krajewski M (ed), *Services of General Interest Beyond the Single Market* (TMC Asser Press 2015) 226.
13 Such field studies look at actual SD implications in the country, namely social protection development, economic development or enhanced environmental protection. See

It should further be noted that the focus of the book is the analysis of IIAs.¹⁴ Post-Lisbon EU IIA practice is, in this respect, the main object of assessment.¹⁵ At the centre of analysis are the trade and investment agreements with Singapore, Vietnam, Canada and Mexico. As far investment liberalisation and SD provisions are discussed, the agreements with Korea, Japan and Mercosur are also covered.¹⁶

The remainder of the present introduction recalls the EU's particularities as a global actor and exposes the underpinning (economic) assumptions of the book's analysis. It closes with the presentation of the outline of the book's argument.

---

eg Harrison J et al, 'Governing Labour Standards through Free Trade Agreements: Limits of the European Union's Trade and Sustainable Development Chapters', 57 (2018) JCMS: Journal of Common Market Studies 2, 260–277.

14 The study's scope is thus limited to IIAs. This is notwithstanding the fact that other instruments regulating foreign investment are highly relevant for SD. In particular, investment contracts concluded between an investor and a host State are crucial for SD; likewise, domestic legislation applicable to investment activities is important and plays a fundamental role for SD. For the negative impact on investment contracts, see, Crockett A, 'Stabilisation Clauses and Sustainable Development: Drafting for the Future', in: Brown C and Miles K, *Evolution in Investment Treaty Law and Arbitration* (Cambridge University Press 2011) 516–538. Moreover, development financing and other credit facilities for private investors seeking to invest in developing countries also fall outside the present study's scope. See also, Chapter 8.3.

15 The present book reflects law and policy developments as of 30 Nov 2020. Therefore, the EU-China Comprehensive Agreement on Investment could only be addressed to a limited extent.

16 Hereafter the acronyms of the agreements are used. Comprehensive Economic and Trade Agreement between Canada, of the one part, and the European Union and its Member States, of the other part, [2017] OJ L 11/23 (CETA); Economic Partnership Agreement between the European Union and Japan, [2018] OJ L 330/3; (EUJFTA); Free Trade Agreement between the European Union and Singapore, [2019] OJ L 294; (EUSFTA); Investment Protection Agreement between the European Union and Singapore, (authentic text of April 2018; not yet in OJ) (EUSIPA); Free Trade Agreement between the European Union and Mexico (authentic text of April 2018; not yet in OJ) (EUMFTA); Free Trade Agreement between the European Union and Vietnam, [2019] OJ L 186; (EUVFTA). Investment Protection Agreement between the European Union and Vietnam, (authentic text as of August 2018; not yet in the Official Journal), (EUVIPA); Free Trade Agreement between the European Union and MERCOSUR, (text of July 2019; not yet in OJ) (EUMERFTA); Comprehensive Agreement on Investment (CAI) between the European Union and China, (text of January 2021; not yet in the OJ) (EUCCAI).

1.1 The Distinctiveness of the EU as a Global Actor

When considering the EU as a "global actor" or "normative power",[17] it is important to bear in mind that the EU is not a State and thus its capacity to act in the international system depends on a number of conditions, such as an international legal personality, external recognition, as well as necessary competence that has been attributed to it by its Member States.[18] The most complex issues surrounding the EU as a global actor remains those related to questions of competences. Unlike a State, the EU does not have unlimited competences flowing from recognised sovereign statehood but is an organisation of attributed powers.[19] EU primary law states specifically that the EU "shall only act within the limits of the competences conferred upon it by the Member States in the Treaties to attain the objectives therein".[20] The principle of conferral sets two clear limitations on any EU legislative act including the adoption of an international agreement: first, the requirement of the existence of a substantive competence, and second, the need of choice of an appropriate legal basis.[21] There are legal requirements and limits of the EU as a global actor that constitute the distinctiveness of the EU's mode of governance with respect to external action.[22] It becomes apparent that concepts such as the EU as a

---

17   The idea of "Normative Power Europe" has been developed by Ian Manners. See Manners I, 'Normative Power Europe: A Contradiction in Terms?' 40 (2002) Journal of Common Market Studies 2, 235–258. See at 252: "Thus my presentation of the EU as a normative power has an ontological quality to it—that the EU can be conceptualized as a changer of norms in the international system; a positive quantity to it—that the EU *acts* to change norms in the international system; a normative quantity to it—that the EU *should* act to extend its norms to the international system." Emphasis in original.

18   Before the Lisbon Treaty, the international legal personality of the EU was recognised *de facto*. With the Lisbon Treaty, the EU was granted an explicit international legal personality; see TEU, Art 47: "The Union shall have legal personality". See also, Marín Durán G and Morgera E, *Environmental Integration in the EU's External Relations: Beyond Multilateral Dimensions* (Hart Pub 2012) 6.

19   Cremona M, 'Structural Principles and Their Role in EU External Relations Law' (2016) 69 Current Legal Problems 35, 12.

20   TEU, Art 5(2). See also TEU, Art 5(3) on subsidiarity and (4) on proportionality.

21   Marín Durán and Morgera, above note 18, 8.

22   For these reasons, the EU has also been described as a rule-based international actor, see Cremona, above note 109, 12. See also De Witte B, 'Too Much Constitutional Law in the European Union's Foreign Relations?' in: Cremona M and De Witte B (eds), *EU Foreign Relations Law: Constitutional Fundamentals* (Hart Pub 2008), 11; Cremona M, 'Values in EU Foreign Policy', in: Evans M and Koutrakos P (eds), *Beyond the Established Legal Orders: Policy Interconnections between the EU and the Rest of the World* (Hart Pub 2011), 276.

"normative power" or the EU as a "global actor" serve to analyse the content, meaning and importance of the EU action and law-making at the international scene.[23] The essential idea is that the EU promotes international norms in a non-coercive normative way based on its values and principles enshrined in its founding treaties.[24] The legal interest lies within the EU's commitment to act externally in accordance with its own determined normative basis.[25]

The newly gained competence over foreign direct investment (FDI)[26] has allowed the EU to assert a proactive role in developing its own international investment policy. However, the policy cannot be fully considered autonomous and a number of practical and legal challenges remain to be overcome to establish a functional EU investment policy.[27] The main factor impeding the policy's autonomy derives from the complex division of competences between the EU and its Member States. Whilst FDI fully falls under the EU's exclusive external competence, the EU has only shared competences over portfolio investment and investor-State dispute settlement.[28] Therefore, the EU cannot conclude comprehensive IIAs alone but must cooperate with its Member States. The EU's effectiveness as a global actor in the field of international investment law thus depends on cooperation with its Member States. The split of competences certainly heightens the complexity of the governance model of the EU concerning international investment regulation.

1.2 Assumptions Regarding Investment Treaties

Legal scholarship dealing, one way or the other, with the relationship between international investment law and SD implies certain economic assumptions. The present book is no exception in this regard as two fundamental

---

[23] Wessel RA, 'The Meso Level: Means of Interaction between EU and International Law: Flipping the Question: The Reception of EU Law in the International Legal Order' (2016) 35 Yearbook of European Law 533.

[24] De Burca G, 'EU External Relations: The Governance Mode of Foreign Policy', in: Van Vooren B, Blockmans S and Wouters J (eds), *The EU's Role in Global Governance: The Legal Dimension* (Oxford University Press 2013) 40.

[25] Eeckhout above note 12, 226.

[26] TFEU, Art 207(1) in combination with Art 3(1)(e). See also, Opinion 2/15, above note 2, paras 33–37 and 109.

[27] Such as the organisation of the transition from Member States bilateral investment treaties (BITs) to EU IIAs and the repartition of roles and responsibilities between the EU and the Member States in the context of investor-State dispute settlement.

[28] Opinion 2/15, above note 2, paras 244 and 293.

assumptions are underpinning its methodology. The first assumption is that IIAs can effectively address issues of SD. Thus, they can be beneficial for SD. The second assumption is that traditional international investment law did not, or not sufficiently, address issues of SD.

To explain the first assumption, it is necessary to reflect back to the economic premises that have shaped modern international investment law since its beginnings in the 1950s. IIAs were since their inceptions considered as legal instruments that bring about development, economic growth and welfare to host and home countries.[29] There is a traditional twofold causal link presumed by States that have been keen to negotiate investment agreements. To begin with, these instruments increase foreign investment (first causality). Subsequently, such foreign investment leads to economic growth-enhancing public welfare of States and their populations (second causality). In this sense, host States are coveted to attract investments—especially foreign direct investment (FDI)—due to capital injections, transfer of knowledge and technology, access to international markets, and other associated benefits.[30] Home States seek to enhance outward foreign investment because their companies can expand abroad and gain access to resources. This can increase the companies' competitiveness and profitability, which is beneficial for the home country's employment rate and tax revenue.[31] Thus, there are expectations that foreign investment has a number of positive impacts on economic development at a macro-economic level for both the host and the home State.[32] Insights from economics, however, reveal that both of these causal links cannot that easily be presumed.[33]

---

29 Germany-Pakistan BIT [1959], Preamble, recital 3: "RECOGNIZING that an understanding reached between the two States is likely to promote investment, encourage private industrial and financial enterprise and to increase the prosperity of both the States." See also ICSID Convention [1965], Preamble, recital 1: "Considering the need for international cooperation for economic development, and the role of private international investment therein".

30 See eg, Alfaro L, 'Gains from Foreign Direct Investment: Macro and Micro Approaches World Bank's ABCDE Conference' (2016) The World Bank Economic Review, S2-S15.

31 Johnson L, 'FDI, International Investment and the Sustainable Development Goals', in: Krajewski M and Hoffmann RT (eds), *Research Handbook on Foreign Direct Investment* (Edward Elgar Pub 2019) 127–128; See also, Sauvant KP et al, 'Trends in FDI, Home Country Measures and Competitive Neutrality', in: Bjorklund AK (ed), *Yearbook on International Investment Law and Policy 2012–2013* (Oxford University Press 2014) 6–10.

32 Schill S, Tams CJ and Hofmann R (eds), *International Investment Law and Development: Bridging the Gap* (Edward Elgar Publishing 2015) 3.

33 Without attempting to provide a full review of the existing literature, the following shall summarise the main findings from economics.

The existing literature has provided mixed answers to the question of whether IIAs increase foreign investment.[34] Whilst, a minority of studies finds that there is no significant impact of entering into an IIA on the total inflows of foreign investment,[35] a majority does observe that IIAs have a "positive and statistically significant impact" on inward foreign investment.[36] Especially more recent studies tend to confirm the overall positive impacts of IIAs on the investment inflows by using new estimation techniques, long-term data, and bilateral data on investment flows rather than general data.[37] However, several authors still highlight the limits of the current economic studies. Despite their improved methodology, their scope remains too limited.[38] Namely, most of the existing studies do not distinguish between the different types of investment according to their economic sectors. The rare studies that integrate this differentiation show that IIAs can have very different impacts depending on the economic sectors.[39] Typically, IIAs have bigger effects on investment decisions for those economic activities that involve important sunk costs for investors and are susceptible to expropriation, such as the mining and utilities sectors.[40]

---

34 Bonnitcha J, Poulsen LNS and Waibel M, *The Political Economy of the Investment Treaty Regime* (Oxford University Press 2017) 158. The authors came to this conclusion by having analysed thirty-five published quantitative studies of how investment treaties affect FDI. The same finding was also made in the following articles: Colen L and Guariso A, 'What Type of Foreign Investment is attracted by Bilateral Investment Treaties?' in De Schutter O, Swinnen JFM and Wouters J (eds), *Foreign Direct Investment and Human Development: The Law and Economics of International Investment Agreements* (Routledge 2013) 138; Salacuse JW and Sullivan NP, 'Do BITs Really Work?: An Evaluation of Bilateral Investment Treaties and Their Grand Bargain', in: Sauvant KP and Sachs LE (eds), *The Effect of Treaties on Foreign Direct Investment* (Oxford University Press 2009) 109–170; UNCTAD, *The Role of International Investment Agreements in Attracting Foreign Direct Investment to Developing Countries* (United Nations 2009); Van Aaken A and Lehmann TA, 'Sustainable Development and International Investment Law' in: Echandi R and Sauvé P (eds), *Prospects in International Investment Law and Policy* (Cambridge University Press 2013) 319–321.

35 Eg Hallward-Driemeier M, 'Do Bilateral Investment Treaties Attract Foreign Direct Investment? Only a Bit—and They Could Bite', (2003) World Bank Policy Research WPS No 3121. See also, Bonnitcha, Poulsen and Waibel, above note 34, 159.

36 It should be mentioned that the degree of the impact can vary remarkably depending on the circumstances, see Bonnitcha, Poulsen and Waibel, above note 34, 159.

37 Colen and Guariso, above note 34, 139.

38 Ibid, 140.

39 Ibid, 148–155. Colen and Guariso established tables that show the different impacts of IIAs depending on economic sectors (agriculture, mining, manufacturing, utilities, services and banking).

40 Ibid. The leading micro-economic justification for the conclusion of IIAs is the argument that they solve hold-up problems. For more details, see Bonnitcha, Poulsen and Waibel, above note 34, 128–137.

In addition to that, most studies reveal that a companies' decision to invest in a given country is, to a large extent also influenced by elements that are independent of the existence of an IIA. Examples hereto are market potential, human capital and existing infrastructure in the host State.[41] It becomes apparent that the assessment on the effectiveness of IIAs depends on answers that are to be provided by empirical studies, many of them are yet ongoing.[42] What can be said is that—in general—IIAs can have an impact on the increase of foreign investment inflows.[43]

Considering now the second question on whether foreign investment leads to economic growth. This question is more controversial and complex.[44] In theoretical terms, it is widely accepted that foreign investment (especially FDI) entails economic benefits, encompassing a bundle of capital stock, know-how, technology and access to international markets. Therefore, impacts on economic growth are expected to be diverse.[45] Empirical studies focusing on the micro-economic benefits of foreign investment confirm the theoretical assumption and show that foreign firms are in general more productive than domestic firms.[46] Yet, in macro-economic terms, the empirical findings on the foreign investment impacts on the host State economy are less clear.[47] Whilst

---

41 Salacuse and Sullivan, above note 34, 109–170; UNCTAD, above note 34.
42 Bonnitcha, Poulsen and Waibel, above note 34. The authors highlight that many economic studies only engaged with the question whether IIAs increase foreign investment even though "any evaluation of the investment treaties' economic impact depends not only on *whether* investment treaties increase aggregate inward foreign investment, but also on *how* and *why* investment treaties affect different types of investment" (at 57 and 166). Emphasis in original. The authors add that "the microeconomic analysis of investment treaties cannot divorce form the underlying empirical questions about the legal system and government decision-making in the states that are bound by them. Empirical questions about the firms' decision-making are also an important consideration" (at 154).
43 In many policy instruments, UNCTAD expresses this view. See eg UNCTAD, above note 34, xii: "IIAs add a number of important components to the policy and institutional determinants for FDI, and thereby contribute to enhancing the attractiveness of countries. In particular, they improve investment protection and add to the security, transparency, stability and predictability of the investment framework. By liberalizing market access for non-tradable services, and effectively creating a 'market' for such services, IIAs also improve an important economic determinant of foreign investment."
44 De Schutter O, Swinnen JFM and Wouters J (eds), *Foreign Direct Investment and Human Development: The Law and Economics of International Investment Agreements* (Routledge 2013) 2.
45 Colen L, Maertens M and Swinnen J, 'Foreign Direct Investment as an Engine for Economic Growth and Human Development', in De Schutter et al, above note 44, 80 and 85.
46 Ibid, 85.
47 See eg De Mello L 'Foreign Direct Investment in Developing Countries', (1997) Journal of Development Studies, vol 34, issue 1, 10: "whether FDI can be deemed to be a catalyst

in theory, the increased productivity of foreign companies, may enhance economic growth in host States through indirect spill-over effects, empirical studies reveal that actual outcomes are very heterogeneous.[48]

This can be explained by the fact that several factors are conditioning the growth effect of foreign investment. First, the technological gap that exists between the home and the host State has an impact. Less developed countries will grow relatively faster and catch up with developed nations because the imitation of technology is cheaper than the invention of new ideas.[49] In principle, the wider the technological gap, the bigger are the growth expectations. Studies have also found that where the gap is too important, host States cannot absorb the knowledge and technology spill-over effects due to a lack of human capital and education.[50] The second factor relates to the host State's macro-economic conditions and plays a crucial role for the growth effect of foreign investment. For instance, countries with an outwardly oriented trade policy are more likely to benefit foreign companies than countries pursuing an inwardly oriented policy.[51] In addition, an increase in competition through the presence of foreign companies is only beneficial for those economies that already dispose of relatively competitive firms. Otherwise, the presence of foreign firms is likely to lead to the crowding out domestic firms in the host country.[52] Moreover, the investment's economic sector also plays an important role for the growth effects of foreign investment. For instance, the manufacturing sector bears more potential for growth than investments in natural resources.[53] Lastly, the entry mode of foreign investment also plays in. As such, greenfield investments have more economic potential by adding to the industrial capacity of host States than mergers and acquisition transfers, which only provoke a shift in ownership. In sum, it can be noted that foreign investment

---

for output growth, capital accumulation, and technological progress, seems to be a less controversial hypothesis in theory than in practice."

48   Colen, Maertens and Swinnen, above note 45, 71. According to the authors, such spill-over channels imitate technology and technical skills, the formation of human capital, competition, crowding in domestic firms, and positive export effects (see 86–89).
49   Ibid, 95.
50   Ibid.
51   OECD, 'Foreign Direct Investment for Development—Maximising Benefits, Minimizing Costs' (OECD Publications 2002) 11.
52   See eg, Driffield N and Hughes D, 'Foreign and Domestic Investment: Regional Development or Crowding out?' (2003) 37 Regional Studies, 277.
53   A distinction is moreover made between labour-intensive and technology-intensive investments, where the former is expected to be more growth-enhancing, see Colen, Maertens and Swinnen, above note 45, 71.

may produce wide-ranging economic benefits even though they are not automatic and depending on a number of factors.

So far, the stated assumption relates to the economic benefits of IIAs. It is now important to question their impact on SD. The main difference in questioning SD impacts rather than economic impacts is to look beyond the purely economic implication and take into account a series of non-economic factors, such as impacts on the environment, education, health, employment, human rights and good governance.[54] Comprehensive studies specifically on the correlation between IIAs and SD are yet seldom, but the existing ones indicate, with respect to SD too, that the benefits of an increase in investment are mixed.[55] For instance, there are positive instances where foreign investment can improve industries' environmental performance in host countries by using newer and cleaner technology.[56] At the same time, an increase in foreign investment can cause or exacerbate environmental challenges. There are numerous examples, especially in the area of natural resources, such as oil and gas exploitation and mining, where actions of foreign companies have resulted in huge damage to the environment, including the health of local populations.[57] On the social impacts, the economic potential of foreign investment leading to greater profitability of companies should result in more employment, more education as well as an increase in public spending for other social ends. Yet, empirical studies also show that investment's negative social effects can range from increasing unemployment through the crowding-out of local firms, contributing to inequalities and even increasing corruption.[58] As a result, it is noted that IIAs can be beneficial for SD, but SD outcomes are not automatic.

All this leads to the next central assumption and relates to whether the way in which IIAs are drafted, namely their design and wording, has a bearing on influencing SD outcomes. This question relates to the reasons for the current

---

54 In this respect, a work of reference are the annual 'Sustainable Development Reports' that present the SD Index and Dashboards for all UN member states and frames the implementation of the Sustainable Development Goals (SDGs). Report are available at <https://www.sdgindex.org>.
55 It can have positive as well as negative effects on SD-related issues. Johnson, above note 31, 128.
56 Kozuluk T and Timiliotis C, 'Do Environmental Policies Affect Global Value Chains' (OECD Publications 2016).
57 It is sufficed to mention the oil pollution in Ecuador by Chevron and in Nigeria by Shell. See also, Kareem SD, et al, 'Impacts of Oil Foreign Direct Investment on Environment and Poverty Level in Niger Delta Oil Producing Region: A Structural Equation Modeling Approach', (2014) International Journal of Energy Economics and Policy, Vol 4, No 4, 679–692.
58 Johnson, above note 31, 129.

reform of international investment law. States perceive today that traditional international investment law[59] did not fulfil their long-term expectations, also with respect to SD.[60] The lessons from the past twenty years are that real costs exist to the conclusion of IIAs, which may or may not be compensated by its gains.[61] The "sovereignty costs" or the loss of "policy space" started to be increasingly perceived by States with the surge in investor claims during the last decade. Accordingly, most States consider earlier IIAs being drafted too broadly and vaguely. In addition, the idea of using IIAs to harness foreign investment towards environmental and social ends did not yet exist when the early IIAs have been concluded. The following sums up very well the shift, which has taken place:

> "Indeed, even where the arrival of FDI is beneficial for economic growth and poverty reduction of the host country in aggregate terms. The debate has devoted increasing attention to the opportunities and threats it may pose [...] The question in the past was how to increase the attractiveness of one jurisdiction to foreign investors, and the conclusion of IIAs was seen as an obvious means towards that end. *The question is now how to align the incentives in order to maximise the positive impacts of FDI while minimising the potential negative impacts.*"[62]

The reorientation has manifested itself empirically. The conclusion of IIAs remains a key strategy of countries in attracting foreign investment but are adding new provisions or clarifying existing disciplines, thereby seeking to integrate SD. States are, in fact, assuming that by developing new legal approaches for the design of their IIAs, SD issues can be addressed. In other words, how IIAs are drafted and shaped does make a difference for, on the one

---

59 [Definition of traditional IIAs?] The large bulk of IIAs only mention economic objectives in their preambles and contain no reference to social or environmental standards. Eg German Model BIT, preamble: "desiring to intensify economic co-operation between the two States, intending to create favourable conditions for investments by investors of either State in the territory of the other State, recognizing that the encouragement and contractual protection of such investments are apt to stimulate private business initiative and to increase the prosperity of both nation". See, UNCTAD's Database, Investment Policy Hub.

60 The expected long-term benefits did not occur. See Columbia Center on Sustainable Investment, 'Costs and Benefits of Investment Treaties—Practical Considerations for States', (2018) Policy Paper, 15.

61 De Schutter, Swinnen and Wouters, above note 44, 7.

62 Ibid. Emphasis added.

INTRODUCTION

hand, maximising the positive impacts of foreign investment, and on the other hand, minimising its negative impacts. The assumption is thus twofold. First, it is assumed that there is a link between treaty design and the risk of attracting claims for investor-State dispute settlement. Second, it is assumed that there is a link between treaty design and positive SD spill-over effects. Both causal links are not yet proven and therefore assumed. Based on the assumption, however, the integration of SD in international investment law is a worthwhile cause.[63] Whilst, the present book shares the assumption, its analysis highlights the limits of treaty drafting and indicates how certain clauses are likely to perform in practice.

1.3 Outline of the Argument

Building on these premises, the present book is divided into 7 chapters and grouped into two parts. Part 1, consisting of Chapters 2 to 4, provides the conceptual and normative framework of SD integration in international law and EU law. Part 1, serves in setting the benchmarks by which EU IIAs will be assessed in Part 2 of the study. Thus, Part 2 concerns the legal effects of SD and the emerging transformation of international investment law and governance.

Chapter 2 has the purpose first to analyse the concept of SD within the international legal order seeking to provide answers on the concept's origins, meaning(s) and legal status. Key instruments, such as the 1992 Rio Declaration as well as the 2015 Sustainable Development Goals (SDGs) are looked at. The focus is on the extent to which SD can guide law-makers in their decisions. In a second step, Chapter 2 will present and discuss the main features of the debate on the difficult relationship between SD and international investment law. By depicting how the concept challenges many of the traditional aspects of IIAs and introduces opportunities of better balancing their costs and benefits, the analysis has the purpose of drawing a line between those arguments that are normative and those that are political.

Chapter 3 analyses SD in the EU legal order. It considers the normative nature of Union objectives and their legal effects. While Union objectives are binding, they provide the EU institutions with direction on how to concretely

---

63   It is certain that domestic law and investment contracts simultaneously play a fundamental role in assuring that investment activities respect environmental standards, social protection at work and basic human rights. In the understanding of the present study, IIAs have a *complementary* role to domestic regulation on foreign investment and thus impact on the overall framework.

implement them. Chapter 3 examines, in particular, the requirements of policy integration and policy coherence, which are principles of EU constitutional law. Both are key for the realisation of SD under EU law. The chapter concludes with examining of how differently SD is articulated in the various internal and external EU policies.

Chapter 4 first discusses the evolution of EU international investment law-making before and after the entry into force of the Lisbon Treaty. Subsequently, the scope of post-Lisbon EU competence over foreign investment and SD are examined. The chapter then turns to the orientation of EU international investment law-making as being part of the EU's Common Commercial Policy (CCP). It looks at the obligation for EU institutions to integrate SD into EU IIAs, their discretion to do so and the soft law instruments that point out the policy intentions of how SD integration under the CCP should unfold. The chapter also considers the adoption and the content of EU IIAs, and it reveals why issues around the autonomy of the EU legal order have become directly linked to SD.

Chapter 5, the first chapter of Part 2, focuses on specific SD tools establishing SD integration through regulatory linkages of investment, social standards and environmental protection under EU IIAs. In other words, how the EU uses its SD objective and strategies to shape IIAs concretely is the main object of Chapter 5. "Sustainable Development and Trade Chapters" contained in EU free trade agreements (hereafter: TSD chapters) is of central importance as most of the legal tools used by the EU to create regulatory linkages can be found in TSD chapters of comprehensive FTAs. Chapter 5 mainly examines their content, such as commitments not to lower social and environmental standards to attract investments, or the reaffirmation of international commitments in the field of environmental protection and social standards, as well as the commitment to ensure a high level of protection within domestic law. Furthermore, Chapter 5 analyses the institutional and procedural arrangements seeking to ensure that SD concerns are taken into account in the application of the agreement, as well as the enforcement mechanisms, which seek to ensure the respect of the provisions contained in the TSD chapter. Chapter 5 also addresses additional fields of cooperation on SD and investment linkages, such as climate change mitigation and the fight against corruption. The chapter considers how and to what extent EU IIAs foster the responsibilities of foreign investors to achieve SD. Finally, the chapter assesses Sustainability Impact Assessments (SIAs) that are conducted during the negotiations of trade and investment agreements.

The subsequent Chapter 6 analyses those provisions of EU IIAs dealing with investment liberalisation and protection. It first looks at the main investment protection standards, which are under EU IIAs, subject to investor-State dispute resolution. Chapter 6 discusses the reaffirmation clauses on the right to regulate and the set of general exceptions in EU IIAs. It then turns to the issue of investment liberalisation. Subsequently, the definition of investment is analysed. Lastly, the chapter discusses certain procedural aspects of investor-State dispute resolution, mainly the issue of transparency and *amicus curiae* participation. Chapter 6 is concerned with how the EU contributes to the ongoing debate on finding the right balance between SD public interests and the interests of private investors.

At the heart of Chapter 7 are issues around the interpretation of EU IIAs. Given that SD is one of the main objectives of EU IIAs, the concept ultimately plays a central role in the interpretation of the norms and standards regulating foreign investment. The chapter starts off by considering the references to SD in the preambles of EU IIAs and points out the relationship and legal interactions between TSD chapters and investment liberalisation and protection provisions. In a final step, Chapter 7 considers more concretely the interpretative tools and methods of SD integration at the moment of interpretation of EU IIAs.

Chapter 8 serves as the general conclusion of the enquiry. It provides answers to the research question by commenting on whether and to what extent the EU has become a global actor that integrates SD in international investment law. The conclusion also resumes the finding on the nature, limits and benefits of discretion in the context of SD. Finally, the present book suggests an outlook pointing to additional and complementary legal frameworks that also have to play an increased role to achieve sustainable investment activities globally.

PART 1

Conceptual and Normative Framework of SD
Integration in International Law and EU Law

∴

CHAPTER 2

Sustainable Development in the International Legal Order

Sustainable development (SD) has become a constitutive paradigm of our modern times. In 2015, the United Nations General Assembly reaffirmed[1] with its Agenda 2030 the commitment to SD and embarking on the path of "transforming our world" to secure us the *People*, our *Planet*, world *Peace* and our common *Prosperity* through a global *Partnership* in order to achieve SD.[2] The concept of SD serves in describing a global aspiration for welfare and decent life, combining economic development, social development and environmental protection.[3] SD has consequences affecting all areas of human activity. It pervades the discourses of the public and the private sector on current global challenges.[4] SD has, moreover, found its way into the international law domain. An increasing number of international treaties enshrines the concept, including international investment agreements (IIAs).

This opening chapter revisits the origins, content and legal status of SD under international law. In its first part, it seeks to capture the normative content of SD by distinguishing between legal obligations and those for which the legal status is yet uncertain. The ambition is not to enter into an exhaustive analysis of SD under international law as there exists abundant literature on the topic.[5] Rather, the main aspects of the concept are presented here as they

---

1   The international community first stated its commitment to SD at the 1992 Rio Conference on Environment and Development. See UN Conference on Environment and Development, 'Rio Declaration on Environment and Development and Agenda 21', [1992] Doc A/CONF.151/26Rev 1.
2   UN General Assembly, 'Transforming our world: the 2030 Agenda for Sustainable Development', [2015] A/RES/70/1 (hereafter: Agenda 2030).
3   Sachs J, *The Age of Sustainable Development* (Columbia University Press 2015) xiii.
4   Such challenges encompass climate change, food safety, biodiversity loss, immigration prompted by natural disasters, poverty and social inequalities, and the depletion of natural resources. They are with the world's population and global temperature steadily rising aggravated. The world population continues to rise rapidly by around 75 million people each year. Estimations indicate by the 2020s it will be: 8 billion; by the 2040s: 9 billion, and by 2100: 11 billion. An average global temperature increase between 1.8 and 4.0 degrees Celsius is expected by 2100.
5   The legal controversies around SD lay mainly in three areas: origin, content and legal status under international law. To name just a few previous works: Barral V, *Le développement durable en droit international: essai sur les incidences juridiques d'une norme évolutive* (Bruylant

allow setting its legal characteristics. In its second part, the chapter turns to the question, which concerns—in more concrete terms—what the SD paradigm entails for international investment law. As the debate on the SD-investment nexus is ongoing, the chapter aims to clarify where the debate stands and what the arguments are.

2.1   Historical Developments

The modern understanding of the concept of SD was only construed towards the end of the 20th century and, to a large extent, as a result of UN-led promotion.[6] Whilst the 1972 Stockholm Conference on the Human Environment[7] launched the era of environmental awareness, the concept of SD was yet mentioned. States were not yet agreeing to put environmental protection on an equal footing with development concerns.[8] However, form 1972 onwards,

---

2016); Boyle AE and Freestone D (eds), *International Law and Sustainable Development: Past Achievements and Future Challenges* (Oxford University Press 1999); Cordonier Segger M-C and Khalfan A, *Sustainable Development Law Principles, Practices, and Prospects* (Oxford University Press 2004); Gehne K, *Nachhaltige Entwicklung als Rechtsprinzip: Normativer Aussagegehalt, rechtstheoretische Einordnung, Funktionen im Recht* (Mohr Siebeck 2011); Schrijver N, *The Evolution of Sustainable Development in International Law: Inception, Meaning and Status* (Martinus Nijhoff 2008).

6   The idea of SD is reportedly much older. First, SD has been traced back to ancient agricultural systems in the Americas, Africa, the Middle East and Asia; see *Case Concerning the Gabcíkovo-Nagymaros Project* (Hungary/Slovakia), Separate Opinion of Vice-president Weeramantry, ICJ Rep 1997, 88. Second, SD also appeared in continental Europe in medieval times, when, between 1300 and 1350, timber use reached a peak leading to almost complete deforestation in Europe. Thus, legislation was adopted based on the principle of sustainability; see Bosselmann K, *The Principle of Sustainability: Transforming Law and Governance* (Second edition, Routledge 2016) 12–19. Third, by the 18th century, sustainability was a recognised principle of European forestry management. Thus, the practice derived the rule that one cannot take more wood out of the forest than can regenerate. In pre-industrial times, the concept was then also applied to other areas of economic activities, such as fishing and hunting; see Kahl W, 'Einleitung: Nachhaltigkeit als Verbundbegriff', in: Kahl W (ed), *Nachhaltigkeit als Verbundbegriff* (Mohr Siebeck 2008) 17.

7   United Nations Conference on the Human Environment (Stockholm Conference) [1972] adopting the Declaration of the United Nations Conference on the Human Environment (Stockholm Declaration) [1973] A/CONF.48/14/REV.1.

8   In 1972, developing countries, would not have agreed to the Stockholm Declaration if economic development and the environment were on an equal footing; see namely, UN General Assembly, 'Charter of Economic Rights and Duties of States', [1974] A/RES/29/3281, Art 30: "The environmental policies of all States should enhance and not adversely affect the present and future development potential of developing countries". For a different opinion, see Barral, above note 5, 35 et seq.

the basic idea of SD started to float within the international community. The Club of Rome, as the first think tank, announced, in 1972, that there are limits to the ways our economy is working thereby ringing an early alarm clock that environmental considerations must be integrated into development processes.[9] A further early attempt to spell out the idea of SD in Resolution 35/56 on the International Development Strategy for the Third United Nations Development Decade of 1980 as this instrument states that "[t]here is need to ensure an economic development process which is environmentally sustainable over the long run".[10] The first time when SD was referred to in the combination sustainable *and* development then was in the 1980 World Conservation Strategy. The document defined SD as "the integration of conservation and development to ensure that modifications to the planet do indeed secure the survival and well-being of all people".[11] Eventually, SD became prominent in 1987 when the report "Our Common Future" of the World Commission on Environment and Development (better known as the Brundtland Report) was first published.[12] In an alarming manner, the Brundtland Report urged the international community to take concrete actions for the transformation from mere development to development that is sustainable so that development "meets the needs of the present without compromising the ability of future generations to meet their own needs".[13]

2.1.1   *The Rio Conference and Its Follow-Up Process*

Despite the developments of the '70s and '80s, it was the 1992 Rio Conference on Environment and Development that marked the starting-point of the global SD agenda laying the basis for its ongoing follow-up process.[14] One major outcome of the Conference was the Rio Declaration on Environment and Development (hereafter: Rio Declaration) and the action plan Agenda 21.[15]

---

9   Meadows DH et al (eds), *The Limits to Growth: A Report for the Club of Rome's Project on the Predicament of Mankind* (Universe Books 1972).
10 UN General Assembly, 'The International Development Strategy for the Third United Nations Development Decade', [1980] A/RES/35/56, para 41.
11 International Union for Conservation of Nature and Natural Resources (today World Conservation Union), 'World Conservation Strategy: Living Resources for Sustainable Development' (IUCN 1980).
12 UN General Assembly, 'Report of the World Commission on Environment and Development', [1987] A/RES/42/187 (hereafter: Brundtland Report).
13 Ibid, para 27.
14 The Rio Conference is also known as the "World Summit". It reunited, from 3 to 14 June 1992, representatives from 176 countries, around 50 international organisations, and numerous non-governmental organisations.
15 Rio Declaration and Agenda 21, above note 1.

The Rio Conference marks the birth of SD because it was the first time that the international community as a whole officially endorsed the concept of SD and established its political legitimation. The Rio Declaration contains a set of 27 principles providing the basis for a definition of SD as the term SD appears in no less than 12 principles of the instrument. The 27 principles should be read together as they present a "package deal".[16] The significance and authority of the Rio Declaration also come from how the principles have been drafted. The majority of the principles start with the injunction that "States shall ..." and only a few use a "States should ..." formulation. Hence, the principles are drafted in a legalistic way, which can lead to norm-creation and further development of the law. This is why the Rio Declaration is, until today, the most useful reference for any legal analysis about SD and the key document for the conceptual articulation of SD.[17]

The Rio Declaration did, however, not single out one specific definition of SD. Rather, one can find three approaches to SD therein. The first approach can be called anthropocentric approach as the Declaration, in its Principle 1, states "human beings are at the centre of concerns" for SD; this links SD to the right to a healthy environment.[18] The second approach is the equity approach, which is sub-divided into *inter*-generational equity (Principle 3) and *intra*-generational equity (Principles 5, 6 and 7). The former points to the equity between current and future generations, whereas the latter seeks to reduce the gap between developed and developing countries, including the eradication of poverty.[19] Third, the Declaration set out the integrative approach (Principle 4), which requires that environmental protection is an integral part of development processes.[20] As will be discussed hereafter, the principle of integration became the main and most important means to achieve SD.

A number of conferences followed the Rio Conference. In 1997, at the Rio+5, the UN General Assembly strengthened the integrative approach and formulated more clearly the balancing purpose of SD, *i.e.* "[e]conomic development, social development and environmental protection are interdependent and

---

16 Boyle and Freestone, above note 5, 3.
17 Barral V, 'Sustainable Development in International Law: Nature and Operation of an Evolutive Legal Norm' (2012) 23 European Journal of International Law 377, 379; Barral, above note 5, 69 et seq; See also Viñuales JE (ed), *The Rio Declaration on Environment and Development: A* Commentary (Oxford University Press 2015) 8.
18 Sands P and Peel J, *Principles of International Environmental Law* (Fourth edition, Cambridge University Press 2018) 41.
19 The equity approach essentially derived from the Brundtland Report, above note 12, para 27.
20 Rio Declaration, Principle 4.

mutually reinforcing components of [SD]".[21] The third social pillar of SD was confirmed at the 2002 World Summit on SD in Johannesburg.[22] The World Summit had a strong focus on the political implementation of SD but could otherwise not replicate the success of Rio.[23] In 2012, the UN General Assembly convened the Rio+20 Summit with the objective to renew political commitments to SD by assessing the progress and failure of SD implementation and by addressing new challenges.[24] One of the novel concepts that were the outcome of the Rio+20 Summit was the idea of the "green economy in the context of SD".[25] This concept has been criticised for not being sufficiently clear in terms of its meaning and because the concept arguably shifts the SD balance more towards economic prioritisation than environmental and social protection.[26] Yet again, Rio+20 also failed in setting out concrete commitments for States.

In 2015, the world's governments adopted Agenda 2030 to provide SD with new impetus confirming their SD commitments since the Rio Conference.[27] The core components of Agenda 2030 are an overall framework of cooperation provided by "peace" and "partnership", within which social development ("the people"), environmental protection ("the planet"), and economic growth and development ("prosperity") are to be pursued. Agenda 2030 confirms that these three pillars are to be balanced and integrated in order to achieve global SD.[28] The main characteristic of Agenda 2030 is the adoption of 17 Sustainable

---

21   UN General Assembly, 'Programme for the Further Implementation of Agenda 21', [1997] A/RES/S-19/2, para 23. However, even though the social development pillar was not explicitly mentioned in the Rio Declaration, one can find a reference to it in the Agenda 21, above note 1, Ch 8.
22   World Summit on Sustainable Development, 'Johannesburg Declaration on Sustainable Development', [2002] A/CONF.199/20, para 5. See also, 'Plan of Implementation of the World Summit on Sustainable Development', para 140(c): "Strengthen and better integrate the three dimensions of [SD] policies and programmes and promote the full integration of [SD] objectives into programmes and policies of bodies that have a primary focus on social issues. In particular, the social dimension of [SD] should be strengthened [...]".
23   Barral, above note 17, 379–380.
24   UN General Assembly, 'Implementation of Agenda 21, the Programme for the Further Implementation of Agenda 21 and the outcomes of the World Summit on Sustainable Development', [2010] A/RES/64/236, para 20(a).
25   UN General Assembly, 'The Future We Want' (endorsing the outcome document of the Rio+20 Conference), [2012] A/RES/66/288, paras 56 et seq.
26   See eg Viñuales JE, 'The Rise and Fall of Sustainable Development' (2013) 22 RECIEL.
27   Agenda 2030, above note 2, para 11: "We reaffirm the outcomes of all major United Nations conferences and summits which have laid a solid foundation for sustainable development and have helped to shape the new Agenda [...]".
28   Ibid, para 2: "We are committed to achieving [SD] in its three dimensions—economic, social and environmental—in a balanced and integrated manner".

Development Goals (SDGs) and 169 targets. SDGs 1–16 are substantive goals and SDG 17 focuses on their implementation: (1) no poverty; (2) zero hunger; (3) good health and well-being; (4) quality education; (5) gender equality; (6) clean water and sanitation; (7) affordable and clean energy; (8) decent work and economic growth; (9) industry, innovation and infrastructure; (10) reduced inequalities; (11) sustainable cities and communities; (12) responsible consumption and production; (13) climate action; (14) life below water; (15) life on land; (16) peace and strong institutions; and lastly (17) the global partnership for achieving the goals. SDG 17 spells out in order to attain SD, "coherent policies [and] an enabling environment for [SD] at all levels and all actors" is necessary.

Looking at the 17 SDGs, it becomes apparent that Agenda 2030 is a mixture of environmental and socio-economic development concerns with the eradication of poverty and zero hunger being the two first goals.[29] Certainly, a beneficial aspect of the SDGs is that they provide a clear set of political action and law-making areas. Whilst the Agenda underlines the central role of international law and the importance of the Rio Principles, it does itself not provide for new principles, nor does it further clarify the scope of the Rio Principles, let alone confirming their binding nature. Agenda 2030 will presumably not have important impacts on the further development of the law on SD. As a result, the Agenda and its SDGs have to be seen as a framework for action and a confirmation of the world's governments to adopt balanced and integrated measures to achieve SD. The policy dimensions that are "revitalized" and strengthened are important as they underline the necessary global partnership to achieve SD.[30] As recalled by SDG 17, policy coherence across government activities is among the critical guidelines to achieve SD. Policy coherence is a systemic issue of SD governance. It requires decision-makers to seek coherence between national and international SD policies, and between the different national policies, i.e. coherence between environmental and economic law; and likewise, between the different international law regimes, such as international trade law and international law and policies combatting climate change.

---

29 The SDGs are also a successor to the eight Millennium Development Goals (MDGs). Those goals were less comprehensive and focussed on poverty eradication and related issues. See UN General Assembly, 'United Nations Millennium Declaration', [2000] A/RES/55/2.

30 See SDG 17: "Strengthen the means of implementation and revitalize the global partnership for sustainable development".

2.1.2 Legal Effects of SD in International Treaties

SD features in a vast number of international instruments.[31] The concept has especially impacted on the evolution of international environmental law. Starting in 1992, SD was enshrined in all three conventional regimes that derived from the Rio Conference. Firstly, SD found its most prominent incorporation in the climate change regime. The United Nation Framework Convention on Climate Change (UNFCCC) referred to SD as an objective to which the parties have the right to and which they are to promote.[32] The UNFCCC also insists that policies and measures to protect the climate system against human-induced change should be "integrated with national development programmes, taking into account that economic development is essential for adopting measures to address climate change".[33] The subsequent Kyoto Protocol, finalised in 1997, lists a number of policies that parties shall adopt to promote SD.[34] Moreover, SD is the central objective of the 2015 Paris Agreement and informs most of its provisions. Under the Paris Agreement, the measures to be adopted by parties must be taken either in the context of SD[35] or in order to promote or foster it.[36] Secondly, SD has also been integrated into the Convention on Biological Diversity, which states that "each contracting party shall, as far as possible and as appropriate: Promote environmentally sound and sustainable development in areas adjacent to protected areas with a view to furthering protection of these areas".[37] The Convention also requires parties to "integrate, as far as possible and as appropriate, the conservation and sustainable use of biological diversity into relevant sectoral or cross-sectoral plans, programmes and policies".[38] Thirdly, the Convention on Drought and Desertification integrates SD by spelling out that "[t]he objective of the Convention is to combat desertification and mitigate the effects of drought [...] in the framework of an integrated approach [...] with a view to contributing to the achievement of sustainable development in the affected areas."

One can distinguish between two modes of dealing with SD in environmental treaties, either defining SD or providing guidelines on implementing SD.[39]

---

31 The focus here is on its most significant formulations. See also, Barral V and Dupuy PM, 'Sustainable Development and Integration' in Aguila Y and Viñuales JE (eds), *A Global Pact for the Environment—Legal Foundations* (C-EENRG Report 2019-1) 46–48.
32 United Nation Framework Convention on Climate Change (UNFCCC), Art 3(4).
33 Ibid.
34 Kyoto Protocol, Art 2(1).
35 Paris Agreement on Climate Change, Arts 2(1), 4, 6(8).
36 Ibid, Arts 6(1), 6(2), 6(4), 6(9), 7, 8, 10(5).
37 Convention on Biodiversity (CBD), Art 8(e).
38 Ibid, Art 6(b).
39 Barral and Dupuy, above note 31, 47.

For instance, the 2002 Antigua Convention made an attempt to define the concept. It defines SD to describe a process, which places the quality of life of human beings "as the centre and primordial subject of development, by means of economic growth with social equity and the transformation of methods of production and consumption patterns, and which is sustained in the ecological balance and vital support of the region. This process implies respect for regional, national and local ethnic and cultural diversity, and the full participation of people in peaceful coexistence and in harmony with nature, without prejudice to and ensuring the quality of life of future generations."[40] In terms of setting out operational guidelines, the Barcelona Convention for the Protection of the Marine Environment and the Mediterranean Coastal Region is noteworthy. Under this instrument, parties are to protect the environment and contribute to the SD of the Mediterranean Sea Area.[41] The convention lists the measures and principles that parties must adopt and respect to that effect. One finds the enumeration of the precautionary principle, the polluter-pays principle, the duty to undertake environmental impact assessments and the promotion of cooperation. Finally, States must also "commit themselves to promote the integrated management of the coastal zones, taking into account the protection of areas of ecological and landscape interest and the rational use of natural resources."[42]

In current draft instruments of international environmental law that are potentially leading to further law development, SD maintains a central position. Here, the IUCN Draft International Covenant on Environment and Development can be mentioned, which formulates its objective in the following terms: "[t]his Covenant provides a comprehensive legal framework with the aim of achieving environmental conservation, an indispensable foundation for sustainable development".[43] The International Law Commission states in the 2008 Draft Articles on the Law of Transboundary Aquifers that SD figures amongst the principles on the basis of which parties shall pursue cooperation and list the concept next to other fundamental principles such as

---

40 Antigua Convention for Cooperation in the Sustainable Development of the Marine and Coastal Environment of the Northeast Pacific, Art 3(1)(a).

41 Barcelona Convention for the Protection of the Marine Environment and the Coastal Region of the Mediterranean, Art 4.

42 Ibid.

43 International Union for the Conservation of Nature (IUCN), 'Draft International Covenant on Environment and Development', Art 1.

sovereign equality, territorial integrity or good faith.[44] It is worth noting that the draft of the Global Pact for the Environment dedicates one provision to SD that sets out that parties "shall pursue" SD.[45] The Global Pact combines SD with the principle of integration in the same provision.[46] As discussed in the next section, the principle of integration has become the main means of SD operationalisation.

2.2 SD and the Dichotomy of Goals and Means

From the evolution of SD, the concept can be summarised in terms of balance (or reconciliation) and mutual supportiveness between three interdependent pillars: economic development, social development and environmental protection.[47] By tracing back the origins of SD it is difficult to ascertain the normative content and legal function of SD more concretely. Therefore, this section questions how does—and how should the balance operate. Is the balance a goal or a means? If it is a goal, by which means can it be achieved? The argument is being made that the principle of integration is the main means for operationalising the SD balance. At the same time, other SD principles are highly relevant for SD and are thus also discussed before a final assessment on the legal function and status of SD is provided.

2.2.1 *The Importance of the Principle of Integration*
Achieving a balance between social, environmental and economic considerations, requires their respective integration. Hence, it is not surprising that

---

44 International Law Commission (ILC), 'Draft articles on the Law of Transboundary Aquifers' (2008) Official Records of the General Assembly, Sixty-third Session, Supplement No 10 (A/63/10), Art 7 (on "General obligation to cooperate").
45 Global Pact for the Environment, available at <https://globalpactenvironment.org>.
46 The provision currently reads: "Parties shall integrate the requirements of environmental protection into the planning and implementation of their policies and national and international activities, especially in order to promote the fight against climate change, the protection of oceans and the maintenance of biodiversity. They shall pursue sustainable development. To this end, they shall ensure the promotion of public support policies, patterns of production and consumption both sustainable and respectful of the environment."
47 See namely the outcome of the Rio+5 and the Johannesburg Conference, above Section 2.1.1.

there is a strong academic consensus that the principle of integration is the key principle to operationalise SD.[48] Principle 4 of the Rio Declaration provides:

> "In order to achieve [SD], environmental protection *shall* constitute an *integral part* of the development process and cannot be considered in isolation from it."[49]

From a textual interpretation, it becomes apparent that the principle is formulated in a mandatory manner. The principle requires that "development decisions, which fail to take any, or adequate account of the environmental consequences cannot contribute to SD".[50] Although this requirement seems to be the principle's main aspect, it also hints to the requirements that environmental policies may not be used at the expense of fundamental development needs.[51]

From the principle of integration, three different levels of SD operationalisation can be deduced. A first level is the level of decision-making, meaning that all levels of governance—governmental and corporate—when deciding upon a given development measure or project should integrate environmental and social factors.[52] A second level of integration, operates at the moment of norm-creation, this means that when new norms are created, be it at the national or international level, they should reflect and adequately weight all three pillars of SD.[53] A third level of integration then operates at the moment of interpreting norms. The argument here is that the principle of integration

---

48 Dernbach J, 'Achieving Sustainable Development: The Centrality and Multiple Facets of Integrated Decisionmaking', (2003) 10 Indiana Journal of Global Legal Studies 247, 247–285: The author argues that all other SD principles depend on the principle of integration; Viñuales JE, 'Introduction', in: Viñuales, above note 17, 25: "Principle 4 formulates the main expression of the concept of SD in the Rio Declaration"; Kovar JD, 'A Short Guide to the Rio Declaration' (1993) 4 Colorado Journal of International Environmental Law and Policy 119, 127: "the principle reflects a more action-oriented approach toward defining [SD] than many of the Declaration's other principles"; See also Schrijver N and Weiss F (eds), *International Law and Sustainable Development: Principles and Practice* (Martinus Nijhoff Publishers 2004) xii-xiii. See Barral V and Dupuy PM, 'Principle 4 Sustainable Development through Integration', in: Viñuales above note 17, 158 and 177; at 158 "Principle 4 of the Rio Declaration is a key principle in the operation of [SD]".
49 Rio Declaration, Principle 4. Emphasis added.
50 Sands P, 'International Law in the Field of Sustainable Development', (1994) 64 British Yearbook of International Law 303, 338.
51 Ibid.
52 Barral and Dupuy, above note 48, 165–166.
53 International Law Association (ILA), 'International Law on Sustainable Development', Toronto Conference [2006], 4.1.

can, in the hands of adjudicators, be a means by which to achieve SD, namely to resolve a conflict and to reconcile different interests.54 In sum, integration is transversal and relevant for decision and law-making as well as law interpretation. Integration should, moreover, take place at the national, regional and international levels. Even though the origins of the concept are international, its implementation requires the support of national and regional legislators and decision-makers.55

The relevance of the principle of integration for the achievement of SD is further underlined by its use by international courts and tribunals. The International Court of Justice (ICJ) found, in 1997, *Gabcíkovo-Nagymaros* that the "[...] need to reconcile economic development with protection of the environment is aptly expressed in the concept of [SD]".56 The ICJ concluded that this means "the Parties should look afresh at the effects on the environment of the operation of the Gabcíkovo power plant".57 The ICJ then enjoined the parties to give effect to the principle of integration by negotiating an agreed solution *integrating* environmental considerations into the original treaty applicable between the two countries.58 In the 2010 *Pulp Mills* case, the ICJ recalled the need for reconciliation between economic development and environmental protection and further emphasised that the balance between them was the "essence" of SD.59 The clearest application of the principle of integration can be found in the inter-State arbitration between Belgium and the Netherlands on the so-called *Iron Rhine Railway*.60 In its final decision, the arbitral tribunal started with the confirmation that "[...] both international and EC law require the integration of appropriate environmental measures in the design

---

54   Ibid, 4.2; see also Barral and Dupuy, above note 48, 167.
55   Ibid.
56   *Case Concerning the Gabcíkovo-Nagymaros Project* (Hungary/Slovakia), Judgement, ICJ Rep 1997, 7, para 140.
57   Ibid, para 140.
58   Ibid, para 141: "It is for the Parties themselves to find an agreed solution that takes account of the objectives of the Treaty, which must be pursued in a joint and integrated way, as well as the norms of international environmental law and the principles of the law of international watercourses."
59   *Case Concerning Pulp Mills on The River Uruguay* (Argentina v Uruguay), Judgment, ICJ Rep 2010, 14, para 177 *in fine*: "Consequently, it is the opinion of the Court that Article 27 embodies this interconnectedness between equitable and reasonable utilization of a shared resource and the balance between economic development and environmental protection that is the essence of [SD]".
60   *Award in the Arbitration regarding the Iron Rhine ("Ijzeren Rijn") Railway between the Kingdom of Belgium and the Kingdom of the Netherlands*, Decision, 24 May 2005, Reports of International Arbitral Awards XXVII, para 59.

and implementation of economic development activities".[61] The tribunal then explicitly referred to Principle 4 of the Rio Declaration and deduced therefrom:

> "Environmental law and the law on development stand not as alternatives but as mutually reinforcing, integral concepts which require that where development may cause significant harm to the environment there is a duty to prevent, or at least mitigate, such harm [...]"[62]

Applying the principle of integration, the tribunal concluded that both Belgium's economic interests and the Netherland's environmental preoccupation are legitimate and need careful balancing.[63] Based on the just discussed case law, the importance of the principle of integration is ascertained.

Whilst the ICJ was reluctant to give the principle any specific legal status in *Gabcíkovo-Nagymaros* in 1997, the *Iron Rhine* Tribunal in 2005 has affirmed that the principle of integration has become part of customary international law as the latter tribunal found that international law would *require* "the integration of appropriate environmental measures in the design and implementation of economic development activities".[64] The verb "require" suggests that this is not a soft law logic but a binding scenario. In its subsequent case law, the ICJ remained reluctant to set out clearly the legal status of SD but found in the 2010 *Pulp Mills* case that a provision contained in the Statute of the River Uruguay that strikes a balance between environmental concerns and economic development is to be considered as being *consistent* with SD. One can argue that the ICJ derives an obligation that when economic development activities are implemented, they need to be counterbalanced by environmental concerns to be consistent with SD. For these reasons, it seems that with respect to the principle of integration, it is possible to consider it as part of customary law.

One question still needs to be resolved, which relates to the nature of the obligation. Does the principle of integration lay down a procedural or rather a substantive obligation? In other words, do environmental considerations only need to be taken into account without necessarily having an impact or outcome? From the stated case law, it is difficult to deduce a substantive obligation.

---

61 Ibid.
62 Ibid.
63 Ibid, paras 220–221. In this precise case, Belgium could reactivate the Iron Rhine Railway but that such endeavour will, simultaneously, necessitate environmental protection measures. See also Barral and Dupuy, above note 48, 173.
64 *Iron Rhine*, above note 60, para 59. Emphasis added.

Whilst the ICJ and the *Iron Rhine* tribunal underlined that integration serves the purpose of implementing and achieving SD, there is no mention of the means. Both, the ICJ and the Iron Rhine tribunal did, however, refer to substantive principles, such as inter-generational equity in *Gabcíkovo-Nagymaros*,[65] or to the duty "to prevent, or at least mitigate" environmental harm in *Iron Rhine*. Both prevention and inter-generational equity are principles connected to SD and form part of the overall legal framework of SD. The question on whether integration is a procedural obligation thus seems to be appropriate in the sense that SD integration takes place in the broader SD framework. In sum, the principle of integration is binding under general international law and it is a procedural obligation.[66] The discretion on how SD integration should look like substantively is guided by other SD principles. This issue is again addressed after presenting the other SD principles.

2.2.2 *Other SD Principles*

A number of standards and principles, of which some seem *a priori* to be principles of specific legal regimes, are closely connected to the realisation of SD. They play an important role in the integrative and balancing exercise of environmental protection, social development and economic growth. Once again, the Rio Declaration constitutes the best point of departure for discussing the principles related to SD. It combines principles of international environmental law with principles of development cooperation. Attempts have been made to resume and to list the key SD principles[67] but there is not yet a conclusive set of standards and principles. The most relevant SD principles, which are themselves interconnected with each other, shall be presented in the following.

2.2.2.1   Inter-Generational Equity

The basic idea behind the inter-generational equity principle is to ensure the distribution of the quality and availability of the Earth's natural resources

---

65 *Gabcíkovo-Nagymaros Project*, above note 56, para 140.
66 Boyle and Freestone came to the same conclusion, see Boyle and Freestone, above note 5, 16–18. For a different take on this particular matter see Barral and Dupuy, above note 31, 49.
67 International Law Association (ILA), 'New Delhi Declaration of Principles of International Law relating to Sustainable Development', [2002] ILA Res 3/2002. The ILA Declaration lists seven principles, namely: sustainable use of natural resources; equity and the eradication of poverty; common but differentiated responsibility (CBDR); precaution; public participation and access to information and justice; the principle of good governance; integration.

between present and future generations.⁶⁸ Thus, aiming at environmental conservation. The principle emerged before the SD agenda. For instance, the preamble of the 1946 International Convention for the Regulation of Whaling states that it is the interest of "nations of the world in safeguarding for future generations the great natural resources represented by the whale stocks".⁶⁹ As mentioned before, when in 1987, the Brundtland Report introduced the era of SD, the principle of inter-generational equity was at the heart of the definition of SD as the focus was on meeting the needs of present generations without compromising those of future ones.⁷⁰ The Rio Declaration prescribed the principle as "[t]he right to development must be fulfilled so as to equitably meet developmental and environmental needs of present and future generations."⁷¹ In terms of normative aspiration, one can retain first, the responsibility of the present generations (including States) to take the needs of the future generations into account. This responsibility includes a duty to conserve resources as to their availability and their quality. Second, one can deduced from the principle the rights of future generations. However, and despite some significant developments at the national law level,⁷² the legal status of the principle under international law is still debatable.

2.2.2.2 Intra-Generational Equity

Typical development principles related to SD are those based on intra-generational equity, *i.e.* reducing the gaps between developed and developing countries. The Rio Declaration established three principles that, in particular,

---

68   See Rio Declaration, Principle 3. Edith Brown Weiss has written extensively on the principle of inter-generational equity. See eg, Brown Weiss E, 'Climate Change, Intergenerational Equity, and International Law', (2008) 9 The Vermont Journal of International Law 615; Brown Weiss E, 'Intergenerational Equity' in *Max Planck Encyclopedia of Public International Law* (Oxford University Press 2013).

69   1946 International Convention for the Regulation of Whaling, 161 UNTS 361, preamble, para 1.

70   Brundtland Report, above note 12.

71   Rio Declaration, Principle 3. See also *Gabcíkovo-Nagymaros Project*, above note 56, para 140.

72   For instance, in 2017, the Indian Supreme Court examined the principle of intergenerational equity in a mining case. Noting that the National Mineral Policy was almost a decade old, it recommended that the political authorities revisit it to take into account this principle. This was done in 2019 with the adoption of a new National Mineral Policy. Supreme Court of India, *Common Cause v Union of India & Ors*, SC WP 2014, Judgment, 2 Aug 2017, 104–106, paras 205–209. See National Mineral Policy 2019, Section 10 entitled 'Intergenerational equity'.

deal with intra-generational equity. It formulated the more general aim of eradicating poverty and the acknowledgement of the special needs of developing countries, and introduced the more concrete principle of common but differentiated responsibilities (CBDR).[73] Based on the CBDR principle, all countries have a responsibility to cooperate and to participate actively in the development of international law and policy in working towards SD, but developed countries have a heavier responsibility due to their different contributions to global environmental degradation.[74] In addition, developed countries should carry out technology and financial transfers in favour of developing countries.[75] CBDR can have concrete implications for special treatments of developing countries generating differentiated legal commitments.[76] The principle finds its most prominent implementation within the climate change regime but has been introduced in a number of other multilateral environmental agreements.[77]

2.2.2.3 Other Principles of International Environmental Law

The body of law on SD should be understood as the intersections between the legal fields of international economic, social (including human rights) and environmental law.[78] Hence, forming part of the environmental law dimension of SD, the principles of prevention and precaution are crucial for achieving SD. According to the principle of prevention, States have a positive duty to ensure that activities under their control do not cause damage to the environment of another State or in areas beyond the limits of their national jurisdiction.[79] The duty to prevent environmental harm is combined with certain procedural duties, such as to cooperate, notify, seek the consent of concerned persons and groups, and conduct environmental impact assessments (EIAs) on envisaged

---

73 Rio Declaration, Principles 5, 6 and 7.
74 Ibid, Principle 7; see also Principle 11.
75 Ibid, Principle 9.
76 Barral, above note 17, 381.
77 See 1992 Framework Convention on Climate Change (UNFCCC), [1994] OJ L 33/13, Arts 3(3) and 4(1); and 2015 Paris Agreement on Climate Change, [2015] OJ L 282/4, Arts 2(2) and 4(3): see also 1989 Basel Convention on the Control of Transboundary Movements of Hazardous Wastes and their Disposal, [1993] OJ L 39/3, Art 10(2).
78 Grosse Ruse-Khan H, 'A Real Partnership for Development? Sustainable Development as Treaty Objective in European Economic Partnership Agreements and Beyond', (2010) 13 Journal of International Economic Law 139, 152.
79 Stockholm Declaration, above note 7, Principle 21; Rio Declaration, above note 1, Principle 2. See also *Gabčíkovo-Nagymaros*, above note 56, para 140.

economic activities and projects.[80] Another highly relevant principle for SD achievement is the precautionary principle.[81] The idea behind precaution is that a lack of scientific certainty about actual or potential effects of a given activity must not be a reason for a State not to take appropriate measures to avoid environmental damage.[82] Other principles of environmental law relevant for SD relate to the sustainable use of natural resources, which seek to maintain the potential of the resources so that the needs of present and future generations are met;[83] and lastly, the polluter-pays principle provides that environmental damage needs to be rectified at source and that the polluter should pay.[84]

2.2.2.4 Human Rights and Fundamental Labour Principles

Principles related to SD are also those associated with its social dimension. According to Principle 1 of the Rio Declaration, human beings "are entitled to a healthy and productive life in harmony with nature". This wording introduces the idea that SD is inseparable from human health, human welfare and the right to life.[85] The international legal framework dealing with the social dimension of SD comprises the generally accepted human rights instruments, such as the 1948 Universal Declaration of Human Rights and the 1966 International Covenant on Economic, Social and Cultural Rights.[86] At the same time, a specific commitment to the right to a healthy environment in binding human rights instruments has not yet found universal acceptance.[87] Linked to human

---

80   Rio Declaration, Principle 17. This principle has been implemented in the 1991 Convention on Environmental Impact Assessment in a Transboundary Context (Espoo Convention) [1992] OJ C 104/7.
81   Rio Declaration, Principle 15.
82   Boisson de Chazournes L and Mbengue MM, 'The Principles of Precaution and Sustainability' in: Cottier T and Nadakavukaren Schefer K (eds), *Elgar Encyclopedia of International Economic Law* (Edward Elgar Publishing 2017) 621–622.
83   Eg 1992 Convention on Biological Diversity, [1993] OJ L 309/3, Art 2: "'*Sustainable use*' means the use of components of biological diversity in a way and at a rate that does not lead to the long-term decline of biological diversity, thereby maintaining its potential to meet the needs and aspirations of present and future generations."
84   Rio Declaration, Principle 16.
85   Francioni F, 'Principle 1: Human Beings and the Environment', in: Viñuales, above note 23, 97.
86   The list can be extended to the International Covenant on Civil and Political Rights [1966], the Convention on the Elimination of all Forms of Discrimination against Women [1979], and the Convention on the Rights of the Child [1989].
87   See African Charter on Human and Peoples' Rights [1981], Art 24; Additional Protocol to the American Convention on Human Rights in the Area of Economic, Social and Cultural Rights Protocol of San Salvador [1988], Art 11.

welfare, moreover, are social protection standards at work. Therefore, fundamental labour principles are connected to SD. The four most important ones are the freedom of association, the elimination of all form of forced labour, the abolition of child labour and the elimination of all forms of discrimination.[88] Indeed, the International Labour Organization (ILO)' normative framework and guidelines are highly relevant for the achievement of SD, not least the eight fundamental ILO Conventions.[89] Additionally, the current ILO "Decent Work Agenda" is at the heart of SD. The Agenda seeks to foster the integration of social protection standards at work in economic development concerns and employment policies.[90]

2.2.2.5 The Principle of Participation

The principle of participation is a key element for the achievement of SD relevant for each of its pillars and dimensions. Participation in the context of SD includes access to information, public participation in decision-making, and transparency and access to justice.[91] Based on this principle, States have a duty to provide various channels of participation to groups and individuals potentially affected by projects, activities or policies. Its main concern is thus to ensure that the interests of all stakeholders are taken into consideration. The principle has its origin in international environmental law and serves as a procedural tool to ensure people's right to a healthy environment. The principle

---

[88]   ILO Declaration on Fundamental Principles and Rights at Work and its Follow-up, adopted by the International Labour Conference at its Eighty-sixth Session, [1988] (last revision 2010).

[89]   The Eight Fundamental ILO Conventions are: (1) Convention Concerning Forced or Compulsory Labour No 29 [1930]; (2) Equal Remuneration Convention No 100 [1951]; (3) Convention Concerning the Abolition of Forced Labour No 105 [1957]; (4) Freedom of Association and Protection of the Rights to Organise Convention No 87 [1948]; (5) Right to Organise and Collective Bargaining Convention No 98 [1949]; (6) Discrimination (Employment and Occupation) Convention No 111 [1958]; (8) Minimum Working Age Convention No 138 [1973]; (8) Worst Forms of Child Labour Convention No 182 [1999].

[90]   Agenda 2030, SDG 8: "Promote sustained, inclusive and sustainable economic growth, full and productive employment and decent work for all." The Decent Work Agenda goes beyond human rights; it seeks to enhance "fair income, security in the workplace and social protection for families, better prospects for personal development and social integration, freedom for people to express their concerns, organize and participate in the decisions that affect their lives and equality of opportunity and treatment for all women and men"; see ILO, 'Decent work for sustainable development: Ensuring no one is left behind', [2017] GB.329/HL/1.

[91]   Rio Declaration, Principle 10.

has been legally endorsed in Europe through the 1998 Aarhus Convention[92] and in America through the 2018 Escazú Convention.[93]

2.2.2.6 The Principle of Good Governance

A concept that is often linked to SD is good governance even though it has a different origin than SD.[94] It was the World Bank in 1989 that first made reference to good governance in a Report assessing the economic performance of Sub-Saharan Africa.[95] The Rio Declaration was silent on the concept. It was only later, with the 2002 Johannesburg Summit, that good governance was linked to SD.[96] Agenda 2030 encompasses the idea of good governance but uses a different formulation. Its SDG 16 states the need for effective, accountable and inclusive institutions by emphasising the rule of law instead of good governance.[97] Since effective regulations at the national level are essential for SD achievement and putting in place the necessary policies, good governance is a prerequisite for SD and thus inherently linked to SD. Moreover, issues of good governance and the rule of law touch upon another important aspect of the SD Agenda, which is the fight against corruption and bribery in all forms.[98] For the SD of a State, good functioning of its institutions is a prerequisite.[99]

2.2.3 *The Legal Nature of SD*

From the previous sections, it became clear that the legal developments surrounding the concept of SD and the Rio follow-up process are significant and far-reaching. Despite the remarkable career of SD, criticism still exists. Especially when it comes to the legal status of SD, most scepticism is expressed. For many the high level of abstraction of SD constitutes the biggest obstacle to

---

92   Convention on Access to Information, Public Participation in Decision-Making and Access to Justice in Environmental Matters (Aarhus Convention), [1997] OJ C 340/145.

93   Regional Agreement on Access to Information, Public Participation and Justice in Environmental Matters in Latin America and the Caribbean (Escazú Convention) [2018].

94   Gehne, above note 5, 8 et seq; Schrijver and Weiss, above note 48, xi.

95   The World Bank, 'Sub-Saharan Africa, From Crisis to Sustainable Growth, A Long-Term Perspective Study' (1989) xii. In its report, the World Bank affirmed the role of private sector initiative and market mechanisms but found that they must go hand-in-hand with good governance, which means "a public service that is efficient, a judicial system that is reliable, and an administration that is accountable to its public".

96   See World Summit on Sustainable Development, above note 24, para. 5.

97   Agenda 2030, SDG 16 and Target 16.3.

98   Ibid, Target 16.5; see also UN Convention against Corruption, [2008] OJ L 287/1.

99   On the rule of law and economic growth nexus, see Davis ED and Trebilcock MJ, 'The Relationship between Law and Development: Optimists versus Skeptics', (2008) American Journal of Comparative Law 56.

have value for law-making and law application. The concept is often said to be a "buzzword", a "chameleon" or an "all-purpose slogan".[100] The following seeks to question this line of criticism and highlights that the discretion that comes with SD should be understood as a legal process and not as a purely political exercise without any normative dimension.

2.2.3.1   Is SD Part of Customary International Law?

Objection to a customary law status of SD has been fierce.[101] The attempt will, however, be made to depict the legal status of SD. The analysis distinguishes here between SD as the ultimate goal *i.e.* objective that the international community decided to pursue and the main tool to achieve SD, which is, the principle of integration. Looking first at SD as an objective, a strong consensus of the international community exists to aspire SD and accepting the concept as an objective. As highlighted hereabove, States have included SD in a great number of treaty provisions, declarations and other instruments in the past thirty years. However, there is no convincing evidence that SD became customary international law. States have never regarded the concept as having the force of law or as being a legal principle. Therefore, *opinio iuris* is lacking.[102] The reason lays within the formulation of SD. A formula that would require States to develop sustainably could have a norm-creating character.[103] Deducing from the formulations of SD that States must develop sustainably is not logical, and it is generally accepted that such an obligation does not exist under general international law.[104] Even the recent Global Pact on the Environment foresees, that States "shall pursue" SD rather than require that development shall be sustainable.[105] States are thus to pursue SD. This, in return, does not prescribe a specific outcome. Based on its formulation and textual inclusions in international treaties, the concept is considered as an ultimate goal or objective for States leaving them with discretion without "constrain[ing] their conduct".[106] It is also impossible to verify through an objective control such as judicial review whether a State has or has not complied with the obligation.[107] Agenda

---

100   Kahl, above note 6, 2.
101   See, Lowe V, 'Sustainable Development and Unsustainable Arguments', in: Boyle and Freestone, above note 5, 24.
102   Ibid, 24.
103   Ibid, 25.
104   Boyle and Freestone, above note 5, 16–17; see also Barral, above note 17, 386.
105   Global Pact for the Environment, above note 45, Art 3.
106   Lowe, above note 101, 23.
107   See more generally for the purposes of soft law, Abi-Saab G, 'Eloge du « droit assourdi ». Quelques reflexions sur le role de la *soft law* en droit international contemporain',

2030 highlighting the international community's latest intentions, points out that the total of the 169 targets have an "aspirational" character.[108]

The customary law character of SD can also be approached from a different angle. It has been argued that the customary law character of SD was not to be found in an *obligation of result* meaning that States must develop sustainably but in an *obligation of means* by rather asking whether States must implement measures to achieve SD.[109] This idea brings us back to the principle of integration. International courts and tribunals were keen in highlighting that integration is necessary to achieve SD and given the legal effects attached to the principle it is not imprudent to consider it as customary international law. As has been argued before, the principle of integration is binding under general international law.[110] Nevertheless, does this finding also provide SD with a customary law status because SD cannot be achieved without the integration of economic, environmental and social concerns? Arguably the answer is negative. As highlighted throughout this chapter, integration is not the only means to achieve SD. There are several means and principles in order to achieve SD. Consequently, one again arrives at the discretion that States enjoy in executing SD as an obligation of means including the choice among the different means (policy and legal integration, equity approaches, human rights, etc.).

To some extent, the discussion is tedious, and one should rather point out that the actual legal status of the concept does not matter that much as it is undisputed that SD deployed and deploys normative effects.[111] It can be questioned why there would have to be a binding character of SD under customary international law to render SD effective. SD as objective having an aspirational character bears many advantages and arguably renders the concept even more effective as if it would be hard law. There are at least two reasons why this is the case. One reason is that soft law is suitable to capture the evolutive character

---

in: *Nouveaux itinéraires en droit. Hommage à François Rigaux* (Bruylant 1993) 67: "La gradation de la marge de discrétion laissée aux sujets dans l'exécutions des obligations de moyen rend cette exécution, au-delà d'un certain point, invérifiable pas un contrôle objectif externe, tel le contrôle judiciaire."

108   Agenda 2030, above note 2, para 55: "[...] Targets are defined aspirational and global, with each Government setting its own national targets guided by the global level of ambition but taking into account national circumstances."

109   It is, in particular, Virginie Barral answering this question in the affirmative. See Barral, above note 17, 386.

110   See above Section 2.2.1.

111   *Iron Rhine*, above note 60, para 58 "The emerging principles, *whatever their current status*, make reference to conservation, management, notions of prevention and of sustainable development, and protection for future generations." Emphasis added.

of SD given that the content of SD changes according to future needs of the international community and has to adapt according to the different needs and possibilities of States. Another reason is that soft law is the instrument *par excellence* to find a maximum of consensus at the international level, thereby setting out a roadmap for collective action.[112] Soft law has for the achievement of SD integration an important facilitating function, which is not to constrain States but to enable them for action. For a goal that can only be achieved through collective action, it is evident that the facilitating function is crucial.

2.2.3.2 SD and Discretion

Henceforth, it is noted that the abstraction of the SD principle and its legal indeterminacy lead to choices that States and other global actors need to make to achieve SD. In the words of Alan Boyle and David Freestone:

> "[...] given the social and economic value judgements involved in deciding on what is sustainable, and the necessity of weighting conflicting factors, of which environmental protection is only one, states inevitably retain substantial discretion in interpreting and giving effect to the alleged principle, unless specific international action has been agreed."[113]

Concerning the inherent discretion, here again, SD has received criticism. It has been argued that the three-pillar structure and the balance of SD would bring about intrinsic conflicts in itself.[114] Therefore, SD would be an empty aspiration as the concept would seek to encompass opposing issues (namely, development *versus* environment) without clarifying their relations.[115] The lack of a clear hierarchy would not allow effective implementation into decision and law-making. By the same token, adjudicators would have no indication or guideline of how to decide upon concrete solutions as one, for instance, in an environmental-development scenario, inevitably needs to prevail.[116] However, there is no international consensus for any priority between the three pillars

---

112   Abi-Saab, above note 107, 67.
113   Boyle and Freestone, above note 5, 16.
114   International Law Association, above note 53, 18; describing SD as having "intrinsic conflicts". See also Kahl, above note 6; speaking of an "internal conflict" ("Binnenkonflikt").
115   Viñuales, above note 26, 6.
116   Kahl, above note 6, 20. A very clear defender of environmental primacy is Klaus Bosselmann, above note 6, 31: "[...] any talk about the equal importance of development and environment, the two-scale model, three-pillar model or 'magic triangle', is purely ideological. The concern for social justice and economic prosperity are valid and important, but secondary compared to the functioning of the Earth's ecological systems".

of SD. Introducing a hierarchy would indeed not reflect the essence of SD. As a result, decision-makers (governments, legislators, and adjudicators) dispose of discretion to operationalise SD.

The discretion that comes with SD is not as troublesome as it might appear. In fact, decision-makers have discretion but are not entirely free in their decision-making when matters of SD are at stake.[117] The normative framework of SD provides enough benchmarks in order to guide such discretion. First, the concept of SD allows decision-makers to distil interdependencies, synergies and trade-off effects through unbundling the three pillars of SD.[118] This is already quite significant as it allows interlinkages to be seen, and it can avoid the separation of policy fields and legal regimes. Second, is it really true that decision-makers have no indication of how to balance them? As argued before, SD goes beyond the principle of integration. The SD legal framework encompasses several principles that provide further normative content that guides discretion. For instance, it should be recalled that SD has a dominant equity component such as inter-generational equity and intra-generational equity. Both serve as benchmarks for the integrative and balancing process. It is thus, on the one hand, the ability of future generations to meet their own needs (inter-generational equity) and, on the other hand, intra-generational equity that requires a fair distribution of the outcomes of development (social and economic) either within one society or between developed and developing countries that should guide the discretion.[119] In other words, SD invites decision-makers, for the sake of moderation and temperance, not to over-use resources and not to forget those parts of society that are in need. Depending on the subject-matter, other international law principles connected to SD should further guide the exercise of discretion, such as prevention and precaution, or basic labour and human rights.

2.2.3.3 Connecting the Dots

From the above one can conclude that SD is an aspirational and guiding legal principle, and it is not a rule as it does not require States to develop sustainably. Nevertheless, States are to pursue SD, but the means of achieving this

---

117 Hart HLA, 'Direction' [written in 1956], (2013) Harvard Law Review 127, 652–665, at 656: "it would be mistaken to identify the notion of discretion with the notion of choice (tout court) [...] discretion is after all the name of intellectual virtue: it is a near-synonym for practical wisdom or sagacity or prudence; it is the power of discerning or distinguishing what in various fields is appropriate to be done [...]".
118 Gehne, above note 5, 108.
119 Barral, above note 17, 380.

goal allows for discretion for policy and law-maker. It is up to them to decide how the balance between the three SD pillars is most appropriate for their society. SD should thus be understood as an aspirational legal principle. It is a "Leitmotiv" *i.e.* a guiding principle of how humans' and States' development should be designed.[120] SD can be compared with other fundamental legal principles that are highly abstract but less controversial to lawyers, such as democracy, the rule of law, the welfare State, freedom and liberty, and finally equality. As a matter of fact, all of these notions require further concretisation and legal implementation, and all function as basic guiding and structuring principles of a given legal order. Like any other abstract principle, SD depends on "contextual concretization" and "factual elaboration" through law-making otherwise it remains a political aspiration and even an empty concept.[121] The significance of SD thus is not simply phenomenological.[122] The concept poses some of the most relevant challenges to international law-making and offers, at the same time, new and innovative solutions to some of the more systemic problems of the international legal order.[123] These accounts on the general conceptual and normative framework of SD under international law, allow us to discuss the contextual concretisation of SD within international investment law.

2.3 The Integration of SD in International Investment Agreements (IIAs)

International investment law has been based on the premise that a quantitative increase in foreign investment advances development. In recent years this premise has lost much of its credence as the underlying twofold assumption, namely the fact that IIAs increase investment inflows and that more foreign investment is beneficial for development, have proven not to be true in all cases.[124] The single-sided nature of traditional IIAs having the main focus on investment protection has, in addition, led States and other global actors to reconsider the costs and the gains of the regime. Departing from traditional

---

120 Ibid, 9.
121 Ibid, 5. Kahl accurately formulated: "Definitionsmerkmale, Teilprinzipien, Regeln und Instrumente eines offenen Prinzips schrittweise und kooperative herauszuarbeiten, ist eine der vornehmsten Aufgaben der (Rechts-)Wissenschaft, aber auch der Praxis, zumal der Gerichte."
122 Boyle and Freestone, above note 5, 1.
123 Ibid.
124 See Section 1.2.

approaches, States seek to readjust the costs and the gains of IIAs aiming to reconcile the economic growth and profitability credo with environmental protection and social development.[125]

The adoption of the United Nations Agenda 2030 for SD further heightens the need to shift the paradigms in the design of IIAs.[126] Meeting the SDGs requires an important amount of investments, with public investments not being sufficient making additional investment coming from the private sector indispensable.[127] In other words, foreign investment continues to be considered as beneficial and necessary to advance development. The paradigm shift resides in paying increasing attention to the quality of such investment in order not simply to achieve development but development that is sustainable.[128] Just as the relationship between foreign investment and development is not straightforward, so the relationship between foreign investment and SD is a complex one.[129] This makes any discussion on how to design IIAs that better

---

125   OECD, 'Harnessing Freedom of Investment for Green Growth', April 2011; see also Harding T and Javorcik BS, 'Investment Promotion and FDI Inflows: Quality Matters' (2013) 59 CESifo Economic Studies 337.
126   UN General Assembly, Agenda 2030, above note 2.
127   Agenda 2030 recognises the vital need for private investment in order to finance the realisation of SD globally; see, Agenda 2030, above note 2, SDG 17: 'Strengthen the means of implementation and revitalize the Global Partnership for Sustainable Development'. According to UNCTAD: "At the global level, total investment needs are in the order of $5 to $7 trillion per year. Total investment needs in developing countries in key SD sectors [such as basic infrastructure, food security, climate change mitigation and adaptation, health, and education] are estimated at $3.3 trillion to $4.5 trillion per year [...] Current investment in these sectors is around $1.4 trillion implying an annual investment gap of between $1.9 and $3.1 trillion". See UNCTAD, *World Investment Report 2014: Investing in the SDGs: An Action Plan* (United Nations 2014) 140.
128   De Schutter O, Swinnen JFM and Wouters J (eds), *Foreign Direct Investment and Human Development: The Law and Economics of International Investment Agreements* (Routledge 2013) 7. "Indeed, even where the arrival of FDI is beneficial for economic growth and poverty reduction of the host country in aggregate terms. The debate has devoted increasing attention to the opportunities and threats it may pose to the well-being and human rights of more vulnerable groups of the population. [...] the question that now emerges is under which conditions FDI should be encouraged, towards which ends it should be channelled, and which regulatory framework should be imposed in order to ensure that it effectively contributes to human development. The question in the past was how to increase the attractiveness of one jurisdiction to foreign investors, and the conclusion of IIAs was seen as an obvious means towards that end. The question is now how to align the incentives in order to maximise the positive impacts of FDI while minimizing the potential negative impacts".
129   See Section 1.2.

integrate SD highly challenging.[130] This partly explains why there are still no conclusive answers to many of the questions on how IIAs should integrate SD, even though a majority of actors involved agree that international investment law should integrate SD.

In order to conceptualise SD integration into international investment law and governance, the following three perspectives on IIAs and their respective function assist in a better understanding:
- IIAs can be a suitable means to promote investments that are advancing SD
- IIAs should not undermine SD-advancing laws and regulations at the domestic level
- IIAs can enhance international cooperation on SD

All the three aspects are present in modern international investment law-making. The concrete treaty drafting differs however. Some States have started to combine investment liberalisation and protection with more international cooperation to advance SD concerns. Certain States are adding new obligations to their treaties, including obligations on investors' conduct. A majority of States have included clarifications on existing disciplines and procedures. And clearly, we are witnessing a heightened conscientiousness around the importance of policy space under investment treaties.

In the endeavour to find solutions, numerous non-State actors are involved in suggesting new ways to draft IIAs.[131] For instance, the United Nations Conference on Trade and Development (UNCTAD) has adopted the 'Investment Policy Framework for Sustainable Development (IPFSD)' in 2012.[132] The latter became an important instrument of reference in the ongoing reform process in international investment law. It shows that the objective of SD can translate into concrete provisions for foreign investment regulation. Another example, are the G20's 'Guiding Principles for Global Investment Policymaking' which provide that investment policies should be "consistent with the objective of

---

130 As discussed in the introductory chapter, it is difficult to prove exact causation between the adoption of an IIA and foreign investment. A reasonable assessment seems to be that IIAs—next to national regulations, the applicable investment contract and several non-legal factors—are part of the overall investment climate relevant for generating investment in- and outflows. Therefore, IIAs play a role in attracting investment.

131 Eg UNCTAD, Organization for Economic Co-operation and Development (OECD), G20, Commonwealth Secretariat, Association of Southeast Asian Nations (ASEAN), African Union (AU), Southern African Development Community (SADC), International Institute for Sustainable Development (IISD).

132 UNCTAD, 'Investment Policy Framework for Sustainable Development (IPFSD)' (United Nation 2015).

[SD]".¹³³ Moreover, the OECD has a number of policy instruments on investment and SD such as its Policy Framework which has as objective "to mobilise private investment that supports steady economic growth and sustainable development".¹³⁴ The OECD was also one of the first organisations to adopt principles and guidelines on corporate social responsibility (CSR) with its Guidelines for Multinational Enterprises that were first adopted in 1976.¹³⁵

The following examines the purposes of SD integration into IIAs as threefold: IIAs are a suitable means to promote investments that advances SD (2.4.), IIAs should not undermine SD-advancing laws and regulations at the domestic level (2.5.), and IIAs can enhance international cooperation on SD (2.6.). The three ways of examining SD integration into international investment law-making set common grounds based upon which the various actors then deviate according to their policy choices and development needs. The remainder of this chapter provides a succinct yet critical account of the academic and policy debate surrounding the topic of SD integration into IIAs. Many of the aspects discussed are new and to some extent law-making is in a testing phase. For other aspects, such as the debate on the definition of an investment, arguments are more developed and rich arbitral case law exist on the matter. Therefore, in terms of methodology, it should not come as a surprise that the following analysis treats certain questions in the debate in greater detail than others.

2.4 IIAs and SD-Advancing Investment

Foreign private investment is needed to achieve SD in general including the SDGs, in other words, helping to close the financing gaps for SD. The key endeavour is that IIAs should channel sustainable investment as well as stimulating investment in areas where capital is most needed.¹³⁶ Whilst this sounds straightforward, effectively harnessing investment for SD by using IIAs is among the most difficult aspects in practice given that the positive effects of

---

133   G20, 'Guiding Principles for Global Investment Policymaking', Principle V; available at <http://www.oecd.org/daf/inv/investment-policy/G20-Guiding-Principles-for-Global-Investment-Policymaking.pdf>.
134   OECD, 'Policy Framework for Investment 2015 Edition' (OECD Publishing 2015).
135   OECD, 'OECD Guidelines for Multinational Enterprises', annexed to 2000 OECD Declaration on International Investment and Multinational Enterprises, DAFFE/IME(2000)/20; (2001) 40 ILM 237 as amended.
136   Ibid, 131.

international investment are not automatic.¹³⁷ Ideally, IIAs steer investment specifically towards the SDG-related sectors, such as infrastructure, renewable energy, water and sanitation, food security, health and education.¹³⁸ It is largely accepted that channelling and harnessing investment into the SDGs can be realised at the domestic law level, though questions concerning the role of IIAs in this respect remain debated: how can IIAs complement domestic law in making sure that only SD-advancing investments have access to the host State market and enjoy protection under the IIA? Should investment protection be strictly limited to "sustainable" investments? How could this be guaranteed? Can this be ensured by restraining the definition of an investment? How should investment liberalisation be regulated? States have different answers to these questions and States' choices vary in terms of how to use their IIAs to channel sustainable investment. States may favour linking the admission of foreign investment to host countries' SD strategies and limiting, where appropriate, market access for investments that are considered unsustainable. IIAs can restrain investment protection standards for certain investment activities, which are considered not to be beneficial for SD by limiting the definition of covered investments under the IIA. These approaches go beyond States agreeing to merely promote sustainable investment in the preamble of the IIA or through hortatory treaty provisions. At the same time, general statements on the need to promote investment in sectors beneficial for the achievement of SD are not novel and are relatively uncontroversial; additionally, these provisions have not provoked real-life effects.¹³⁹ Therefore, the debate on how to effectively ensure sustainable investment outcomes should focus on how the notion of investment should be defined in IIAs and how and if markets should be liberalised for foreign companies.

2.4.1 Not Subsidising Unsustainable Investment: The Definition of Investment

The starting point for the discussion on how to use IIAs as a beneficial tool for SD originates from those instances where foreign investment activities have

---

137 Johnson L, 'FDI, International Investment and the Sustainable Development Goals' in: Krajewski M and Hoffmann RT (eds), *Research Handbook on Foreign Direct Investment* (Edward Elgar Pub 2019) 128. See Section 1.2.
138 UNCTAD, IPFSD, 6. See also Dupuy PM and Viñuales JE (eds), *Harnessing Foreign Investment to Promote Environmental Protection: Incentives and Safeguards* (Cambridge University Press 2013).
139 For an overview on such treaty language, see Gordon K and Pohl J, 'Environmental Concerns in International Investment Agreements: A Survey' (2011) OECD Working Papers on International Investment 2011/01.

caused clear negative effects. A first step in integrating SD into IIAs is thus to ensure that these treaties do not "subsidise" SD-negative investment.[140] In this vein, they should discourage investments which are harmful for SD by not providing them with treaty protection. SD-negative investments are those that cause important environmental degradation, that result from and continue with corrupt practices and those violating basic labour standards. From a climate policy perspective, this can also include investments in fossil fuel extraction and related infrastructure.

Some governments have started to evaluate which types of investment deserve the protection standards and guarantees offered by the IIA. Not to provide treaty protection to those investment that harm socio-economic or environmental public interests seems logical because the cost-benefit calculation of the treaty conclusion then includes, predominately, costs for the host State.[141] The definition of investment contained in IIAs has been, since the start of the debate on SD and international investment law, amongst the most decisive provisions. This comes with the common trend among States to reduce the scope of the definition so as to more precisely circumscribe what constitutes a "covered" investment under IIAs. Whilst this is also being done for reasons of predictability, the now longer and more nuanced investment definitions contain several aspects that are relevant for SD matters.

2.4.1.1   Foreign Direct Investments versus Financial Investments

IIAs traditionally define investments as meaning "any kind of assets" owned or controlled directly or indirectly by an investor of one of the contracting parties.[142] These definitions reflect the traditional focus of IIAs as being to protect and promote all types of investment on the assumption that any investment is beneficial for economic growth and development. In the context of seeking to channel foreign investment into the SDGs, there is a need to distinguish between the different types of investment and to question if all kinds of assets are in fact likely to promote SD outcomes. A first consideration is the distinction between FDI and portfolio investment. It is mainly business activity in the form of FDI that is relevant for advancing development purposes due to the

---

140   Johnson L, Sachs L and Lobel N, 'Aligning International Investment Agreements with the Sustainable Development Goals' (2020) Columbia Journal of Transnational Law 58, 11. In the words of the authors, IIAs with investment protection standards and stringent enforcement mechanism "act as regulatory incentives that, even if not effective at attracting investment, effectively subsidise foreign investment".
141   Ibid, 11–12.
142   See Section 6.3.

long-term relationship and significant degree of influence over the management of the entity.¹⁴³ FDI is, therefore, not only beneficial due to the injection of long-term capital but it is likely to generate infrastructure and employment in the host State and bring about transfers of knowledge and technology.¹⁴⁴

Portfolio investment is often associated with investment in debt and equity securities that is only intended for financial gains and thus the extent to which this type of investment has the potential to advance the SDGs needs to be scrutinised in particular.¹⁴⁵ From a SD perspective, several arguments can be made in favour of excluding portfolio investment from the scope of IIAs. First, the positive development implications of portfolio investment are very low since this type of investment can include short-term and speculative investment, which often does not generate positive effects on the host State economy.¹⁴⁶ In particular, the above-mentioned positive effects of FDI, such as increased employment possibilities or knowledge and technology transfers are generally not produced through capital commitments in the form of portfolio investment. Second, the volatility of portfolio investment might be problematic for certain States and impact their economic development planning.¹⁴⁷ Third, portfolio investment and investors are less dependent on the protection standards offered under an IIA. The reasons are that portfolio investments generally have no sunk costs and the risk of government interference is relatively lower when compared to FDI.¹⁴⁸ Portfolio investors are more likely to be able to recover the value of their investment and withdraw them from a host country if the host country acts contrary to their interests. Hence, if the correlation between an IIA and attracting portfolio investment is relatively low (compared

---

143   The OECD provides that FDI is "a category of cross-border investment made by a resident in one economy (the direct investor) with the objective of establishing a lasting interest in an enterprise (the direct investment enterprise) that is resident in an economy other than that of the direct investor. [...] The 'lasting interest' is evidenced when the direct investor owns at least 10% of the voting power of the direct investment enterprise." See OECD Benchmark Definition of Foreign Direct Investment (4th ed, OECD 2008) 17.
144   Johnson, above note 137, 127.
145   The International Monetary Fund defines portfolio investment as anything that is not FDI; see, IMF, *Balance of Payments and International Investment Position Manual*, available at <https://www.imf.org/external/pubs/ft/bop/2007/bop6comp.htm>.
146   UNCTAD, IPFSD, 90.
147   Commonwealth Secretariat, prepared by VanDuzer J, Simons P and Mayeda G, *Integrating Sustainable Development into International Investment Agreements: A Guide for Developing Countries* (Commonwealth Secretariat 2012) 61 (hereafter: Commonwealth Secretariat).
148   This is particularly so when compared with investment in the extractive sector, where sunk costs are high and extractive investments bear a higher risk of being subject to regulatory action.

to FDI) then it becomes questionable why IIA protection should be expanded to this type of investment.

At the same time, excluding portfolio investments from the scope of the definition might also have its drawbacks. To exclude them means to considerably narrow the scope of the protection under the IIA and eventually it can result in a country being less attractive for foreign investment.[149] Moreover, it cannot be completely excluded that portfolio investment contributes, to a certain degree, to SD or the SDGs. Whilst the inclusion of portfolio investment extends treaty protection to many relatively small investments, by taking them together these investments may be substantial and complementary. Put differently, for FDI to be successful it may occur that additional portfolio investment is required in order to sustain the business activity.[150] In addition, foreign portfolio investment might also be beneficial for domestic investors in the form of local companies as it can provide the injection of additional capital whilst local companies remain in control of their business. Deciding upon the question of including or excluding portfolio investment ultimately becomes a policy choice for States.

Despite the controversies surrounding the inclusion or exclusion of portfolio investment, there is a growing consensus among the majority of States to exclude certain other assets that should not benefit from IIA protection.[151] This can include sovereign debt instruments, commercial contracts for the sale of goods and services, assets for non-business purposes and might also include intellectual property rights especially when they are not protected under domestic laws.[152] The named assets clearly have a relatively low or no SDG-advancing potential.[153]

2.4.1.2 The Contribution to the Host State's Development

In past arbitral case law, tribunals have repeatedly engaged in defining the concept of investment in general to provide an objective meaning for what constitutes an investment.[154] In particular, ICSID tribunals found that even

---

149 Commonwealth Secretariat, above note 147, 51 et seq.
150 Ibid, 64.
151 Cazala J, 'La réaffirmation de l'Etat en matière de définition des investissements et investisseurs protégés' in: El Ghadban T, Mazuy C-M and Senegacnik A (eds), *La protection des investissements étrangers: vers une réaffirmation de l'État? = The protection of foreign investments: a reaffirmation of the State?: Actes du colloque du 2 juin 2017* (2018) 49.
152 UNCTAD, IPFSD, 90.
153 Commonwealth Secretariat, above note 147, 64.
154 Schreuer C et al (eds), *The ICSID Convention: A Commentary* (2nd ed, Cambridge University Press 2009) 128, pt 152–153.

though the ICSID Convention did not contain a definition of an investment, there existed a definition independent from the applicable IIA or BIT.[155] The tribunal in *Fedax v. Venezuela* first developed certain criteria in order to determine the existence of an investment.[156] According to the *Fedax* tribunal "[t]he basic features of an investment have been described as involving a certain duration, a certain regularity of profit and return, assumption of risk, a substantial commitment and a significance for the host State's development".[157] These four criteria were subsequently reiterated in *Salini v. Morocco* and became from then on the well-known *Salini* test.[158] However, subsequent arbitral case law was divided in terms of what characteristics are to be present and on whether they are mandatory in the sense of constituting a condition for ICSID arbitration. More precisely, the controversial issue is whether the characteristics are jurisdictional conditions under Article 25 of the ICSID Convention. As of today, States have started to explicitly mention the characteristics of an investment in their IIAs. Most States opt for the characteristics of an investment to include: "a certain duration, the commitment of capital or other resources, the expectation of gain or profit or the assumption of risk". Clearly, the most contentious characteristic remains "the contribution to the host State's development", abandoned by many ICSID tribunals in favour of a lighter *Salini* test.[159]

Form an SD perspective the issue of whether or not to mention "the contribution to the host State's development" is a key question. At first sight, it seems to be a tool to promote and channel investments that contribute to SD. By introducing the host State's development into the characteristics of an investment, the definition creates a test of the relationship between the investment activity and the (beneficial, neutral or non-beneficial) impacts for the host State's economy.[160] Adding the characteristic of the contribution to the host

---

155 In the words of the tribunal in *Joy Mining v Arab Republic of Egypt*, ICSID Case No ARB/03/11, Award on Jurisdiction, 6 Aug 2004, para 50: "The parties to a dispute cannot by contract or treaty define as investment, for the purpose of ICSID jurisdiction, something which does not satisfy the objective requirements of Article 25 of the Convention".
156 *Fedax NV v The Republic of Venezuela*, ICSID Case No ARB/96/3, Decision of the Tribunal on Objections to Jurisdiction, 11 July 1997.
157 Ibid, para 43.
158 *Salini Costruttori SpA and Italstrade SpA v Kingdom of Morocco*, ICSID Case No ARB/00/4, Decision on Jurisdiction, 23 July 2001.
159 Sornarajah M, *Resistance and Change in the International Law on Foreign Investment* (Cambridge University Press 2015) 163: "It is not far-fetched to argue that there is an ideological schism that dominates the debate on the definition of investment".
160 SADC Model BIT, Commentary, 13.

State's development seems to be logical as it reads that only those investments that are beneficial for development purposes fall under the scope of the investment definition and thus the scope of IIA protection. Yet, the inclusion of this element, especially if it was to operate as a jurisdictional requirement, must be assessed against its legal predictability and practical feasibility. Indeed, a number of questions arise: How would a tribunal assess a contribution to development? Should the contribution be to development in general or to economic or *sustainable* development? How could a tribunal make an objective assessment given its limited resources and expertise?

These questions have been vigorously debated in arbitral case law. Subsequently to the award in *Salini v. Morocco*, tribunals have referred to the four criteria in a number of cases.[161] In most of these cases, the tribunals were satisfied that the economic activity under scrutiny met these criteria.[162] Based on these cases it is not fully clear if the elements of the *Salini* test were understood as essential requirements, *i.e.* jurisdictional conditions or mere indicators highlighting the typical features of an investment.[163] The contribution to the host State's development was considered to be a jurisdictional condition in the annulment decision in *Patrick Mitchell v. Congo*.[164] In this case, the annulment committee found that the activity of a law firm could not be characterised as an investment under the ICSID Convention given that there was no contribution to the development of the host State.[165] In the case *Malaysian Historical Salvors v. Malaysia*, the sole arbitrator found that a contract dealing with the service of a marine salvage outfit that retrieved pieces of Chinese

---

161 Schreuer et al, above note 154, 130, pt 159. Eg, *Saipem v Bangladesh*, ICSID Case No ARB/05/7, Decision on Jurisdiction, 21 March 2007, paras 99–102, at 99: "(T)he notion of investment implies the presence of the following elements: (a) a contribution of money or other assets of economic value, (b) a certain duration, (c) an element of risk, and (d) a contribution to the host State's development." See also, *Jan de Nul v Egypt*, ICSID Case No ARB/04/13, Decision on Jurisdiction, 16 June 2006, paras 91–96; *Noble Energy v Ecuador*, ICSID Case No ARB/05/12, Decision on Jurisdiction, 5 March 2008, paras 125–135.
162 Ibid.
163 Schreuer et al, above note 154, 130, pt 159.
164 *Patrick Mitchell v The Democratic Republic of Congo*, ICSID Case No ARB/99/7, Decision on the Application for Annulment of the Award, 1 Nov 2006.
165 Ibid, para 33: "The *ad hoc* Committee wishes nevertheless to specify that, in its view, the existence of a contribution to the economic development of the host State as an essential—although not sufficient—characteristic or unquestionable criterion of the investment, does not mean that this contribution must always be sizable or successful; and, of course, ICSID tribunals do not have to evaluate the real contribution of the operation in question. It suffices for the operation to contribute in one way or another to the economic development of the host State, and this concept of economic development is, in any event, extremely broad but also variable depending on the case."

porcelain from the Strait of Malacca was not an investment under the ICSID Convention because the undertaking would not "make any significant contribution to Malaysia's economic development".[166] However, this decision was annulled by an *ad hoc* committee, finding not only that an ICSID tribunal may exceed its powers by failing to exercise jurisdiction, but also that the *Salini* elements did not establish jurisdictional requirements which had to be fulfilled in a cumulative fashion, but rather represented typical characteristics.[167]

The two cases thus gave the criterion of the contribution to the host State's development a decisive role. This approach has been criticised and clearly rejected by most tribunals.[168] For instance, the tribunal in *Saba Fakes v. Turkey*, first considered the three criteria (a substantial contribution of resources, a certain duration and risk) to be "sufficient and necessary to define an investment within the framework of the ICSID Convention".[169] And second, the tribunal explicitly rejected the idea that the contribution to the host State's development would constitute a criterion that has to be taken into account.[170] Along the same lines, the tribunal in *Pey Casado v. Chile* also rejected the said criterion. This tribunal added that it is difficult for such a condition to be established and that the said fourth criterion was in fact absorbed by the three non-controversial elements of the *Salini* test.[171] In this respect, the tribunal pointed to a central element for critique which is the practical feasibility of assessing the impact of

---

166 *Malaysian Historical Salvors v Malaysia*, ICSID Case No ARB/05/10, Award, 17 May 2007, para 143: "The Tribunal finds that [...] the Contract did not make any significant contributions to the economic development of Malaysia. The Tribunal considers that these factors indicate that, while the Contract did provide some benefit to Malaysia, they did not make a sufficient contribution to Malaysia's economic development to qualify as an "investment" for the purposes of Article 25(1) or Article 1(a) of the BIT. [...]".
167 *Malaysian Historical Salvors, SDN, BHD v Malaysia*, ICSID Case No ARB/05/10, Decision on the Application for Annulment, 16 April 2009, paras 74 and 83.
168 *KT Asia Investment Group BV v Republic of Kazakhstan*, ICSID Case No ARB/09/8, Award, 17 Oct 2013; *Saba Fakes v Republic of Turkey*, ICSID Case No ARB/07/20, Award, 14 July 2010; *Victor Pey Casado v Chile*, ICSID ARB/98/2, Award, 8 May 2008.
169 *Saba Fakes v Turkey*, above note 168, para 110.
170 Ibid, para 111.
171 *Pey Casado v Chile*, above note 168, para 232: "[...] L'exigence d'une contribution au développement de l'Etat d'accueil, difficile à établir, lui paraît en effet relever davantage du fond du litige que de la compétence du Centre. Un investissement peut s'avérer utile ou non pour l'Etat d'accueil sans perdre cette qualité. Il est exact que le préambule de la Convention CIRDI évoque la contribution au développement économique de l'Etat d'accueil. Cette référence est cependant présentée comme une conséquence, non comme une condition de l'investissement: en protégeant les investissements, la Convention favorise le développement de l'Etat d'accueil. Cela ne signifie pas que le développement de l'Etat d'accueil soit un élément constitutif de la notion d'investissement. [...]".

the investment on the (economic) development of a host State as an element of jurisdiction *ratione materiae*.[172] Some argue that it is unfeasible to assess the criterion because of the fact that the term "investment" is future-oriented and therefore, the question that comes up is from what point one has to determine whether an investment has contributed or not.[173] This is a question that cannot be answered in the abstract or, as the tribunal in *Phoenix* v. *Czech Republic* put it, "the contribution of an international investment to the *development* of the host State is impossible to ascertain [...]."[174] In the eyes of some authors, the economic development requirement can be assessed and ultimately is relevant for better defining the notion of investment.[175] Their main argument is that there are certain benchmarks that a tribunal can consider in order to determine whether the investment has contributed to the host State's development or not.[176] From this perspective, a reference to the contribution to the host State's development can provide legal grounds for the tribunal to deny treaty protection to investment that clearly does not meet or even undermines development.

In sum, in arbitral case law one finds three different approaches.[177] The first (typical elements) approach, which has been suggested by Christoph

---

172 The feasibility is doubted by a number of authors and tribunals. See, Van Aaken A and Lehmann TA, Sustainable Development and International Investment Law' in: Echandi R and Sauvé P (eds), *Prospects in International Investment Law and Policy* (Cambridge University Press 2013) 335. For instance, LESI v People's Democratic Republic of Algeria, ICSID ARB/03/8, Award, 10 Jan 2005, para 13, last sentence: "Il ne paraît en revanche pas nécessaire qu'il réponde en plus spécialement à la promotion économique du pays, une condition de toute façon difficile à établir et implicitement couverte par les trois éléments retenus"; see also *Victor Pey Casado v Chile*, above note 168, paras 374–375. This tribunal found that from the preamble of the ICSID Convention, one cannot deduce a condition for the existence of an investment.

173 Van Aaken and Lehmann, above note 172, 335.

174 *Phoenix Action, Ltd v Czech Republic*, ICSID Case No ARB/06/5, Award, 15 April 2009, para 85.

175 Jezewski M, 'Development Considerations in Defining Investment', in: Cordonier Segger M-C, Gehring MW and Newcombe AP (eds), *Sustainable Development in World Investment Law* (Kluwer Law International 2011) 234–235.

176 García-Bolívar OE, 'Economic Development at the Core of the International Investment Regime', in Brown C and Miles K (eds), *Evolution in Investment Treaty Law and Arbitration* (Cambridge University Press 2011) 603. The author lists: (a) the extent to which the investment benefits the public interest; (b) whether any transfer of technological knowledge or 'know-how' from investor to the host State has taken place; (c) the degree to which the investment has enhanced the GDP of the host country; (d) whether the investment has had a positive impact on the host State (at 603).

177 Gaillard E, 'Identify or Define? Reflection on the Evolution of the Concept of Investment in ICSID Practice' in: Binder C et al (eds), *International Investment Law for the 21st Century: Essays in Honour of Christoph Schreuer* (Oxford University Press 2009) 406 et seq.

Schreuer is to see the criteria as *flexible*, indicating the typical characteristics of an investment.[178] In this understanding, the contribution to the host State's development becomes a possible element to be looked at, but not a jurisdictional condition. The second (jurisdictional) approach, in contrast, considers each of the four criteria as fixed, meaning that they must be fulfilled in order to find the existence of an investment and thus also the contribution to the host State's development becomes a jurisdictional condition. The third approach explicitly excludes the fourth *Salini* criterion. States are to choose between one of the approaches. The most practical and least radical is the first approach of flexible criteria. It allows tribunals to take all the elements into account not as necessary requirements, but rather as typical features. Making the contribution to the host State's development, a jurisdiction condition presumes that it is possible to legally circumscribed *ex ante* and in abstract terms what constitutes a sustainable investment and is therefore not convincing. The notion of development brings into the analysis a strong economic and social dimension, and in the case of *sustainable development* this is coupled with an additional environmental dimension. Excluding the criterion is also not the right option as it does not take into account the final purpose IIAs ought to have, which is SD. The first approach of flexible criteria thus seems to be the middle ground that would allow tribunals to take all the elements into account not as necessary requirements but rather as yardsticks.

2.4.1.3   The Legality Requirement

Given that an "in accordance with host State's laws" requirement can deprive investors of the remedy of treaty protection including investor-State dispute settlement, it is argued that the requirement could function as an incentive for sustainable foreign investment activities (on the assumption that host State's laws are written and applied to further SD).[179] If the investment was not

---

The author speaks of "two competing methodologies" and hereby distinguishes between those that see the criteria as fixed and those that see them as flexible criteria.

178   Schreuer et al, above note 154, 128, at pt 153: "These features should not necessarily be understood as jurisdictional requirements but merely as typical characteristics of investment under the Convention."; 133, at pt 171: "The development in practice from a descriptive list of typical features towards a set of mandatory legal requirements is unfortunate"; 133, at 172: "A rigid list of criteria that must be met in every case is not likely to facilitate the task of tribunals or to make decisions more predictable."

179   See for more details, Carlevaris A, 'The Conformity of Investments with the Law of the Host State and the Jurisdiction of International Tribunals' (2008) 9(1) The Journal of World Investment and Trade 35; Moloo R and Khachaturian A, 'The Compliance with the Law Requirement in International Investment Law', (2011) 34(6) Fordham International Law Journal 1473.

made in accordance with the applicable law of the host State, a tribunal would consider that an investment was not covered by the treaty. In other words, "in accordance with host State law" provisions concern the legality or "validity" of an investment and not whether there is an investment to begin with.[180] It prevents IIAs from protecting an investment that should not be protected due to its illegality.[181] In this sense, the requirement can function as an incentive for foreign investors to comply with host States' regulations, as in the case of non-compliance, they would no longer benefit from the protections of the treaty.[182]

A legality requirement bears the potential for host States to enact national legislation applicable to the establishment of foreign investment that includes rules and procedures that take into account social and environmental standards. A good example hereto are national law requirements for prospective investors to conduct environmental and social impact assessments (ESIAs).[183] In the absence of the procedural step of obtaining an approved ESIA, the investor's investment is not in accordance with host State laws.[184] In particular, in the case of mining investment, for the granting of mining rights (constituting

---

180   See *Salini v Morocco*, above note 158, para 46: "In focusing on *"the categories of invested assets [...] in accordance with the laws and regulations of the aforementioned party,"* this provision refers to the validity of the investment and not to its definition. More specifically, it seeks to prevent the Bilateral Treaty from protecting investments that should not be protected, particularly because they would be illegal".

181   Ibid. See also, *Fraport v Philippines,* ICSID Case No ARB/03/25, Award I, 16 Aug 2007, para 394: "[...] A failure to comply with the national law to which a treaty refers will have an international legal effect".

182   For more details, see Hepburn J, 'In Accordance with Which Host State Laws? Restoring the "Defence" of Investor Illegality in Investment Arbitration' (2014) 5 Journal of International Dispute Settlement 531.

183   An ESIA refers to the process of environmental authorisation instituted in national legislation and which usually obliges large-scale project to carry out an impact assessment and hold consultations with local stakeholders. For more details, see Intergovernmental Forum on Mining, Minerals, Metals and Sustainable Development (IGF), 'Legal Framework of Environmental and Social Impact Assessment in the Mining Sector', Jan 2019; available at <https://www.iisd.org/sites/default/files/publications/igf-esia-background-en.pdf>.

184   *Cortec Mining Kenya Limited, Cortec (Pty) Limited and Stirling Capital Limited v Republic of Kenya,* ICSID Case No ARB/15/29, Award, 22 Oct 2018, para 319: "The Tribunal concludes that for an investment such as a licence, which is the creature of the laws of the Host State, to qualify for protection, it must be made in accordance with the laws of the Host State. The claims do not relate to bricks and mortar, as earlier observed. The claimed rights flow from a document which has no legal existence or effect, and cannot therefore give rise to compensable rights."

the validity basis of the investment) ESIAs are increasingly an obligatory procedural step under national laws.[185]

In arbitral case law, it has become commonplace for respondent States to allege that investors have not complied with domestic law in making their investment, and therefore, should be prevented from pursuing their claims. Arbitral tribunals have approached the question of whether the compliance with a host State's law is a jurisdictional or admissibility requirement or an issue related to the merits of the dispute.[186] Often, these cases have involved allegations of corruption. As the host State might, in cases of corruption, be likewise in violation of its laws, it has been argued that it would be more beneficial, also from a sustainable development point of view, to consider the illegality of the investment at the merits stage.[187] Otherwise, if jurisdiction is denied the host State could easily escape any legal consequences from an investment tainted by corruption.[188] Arbitral tribunals have indeed been aware of this somewhat unsatisfying solution of denying jurisdiction in the case of corruption; however, their responsibility to promote the rule of law "which entails that a court or tribunal cannot grant assistance to a party that has engaged in a corrupt act" has been underlined.[189]

---

[185] As illustrated in eg *Cortec Mining v Kenya*, above note 184; *William Ralph Clayton, William Richard Clayton, Douglas Clayton, Daniel Clayton and Bilcon of Delaware Inc v Government of Canada*, PCA Case No 2009-04, Award on Jurisdiction and Liability of 17 March 2015; *Bear Creek Mining Corporation v Republic of Peru*, ICSID Case No ARB/14/2, Award, 30 Nov 2017; *Copper Mesa Mining Corporation v Republic of Ecuador*, PCA No 2012-2, Award, 15 March 2016.

[186] For a list of case law, see Diel-Gligor K and Hennecke R, 'Investment in Accordance with the Law' in: Bungenberg M et al (eds), *International Investment Law—A Handbook* (CH BECK; Hart; Nomos 2015) 570–571, pts 11–15; see also, Reinisch A, 'Jurisdiction and Admissibility in International Investment Law', (2017) 16 *The Law and Practice of International Courts and Tribunals* 21.

[187] Van Aaken and Lehmann, above note 172, 335–336.

[188] Ibid. It should be noted that some IIAs deal with corruption and other illegal investments through specific provisions on corruption.

[189] Illustrative on this point is *Metal-Tech Ltd v Republic of Uzbekistan*, ICSID Case No. ARB/10/3, Award, 4 October 2013, para 389: "the conclusion that the claims are barred as a result of corruption, the Tribunal is sensitive to the ongoing debate that findings on corruption often come down heavily on claimants, while possibly exonerating defendants that may have themselves been involved in the corrupt acts. It is true that the outcome in cases of corruption often appears unsatisfactory because, at first sight at least, it seems to give an unfair advantage to the defendant party. The idea, however, is not to punish one party at the cost of the other, but rather to ensure the promotion of the rule of law, which entails that a court or tribunal cannot grant assistance to a party that has engaged in a corrupt act."

A limitation that has been pointed out concerning the provisions on the investment compliance with host State law has been that the clauses generally require compliance with domestic laws only at the establishment phase and are silent on non-compliance during the operation of the investment.[190] It is thinkable to draft provisions in an IIA that require compliance from the investment on an ongoing basis throughout the life of the investment. However, a requirement for continuous legality should not be included in the investment definition. It would make it very easy for the host State to avoid complying with the substantive investment protection standards guaranteed to the investor by changing its laws to make the investor's investment non-compliant. The tribunal in *Copper Mesa v. Ecuador* added that it would be a "harsh result" to deprive the investor of the opportunity to exercise any arbitral remedy "if the investor (or its agents or employees) ever committed a breach of the host State's laws during the life of its investment".[191] To ensure responsible investment throughout the life of an investment activity, in the sense that investment activities operate in compliance with social standards and environmental norms, either national law comes into play or international corporate social responsibility (CSR) standards, or even direct investor obligations enshrined in the IIA.[192] For the purposes of SD, this means that the legality requirement is suitable for promoting and channelling SD at the moment of establishment, e.g. by conditioning the validity for conducting an ESIA though it does not operate as an IIA guarantee for responsible investments in the course of the business activity.

2.4.1.4 Registration and Approval Requirements

An investment definition can also go further than including the requirement that the investment is made in accordance with host State laws, and tie the definition to a registration and approval requirement.[193] As such States can

---

190 See Commonwealth Secretariat, above note 147, 71–72.
191 *Copper Mesa v Ecuador*, above note 185, para 5.55; see also, *Fraport v Philippines*, above note 181, para 345.
192 For more details on investor obligations, see Mbengue MM, 'Les obligations des investisseurs étrangers' in: Société française pour le droit international (Colloque de Paris Vincennes—Saint-Denis), *L'entreprise multinationale et le droit international* (Pedone 2017) 295–337.
193 Bernasconi-Osterwalder N and Malik M, 'Registration and Approval Requirements in Investment Treaties' IISD Best Practice Series, Dec 2012. It is important to note that this type of requirement must not necessarily be included in the investment definition and can also be included in another provision of the IIAs concerned with the scope of the treaty, such as one dealing with the admission of investment.

limit the scope of the treaty to investments that have been registered and approved for the purpose of the treaty. The main difference between legality requirements and approval requirements is that the former are prohibitory in character serving as a "filter" against investments that violate host State law, whilst the latter require the host State's specific acceptance of an investment in order for the investment to be admitted and protected.[194] The procedural requirement for approval and registration can be a useful tool to ensure that investments are only covered when consistent with the SD policies of the host State provided that such policies are in place and well defined. It can allow States to maintain control over what type of investment falls under the scope of an IIA by allowing them to enact laws and procedures that seek to channel sustainable investments.[195]

The tribunal in the *Yaung Chi Oo v. Myanmar* case held that such an "[...] express requirement of approval in writing and registration of a foreign investment [...] is not universal in investment protection agreements [and] goes beyond the general rule that for a foreign investment to enjoy treaty protection it must be lawful under the law of the host State."[196] It declined to exercise jurisdiction over a dispute based on a non-registered investment. In *Desert Line v. Yemen,* the tribunal had to interpret Article 1 of the Oman-Yemen BIT, which provided that a covered investment must be "accepted, by the Host Party, as an investment according to its laws and regulations, and for which an investment certificate is issued".[197] In its decision, the tribunal made a general statement that a treaty requiring "that investors wishing to be protected must identify themselves" and "that only specifically approved investments will give rise to benefits under the relevant treaty" has a "legitimate policy rationale,

---

194 Diel-Gligor and Hennecke, above note 186, 567, pt 6.
195 "Such power will be especially important for a state that has limited capacity to regulate an investor once it has entered the country". See Commonwealth Secretariat, above note 147, 75.
196 *Yaung Chi Oo Trading Pte Ltd v Government of the Union of Myanmar,* ASEAN ID, Case No ARB/01/1, Award, 31 March 2003, para 58. The applicable agreement in this case was the 1987 ASEAN Agreement for the Promotion and Protection of Investments. See its Art II: "This Agreement shall apply only to investments brought into, derived from or directly connected with investments brought into the territory of any Contracting Party by nationals or companies of any other Contracting Party and *which are specifically approved in writing and registered by the host country and upon such conditions as it deems fit* for the purposes of this Agreement." Emphasis added. The 1987 agreement has been replaced by the ASEAN Comprehensive Investment Agreement that contains a similar provision, see, Art 4(a) "Definitions".
197 *Desert Line Projects LLC v The Republic of Yemen,* Award, ICSID Case No ARB/05/17, 6 Feb 2008.

in the sense that the Governments of such States evidently wish to exercise a qualitative control."[198] The reference to the "quality" of the investment shows that through a process of approving investments, States can do more than seeking to increase the quantity of capital inflows by accepting any type of investment. Rather, they have a steering tool for only approving investments that they consider to be beneficial to their development and where applicable, to the achievement of the SDGs. In sum, registration and approval of foreign investment, following a national screening mechanism, bear great potential to define and to channel sustainable investment inflow at the national law level. IIAs can and should, in this respect, leave enough leeway for States to undertake investment screening based on SD criteria. To include a reference in the IIA to the necessity for registration and approval appears to be a good way forward.

2.4.2 Provisions on Investment Liberalisation: Boon or Bane for SD?

The regulation of investment liberalisation is a crucial component with far reaching consequences for States that are liberalising their markets. Liberalisation commitments are those provisions in an IIAs that commit States to allow, restrict, or place conditions on new foreign investment in their own territory. Without conditions set out in an IIA, the admission of new investments is subject to compliance with whatever requirements are imposed under the national law of the host State. There is no right *per se* for foreign investors to enter the host State or to establish themselves.[199] Whether a State seeks to grant such rights under an international agreement depends on its

---

198 Ibid, para 108: "Some States sign BITs without any regard to the *ex ante* identification of investors who may be covered by the treaty in question. This option ensures broader coverage and may be thought to maximize the stimulation of investment flows between the two countries. Others require that investors wishing to be protected must identify themselves, on the footing that only specifically approved investments will give rise to benefits under the relevant treaty. This is a different approach, but it too has a legitimate policy rationale, in the sense that the Governments of such States evidently wish to exercise a qualitative control on the types of investments which are indeed to be promoted and protected." In the present case, Yemen tried to argue that the investment was not covered because no certificate had been issued. The tribunal, however, rejected this formal argument finding that Article 1 of the applicable BIT should be interpreted as having a "material objective". The tribunal further underlined that based on the facts of the case, the investment has been accepted and welcomed by the Head of State in good faith, see para 119.

199 De Mestral A, 'Pre-Entry Obligations under International Law', in: Bungenberg M et al, *International Investment Law—A Handbook* (BECK; Hart; Nomos 2015) 685.

economic interests, and thus usually stark differences exist between capital-importing and capital-exporting countries.[200]

Investment liberalisation has received less attention in the debate on how to integrate SD into IIAs. One reason for this is that a majority of IIAs still do not contain such provisions.[201] Another reason is that, even where provisions on investment liberalisation are included in an IIA, they are mostly not subject to investor-State dispute settlement. Yet, more attention should be given to liberalisation commitments as they have crucial development impacts, especially host States with developing economies. Using economic insights, it has been shown that the benefits of foreign capital inflows depend on a number of aspects, including the characteristics of the investment, the nature of its linkages to the host State's economy and the extent to which positive spill-over effects can be absorbed by the host State's economy.[202] For investment liberalisation provisions too, much depends on how they are designed and crafted in order to channel sustainable investment.

A key argument of the proponents of SD integration into investment liberalisation is that through the relevant provisions, encompassing provisions on pre-establishment rights, market access commitments and performance requirements, States can opt for selective liberalisation.[203] The main idea is that only SD-beneficial investment should be allowed to enter the market of host States. IIAs typically limit the scope of the right of establishment by expressly excluding certain sectors. There are two approaches to control and limit the scope of establishment rights: the "negative-list" approach and the "positive-list" approach.[204] Positive lists compared to negative lists are considered to be less burdensome from an administrative point of view.[205] They are, in general, less complex for States because a State needs to consciously name the sector it agrees to liberalise thereby ensuring more control over the scope of liberalisation. Each State has to determine the SD sensitive sectors that require more foreign capital inflow and for which it makes sense to open the market with the aim of attracting more foreign investment. There is hence potential to

---

200   Sacerdoti G, 'The Admission and Treatment of Foreign Investment under Recent Bilateral and Regional Treaties', 105 (2000) Journal of World Investment 1, 105.
201   De Mestral, above note 199, 696–698.
202   See Section 1.2.
203   Pre-establishment rights granted to foreign investors are never absolute. See also, Sacerdoti, above note 200, 105.
204   Mann H, 'Investment Liberalization: Some Key Elements and Issues in Today's Negotiating Context' Issues in International Investment Law (IISD 2007).
205   UNCTAD, IPFSD, 117.

align the opening of economies to foreign investment with national social and economic development strategies and priorities.

Most of the discussion on SD and investment liberalisation is concerned with the multiple risks that come, especially for developing countries, with opening up markets. If the market access requirements are restrictive in the sense that they constrain host State's to maintain the same openness without the possibility of adapting to development needs, liberalisation commitments often enough constitute a hurdle for SD. In particular, they can run counter to the benefits of SD investment screening processes mentioned in the previous section. Despite the often-lacking possibility of direct enforcement against a State by a foreign investor, investment liberalisation provisions can have an impact on the host State's policy space needed for SD.[206] Therefore, one aspect of the debate concerns which type of sectors should be liberalised. For instance, the liberalisation of investment in certain public interest sectors, which provide essential goods and services to the population, such as water, electricity, transport, education, and health services, can run counter to the State's long-term interest and those of its population.[207] The control of the entry of foreign investment is for those public interests areas even more important for developing countries, where foreign investment is often poorly regulated and subsequent legal control mechanisms are missing or ineffective.[208] International obligations to liberalise specific sectors, can put the host State at risk of an improper commitment that may constrain future government measures, such as the ability to change its domestic law later because domestic economic needs should require to close a sector that is listed as open in the agreement to be closed.[209] For developing countries, in particular, limiting States' discretion in terms of accepting or refusing foreign investment can preclude the adoption of economic development measures and might constrain the development of infant industries.[210] From that perspective, "in order to develop a strong domestic presence in a particular sector, it is sometimes necessary to give that sector temporary support and/or protection—assistance to help compete with, or a shelter behind which to develop free from, the potentially crushing

---

206 Ibid, 81.
207 Dimopoulos A, 'EC Free Trade Agreements: An Alternative Model for Addressing Human Rights in Foreign Investment Regulation and Dispute Settlement?', in: Dupuy PM, Petersmann EU and Francioni F (eds), *Human Rights in International Investment Law and Arbitration* (Oxford University Press 2009) 572.
208 Commonwealth Secretariat, above note 147, 106.
209 SADC Model BIT, Commentary, 15.
210 UNCTAD, 'Admission and Establishment', in: UNCTAD, *Series on Issues in International Investment Agreements* (United Nations 2002) 37.

competition of more efficient and/or more powerful foreign producers."[211] In other words, newly arrived investors can threaten local companies, especially in countries where there are not yet well-established competition laws.

Another aspect of investment liberalisation is performance requirements. In simple terms, performance requirements are obligations that a State may inflict on investors to take certain actions with a view to achieving domestic policy objectives.[212] Performance requirements have been used by many countries to further (with varying levels of success) diverse policy goals such as improving the competitiveness of domestic industries.[213] As the imposition of performance requirements is often presented as an obstacle to (trade and) investment liberalisation, an increasing number of States include treaty restrictions against performance requirements. Thus, even though provisions on performance requirements are not among the traditional clauses of IIAs, they are more and more included into IIAs. Several IIAs reiterate the prohibition of those performance requirements that are inconsistent with the WTO's Agreement on Trade-Related Investment Measures (TRIMS Agreement). The TRIMS Agreement prohibits certain categories of trade-related performance requirements such as requirements for domestic sourcing of inputs, and restrictions on imports and exports related to local production. Certain IIAs go beyond the requirements of the TRIMS Agreement and also prohibit other performance requirements. Here a typical additional prohibition is the performance requirement that seeks to guarantee that foreign companies will have no obligation concerning a transfer or sharing of technology, production processes, or other proprietary knowledge.

In the debate on SD integration in IIAs, one cannot oversee that certain performance requirements oblige investors in terms of what sustainable investment activities are supposed to bring about, *i.e.* technology transfer, employment creation and local content enhancement. From an SD perspective, the question that is raising concerns is whether performance requirements are a necessary policy that infringes investment flows and thus investment

---

211 Bernasconi-Osterwalder N et al, 'Investment Treaties and Why They Matter to Sustainable Development: Questions and answers' (IISD 2012) 23.
212 Commonwealth Secretariat, above note 147, 194. Performance requirements can include, for example: requirements to export a certain percentage of total sales, or total production; requirements to enter into joint venture arrangements with domestic partners; requirements to transfer or share technology; requirements that a certain amount of inputs be locally sourced; requirements to expend a certain amount on research and development; and requirements to hire a certain number or percentage of local employees.
213 Bernasconi-Osterwalder N et al, 'Investment Treaties and Why They Matter to Sustainable Development: Questions and answers' (IISD 2012) 27–28.

liberalisation. From empirical evidence, the results of performance requirements are mixed and not all performance requirements are equal in terms of effect.[214] Nonetheless, performance requirements have historically served as policy tools for States to facilitate national industrialisation through, for example, augmenting the value of production, productivity rates and employment creation in domestic economic activities; diversifying economic sectors; creating domestic links between the various stages of manufacturing; and, incentivising the innovation and development of technology, which can also include clean technology.[215] The latter aspect is highly relevant for SD, more precisely for sustainable industrial development.[216] For these reasons and for the purpose of aligning IIAs with SD, the argument that performance requirements should be prohibited under IIAs needs to be dismissed. Rather, IIAs should allow for flexibility to use some types of performance requirements. The commitment to a list of certain prohibited performance requirements limits host States in their (future) policy options. In the current debate, a new approach, which stands in clear contrast to the prohibitive approach has been developed. Some IIAs promote the use of performance requirements, including local content initiatives, where warranted, as an important tool for enhancing the quality/sustainability of investments. In the debate on SD and performance requirements, the bottom line should be that States retain flexibility within their choice to use certain performance requirements as a policy tool that can help maximise SD benefits from foreign investment.

2.5 IIAs and Domestic Regulation on SD

Regulation, be it at the national, regional or international level, is essential for achieving SD. National law plays the central role in the implementation of the SDGs.[217] The interrelationship between SD and IIAs thus boils down to the issue of public policy flexibility for domestic legislators to fulfil their SD commitments and objectives through regulations and other policy measures.

---

214   Ibid.
215   Bhumika M, 'International Investment Agreements and Industrialization: Realizing the Right to Development and the Sustainable Development Goals', Human Rights Council [2018] A/HRC/WG.2/19/CRP.5, paras 34–35.
216   SDG 9: "Build resilient infrastructure, promote inclusive and sustainable industrialization and foster innovation".
217   SDG 17 seeks to "strengthen the means of implementation"; target 17.15 in particular: "Respect each country's policy space and leadership to establish and implement policies for poverty eradication and sustainable development."

One of the key functions of SD integration within international investment law remains to ensure that investment protection standards do not infringe or override the policy space of States. The debate on "regulatory space", the "right to regulate" or "regulatory autonomy" of States has been dominating the reform debate.

The debate on regulatory flexibility originates from past investment disputes. Investors have challenged a range of regulatory measures adopted by host States, *inter alia* measures that are relevant for SD, such as to regulate the use of pesticides, the discharge of pollutants, the sale of tobacco products and the phase-out of nuclear power.[218] Not all claims have been successful but the important amounts of money involved and the range of government conduct disputes have led to questioning about whether the asymmetrical nature of IIAs grant overly expansive rights to foreign investors but do not sufficiently counterbalance these rights with the States' right to regulate in the general public interest, including for the benefit and promotion of SD. In the debate on issues touching on the right to regulate, one finds four recurrent arguments:

– The provisions are imprecise leaving too much discretion to adjudicators, which creates uncertainties and what in return chills down the adoption of SD-relevant legislation
– There is not enough flexibility for States to respond to current and future SD challenges
– ISDS through arbitration is not suitable for disputes that involve SD matters
– Tribunals have adopted pro-investor interpretations and accorded higher protection standards than under national law, thereby, they diminish SD and public interests

---

218   Eg *Bilcon v Canada*, above note 185; *Pac Rim Cayman LLC v El Salvador*, ICSID Case No ARB/09/12, Award, 14 Oct 2016; *Bear Creek Mining Corporation v Republic of Peru*, ICSID Case No ARB/14/2; *Burlington v Ecuador*, ICSID Case No ARB/08/5, Decision on Jurisdiction, 2 June 2010, Decision on Liability, 14 Dec 2012; *Perenco v Ecuador*, Decision on Jurisdiction, 30 June 2011; *Urbaser v Argentina*, ICSID Case No ARB/07/26, Award 8 Dec 2016, *Philip Morris v Uruguay*, ICSID Case No ARB/10/7, Award, 8 July 2016; *Philip Morris v Australia*, PCA Case No 2012-12, Award on Jurisdiction and Admissibility, 17 Dec 2015. The two latter cases are considered to be of interest for SD despite the fact that the concept is not mentioned explicitly in the awards. The reason is that the respective State measures under scrutiny in both cases sought to mitigate undisputed public health risks linked to tobacco consumption and public health being part of the SDGs. See SDG 3 on ensuring "healthy lives and promote well-being of all at all ages". For more SD-relevant cases, see also, Bernasconi-Osterwalder N and Johnson L, *International Investment Law and Sustainable Development. Key Cases from 2000–2010* (IISD 2011); Schacherer S, *International Investment Law and Sustainable Development. Key Cases from the 2010s* (IISD 2018).

Concerns about the right of States to regulate and the protection of foreign investor are no longer a novelty and contours, details and the drafting of investment protection standards evolve more and more over time. At the same time, the stated arguments are controversial to different degrees.[219] The argument on the drawbacks of having imprecise standards have found widespread acceptance. States agree that regulatory flexibility is fundamental and must be safeguarded. Yet there is no consensus on how IIAs should provide such flexibility and how this is best integrated into concrete treaty language. Among the most controversial aspects are the approaches on ISDS and whether they actually relate to SD. As will be shown hereafter, the ISDS reform discussion is not primarily of SD relevance but should be distinguished from it and classified as issues relating to concerns of legitimacy.

2.5.1 *More Precise Provisions*

One of the specificities of IIAs and in particular of traditional BITs has been that their treaty provisions display a particularly high degree of generality and vagueness.[220] The traditional open-textured provisions give, and gave in the past, investment tribunals' significant discretion over the interpretation of the protection standards. The prevailing rationale underlying more precise IIA standards is for States to regain control over the interpretation of the IIA by providing more guidance to future adjudicators.[221] All the substantive protection standards and related provisions are being framed with greater precision. This includes fair and equitable treatment (FET), expropriation, transfer of funds and also exceptions clauses and carve-outs. The issues around having more precise treaty provisions are directly connected to regulatory flexibility since through more precise treaty language, States seek to exert and to regain greater control over the manner in which investment treaty provisions are interpreted thereby allowing them more flexibility as the outcome of the interpretation becomes more certain.

Much of the debate on more precise treaty language has surrounded FET. Old-generation treaties contained broadly worded and unqualified FET clauses.

---

219 Here too, the different categories interrelate yet they allow the debate and its objectives to be structured.
220 On the benefits of broadly drafted IIA standards, see Tietje C and Crow K, 'The Reform of Investment Protection Rules in CETA, TTIP, and Other Recent EU FTAs: Convincing?', in: Griller S, Obwexer W and Vranes E (eds), *Mega-Regional Trade Agreements: CETA, TTIP, and TiSA ; New Orientations for EU External Economic Relations* (Oxford University Press 2017) 91 et seq.
221 Henckels C, 'Protecting Regulatory Autonomy through Greater Precision in Investment Treaties: The TPP, CETA, and TTIP', Journal of International Economic Law (2016) 32.

A typical BIT, for instance, merely provides on FET that "[each] Contracting State shall in its territory in every case accord investments by investors of the other Contracting State fair and equitable treatment [...] under this Treaty".[222] The notions of fairness and equity lack clear legal prescriptions in international law and, traditionally, IIAs did not further define them. FET is the most frequently invoked and the most often successfully argued protection standard.[223] Investors have often considered them as blanket protection and systematically used them to challenge host State measures that they deemed to adversely affect their investments.[224] The recurrent issues in these cases used to be questions on the elements that constitute a breach of the standard and on the threshold to be attained for the standard to be breached.[225] Due to the lack of clear textual guidance, investment tribunals have developed over the years core elements constituting a breach of FET.[226] Certain elements are widely accepted, such as that investors should not receive treatment that is "arbitrary, grossly unfair, unjust or idiosyncratic, is discriminatory and exposes the claimant to sectional or racial prejudice, or involves a lack of due process leading to an outcome which offends judicial propriety".[227] Whilst the *jurisprudence*

---

222   2008 German Model BIT, Art 2(2).
223   Henckels, above note 221, 33.
224   OECD, 'Fair and Equitable Treatment Standard in International Investment Law', vol 2004/03 (2004) OECD Working Papers on International Investment 2004/03.
225   The is extensive literature on the FET standard, see the analysis of: Kläger R, 'Fair and Equitable Treatment' in International Investment Law (Cambridge University Press 2011); Bonnitcha J, *Substantive Protection under Investment Treaties: A Legal and Economic Analysis* (Cambridge University Press 2014) 143–228; Dumberry P, Fair and Equitable Treatment: Its Interaction with the Minimum Standard and Its Customary Status (Brill 2018); Levashova Y, *The Right of States to Regulate in International Investment Law: The Search for Balance between Public Interest and Fair and Equitable Treatment* (Kluwer Law International, BV 2019).
226   See especially the case law under NAFTA eg *Glamis Gold, Ltd. v United States*, Award, 8 June 2009, UNCITRAL, para 627; Cargill Inc v Mexico, Award, 18 September 2009, ICSID No ARB(AF)/05/02, para 296; *Mobil Investments Canada Inc. and Murphy Oil Corporation v Canada*, Decision on Liability and on Principles of Quantum, 22 May 2012, ICSID No ARB(AF)/07/4, para 152; *Eli Lilly and Company v Canada*, Final Award, 16 March 2017, UNCITRAL Case No UNCT/14/2, para 222; *Bilcon v Canada*, above note 185, paras 442–3; *Mesa Power Group, LLC v Canada*, Award, 24 March 2016, PCA Case No 2012-17, para 502.
227   In *Waste Management v. Mexico*, the tribunal summarised that "[...] minimum standard of treatment of fair and equitable treatment is infringed by conduct attributable to the State and harmful to the claimant if the conduct is arbitrary, grossly unfair, unjust or idiosyncratic, is discriminatory and exposes the claimant to sectional or racial prejudice, or involves a lack of due process leading to an outcome which offends judicial propriety—as might be the case with a manifest failure of natural justice in judicial proceedings or a

constante is, in principle, beneficial in terms of clarity of the standards, the risks of extensive interpretations remain. The concept of legitimate expectations, in particular, troubles those that argue in favour of more predictability as regards the scope of protection offered by the FET standard. The conditions for when legitimate expectations of investors exist are controversial and different tribunals have found different answers to this question.[228] Some tribunals have found that investors' legitimate expectations can be based on what they expected to be their future business prospects; other tribunals have agreed with the investors that certain commitments or promises given by government officials, even when given orally, can create legitimate expectations. In sum, whilst arbitral case law has developed over the years, a list of elements that fall under the FET standards, uncertainties for States remain, especially when it comes to the scope of the concept of legitimate expectations.

Past investment arbitration cases have led States to seek to prevent the possibility of overly expansive interpretations of the scope of FET. At this point, certain key approaches can be identified. A first approach is to keep the provision vague providing large discretion to future arbitrators. A second approach consists of seeking to draft clearer and more predictable FET provisions in IIAs.[229] A third approach is not to include a provision on FET in the treaty.[230]

---

complete lack of transparency and candour in an administrative process. In applying this standard, it is relevant that the treatment is in breach of representations made by the host State which were reasonably relied on by the claimant. Evidently the standard is to some extent a flexible one which must be adapted to the circumstances of each case." See, *Waste Management, Inc. v Mexico II*, ICSID No ARB(AF)/00/3, Award, 30 April 2004 para 98.

[228] The concept of legitimate expectations is probably the most polarising element of FET; see, *Tecnicas Medioambiantales Tecmed SA v Mexico*, ICSID Case No ARB(AF)/00/2, 29 May 2003, para 154; *SAUR International v Argentina*, ICSID Case No ARB/04/4, Award, 22 May 2014, paras 495 et seq; *Marion Unglaube und Reinhard Unglaube v Costa Rica*, ICSID Case No ARB/08/1, Award, 16 May 2012, para 249; *Crystallex International Corporation v Bolivarian Republic of Venezuela*, ICSID Case No ARB(AF)/11/2, Award, 4 April 2016, para 546: "As already stated, the Tribunal agrees with the majority of investment tribunals which have concluded that protection of legitimate expectations is now considered part of the FET standard." Arbitral tribunals have concluded that the doctrine of legitimate expectations is "firmly rooted in arbitral practice [...]". See also, *Bilcon v Canada*, above note 185, paras 444 et seq. See also, Kläger, above note 225, 165–187; Commonwealth above note 147, 145–147.

[229] Schill S and Jacob M, 'Trends in International Investment Agreements, 2010–2011: The Increasing Complexity of International Investment Law' in: Sauvant KP (ed), *Yearbook on International Investment Law & Policy 2011–2012* (Oxford University Press 2013) 142.

[230] Eg Brazil-Malawi CIFA; PAIC; and recommendation made in the SADC Model BIT, Commentary, 22.

The latter approach certainly is the safest way to preclude unwarranted interference with a State's regulatory autonomy and the way in which it engages in pursuing SD objectives.[231] A fourth approach is to include FET but to exclude the standard from being invoked in an investor-State dispute.[232] The treaty practice of combining FET clauses with a reference to the minimum standard of treatment under customary international law is not a novel treaty practice and the approach remains controversial. It is namely unclear whether any such reference to the minimum standard of treatment is beneficial for better prescribing the scope of the standard. The reason is that it is unclear what the customary minimum standard of treatment requires in cases of regulatory changes.[233] From an SD perspective, an FET clause should be drafted so as to reduce uncertainties. They make it hard for States to implement the FET obligation and could, therefore, encourage regulatory constraints as States may seek to avoid any action that might be in breach of the standard.[234] In light of the uncertainties with respect to the elements, it is an effective way forward to indicate in the IIA the elements that constitute a breach of the FET standard. As shown in Chapter 6, there are no easy solutions and States should assess the costs and benefits of either better prescribing the FET standard, or not including it altogether. Certain States and regions might come to the conclusion that the guarantee of FET is too important for foreign investors such that its non-inclusion would be impossible. One way of reducing the costs is to exclude the standard from ISDS but to keep it in the treaty as a guarantee, thereby infusing confidence among foreign investors.

The goal of achieving more precise treaty standards also touches upon States' commitments on non-discrimination treatment. From an SD perspective, it is important to ensure that States retain the right to distinguish SD-friendly investments from those investments and operations that will or may potentially harm the environment, social standards or development interests of the host State.[235] Under non-discrimination clauses, a State guarantees to

---

231   See PAIC, as well as the CIFAs of Brazil, see eg Brazil-Malawi CIFA.
232   The USMCA contains an FET clause, see Art 14.6 (Minimum Standard of Treatment) and Annex 14-A. However, the USMCA eliminates ISDS between the United States and Canada, and between Mexico and Canada; for the relation between Mexico and the United States, ISDS still exists but FET is excluded from its scope, see USMCA, Annex 14-D, Art 14.D.3.
233   Kläger R, 'Fair and Equitable Treatment' in International Investment Law (Cambridge University Press 2011) 53 et seq.
234   Commonwealth Secretariat, above note 147, 140.
235   The large bulk of investor claims on discrimination are based on the national treatment standard, but for cases where an MFN treatment clause is at stake, there should be no difference in approaching the question of the appropriate comparator.

treat investors from the partner State no less favourably than it treats investors in *like circumstances* from other States or domestic investors.[236] However, the provisions on non-discrimination generally do not elaborate further on the scope of the obligation or on how public welfare measures should be analysed in the case of an alleged breach of the standard.[237] Due to the lack of guidance within the standard, arbitral tribunals have developed a number of different approaches, which have resulted in extending the scope of the obligation and thus potentially affecting the regulatory space of host States to promote public welfare objectives.[238] Past arbitral case law not only shows that tribunals have developed a wide range of approaches to determine likeness, they also reveal that tribunals assessed likeness on a factual assessment of the extent to which a foreign investor is adversely affected by the measure in comparison to (like) domestic investors.[239] Yet the purely factual assessment of likeness between investors/investments does not take the regulatory purpose into account in the assessment. Since the key issue of the condition of the non-discrimination standard to apply is that the investor/investment compared are "like" or in "like circumstances", the fewer factors that are taken into account for the establishment of likeness, the broader the definition of likeness becomes and the easier it is for the host State to afford equal treatment.[240] Therefore, certain IIAs have started to circumscribe likeness. In order to better guide tribunals, a set of elements that are to be taken into account have started to be included in IIAs; a key element of such a list is the regulatory purpose of a State measure.

2.5.2 *Flexibility Clauses*

Flexibility and adequate policy space are needed for SD-advancing domestic measures and laws. Flexibility is required for good faith regulations that are adopted in the public interest, including SD purposes. In the words of Anne van Aaken,

---

236 A reference to "in like circumstance" has traditionally been included in North American IIAs. See, NAFTA, Arts 1102 and 1103; 2004 Canadian Model BIT, Arts 3 and 4; 2012 US Model BIT, Arts 3 and 4.
237 Henckels, above note 221, 43.
238 Mitchell AD, Heaton D and Henckels C, *Non-Discrimination and the Role of Regulatory Purpose in International Trade and Investment Law* (Edward Elgar Publishing 2016) 135.
239 Mitchell, Heaton and Henckels, above note 115, 65–66 and 135.
240 In *Occidental v Ecuador* the tribunal took an extensively broad definition, by considering that the oil exporter Occidental was in like circumstances with national flower exporters. See, *Occidental Exploration and Prod. Co. v Republic of Ecuador*, UNCITRAL, LCIA Case No UN3467, Final Award, 1 July 2004, paras 173–179.

"[a] good faith regulation or measure is unlikely to be the result of an opportunistic behaviour by the government but rather a demand of evolving factual legal circumstances, that is, it is to be assumed that a purpose enhancing the welfare of citizens is behind the measure. Would state parties have known *ex ante*, they would have excluded the measures from the need for compensation."[241]

SD is precisely concerned with this type of measures as often enough, the achievement of SD requires constant adaptation and is subject to social changes and scientific innovation. Both display a relatively high degree of volatility. This means that at the moment of concluding a treaty, it is impossible for States to foresee the measures they will need to take in the future. In order to distinguish good faith regulation and opportunistic behaviour of States, the intent of the measures becomes highly critical. Discriminatory conduct often serves as an indicator of opportunistic behaviour but intent plays an "exculpatory role" since even discriminatory conduct may be permissible if the effect is discriminatory but the intent is benevolent.[242] In this logic, the intent of the regulation (for instance environmental protection) should prevail over the discriminatory effect, unless discriminatory intent can be proven against the face of the regulation.[243] As the *Saluka* tribunal acknowledged, international investment law has yet to identify in a comprehensive and definitive fashion precisely what regulations are considered 'permissible' and 'commonly accepted' excluding State liability under IIAs.[244] In this vein, IIA treaty practice shows that exceptions, such as the police powers doctrine and general exception clauses are increasingly included and serve to better define the line between treaty breach and valid regulatory activity. Another, yet softer approach to increasing flexibility for regulatory State action, is achieved through restatements of the parties' right to regulate.

---

241 Van Aaken A, 'Smart Flexibility Clauses in International Investment Treaties and Sustainable Development' (2014) The Journal of World Investment & Trade 827, 852.

242 Ibid, 854. See also, Mitchell AD, Heaton DOF and Henckels C, *Non-Discrimination and the Role of Regulatory Purpose in International Trade and Investment Law* (Edward Elgar Publishing 2016) 138 et seq.

243 Van Aaken, above note 241, 853: "If investment is as trade about competitive opportunities, a special scrutiny should be applied to discriminatory conduct of the state but non-discriminatory conduct should, as good faith measure, get the benefit of doubt". She further argues that past arbitral tribunals did not always clearly distinguish between intent and effect of the measure.

244 See, *Saluka Investments BV v Czech Republic*, UNCITRAL, Partial Award, 17 March 2006, para 263–264.

2.5.2.1 Police Powers Exception

In regulatory disputes, host States are frequently confronted with claims of indirect expropriation. In light of the public interests that are at stake, a number of tribunals have considered the police powers doctrine that allows a State to regulate without paying compensation even though the regulatory measures have effects equivalent to expropriation.[245]

The police powers doctrine "[i]s an accepted principle of customary international law that where economic injury results from a *bona fide* non-discriminatory regulation within the police power of the State, compensation is not required".[246] However, arbitral practice has been inconsistent in applying the exception. In the past, several awards have arguably been encroaching too far on States' rights under customary international law to exercise their police powers by failing to consider the purpose of a challenged

---

245 See eg, *Tecmed v Mexico*, above note 228, para 119: "[t]he principle that the State's exercise of its sovereign powers within the framework of its police power may cause economic damage to those subject to its powers as administrator without entitling them to any compensation whatsoever is undisputable"; *Methanex Corp v United States of America*, NAFTA/UNCITRAL, Award, 3 Aug 2005, part IV, Ch D, para 7: "as a matter of general international law, a non-discriminatory regulation for a public purpose, which is enacted in accordance with due process and, which affects, *inter alios*, a foreign investor or investment is not deemed expropriatory and compensable unless specific commitments had been given by the regulating government to the then putative foreign investor contemplating investment that the government would refrain from such regulation"; *Chemtura Corp v Canada*, UNCITRAL, Award, 2 Aug 2010, para 266: "[T]he Tribunal considers in any event that the measures challenged by the Claimant constituted a valid exercise of the Respondent's police powers. As discussed in detail in connection with Article 1105 of NAFTA, the PMRA took measures within its mandate, in a non-discriminatory manner, motivated by the increasing awareness of the dangers presented by lindane for human health and the environment. A measure adopted under such circumstances is a valid exercise of the State's police powers and, as a result, does not constitute an expropriation". See also, *CME Czech Republic BV v Czech Republic*, UNCITRAL, Partial Award, 13 Sep 2001, para 603; *Total SA v Argentine Republic*, ICSID Case No ARB/04/01, Decision on Liability, 27 Dec 2010, para 197; *Tza Yap Shum v Republic of Peru*, ICSID Case No ARB/07/6, Award, 7 July 2011, para 145; *El Paso Energy International Company v Argentine Republic*, ICSID Case No ARB/03/15, Award, 31 Oct 2011, paras 236–241, 243; *SAUR International SA v Argentina*, ICSID Case No ARB/04/4, Decision on Jurisdiction and Liability, 6 June 2012, paras 396–401.

246 See OECD, '"Indirect Expropriation" and the "Right to Regulate" in International Investment Law' OECD Working Papers on International Investment 2004/04, 5. For an overview on the police powers doctrine, see *Philip Morris v Uruguay*, above note 218, paras 288 et seq. See also, *Saluka Investments BV v Czech Republic*, UNCITRAL, Partial Award, 17 March 2006, para 262: "the principle that a State does not commit an expropriation and is thus not liable to pay compensation to a dispossessed alien investor when it adopts general regulations that are 'commonly accepted as within the police powers of States' forms part of customary law today."

measure when determining whether it constituted an indirect expropriation. For instance, the NAFTA tribunal in *Metalclad v. Mexico*, held that it "need not decide or consider the motivation or intent of the adoption of the Ecological Decree", but only whether it had the effect of depriving the foreign investor "of the use or reasonably-to-be-expected economic benefit of property".[247] For the tribunal in *Azurix v. Argentina*, the issue was "not so much whether the measure concerned is legitimate and serves a public purpose, but whether it is a measure that, being legitimate and serving a public purpose, should give rise to a compensation claim".[248] Conversely, the practice of investment tribunals also provides several examples of cases where this concept has been discussed and often applied to dispose of the claim.[249] The tribunal in *Methanex v. United States*, is well-known for its interpretation of the police powers as being very favourable to the State's regulatory powers. It found that, in determining whether a regulation had resulted in an indirect expropriation, the primary issue was whether the measure concerned was legitimate and served a public purpose. In support of the customary international law police-powers concept, the tribunal held that, "as a matter of general international

---

247 *Metalclad Corporation v Mexico*, ICSID Case No ARB(AF)/97/1, Award, 30 Aug 2000, paras 103 and 111.
248 *Azurix Corp. v Argentina*, ICSID Case No ARB/01/12, Award, 14 July 2006, para 115–117.
249 See eg, *Tecmed v Mexico*, above note, para 228: "[t]he principle that the State's exercise of its sovereign powers within the framework of its police power may cause economic damage to those subject to its powers as administrator without entitling them to any compensation whatsoever is undisputable"; *Methanex Corp v United States of America*, above note 245, part IV, Ch D, para 7: "as a matter of general international law, a non-discriminatory regulation for a public purpose, which is enacted in accordance with due process and, which affects, *inter alios*, a foreign investor or investment is not deemed expropriatory and compensable unless specific commitments had been given by the regulating government to the then putative foreign investor contemplating investment that the government would refrain from such regulation"); *Chemtura Corp v Canada*, UNCITRAL, Award, 2 Aug 2010, para 266: "[T]he Tribunal considers in any event that the measures challenged by the Claimant constituted a valid exercise of the Respondent's police powers. As discussed in detail in connection with Article 1105 of NAFTA, the PMRA took measures within its mandate, in a non-discriminatory manner, motivated by the increasing awareness of the dangers presented by lindane for human health and the environment. A measure adopted under such circumstances is a valid exercise of the State's police powers and, as a result, does not constitute an expropriation". See also, *CME Czech Republic BV v Czech Republic*, UNCITRAL, Partial Award, 13 Sep 2001, para 603; *Total SA v Argentine Republic*, ICSID Case No ARB/04/01, Decision on Liability, 27 Dec 2010, para 197; *Tza Yap Shum v Republic of Peru*, ICSID Case No ARB/07/6, Award, 7 July 2011, para 145; *El Paso Energy International Company v Argentine Republic*, ICSID Case No ARB/03/15, Award, 31 Oct 2011, paras 236–241, 243; *SAUR International SA v Argentina*, ICSID Case No ARB/04/4, Decision on Jurisdiction and Liability, 6 June 2012, paras 396–401.

law, a non-discriminatory regulation for a public purpose, which is enacted in accordance with due process and, which affects, inter alios, a foreign investor or investment is not deemed expropriatory and compensable".[250] The tribunal did not take into account the economic impact of the regulation at issue or the degree of interference with the investor's legitimate expectations. The inconsistency in arbitral case law led States, especially the United States and Canada to respond to the controversy surrounding the content of the indirect expropriation standard. Both countries revised their model BITs to provide some guidance to tribunals. Each added an interpretive annex subjecting claims of indirect expropriation to a "case-by-case" and fact-specific inquiry. The North-American treaty practice introduced the formulation of "[e]xcept in rare circumstances, such as when a measure or series of measures are so severe in the light of their purpose that they cannot be reasonably viewed as having been adopted and applied in good faith, non-discriminatory measures of a Party that are designed and applied to protect legitimate public welfare objectives, such as health, safety and the environment, do not constitute indirect expropriation". In this approach, which has been followed widely in other IIAs and by other States, the interference with the property plays a role as far as its effects are "severe", and tribunals are to take it into account. The formulation in an IIA could also be different and it could be stated that "[n]on-discriminatory state measures that are designed and applied to protect legitimate public welfare objectives do not constitute indirect expropriation".[251] A certain number of States is currently introducing this formulation in their IIAs, providing broader scope for the police powers exception.[252] In other words, a majority of States are keen today to codify the police powers doctrine within provisions on the protection against indirect expropriation but differences can exist in terms of whether or not the effects of the measure are to be taken into account. From an SD-perspective, the police power doctrine is appraised as being beneficial to better safeguard the regulatory space of States allowing for a better balancing of investor and State interests when claims of indirect expropriation are at stake.[253]

---

250   *Methanex v United States of America*, above note 245, para 278.
251   Commonwealth Secretariat, above note 147, 167. See also, De Nanteuil A, 'Expropriation', in: Mbengue MM and Schacherer S (eds), *Foreign Investment Under the Comprehensive Economic and Trade Agreement (CETA)* (Springer International Publishing 2019) 150.
252   See Section 6.1.1.2.
253   UNCTAD, IPSFD, 99; Commonwealth Secretariat, above note 147, 173; Nikièma S, 'Indirect Expropriation' IISD Best Practice Series, 2012.

2.5.2.2 General Exceptions

General exceptions have gained prominence as strong flexibility mechanisms for States to safeguard their regulatory space. If a measure falls under them, States act within the legal frame of the IIA without breaching it and are thus exempted from liability. In IIA practice, general exceptions are relatively new but they are on the rise. According to Alschner and Berge, around 100 treaties of the current IIAs contain general exception clauses, of which two thirds are inspired by Article XX of the GATT[254] or Article XIV of the GATS,[255] and one third follows the model of prohibition and restriction clauses first included in the 1985 Singapore-China BIT.[256] The inclusion of general exception clauses is part of the panoply of SD integration. The argument is that general exception clauses can "safeguard policy space" or domestic regulatory measures that aim to pursue legitimate public policy objectives and "limit State liability".[257] However, their utility and effectiveness, in order to provide greater or clearer policy space for States to enact SD legislation, needs yet to be tested in practice.

So far, their suitability in practice has already led to the occurrence of counter-arguments. The reasons are highlighted by, at least, two investment arbitration cases, where the inclusion of general exception clauses was not

---

254 Alschner W and Berge TL, 'Reforming Investment Treaties: Does treaty design matter?' IISD ITN 17 Oct 2018. An example of a GATT-inspired chapeau of a general exception clause is CETA, Art 28.3(1): "For the purpose of [...] Sections B (Establishment of investment) and C (Non-discriminatory treatment) of Chapter Eight (Investment), *Article XX of the GATT 1994 is incorporated into and made part of this Agreement.* The Parties understand that the measures referred to in Article XX (b) of the GATT 1994 include environmental measures necessary to protect human, animal or plant life or health. The Parties understand that Article XX (g) of the GATT 1994 applies to measures for the conservation of living and non-living exhaustible natural resources."

255 An example of a GATS-inspired chapeau of a general exception clauses can be found in the ASEAN-Hong Kong, China SAR Investment Agreement, Art 9(1): "Subject to the requirement that such measures are not applied in a manner which would constitute a means of arbitrary or unjustifiable discrimination between the Parties or their investors, where like conditions prevail, or a disguised restriction on investors of another Party or their investments, nothing in this Agreement shall be construed to prevent the adoption or enforcement by any Party of measures".

256 Singapore-China BIT, Art 11 'Prohibitions and restrictions', "The provisions of this Agreement shall not in any way limit the right of either Contracting Party to apply prohibitions or restrictions of any kind or take any other action which is directed to the protection of its essential security interests, or to the protection of public health or the prevention of diseases and pests in animals or plants."

257 UNCTAD, IPFSD, 85.

beneficial. The first case dealing with general exceptions in relation to investment protection standards was *Copper Mesa v. Ecuador*.[258] The tribunal found that the arbitrariness and lack of due process in Ecuador's withdrawal of a mining license not only violated the expropriation and FET clauses of the Canada-Ecuador BIT, but also rendered the treaty's general exception clause inapplicable.[259] The tribunal justified the non-application of the general exceptions clause by stating that liability would only be exempted for measures that were "not applied in an arbitrary or unjustifiable manner".[260] Another case that shows the limits of general exceptions is *Bear Creek v. Peru*.[261] In this case, the tribunal refused to apply the police powers doctrine due to the existence of an exhaustive list of general exceptions under the applicable agreement, which would render it impossible to add any further exception, such as the police powers doctrine.[262] Both tribunals, without providing much reasoning, adopted an interpretation that limits the intended effects of the clauses. If general exceptions are inapplicable on the same grounds that gave rise to a violation of the primary obligations in the first place, they will rarely save respondent States from liability.[263] Similarly, if they operate as replacements rather than complements to the flexibility already offered, such as through the

---

258 *Copper Mesa Mining Corporation v Republic of Ecuador*, PCA No 2012-2, Award, 15 March 2016.
259 Ibid, paras 6.58–6.67.
260 Ibid. See also Canada-Ecuador BIT, Art XVII(3).
261 *Bear Creek Mining Corporation v Republic of Peru*, ICSID Case No ARB/14/2, Award, 30 Nov 2017.
262 Ibid, paras 473–474; at 473: "[…] Further, the list is not introduced by any wording (e.g. "such as") which could be understood that it is only exemplary. It must therefore be understood to be an exclusive list. Also in substance, in view of the very detailed provisions of the FTA regarding expropriation (Article 812 and Annex 812.1) and regarding exceptions in Article 2201 expressly designated to "Chapter Eight (Investment)", the interpretation of the FTA must lead to the conclusion that no other exceptions from general international law or otherwise can be considered applicable in this case."
263 Several authors have likewise underlined these shortcomings. See eg Henckels C, 'Should Investment Treaties Contain Public Policy Exception' (2018) 59 BC L Rev 2825; Alschner and Berge, above note 254; Newcombe A, 'General Exceptions in International Investment Agreements', in: Cordonier Segger M-C, Gehring MW and Newcombe AP (eds), *Sustainable Development in World Investment Law* (Kluwer Law International 2011) 355–361. Another issue that has come up in practice so far, is that in some instances, respondent States did not make use of the general exception clause. This has occurred in *Gold Reserve Inc v Bolivarian Republic of Venezuela*, ICSID Case No ARB(AF)/09/1, Award, 22 Sep 2014; *Crystallex v Venezuela*, above note 228; *Rusoro Mining Ltd v Bolivarian Republic of Venezuela*, ICSID Case No ARB(AF)/12/5), Award, 22 Aug 2016.

police powers doctrine, they will provide little additional policy space or may even detract from it.²⁶⁴

Given these elements, introducing general exceptions as a means of SD integration should be done cautiously.²⁶⁵ Three aspects should be considered. A first question thus relates to whether or not general exception should apply to all investment protection standards, especially to those that already contain policy flexibility mechanisms, such as the codification of the police powers within the indirect expropriation provision. A second questions relates to the list of general exceptions, i.e. which policies and policy measures should be included in the list of measures. In most IIAs, these lists are often relatively narrow in scope and imported from trade law with limited relevance to the issues raised in ISDS proceedings. One can thus argue that it would be beneficial, in order to provide policy space for SD, to add more explicit language, such as to include a clear exception for measures with human rights or labour protection objectives. In addition, exhaustive lists are likely to reduce the scope and potential impact of general exceptions given that a measure at issue needs to fit into a specific category.²⁶⁶ Restrictive interpretations by future adjudicators can certainly not be presumed, but there are important areas of SD regulation going beyond the GATT and the GATS, such as human rights climate change mitigation and, in particular, measures that seek to address the transition from fossil to renewable energy sources. A final question relates to the nexus requirement between the exception and the relevant substantive norm. The nexus requirement can be more or less stringent. General exceptions clauses that require that government action "be necessary" based to achieve the particular objective are the least restrictive for investors.²⁶⁷ Past arbitral case law shows that tribunals have not elaborated a consistent approach to what the

---

264 Lévesque C, 'The Inclusion of GATT Article XX Exceptions in IIAs: A Potentially Risky Policy', in: Echandi R and Sauvé P (eds), *Prospects in International Investment Law and Policy* (Cambridge University Press 2013) 365.
265 Mitchell AD, Munro J and Voon T, 'Importing WTO General Exceptions into International Investment Law', in: Sachs L, Johnson L and Coleman J, *Yearbook on International Investment Law & Policy 2017* (Oxford University Press 2019) 310–311: "[…] we urge treaty drafters and negotiators to act cautiously in introducing general exceptions from the WTO context into IIAs. The impact on the interpretation of investment obligations is not always foreseeable, and the expected interaction between different treaty provisions as well as the underlying WTO/investment treaty case law must be considered in detail".
266 Martini C, 'Avoiding the Planned Obsolesce of Modern International Investment Agreements: Can General Exception Mechanisms be Improved, and How?' (2018) 59 BC L Rev 2877, 2894.
267 Henckels, above note 263, 2837.

concept of necessity entails as highlighted in the Argentinean crisis cases.[268] Some tribunals have applied a strict interpretation of the concept as meaning the "only way available".[269] Meanwhile, other tribunals have adopted a more deferential approach stating that States are allowed to adopt any "legitimate measure" if necessary.[270] Different hereto the WTO Appellate Body interpreted the concept of necessity as meaning that there was no "reasonably available alternative" to the adopted State measure, which would have been less restrictive to trade.[271] The nexus requirement is an important part of general exception clauses as it sets out the scope of review.[272]

Consequently, the relationship between the standards of investment protection and general exceptions requires further analysis and debate. As it seems currently, general exception clauses might not be the most effective way to shield *bona fide* public welfare measures from liability given the uncertainties around their interpretation. Lastly, one should not overlook that having general exceptions singles out to some extent the assessment of the regulatory purpose of a challenged measure once a *prima facie* breach of investment obligations has been established.[273] Through general exception provisions, laws and other government actions taken to promote public welfare are approached as exceptional rather than something that takes place in the ordinary course of governance, which undermines this objective.[274] From an SD perspective, however, regulation is essential and should not be seen as exceptional.

2.5.2.3 Other Flexibility Clauses

Also among the treaty clauses that seek to enhance the regulatory flexibility of States are those clauses stating the "right to regulate" of the contracting parties. These provisions reaffirm States' right to regulate within their territories to

---

268 Alvarez JE, *The Public International Law Regime Governing International Investment* (AP All-Pocket 2011) 266–268.
269 See also, *CMS Gas Transmission Company v Argentina*, ICSID Case No ARB/01/8, Award, 12 May 2005, para 323; *Sempra Energy International v Argentina*, ICSID Case No ARB/02/16, Award, 18 Sep 2007, para 339, 351; *Enron Corporation v Argentina*, ICSID Case No ARB/01/3, Award, 15 May 2007, para 308.
270 *LG&E Energy Corp v Argentine Republic*, ICSID Case No ARB/02/1, Decision on Liability, 3 Oct 2006, paras 239–257. The tribunal affirmed that necessity "should be only strictly exceptional and should be applied exclusively when faced with extraordinary circumstances".
271 *EC—Measures Affecting Asbestos and Products Containing Asbestos*, Panel Report, (2000) WT/DS135/R, para 8.222.
272 Van Aaken, above note 241, 850.
273 Henckels, above note 263, 2843.
274 Ibid.

achieve "legitimate policy objectives, such as the protection of public health, safety, the environment or public morals, social or consumer protection or the promotion and protection of cultural diversity".[275] They have been included in order to better safeguard regulatory space for a legitimate public welfare objective in the case of an investor claim alleging a breach of its investment guarantees, but they are no exception as such, meaning on their basis liability can on be excluded. In the context of international investment law, the State's right to regulate can be resumed as to encompass two elements.[276]

The concrete benefits of having provisions on the right to regulate should, however, not be overestimated.[277] Whilst they set the tone for the application and interpretation of the investment protection standards, they add little to how to weigh the stated objectives in relation to investors' rights. In the past, the pivotal issue in arbitral cases concerning the right to regulate of States has not been that legitimate regulatory objectives were not sufficiently recognised but how to strike an adequate balance between the regulatory purposes and investment protection. Therefore, it is important to underline that most of the recent right to regulate provisions simply state that governments may adopt and maintain the measure but are obliged to pay compensation if they violate any of the investment protection standards. A right to regulate clause still leaves it to the adjudicators to interpret the treaty to strike the balance. Those provisions that are dealing with the actual balancing are and remain the substantive treaty provisions. Given that this type of clause does not entail concrete obligations, it is not controversial among States. From an SD-perspective and despite the fact that right to regulate provisions are not operating as exceptions, these provisions are still a welcome feature of modern IIAs since these clauses most likely impact on how arbitrators will use their discretion, namely in light of broader policy objectives.

2.5.3   SD and Investor-State Dispute Settlement

The beginning of the 21st century is not only the era of SD integration into international investment law but also a time in which international investment arbitration finds itself in a "legitimacy crisis".[278] It has become widely accepted

---

275 Eg CETA, Art 8.9(1).
276 Mann H, 'Investment Liberalization: Some Key Elements and Issues in Today's Negotiating Context' Issues in International Investment Law (International Institute for Sustainable Development (IISD) 2007); See generally, Titi C, *The Right to Regulate in International Investment Law* (Nomos 2014).
277 See hereto also, Johnson, Sachs and Lobel, above note 140, 31.
278 Causes and effects of the legitimacy crises go beyond the scope of the present book. There is extensive literature on the topic, eg Dietz T, Dotzauer M and Cohen ES, 'The

that ISDS through arbitration needs to be reformed. The criticisms of States and other stakeholders culminated in the 2017 mandate given to the Working Group III of the UN Commission for international Commercial Law (UNCITRAL) to evaluate the criticisms made to ISDS, to consider whether a reform is necessary and in the affirmative, to suggest solutions for the reform.[279]

The SD reform approaches and those that seek to mitigate the legitimacy crisis are sometimes put under the same umbrella; by doing so, the link between SD and ISDS might however be too easily assumed. Whilst there are communalities between the two reform agendas, such as addressing the concerns related to the right to regulate, there are however differences as regards the causes of reform as well as their intended effects. In order to shed some light on the differences between the two reform agendas and to comment on the relationship between SD and ISDS, two questions are briefly addressed here.[280] First, does ISDS undermine SD, and second, is it possible to design a system of ISDS that is consistent with and supportive of SD?

2.5.3.1 Debates about Whether ISDS Undermines SD

The past thirty years of ISDS through arbitration have shown up the many issues and flaws of ISDS. The wave of arbitration claims that succeeded the 1990s' boom in investment treaty signing triggered States' current understanding that ISDS can impose important financial and political costs for States. One recurrent argument of the debate that directly affects SD is to say that a State's exposure to ISDS creates "regulatory chill".[281] The term refers to the possibility

---

Legitimacy Crisis of Investor-State Arbitration and the New EU Investment Court System' (2019) 26 Review of International Political Economy 749; Schill SW, Authority, Legitimacy, and Fragmentation in the (Envisaged) Dispute Settlement Disciplines in Mega-Regionals, in: Griller S, Obwexer W and Vranes E (eds), *Mega-Regional Trade Agreements: CETA, TTIP, and TiSA ; New Orientations for EU External Economic Relations* (Oxford University Press 2017) 111; Schneiderman D, 'Legitimacy and Reflexivity in International Investment Arbitration: A New Self-Restraint?' (2011) 2 Journal of International Dispute Settlement 471.

279 The UNCITRAL consensus displays the desirability to address concerns of consistency, coherence, predictability, and correctness of arbitral rulings; independence, impartiality, and diversity of decision-makers; and costs and duration of proceedings. See, United Nations Commission on International Trade Law (UNCITRAL) 'Report of Working Group III (Investor-State Dispute Settlement Reform) on the Work of its Thirty-Sixth Session (Vienna, 29 Oct-2 Nov 2018)'. Another reform is underway at ICSID, see ICSID Secretariat, 'Proposals for Amendment of the ICSID Rules', Working Paper on proposals for rule amendments, building on proposals that were originally published in August 2018.

280 It is not the aim to go through all the points of critique that are discussed at UNCITRAL.

281 On the debates on regulatory chill, see Tienhaara K, 'Regulatory Chill and the Threat of Arbitration: A View from Political Science', in Brown C and Miles K (eds), *Evolution in Investment Treaty Law and Arbitration* (Cambridge University Press 2011) 606; Bonnitcha

that investment treaties discourage States from adopting legitimate measures in practice. The extent to which ISDS and IIAs in general cause regulatory chill is among the most controversial issues.[282] Regulatory chill can derive from a number of ISDS characteristics, such as its high costs or the traditional broadly worded provisions that give incentives for investors to bring a claim.[283] The issue here is not whether host States frequently win or lose the cases but the mere fact of risks that claims may be brought and that a State might be held responsible as both of these factors can lead States to decide not to engage into certain regulatory action. Evidence with respect to regulatory chill is, however, mixed. There is evidence that regulatory chill has occurred[284] but there is also evidence that many claims have been the result of States actually maintaining regulatory measures and not shying away from the risks of ISDS.[285] In other words, the extent of regulatory chill is difficult to measure.[286] Yet the issue has a clear connection with SD. As discussed throughout this book, regulation is essential for SD and the implementation of the SDGs. Therefore, the extent to which a dispute settlement system undermines or threatens a State's rights to regulate has a bearing on SD. Given the risk of ISDS claims, certain States might be reluctant to introduce new and ambitious SD legislation as it might

---

J, Poulsen LNS and Waibel M, *The Political Economy of the Investment Treaty Regime* (Oxford University Press 2017) 238–244.

[282] Ibid, 239. Bonnitcha et al find that "[d]espite the centrality of regulatory chill to public debate and treaty practice, however, there is surprisingly little research on whether and to what extent concerns of regulatory chill are justified." For ISDS cases including issues of environmental protection, Behn and Langofrod have shown that "only in a small minority of cases (four of 47 cases where information is available) did claimants challenge domestic legislation, rather than executive or judicial action, and they lost in each of these cases". See Behn D and Langford M, 'Trumping the Environment? An Empirical Perspective on the Legitimacy of Investment Treaty Arbitration' [2017] The Journal of World Investment & Trade 14, 48.

[283] Commonwealth Secretariat, above note 147, 401.

[284] Eg New Zealand delayed the implementation of tobacco plain packaging for several years while the ISDS case against Australia's tobacco plain packaging was pending. Once Australia successfully defended its measures, New Zealand enacted the measure. Another example, is the *Vattenfall v Germany I* arbitration, which was settled but it resulted in the city of Hamburg watering down the environmental protection requirements for the Elbe river area.

[285] Eg South Africa in *Piero Foresti, Laura de Carli & Others v The Republic of South Africa*, ICSID Case No ARB(AF)/07/01, Award, 4 Aug 2010; Canada in *Chemtura Corporation v Government of Canada*, UNCITRAL, Award, 2 Aug 2010; or the USA in *Methanex v United States*, above note 245.

[286] Van Harten G and Scott DN, 'Investment Treaties and the Internal Vetting of Regulatory Proposals: A Case Study from Canada' [2015] SSRN Electronic Journal, available at <http://www.ssrn.com/abstract=2700238>.

harm foreign investors and provoke an increase in claims. This alone is problematic for the realisation of the SDGs.

Based on the financial costs of ISDS only, it is often argued that they undermine SD, especially when developing countries are involved.[287] The argument is that public funds that need to be used on ISDS are then missing for SDGs-advancing policy measures in host States, assuming that they intend to enact such legislation. Either way, the question of how costly a system of justice can and should be is an important one. One can argue, however, that since SD-relevant spending can only be assumed, discussions on the high costs of procedure and compensation and whether they are justified or not would better fit into discussions related to the legitimacy crisis of ISDS, meaning that it is more a question of legitimacy (in the sense of what States and other stakeholders accept) having compensation awards that regularly cost several million dollars and often over one billion. By the same token, other flaws of the ISDS system, such as treaty shopping or issues around third-party funding should rather be linked to the legitimacy debate.[288]

Finally, the asymmetrical nature of ISDS, i.e. the fact that only investors can bring a claim highlights that the current system is failing to provide remedies when investment disputes are around the wrongful acts of corporations rather than of the host State. The possibility of a State filing a counterclaim is an exceptional rather than the rule. The result has been that, in several instances, it has been difficult to hold multinational corporations accountable.[289] In addition to the limited remedies offered to States to file a claim against an investor at

---

287   For instance, the $4 billion compensation award in the *Tethyan Copper v Pakistan* in July 2019 was 2/3 of the bailout sum of the International Monetary Fund (IMF) that had been agreed two months earlier with the intention of saving the Pakistani economy from collapse. See Bonnitcha J and Brewin S, 'Compensation Under Investment Treaties' (2019) IISD Best Practice Series. See *Tethyan Copper Company Pty Limited v Islamic Republic of Pakistan*, ICSID Case No ARB/12/1, Award, 12 July 2019. In addition, the example of Ecuador is a telling one; on 5 Oct 2012, an investment arbitration tribunal ordered the government of Ecuador to pay $2.3 billion to the US oil company Occidental. It was the largest amount a State had been ordered to pay by an investor-State tribunal up to that point. For Ecuador, that sum represented 59% of the country's 2012 annual budget for education and 135% of the country's annual healthcare budget. See, <https://www.tni.org/en/article/why-did-ecuador-terminate-all-its-bilateral-investment-treaties>.
288   Discussion at UNCITRAL. See also, Baumgartner J, *Treaty Shopping in International Investment Law* (Oxford University Press 2017) 59–61. Despite linking SD to treaty shopping and the increased risks for States to face ISDS claims, Jorun Baumgartner highlights that this issue rather relates to concerns of legitimacy than to SD.
289   The governance gap has been demonstrated by Steinitz M, *The Case for an International Court of Civil Justice* (Cambridge University Press 2019).

the international level, there is evidence that ISDS undermines human rights protection in the host State especially with respect to access to justice for vulnerable communities.[290] Local communities that suffer from human rights violations of MNEs have no to very few procedural means to enforce their human rights. The fact that traditional ISDS through arbitration only grants privileges to one actor, the private investor impacts SD. If modernising ISDS should be undertaken in light of SD, these concerns cannot be overlooked.

2.5.3.2 Is It Possible to Design an ISDS System Consistent with SD?

The current reform of ISDS is mainly based on legitimacy concerns and not primarily but rather coincidently with certain concerns and impacts on SD. But what would an ISDS system that is consistent with SD look like? Does SD require bolder and more systemic shifts in how investment-related disputes should be tackled going beyond the investor-State relationship? Certainly, an ISDS reform in light of SD should ensure that solutions are consistent with and supportive of the SDGs. This means, for instance, being mindful of implications of reform solutions for legal, political, and economic inequality between States, and between different groups and actors in society. It means that the ability of governments to regulate in the public interest is not undermined. More concretely, the guiding SD principles should be the principle of public participation that requires transparency of proceedings and the possibility for local communities that are affected by investment activities to be informed and to be, at least, allowed to participate in the proceedings.[291] Moreover, SD gives special attention to the needs of developing countries and requires a global partnership that seeks to balance the rights and obligations of all stakeholders. In this respect, SD demands that States strengthen the responsibility of multinational corporations and improve accountability mechanisms, which could be legal solutions at the international level. The most important linkages between ISDS and SD are to be explored in this triangular setting of investor, host State and local population.

In contrast, procedural questions of ISDS and questions such as whether it is more suitable to have arbitration or a standing investment court (where

---

290 CCSI, research ongoing on this question; <http://ccsi.columbia.edu/work/projects/access-to-justice/?utm_source=CCSI+Mailing+List&utm_campaign=a20b86dd19-ISDS+Reform+at+UNCITRAL&utm_medium=email&utm_term=0_a61bf1d34a-a20b86dd19-62934621>.

291 On the principle of participation, see above Section 2.2.2.4.

still only investors can bring a claim against a host State) do not have SD as a guiding objective. For instance, considering the approaches and solutions discussed within Working Group III of UNCITRAL, it appears that they are not directly connected to SD; rather, they all seek to improve the effectiveness of an adjudicative system and to infuse it with legitimacy in various ways.[292] As argued before, it is helpful to distinguish between legitimacy-improving reform and SD-guided reform. SD would require certain systemic shifts in how investment-related disputes are tackled. It would imply discussions on how to give standing for affected communities and how to better hold international corporations accountable for wrongful acts in the course of their investment activity.[293] Yet, States and other global actors currently focus on the procedural improvements and some systemic adjustments, such as the introduction of an appeals mechanisms. The UNCITRAL consensus does not include the objective of rendering the system more inclusive. This means that the privileged legal position for international investors remains untouched. For the present book, this means that the choice has been made not to deal with the reform discussion surrounding ISDS in the next chapters, with the exception of the few SD-relevant procedural aspects introduced by the EU in its IIAs. Otherwise, there is still a very limited amount of concrete State practice that seeks to build a comprehensive investment-related dispute settlement system.[294] Nonetheless, important research should be done on inclusive investment-related dispute settlement mechanisms supportive of the SDGs.

2.5.4 *Ensuring Interpretation in Light of SD*

Finally, the interaction of IIAs and domestic regulations for the purpose of SD also concerns the interpretation of IIAs when applied in investor-State dispute proceedings. In other words, IIA design in light of SD does not end at the signature table but is a process that continues into a treaty's application.

---

292   It has been argued that SD can be beneficial for legitimacy purposes, Schill SW, 'Reforming Investor-State Dispute Settlement (ISDS): Conceptual Framework and Options for the Way Forward' E15Initiative, Geneva: International Centre for Trade and Sustainable Development (ICTSD) and World Economic Forum, 2015. But then again how would that look in more concrete terms?

293   IISD, 'Investment-Related Dispute Settlement: Towards a comprehensive multilateral approach' Workshop in Montreux 2016, <https://www.iisd.org/events/investment-related-dispute-settlement-towards-comprehensive-multilateral-approach>.

294   Brazil is one of the few countries that deviates from the traditional ISDS; instead, its CIFAs establish a system that combines dispute prevention mechanisms, creating institutions to ensure continued communication and foster cooperation, and State-to-State arbitration.

Investment arbitrators are to give weight to specific treaty design innovations. Arguably, setting out more precise investment protection standards and criteria that adjudicators have to take into account provides greater constraints on their decision-making and narrows down their discretion.[295] Law-making thus has an impact on the interpretation of the law as SD integration may assist and encourage a tribunal to interpret rules in light of SD.[296] The concept of SD affects the interpretation mainly through the inclusion of the concept in the preamble of an IIA, most of which state a "commitment to promote [SD]".[297] Yet, in order to fully integrate the SD rationale, a preambular reference and more detailed provisions are not sufficient to take away all adjudicatory discretion or to prescribe a given outcome or ensure outcomes in compliance with SD. Therefore, SD can be additionally integrated through interpretative techniques and methods, such as systemic integration and proportionality analysis. In this sense, SD can guide the interpretation and judicial discretion can be used in light of SD and its connected principles. The remaining discretion should not be considered as a negative element; it permits flexibility and a "degree of adaptability" for unforeseen situations that could not have been anticipated when an IIA was drafted.[298] In the reform debate, allowing SD to enter at the stage of treaty interpretation is not a controversial topic, and most IIAs refer, one way or another to SD.[299]

2.6   IIAs and International Cooperation on SD

The third and final perspective on how SD integration into international investment law and governance can unfold, relates to the question of how IIAs can be supportive of the international cooperation on SD. The said international cooperation on SD emerged with the 1992 Rio Conference. What became the SD agenda had, from the beginning, the aim to shape the legal framework and

---

295   Tietje and Crow, above note 220, 91–93.
296   International Law Association (ILA), 'International Law on Sustainable Development', Toronto Conference [2006] 13.
297   CETA, preamble, recital 9: "Reaffirming their commitment to promote sustainable development and the development of international trade in such a way as to contribute to sustainable development in its economic, social and environmental dimensions."
298   Henckels, above note 263, 33. See Chapter 7 on the interpretation of EU IIAs.
299   Out of the 2577 IIAs mapped by UNCTAD, 78 contain a specific reference to SD; 45 to the right to regulate; 223 contain a reference to human rights, labour, health, CSR or poverty reduction; and 143 IIAs' preamble makes reference to environmental protection, plant or animal, climate change or biodiversity.

governance structures supportive of SD at the national and the international levels. This means that IIAs also play a role in the bigger endeavour of implementing the SD agenda through international cooperation. Even though these questions are less discussed in the current reform, they are highly critical for SD. For instance, IIAs can be beneficial for the SD agenda by strengthening SD legislation at the national level. In this vein, IIAs can support efforts related to the challenge of establishing a robust legal framework that ensures sustainable economic activities within a country. In this respect, IIAs fill governance gaps where social and environmental regulations are non-existent or incomplete at the national level. Given that in some countries national regulatory regimes are underdeveloped, it is therefore beneficial to support their efforts through international instruments. IIAs can include provisions on commitments to ensure high levels of environmental and social protection as well as commitments not to lower environmental and labour standards in order to attract foreign investment. In principle, IIAs can go beyond incentivising by complementing national legislation applicable to investment activities. Here the IIAs themselves set out binding SD commitments applicable to the contracting parties.[300] Next to strengthening national legislative measures, IIAs can also set incentives for common action for the contracting parties in different international fora, such as the ILO or under MEAs. In this respect, IIAs can be used in order to support international cooperation on SD and allow the international investment regime to be connected with other branches of international law, such as environmental law and climate change mitigation, international labour law and the evolving standards of CSR and good governance.

2.6.1   *Avoiding a Race to the Bottom and Enhancing SD Standards*

One way of cooperating on SD through an IIA is to prevent States from lowering their social and environmental standards in order to attract more foreign capital inflow. Sustainable investments can be undermined when States seek to attract foreign investment that is environmentally damaging or fails to address violations of fundamental labour standards as an incentive to attract foreign investment. So-called non-lowering of standards clauses aim to prevent SD-harming and unfair competitive advantages between contracting parties. They are intended to respond to the "pollution heaven" hypothesis and the

---

300   Commonwealth Secretariat, above note 147, 255: "Many developing states do not possess the technical capacity or the physical and institutional infrastructure to regulate the environment or social effects of foreign investments effectively."

phenomenon of "social dumping".³⁰¹ These treaty provisions place an international bottom line on States' freedom to regulate in the relevant SD areas. Moreover, foreign investors are discouraged from seeking or putting pressure on States for the adoption of measures that would lower important SD standards.³⁰² It has further been noted that the creation by foreign investors of legitimate expectations on the adoption of less stringent measures is prevented through the existence of such clauses.³⁰³ Non-lowering of standards clauses have appeared in IIAs since the 1990s.³⁰⁴ Mostly, these provisions are written in a non-binding manner.³⁰⁵ And even though some recent IIAs make the obligation binding, the inclusion of non-lowering of standards clauses is not a controversial issue in the current debate on how to integrate SD in IIAs. The main reason is that these provisions are generally not subject to ISDS or another form of stringent enforcement mechanism.³⁰⁶ In fact, the biggest issue related to non-lowering of standards clauses, is their effective implementation and enforcement. Disagreements between contracting parties concerning alleged infringements of the clauses, are mainly resolved through consultation. This explains why it is not controversial to have them in an IIA but why controversy and debate exist in terms of how to enforce these clauses and thus how to make them more effective.³⁰⁷ Different arguments are being made. Kathleen

---

301   Johnson, Sachs and Lobel above note 140, 35. The authors underline that if such incentive language is not present then the "agreements miss a crucial opportunity to combat costly and often wasteful beggar-thy-neighbour incentive schemes that can erode the benefits FDI otherwise might offer." On the effects of employment regulations on FDI, see Olney WW, 'A Race to the Bottom? Employment Protection and Foreign Direct Investment' (2013) 91 Journal of International Economics 191.

302   Gazzini T, 'Bilateral Investment Treaties and Sustainable Development' [2014] The Journal of World Investment & Trade 929, 930. Gazzini highlights that the most often stated policy areas that are SD relevant where risks of race to bottom can exist are environmental and labour policy.

303   Ibid.

304   Gordon and Pohl, above note 139, 21.

305   NAFTA, Art 1114(2): "The Parties recognize that it is inappropriate to encourage investment by relaxing domestic health, safety or environmental measures. Accordingly, a Party should not waive or otherwise derogate from, or offer to waive or otherwise derogate from, such measures as an encouragement for the establishment, acquisition, expansion or retention in its territory of an investment of an investor." Such best-efforts clauses can also be found in the model BITs of the United States and of Canada.

306   UNCTAD, IPFSD, 119.

307   Claussen K, 'Reimagining Trade-Plus Compliance: The Labor Story' (2020) 23 Journal of International Economic Law 25. See also, Zimmer R, 'Sozialklauseln im Freihandelsabkommen der Europäischen Union mit Kolumbien und Peru', Recht der Internationalen Wirtschaft 2011, 625–632; Marx A et al, *Dispute Settlement in the Trade and Sustainable Development Chapters of EU Trade Agreements* (Leuven Centre for Global

Claussen, for instance, argues that commitments on labour protection standards should not be treated as "ordinary" trade and investment issues. She suggests that the institutional design and enforcement for these commitments must "strike the right balance between legalization and management to build confidence".[308] From this perspective, to gain SD-beneficial spill-over effects, it would be more effective to work out more stringent enforcement mechanisms. Others argue that environmental and labour commitments are more effectively implemented when the enforcement remains cooperative.[309] And yet others suggest that non-lowering of standards should be accompanied by transparency requirements and enforcement mechanisms that include citizen complaint processes allowing their monitoring and implementation.[310] There are no easy solutions for treaty-drafting as demonstrated by IIA practice, which is analysed in Chapter 5 of this book.[311]

2.6.2 *Addressing SD-Investment Issues of Global Concern*

A logical reason why States should cooperate on SD through their IIAs is that many of the risks for SD that come with global investment are best dealt with at the international and not at the domestic law level. Unilateral State regulation and policy measures are not efficient for many issues of environmental protection and definitely not for climate change mitigation. Creating a better nexus between investment and SD concerns considers IIAs as being able to promote more sustainable production and consumption patterns that are consequently to the benefit of all countries. Illustrative areas of action promote respect for internationally agreed standards in the fields of labour rights and environmental protection, and coordinating on regulations in the fight against corruption as well as climate change mitigation. IIAs can establish baselines of internationally-agreed standards in SD-relevant policy areas. Typically, this is achieved by reinforcing and integrating commitments under international agreements. In this vein, the idea is that IIAs provide support for the

---

Governance Studies 2017) 10; Bartels L, 'Human Rights and Sustainable Development Obligations in EU Free Trade Agreements' in: Wouters J et al (eds), *Global Governance through Trade: EU Policies and Approaches* (Edward Elgar Publishing 2015) 89; Ebert FC, 'The Comprehensive Economic and Trade Agreement (CETA): Are Existing Arrangements Sufficient to Prevent Adverse Effects on Labour Standards?' [2017] International Journal of Comparative Labour Law and Industrial Relations 295, 307.

308   Claussen, above note 307, 43.
309   Eg Marín Durán G, 'Sustainable Development Chapters in EU Free Trade Agreements: Emerging Compliance Issues' [2020] Common Market Law Review 1031, 1055.
310   Johnson, Sachs and Lobel, above note 140, 41.
311   See, Section 5.2.2.

implementation of SD standards since contracting parties agree to reinforce their existing commitments, for instance under key MEAs and labour conventions. Moreover, under IIAs, the contracting parties can also agree to increase the level of ambition with respect to their commitments and strengthen the resources they put into effective enforcement. Integrating those international agreements that form part of the global SD framework is one of the central aspects to align the international investment regime with the international cooperation on SD.

The alignment between the legal framework on the fight against global warming and international investment law is an illustrative example in this respect.[312] As one of the most pressing SD imperatives that require international concerted action, the question of how IIAs could serve as an enabling instrument for climate change mitigation is fundamental.[313] Debates of States, governmental organisations, scholars and think tanks on how this should be done are increasingly appearing. One aspect of the debate linked to climate change mitigation is energy transition from fossil fuels to renewable energies.[314] The main idea is that IIAs should be used as complementary instruments to support responsible action on climate change by providing incentives to encourage investments that support mitigation goals, including targeted financial or technical supports for forest conservation or clean energy investment.[315] The specific barriers to investment in climate change mitigation and adaptation encompass the reluctance of companies to invest in green products. The reasons are market distortion and regulatory uncertainties, such as those resulting from fiscal measures and subsidies but also technological

---

312 Climate change typically creates a "transnational cooperation dilemma" since cross-border externalities render unilateral action by States largely ineffective in solving the problem. See, Barrett S, *Environment and Statecraft: The Strategy of Environmental Treaty-Making* (Oxford University Press 2005) 49.

313 Mitigation means action to limit emissions and to preserve or enhance drawdown of emissions. See, Paris Agreement, Art 4(7): "Mitigation co-benefits resulting from Parties' adaptation actions and/or economic diversification plans can contribute to mitigation outcomes [...]".

314 Eg, Boute A, 'The Potential Contribution of International Investment Protection Law to Combat Climate Change' (2009) 27 Journal of Energy & Natural Resources Law 333; OECD, 'How to Unlock Private Investment in Support of Green Grwoth?' (OECD 2013); International Finance Corporation, *Climate Investment Opportunities in Emerging Markets* (World Bank 2016). These publications are to be distinguished from those that focus on the normative conflicts between the investment regime and the climate change regime, see eg, Viñuales JE, Foreign Investment and the Environment in International Law (Cambridge University Press 2012) 253–278.

315 Johnson, Sachs and Lobel, above note 140, 41.

risks and limited short-term returns on investment.[316] In addition, IIAs could go further and discipline continued fossil fuel dependence.[317] Through IIAs, contracting parties can agree on common policies and regulations in areas such as product energy efficiency standards or technical requirements for climate-friendly infrastructure and thereby contribute to a more predictable legal framework for foreign investors in relevant sectors. At the very least, IIAs can contain provisions that generally state the parties' will to promote climate-friendly investment, such low-carbon FDI flows.

Most of the approaches addressing issues of global concern are nascent and not many IIAs contain provisions going in this direction. It can be expected that these approaches will gain more and more importance in the next few years. A characteristic of all these approaches is that they go beyond the debate on interference with regulatory SD measures at the national level, for instance national climate change mitigation measures.[318] Yet having robust international cooperation on SD matters and a reference in the IIA to the cooperative agendas of the two parties can provide backing for States when they need to justify treatment accorded to foreign investors in an investment arbitration case. International SD cooperation can relieve States, to some extent, of the burden of individually justifying such measures. An example hereto is the case of *Philip Morris v. Uruguay*, where the international cooperation on public health, i.e. the WHO Framework Convention on Tobacco Control and the studies of the PAHO, precisely had these benefits.[319] In sum, IIA provisions with the

---

316 Boute, above note 314, 337.
317 Nathalie Bernasconi-Osterwalder and Martin Dietrich Brauch argue that a "modernized ECT should abandon its energy-source neutrality and, instead, expressly discriminate between carbon-intensive energy investments, which should receive less favourable treatment and ultimately be eliminated, and low-carbon energy investments, which should be encouraged". See, Bernasconi-Osterwalder N and Brauch MD, 'Redesigning the Energy Charter Treaty to Advance the Low-Carbon Transition' TDM 1 (2019) 11.
318 In a number of cases, climate change regulation has come under threat. The debate on IIAs and national climate policies and hereto the risk when the two can enter into conflict will be dealt with under the right to regulate umbrella in the present book.
319 *Philip Morris v Uruguay*, ICSID Case No ARB/10/7, Award, 8 July 2016, paras 38 and 43. As the WHO and FCTC Secretariat noted, large graphic health warnings are an effective means of informing consumers of the risks of tobacco consumption and of discouraging tobacco consumption. Therefore, the submissions supported that the Uruguayan measures are effective means of protecting public health. The PAHO amicus brief stated that "Uruguay's tobacco control measures are a reasonable and responsible response to the deceptive advertising, marketing and promotion strategies employed by the tobacco industry, they are evidence based, and they have proven effective in reducing tobacco consumption". Anne van Aaken has, moreover, argued that if there is international

aim to address SD-investment issues of global concern are not at the centre of a controversial debate despite their practical relevance and benefits for SD.

2.6.3 *Responsible Investment and the Balancing of Rights and Obligations of Investors*

A comprehensive reform discussion on SD integration in international investment governance includes the role and the responsibilities of foreign investors. How corporate activities can be prevented from having negative effects on the local environment or the human rights situation in a host State has been the starting point of the discussion. Today, the debate goes beyond mere questions of compliance and also involves the question of how foreign investors can actively contribute to SD. Whilst States agree that foreign investor are required to comply with their national laws and are to adopt a certain level of diligence when exercising their business,[320] there is controversy around whether foreign companies have a responsibility to contribute more actively to development purposes, such as technical education and social inclusion. In addition, whether international law, and namely IIAs, are the appropriate instrument to ensure a better accountability mechanism for MNEs is not unanimously admitted. In contrast, States adopt, in this respect, quite different strategies and approaches.

One strand of the argument consists of stressing the need to better articulate international provisions and processes to ensure that investors adhere to SD standards.[321] The reason for such concerns is that even though investment activities fall under a set of jurisdictions, including the domestic legal order of the home and the host State, the regulation applicable is often not sufficient to ensure CSR practices.[322] Moreover, the standards for the protection of the environment, as well as social and economic rights, can differ from country to country.[323] And depending on the economic leverage of a given foreign

---

consensus on the requirement to regulate on certain [SD] issue areas; it needs to be presumed that this happens in good faith. See, Van Aaken, above note 241, 856.

320   Investment in accordance with host State law is discussed under Section 6.3.1.
321   Commonwealth Secretariat, above note 147, 287 et seq. Agenda 2030 promotes a multi-stakeholder partnership on SD, which, in particular, seeks to mobilise and to share "knowledge, expertise, technology and financial resources". Multinational enterprises (MNEs) investing in foreign countries are part of the global SD partnership. See, Agenda 2030, targets 17.16 and 17.17.
322   Waleson J, 'Corporate Social Responsibility in EU Comprehensive Free Trade Agreements: Towards Sustainable Trade and Investment' (2015) 42 Legal Issues of Economic Integration 2, 147.
323   Ibid.

investor, countries might turn a blind eye to domestic law violations relating to SD matters. International human rights treaties are also only of very limited help for host countries. This was highlighted in the case *Urbaser v. Argentina*.[324] Even though the tribunal found, by citing international human rights instruments, that human rights obligations such as the right to water can be directly imposed on international corporations, it concluded that international human rights obligations are primarily addressed to States and are not drafted in a way as to contain obligations on corporations.[325]

The procedural dimension of the reform debate on investors' conduct concerns the question of how to provide mechanisms for communities, individuals and sometimes governments adversely affected by investors' corporate behaviour to seek and to obtain redress for harm suffered.[326] International law does not provide many effective ways of holding to account foreign investors who violate international human rights, labour rights or norms for environmental protection. As Johnson et al. have highlighted, often enough, the domestic law of host States does not provide effective remedies that allow individuals to sue foreign investors for harms they have suffered as a consequence of the investment activity.[327] All this is corroborated by the lack of resources of many States to follow up on complaints. Beyond the host State, litigation against corporations faces difficult legal hurdles for harmed individuals and communities to bring civil suits against a parent corporation in the home State for acts of its foreign subsidiaries that commit human rights and other violation in the host State. Finally, corporate defendants have seemingly endless resources to pour into legal defence and often enough take benefit from the complex web of legal structuring across borders as single legal entities, each with carefully crafted holdings of assets and liabilities.[328] In this area of international law, much still needs to be done.

---

324 *Urbaser v Argentina*, above note 218, paras 1194–1195. Interestingly, the tribunal also held that, even if a BIT does not contemplate investors as subjects of international law, this would not undermine the idea that foreign investors could be subjected to international law obligations. Moreover, the tribunal stressed that, in the light of recent developments in international law, it could no longer be admitted that companies operating internationally would be immune from becoming subjects of international law.

325 Ibid, paras 1205–1207.

326 IISD, 'Integrating Investor Obligations and Corporate Accountability Provisions in Trade and Investment Agreements', Report of the expert meeting, Versoix, Switzerland, January 2018, available at <https://www.iisd.org/sites/default/files/publications/report-expert-meeting-versoix-switzerland-january-2018.pdf>.

327 Johnson, Sachs and Lobel, above note 140, 37.

328 Ibid.

At present, both, the scope and nature of obligations for foreign investors, as well as the procedural implementation of investor obligations are subject to debate.[329] On the question of how IIAs can handle these issues, the answer used to be by making reference to CSR instruments in IIAs.[330] Such CSR standards have been enshrined and further elaborated in numerous international guidelines and soft law instruments. For instance, the OECD Guidelines for Multinational Enterprises consist of a set of recommendations jointly addressed by governments to multinational enterprises. They provide principles and standards of good practice. The observance of the Guidelines by enterprises is, however, voluntary and not legally enforceable, whereas, the countries adhering to the Guidelines make a binding commitment to implement them, in particular to set up National Contact Points.[331] The UN Global Compact is another CSR instrument that sets out ten key principles addressed to multinational enterprises, which relate to human rights, labour, environment and anti-corruption.[332] These principles are derived from the Universal

---

[329] The international community is struggling to negotiate and adopt a binding international treaty on MNEs. For instance, the process that was started in 2014 by the Human Rights Council on the initiative of Ecuador and entrusted to an Open-ended Intergovernmental Working Group on transnational corporations and other business enterprises with respect to human rights, as received opposition from several States. See, UN Human Rights Council, 'Elaboration of an international legally binding instrument on transnational corporations and other business enterprises with respect to human rights', [2014] A/HRC/RES/26/9.

[330] The concept of CSR still awaits a uniform definition at the international level. Miles K, *The Origins of International Investment Law—Empire, Environment and the Safeguarding of Capital* (Cambridge University Press 2013) 217. See also Hepburn J and Kuuya V, 'Corporate Social Responsibility and Investment Treaties', in: Cordonier Segger M-C, Gehring MW and Newcombe AP (eds), *Sustainable Development in World Investment Law* (Kluwer Law International ; Aspen Publishers 2011) 590–592, at 592: "a corporation is expected to attain its profit-making goals while also ensuring that it behaves like a good corporate citizen whose activities enhance the enjoyment of human and environmental rights and reflect positive business ethics." A survey of a broad range of such standards is found in Sauvant K and Mann H (2017), *Towards an indicative list of FDI sustainability characteristics* (E15 Task Force on Investment Policy Think Piece, October 2017); available at <http://e15initiative.org/publications/towards-an-indicative-list-of-fdi-sustainability-characteristics/>.

[331] The contact points are implemented in domestic legislation, but States dispose of flexibility concerning their precise organisational form. OECD, 'OECD Guidelines for Multinational Enterprises', annexed to 2000 OECD Declaration on International Investment and Multinational Enterprises, DAFFE/IME(2000)/20); (2001) 40 ILM 237 as amended, part A. "An NCP may be a governmental unit, or an organisation consisting of government representatives, independent experts and representatives of business, worker organisations and other non-governmental organisations".

[332] The ten principles are: (1) Businesses should support and respect the protection of internationally proclaimed human rights; and (2) Make sure that they are not complicit in

Declaration of Human Rights, the ILO Declaration, and the UN Convention against Corruption (UNCAC). They are addressed directly to businesses, but they do not foresee any enforcement mechanism. However, the UN Global Compact secretariat compiles lists of companies and progress reports showing the level of engagement in applying the ten principles.[333] Another recurrent standard-setting instrument is the UN Guiding Principles on Business and Human Rights,[334] setting out that enterprises should respect human rights, have responsibilities towards human rights and should implement policies in this respect, including conducting due diligence processes in order to identify potential risks. Lastly, the Tripartite Declaration of Principles for Multinational Enterprises and Social Policy of the ILO[335] features a list of key CSR instruments. It provides guidance and good practices regarding socially oriented principles for multinational enterprises as it is grounded in the principles contained in international labour conventions and recommendations.

All of these instruments have their benefits, especially as they set out a comprehensive set of areas of compliance and of actions for MNEs. These instruments can also inspire national legislators to adopt and implement the standards in their domestic laws. IIAs have been used to promote CSR standards and the compliance thereof. Typically, IIAs incorporate a provision recommending States to include internationally recognised CSR standards into their corporate policies.[336] However, the experience of the last decades has also shown that merely voluntary standards are not sufficient to ensure sustainable investment

---

human rights abuses. Labour: (3) Businesses should uphold the freedom of association and the effective recognition of the right to collective bargaining; (4) The elimination of all forms of forced and compulsory labour; (5) The effective abolition of child labour; and (6) The elimination of discrimination in respect of employment and occupation. Environment: (7) Businesses should support a precautionary approach to environmental challenges; (8) Undertake initiatives to promote greater environmental responsibility; and (9) Encourage the development and diffusion of environmentally friendly technologies. Anti-Corruption: (10) Businesses should work against corruption in all its forms, including extortion and bribery.

333   The initiative gathers around 8,000 companies and 4,000 non-business participants located in more than 160 countries, see UN Global Compact, 'Guide to Corporate Sustainability', available at <https://www.unglobalcompact.org/docs/publications/UN_Global_Compact_Guide_to_Corporate_Sustainability.pdf>.

334   UN Human Rights Council, 'Guiding Principles on Business and Human Rights: Implementing the United Nations 'Protect, Respect and Remedy' Framework" [2011] A/HRC/17/31.

335   ILO, 'Tripartite Declaration of Principles concerning Multinational Enterprises and Social Policy' [1977; last amended 2017].

336   UNCTAD, *World Investment Report 2011: Non-Equity Modes of International Production and Development* (United Nations 2011) 111.

activities.³³⁷ Therefore, certain States are in favour of direct investor obligations in IIAs as a means to complement their domestic law and to better balance the rights and obligations of foreign investors at the international level. This approach appears to be straightforward and logical but is practically and politically complex and controversial. Counter-arguments and scepticism towards direct investor obligations often relate to their enforcement: should they be enforceable in national courts? Or in ISDS proceedings through counter-claims? There is no doubt that the effectiveness of direct investor obligations in IIAs goes hand in hand with effective procedural mechanisms including the possibility for communities, individuals and governments to invoke the potential violation of them.³³⁸ Whilst ensuring such effectiveness requires political will and resources, it seems clear from an SD perspective that more than the promotion of CSR through dozens of voluntary standards, guidelines, principles and norms is needed to address the environmental, economic and social impacts of multinational enterprises. A positive impact of CSR standards is that investors cannot reasonably expect that they will be able to operate under lower standards, which, in return, limits the range of what they can reasonably claim (and obtain) in investment proceedings.³³⁹ Whether an IIA is a well-suited instrument for direct investor obligations requires further discussion. At the same time, using IIAs for the inclusion of direct investor obligations would not substitute investor obligations contained in the investment contract or national law. In this respect, IIAs work as complementary legal instruments. As mentioned before, the complementary benefits of IIAs are even more important for developing countries.

2.6.4 *Measuring the SD Impacts of IIAs*

If the ultimate goal of IIAs is SD, the debate on how to better ensure such an outcome also encompasses impact assessments of IIAs themselves. Thus, SD integration can take place at the moment of the negotiation of an IIA, namely through the conduct of a sustainability impact assessment of the agreement.³⁴⁰

---

337   See Daniel C, Wilde-Ramsing J, Genovese K and Sandjojo V, *Remedy Remains Rare: An analysis of 15 years of NCP Cases and Their Contribution to Improve Access to Remedy for Victims of Corporate Misconduct* (OECD Watch 2015). See also, Daniel C et al (eds), *Glass half full? The State of Accountability in Development Finance* (Centre for Research on Multinational Corporations (SOMO) 2016).
338   See Section 5.4.2.
339   Viñuales JE, 'Investor Diligence in Investment Arbitration: Sources and Arguments' (2017) ICSID Review 32(2) 355.
340   There are also other designations, which mostly designate a more restrictive impact assessment, such as human rights impact assessment, or environmental impact

Such impact assessments take into account the IIA's potential future effects on the environment, the economy and the guarantee of social protection within the negotiating partner countries, and in some cases also third countries. The inquiry is a factual assessment of the potential impacts and is either conducted by independent consulting agencies or by State agencies. Assessments usually take place alongside the negotiations of investment agreements. Their function is to avoid that the IIAs having negative impacts on SD. In some cases, impact assessments of IIAs also seek to facilitate the outreach to stakeholders within the partner countries through consultations with them. Another function of SD integration, at the point of negotiation, is that impact assessments can be an important tool in making sure that the negotiating parties do not make concessions that will later make it more complicated for them to comply with other international obligations, such as those based on human rights treaties or MEAs.[341] Whilst it is crucial to do the impact assessment before the IIA is finalised (before or whilst negotiating the treaties), it is also important to consider the impact of IIAs during their application, and to develop and implement policy responses where necessary.[342] In this vein, *ex ante* SIAs can be combined with *ex post* evaluations of trade and investment agreements. Impact assessments are certainly a way to capture how IIAs effect changes in investment flows and practices, and are generally considered to be a beneficial tool to enhance SD integration in terms of trade and investment relations between States.[343] The practice of conducting impact assessment of trade and investment agreements has become common practice of certain yet few States.[344] The practice is, thus, far from being universally applied. Since it is mostly done unilaterally and does not impose additional obligations on States or investors, it is among the less controversial issues of international investment law-making. In terms of ensuring concrete SD outcomes, States should evaluate the projected environmental, social, economic and human rights

---

assessment, social impact assessment, etc. See, International Association for Impact Assessment. However, impact assessments of agreements are to be distinguished from impact assessments of projects.

341   UNGA, A/HRC/19/59/Add.5, Human Rights Council, Report of the Special Rapporteur on the right to food, De Schutter O, 'Guiding principles on human rights impact assessments of trade and investment agreements,' para 2.

342   The rationale behind *ex post* SD reviews is that contracting partners can react to negative impacts, and, if need be, amend the agreement. For more details, see Ebert, above note 307, 323.

343   Marín Durán G and Morgera E, *Environmental Integration in the EU's External Relations: Beyond Multilateral Dimensions* (Hart Pub 2012) 234.

344   Especially, the EU, Canada and the USA. See Section 5.5.

impacts of the agreements as well as the factors that make those impacts more or less likely to occur.[345] The results of the impact assessment should be taken seriously by negotiators and other decision-makers whilst the impact assessment process also needs also to be clearly defined and continuously updated according to the latest scientific insights.

2.7   Concluding Remarks

With the 1992 Rio Conference, SD became one of the key guiding principles for the international community. The concept is not readily apprehensible as it is evolutive in nature and is associated with a large bulk of aspects, sub-principles and policy goals, which all—one way or the other—concern the general welfare of humanity. The clearest manner to define and describe SD is the balance between economic development, social development and environmental protection as interdependent and mutually reinforcing components. This is not withstanding the fact the SD comes with a much larger and more complex normative framework under which fall a number of principles and approaches. In the present chapter, it has been argued that the principle of integration plays a central role in achieving SD because the balance between social, environmental and economic considerations requires their respective integration. In this way, the principle of integration is a procedural principle requiring States and decision-makers to adopt integrated approaches to policy areas and to consider the inter-connectedness of the issues at hand. SD, in this logic, is not an equivalent to the principle of integration since this finding neglects the other SD principles and goals of the Rio Declaration and Agenda 2030, such as the equity principles, prevention or precaution. A more appropriate understanding appears to be that integration is the main means to achieve SD given that it has important benefits for the operationalisation of SD. The objective of SD, in return, is a goal or policy aim. By their nature, goals resemble idealistic visions and are hard to achieve. SD is not different in this respect. Rather it is helpful to see the concept as a process. Thus, the question is not whether we actually develop sustainably but whether decision-makers use their powers to thrive for SD. More concretely, the normative SD framework seeks to guide decision-makers to fix certain misalignments between the scope and impact of economic forces and actors and the integration of environmental and social protection. Whilst States pursue SD, the concrete means of achieving it allows

---

345   Commonwealth Secretariat, above note 147, 273–274.

for discretion in policy approaches and law-making. States decide how to balance the three SD pillars is most appropriately for their society. The discretion must, however, be exerted against the normative SD framework. Finally, law-making and regulation on SD matters is necessary for the legal development of the concept. Whether SD deploys concrete effects depends on contextual concretisation and factual elaboration through law-making otherwise, it remains a political aspiration. SD does not promise perfect solutions but it poses new and challenging questions for international law-making and, at the same time, offers innovative guidelines to some of the more systemic problems of international law.

International investment law is one of the regimes for which the integration of SD is vividly discussed, debated and further developed by States. The paradigm shifts that are taking place within international investment law and governance show the extent to which SD can translate into concrete treaty drafting. The present chapter had the purpose of providing a succinct overview of the pros and cons of the most relevant approaches of SD integration in IIAs. The analysis suggested three functions of SD integration in international investment law-making, which help to apprehend the panoply of treaty drafting approaches. The issues, presented through the lens of three SD functions, reflect the normative questions that States, intergovernmental organisations, NGOs and scholars try to answer on how IIAs should be drafted to best guarantee SD outcomes.

A first function is that IIAs can be a suitable means by which to promote SD-friendly investments. In other words, IIAs should ensure that they do not "subsidies" SD-negative investment. In this vein, they should discourage investment which is harmful for SD by not providing them with the IIA's treaty protection. Therefore, arguments are made to draft the investment definition in such a way as to only guarantee protection to investments that are SD-friendly. As discussed, investment in the form of FDI is in principle the most beneficial form for SD due to the more concrete spill-over effects. At the same time, it cannot totally be excluded that portfolio investments can never bear benefits for SD, namely when they operate as a financial support to local companies. Moreover, including a reference to the contribution to the host State's development remains highly controversial. Making a contribution to the host State's development a *sine qua non* condition for treaty protection and access to ISDS might be an interesting policy approach but it comes with drawbacks as it is, in practice, not clear how such a contribution would be assessed. It has been argued that the criteria should be referred to while keeping their fulfilment flexible in a concrete case. The debate on sustainable investment also covers *ex ante* screening mechanisms of investments. Here, treaty protection is subject to approval of an investment. States can elaborate a list of criteria that allow them to evaluate an investment and that they consider particularly useful to advance SD in their country. Next to the definition of an investment, it has been argued that liberalisation commitments bear potentials for channelling sustainable investment activities into a country. Even though this topic receives less attention in the debate, provisions concerning market liberalisation have the potential to align the opening of economies to foreign investment with national social and economic development strategies and priorities. *A fortiori*, IIAs should, therefore, not undermine the capacity of States to unilaterally set conditions and make decisions on which sectors are liberalised. In particular, developing countries should not be burdened with performance requirements that go beyond what has been agreed at the WTO.

The second and most prominently discussed function of SD integration in IIAs concerns the States' regulatory space for SD-advancing laws and regulations at the national level. The idea is that investment protection standards are drafted in such a way as to better safeguard policy areas promoting SD and avoiding a scenario whereby IIAs pose obstacles to the realisation and implementation of domestic SD legislation. Several approaches are being discussed to introduce safeguards into IIAs. One way is to draft investment protection standards with greater precision, as the example of FET reveals. An important aspect of the debate is to enhance regulatory flexibility through exceptions. The codification of the police power doctrine appears to be a good way forward as it allows for a balancing when claims based on an indirect expropriation are at stake. In contrast hereto, the inclusion of general exception clauses in IIAs has already been proven to be less effective in introducing more regulatory flexibility. Also, it might be preferable to frame the substantive obligations in such a way as to provide greater clarity about the types of government action that are permitted and proscribed and to allow flexibility within the treaty's substantive provision. Considering the resolution of investor-State disputes, it is well-known that investment arbitration has had an important triggering effect for the reform and reorientation of the investment regime. In this chapter, it has, however, been argued that the correlation between ISDS and SD requires a closer look. Under two scenarios, ISDS harms SD. First, SD is undermined when a State has to pay large sums on ISDS proceedings and compensation payments to investors, and that money is then missing for SD-advancing policy measures assuming that the defaulting State has such intentions. Second, SD is undermined when the threat of an ISDS claim thwarts the adoption of national SD legalisation. In the reform debate, these two assumptions are presented as true in all cases, even though only mixed evidence exists for both scenarios.[346]

Finally, the third function concerns the IIAs' potential to enhance international cooperation on SD that has the general purpose of strengthening the regulation on environmental protection and social standards including human rights at the national and the international law level. IIAs can be beneficial for advancing the SD agenda if they include commitments for States not to lower environmental and labour regulations to attract investment, if they require from State to adhere to certain internationally agreed standards or if they contain commitments to ratify international environmental and labour conventions. An increasingly important topic is collaboration and promotion commitments on global SD issues that can encompass for instance climate change mitigation and anti-corruption measures. Such environmental and social clauses are less controversial in the reform debate. On the one hand, these provisions are still new in international investment governance, and on the other hand, they are not subject to stringent inter-State enforcement or ISDS. As discussed in this chapter, better enforcement mechanisms might be necessary to render the provisions effective. At the same time, the debate has just started and more research is needed in this respect. Lastly, IIAs can also include commitments to increase the accountability of MNEs. The question of how IIAs can ensure CSR and other obligations, deriving from human rights, good governance, labour standards and environmental protection laws, is a controversial issue in the debate on SD integration in IIAs. From an SD perspective, the asymmetric nature of IIAs that only provides rights and no obligations for foreign investors can hardly be maintained. Investor obligations should be included in IIAs especially because there is no other binding legal instrument for MNEs in force and voluntary standards have not been sufficient. The debate is ongoing about how to best enforce such obligations under IIAs but given that the SD agenda promotes multi-stakeholder responsibility for SD that includes MNEs, IIAs should not be silent on corporate behaviour in host States.

The three different functions and ways to consider SD integration in international investment law-making lay out the common grounds on which many States and other actors agree. So far, several of the described approaches are nascent or have only been included in model treaties. Others are contained in treaties but that have not yet found concrete application or have not yet been subject to legal interpretation in an investment dispute. Therefore, one needs to be careful in making final judgements on their effectiveness. For the present

---

346 See Section 2.5.3.

analysis, presenting the normative discussion surrounding the integration of SD into IIAs is an important step as it allows to position the EU in the current debate setting the international law benchmarks against which the EU investment law-making is scrutinised. For these reasons, the chapter's main purpose has not been to provide normative answers to all the questions and challenges SD poses to international investment law-making. Rather it has conceptualised the reform approaches and set out the trends and benchmarks for international investment law-making. In this framework of new approaches and SD-led policies for IIAs, the EU has to define its investment law-making. The normative framework on SD and the developments in international investment law to align IIAs with SD imperatives create legal obligations and expectations that the EU cannot disregard. In other words, the EU should not depart from such a politico-legal setting. Not engaging with the debate would undermine the position of the EU as a global actor.

CHAPTER 3

Sustainable Development in the EU Legal Order

SD deploys different legal impacts depending on the legal status it has been assigned to in a given legal order.[1] Within the EU legal order, SD forms part of the Union objectives applicable to the internal and external actions of the EU. The concept has constitutional rank and consequently, has shaped the legislative and policy measures taken by the EU. Given that SD is primarily an international construct, international law and global policy instruments influenced to a considerable extent the content of SD within the EU legal order, yet those that expect SD to be defined under EU law will be disappointed. The concept is not a well-defined notion under international law, and under EU law, it appears to be equally difficult to determine the substantive content of the concept in abstract and absolute terms.[2] The reasons are that the EU treaties do not define SD and the Court of Justice of the European Union (CJEU) did not define the concept either.[3] An additional difficulty for determining the content of SD within the EU legal order is the sometimes "inflatory use" of the term by the EU institutions.[4] However, if one takes a more policy-specific and context-specific approach to SD, the contours of the concept become indeed apparent. The increasing crystallisation of SD in specific policies is also due to the fact that SD has become a general objective of trans-political application. This chapter looks at both internal and external objectives with a focus on external issues.

---

1 Gehne K, *Nachhaltige Entwicklung als Rechtsprinzip: normativer Aussagegehalt, rechtstheoretische Einordnung, Funktionen im Recht* (Mohr Siebeck 2011) 257.
2 For SD in international law, see Section 2.1.
3 Even though the Court arguably had the opportunity to do so. See ECJ, Case C-142/95 P *Associazione degli Agricoltori della provincia di Rovigo v Commission*, EU:C:1996:493; and ECJ, Case C-371/98 *R v Secretary of State for Environment, Transport and the Regions, ex p First Corporate Shipping*, EU:C:2000:108. In the latter case, Advocate General Léger attempted to define SD: "[SD] does not mean that the interest of the environment must necessarily and systematically prevail over the interests defended in the context of their policies pursued by the Community [...]. On the contrary, it emphasizes the necessary balance between various interests which sometime clash, but which must be reconciled", see AG Léger, Opinion, para 54. In its judgement, the Court did not refer to this passage of the AG's opinion.
4 Krämer L, 'Sustainable Development in the EC' in: Bugge H and Voigt C (eds), *Sustainable Development in International and National Law: What Did the Brundtland Report Do to Legal Thinking and Legal Development, and Where Can We Go from Here?* (Europa Law Publishing 2008) 377.

The chapter aims to analyse SD within the EU legal order and show how the objective operates therein. After a presentation of the reception of the concept in EU law, the chapter considers the normative nature of Union objectives and the legal effects that derive from them. The normative framework of SD providing discretion to the EU's institutions has the benefit of policy-specific adaption. Subsequently, the analysis turns to the legal principles and requirements of EU constitutional law that are supportive of SD. The requirements of policy integration and policy coherence receive special attention. The principle of integration is key for the realisation of SD within the EU. The latter also reveals interesting similarities when looking at the legal functions of SD in EU law and international law.[5] The chapter concludes with the examination of how differently SD is articulated in the various EU policies. It thereby lays the conceptual building block after which the Common Commercial Policy is examined in Chapter 4.

3.1 The Reception of SD as a Union Objective

With the 1992 Rio Conference on Environment and Development, countries and other international actors, including the EU, began to elaborate policy measures on SD seeking to implement the principles of the Rio Declaration and Agenda 21.[6] Over the years, SD has had an apparent impact on EU laws and policies. Even up to the present day, the EU seeks to follow international developments concerning SD closely. The EU's current endeavour is to implement

---

5 It should also be mentioned that the legal status and function of objectives is, in the present chapter, understood purely from the perspective of EU primary law. This perspective does, however, not neglect the possible binding nature of SD as an objective based on general international law or customary international law as far as the customary law status is admitted (with reference to the relevant section of the work). In a case such as the latter, the EU would additionally be bound by the objective of SD derived from the international legal order; ECJ, Case C-162/96 *A Racke GmbH & Co v Hauptzollamt Mainz*, EU:C:1998:293, paras 45–46. Confirmed in ECJ, Case C-366/10 *Air Transport Association of America and others v Secretary of State for Energy and Climate Change*, EU:C:2011:864, para 101. As the following reasoning will show, Union objectives are binding on EU institutions, the impacts of SD as a customary international law rule are in any case rather supplementary. See also Art 3(5) TEU: the EU shall contribute to "the strict observance and the development of international law" including customary international law.
6 UN Conference on Environment and Development, 'Rio Declaration on Environment and Development and Agenda 21', [1992] Doc A/CONF.151/26Rev 1 (hereafter: Rio Declaration). See Section 2.1.

Agenda 2030 and to contribute to the achievement of the SDGS in Europe as well as globally.[7]

Tracing back history, it is interesting that some elements of SD were, in the European context, already present at the start of the environmental policy initiatives of the European Community (EC) in the 1970s.[8] That decade was characterised by growing public and scientific awareness of the need for environmental protection and the awareness of the wider public that there are limits to the growth model was rising. The run-up to the 1972 Stockholm Conference on the Human Environment gave a strong impetus for EU Member States to establish an environmental policy at the European level. Reportedly, the original six Member States tried to gain international support for more stringent environmental obligations during the Stockholm Conference, which has failed for political reasons.[9] The outcome declaration of the Stockholm Conference, despite being a milestone document for international environmental law, still subordinated environmental protection to economic development, whereas for the EC, at least in the initial stages of its environmental policy, economic development and environmental protection were considered to be on an equal footing. In the aftermath of the Stockholm Conference, the EC head of States and governments made an early allusion to the main concerns of SD without, however, mentioning the term. They set out that "[e]conomic expansion is not an end in itself", but must be beneficial to humanity, which can ultimately only be achieved by also protecting the environment.[10] Shortly after, the European Commission elaborated the first

---

7   UN General Assembly, 'Transforming our world: the 2030 Agenda for Sustainable Development', [2015] A/RES/70/1 (hereafter Agenda 2030); European Commission Communication, 'Next steps for a sustainable European future. European action for sustainability', COM (2016) 739 final; European Parliament, 'Resolution of 6 July 2017 on EU action for sustainability', 2017/2009(INI).

8   The first communication of the Commission concerning the Community's policy on the environment was issued on 22 July 1971, see Commission of the European Communities, 'First Communication of the Commission about the Community's policy on the environment', SEC (71) 2616 final.

9   Langlet D and Mahmoudi S, *EU Environmental Law and Policy* (Oxford University Press 2016) 27.

10 'Statement from the Paris Summit', Bulletin of the European Communities, [1972] No 10, 14–26, para 3: "Economic expansion is not an end in itself. Its first aim should be to enable disparities in living conditions to be reduced. It must take place with the participation of all the social partners. It should result in an improvement in the quality of life as well as in standards of living. As befits the genius of Europe, particular attention will be given to intangible values and to protecting the environment, so that progress may really be put at the service of mankind."

Environment Action Programme (EAP).[11] This first EAP of 1973 contained the rationale that economic development, prosperity and the protection of the environment are mutually interdependent and highlights that for the EU, at that time already, economic development and environmental protection were in principle on an equal footing.

The third and fourth EAP adopted in 1982 and 1987 respectively, marked a certain shift as the European Commission started to link environmental protection to the internal market, highlighting the potential economic risks and benefits of enhanced environmental protection.[12] Henceforth, the interlinkages between the regulation of environmental protection and the internal market became the main focus of the still young EU environmental policy. In this vein, environmental regulations should be harmonised in order to avoid distortion of competitiveness. In 1985, the Court of Justice held that environmental protection had become an "essential objective" of the Community.[13] Moreover, since the fourth EAP of 1987, environmental protection was no longer seen as an independent policy but as an integrated activity within economic processes and decision-making. The idea of integration then found its way into the Single European Act adopted in 1986, which included for the first time the environmental integration clause.[14] The approach of environmental integration into economic development marked the prelude to the era of SD at the European level. Only one year later, the Brundtland Report was adopted, mentioning SD as a response to the planet's urgent ecological and development challenges.[15] As a reaction to that, the European Council in 1988 declared that SD "must be one of the overriding objectives of the Community policy".[16] In its 1990 Dublin

---

11 First Environmental Action Programme (EAP) was adopted by the European Council in 1972 and covered the period 1973–1976. EAPs are until today important instruments setting out the fundamental principles of EU environmental policy and have consequently been enshrined in Member States' and EU legislation. For more details on the various Environment Action Programmes, see Langlet and Mahmoudi, above note 9, 28–32. The seventh EAP has been adopted in 2013 and covers the period up to 2020.

12 The Second EAP was adopted in 1977 and covered the period 1977–1981. The Third EAP was adopted in 1983 and covered the period 1982–1986.

13 ECJ, Case 240/83 *Procureur de la République v ADBHU*, EU:C:1985:59, para 13. For more details, see Jans JH and Vedder HHB, *European Environmental Law: After Lisbon* (4 ed, Europa Law Publ 2012) 3–6.

14 Environmental protection was only explicitly introduced into the EU treaties with the Single European Act (SEA) in 1986.

15 UN General Assembly, 'Report of the World Commission on Environment and Development', [1987] UN-Doc A/RES/42/187 (Brundtland Report). See Section 2.1.1.

16 European Council, Presidency Conclusions (Rhodes), 'Declaration on the Environment' [1988] SN 4443/1/88 annexe 1, para 2.

Declaration, the European Council then defined SD as a "tool" for improving the state of the environment, social efficiency and competitiveness simultaneously.[17] Moreover, it urged the Commission to take action to bring the internal market into compliance with SD. Henceforth, the development of the internal market must be "sustainable and environmentally sound".[18] The subsequent fifth EAP, adopted in 1993, in the aftermath of the Rio Conference, was entitled "Towards Sustainability". The instrument finally connected the concept of SD to the EU's environmental policy.[19]

3.1.1 SD in EU Primary Law

With the 1992 Maastricht Treaty,[20] the concept of SD was first introduced into the EU treaties. Former Article B TEU provided that the EU shall promote "economic and social progress which is balanced and sustainable".[21] In former Article 2 TEC, the objective was set out that the European Community promotes "sustainable and non-inflationary growth respecting the environment".[22] It becomes apparent that the first formulations of SD within EU primary law were not a fully-fledged recognition of SD as the term "sustainable development" was not used but only the adjective sustainable in combination with progress and growth. Consequently, the first references were restrictive, and SD did not yet become an overarching objective of the EU.[23] The first formulations in EU primary law deviated from the international formulations of SD, in particular, those contained in the 1992 Rio Declaration. The combination of "sustainable" and "growth" has not been formulated as such in the Rio Declaration. In the context of the EU treaties, sustainable growth is meant for economic growth, which is one of the objectives of European integration, in general, adding the qualifier of "respecting the environment" in order to make

---

17   European Council, Presidency Conclusions (Dublin), 'The Environmental Imperative' [1990] SN 60/1/90.
18   Ibid, annexe II, 24.
19   The Fifth EAP was adopted in 1993 and covered the period 1993–2000.
20   The Treaty of Maastricht, signed on 7 Feb 1992, entered into force on 1st Nov 1993.
21   TEU (Maastricht), Art B.
22   TEC (Maastricht), Art 2.
23   See, Krämer, above note 4, 377; see also Pallemaerts M, 'The EU and Sustainable Development: An Ambiguous Relationship', in: Pallemaerts M and Azmanova A (eds), *The European Union and Sustainable Development: Internal and External Dimensions* (VUB Press 2006) 22–23: "While there was obviously a debate on sustainability, no consensus could be reached on recognizing sustainable development as an objective of the Community, and the compromise ultimately made was to refer to 'sustainable growth' instead."

growth sustainable.²⁴ Moreover, Article 2 TEC also referred, in a separate sentence, to "a high level of employment and of social protection" as well as "social cohesion".²⁵ To date, these elements are part of the EU's understanding of SD and are further discussed hereafter. Lastly, the Maastricht Treaty contained one complete reference to the term "sustainable development" in the provision of development cooperation. Former Article 130(1) TEC provided that the objective of the Community's development cooperation was to "foster the sustainable economic and social development of the developing countries".

It was the Treaty of Amsterdam²⁶ that made SD in 1997 a general and overarching objective of the EU.²⁷ SD was added to former Article B TEU providing that the EU shall set itself the objectives, such as "to promote economic and social progress and to achieve balanced and sustainable development". According to Article 2 TEC, as amended by the Treaty of Amsterdam, the EU shall promote *inter alia* "a harmonious, balanced and sustainable development of economic activities" as well as "sustainable and non-inflationary growth".²⁸ The modified Article 2 TEC did not replace the notion of "sustainable and non-inflationary growth" as introduced by the Maastricht Treaty but the reference to "respecting the environment" was taken out. Article 2 TEC made environmental protection an explicit objective as it added that the European Community seeks to promote "a high level of protection and improvement of the quality of the environment".²⁹ The Amsterdam Treaty further introduced an amendment to a central provision of environmental protection: the so-called "environmental integration clause", which was first introduced in the Single European Act in 1986.³⁰ Under the Amsterdam Treaty, former Article 6 TEC set out the obligation to integrate environmental protection into the definition and implementation of other Community policies and activities "in

---

24   Ibid.
25   TEC (Maastricht), Art 2.
26   The Treaty of Amsterdam, signed on 2 Oct 1997, entered into force on 1ˢᵗ May 1999.
27   TEU (Amsterdam), Preamble, recital 7: "[...] determined to promote economic and social progress for their peoples, taking into account the principle of sustainable development and within the context of the accomplishment of the internal market"; See also
28   TEC (Amsterdam), Art 2.
29   TEC (Amsterdam), Art 2; Pallemaerts and Azmanova, above note 23, 24.
30   The duty of environmental integration was first introduced in the Single European Act of 1986, see TEC (SEA), Art 130r(2). However, even before that, the third EAP has indicated the EU's willingness and its Member States to integrate the environmental dimension into economic development processes.

particular with a view to promoting sustainable development".³¹ This provision clearly emphasises the environmental dimension of SD by stressing that other policies must take into account environmental and ecological constraints to achieve SD. The requirement of environmental integration under EU primary law from then on fully "translated" Principle 4 of the Rio Declaration.³² Given all these elements, the Amsterdam Treaty was an improvement in fostering SD within the EU legal order.³³

The 2009 Lisbon Treaty gave further impetus for the evolution of SD as an objective and guiding principle of the EU. Under the Lisbon Treaty, SD kept its position in Article 3 TEU, which is the provision that enshrines the main objectives of the EU. Article 3 TEU emphasises, in a specific provision, the objectives set out in the TEU preamble, thereby giving them more significance.³⁴ Just as under the Treaty of Amsterdam, SD remained one of the EU's overarching general objectives, but the scope of the commitment has been broadened. Article 3(3) TEU provides that the EU:

> "shall work for the sustainable development of Europe based on balanced economic growth and price stability, a highly competitive social market economy, aiming at full employment and social progress, and a high level of protection and improvement of the quality of the environment."

The provision highlights SD as being achievable through meeting several goals that are related to the internal market of the EU, such as price stability or a highly competitive social market economy. The "rising living standard" and the "quality of life" were taken out, whereas, the "high level of protection and

---

31 TEC (Amsterdam), Art 6: "Environmental protection requirements must be integrated into the definition and implementation of the Community policies and activities referred to in Article 3, in particular with a view to promoting sustainable development."

32 Rio Declaration, above note 6, Principle 4: "In order to achieve sustainable development, environmental protection shall constitute an integral part of the development process and cannot be considered in isolation from it". See Section 1.1.2. See also Barral V and Dupuy PM, 'Principle 4: Sustainable Development through Integration', in: Viñuales JE (ed), *The Rio Declaration on Environment and Development: A Commentary* (Oxford University Press 2015) 157 et seq.

33 See also, Jans and Vedder, above note 13, 9.

34 TEU, Preamble, recital 9: "Determined to promote economic and social progress for their people, taking into account the principle of sustainable development and within the context of the accomplishment of the internal market and of reinforced cohesion and environmental protection, and to implement policies ensuring that advances in economic integration are accompanied by parallel progress in other fields". See also, EUCFR, Preamble, recital 3.

improvement of the quality of the environment" has been maintained. The Lisbon Treaty also maintains the requirement for integration of environmental protection that can be found in Article 11 TFEU. The provision states "[e]nvironmental protection requirements must be integrated into the definition and implementation of the Union's policies and activities, in particular with a view to promoting sustainable development".[35] A similar provision can be found in the EU Charter of Fundamental Rights (EUCFR). Article 37 thereof on "Environmental Protection" provides "[a] high level of environmental protection and the improvement of the quality of the environment must be integrated into the policies of the Union and ensured in accordance with the principle of sustainable development". SD and environmental concerns were thus linked to other fundamental rights.[36] At the same time, this does not mean that the provision would confer a right *per se*, as it is not drafted as such. The EUCFR operates a distinction between "rights" and "principles".[37] The environmental integration falls under the latter category deploying no direct rights for EU citizens but instead describing an objective addressed to the EU institutions.

An important novelty that has been introduced with the Lisbon Treaty is the strengthening of the external dimension of the objective of SD. Article 3(5) TEU has been introduced with the purpose of setting out a number of values, objectives and principles, which the EU must pursue in its international relations. It adds, namely, that the EU shall "in its relations with the wider world [...] contribute to [...] the sustainable development of the Earth [...]".[38] Also, Article 21 TEU provides an even more extensive set of general external objectives, with SD having a central position. According to Article 21(2) TEU:

"The Union shall define and pursue common policies and actions, and shall work for a high degree of cooperation in all fields of international

---

35   TFEU, Art 11 (TEC, Art 6).
36   A minor difference must be stressed; the Charter uses only the term "policies" and not "activities". Since the Lisbon Treaty, the Charter has the same legal value as the treaties, see TEU, Art 6(1).
37   EUCFR, Art 52(5). For an analysis of the distinction between rights and principles, see ECJ, Case C-176/12 *Association de Médiation Sociale*, EU:C:2014:2, Opinion of AG Cruz Villalon, paras 43–80.
38   TEU, Art 3(5): "In its relations with the wider world, the Union shall uphold and promote its values and interests and contribute to the protection of its citizens. It shall contribute to peace, security, the sustainable development of the Earth, solidarity and mutual respect among peoples, free and fair trade, eradication of poverty and the protection of human rights, in particular the rights of the child, as well as to the strict observance and the development of international law, including respect for the principles of the United Nations Charter".

relations, in order to: [...] foster the sustainable economic, social and environmental development of developing countries, with the primary aim of eradicating poverty [letter d]; and help develop international measures to preserve and improve the quality of the environment and the sustainable management of global natural resources, in order to ensure sustainable development [letter f]"

In sum, SD figures—as an objective—prominently within EU primary law. Since the Amsterdam Treaty, the concept is part of the key constitutional principles of the EU legal order.

3.1.2 *Legal and Political Impacts of SD*

The Rio Declaration and Agenda 21 also marked the beginning of the introduction of SD into EU secondary law.[39] From 1992 until today, the EU has adopted over 250 regulations and directives containing references to SD.[40] In the large majority of instruments SD functions as an objective of the legislative act. It is mentioned either in the preamble or in one of the first articles thereof. The most important internal EU policy areas, in which the concept of SD has been incorporated, are the Fisheries Policy, the Regional Policy, the Common Agricultural Policy, as well as the policies of Energy and Transport.[41] Concerning EU secondary law on environmental protection, it is interesting to note that SD is not systematically included in all areas of EU environmental law; here the main areas of SD integration are found in the use of water, the conservation of biodiversity and climate change.[42] For its external field of action, the EU integrated SD in a number of legislative acts dealing with its policy on Development Cooperation.[43] In addition, SD has, since the beginning of the 1990s, been enshrined in numerous bilateral and multilateral treaties

---

39 De Sadeleer N, *EU Environmental Law and the Internal Market* (Oxford University Press 2014) 18. The first Regulation mentioning SD was Regulation No 443/92 of the Council of 25 Feb 1992 on financial and technical assistance to, and economic cooperation with, the developing countries in Asia and Latin America, [1992] OJ L 52/1.
40 Status Jan 2019.
41 See for more details, Krämer, above note 4, 379–387.
42 Ibid. Eg Directive 2000/60 of 23 Oct 2000 establishing a framework for Community action in the field of water policy, [2000] OJ L 327/1; and Directive 92/43 of the Council of 21 May 1992 on the conservation of natural habitats and of wild fauna and flora [1992] OJ L 206 (Habitats Directive).
43 On development cooperation, see eg Regulation No 443/92, above note 39. See also eg Regulation No 980/2005 of the Council of 27 June 2005 applying a scheme of generalised tariff preferences, [2005] OJ L 169/1.

concluded by the EU.⁴⁴ In particular, SD references can be found in agreements with developing countries, in economic agreements and in multilateral environmental agreements (MEAs). A common strand, also for international agreements to which the EU is a contracting party, is that SD mainly serves as an objective and ultimate goal of a given treaty arrangement. Hence, the references made to SD in various policy areas of the EU highlight that SD is used in a flexible way by the EU institutions. And as discussed hereafter, the contours of SD have regularly been adapted according to the policy area in which it operates.

Next to the traditional sources of EU law, the role of soft law instruments with respect to SD should not be overseen.⁴⁵ The instruments used by the EU vary from action plans and action programmes to policy strategies and communications. These medium-term programmes and policy documents mirror a general political climate and, for the EU, they mostly constitute a reaction to the developments on SD at the international level. They are non-binding, yet they deploy certain legal effects in the sense that they can lead to new EU legislation or impact the amendment of the EU treaties.⁴⁶ The following shall provide an overview of some of the most important instruments adopted by the EU institutions shaping the evolution of SD integration within the EU legal order.

A central policy instrument of the EU seeking to mainstream SD in all EU policies was the so-called Sustainable Development Strategy (SDS).⁴⁷ The European Council initiated the Strategy in 2001. The head of States and

---

44   Eg Cotonou Agreement, [2000] OJ L 317/3; Convention on Biological Diversity [1993] OJ L 309/3; Nagoya Protocol on Access to Genetic Resources and the Fair and Equitable Sharing of Benefits Arising from their Utilization to the Convention on Biological Diversity, [2014] OJ L 150/234.

45   At the international level, soft law instruments play a particularly important role in the context of international social standards and environmental law. See eg, Redgwell C, 'Sources of International Environmental Law: Formality and Informality in the Dynamic Evolution of International Environmental Law Norms' in: Besson S and d'Aspremont J (eds), *The Oxford Handbook on the Sources of International Law* (Oxford University Press 2017) 940–958.

46   See for more details on soft law within the EU, Eliantonio M and Stefan O, 'Soft Law Before the European Courts: Discovering a "Common Pattern"?' (2018) 37 Yearbook of European Law 457.

47   The strategy has been prepared by the Commission and at the 2001 Göteborg summit approved by the European Council. See European Commission Communication, 'A Sustainable Europe for a better World—A European Union Strategy for Sustainable Development', COM (2001) 264 final; and European Council, Presidency Conclusions (Göteborg), [2001] SN 200/1/01 REV 1.

governments reiterated that SD is "a fundamental objective under the Treaties", which "requires dealing with economic, social and environmental policies in a mutually reinforcing way".[48] Otherwise however, the European Council failed to adopt a more concrete definition of SD.[49] In 2002, the first SDS was complemented by an additional strategy that focused on the external dimension of SD.[50] In 2006, the European Council then adopted a Review of the SDS.[51] The latter instrument reiterated that the main components of SD were environmental protection, social equity and cohesion as well as economic prosperity.[52] The Review of the SDS later had an impact on the elaboration of the Lisbon Treaty and the strengthening of SD therein.[53] In terms of monitoring the implementation of the SD objective, the 2006 Strategy led the EU to mandate Eurostat to prepare monitoring reports on the progress of the EU with respect to SD.[54] The Strategy was subsequently once more subject to review. The last update of the Strategy emphasised that many "unsustainable" trends required "urgent action, such as to curb and adapt to climate change, to decrease high energy consumption in the transport sector and to reverse the current loss of biodiversity and natural resources".[55]

In a number of additional policy instruments, the EU made statements on the development of the SD concept at the international level, mostly in terms of the Rio follow-up process.[56] Lately, as a reaction to Agenda 2030 and the SDGs, the European Commission and the European Parliament issued a statement

---

48   Ibid (Conclusion of the Council), para 19.
49   Langlet and Mahmoudi, above note 19, 44. The SDS makes a reference to the SD definition of the Brundtland Report, above note 17, ("to meet the needs of the present generation without compromising those of future generations").
50   European Commission Communication, 'Towards a world partnership for sustainable development', COM (2002) 82 final.
51   European Council, Review Sustainable Development Strategy, [2006] Doc 10917/06.
52   Pallemaerts M, 'Developing More Sustainability?' in: Jordan A and Adelle C (eds), *Environmental Policy in the EU: Actors, Institutions and Processes* (Earthscan New York 2012) 358, Box 19.2.
53   Ibid, 354–359; see also Lee M, *EU Environmental Law, Governance and Decision-Making* (Second edition, Hart Pub 2014) 63–64.
54   Since 2007, Eurostat conducts monitoring reports on the implementation of SD within the EU. The latest report is available at <https://ec.europa.eu/eurostat/web/products-statistical-books/-/KS-04-17-780>.
55   European Council, Review Sustainable Development Strategy, [2009] Doc 16818/09.
56   European Council, above note 47; World Summit on Sustainable Development, 'Johannesburg Declaration on Sustainable Development', [2004] A/CONF/199/20; European Commission, Communication, 'Rio+20: towards the green economy and better governance', COM (2011)363 final. UN General Assembly, 'The Future We Want', Outcome Document Adopted at Rio+20', [2012] A/RES/66/28.

dealing with how SD integration should look at the EU level.⁵⁷ Its adoption illustrates that the EU seeks to follow closely international developments on SD. Finally, SD also deploys a central role in sectoral policy instruments, of which three shall be mentioned here.⁵⁸ First, EAPs play a significant role in EU environmental policy. The Fifth EAP, adopted in 1993, first focused on SD and formulated in greater detail the environmental components of SD. Under the current Seventh EAP that was adopted in 2013, SD is mainly understood in the context of transforming economic activities into a resource-efficient green economy.⁵⁹ Second, the Strategy Europe 2020 on "smart, inclusive and sustainable growth" should also be mentioned.⁶⁰ The strategy's main goal is to strengthen economic growth and employment in the EU, by stressing the need to render the EU a more resource-efficient and more competitive economy. Third, another policy instrument with a strong SD component is the 2017 European on Development.⁶¹ The European Consensus on Development is a high-level policy document jointly adopted by all the main EU institutional actors as well as the Member States. The instrument focuses on eradicating poverty promoted in the context of the EU's development cooperation policy.

3.2   SD—A Union Objective Unlike Any Other?

The legal status under EU law is determined by the position it holds within the EU treaties. SD is located in the provisions of the treaties that set out the fundamental principles and objectives of the EU legal order. The concept figures next to other Union objectives such as peace, democracy, human rights, as well as security and justice. Article 3(3) TEU contains the economic, social, and cultural principles for the EU internal order. SD as an external Union objective can be found in Articles 3(5) and 21 TEU setting out a number of values, objectives

---

57   European Commission, above note 7; and European Parliament, above note 7. The content of the instrument is further discussed hereafter.
58   The common commercial policy is not mentioned here because it will be discussed in detail under Section 3.5.
59   Decision No 1386/2013 of the European Parliament and the Council, [2013] OJ L 354/171. See also UN Rio+20, above note 56.
60   European Commission Communication, 'Europe 2020—A strategy for smart, sustainable and inclusive growth', COM (2010) 2020 final.
61   The New European Consensus on Development 'Our World, Our Dignity, Our Future', Joint Statement by the Council and the representatives of the Governments of the Member States meeting within the Council, the European Parliament and the European Commission, [2017] (hereafter: New European Consensus on Development).

and principles of EU external action.⁶² As such, Article 3(5) TEU indicates that the EU "shall uphold and promote its values and interests". Article 21(1) TEU states that "the Union's action on the international scene shall be guided by the principles which have inspired its own creation, development and enlargement".⁶³ SD hence falls under the norm category of Union objectives within the EU legal order. This section seeks to examine more closely the normativity of SD as a Union objective and to show that Union objectives are a purposeful norm category in the EU legal order.⁶⁴

3.2.1   *The Changing Position of Objectives in the EU Legal Order*

To understand the norm category of Union objectives, it is essential to contrast them with competences. Objectives and competences are two components of the principle of attribution and its corollary, the principle of speciality. Both principles are not proper for the EU. Any international organisation is based on attributed powers conferred by its creators to achieve the objectives assigned to it in the organisation's founding treaty.⁶⁵ At the same time, in the course of the integration process of the EU, it became questionable whether Union objectives still have their original function.⁶⁶

At the origins of the EU stand three specialised international organisations: the European Coal and Steel Community, the European Economic Community and the European Atomic Energy. The so-called Communities

---

62   Since the Treaty of Amsterdam, when SD became an objective in its own right, there was a distinction between SD internally and externally.
63   TEU, Art 21(1).
64   The internal and external Union objectives are considered together here given that their functions and legal consequences are essentially the same. See Sommermann KP, 'Article 3 TEU' in: Blanke HJ and Mangiameli S (eds), *The Treaty on European Union (TEU)* (Springer 2013) 179, pt 51; see also Larik J, *Foreign Policy Objectives in European Constitutional Law* (Oxford University Press 2016) 126. For a definition of normativity see, Amselek P, *Méthode phénoménologique et théorie du droit* (L.G.D.J. 1964) 257: Une "proposition est normative en tant qu'elle formule un modèle"; Ost F and van de Kerchove M, *De la pyramide au réseau? Pour une théorie dialectique du droit* (Publications des Facultés universitaires Saint-Louis 2002) 33: "est effective la règle utilisée par ses destinataires comme modèle pour orienter leur pratique".
65   Campbell AIL, 'The Limits of the Powers of International Organisations' (1983) 32 International and Comparative Law Quarterly 523. See also PCIJ, *Jurisdiction of the European Commission of the Danube* (Advisory Opinion) [1927] PCIJ Rep Series B No 14, 64; ICJ, *Legality of the Use by a State of Nuclear Weapons in Armed Conflicts* (Advisory Opinion) [1996] ICJ Rep 66, paras 19 and 25.
66   Larik J, 'From Speciality to a Constitutional Sense of Purpose: On the Changing Role of the Objectives of the European Union' (2014) 63 International and Comparative Law Quarterly 935, 938.

constituted, like any international organisations, derivate subjects of international law with only a limited set of powers and a set of specific (and limited) objectives.[67] Objectives are particularly important for international organisations as they state the purpose and function of the entity. In other words, international organisations are, in principle, "functional entities" with limited powers that are connected to the pursuance of specific and preformulated objectives.[68] Moreover, unlike States that have the capacity to establish their own competences (*Kompetenz-Kompetenz*), the powers of international organisations are restricted to those powers that have been attributed to them to pursue the specific objectives for which they were created, according to the principle of attribution.[69] In this respect, objectives are also an important element for the determination of potential *ultra vires* actions taken by a given international organisation in the exercise of their mandate.[70]

The EU started as an international organisation with few specific objectives, namely "limited economic integration with a view to securing greater peace and prosperity for the Member States".[71] However, more and more competences were shifted from the Member States to the EU with the result of deepening integration. The EU has become, over the last decades, an entity with manifold objectives, functions and areas of action. It has evolved into something much larger and more complex and can hardly be qualified as an ordinary international organisations given that its functions are no longer "specialised" and confined to one single area of activity.[72] Whilst the process of European integration did not discard the principle of attributed competences, it affected the relationship between competences and the objectives.[73] The

---

67   According to the usual definition, international organisations are entities based on an international agreement and governed by international law, with States (and/or other organisations) as their members and equipped with at least one organ with a will of its own. See, Schermers H and Blokker N, *International Institutional Law* (4th edn, Martinus Nijhoff 2003) 36–47.
68   Larik, above note 66, 939.
69   Larik, above note 64, 151–152.
70   *Certain Expenses of the United Nations* (Advisory Opinion), ICJ Rep 1962 151, 168.
71   De Búrca G, 'Europe's *raison d'être*' in: Kochenov D and Amtenbrink F (eds), *The European Union's Shaping of the International Legal Order* (Cambridge University Press 2014), 21.
72   Ibid. Larik, above note 66, 939.
73   Larik, above note 64, 129. This transformation of the EU into a *sui generis* entity is, according to the legal culture and language of scholars, either described by the terms "specificity" i.e. *spécificité* or by the process of "constitutionalisation" of the EU legal order. French scholars refer to *spécificité*, see eg Mégret J, 'La spécificité du droit communautaire', Revue internationale de droit comparé (1967) 19–3, 565–577. German and Anglo-Saxon scholarship mainly uses "constitutionalisation", see eg Weiler J, *The Constitution of Europe: 'Do the New Clothes Have an Emperor?' And Other Essays on European Integration* (Cambridge

Treaty of Lisbon marked the further broadening of the scope of the principle of speciality because more competences have been attributed to the EU and the breadth of objectives has again been widened.

At the same time, the EU still needs to be understood through the lenses of an international organisation mostly so because competences need to be conferred by its Member States. The allocation of competences is, under EU law, governed by the principle of conferral (*i.e.* the principle of attribution). Article 5(2) TEU provides that the EU "shall act only within the limits of the competences conferred upon it by the Member States in the Treaties to attain the objectives set out therein".[74] Article 3 TEU (containing the general objectives of the EU) provides, in its paragraph 6, that the EU "shall pursue its objectives by appropriate means commensurate with the competences which are conferred upon it in the Treaties". In addition, Article 5(2) TEU also adds that "[c]ompetences not conferred upon the Union shall remain with the Member States". In order to pursue its functions and objectives, the EU disposes of a number of sectoral competences. The principles of proportionality and subsidiarity govern the exercise of competences in relation to objectives.[75] Namely, through the principle of proportionality, objectives condition the impact of an intervention of a given EU action. Article 5(4) TEU provides that "the content and form of the Union action shall not exceed what is necessary to achieve the objectives of the Treaties". According to the CJEU, the principle of proportionality requires the EU to adopt measures that are appropriate for ensuring the attainment of the objective, whereby they pursue and do not go beyond what is necessary for that purpose.[76] The principle of subsidiarity, in return, seeks to condition the exercise of the competences that are shared between the EU and its Member States. Article 5(3) TEU, for its part, provides that "the Union shall act only if and in so far as the objectives of the proposed action cannot be sufficiently achieved by the Member States".

The principle of conferral has not lost its importance within the EU legal order. Members States remain attentive to oversee the exercise of the competences of the EU institutions and legal quarrels between the Member States and

---

University Press 1999); Peters A, *Elemente Einer Theorie Der Verfassung Europas* (Duncker & Humblot 2001).

74 See also, TEU, Art 1: "By this Treaty, the HIGH CONTRACTING PARTIES establish among themselves a EUROPEAN UNION, hereafter called 'the Union' on which the Member States confer competences to attain objectives they have in common. [...]"

75 Neframi E, 'Le rapport entre objectifs et compétences: de la structuration et de l'identité de l'Union européenne', in: Neframi E (ed), *Objectifs et compétences dans l'Union européenne* (Bruylant 2013) 8.

76 See eg ECJ, Case C-106/91 *Ramrath v Ministre de la Justice*, EU:C:1992:230, paras 29 and 30.

the EU institutions over competence questions still are among the everyday business of the CJEU. In this respect, the scope of application of Union objectives still defines the extent to which conferred competences can be exercised, but the increase in objectives makes it more and more challenging to frame a clear relationship between competence and objective(s), mainly because a given competence in one field can come with a multiple set of objectives, and a given objective, in contrast, can also find its expression in a series of provisions attributing competences under the EU treaties.[77] Especially general objectives have implications on the determination of the appropriate legal basis of EU measures and are further discussed in the section on the legal effects of SD. In the past, the relationship between competences and objective was blurred by the flexibility clause enshrined in Article 352 TFEU.[78] The latter provision allows EU institutions to warrant powers that are not foreseen in the treaties in order to pursue an objective. A given objective of the EU could lay the basis for a modality of action "within the framework of the policies defined in the Treaties".[79] In the course of the integration process, EU institutions have generously used this provision, a practice that has occasionally been sanctioned by the CJEU.[80] A specific declaration of the Member States to the Lisbon Treaty sets out that Article 352 TFEU cannot serve as a basis for widening the scope of competences.[81] Moreover, since the Lisbon Treaty, the recourse to this

---

77 ECJ, Opinion 2/13, *Accession of the European Union to the European Convention for the Protection of Human Rights and Fundamental Freedoms*, EU:C:2014:2454, para 172: "The pursuit of the EU's objectives, as set out in Article 3 TEU, is entrusted to a series of fundamental provisions, such as those providing for the free movement of goods, services, capital and persons, citizenship of the Union, the area of freedom, security and justice, and competition policy. Those provisions, which are part of the framework of a system that is specific to the EU, are structured in such a way as to contribute—each within its specific field and with its particular characteristics—to the implementation of the process of integration that is the raison d'être of the EU itself."

78 TFEU, Art 352(1): "If action by the Union should prove necessary, within the framework of the policies defined in the Treaties, to attain one of the objectives set out in the Treaties, and the Treaties have not provided the necessary powers, the Council, acting unanimously on a proposal from the Commission and after obtaining the consent of the European Parliament, shall adopt the appropriate measures. Where the measures in question are adopted by the Council in accordance with a special legislative procedure, it shall also act unanimously on a proposal from the Commission and after obtaining the consent of the European Parliament."

79 Ibid.

80 ECJ, Case 8/73 *Massey-Ferguson*, EU:C:1973:90, para 4; ECJ, Joined Cases C-402/05 P and C-415/05 P *Kadi and Al Barakaat*, EU:C:2008:461, para 235.

81 Lisbon Treaty, Declaration No 42: "The Conference underlines that, in accordance with the settled case law of the Court of Justice of the European Union, Article 352 of the Treaty on the Functioning of the European Union, being an integral part of an institutional system

provision has dramatically declined not least because competences are, under the current treaties, better defined and explicitly listed. Nevertheless, the Lisbon Treaty did not reintroduce a strict functionality relationship between competences and objectives as it increased the number of general objectives that operate in a transversal and horizontal manner.

3.2.1.1 SD as a General and Horizontal Objective

SD operates as a general objective for all EU action, internally as well as externally due to its incorporation in Article 3 TEU. General objectives are considered general as they apply (in principle) to all EU action *i.e.* they are detached from a specific sector or policy area.[82] Article 21 TEU adds further general objectives for EU external actions. They are also general as the list of Article 21 TEU applies to any EU external policy area. General objectives thus have a transversal character by being relevant across all EU actions. Due to the transversal character of general objectives, they are closely connected to horizontal objectives. Such horizontal objectives are expressed and formalised by horizontal clauses—also called integration clauses.[83] The most important example in this respect is Article 11 TFEU on environmental integration setting out that "environmental protection requirements must be integrated into the definition and implementation" of all EU policies and activities "in particular with a view to promoting [SD]".[84] For this latter provision, SD is a horizontal objective operationalised by the horizontal clause on environmental integration. Since the Lisbon Treaty, the number of horizontal clauses has increased. Two of them, environmental protection (Article 11 TFEU) as well as social standards and protection (Article 9 TFEU) are linked to SD. For the social integration clause, the link to SD has been established by the CJEU.[85] The horizontal

---

based on the principle of conferred powers, cannot serve as a basis for widening the scope of Union powers beyond the general framework created by the provisions of the Treaties as a whole and, in particular, by those that define the tasks and the activities of the Union. In any event, this Article cannot be used as a basis for the adoption of provisions whose effect would, in substance, be to amend the Treaties without following the procedure which they provide for that purpose".

82 Michel V, 'Les objectifs à caractère transversal' in: Neframi E (ed), *Objectifs et compétences dans l'Union Européenne* (Bruylant 2013) 180.
83 Ibid.
84 See also CFREU, Art 37: "A high level of environmental protection and the improvement of the quality of the environment must be integrated into the policies of the Union and ensured in accordance with the principle of sustainable development."
85 ECJ, Case C-201/15 *AGET Iraklis*, EU:C:2016:972, paras 76–78. At para 76: "[…] as is apparent from Article 3(3) TEU, the European Union is not only to establish an internal market but is also to work for the sustainable development of Europe, which is based, in particular,

effects of these clauses (through integration) serve SD and makes it a horizontal objective within the EU treaties. Even though a distinction between general and horizontal objectives can be made on the basis of their genesis and their different positions in the treaties, their common feature is that they apply to all EU action, independently of the policy field and competences in question. The *transversal* character is a common feature for both, but one distinction should be underlined: while general objectives either apply internally or externally, horizontal objectives (as expressed in Articles 9 and 11 TFEU) apply to both internal and external action.

Moreover, general objectives constitute, an important pillar in the EU legal order because they reflect the multiplicity of EU actions and the growing numbers of sectors, in which the EU operates. In practice, an action taken for one sector has implications for another sector. For instance, regulations in the agricultural sector also have implications for the environment and often for human health, or regulations seeking to combat climate change can have considerable economic implications. It is therefore important that the focus of laws and regulations is not merely sectoral or concerned with one objective only as this can endanger the realisation of other objectives. General objectives contained in the EU treaties seek to mediate such risk of isolated and purely sectoral lawmaking by requiring the EU institutions to take all the (relevant) objectives into account in any policy field.[86] SD, as a three-dimensional concept, is a well-suited Union objective for addressing the risk of sector-specific legislation and serves to guide the EU institutions to adopt measures that reflect the interconnectedness between the interests at stake. The balancing purpose of transversal objectives is thus aptly expressed in SD. Cross-sectorial legislation can, for the EU, however, be a burdensome undertaking because the nature and scope of its attributed competences vary from one policy to the other. Objectives of transversal character, such as SD, can, in this respect, allow for broad interpretations of a legal basis, which can help to find a solution in a quarrel on the right legal basis but it can also lead to *ultra vires* action by the EU institutions.[87]

---

on a highly competitive social market economy aiming at full employment and social progress, and it is to promote, inter alia, social protection [...]". See also ECJ, Opinion 2/15 *Free Trade Agreement with Singapore*, EU:C:2017:376, para 146.

86 Michel, above 82, 183.

87 Consider also ECJ, Case 62/88 *Greece v Council (Chernobyl I)*, EU:C:1990:15329, pt 18: "The fact that maximum permitted levels of radioactive contamination are fixed in response to a concern to protect public health and that the protection of public health is also one of the objectives of Community action in environmental matters, in accordance with the Article 130r(1), likewise cannot remove Regulation No 3955/87 from the sphere of the common commercial policy."

Finally, general objectives within the EU legal system can help to encourage the migration of legal principles from one policy to another. An illustrative example here would be the migration of the precautionary principle applied in environment policy[88] to laws and regulations dealing with workers' health.[89]

The benefits of Union objectives are thus integrated legal approaches, which should lead to more coherence between the various policies of the EU. These beneficial integrative approaches fostered through the general Union objectives are precisely what the concept of SD seeks to achieve through its three-pillar structure (encompassing economic development, social progress as well as environmental protection) and the interrelationship and reinforcing character of the three pillars.[90]

3.2.1.2 SD and the Values of the EU

Finally, SD operating as a general objective within the EU treaties should also be considered in the broader context of the values of the EU that are set out in Article 2 TEU.[91] This underlines that the concept roots in many of the principles and values on which the EU was funded. SD can, in particular, be deduced from values such as "solidarity" and "justice".[92] Internally, the concept of justice and solidarity in Article 2 TEU are expressed in "the sustainable development of Europe", and promoting, among other things "social justice" and "economic, social and territorial cohesion and solidarity among the Member States" as set out in Article 3(3) TEU. Externally, these values are mirrored in the expression of the objective to contribute to "the sustainable development of the Earth, solidarity and mutual respect among people" as well as the "eradication of poverty as set out in Article 3(5) TEU. In the external context, the value promotion of "solidarity" also encompasses the aim "to encourage the integration of all countries into the world economy", to "help develop international measures to preserve and improve the quality of the environment and the sustainable management of global natural resources, in order to ensure [SD]", and to "assist populations, countries and regions confronting natural or man-made disasters"

---

88 TFEU, Art 191.
89 Eg ECJ, Case C-180/96, *United Kingdom of Great Britain and Northern Ireland v Commission of the European Communities*, EU:C:1998:192.
90 See Section 2.1.
91 TEU, Art 2: "The Union is founded on the values of respect for human dignity, freedom, democracy, equality, the rule of law and respect for human rights, including the rights of persons belonging to minorities. These values are common to the Member States in a society in which pluralism, non-discrimination, tolerance, justice, solidarity and equality between women and men prevail."
92 Larik, above note 64, 118–119.

as expressed in Article 21(2) TEU. SD as an expression in the EU treaties of the values of solidarity, justice and also equity[93] is closely linked to a number of other general objectives and, to a certain extent, absorbs those more specific objectives.[94] It can be added that other EU values, such as democracy, good governance, the rule of law and human rights operating as preconditions of SD also form part of the bigger framework of SD within the EU legal order. In the external sphere, the treaties direct the EU to promote these values and the EU generally presents itself as a value-driven actor.[95] Article 3(5) and 21 TEU are assisting that EU action on the international scene is guided by the values set out in Article 2 TEU.[96] The specificity with SD is that the concept has an international origin different from many other values that the EU typically upholds externally, such as democracy. By promoting and engaging with the concept of SD the EU promotes the multilaterally agreed values of equity and ecological sustainability that are inherent in SD.

3.2.2 *The Legal Effects of SD and Its Limits*

There is little controversy that Union objectives are to be considered as a norm category of EU law and are to be distinguished from non-binding (policy) guidelines.[97] Such findings are not only based on the wording of the provisions stating "shall contribute to"[98] but, additionally, the bindingness of Union objectives was confirmed from early on by the CJEU. In a judgement of 1957, the Court already found that the High Authority of the European Coal and Steel Community was under "a duty to observe" other provisions of the treaty establishing the Community, namely those setting out objectives as they would "establish the fundamental objectives of the Community."[99] In a later case in 1973, in relation to the former Article 3(f) TEC on the objective of ensuring

---

93 Equity is not mentioned in the EU treaties, yet in the international context, SD is mostly linked to equity, namely inter-generational equity and intra-generational equity as expressed in the Rio Declaration, above note 6, Principles 3, 5, 6 and 7. See also Brundtland Report, above note 15, paras 16–26 on "Equity and Common Interest".
94 See Section 4.3.1.1.
95 See TEU, Art 3(5). Whilst this reflects to some extent a euro-centric world view, the strand of thinking derives from EU policy instruments, such as the 2001 Laeken Declaration or the renewed European Development Consensus of 2017. Eg, European Development Consensus, above note 61, paras 2 and 13–15.
96 Cremona M, 'Values in EU Foreign Policy', in: Evans MD and Koutrakos P (eds), *Beyond the Established Legal Orders: Policy Interconnections between the EU and the Rest of the World* (Hart Pub 2011) 314.
97 Larik, above note 64, 154.
98 Eg TEU, Art 3(5).
99 ECJ, Case 8/57 *Groupement des hauts fourneaux et aciéries belges*, EU:C:1958:9, page 253.

competition within the European Economic Community, the Court refused that this provision would merely contain a "general programme devoid of legal effect".[100] On the contrary, it held that "[former] Article 3 [TEC] considers the pursuit of the objective which it lays down to be indispensable for the achievement of the Community's task."[101] Union objectives have "obligatory force".[102] The Court has also stressed that the stipulation of objectives "requires" the EU to take them into account in their various policy fields.[103]

Union objectives thus obtain their binding nature from their embedment in EU primary law. Their effectiveness as a binding norm, however, also depends on the degree of assertiveness. This difference between "formal" bindingness based on the constitutional rank of objectives in the EU treaties and the disputed "material" bindingness based on questions of effectiveness can make it difficult to apprehend the legal function of Union objectives. Those scholars that were concentrating on the material bindingness argued that Union objectives should not be considered to be binding because of their high level of abstraction and vagueness. After the entry into force of the Lisbon Treaty, in particular, doubts were raised on the bindingness of the external objectives as they are, according to some, formulated in an overly ambitious manner.[104] However, the wording of Articles 3(5) and 21 TEU is not vague as to its binding nature, "shall pursue" and "shall contribute" give enough grounds to understand these provisions as an obligation for the EU.[105] Therefore, most scholars generally agreed that internal and external Union objectives are fundamental treaty provisions, which are clearly drafted in a mandatory language despite their programmatic aspects.[106] This latter finding is the convincing one. In

---

100 ECJ, Case 6/72 *Europemballage Corporation and Continental Can Company Inc v Commission*, EU:C:1973:2, para 23.
101 Ibid; see also Larik, above note 64, 154–155.
102 *Continental Can*, above note 100, para 18.
103 Eg ECJ, Case C-268/94 *Portugal v Council*, EU:C:1996:461, para 23.
104 See Drescher W, 'Ziele und Zuständigkeiten', in: Marchetti A and Demesmay C (eds), *Der Vertrag von Lissabon: Analyse und Bewertung* (Nomos 2010) 68; Leino P, 'The Journey Towards All that is Good and Beautiful: Human Rights and 'Common Values' as Guiding Principles of EU Foreign Relations Law', in: Cremona M and Witte B de (eds), *EU Foreign Relations Law: Constitutional Fundamentals* (Hart 2008) 259.
105 Dimopoulos A, 'Integrating Environmental Law Principles and Objectives in EU Investment Policy: Challenges and Opportunities', in: Levashova Y, Lambooy T, Dekker I (eds), *Bridging the Gap between International Investment Law and the Environment* (Eleven International Publishing 2016) 253.
106 Eeckhout P, 'A Normative Basis for EU External Relations? Protecting Internal Values Beyond the Single Market' in: Krajewski M (ed), *Services of General Interest Beyond the Single Market* (Springer International Publishing 2015) 220. Krajewski M, 'Normative Grundlagen der EU-Außenwirtschaftsbeziehungen: Verbindlich, umsetzbar und

other words, in order to decide upon the binding nature of Union objective it is more relevant to take into account their constitutional rank (formal bindingness) and only question in a second step the effectiveness of the norm category. The reason is that the CJEU has constantly confirmed the bindingness of internal and external Union objectives. In Opinion 2/15, the Court reiterated the bindingness and found, in particular, that the EU has an obligation to integrate the SD objective "into the conduct of its [CCP]".[107]

In a next step, one needs to question for whom Union objectives are binding. The principal addressees of Union objectives are the institutions of the EU.[108] This means that they have to follow the orientation that is provided for through the Union objectives when legislating or adopting other acts and measures.[109] More specifically concerned are thus the Council and the European Parliament due to their co-legislative function, as well as the European Commission as it is the latter that proposes new law-making.[110] They have to seek the attainment of the objectives through coordinated action. A more controversial question is whether the Member States can also be addressees of Union objectives.[111] The CJEU held that "Articles 3 and 4 TEC specify fields and objectives to which the activity of the European Community are to relate, and do not lay down obligations on the Member States or public or private bodies".[112] At the same time, Member States are indirectly bound by Union objectives when they implement Union policies.[113] This is based on the principle of sincere cooperation stipulating that the Member States "shall facilitate the achievement of the Union's tasks and refrain from any measures which could jeopardise the attainment of the Union objectives".[114] Member States have a positive obligation to fulfil these Union objectives as far as they act within the framework of the EU. It does not depend on whether the EU's competences are exclusive or shared. As such, it operates as a constitutional safeguard for the protection of the EU's

---

angewandt?' (2016) EuR Heft 3, 242–243, Larik J, *Foreign Policy Objectives in European Constitutional Law* (Oxford University Press 2016) 153–173.

107 Opinion 2/15, above note 85, para 143.
108 See eg, *Continental Can Company*, above note 100, paras 24 et seq.
109 Sommermann, above note 64, 161, pt 6.
110 TEU, Arts 14(1) (Council); 16(1) (Parliament); 17(2) TEU (Commission).
111 Larik, above note 64, 155.
112 ECJ, Case C-181/06 *Deutsche Lufthansa AG v ANA—Aeroportos de Portugal SA*, EU:C:2007:412, para 31.
113 Ruffert M, 'Art. 3 (ex-Art. 2 EUV) [Ziele der EU]' in: Calliess C and Ruffert M (dir), *EUV/AEUV Das Verfassungsrecht der Europäischen Union mit Europäischer Grundrechte Charta—Kommentar* (4. Auflage, Beck 2011) 43; Larik, above note 64, 155.
114 TEU, Art 4(3).

interests.[115] Within the sphere of EU internal policies, the principle of sincere cooperation may require, from the Member States, the passing of specific implementing legislation and the adoption of associated administrative regulations to establish conditions necessary for the achievement of the objective pursued by the EU action.[116] In the sphere of EU external action, the principle of sincere cooperation is particularly relevant for those areas where the Union is internationally disabled from exercising its competences. For instance, when international organisations only recognise States as participating members.[117] Finally, Union objectives generally do not bind legal persons or individuals and do not convey rights to them.[118] Yet, legal persons and individuals are indirectly bound by or can benefit from Union objectives whenever they are concretised in EU law or national implementing legislation.[119] They might namely become relevant for individuals when relevant norms are interpreted in light of the objectives applicable to them and thereby be beneficial.[120]

3.2.2.1 Discretionary Powers of the EU Institutions

The effectiveness of Union objectives depends on their assertiveness. In order for the addresses of the norm, *i.e.* the EU institutions, to fulfil their mandate given by the treaties to pursue the objectives, including SD, one needs to consider the scope of the obligation. Generally, they impose on EU institutions a "constant duty to pursue the objectives within the margin of feasibility".[121] As argued by Laris Jorik, Union objectives are mostly of "imperfectible" nature meaning they cannot be fully achieved and require continuous efforts.[122] One can further query whether EU measures must *be in compliance* with the objectives or, more proactively, whether EU measures must seek to *promote*

---

115 See eg Klamert M, *The Principle of Loyalty in EU Law* (Oxford University Press 2014) 18.
116 Hofmann HCH, 'General Principles of EU Law and EU Administrative Law' in: Barnard C and Peers S (eds), *European Union Law* (2nd ed, Oxford University Press 2017) 200. See also ECJ, Case 33/76 *Rewe-Zentralfinanz EG v Landwirtschaftskammer für das Saarland*, EU:C:1976:188, para 5.
117 See specifically on the EU in the International Labour Organisation (ILO), ECJ, Opinion 2/91 *ILO Convention*, EU:C:1993:106, para 37. See also, Blanquet M (ed), *La prise de décision dans le système de l'Union européenne* (Bruylant 2011).
118 *Deutsche Lufthansa AG v ANA—Aeroportos de Portugal SA*, above note 112, para 31; see also Larik, above note 64, 156.
119 Ruffert, above note 113, 44.
120 Sommermann, above note 64, 162, pt 8.
121 Larik, above note 64, 157.
122 Ibid. Counter-examples hereto are, according to Larik, perfectible objectives such as the completion of the Common Market.

the achievement (even though imperfectible in nature) of the objective.¹²³ At the same time, all objectives are formulated as promotional obligations and thus require the EU to take proactive action.¹²⁴ Conceptually, however, a measure that complies with an objective, for instance with SD, also promotes such an objective. Such discretion also encompasses the choice of prioritising one objective over another in a case of conflict between them especially where a set of general objectives apply to a policy area.¹²⁵ The weighting of various objectives is possible given that there is, in general, no hierarchy between Union objectives.¹²⁶ Clearly, the bindingness of the Union objectives requires that each time an organ of the EU disposes of a margin of appreciation, it needs to be guided by the Union objectives.¹²⁷ EU institutions always have to use their discretion according to the Union objectives.¹²⁸ Therefore, the question on compliance is not whether a measure ultimately fails to achieve an objective but whether the EU institutions did or did not consider the relevant objectives or obviously contravenes the core of them.¹²⁹

Nevertheless, the extent to which it is possible to enforce respect for Union objectives can be questioned given the large margin of appreciation that EU institutions enjoy for the realisation of the objectives.¹³⁰ From CJEU case law, one can deduce that compliance of EU acts with the objectives is required. In the case *Air Transport Association of America*, the Court made clear that the overarching policy objectives are yardsticks for the validity of EU action.¹³¹ Indeed, objectives have played a role in the case law of the CJEU, mostly so with respect to proportionality analyses.¹³² Any action by the EU shall not go beyond what is necessary to achieve the objectives of the treaties.¹³³ In a

---

123 See language in the treaties: EU "shall uphold and promote" in TEU, Art 3(5).
124 Sommermann, above note 64, 162, pt 8.
125 See ECJ, Case 139/79 *Maizena GmbH v Council of the European Communities*, EU:C:1980:250, para 23.
126 Terhechte JP, 'Art. 3 EUV', in: Grabitz E, Hilf M and Nettesheim M (dir), *Das Recht der Europäischen Union: Band I: EUV/AEUV, Rechtsstand: Juli 2010* (41 Aufl, Beck, CH 2010, mit Ergängzungen bis 2017) 9.
127 Ruffert, above note 113, 44.
128 See ECJ, Case 1/69 *Italy v Commission*, EU:C:1974:71, paras 4 and 5.
129 Sommermann, above note 64, 161, pt 6.
130 Larik, above note 64, 159.
131 *Air Transport Association of America*, above note 5, para 101.
132 Sommermann KP, *Staatsziele und Staatszielbestimmungen* (Mohr Siebeck 1997) 423–425. Eg ECJ, Case 11/70 *Internationale Handelsgesellschaft mbH v Einfuhr- und Vorratsstelle für Getreide und Futtermittel*, EU:C:1970:114, para 12.
133 TEU, Art 5(4); Protocol (2) on the Application of the Principles of Subsidiarity and Proportionality.

proportionality analysis, the CJEU thus assesses whether a given EU measure is "appropriate and necessary for meeting the objectives legitimately pursued by the legislation in question".[134] According to the Court, "when there is a choice between several appropriate measures, the least onerous measure must be used and the charges imposed must not be disproportionate to the aims pursued".[135] Consequently, the legality of a measure can only be affected by a given Union objective if the measure is *manifestly inappropriate* with regard to the achievement of the objective the competent institution intends to pursue.[136] Manifest inappropriateness is a very high threshold and indeed, the Court's interference on the concrete choices based on the institutions' discretion is unlikely. Namely, in areas of EU action for which the institutions dispose of broad discretion, such as in the context of external action, the CJEU applies a limited review of the policy choices made.[137] In its post-Lisbon case law, the CJEU reiterated that the EU institutions dispose of "wide discretion in the field of external economic action".[138] In the external sphere flexibility in negotiations with third countries can be essential and discretionary powers are required. For instance the Common Commercial Policy (CCP), the Court could in theory review CCP measures on whether it actually pursues SD and whether the measure is proportionate, given the other objectives at stake, such as trade liberalisation.[139]

To conclude, due to the discretion enjoyed by the EU institutions to pursue Union objectives within the margin of feasibility, this norm category has low justiciability.[140] Arguably, for the purposes and functions of Union objective it

---

134   See eg ECJ, Case 265/87 *Hermann Schräder HS Kraftfutter GmbH & Co KG v Hauptzollamt Gronau*, EU:C:1989:303, para 21.
135   Ibid, para 22.
136   Ibid. See also ECJ, Case 179/84 *Bozzetti v Invernizzi*, EU:C:1985:306.
137   See eg, ECJ, Case C-272/15 *Swiss International Air Lines*, EU:C:2016:993, para 24. The Court stated that "the institutions and agencies of the Union have available to them, in the conduct of external relations, a broad discretion in policy decisions" and that "the conduct of external relations necessarily implies policy choices".
138   GC, Case T-512/12 *Front Polisario v Council*, EU:T:2015:953, para 164. The General Court referred to the case Odigitria of 1995; see CFI, Case T-572/93 *Odigitria v Council and Commission*, EU:T:1995:131, para 38.
139   Dimopoulos, A, 'The Effects of the Lisbon Treaty on the Principles and Objectives of the Common Commercial' (2010) Policy European Foreign Affairs Review, 15(2), 169.
140   Ruffert, above note 113, 44, pt 7. However, it should be noted, that the CJEU is generally willing to use objectives as a tool for the interpretation of EU law and stressed the importance thereof. In this respect, the EU treaties are not different from other international treaties. The quite often-used teleological approach of interpretation by the CJEU relies on the recourse of Union objectives. They have become an important tool for the legal development of EU law in general. The CJEU held from early on that EU law is to be

is less significant whether there are enforceable by the Court or not as Union objectives' functions rather are to provide a law-making instruction, to set out a directive for the use of the decision-makers' discretion and to serve as a interpretative tool for the CJEU.[141]

3.2.2.2   The Choice of the Appropriate Legal Basis

A further question that needs to be addressed when considering the legal effect of general objectives is whether and to what extent they impact on the choice of the appropriate legal basis for a specific EU measure. As mentioned before, the general objectives have modified the competence-objective nexus in the course of the European integration process. Competences of the EU and their nature is closely related to the question over correct legal bases. In practical terms, the choice of legal base used is crucial. It affects the determination of the nature and scope of the competence and it will determine which legislative procedure must be used. In turn, this defines the extent of involvement of each institution and the legality of any decision made by an EU institution.[142] In Opinion 2/00, the Court has pointed out that the choice of legal basis has "constitutional significance".[143] Unsurprisingly, the CJEU regularly has judged

---

"interpreted and applied in the light" of Union objectives. See eg ECJ, Joined Cases 6 and 7/73 *Istituto Chemioterapico Italiano S.p.A. and Commercial Solvents Corporation v Commission*, EU:C:1974:18, para 32; and ECJ, Case 15/81 *Gaston Schul Douane Expediteur BV v Inspecteur der Invoerrechten en Accijnzen*, EU:C:1982:135, para 33. For a case relating to SD, see ECJ, Case C-43/10 *Nomarchiaki Aftodioikisi Aitoloakarnanias and Others*, EU:C:2012:560. See, Calliess C, 'Kollektive Ziele und Prinzipien im Verfassungsrecht der EU—Bestandsaufnahme, Wirkungen und Perspektiven', in: Hiebaum C, Koller P and Internationale Vereinigung für Rechts- und Sozialphilosophie (eds), *Politische Ziele und juristische Argumentation: Symposium der Internationalen Vereinigung für Rechts- und Sozialphilosophie* (Steiner 2003) 92.

141 Kahl W, 'Einleitung: Nachhaltigkeit als Verbundbegriff', in: Kahl W (ed), *Nachhaltigkeit als Verbundbegriff* (Mohr Siebeck 2008) 11.

142 Neframi, above note 75, 15. On occasion, the choice of legal basis has proved controversial, see, ECJ, Case C-300/89 *Commission v Council (Titanium Dioxide)*, EU:C:1991:244. In this case, the Court was mindful of the need to guarantee the EU Parliament's rights under the Treaty to participate in the legislative process.

143 ECJ, Opinion 2/00 *Cartagena Protocol*, EU:C:2001:664, para 5: "The choice of the appropriate legal basis has constitutional significance. Since the Community has conferred powers only, it must tie the Protocol to a Treaty provision which empowers it to approve such a measure. To proceed on an incorrect legal basis is therefore liable to invalidate the act concluding the agreement and so vitiate the Community's consent to be bound by the agreement it has signed. That is so in particular where the Treaty does not confer on the Community sufficient competence to ratify the agreement in its entirety, a situation which entails examining the allocation as between the Community and the Member States of the powers to conclude the agreement that is envisaged with non-member

on legal basis litigation. Since the EU enjoys conferred powers only, it must always link a measure which it adopts to a treaty provision empowering it to approve that measure.¹⁴⁴ According to established case law of the Court, "the choice of the legal basis for a measure must be based on objective factors which are amenable to judicial review. Those factors include in particular the aim and content of the measure."¹⁴⁵ The traditional test applied by the Court is to consider the aim of the agreement and its content.

The well-settled case-law of the Court further sets out that where an international agreement of the EU pursues more than one purpose or comprises two or more components of which one is identifiable as the main or predominant purpose or component, whereas the other(s) is (or are) merely incidental or extremely limited in scope, the EU has to conclude that agreement based on a single legal basis, namely the one required by the main or predominant purpose or component.¹⁴⁶ Conversely, if it can be established that an agreement "simultaneously" pursues a number of objectives, or has several components, which are inextricably linked without one being incidental to the other, such that various provisions of the Treaties are applicable, the EU's act concluding that agreement would need to be founded on the various legal bases corresponding to those components.¹⁴⁷

With general objectives, the line between the different policy areas gets more blurred, and this might have implications on the number of legal bases that have to be used for a given measure or it leads to broader interpretations

---

countries, or where the appropriate legal basis for the measure concluding the agreement lays down a legislative procedure different from that which has in fact been followed by the Community institutions."

144 ECJ, Opinion 1/08 *Agreements modifying the Schedules of Specific Commitments under the GATS*, EU:C:2009:739, para 111: "As regards the order in which the two questions referred to the Court must be considered, the Court accepts that, as most of the interveners have stated and as the Commission itself indeed acknowledges, the character, whether exclusive or not, of Community competence to conclude the agreements at issue and the legal basis to which recourse must be had for that purpose are two questions which are closely linked." In other words, the principles governing the allocation of (external) competences and those governing the choice of legal basis of EU action are different but interconnected questions.

145 ECJ, Case C-268/94 *Portugal v Council*, above note 103, para 22; Case C-300/89 *Commission v Council (Titanium Dioxide)*, above note 142, para 10; Case C-84/94 *United Kingdom v Council* EU:C:1996:431, para 25. See, more recently, Case C-263/14 *Parliament v Council*, EU:C:2016:435, para 43.

146 See, ECJ, Case C-281/01 *Commission v Council (Energy Star)*, EU:C:2002:761, para 43; and Case C-137/12 *Commission v Council*, EU:C:2013:675, para 76.

147 *Parliament v Council*, above note 144, para 44; *Commission v Council (Rotterdam Convention)*, above note 145, para 51.

of the competence scope of a given policy. Especially, with Articles 3(5) TEU and 21 TEU, the EU treaties require that the same general objectives are to be pursued in all external policies. Determining one or eventually only two appropriate legal bases could be more difficult as an increased number of provisions enter into account. While the delimitation between different foreign policies has never been straightforward due to the fact that international agreements rarely fall within one policy area only,[148] the Lisbon Treaty leads to reconsidering or at least to questioning whether the traditional test of aim and content of the measure should still be the appropriate one. It seems that taking into account the aim of the agreement does no longer make sense given that multiple objectives enter into account. In this sense, only the content of a specific measure would determine the legal basis under which it should be adopted. However, a counter-argument to this is that a single-sided test would give too much weight to the content of the measure and thereby undermining the objectives pursued. One solution could be to consider next to the content of the measure, the specific objective of the policy under which the measure is adopted. If one takes the example of the CCP, it would mean that the general objectives do not override the specific objectives of the CCP, which are most prominently trade and investment liberalisation.[149] Whilst a trade agreement can contain non-economic components, the core of the content and aim mostly remains trade and investment liberalisation and the regulation thereof. Put differently, an EU trade and investment agreement could have important social and environmental provisions as well as SD as an objective but could still be based on the CCP competence.

In Opinion 2/15, the Court adopted a different approach.[150] The Court did not use its traditional test of aim and content concerning the legal basis for TSD chapter of the EU-Singapore FTA but adopted a reasoning of subsuming SD under the CCP and considered Article 207(1) TFEU to be the sole legal basis necessary as regards the FTA's TSD chapter. The question to what extent this meant stretching the scope of the CCP competence is discussed in the next chapter.[151] However, the reasoning in Opinion 2/15, would more generally mean

---

148 An illustrative example is the CJEU's case law on delimiting the CCP from the EU's environmental policy. See, ECJ, Case C94/03 *Commission v Council (Rotterdam Convention)*, EU:C:2006:2; Opinion 2/00 *Cartagena Protocol,* above note 143. On development cooperation see eg *Portugal v Council*, above note 103. On the CFSP see eg ECJ, C-91/05 *Commission v Council*, EU:C:2008:288, and ECJ Case C-130/10 *Parliament v Council*, EU:C:2012:472.
149 Dimopoulos, above note 139, 165–166.
150 Opinion 2/15, above note 85, para 139 et seq.
151 See Section 4.2.1.

a tendency that the broader objectives of a legislative acts and international agreements can be subsumed under the umbrella of a policy without the need to be categorised as ancillary or incidental to the predominant purpose. As a result, the broadening of the scope of a competence takes place. Whether this tendency of widening the scope of a competence will be more widely applied by the Court is not certain. Any legal measure of the EU requires a case-by-case assessment in order to decide on the appropriate legal basis and whether the action falls within the scope of the competence provided for under that legal basis. From EU constitutional law, these tendencies are highly relevant as its shakes the basic principle of conferral and attributed powers. Taking a purely SD-promotional perspective beyond the constitutional implications, one can note that SD gains weight and importance if it leads to the adaptation of the competence at stake. It facilitates EU action integrating SD, especially when the competence subsuming SD is exclusive.

3.3 Legal Means of EU Law Supportive of SD

EU law contains two key constitutional requirements, which can directly be connected to SD operating as an enabling means to achieve the objective of SD. Namely, the social and environmental requirements as well as policy coherence. Interestingly, in its political response to Agenda 2030, the European Commission precisely referred to these two features of the EU legal order. It acknowledged that the three dimensions of SD must be "*integrated* in a balanced manner"[152] and highlighted that "achieving *coherence across all EU policies* is crucial for achieving the SDGs".[153]

Regarding the integration under EU law, its legal function reveals several similarities with the SD objective itself. Under EU law as under international law, it is, more accurate conceptually and more useful practically to distinguish between them and consider one as the overarching goal and the other as one of the means to achieve it.[154] According to Article 11 TFEU, SD is the

---

[152] European Commission, 'Next steps for a sustainable European future', above note 7, 3: "The 2030 Agenda integrates in a balanced manner the three dimensions of sustainable development—economic, social and environmental—and reflects for the first time an international consensus that peace, security, justice for all, and social inclusion are not only to be pursued on their own but that they reinforce each other".

[153] European Commission, 'Next steps for a sustainable European future', above note 7, 14. Emphasis added.

[154] See Section 2.2. Consider Marín Durán G and Morgera E, *Environmental Integration in the EU's External Relations: Beyond Multilateral Dimensions* (Hart Pub 2012) 155. The authors

objective of environmental integration. A key question is whether the integration requirement under EU law is of procedural nature requiring the EU institutions to take social and environmental aspects into account or whether the requirement further dictates the content of the relevant social and environmental standards. The following argues that the bottom line of the integration requirements under EU law is a procedural obligation in the sense that social and environmental aspects must be taken into account in any decision-making of the EU intuitions. Setting out a procedural obligation of integration within the EU treaties provides the SD objective with a strong normative directive. Conversely, the substantive scope of the obligation to integrate social and environmental aspects depends on other EU law principles and the EU institutions' concrete policy guidelines.

3.3.1 Social and Environmental Integration

The balance, which is inherent to the concept of SD, understands economic development, social development and environmental protection as being interdependent and mutually reinforcing. Therefore, integration is an important tool for the achievement of SD.[155] EU primary law enshrines the idea of integration, as it contains several integration clauses. Environmental integration was first included in the treaties under the 1986 Single European Act (SEA),[156] and since the Treaty of Amsterdam, environmental integration serves to achieve SD. Under the Treaty of Lisbon, the requirement of environmental integration can be found in Article 11 TFEU, and has also been included in Article 37 EUCFR. Since the Lisbon Treaty, EU primary law contains several other integration clauses next to environmental integration. Their common strand is that they figure among the general principles of EU law and apply to all EU policies. These clauses range from the equality between men and women, social protection, non-discrimination, consumer protection and animal welfare.[157]

The environmental integration provision is explicitly linked to SD under Article 11 TFEU. The social integration clause of Article 9 TFEU has been linked to SD by the CJEU in the *AGET Iraklis* case.[158] The CJEU even more clearly stated

---

likewise consider the environmental integration requirement as a means to achieve SD in both EU internal and external measures.
155 Ibid.
156 Eg TEC, Art 130r.
157 See TFEU, Art 8 (equality between men and women); Art 9 (social protection); Art 10 (non-discrimination); Art 11 (environmental protection); Art 12 (consumer protection).
158 *AGET Iraklis*, above note 85. From early on the CJEU emphasised the integration into the internal market of social protection standards and environmental protection. As such,

the reference to the principle of integration in relation to SD in its Opinion 2/15..[159] The Court found that the integration of SD in EU external action was further enhanced in Articles 9 and 11 TFEU.[160] The Court emphasised also, in Opinion 2/15, that these provisions respectively provide that, "in defining and implementing its policies and activities, the Union shall take into account requirements linked to [...] the guarantee of adequate social protection" and also "environmental protection requirements must be integrated into the definition and implementation of the Union's policies and activities, in particular with a view to promoting [SD]".[161] From the reasoning of the CJEU, both with respect to SD internally and SD externally, the three-pillar approach leads to an integrative exercise.

The CJEU's case law highlights the logical nexus between SD and integration. The integration clauses contained in EU primary law have the main purpose of requiring integrative law and policy-making from the EU institutions.[162] With respect to environmental integration, the two relevant provisions, Article 11 TFEU and 37 EUCFR, are clearly framed in mandatory language, *i.e.* "must be

---

the Court held already in 1976 that the Union has an economic but also a social purpose, see ECJ, Case 43/75 *Gabrielle Defrenne v Sabena*, EU:C:1976:56, para 12. It was only in 2007, in the case *Viking Line* when the Court linked social protection standards that are to be taken into account for the EU internal market with the overall objective of SD. ECJ, Case C-438/05 *International Transport Workers' Federation and Finnish Seamen's Union v Viking Line ABP and OÜ Viking Line Eesti*, EU:C:2007:772, para 78: "It must be added that, according to Article 3(1)(c) and (j) EC, the activities of the Community are to include not only an 'internal market characterized by the abolition, as between Member States, of obstacles to the free movement of goods, persons, services and capital', but also 'a policy in the social sphere'. Article 2 EC states that the Community is to have as its task, inter alia, the promotion of 'a harmonious, balanced and [SD] of economic activities' and 'a high level of employment and of social protection'."

159 Opinion 2/15, above note 85. For a detailed discussion, see Section 4.3.
160 Ibid, para 146.
161 Ibid. See also the wording of TFEU, Arts 9 and 11; and *AGET Iraklis*, above note 85, paras 76–78; at para 76: "[...] as is apparent from Article 3(3) TEU, the European Union is not only to establish an internal market but is also to work for the [SD] of Europe, which is based, in particular, on a highly competitive social market economy aiming at full employment and social progress, and it is to promote, inter alia, social protection [...]".
162 The CJEU often had to deal with the environmental integration clause in cases on the appropriate legal basis, such as *Greece v Council (Chernobyl I)*, above note 87; ECJ, Opinion 2/00 *Cartagena Protocol*, EU:C:2001:664; ECJ, Case C336/00 *Republik Österreich v Martin Huber*, EU:C:2002:509; *Commission v Council (Rotterdam Convention)*, above note 145. For an overview of this case law, see Dhondt N, *Integration of Environmental Protection into Other EC Policies: Legal Theory and Practice* (Europa Law Publ 2003) 169–75.

integrated".¹⁶³ In fact, Article 11 TFEU is the only integration clause that uses this formulation. Conversely, the social integration clause, Article 9 TFEU, states, "shall take into account". Despite being formulated in a somewhat less binding manner, for the promotion of SD, both environmental, as well as social integration, are fundamental.¹⁶⁴ The CJEU brought both integration clauses under the umbrella of SD and did not place great importance in the differences in the formulations of the two clauses. To bring them together instead suggests that to promote SD, EU institutions must integrate social and environmental concerns.¹⁶⁵ Thus, the integration principle legitimises the relevance of social and environmental considerations to other policy areas, and EU primary law creates an obligation on decision-makers to take them into account systemically. Based on the bindingness of the integration clause, one can argue that any piece of legislation that does harm to social or environmental protection violates this treaty obligation and may, therefore, be subject to annulment by the CJEU.¹⁶⁶

At the same time, and as is the case with Union objectives, the bindingness of the social and environmental integration requirements is relativized by the discretion that the EU institutions enjoy in deciding whether and to what extent social and environmental concerns are to be taken into account for measures adopted in the context of a given policy. For instance, in cases related to disputes over the lawfulness of an ozone depletion regulation, the CJEU confirmed the wide discretionary powers of the EU institutions with respect to the Treaty-based environmental objectives and principles.¹⁶⁷ The Court justified the need for institutional discretion by highlighting the fact that the

---

163 TFEU, Art 11: "Environmental protection requirements must be integrated into the definition and implementation of the Union's policies and activities, in particular with a view to promoting sustainable development." This principle is also enshrined in the Charter of Fundamental Rights of the EU (CFREU). See CFREU, Art 37: "A high level of environmental protection and the improvement of the quality of the environment must be integrated into the policies of the Union and ensured in accordance with the principle of sustainable development."
164 The concept of SD itself does not provide for any prioritisation between its three pillars. Gehne, above note 1, 107; De Sadeleer, above note 39, 17. See also, *R v Secretary of State for Environment, Transport and the Regions, ex p First Corporate Shipping*, above note 3, AG Léger, Opinion, para 54.
165 On environmental integration, see Morgera E and Marin Duran G, 'Article 37', in: Peers S et al, *The EU Charter of Fundamental Rights a Commentary* (Hart Pub 2014) 996.
166 See Dhondt, above note 162, 144–64. See also Marín Durán and Morgera, above note 154, 32.
167 See ECJ, Case C-284/95 *Safety High-Tech v S & T Srl*, EU:C:1998:352, paras 34–37; and EJC, Case C-341/95, *Gianni Bettati v Safety High Tech*, EU:C:1998:353, paras 32–35.

institutions have to make complex assessments of and balance between these objectives and principles.[168] Therefore, its judicial review of the implementation of integration clauses is limited to verifying that the competent institution's action was not "vitiated by a *manifest error or a misuse of powers* and that it did not clearly exceed the bounds of its discretion".[169] The social and environmental integration requirements have, like Union objectives, relatively low justiciability.

This leads to the question, what—through the environmental and social clauses—needs to be integrated? In other words, what are the elements of environmental or social law and policy that should guide the discretion of decision- and policy-makers? First, environmental integration relates to the principles and objectives of EU environmental policy as enshrined in Article 191 TFEU. The latter provision lists the objectives of the general protection of the environment and the improvement thereof, human health, prudent and rational utilisation of natural resources, the promotion of international measures, and combating climate change.[170] In addition, EU environment policy rests on the principles of precaution, prevention rectifying pollution at the source, and the "polluter-pays" principle.[171] Second, concerning the social integration clause, the objectives and principles of EU social policy are to be integrated.[172] Based on Article 151 TFEU, this policy has the objectives to promote employment, improve living and working conditions, proper social

---

168   Eg *Bettati v Safety High Tech*, above note 167, paras 32–35, at para 35: "However, in view of the need to strike a balance between certain of the objectives and principles mentioned in Article 130r and of the complexity of the implementation of those criteria, review by the Court must necessarily be limited to the question whether the Council, by adopting the Regulation, committed a manifest error of appraisal regarding the conditions for the application of Article 130r of the Treaty."

169   See eg ECJ, Case C331/88 *The Queen v Minister of Agriculture, Fisheries and Food and Secretary of State for Health, ex parte: Fedesa and others*, EU:C:1990:391, para 8. See also, ECJ, Case C-120/97 *Upjohn v The Licensing Authority*, EU:C:1999:14, para 34: "According to the Court's case-law, where a Community authority is called upon, in the performance of its duties, to make complex assessments, it enjoys a wide measure of discretion, the exercise of which is subject to a limited judicial review in the course of which the Community judicature may not substitute its assessment of the facts for the assessment made by the authority concerned. Thus, in such cases, the Community judicature must restrict itself to examining the accuracy of the findings of fact and law made by the authority concerned and to verifying, in particular, that the action taken by that authority is not vitiated by a *manifest error or a misuse of powers* and that it did not *clearly exceed the bounds of its discretion*." Emphasis added.

170   TFEU, Art 191(1).

171   TFEU, Art 191(2).

172   Anderson KM, *Social Policy in the European Union* (Palgrave Macmillan 2015) 14–48.

protection, dialogue between management and labour, the development of human resources with a view to lasting high employment and finally, the combating of exclusion of certain groups.[173] Furthermore, Article 151 TFEU explicitly opts into the EU social policy the European Charter for Social Rights, which has been elaborated under the auspices of the Council of Europe and the Community Charter of the Fundamental Social Rights of Workers.[174] In the exercise of their discretion, EU institutions should also make recourse to the policy documents and strategies adopted for the specific policies.

As a result, the principle of integration provides SD with more legal weight because it provides a clear tool for operationalising SD.[175] Integration clauses have the advantage of provoking spill-over effects between the various EU policies and thereby can lead to integrated law-making and policy coherence. As far as concretisation of the integration requirements is concerned one arrives at the same observation as for the SD objective itself. How and the extent to which social and environmental standards, objectives and principles are integrated is part of the discretionary powers of the EU institutions.

3.3.2 *The Requirement of Policy Coherence*

Conceptionally, policy coherence is directly linked to SD if not inherent to the concept. Given that the three pillars of SD shall be mutually reinforcing, the need for harmonisation and reconciliation between the different sub-sets and policy areas (economic, social and environmental) is indicated.[176] The quest for coherence figures prominently in EU primary law. The EU has a formal requirement for its policy and law-making to ensure coherence and consistency.[177] Article 7 TFEU states that the EU "shall ensure consistency between its

---

173 TFEU, Art 151.
174 European Social Charter (ETS No 35), adopted in 1961, the Revised European Social Charter (ETS No 163), [1996]; see also Community Charter of Fundamental Social Rights of Workers [1989].
175 Jans and Vedder, above note 13, 23.
176 Agenda 2030 underlines the need for policy coherence. See SDG 17 and its targets. The European Commission, for its parts, is convinced that the EU's implementation of the 2030 Agenda will further catalyse the joined-up approach between the EU's external action and internal policies. See European Commission, 'Next steps for a sustainable European future', above note 7, 3.
177 For present purposes, the concepts of "coherence" and "consistency" will be used interchangeably. A distinction between these two terms has been made in legal scholarship on EU external relations. See eg, Hillion C, 'Tous pour un, un pour tous ! Coherence in the External Relations of the European Union' in: Cremona M (ed), *Developments in EU External Relations Law* (Oxford University Press 2009) 12–16.

policies and activities, taking all of its objectives into account and in accordance with the principle of conferral of powers". This provision applies to both EU internal and external action. For external action in particular, Article 21(3) TEU further reiterates the objective of coherence and consistency. In this vein, the Council and the European Commission are entrusted with the responsibility of ensuring coherence between the different areas of the EU's external action, as well as between these and its other policies.[178]

The concept of coherence under EU law has attracted much interest among legal scholars.[179] In order to break down the different aspects of coherence, a distinction is mostly made between horizontal and vertical coherence. Horizontal coherence concerns the coherence between the different policies and actors at EU level, whereas vertical coherence concerns coherence between the EU's policies and those of its Member States. In addition, the function and purpose of coherence have further been described.[180] First, coherence within the EU legal order should be understood as legal consistency, which means, in other words, the avoidance of conflicts between different sets of EU law. Second, coherence serves as a delimitation and thus effective "allocation of tasks between actors, norms and instruments".[181] Third, coherence should also be understood as a tool for "synergy between actors, norms and instruments through cooperation and complementarity".[182] It is interesting to question to what extent coherence fosters SD and to what extent SD as a Union objective brings about coherence.

A first positive aspect of coherence is that the concept seeks to establish legal consistency within a given legal system. Legal consistency means for the EU that legislative measures adopted under the different policies of the EU are consistent in the sense that there is no legal conflict between them, which would need

---

178   TEU, Arts 21(3) and 26(2).
179   See for instance the various contributions in Michel V (dir), *Le droit, les institutions et les politiques de l'Union européenne face à l'impératif de cohérence: Actes du colloque des 10 et 11 Mai 2007* (Presses universitaires de Strasbourg 2009).
180   Cremona M, 'Coherence in European Union Foreign Relations Law', in: Koutrakos P, *European Foreign Policy: Legal and Political Perspectives* (Edward Elgar 2011) 60–61. This has been further developed by Bart Van Vooren stating that coherences can serve "[t]o attain coherence between norms, actors and instruments towards a common objective, between them conflicts should be avoided and resolved (first level), tasks should be allocated effectively (second level), and positive synergy should be achieved (third level)"; see Van Vooren B, *EU External Relations Law and the European Neighbourhood Policy: A Paradigm for Coherence* (Routledge 2012) 69. See also Larik, above note 64, 189–190.
181   Cremona, above note 180, 60.
182   Ibid.

to be resolved through the conflict of norms rules.¹⁸³ In the context of SD, it is interesting to notice that the concept itself seeks to foster such legal consistency through systemic integration (a term more often used for international law), as well as mutual reinforcement between the three pillars (of economic development as well as social and environmental protection). For EU law, consistency first and foremost requires coherence between the various policies. In this vein, general and horizontal Union objectives with transversal effects applying to all EU policies have a structuring purpose. By orienting all EU policies to common objectives, a coherent legal and political structure should be established.¹⁸⁴ The three pillars of SD require that harmonisation be found between economic development, social development, and environmental protection. Thus, SD like the general objective of coherence, seeks that law-making is not sector-specific and isolated but operates in a coherent and systemically integrated manner to avoid legal conflicts and foster synergies.¹⁸⁵ Consequently, SD as a Union objective can foster coherence within the EU legal order, but likewise, the principle of coherence under EU law is well suited for SD promotion.

The rather complex governance structure of the EU makes the quest for coherence of particular importance. Competences differ from one policy to the other and EU action requires constant cooperation with its Member States. For effective SD promotion, coherence between different governance levels, such as internal and external policies, is fundamental. The reason is that incoherent national policies should not undermine international commitments but to the contrary, be consistent with them to implement the SD commitments taken at the international level. The international SD agenda is dependent on effective national SD transposition into policy measures and legislation. In addition hereto, the quest for (vertical) coherence between the measures taken by the EU and its Member States is, for effective SD promotion, likewise decisive and highlights the need for effective allocation of tasks in the pursuit of SD. For EU external action in particular, the EU's action is subject to an extended and general set of objectives, with the consequence that for one policy, multiple objectives should be taken into account.¹⁸⁶ Coherence here mandates the EU

---

183 Report of the Study Group of the International Law Commission finalised by Martti Koskenniemi, Fragmentation of International Law: Difficulties arising from the Diversification and Expansion of International Law, [2006] UN Doc A/CN.4/L.682.
184 Michel, above note 82, 181.
185 Gehne, above note 1, 261; Grosse Ruse-Khan H, 'A Real Partnership for Development? Sustainable Development as Treaty Objective in European Economic Partnership Agreements and Beyond' (2010) 13 Journal of International Economic Law 139.
186 TEU, Art 21(1–2).

institutions to take all the objectives into account and to build synergies and mutually reinforcing outcomes. This means for the EU that there is a need for permanent conciliation between the different objectives, as there is no hierarchy between them.[187] Lastly, coherence between the different EU's external policies also impacts the credibility of the EU as a global actor in pursuing SD in the sense that SD is not reduced to development cooperation or environmental protection but also economic policies, namely the CCP are mainstreamed by SD.

3.4 Contours of the Substantive Scope of SD under EU Law

The treaties require the EU and its institutions to take general objectives into account in various policy fields but allow, at the same time, for discretion to determine which measures should be taken to attain such objectives.[188] The question that occupies international and EU lawyers likewise is whether SD provides for substantive obligations or whether it is possible to outline the principles and specific objectives that form the broader normative framework on SD. In the previous section it has been argued that the social and environmental requirements, together with policy coherence, form part of the normative SD framework. This section aims to shed further light on the substantive contours of the SD framework within the EU legal order, not in an exhaustive manner but rather with the intent to show how SD as a Union objectives operates and unfolds differently depending on the subject matter of the policy at stake. Therefrom, the argument is derived that the SD policy directions and guidelines applicable to the exercise of the policy discretion of the EU institutions varies depending on the subject matter, on the policy area, and on the competences enjoyed by the EU.

Finding the substantive contours of SD within the EU legal order depends on how well a policy area is developed in the sense of how well are the specific objectives and fundamental principles thereof formulated in the treaties, to what extent the CJEU has had occasion to provide further law development to those specific aims and principles, and also how EU soft law instruments turn SD into strategies. The extent to which the EU can pursue general objectives through a given policy also depends on the nature and scope of the competence attributed for that policy. Or put differently, the discretion of the EU

---

187   Michel, above note 82, 180–181.
188   Larik, above note 66, 953.

institutions can be more or less important depending on the competences the EU enjoys for a specific field of action. In policy fields of shared competences, such as in the area of transportation, EU institutions enjoy less margin of appreciation to implement general Union objectives and to transpose them into concrete legislation or policy measures.[189] This margin is arguably wider, for those policies where the EU disposes of exclusive competences and the scope for action is more important and thus the impact of the objective.

Virginie Barral has in a comprehensive study shown that SD is of an intrinsically evolutionary nature and therefore any strict and *a priori* identification of measures for its pursuit is precluded, on the contrary, the adaptation of standards according to the circumstances of each situation is consistent with the concept's nature.[190] As a result soft law instrument play a key role in the normative framework on SD. And any outline of the substantive contours of SD relies on soft law instruments. This is particularly true for the international law level but it is likewise the case within the EU legal order. As a response to the United Nations Agenda 2030 and its SDGs, the European Commission adopted a communication on "Next steps for a sustainable European future— European action for sustainability".[191] The document serves as the current references point in setting out the actions that the EU should take. In this non-binding instrument, the Commission firstly emphasises that Agenda 2030 is consistent with the vision of the EU,[192] and then presents a work stream, which is to "fully *integrate* the SDGs in the European policy framework" through an assessment of how much SD integration has already been achieved in various policy fields of the EU and to examine what further action might be needed.[193] The mapping exercise of the European Commission came to the conclusion that all 17 SDGs are addressed through already existing EU policy initiatives.[194] The reading of the document thus further corroborates that SD action and concretisation is a policy-specific issue. The substantive contours of SD always need to be understood in the context of a policy and cannot readily be transposed from one policy to another.

---

189   TFEU, Art 4.2(g).
190   Barral V, *Le développement durable en droit international : essai sur les incidences juridiques d'une norme évolutive* (Bruylant 2016).
191   Agenda 2030, above note 7; and European Commission, 'Next steps for a sustainable European future', above note 7.
192   European Commission, 'Next steps for a sustainable European future', above note 7, 3.
193   Ibid, 3. Emphasis added.
194   For more details on the mapping, see Commission Staff Working Document, 'Key European action supporting the 2030 Agenda and the Sustainable Development Goal, Accompanying Document to the Communication', SWD (2016) 390 final.

3.4.1 *Articulation of SD within EU Internal Policies*

As discussed, with the beginning of the global SD agenda in 1992, the institutions of the EU started to integrate the concept into a number of EU legal measures and policy instruments. Notwithstanding, the EU's intention to closely follow the international development concerning the content of SD and the means to achieve it, the concept of SD had regularly been adapted to the European context and according to the policy area in which it operates.

3.4.1.1 Key Internal Policy Areas with SD Components

Several EU policies have used SD as a core principle or main guiding objective. It might come as a surprise that the environmental policy of the EU does not refer to SD in a systemic way.[195] EU environmental legislation encompasses a number of issues, ranging from climate change, biodiversity, water, air pollution, noise, dangerous substances, genetically modified organisms, waste, nuclear safety, and environmental liability. Nevertheless, the majority of the legislation in these fields does not contain a reference to SD. A reason seems to be that Article 191 TFEU establishing the environmental policy of the EU does not mention SD.[196] Moreover, the EU was actively legislating in environmental protection prior to the beginning of the global SD agenda in 1992, which can also explain that certain areas of EU's environmental policy rely less on SD. Despite the sometimes missing explicit link to SD, the principles and specific objectives of the EU's environmental policy are among the contours that allow outlining the substantive scope of SD. Henceforth, the four specific objectives, set out in Article 191(1) TFEU, enter into consideration, namely preserving, protecting and improving the quality of the environment (1), protecting human health (2), prudent and rational utilisation of natural resources (3), and promoting measures at international level to deal with regional or worldwide environmental problems, and in particular combating climate change (4). Three key principles of EU's environmental law are the principles of prevention, precaution, and the polluter-pays principle.[197]

An illustrative example of an internal EU policy, where SD has been used more systematically is the Fisheries Policy. The measures adopted under the said policy show that SD found a specific articulation in the context of the fisheries sector. For instance, the Regulation No 2371/2002 on the conservation and sustainable exploitation of fisheries resources in the EU attempted to define

---

195 Morgera E, 'Environmental Law', in: Barnard C and Peers S (eds), *European Union Law* (2nd ed, Oxford University Press 2017) 669.
196 See also Krämer, above note 4, 378–379.
197 TFEU, Art 191(2).

SD as to mean, in this particular context, "the exploitation of a stock in such a way that the future exploitation of the stock will not be prejudiced and that it does not have a negative impact on the marine eco-systems."[198] This definition clearly emphasises the inter-generational equity principle, which is one of the main aspects of the definition of SD and which is also included in the Rio Declaration.[199] Regulation No 2371/2002 also provides that the common fisheries policy is to apply the precautionary principle in taking measures to minimise the impact of fishing activities on marine ecosystems.[200] As part of its Fisheries Policy, the EU regularly concludes bilateral agreements with third countries with a view to giving the European fishing fleet access to their fishing grounds. These agreements do not contain any further definition of SD but generally, refer to "sustainable exploitation of fishery resources".[201] Depending on the partner country, the reference to sustainable exploitation can be combined with the objective of developing the fisheries sector of that country.[202] This latter element shifts the understanding of SD in the fisheries context more closely to the partner country's socio-economic development.

Another policy area in which SD comes into play is the Regional Policy of the EU, which is the policy that seeks to reduce "disparities between the levels of development of the various regions and the backwardness of the least favoured regions or islands, including rural areas" of the EU.[203] In the Framework Regulation No 1083/2006 on the Regional -, Social -, and Cohesion Fund, SD has not been defined but, to some extent, described.[204] At the outset, the regulation provides that the Funds are to be pursued in the "framework" of SD and the "promotion of the goal of protection and improving the environment". The explicit reference to the environment does, however, not change

---

[198] Regulation No 2371/2002 of the Council of 20 December 2002 on the conservation and sustainable exploitation of fisheries resources under the Common Fisheries Policy, [2002] OJ L 358/59, Art 3(e).
[199] Rio Declaration, above note 6, Principles 3, 5, 6 and 7. See also Brundtland Report, above note 15, paras 16–26 on "Equity and Common Interest".
[200] Regulation No 2371/2002, above note 198, Art 2.
[201] Eg Agreement between the European Union and the Republic of the Seychelles on access for fishing vessels flying the flag of the Seychelles to waters and marine biological resources of Mayotte, under the jurisdiction of the European Union, [2014] OJ L 167/4, Art 1.
[202] Ibid, Art 3.
[203] TFEU, Art 174.
[204] Regulation No 1083/2006 of the Council of 11 July 2006 laying down general provisions on the European Regional Development Fund, the European Social Fund and the Cohesion Fund, [2006] OJ L 210/25, Art 1.1(2); see also Regulation No 1084/2006 of the Council of 11 July 2006 establishing a Cohesion Fund, [2006] OJ L 210/79, Arts 1.1 and 2.1(b).

the impression that under the Regulation, SD mainly plays a socio-economic role. This is further underlined by the fact that, in particular, the Regional Fund has the objective of the promotion of "sustainable integrated regional and local economic development". Moreover, the regulation describes the priorities of the EU "in favour" of SD so as to include "strengthening growth, competitiveness, employment and social inclusion" as well as "protecting and improving the quality of the environment".[205] Yet in the rest of the operative provisions, sustainability language is then used in a non-coherent way as references are made to "sustainable tourism"; "clean and sustainable public transport"; "[SD] of coastal fishing" or even "sustainable inclusion in the labour market of job seekers and inactive persons".[206] The example of the Regional Policy shows that the concept of SD or the adjective sustainable is used in numerous ways, which is regrettable, as it does not lead to a coherent understanding of the concept.

Lastly, SD became highly relevant in the context of the EU's Energy Policy.[207] The policy's aim is to ensure access to secure, affordable and sustainable energy supplies and includes the promotion of the use of renewable energy. SD became one of the objectives of EU Energy Policy and Law.[208] A key legal instrument is the Directive 2009/28 on the promotion of renewable energy sources.[209] The directive does not contain a definition of SD, but in the elaborated considerations of the instrument, one can find elements related to SD, namely "sustainable competitive energy policy" (consid. 3), "sustainable investment" (consid. 8); "sustainable production" (consid. 9) as well as that the transition to renewable energy can "contribute significantly to [SD] in rural areas and offer farmers new income opportunities" (consid. 12). These examples highlight that in the context of the EU Energy Policy, SD is to be understood in the logic of the "green economy".[210] Finally, the directive underlines the need

---

205   Ibid.
206   See also Regulation No 1081/2006 of the European Parliament and of the Council of 5 July 2006 on the European Social Fund, [2006] OJ L 210/18, Art 3(1)(b); and following provision Art 3(1)(c) "sustainable integration in employment of disadvantaged people".
207   TFEU, Art 194. For more details see Talus K, *Introduction to EU Energy Law* (Oxford University Press 2016).
208   European Commission Communication, 'A policy framework for climate and energy in the period from 2020 to 2030', COM/2014/015 final.
209   Directive 2009/28 of the European Parliament and of the Council of 23 April 2009 on the promotion of the use of energy from renewable sources and amending and subsequently repealing Directives 2001/77 and 2003/30, [2009] OJ L 140/16.
210   The "green economy" concept was namely promoted at the Rio+20 conference. See above note 56.

for the elaboration of clear sustainability criteria for biofuels, bio-liquids and biomass fuels used for heat and power seeking to ensure that energy production is in compliance with SD requirements.[211] The instrument does not define SD but rather delegates the question of the most SD-friendly approach to a factual assessment and the national legislator implementing the directive.

3.4.1.2 The Concept of "Sustainable Growth"

The genesis of the current Article 3 TEU showed that since the inception of SD in the EU legal order did not have a focus on environmental aspects.[212] Under the Maastricht Treaty, SD fell under the umbrella of "sustainable and non-inflationary growth respecting the environment".[213] This wording was maintained under the amendments of the Amsterdam Treaty. It was the Lisbon Treaty that modified Article 3 TEU, which situates, in the current wording of paragraph 3, that the SD of Europe is founded "on balanced economic growth and price stability, a highly competitive social market economy, aiming at full employment and social progress, and a high level of protection and improvement of the quality of the environment".[214]

Even though the reference to "sustainable growth" disappeared, the provision as such lets it be readily understood that SD as a general internal Union objective has an important emphasis on economic aspects, such as economic growth, price stability as well as a competitive market economy. The CJEU confirmed, "that, as is apparent from Article 3(3) TEU, the [EU] is not only to establish an internal market but is also to work for the [SD] of Europe, which is based in particular, on a highly competitive social market economy aiming at full employment and social progress, and it is to promote, inter alia, social protection."[215]

Moreover, the concept of "sustainable growth" did not disappear despite no longer figuring in the treaties. The Lisbon Strategy[216] and the subsequent Strategy Europe 2020 with the title "A Strategy for Smart, Sustainable and Inclusive Growth",[217] made "sustainable growth" one of the central concepts. According to Strategy Europe 2020, sustainable growth constitutes the process

---

211 Directive 2009/28, above note 210.
212 See also Langlet, above note 19, 43.
213 TEC (Maastricht, 1992), Art 2.
214 TEU, Art 3(3).
215 *AGET Iraklis*, above note 85, para 76. Emphasis added.
216 During the European Council in Lisbon in March 2000, EU leaders launched a Lisbon Strategy aimed at making the EU the world's most competitive economy by 2010.
217 European Commission, Communication from the Commission—Europe 2020—A strategy for smart, sustainable and inclusive growth, COM (2010) 2020. For more details see, Kaddous C, 'Une confrontation des perspectives: La stratégie de l'Europe 2020 et la

of "building a resource efficient, sustainable and competitive economy".[218] Sustainable growth is to be achieved through a number of initiatives and actions: the exploitation of "Europe's leadership in the race to develop new processes and technologies, including green technologies, accelerating the roll out of smart grids using [information communication technologies]"; the exploitation of "EU-scale networks, and reinforcing the competitive advantages of [the EU's] businesses, particularly in manufacturing and within [the EU's small and medium-sized enterprises]"; and finally the assistance of "consumers to value resource efficiency".[219] The targeted outcome of the EU is to prosper in "a low-carbon, resource-constrained world while preventing environmental degradation, biodiversity loss and unsustainable use of resources. It will also underpin economic, social and territorial cohesion."[220] For the EU internally, the concept of SD serves in particular to advance the pursuit of economic development and growth of the EU.[221] The Europe 2020 Strategy stresses the priority of economic growth in particular as a response to the financial crisis of 2008. The main social concern is employment, and the main environmental concern is climate change. In the context of sustainable growth, both employment and climate change are considered to be beneficial for the economy.[222] As such, policy initiatives against global warming are mainly understood with respect to its business opportunities. From a balancing SD perspective, the Europe 2020 Strategy certainly provides priority to the economic component of SD and, to a lesser extent, to environmental protection. At the same time, the current 7th EAP, even though it is an environmental policy instrument, also promotes the importance of the "socio-economic benefits" of environmental protection, including employment and the exploitation of the global market for "eco-industries".[223] The EU clearly brings in the idea of a "green economy" that was developed at the Rio+20 conference in 2012.[224] The idea of the green economy is to achieve synergy between economic interests and environmental

---

relance du marché intérieur' in: Moreiro González CJ (ed), *EU2020: the Lisbon Process revisited = EU2020 = le Processus de Lisbonne revisité* (Difusión Jurídica 2012) 15 et seq.

218 Ibid, 14.
219 Ibid.
220 Ibid.
221 Lee, above note 53, 63.
222 Ibid, 64.
223 Seventh EAP, above note 13. Some others have argued that SD provides an opportunity to give preference to economic development and may, therefore, work against environmental protection. See Krämer, above note 4, 378–379; Ross-Robertson A, 'Is the Environment Squeezed out of Sustainable Development?' 2000, Public Law, 249.
224 UN Rio+20, above note 56.

protection. The current EU's climate change policy seeks to combine "competitiveness and sustainable growth".[225]

3.4.2 *Articulation of SD within EU External Action*

Through Articles 3(5) and 21 TEU, SD holds a prominent position among the Union's external objectives. Development cooperation was the first external policy in which SD found strong incorporation. Today, the concept found an echo in numerous key external policy actions, among the EU's external environmental policy, the Common Foreign and Security Policy (CFSP), and the CCP, which is analysed in the subsequent chapter.

3.4.2.1 Key External Policy Areas with SD Components[226]

Contrary to its internal policy, the EU's external environmental policy made SD one of its key objectives.[227] The EU external environmental policy shows that the EU has been keen to adopt the SD language within international environmental law since the 1990s. Regarding global environmental protection and climate change mitigation, the EU regularly and actively participates in the various multilateral treaty frameworks, and bilateral agreements are seldom. This means that the substantive contours of SD within this policy fields are the same as those principles and sub-objectives formulated at the international level. In other words, the EU's external environmental policy is likely to be the policy where one finds the least EU-specific adaptation of the content of SD and consistency in the understanding of SD can be assumed. This is mainly highlighted by numerous multilateral environmental agreements (MEAs) concluded by the EU that enshrine SD.[228] For instance, the Convention on

---

225 European Commission, 'Next steps for a sustainable European future', above note 8, 4. Including the promotion of a Circular Economy; see in this respect European Commission Communication, 'Closing the loop—An EU action plan for the Circular Economy', COM (2015) 614 final.
226 The Common Commercial Policy is a key external policy and is dealt with in greater detail in the subsequent chapter.
227 Marín Durán G and Morgera E, *Environmental Integration in the EU's External Relations: Beyond Multilateral Dimensions* (Hart Pub 2012) 2.
228 The full list of MEA to which the EU is a Contracting Party or a Signatory is available at <http://ec.europa.eu/environment/international_issues/agreements_en.htm> The Rio Declaration is not an MEA. At the international level, no convention could be found that would combine social protection with SD. International agreements concluded by the EU are an integral part of the EU legal order, see TFEU, Art 216(2). MEAs generally do not contain any definition of SD. A rare example is the Antigua Convention, Art 1(a), to which the EU is not a contracting party.

Biological Diversity[229] describes the term "sustainable use" as meaning "the use of components of biological diversity in a way and at a rate that does not lead to the long-term decline of biological diversity, thereby maintain[ing] its potential to meet the needs and aspirations of present and future generation".[230] The 2015 Paris Agreement[231] serves as a further example that has SD as its general objective, but it also finds that "climate change policy [...] must support economic growth and the broader sustainable development agenda". Also, the Barcelona Convention[232] is an interesting example because it lists in its Article 4, principles that are to be applied by the Parties in order to contribute to the SD of the Mediterranean Sea. Among these principles, one can find the precautionary principle, the polluter-pays principle as well as the obligation to conduct environmental impact assessments.[233] Without entering in a detailed analysis, one can retain that the EU generally and systemically uses its external environmental policy to promote SD.

The second policy with strong SD components is the CFSP.[234] The plan for action established by the European External Action Service, draws a link between the concept of SD and peace. As such, the aim of a "peaceful and sustainable world" became one of its objectives.[235] According to the document, a "resilient society" features democracy and trust in institutions, and SD "lies at the heart of a resilient state."[236] The link between SD and the CFSP is interesting as it reflects the EU's understanding that the fostering of SD in third—and mostly neighbouring—countries is ultimately beneficial for its own security.

3.4.2.2 The "Eradication of Poverty"

For the EU's external action, SD serves as a concept to tackle the global issue of eradicating poverty in developing countries. It was the EU's policy on development cooperation, which, from its beginning, has integrated SD as one of its key principles and objectives.[237] The 2017 European Consensus on

---

229 Convention on Biological Diversity, above note 44.
230 Ibid, Art 2.
231 Paris Agreement on Climate Change, [2015] OJ L 282/4.
232 Convention for the Protection of the Marine Environment and the Coastal Region of the Mediterranean, [1977] OJ L 240 ("the Barcelona Convention").
233 Ibid, Art 4(3).
234 TEU, Arts 23–41.
235 European External Action Service, 'Shared Vision, Common Action: A Stronger Europe, A Global Strategy for the European Union's Foreign and Security Policy' [2016].
236 Ibid, 23.
237 TFEU, Art 208. See Regulation No 2494/2000 of the European Parliament and of the Council of 7 November 2000 on measures to promote the conservation and sustainable management of tropical forests and other forests in developing countries, [2000] OJ

Development is the current framework for the development cooperation of the EU.[238] In line with Agenda 2030 that makes the eradication of poverty the first SDG, the renewed Consensus also underlines the pressing need for poverty eradication.[239]

The EU understands poverty eradication as a "multidimensional" issue that relates to "economic, social, environmental, cultural and political aspects".[240] The specific sub-objectives are the "end to hunger and all forms of malnutrition as well as [to] promote universal health coverage, universal access to quality education and training, adequate and sustainable social protection, and decent work for all within a healthy environment".[241]

Under the policy of development cooperation, the concept of SD has been integrated into several agreements with third countries. The Cotonou Agreement concluded between the EU and the African, Caribbean, and Pacific Group of States (ACP) is an illustrative example in this respect. The agreement's main objective is to eradicate poverty and to integrate the ACP countries into the world economy.[242] The Cotonou Agreement is also remarkable for the way in which it combines SD with human rights as well as for how it promotes good governance in the ACP countries, stating that the respect for "human rights and fundamental freedoms, including respect for fundamental social rights, democracy based on the rule of law and transparent and accountable governance are an integral part of [SD]".[243] In addition, the Cotonou Agreement lays the basis for Economic Partnership Agreements (EPAs) with countries or regions of the ACP. One of those is the EPA with the Southern African

---

L 288/6, Art 2(4); and Regulation No 2493/2000 of the European Parliament and of the Council of 7 November 2000 on measures to promote the full integration of the environmental dimension in the development process of developing countries, [2000] OJ L 288/1, Art 2. Both regulations are no longer in force. Under the two regulations, however, SD has been defined as meaning "the improvement of the standard of living and welfare of the relevant populations within the limits of the capacity of the ecosystems by maintaining natural assets and their biological diversity for the benefit of present and future generations".

238 New European Development Consensus, above note 61.
239 Ibid. See also Agenda 2030, above note 7, SDG 1: "End poverty in all its forms everywhere".
240 New European Development Consensus, above note 61, para 22.
241 Ibid.
242 Cotonou Agreement, above note 44, Arts 1, 2 and 9.
243 Ibid, Art 9(1): "Cooperation shall be directed towards sustainable development centred on the human person, who is the main protagonist and beneficiary of development; this entails respect for and promotion of all human rights. Respect for all human rights and fundamental freedoms, including respect for fundamental social rights, democracy based on the rule of law and transparent and accountable governance are an integral part of sustainable development."

Development Community.²⁴⁴ Therein the Parties stated to "understand [SD] to apply in the case of this Agreement as a commitment that: (a) the application of this Agreement shall fully take into account the human, cultural, economic, social, health and environmental best interests of their respective populations and of future generations [...]."²⁴⁵

3.5 Concluding Remarks

SD as a general objective of all EU policies operates and interacts with a number of other legal principles and requirements of EU constitutional law. The key finding of the present chapter is that SD, as regards its legal function and implications, is best understood as a framework in which the EU institutions are to make decisions and take action. In this respect, EU institutions dispose of discretion but cannot disregard SD. The other key finding is that the substantive implications of SD, i.e. what the objective entails more concretely in terms of substantive benchmarks is policy-specific.

SD figures among the Union objectives. As such it is part of those norms that provide guidance and direction to the constitutional setting connecting the values of a society with legal principles and policy implementation. They are the link between the non-legal and the legal. From early on, the Court of Justice held that Union objectives are binding upon all EU institutions. Based on their binding nature, it has been argued that SD has to be considered in any—internal or external—policy and law-making. The purposes and functions of Union objective are to provide a law-making instruction and to set out a directive for the use of the decision-makers' discretion. Put differently, Union objectives are a matter of legislative and executive discretion, with which the CJEU is generally unlikely to interfere. The discretion relating to objectives does not represent a weakness but rather a strength since it allows decision-makers with flexibility and leeway of adaptation. Therefore, for the purposes and functions of Union objective it is less significant whether they are actually enforceable by the Court in the sense that the Court would annul a measure based on the finding that it does not pursue a given objective. SD as a Union objective is addressed to the EU executive and legislative institutions.

---

244 Economic Partnership Agreement between the European Union and its Member States, of the one part, and the SADC States, of the other part, [2016] OJ L 250/3.
245 The agreement as a whole also has SD as main the objective. See EU-SADC EPA, Art 7(2); Art 7(3) states: "As a result, the Parties agree to work cooperatively towards the achievement of people-centred [SD]".

The broader legal framework of EU law that interacts with the SD objective is rich and enabling. It has namely been argued that the requirement of social and environmental integration is a central tool under EU law to pursue and implement the objective of SD. Moreover, the objective of coherence under EU law corresponds to the benefits that the concept of SD seeks to establish and thus, also serves as a legal tool under EU law to foster SD implementation. Substantively, EU law contains many policy specific principles that further form part of the SD normative framework. For the environmental pillar, this includes the principles of prevention, precaution, the polluter-pays principle, and human health and the conservation of natural resources. For the social pillar, the EU law substantive frameworks highlight the promotion of employment, improvement of living and working conditions, social protection, dialogue between management and labour, and decent work.

The occurrences of SD, namely within EU secondary law and international treaties concluded by the EU, are a declination of the SD objective and highlight different articulations of the same concept. The examples of concrete SD implementation in various EU policies shows that the concept plays out differently in different contexts. Also, non-binding instruments adopted by the EU institutions include several references to SD and guide on how SD could be achieved in a specific context. These soft law instruments not only play a role in understanding SD within the EU legal order but they serve as a tool for the EU to update and adapt the measures to be taken according to new developments and challenges. The soft law instruments are a consequence of the discretion enjoyed by the EU institutions and express their intention on how SD is to be implemented in a given policy.

The general examination of SD within the EU legal order has allowed setting the constitutional foundations of the assessment of the EU as a global actor in international investment governance. The EU law benchmark has its starting position in the normative framework of SD under EU law. In particular, the requirements of integration and coherence provide normative yardsticks against which the EU's investment law-making policy can be assessed. The next chapter takes a closer look at SD within the CCP. It explores how SD impacts and shapes the EU's trade and investment law-making.

CHAPTER 4

Sustainable Development—An Integral Part of EU Investment Law-Making

The Common Commercial Policy (CCP) is one of the most important policies of the EU. It allows the EU to be a key actor in international economic governance. Traditionally, the EU purses a trade agenda that seeks to establish a rules-based order with open markets and free trade. To this end, a variety of goals are pursued within the EU's external trade regime to liberalise trade. Such agenda reflects the paradigm that increased global trade through greater liberalisation is a foremost path toward economic growth. SD does not negate that economic growth is often a pre-condition for development. However, the concept reveals that, alongside economic growth, trade liberalisation can create environmental degradation and social challenges and that the benefits of trade are not always equally distributed. Since the entry into force of the Lisbon Treaty, the EU's CCP has to pursue, next to trade and investment liberalisation also broader societal objectives, and namely so SD. The CJEU held in 2017 that "the objective of [SD] henceforth forms an integral part of the [CCP]."[1] The Court's statement has arguably far-reaching consequences for the EU's CCP. Does SD integration require a shift away from the EU's traditional trade agenda? Is free trade no longer the ultimate goal but somewhat has become a means to achieve SD? In other words, what does it entail for the CCP to have SD as one of its key objectives?

With the entry into force of the Lisbon Treaty in 2009, the scope of the CCP was extended to include FDI. The EU was attributed an express and exclusive external competence over FDI as forming part of the CCP. Since that time, the EU institutions have shaped an autonomous and comprehensive "European international investment policy".[2] With the landmark Opinion 2/15, the CJEU further defined the scope of the EU's competence over foreign investment.[3] And over the last decade, the content of EU IIAs[4] has been further crystallised

---

1 ECJ, Opinion 2/15 *Free Trade Agreement with Singapore*, EU:C:2017:376, para 147.
2 European Commission Communication, 'Towards a comprehensive European international investment policy', COM (2010) 343 final.
3 Opinion 2/15, above note 1.
4 The term international investment agreement (IIA) is defined broadly. As such an IIA is considered to be an international agreement containing provisions relating to the regulation of foreign investment. This namely includes agreements with obligations commonly found

as the EU successfully concluded negotiations with key trade and investment partners, such as Canada and Mexico. Except for the ECT, only post-Lisbon IIAs contain investment protection standards and a dispute settlement mechanism for investor-State disputes.

Against this backdrop, the purpose of the present chapter is to analyse how SD impacts the CCP and the EU's international investment policy and law-making. It seeks to show the constitutional requirements addressed to the EU institutions when further shaping the investment policy and their intentions on how to use the discretion they enjoy when implementing the policy. In going about these issues, the chapter starts off with the evolution of EU international investment law-making before and after the entry into force of the Lisbon Treaty. It then analyses the scope of post-Lisbon EU competence over foreign investment as well as trade-related SD matters. Subsequently, the set of general objectives applicable to the CCP are analysed. It is argued that SD bears a central position among the objectives, such as to impact EU strategies on trade and investment agreements. Finally, the chapter discusses the implications of Opinion 1/17 in light of SD.[5] Whilst the opinion was mainly concerned with procedural issues related to the Investment Court System enshrined in the CETA, the Court's statements on the regulatory autonomy of the EU institutions have a direct link with the endeavours to integrate SD within IIAs. All these elements allow setting the EU law benchmark that is deployed in the present book as they set out the key components that should be present in EU IIAs for the EU to live up to its legal framework and policy ambitions.

4.1   The Evolution of International Investment Law-Making of the EU

Looking at pre-Lisbon IIA practice of the EU allows for a full picture of the gradual expansion of the EU in the field of foreign investment regulation.[6] It also leads to an understanding about why the content and scope of EU IIAs is

---

    in bilateral investment treaties (BITs) having substantive investment protection standards and (mostly) an investor-State dispute settlement through arbitration; but also agreements that only contain provisions on market access, national treatment and most favoured nation treatment (MFN) with respect to commercial presence in the host State, provisions on the free movement of capital as well as agreements establishing an institutional framework between the parties to promote and cooperate on investment.

5 ECJ, Opinion 1/17 *EU-Canada CET Agreement,* EU:C:2019:341.

6 For a more detailed historical overview see, Basedow R, 'A Legal History of the EU's International Investment Policy' (2016) 17 The Journal of World Investment & Trade 743.

different and more comprehensive than is the case for the BITs of EU Member States.[7]

4.1.1 Pre-Lisbon EU Investment Law-Making

The pre-Lisbon EU IIA practice was relatively unnoticed not least because several EU Member States, such as France, Germany and the Netherlands were among the most important global actors regarding the conclusion of traditional BITs regulating the protection of foreign investors in third countries.[8] Given the predominance of the Member States in this field, proposals on amending the EU treaties to add to the CCP an express external competence for the regulation of foreign investment failed when the treaties were amended at Amsterdam and Nice.[9]

Even though before Lisbon, an express reference to foreign investment was not added to the CCP, the question of whether "international trade" could also encompass some aspects of foreign investment regulation was a controversial issue in the pre-Lisbon era. In the course of negotiation on the establishment of the World Trade Organization (WTO) in 1994, the international community discussed the expansion of international trade to other economic activities, such as trade in services.[10] At the time, the EU could become a full member of the WTO due to its competence based on the CCP. However, whether the scope of the CCP also extended to the conclusion of the General Agreement

---

[7] In the main text, the term 'EU' is generally used irrespective of whether it was the EC in the past. Likewise, the main text only refers to the current numbering of articles under the TEU and TFEU.

[8] To date, France has concluded 115 BITs; Germany 131 BITs; and the Netherlands 93 BITs.

[9] In the course of the elaboration of the Treaty of Amsterdam, the proposal to include FDI was mainly rejected by France. In the later negotiations on the Treaty of Nice, the inclusion of FDI was again discussed and yet again rejected by the majority of Member States. See Johannsen S, 'Die Kompetenz der Europäischen Union für Ausländische Direktinvestitionen nach dem Vertrag von Lissabon', (2009) Beiträge zum Transnationalen Wirtschaftsrecht 46, 8. With the Nice amendments, the EU had arguably obtained powers to regulate the initial establishment of foreign investors, however, with important limitations. The limitations concerned the non-service sector and certain specific other service sectors, such as transportation. See Dimopoulos A, *EU Foreign Investment Law* (Oxford University Press 2011) 89.

[10] The Uruguay Round at the World Trade Organization (WTO), marks the change in international economic relations such as that international trade was no longer only linked to trade in goods but encompasses also matters of trade in services and the protection of intellectual property. Issues of investments were discussed but did ultimately not lead to the development of comprehensive rules on the liberalisation and protection of investment. See Kurz J, *The WTO and International Investment Law: Converging Systems* (Cambridge University Press 2016) 48–53.

on Trade in Services (GATS) had to be settled by the CJEU.[11] In Opinion 1/94, the Court found that the first mode of supply of services under the GATS (a service supplier established in one country renders the service to a consumer residing in another) fell under the scope of the CCP.[12] The Court then, however, denied that the same would hold true for the three other modes of service supply, namely consumption aboard, commercial presence and the presence of natural persons.[13] These modes fell according to the Court entirely outside the scope of the CCP.[14] As foreign investment usually entails a lasting establishment, i.e. commercial presence or the presence of natural persons, in the host State and not merely a cross-border economic supply, it followed from Opinion 1/94 that foreign investment in the service sector was excluded from the CCP.[15] In Opinion 2/92 rendered shortly after Opinion 1/94, the Court also denied the existence of EU competence under the CCP to participate in an instrument of the Organisation of Economic Cooperation and Development (OECD) concerned with the treatment accorded to foreign-controlled undertakings established in the territory of OECD member countries.[16] Whilst, the CJEU accepted that the conditions for the participation of foreign-controlled undertakings in trade between the Member States and third countries are subject to the CCP,[17] it held that issues relating to their establishment did not.[18] Opinions 1/94 and 2/92, both show the extent to which the Court was, at the time, reluctant to extend the scope of the CCP by stretching the notion of international trade to the establishment of rules on investment.[19]

Without any explicit legal basis providing the EU with competence to enact measures in the field of foreign investment, the EU was limited to acting externally either based on implied external competence derived from internal competences or to ground its action in alternative legal bases setting out

---

11   The GATS deals *inter alia* with services that are supplied by means of commercial presence, which is essentially foreign direct investment in the service sector; see GATS Art I(2)(c).
12   ECJ, Opinion 1/94 *Agreement establishing the World Trade Organization*, EU:C:1994:384, para 44.
13   Ibid, para 45.
14   Ibid, paras 48–53.
15   See also, Ceyssens J, 'Towards a Common Foreign Investment Policy?—Foreign Investment in the European Constitution' (2005) 32 Legal Issues of Economic Integration 259, 260; Strik P, *Shaping the Single European Market in the Field of FDI* (Hart Pub 2014) 70.
16   ECJ, Opinion 2/92 *Third Revised Decision of the OECD*, EU:C:1995:83, para 4.
17   Ibid, para 24.
18   Ibid, para 28.
19   Dimopoulos, above note 9, 86.

other external policies.[20] EU measures on international investment rules, to the extent that it was possible, were consequently based on a set of dispersed and limited competences.[21] The provisions that provided competence to the EU in the field are alternative and do not provide a complete or targeted basis for action.[22] For the sake of clarity, the three main competence areas are discussed in the following.[23] Yet, it is important to notice that pre-Lisbon EU investment law-making reveals "no clear link" between the legal basis upon which the external agreements have been based and the investment-related commitments contained in these agreements.[24]

First, the EU relied on its competences with respect to the EU internal market, namely those competences on free movements of capital and the freedom of establishment, to conclude international agreement regulating foreign investment. The EU thus considered disposing of implied external competence for foreign investment based on its internal competences. For the EU internal market, the freedom of establishment enshrined in Article 49 TFEU, concerns the "establishment of nationals of a Member State in the territory of another Member State". Even though the formulation clearly regulates a purely intra-EU situation, this provision could serve as a basis for implied external competence for the initial establishment of investments.[25] It can be highlighted by a number of EU IIAs that they were concluded on implied external competence of the EU based on the freedom of establishment. The nature of such competence was however shared.[26] In Opinion 1/94, the Court found in its analysis on the GATS that the EU did not dispose of implied *exclusive* external competence based on the provisions on the freedom of establishment so far as FDI in the service sector was concerned.[27] Yet, whether *shared* implied external competence existed was neither confirmed nor denied by the Court.[28] Moreover, Articles 63 and 64(2) TFEU provide the EU with internal competence

---

20 TFEU, Art 64 (TEC, Art 57(2)); TFEU, Art 207 (TEC, Art 133); TFEU, Arts 211 and 211 (TEC, Arts 181 and 181a); TFEU, Art 217 (TEC, Art 319); TFEU, Art 352 (TEC, Art 308).
21 Dimopoulos, above note 9, 19 et seq.
22 Strik, above note 15, 73–78.
23 TFEU, Art 352 (TEC, Art 308) will not be further analysed. The so-called "flexibility clause" can as a last resort establish EU competence.
24 Strik, above note 15, 100.
25 Karl J, 'The Competence for Foreign Direct Investment, New Powers for the European Union?' (2004) 3 Journal of World Investment and Trade 413.
26 TFEU, Art 4(1) and (2)(a).
27 Opinion 1/94, above note 12, para 86.
28 It is interesting to note that the WTO Agreement was ultimately amongst other provisions concluded on the basis of the freedom of establishment. See Decision 94/800 of the Council of 22 December 1994 concerning the conclusion on behalf of the European

on the matter of the free movement of capital within the EU internal market. However, these provisions also apply to capital transfers to and from third countries. According to Article 63(1) TFEU, any restrictions on the movement of capital between the Member States and between the Member States and non-Member States are prohibited. In the pre-Lisbon era, it has been argued that the competence of the EU under these provisions would be an explicit and shared external competence in the field of foreign investment.[29] At the same time, the free movement of capital did and still does not deal comprehensively with the phenomenon of investments.[30] The free movement of capital does not concern the establishment of an FDI, but only the capital transfers relating to FDI and portfolio investments. However, EU IIA practice shows that Articles 63 and 64(2) TFEU have been used repeatedly by the EU to ground its actions in the field of foreign investment. The most prominent example hereto certainly is the Energy Charter Treaty (ECT). Based on the combination of internal market provisions, the EU (i.e. the European Community at the time) signed in December 1994, the ECT together with the then twelve EU Member States, and EURATOM.[31] The treaty, which entered into force in April 1998, has become one of the most important multilateral investment treaties. For the EU, the ECT is the only pre-Lisbon IIAs that contains investment protection standards and ISDS through arbitration.

Second, a further provision used by the EU as a legal basis for its action in the field of foreign investment has been Article 217 TFEU on association agreements with third countries.[32] This provision provides the EU with relatively extensive external competences since the term of association is not defined in the EU treaties. Therefore, EU institutions dispose of a wide margin of discretion in defining the subject-matter of such an association agreement with third countries. According to the CJEU, association agreements involve creating "special, privileged links with non-member countries which must, at least to a certain extent, take part in the [EU] system".[33] The Court moreover held

---

Community, as regards matters within its competence, of the agreements reached in the Uruguay Round multilateral negotiations (1986–1994), [1994] OJ L 336/1.
29   Karl, above note 25, 415 et seq; Shan W, 'Towards a Common European Community Policy on Investment Issues' (2001) 3 Journal of World Investment and Trade 604, 608.
30   Strik, above note 15, 75; Dimopoulos, above note 9, 82.
31   Such as the Energy Charter Treaty (ECT); see Decision 98/181 of the ECSC, Euratom, Council and Commission of 23 Sep 1997 on the conclusion, by the European Communities, of the Energy Charter Treaty and the Energy Charter Protocol on energy efficiency and related environmental aspects, [1997] OJ L 69/1. See for an overview, Ceyssens, above note 15, 266.
32   TFEU, Art 217 (TEC, Art 310).
33   ECJ, Case C-12/86 *Demirel v Stadt Schwäbisch Gmünd*, EU:C:1987:400, para 9.

that the EU could conclude association agreements covering "all the fields" of EU primary law.[34] The EU thus had the competence to include provisions similar to those of the internal market in such agreements. Consequently, Article 217 TFEU only allowed the EU to assume commitments in the field of investment with third countries mirroring the extent to which the EU is competent to regulate investment internally. As has just been mentioned, based on internal powers, the EU only disposed of shared competences; and the scope of the competence was for foreign investment regulation limited to the freedom of establishment and the free movement of capital.[35] However, due to the flexibility of Article 217 TFEU, numerous EU IIAs have been concluded on this legal basis.[36]

Third, Articles 211 and 212 TFEU provide the EU with competence to conclude development and technical cooperation agreements with third countries.[37] The EU also used those provisions as legal bases to conclude international agreements containing investment-related provisions. The relevance of using Articles 211 and 212(3) TFEU lies within the existence of linkages between, on the one hand, foreign investment and, on the other hand, the economic development of developing countries, as well as technical cooperation for improving investment flows in those countries.[38] Thus, these types of agreements must have, as their main objective, the development of developing countries. Therefore, it becomes apparent that Articles 211 and 212(3) TFEU only allow for limited action in the field of foreign investment and are, in particular, not suitable for IIAs with developed countries. In other words, whilst, development cooperation agreements can provide a general framework for cooperation in foreign investment matters, they cannot have the regulation of foreign investment as a central (or unique) element.[39] At any rate,

---

34 Ibid.
35 Dimopoulos, above note 9, 120–121; Strik, above note 15, 76–77; Ceyssens, above note 15, 262.
36 Eg EC-Jordan EMA, [2002] OJ L 129/3; EC-Lebanon EMA, [2006] OJ L 143/2; EC-Egypt EMA, [2004] OJ L 345/115.
37 TFEU, Arts 211 and 212 (TEC, Arts 181 and 181a).
38 Dimopoulos, above note 9, 121.
39 Ibid. See also for the limitations imposed by the ECJ, Case C-268/94 *Portugal v Council*, EU:C:1996:461, para 45: "As regards more particularly the provisions of the Agreement which relate to specific matters, those provisions establish the framework of cooperation between the contracting parties. Taken as a whole, they are limited to determining the areas for cooperation and to specifying certain of its aspects and various actions to which special importance is attached. By contrast, those provisions contain nothing that prescribes in concrete terms the manner in which cooperation in each specific area envisaged is to be implemented."

for its relations with developing countries, the EU has used the legal basis on development cooperation extensively, allowing it to conclude agreements that contain investment-related provisions.⁴⁰

In sum, pre-Lisbon EU IIA practice was based on a restricted set of competences, which, in return, were of limited scope to regulate international investment excluding, namely, provisions on investment protection that can be found in the BITs of EU Member States. With the exception of the ECT, it is interesting to note that most pre-Lisbon EU IIAs mirror the EU internal market framework for intra-EU investments.⁴¹ Thus, it is not surprising that pre-Lisbon EU IIAs are characterised by provisions on non-discrimination requirements and investment liberalisation provisions. For those EU IIAs that have been concluded in the context of the EU's development cooperation, the emphasis is on the development aspects of foreign investment as an element of economic assistance and cooperation.⁴² The beginning of the millennium was marked by the continuation of the liberalisation agenda of the EU.⁴³ The opening of third country markets to EU nationals has been explicitly considered a fundamental objective of EU external economic strategy.⁴⁴ This meant that, not long before the adoption of the Lisbon Treaty, the EU was pushing for a more extended scope of action relating to the regulation of investment.⁴⁵

---

40 The EU did so from early on. See Report from the Commission to the Council, Investment Protection and Promotion Clauses in Agreements between the Community and Various Categories of Developing Countries: Achievements to Date and Guidelines for Future Action, COM (80) 24 final, 8 May 1980, 17–18. See for an overview, Voss J, 'The Protection and Promotion of European Private Investment in Developing Countries—An Approach Towards a Concept for a European Policy on Foreign Investment: A German Contribution', 18 CMLR (1981), 363–395; the author refers to the 1980 EU-ASEAN Cooperation Agreement, which contains a general references to the objective of strengthening the economic relations between the parties through investments and promotes the adoption for investment protection arrangements between EU Member States and the ASEAN region.
41 Dimopoulos, above note 9, 17.
42 The main objectives of EU development cooperation are SD and the eradication of poverty; see Section 2.4.3.
43 As highlighted by the Commission strategy 'Global Europe'. See European Commission Communication, 'Global Europe: Competing in the world', COM (2006) 567 final.
44 Dimopoulos, above note 9, 19.
45 The last significant development before the entry into force of the Lisbon Treaty was in 2006 the so-called 'Minimum Platform on Investment', which is an internal EU instrument that served as a negotiating template for EU IIAs. See Council, 'Minimum Platform on Investment', [2006] Doc 15375/06. The platform has never been made publicly available, but reportedly the template focused on securing additional market access commitments and namely served as a basis for the FTA with Korea as well as for the EPA with the CARIFORUM States. See EUKFTA, [2010] OJ L 127/6; EU-CARIFORUM EPA, [2008] OJ L 289/3.

4.1.2 Post-Lisbon: Building an Autonomous EU Investment Policy

With the entry into force of the Lisbon Treaty, an express reference to FDI was finally added to the CCP under Article 207 TFEU. Yet, right after the treaty reform, it became apparent that the new competence raised important practical and legal challenges that would need to be overcome within the upcoming years to establish a functional EU investment policy. The legal challenges have provoked a magnitude of contributions by scholars of EU law and international investment law.[46] They, in particular, have discussed the scope of EU competence over FDI, the organisation of the transition from Member States' BITs to EU IIAs,[47] as well as the repartition of roles and responsibilities between the EU and the Member States in the context of investor-State dispute settlement.[48] The extent of the attention is not surprising when considering that EU Member States' BITs account for almost half of the global IIA network. Having the EU take over competences in FDI has implied the emergence of an important new actor.

As an initial step, EU institutions positioned themselves and set out their respective understandings for the main orientations of the newly gained policy. The Commission did so through a well-known Communication with the title "Towards a comprehensive European international investment policy".[49]

---

46   To mention a few, eg Bungenberg M, 'The Division of Competences Between the EU and Its Member States in the Area of Investment Politics' in: Bungenberg M, Griebel J and Hindelang S (eds), *International Investment Law and EU Law* (Springer 2011); Burgstaller M, 'European Law and Investment Treaties' (2009) Journal of International Arbitration 181; Calamita NJ, 'The Making of Europe's International Investment Policy: Uncertain First Steps' (2012) Legal Issues of Economic Integration 301; De Luca A, 'New Developments on the Scope of the EU Common Commercial Policy under the Lisbon Treaty, Investment liberalization vs. investment protection?', in: Sauvant, K (ed), Yearbook on International Investment Law & Policy 2010/2011 (Oxford University Press 2012) 165–215; Reinisch A, 'EU on the Investment Path, Quo Vadis Europe—The Future of EU BITs and Other Investment Agreements' (2013) Santa Clara Journal of International Law 12, 111–158. Weiss F and Steiner S, 'The Investment Regime under Article 207 TFEU: A Legal Conundrum, the Scope of 'foreign direct investment' and the Future of intra-EU BITs', in: Beatens F, *Investment Law within International Law* (Cambridge University Press 2013) Ch 16.

47   The organisation of a smooth transition is a core practical challenge and regulated by Regulation No 1219/2012. See Regulation No 1219/2012 of the European Parliament and the Council, on establishing transitional arrangements for bilateral investment agreements between Member States and third countries, [2012] OJ L 351/40.

48   See Regulation No 912/2014 of the European Parliament and of the Council of 23 July 2014 establishing a framework for managing financial responsibility linked to investor-to-State dispute settlement tribunals established by international agreements to which the European Union is party, [2014] OJ L 257/121.

49   European Commission, above note 1.

The Commission had proposed that future EU IIAs should include investment protection standards, such as fair and equitable treatment, expropriation as well as investor-State dispute settlement through arbitration taking inspiration from the BIT network of the Member States. The Commission moreover defined criteria for the selection of countries with which the EU should envisage starting IIA negotiations. Shortly after the publication of the Communication, the Council[50] and the European Parliament[51] also took a position on the future of the EU's investment policy. The position of the Parliament differs from those of the other two institutions, namely in terms of the definition of the notion of investment under future EU IIAs. In the eye of the Parliament, such definition needs to avoid the possibility for extensive interpretations as it could undermine the States' right to regulate.[52] Conversely, the Council's emphasis was more on the need to ensure a high level of protection and legal security of EU investors in third countries.[53] A common concern of all the three institutions was the importance given to the general objectives of EU external action serving as guidance for the future orientation of the investment policy. All three institutions moreover stressed the need to ensure corporate social responsibilities and the use and implementation of the OECD Guidelines for Multinational Enterprises.[54]

The EU institutions were, right from the start of the investment policy, also aware of the necessity for the legal arrangement of the gradual transition from Member States BITs to EU IIAs and adopted Regulation No 1219/2012, which regulates the transition.[55] The EU seeks to substitute the Member States in the exercise of their foreign investment policies, by gradually setting aside Member State BITs with third countries. Regulation No 1219/2012, more superficially, regulates two aspects of the transitional arrangements. It addresses the status under EU law of EU Member States' BITs that existed before the entry into force of the Lisbon Treaty. Moreover, it allows the Member States to amend existing BITs or conclude new ones with third

---

50   Council of the European Union, 'Council Conclusions', 3041st Foreign Affairs Council Meeting, Luxembourg, 25 Oct 2010.
51   European Parliament resolution of 6 April 2011 on the future European international investment policy 2010/2203(INI), [2012] OJ C 296E.
52   Ibid, para D.
53   Council of the European Union, above note 50, para 8.
54   OECD, 'OECD Guidelines for Multinational Enterprises', annexed to 2000 OECD Declaration on International Investment and Multinational Enterprises, DAFFE/IME(2000)/20); (2001) 40 ILM 237 as amended.
55   Regulation No 1219/2012, above note 47.

countries provided that the terms, conditions and procedures set out in the regulation are respected.[56] In particular, to open negotiations or sign a BIT, Member States must obtain authorisation from the European Commission. Next to the transitional arrangement Regulation, the EU adopted another regulation that is important for the development of a functional EU investment policy. Regulation No 912/2014,[57] the so-called "Financial Responsibility Regulation", sets out the rules concerning the allocation of financial responsibility between the EU and its Member States, and provides for situations in which the EU and/or one of its Member States can act in investor-State dispute settlement.[58]

Building an autonomous investment policy also meant that the EU sets out its priority countries with which it seeks to conclude IIAs. From the start, EU-led negotiations included those with Canada and Singapore.[59] Based on the mandates from the Council, the Commission is active in initiating new negotiations on IIAs mainly in the form of investment chapters contained in broad FTAs.[60] The main FTA negotiations that can be mentioned are those with the United States of America, India and Mexico. At the time of writing, four IIAs of the EU have been successfully concluded, the FTAs with Japan, Mexico, Singapore and Vietnam as well as the Comprehensive Economic and Trade Agreement (CETA) with Canada. The successful conclusion of these IIAs is a first key stage of the investment policy of the EU. However, the effectiveness of the EU investment policy has already been put into test.

In particular, the process of adopting the CETA with Canada has shown the difficulties of establishing an autonomous EU investment policy. The negotiations for CETA began in May 2009 and were completed in August 2014. In July 2016, the European Commission proposed that the agreement be concluded and signed as a mixed agreement, meaning not only the EU but also all its Member States have to sign and ratify the agreement. The CETA was finally signed in October 2016. The signature was jeopardised and delayed for a few days by objections from the Walloon Parliament, which refused to give its

---

56 Ibid, Art 1(1).
57 Regulation No 912/2014, above note 48.
58 For more detail see Dimopoulos A, 'The Involvement of the EU in Investor-State Dispute Settlement: A Question of Responsibilities' (2014) Common Market Law Review 1671.
59 European Commission, 'Trade for All', above note 2, 7.
60 However, the EU is negotiating a stand-alone investment agreement with China. More information available at <http://ec.europa.eu/trade/policy/countries-and-regions/countries/china/>.

consent to the federal Belgian government to sign the agreement.⁶¹ In order to convince the Walloons, the EU and Canada had signed a "Joint Interpretative Instrument" on CETA.⁶² This document having legal force clarifies what has been agreed by Canada and the EU in a number of controversial areas such as the Investment Court System, governments' right to regulate, and labour and environmental standards. In February 2017, the European Parliament gave its consent to the agreement.⁶³ Those parts of CETA that fall under the competence of the EU entered into force provisionally.

The CETA had to pass a further significant legal test as Belgium submitted a request to the CJEU for an opinion on the agreement's compatibility with EU law.⁶⁴ Part of the compromise with the Walloons was Belgium's subsequent request to the CJEU for an opinion on the agreement's compatibility with EU primary law. In its submission to the Court, Belgium asked a set of three questions concerning the CETA Investment Chapter and more specifically its Section F on the Investment Court System (ICS). Belgium highlighted three risks of incompatibility of the mechanism for settling investment disputes between investors and States: firstly, the risk of undermining the autonomy of the Union's legal order; secondly, the risk of violating the general principle of equal treatment and the need for Union law to be effective⁶⁵ and thirdly, compatibility with the right of access to an independent tribunal.⁶⁶

Dealing with this set of issues, the Court found that the CETA Investment Court was compatible with each of them. On equal treatment, the Court found that the ICS does not infringe this fundamental principle. The argument was that CETA, like IIAs in general, only entitles foreign investors to bring an

---

61   See also Kaddous C, 'De quelques défis liés à la conclusion des accords mixtes', in: *Liber amicorum Antonio Tizzano: de la Cour CECA à la Cour de l'Union: le long parcours de la justice européenne* (G Giappichelli 2018) 458–459.
62   Joint Interpretative Instrument on the Comprehensive Economic and Trade Agreement (CETA) between Canada and the European Union and its Member, [2017] OJ L 11/3.
63   See European Parliament legislative resolution of 15 February 2017 on the draft Council decision on the conclusion of the Comprehensive Economic and Trade Agreement (CETA) between Canada, of the one part, and the European Union and its Member States, of the other part, 10975/2016-C8-0438/2016-2016/0205(NLE).
64   More precisely, Belgium has asked the CJEU to rule on the compatibility of the Investment Court System (ICS) that is contained in CETA, first with the principles of EU law; second, with the general principle of quality and "practical effect" requirement of EU law; third, with the right of access to the courts; and finally, with the right to an independent and impartial judiciary. The provisions that are relevant in this respect are Art 191(1) TEU, and Art 344 TFEU; autonomy of the EU legal order.
65   CFREU, Art 20.
66   CFREU, Art 47.

action before a dispute settlement body. Such right does not exist for domestic companies. The Court smashed this argument as it did not consider domestic and foreign companies to be comparable, so that the principle of equal treatment does not apply.[67] Rather, Canadian investors in the EU and EU investors in Canada are comparable.[68] As far as the third argument of Belgium is concerned, the Court also assessed the ICS's compatibility with the principle of access to an independent court in accordance with Article 47(3) of the EU Charter of Fundamental Rights.[69] Here, the Court examines both the access of small and medium-sized enterprises to the CETA Court and the personal independence of the members of the CETA Court. With regard to the former, the Court states that the CETA Court system is only compatible with EU law if the support mechanism for small or medium-sized investors planned by the contracting parties is implemented before the CETA is approved by the EU.[70] With regard to the independence of judges, the mechanism of appointment provided for in the CETA is sufficient for the Court.[71] The Court's reasoning on the principle of autonomy is noteworthy and is discussed in greater detail hereafter together with the implications of Opinion 1/17 for the EU as a global actor.[72]

---

67 Opinion 1/17, above note 5, para 180.
68 See also the same reasoning of AG Bot, Opinion, para. The reasoning of the Court can be seriously questioned because it disregards the actual rationale of the principle of equal treatment, since the reference value should be the same sovereign act. See on this point Krajewski M, 'Ist CETA der „Golden Standard"? EuGH hält CETA-Gericht für unionsrechtskonform', *VerfBlog*, 2019/4/30. He argued that In this respect, EU companies and Canadian companies affected by an EU measure are in a comparable situation. EU companies in Canada and Canadian companies in the EU, on the other hand, do not constitute a comparable pair in terms of the principle of equality.
69 Opinion 1/17, above note 5, para 189. The EU has in Statement No 36 underlined that 2There will be better and easier access to this new court for the most vulnerable users, namely SMEs and private individuals. To that end: (1) The adoption by the Joint Committee of additional rules, provided for in Article 8.39.6 of the CETA, intended to reduce the financial burden imposed on applicants who are natural persons or small and medium-sized enterprises, will be expedited so that these additional rules can be adopted as soon as possible. (2) Irrespective of the outcome of the discussions within the Joint Committee, the Commission will propose appropriate measures of (co)-financing of actions of small and medium-sized enterprises before that Court and the provision of technical assistance.
70 Opinion 1/17, above note 5, para 221. See also Statement No 36 of the EU, which stresses the following objective: "The system should progress towards judges who are employed full time."
71 Eg, the Court does not see any fundamental problem in the possibility of case-related payment, which may still be possible in the initial phase Opinion, 1/17, above note 5, para 239.
72 See below Section 4.5.

4.2 EU Competence over Foreign Investment and SD

The CCP has been, since its inception in 1958, the most important and most dynamic external policy of the EU, allowing it to be among the key actors in the global economic system.[73] One reason for the success of the CCP was the early recognition of EU exclusive competence in this field.[74] Since the entry into force of the Lisbon Treaty, FDI falls under the range of issues of EU's trade policy enshrined in Article 207(1) TFEU. It follows that the EU's competence in this field is exclusive.[75] Yet, the scope of the competence was controversial and raised a number of legal questions. First, how to define FDI in the absence of such a definition in the treaties' provisions has been discussed. Second, whilst it was rather clear that the term FDI could not encompass non-direct investment, namely portfolio investment, the debate was whether the EU disposes of exclusive external implied competence to conclude international agreements regulating non-direct investment. Shortly after the entry into force of the Lisbon Treaty, the Commission was arguing in favour of implied exclusive competence in the field, to the extent that IIAs affect the scope of the "common rules", such as the provisions of the treaties on capital and payments.[76] Yet the majority of scholars denied the Commission's argumentation and concluded that the competence for non-direct investment remained, also under the Lisbon Treaty, an implied but shared external competence. Third, the debate also revolved around the question of what type of regulation of FDI falls under the exclusive competence of the CCP. The reason was that the international regulation of FDI not only covers issues of liberalisation (such as admission and non-discriminatory pre-establishment treatment of FDI) but also standards of protection such as fair and equitable treatment, expropriation clauses as well as investor-State dispute settlement provisions. The question of whether the EU has been empowered by the Lisbon Treaty to regulate

---

73 Kaddous, above note 62, 225; see also, Koutrakos P, *EU International Relations Law* (Second edition, Hart Pub 2015) 29.
74 The Court had already asserted in 1975 the exclusivity of the EU's competence with respect to the CCP. In the case *Donckerwolcke* it then highlighted the practical implications of exclusivity in terms of the position of the EU Member States. See ECJ, Opinion 1/75 *Local Cost Standard,* EU:C:1975:145; ECJ, Case 41/76 *Donckerwolcke and others v Procureur de la République,* EU:C:1976:182, paras 33–35.
75 TFEU, Art 3(e).
76 European Commission, 'Trade for All', above note 2, 8; See also Kaddous C, 'Reflections on the Changes in the European Union's Common Commercial Policy', in: Biaggini G, Diggelmann O and Kaufmann C (eds), *Polis und Kosmopolis Festschrift für Daniel Thürer* (Dike; Nomos 2015) 346–347.

aspects of investment other than the liberalisation was controversial. Some favoured a restrictive approach, mainly referring to the negotiating history of the Lisbon Treaty.[77] Others argued for a more functionalist understanding on the scope of the FDI competence also in order to cover post-establishment treatment and protection of FDI as well.[78]

The CJEU's Opinion 2/15 on the EU-Singapore FTA settled most of these initial controversies.[79] The agreement is one of the first FTAs negotiated by the EU on the basis of Article 207 TFEU that contained a chapter on substantive investment protection provisions as well as a system for investor-State dispute settlement.[80] Thus the initial chapter on investment, which became—as a consequence of Opinion 2/15—the Investment Protection Agreement (IPA), is closer to the scope and content of traditional BITs of the EU Member States. At the end of the negotiations of the said FTA, and before the agreement's signature, the Commission submitted a request to the CJEU for an opinion to determine whether the EU had exclusive competence enabling it to sign and conclude the agreement without the participation of the Member States.[81]

In essence, the Court found that the EU could not conclude the FTA with Singapore alone because some of its provisions fall within the scope of competences shared between the EU and the Member States. With respect to the investment chapter of the agreement, the Court found that the EU had exclusive competence over FDI but not over other non-direct foreign investments.[82] The FTA with Singapore, like most of the IIAs, contains a broad, so-called asset-based definition of investment, which is clearly not limited to FDI but which includes portfolio investment as well.[83] The distinction between direct and non-direct investment was then decisive for the substantive standards under the agreement in order to determine whether they fall or not under the CCP. The same substantive standard is of exclusive EU competence, if it relates

---

77   Krajewski M, 'The Reform of the Common Commercial Policy' in: Biondi A, Eeckhout P and Ripley S (eds), *EU Law after Lisbon* (Oxford University Press 2012) 303–305.
78   See especially European Commission, 'Trade for All', above note 2.
79   See also, Kaddous C and Piçarra N, 'Topic 3: The External Dimension of EU Policies. An Update on the Roles of the EU institutions and Member States. An Assessment of the Current Challenges on Trade, Investment Protection and the Area of Freedom, Security and Justice', XXVIII FIDE Congress, Estoril 23–26 May 2018, Final Report, 106–108.
80   Opinion 2/15, above note 1, paras 5–8. The investor-State dispute settlement through arbitration has after Opinion 2/15 been replaced by an Investment Court System (ICS) under the EUSIPA, see below Section 4.4.3.
81   TFEU, Art 218(11).
82   Opinion 2/15, above note 1, paras 81 and 243.
83   Reinisch A, 'The Division of Powers Between the EU and Its Member States "After Lisbon" ' in: Bungenberg M et al (eds), *International Investment Law and EU Law* (Springer 2011) 49.

to FDI and of shared competence if it relates to other non-direct investments. Opinion 2/15 is a milestone for the delimitation of the scope of the competence of the EU with respect to investment law-making.[84]

4.2.1 Exclusive Competence over Foreign Direct Investment

Under Article 207 TFEU, the notion "foreign", first of all, refers to investments from the EU into third countries, and also to investments of third-country nationals into the EU.[85] The subsequent term "direct investment" is a well-known concept of EU law. This is especially the case under the internal market provisions of the EU treaties that guarantee the free movement of capital and payments between Member States, and between a Member State and third counties.[86] The term "direct investment" can be found in Article 64 TFEU, which allows existing restrictions to be maintained "in respect of the movement of capital to or from third countries involving direct investment—including in real estate".[87] In a series of cases, the CJEU has set out more precisely the meaning of direct investment, *i.e.*:

> "investments of any kind made by natural or legal persons which *serve to establish or maintain lasting and direct links* between the persons providing the capital and the undertakings to which that capital is made available in order to carry out an economic activity. Acquisition of a holding in an undertaking constituted as a company limited by shares is a direct investment where the shares held by the shareholder enable him to *participate effectively in the management* of that company *or in its control.*"[88]

The origin of this definition is taken from the Directive 88/361 on capital movements, which is no longer in force.[89] The Directive relied on the widely accepted definitions on direct investment of the International Monetary Fund

---

84 Opinion 2/15, above note 1, para 30.
85 Eeckhout P and Ortino F, 'Towards an EU Policy on Foreign Direct Investment' in: Biondi A, Eeckhout P and Ripley S (eds), *EU Law after Lisbon* (Oxford University Press 2012) 314.
86 TFEU, Art 63.
87 TFEU, Art 64(1). See also its previous version, TEC, Art 57(1).
88 ECJ, Case C-446/04 *Test Claimants in the FII Group Litigation v Commissioners of Inland Revenue*, EU:C:2006:774, paras 181 and 182; ECJ, Case C-326/07 *Commission v Italy*, EU:C:2009:193, para 35; ECJ, Case C-464/14 *SECIL*, EU:C:2016:896, paras 75 and 76. See also Opinion 2/15, above note 1, para 80. Emphasis added.
89 Directive 88/361 of the Council of 24 June 1988 for the implementation of Article 67 of the Treaty, [1988] OJ L 178/5.

(IMF) and the OECD.⁹⁰ In Opinion 2/15, the Court used its settled case law to define FDI under Article 207 TFEU. The Court concluded that FDI falls under the exclusive competence of the EU.⁹¹

Conversely, non-direct investments have to fall outside the scope of Article 207 TFEU. The precise mention of "foreign direct investment" has to be understood, according to the Court, as an "unequivocal expression of intention" of the Member States.⁹² Therefore, other investments cannot fall under the exclusive competence of the EU. Moreover, to sustain its findings, the Court applied its general test of "direct and immediate effects on trade" to determine whether non-direct investment could still fall under the notion of international trade and thus under the CCP. It first underlined that so far FDI is concerned the link existed because the fact that the FTA with Singapore regulates the participation by a natural or legal person of a third State in the EU and vice versa in the management and control of a company that carries out business activities has "direct and immediate effects on trade".⁹³ However, the Court saw no link of that kind in the case of non-direct investments, which do not have a participatory share allowing the management and control of the company.⁹⁴ Consequently, Opinion 2/15 confirmed that the EU has exclusive external competence to approve commitments vis-à-vis a third State only relating to FDI.⁹⁵

4.2.2 Shared Implied External Competence over Non-Direct Investment

A much more controversial issue to be solved in Opinion 2/15 was the question of whether the EU had implied exclusive competence over non-direct investments under Article 3(2) TFEU or whether this competence was an implied but shared competence between the EU and the Member States. In order to tackle this issue, the term non-direct investment needed to be defined. Like

---

90   OECD, 'Code of Liberalisation of Capital Movements' [first version 1961, last update 2018]; and International Monetary Fund (IMF), 'Balance-of-Payments-Manual' [1993]. The IMF manual expresses the lasting interest element, which is a crucial element of direct investment in terms of a 10% minimum ownership requirement (see para 362 thereof). See also Ceyssens, above note 15, 274, Reinisch, above note 84, 46–50; Hinojosa-Martínez LM, 'The Scope of the EU Treaty-Making Power on Foreign Investment: Between Wishful Thinking and Pragmatism' (2016) 17 The Journal of World Investment & Trade 86, 88–94.
91   Opinion 2/15, above note 1, para 81.
92   Ibid, para 83.
93   Ibid, paras 36 and 84; See also ECJ, Case C-414/11 *Daiichi Sankyo and Sanofi-Aventis*, EU:C:2013:520, para 51; ECJ, Case C-137/12 *Commission v Council*, EU:C:2013:675, para 57; ECJ, Opinion 3/15 *Marrakesh Treaty*, EU:C:2017:114, para 61.
94   Opinion 2/15, above note 1, para 84.
95   TFEU, Art 3(1)(e).

the notion of direct investment, the term non-direct investment is known under EU law. In constant case law, the CJEU defined it as follows:

> [N]on-direct foreign investment may, inter alia, take place in the form of the acquisition of company securities with the *intention of making a financial investment without any intention to influence the management and control of the undertaking* ('portfolio' investments), and that such investments constitute movements of capital for the purposes of Article 63 TFEU.[96]

Accordingly, the distinctive feature between direct and non-direct investment is that for a direct investment the investor is placed in a position whereby he/she can pursue entrepreneurial aims, such as the control and management of the company, meaning that major or important entrepreneurial decisions cannot be reached without his or her consent. In contrast, if the investor does not acquire such control within a company, one speaks of portfolio investment.[97] In order to assess whether the investor is in such a position often depends on a number of circumstances and therefore needs to be assessed on a case-by-case basis.[98] A regularly important benchmark in this respect is the minimum threshold of 10% participation in the company in order to be considered as a direct investment.[99]

Concerning non-direct investment, the Court in Opinion 2/15 started its analysis on whether the EU disposes of implied *exclusive* competence pursuant to Article 3(2) TFEU. This provision foresees three possible conditions under which external competence of the EU can be exclusive.[100] In the Opinion, the Court focused on the final limb,[101] which sets out that the EU "shall have

---

[96] Opinion 2/15, above note 1, para 227. Emphasis added. See also, ECJ, Joined Cases C-282/04 and C-283/04, *Commission v Netherlands*, EU:C:2006:208, para 19; ECJ, Case C-81/09 *Idryma Typou v Ypourgos Typou*, EU:C:2010:622, para 48; ECJ, Case C-212/09 *Commission v Portugal*, EU:C:2011:717, para 47.

[97] Hindelang S, *The Free Movement of Capital and Foreign Direct Investment: The Scope of Protection in EU Law* (Oxford University Press 2009) 79.

[98] Ibid.

[99] International Monetary Fund, above note 79. See also *Plama Consortium Limited v Bulgaria*, ICSID Case No ARB/03/24, Decision on Jurisdiction, 8 Feb 2005, para 170; *Saba Fakes v Turkey*, ICSID Case No ARB/07/20, Award, 14 July 2010, para 134.

[100] TFEU, Art 3(2): "The Union shall also have exclusive competence for the conclusion of an international agreement when its conclusion is provided for in a legislative act of the Union or is necessary to enable the Union to exercise its internal competence, or in so far as its conclusion may affect common rules or alter their scope."

[101] Opinion 2/15, above note 1, para 235. The Court excluded the two other hypotheses of Article 3(2) TFEU, i.e. the conclusion of the international agreement is provided for

exclusive competence for the conclusion of an international agreement [...] in so far as its *conclusion may affect common rules or alter their scope*".[102] This provision was introduced with the Lisbon Treaty and essentially codified the AETR principle.[103] In essence, the principle sets out that when "common rules", meaning EU laws and measures, come into existence at the internal EU level, only the EU is in the position to assume and carry out obligations towards third countries affecting the sphere of application of such EU laws and measures.[104] In Opinion 2/15, the European Commission argued that the term "common rules" would also relate to treaty provisions, namely Articles 63 to 66 TFEU on the free movement of capital. The Court disagreed and underlined that "common rules" only refer to secondary law that the EU has adopted in the exercise of its internal competence.[105] According to the Court, if "common rules" should have been extended to EU primary law, the treaty drafters would have done so in the revision process of the Lisbon Treaty.[106] In addition, given the primacy of the TEU and TFEU over international agreements concluded on their basis, such international agreements cannot have an impact on the meaning or scope of the EU treaties or in any way "alter their scope" pursuant to Article 3(2) TFEU.[107]

After having excluded implied exclusive competence based on Article 3(2) TFEU, the Court went on to use the similarly worded provision of Article 216 TFEU.[108] Unlike Article 3(2) TFEU, Article 216 TFEU can provide the EU with external implied competence without distinguishing between exclusive

---

in a legislative act of the EU; or it is necessary to enable the EU to exercise its internal competence.

102   Ibid. Emphasis added.
103   ECJ, Case 22/70 *Commission v Council* (AETR), EU:C:1971:32, paras 17–19. The AETR principle was subsequently followed in numerous cases and opinions. See eg, Opinion 2/91 *ILO Convention*, EU:C:1993:106, para 9; Opinion 1/94, above note 10, para 48; ECJ, Case C-467/98 *Commission v Denmark* (Open Skies), EU:C:2002:625, para 44.
104   AETR, above note 103, para 18.
105   Opinion 2/15, above note 1, para 233.
106   Ibid, para 234.
107   AG Sharpston adopted a different reasoning in this respect. See Opinion of AG Sharpston (Opinion procedure 2/15), EU:C:2016:992 para 358.
108   TFEU, Art 216(1): "The Union may conclude an agreement with one or more third countries or international organisations where the Treaties so provide or where the conclusion of an agreement is necessary in order to achieve, within the framework of the Union's policies, one of the objectives referred to in the Treaties, or is provided for in a legally binding Union act or is likely to affect common rules or alter their scope." See also ECJ, Opinion 1/03 *New Lugano Convention*, EU:C:2006:8, para 114; ECJ, Opinion 1/13 *Accession of third States to the Hague Convention*, EU:C:2014:2303, para 67; ECJ, Case C-600/14 *Germany v Council*, EU:C:2017:935, para 45.

and shared competences.[109] For its analysis of the said provision, the Court focused on the necessity condition, which means that the EU can possess external competences to conclude an international agreement when such a conclusion is *necessary* to achieve one of the objectives referred to in the treaties. As regards non-direct investment, the Court found that "in the light of the fact that the free movement of capital and payments between Member States and third States, laid down in Article 63 TFEU, is not formally binding on third States, the conclusion of international agreements which contribute to the establishment of such free movement on a reciprocal basis may be classified as necessary in order to achieve fully such free movement".[110] As a consequence, the EU possesses implied external competence based on 216(1) TFEU in combination with Article 63 TFEU. The nature of the competence is shared pursuant to the competence of the EU for the internal market based on Article 4(1) and (2)(a) TEFU.[111] Without entering into detail on the relationship between the Articles 3(2) and 216(1) TFEU, it should be noted that in Opinion 2/15, the Court has not contributed to a more precise delimitation between the two provisions. In particular, it is unclear why the necessary requirement under 216(1) TFEU was satisfied but not so under Article 3(2) TFEU.[112]

4.2.3   *Forms of Investment Regulation Falling under EU Competence*

The next question in Opinion 2/15 was whether the measures that fall under EU competence only relate to the admission of investment or whether the scope of the competence also encompasses the treatment accorded to investment after their admission into the host State.[113] The Court held that not only the admission of FDI but also the protection of FDI falls within the CCP when they display a "specific link" with trade between the EU and third States. The specific link to trade is, as mentioned before, defined so as to mean that a measure

---

109   *Germany v Council,* above note 108, para 49: "It follows from the very wording of [Article 216(1) TFEU], in which no distinction is made according to whether the European Union's external competence is exclusive or shared, that the Union possess such competence in four situations. [...]".

110   Opinion 2/15, above note 1, para 240.

111   Ibid, paras 239–242.

112   See also on this point Cremona M, 'Shaping EU Trade Policy Post-Lisbon: Opinion 2/15 of 16 May 2017' (2018) 14 European Constitutional Law Review 231, 249. At the same time, exclusive external competence for the EU based on necessity has been accepted only once by the CJEU. See, ECJ, Opinion 1/76 *Draft Agreement establishing a European laying-up fund for inland waterway vessels*, EU:C:1977:63.

113   It has been uncontested that the FDI competence covers the admission of FDI.

"is essentially intended to promote, facilitate or govern" trade and has a "direct and immediate effect" on trade.[114]

The Court underlined that Article 207(1) TFEU does not make any such distinction but refers generally to acts concerning FDI independent of whether they relate to the admission or the protection of FDI.[115] By defining the scope in this way, the Court agreed with the Commission in the sense that all investment protection standards of foreign investors are part of the CCP.[116] This includes non-discrimination standards, such as national and most-favoured nation treatment. It also includes fair and equitable treatment and the compensation of losses in case of war or other armed conflicts. It furthermore includes the right of foreign investment concerning the free transfer of their funds as well as the clause on subrogation, which is the guarantee that investors may transfer rights or titles, and the assignment of claims in respect of investments made in a host State's territory.

Likewise, the provisions on expropriation also fall under EU competence and, in particular, do not impinge Member States' powers guaranteed under Article 345 TFEU.[117] The article foresees that the EU treaties shall in no way prejudice the rules in Member States governing the system of property ownership. In Opinion 2/15, the Court further confined the scope of this provision. It stressed that Member States are free to exercise their powers concerning property ownership, but that would not mean that those Member States' actions and measures are not subject to the fundamental rules of the EU, in particular the principle of non-discrimination.[118] The Court thus concluded that the EU has external competence over the provision on the protection against unlawful expropriation in the FTA with Singapore, because the provision "reflects the simple fact that whilst the Member States remain free to exercise their competence regarding property ownership so far as they are concerned, they are

---

114 Opinion 2/15, above note 1, para 36. *Daiichi Sankyo and Sanofi-Aventis*, above note 82, para 51; ECJ, Case C-137/12 *Commission v Council*, EU:C:2013:675, para 57; ECJ, Opinion 3/15, above note 94, para 61.
115 Opinion 2/15, above note 1, para 87.
116 Ibid, paras 88–93.
117 Before the CJEU gave Opinion 2/15, arguments were made that any clause on expropriation could not fall under EU competence by making reference to Article 345 TFEU. See Ceyssens, above note 15, 279–280; Dimopoulos, above note 9, 108 et seq; Bischoff JA, 'Just a Little Bit of "Mixity"? The EU's Role in the Field of International Investment Protection Law' (2011) Common Market Law Review 1527, 1543 et seq.
118 Opinion 2/15, above note 1, para 107. See also ECJ, Joined Cases C-105/12 to C-107/12 *Nederlanden v Essent NV and Others*, EU:C:2013:677, paras 29 and 36.

nonetheless not absolved from compliance with those principles and fundamental rights".[119]

Lastly, while the EU has external competence relating to all investment protection measures, a distinction must be made depending on whether the measure applies to FDI or non-direct investment. First, for FDI, the Court accepted the link between the investment protection measures and trade. It stated that "[t]he establishment of such a legal framework is intended to promote, facilitate and govern trade between the [EU] and the Republic of Singapore, within the meaning of [the Court's] case-law."[120] Thus, only those measures that relate to FDI are part of the CCP as it is only them that have direct and immediate effects on trade.[121] Second, for the investment protection standards applying to non-direct investments, this logically meant that they fall outside the CCP and are of shared competence between the EU and its Member States.[122]

4.2.4 *Investor-State Dispute Settlement*

The initial FTA with Singapore contained a traditional investor-State dispute settlement through arbitration.[123] Hence, the Court also needed to decide whether the EU has external competence in this respect. In its previous case law, the Court recognised that institutional and dispute settlement provisions designed for the effective implementation of an international agreement will be regarded ancillary to the substantive obligations and will therefore "follow" the competence attributed to those substantive provisions and share their legal bases.[124] In Opinion 2/15, the Court adopted a different reasoning. It found that investor-State dispute settlement through arbitration falls not within the exclusive competence of the EU, but within the shared competence of the EU and its Member States. The Court drew this conclusion irrespective of whether the dispute concerns a direct investment or an indirect investment. The Court's

---

119 Opinion 2/15, above note 1, para 107.
120 Ibid, para 94.
121 Ibid, para 95. See also ECJ, Case C-414/11 *Daiichi Sankyo and Sanofi-Aventis*, above note 82, para 51–53; ECJ, Case C-281/01 *Commission v Council* (Energy Star), EU:C:2002:761, paras 40–41; ECJ, Opinion 2/00, EU:C:2001:664, para 37; ECJ, Case C 94/03 *Commission v Council* (Rotterdam Convention), EU:C:2006:2, para 46.
122 Opinion 2/15, above note 1, para 109.
123 The investor-State dispute settlement through arbitration has after Opinion 2/15 been replaced by an Investment Court System (ICS) under the EUSIPA, below note 141, see Art 3.9 et seq.
124 ECJ, Opinion 1/91 *EEA Agreement*, EU:C:1991:490, paras 40 and 70; Opinion 1/09 *Patents Court*, EU:C:2011:123, para 74; ECJ, Opinion 2/13, above note 77, para 182. See also Cremona, above note 112, 255.

reasoning was mainly concerned with the issue of whether, under the terms of the FTA with Singapore, the Member States and the EU are deemed to consent to the investor-State dispute settlement. The Court found that Member States were unable to oppose a foreign investor's decision to submit a claim under the dispute settlement foreseen in the agreement.[125] In other words, the consent of the Member States does not exclude the possibility for an investor to seek judicial relief within the jurisdiction of the Member State concerned. This decision, however, solely depends on the discretion of the claimant investor. If the investor chooses investment arbitration, a Member State has no possibility to oppose as its consent was given forehead.[126] In the eye of the Court, such a regime cannot be of "purely ancillary nature" in the sense of the previous CJEU case law.[127]

In contrast hereto was the reasoning of Advocate General Sharpston. She applied previous CJEU case law and concluded that the EU's competence is shared with the Member States as regards the investor-State dispute settlement provisions, in so as far as non-direct investment is at stake, and that the EU's competence is exclusive competence as regards the investor-State dispute settlement provisions, in so far as an FDI is at stake.[128] The reasoning of the Advocate General seems indeed to be more logical. At the same time, it seems that, for the Court, the specificities of investor-State dispute settlement, namely the unconditional offer to investors for direct enforcement of their rights against EU Member States, was a key element in not following its previous case law.[129] For these reasons, the Court concluded that the EU's external competences are shared. The Court's reasoning must still be criticised because it remained silent on the legal basis that provides the grounds for the EU's shared competence. Given that the Court refused that the procedural provisions follow the competences on the substantive provisions of the FTA, the EU would need another legal basis for the provisions on investor-State dispute settlement.[130] On this point indeed, the Court is not clear.

---

125 See also Regulation No 912/2014, above note 48.
126 Opinion 2/15, above note 1, paras 292–293.
127 Ibid, para 292.
128 Opinion of AG Sharpston, above note 107, paras 523–544.
129 It should be noted that in Opinion 1/09, above note 124, and Opinion 2/13, above note 77, the issue was about judicial procedures; here the question relates to an arbitral procedure. This might have also been a reason why, for the Court, the transposition of its previous case law was inappropriate in Opinion 2/15.
130 Cremona, above note 112, 256.

4.2.5 SD—*Stretching the Scope of the CCP*

In Opinion 2/13, the Court had to examine whether Chapter 13 of the FTA with Singapore, entitled "Sustainable Development"[131] fell under the exclusive competence governing the CCP or rather within the shared competence of environmental and social policy and thus fell outside the CCP.[132] The Court responded in the affirmative, albeit the fact that some of the elements contained therein are not trade instruments in the traditional sense.

In order to decide whether a trade agreement solely or only partially falls under the exclusive competence of the CCP, the Court applies its well-established test of "specific link" and "direct and immediate effects" on trade.[133] As discussed in the previous chapter, the question on competences can hardly be separated from the question over the appropriate choice of legal basis.[134] Hence, even though the Commission did not pose the question over the correct legal basis in Opinion 2/15, the Court still had to address the issue as a matter of practical necessity since it had to determine whether Article 207(1) TFEU alone was the appropriate legal basis for Chapter 13 of the FTA.[135] In the words of the Court:

> "It is settled case-law that the mere fact that an EU act, such as an agreement concluded by it, is liable to have implications for trade with one or more third States is not enough for it to be concluded that the act must be classified as falling within the common commercial policy. On the other hand, an EU act falls within that policy if it relates specifically to such trade in that it is essentially intended to promote, facilitate or govern such trade and has direct and immediate effects on it [...]".[136]

---

131   Chapter 13 of the said FTA is a typical chapter on SD matters that the EU regularly includes in its trade and investment agreements with third countries. It seeks to ensure that contracting partners follow international requirements in the three pillars that comprise SD: economic, environmental and social. The content of TSD chapters is discussed in Chapter 5.
132   Environmental policy: TFEU, Arts 191–192 and 4(1)(e); Social policy: TFEU, Arts 153 and 4(1)(b).
133   Koutrakos, above note 73, 53 et seq.
134   On general objectives and the choice of legal basis, see Section 3.2.2.2.
135   See on this point, Kleimann D, 'Reading Opinion 2/15: Standards of Analysis, the Court's Discretion, and the Legal View of the Advocate General', EUI RSCAS 2017/23, 4–5. David Kleimann points out that it is not readily apparent "[w]hether the Court, for the purpose of its competence analysis, applies the same analytical standards it employs for pure legal basis case [...]".
136   Opinion 2/15, above note 1, para 36. See also *Daiichi Sankyo and Sanofi-Aventis Deutschland*, above note 82, para 51. See also Opinion 3/15, above note 82, 61.

For the Court, Chapter 13 of the FTA with Singapore meets the conditions of having a specific link to international trade as well as direct and immediate effects on it. With respect to the specific link, the Court refers to three reasons. First, the preamble of the FTA, in combination with the definition of SD within Chapter 13, establishes a link between trade and these SD components through the legal context of the agreement.[137] Second, a specific link also derives from the "reciprocal commitment of the Parties that they will not take advantage of their international social and environmental obligations to introduce arbitrary discriminations or disguised restrictions into their trade relations". Third, the Court additionally saw a specific link between trade and Chapter 13 in the fact that a "breach of the provisions concerning social protection of workers and environmental protection" would allow one of the Parties to suspend the execution of other provisions of the FTA with Singapore. The Court found that "[the SD] Chapter plays an essential role in the envisaged agreement".[138] Concerning the effects that Chapter 13 may have on the trade relationship between Singapore and the EU, the Court again advanced three aspects. First, the provisions of Chapter 13 "condition trade insofar as the Parties agree not to encourage trade through the diminution of social and environmental protection under an internationally agreed threshold, and not to use the latter for protectionist purposes".[139] Second, they would reduce the risk of major disparities between the costs of producing goods and supplying services and thus favour trade. Third, the Court found that the Parties' commitment to introducing documentation, verification and certification systems to fight against the illicit trade of timber and to combat illegal unreported and unregulated fishing will affect the trade in these products.[140]

While some arguments of the reasoning are little troublesome, two reasons on which the Court established a specific link with trade require further consideration.[141] A first critical point concerns the question of whether all

---

137 Kleimann, above note 135, 12.
138 Opinion 2/15, above note 1, paras 162.
139 Opinion 2/15, above note 1, para 158: "Such effects result, first, from the commitment of the Parties, stemming from Article 13.1.3 of the envisaged agreement, on the one hand, not to encourage trade by reducing the levels of social and environmental protection in their respective territories below the standards laid down by international commitments and, on the other, not to apply those standards in a protectionist manner."
140 Opinion 2/15, above note 1, para 160.
141 Eg, Ankersmit L, 'Opinion 2/15: Adding Come Spice to the Trade & Environment Debate' (European Law Blog 2017); Beaucillon C, 'Opinion 2/15: Sustainable Is the New Trade. Rethinking Coherence for the New Common Commercial Policy' (European Papers 2017); Marín Durán G, 'Sustainable Development Chapters in EU Free Trade

the substantive provisions of the TSD chapter have a specific link with trade in that they have direct and immediate effects on it.[142] As highlighted by the Advocate General, some provisions in the TSD chapter had a specific link and direct effects on international trade, such was namely the case for the promotion of climate-friendly goods and services, as well as those provisions that set out non-lowering of standards clauses as those provisions seek to establish a level-playing field. The latter type of provisions only apply in the context of trade and investment as the Parties are required not to lower their standards in order to attract trade and investment.[143] Other provisions were, according to the Advocate General, standard-setting and therefore required separate legal bases next to Article 207 TFEU. Such was the case for the provisions that refer to the Conventions of the International Labour Organization (ILO) and multilateral environmental agreements, which both the EU and Singapore have ratified: these commitments "essentially seek to achieve in the [EU] and Singapore minimum standards of (respectively) labour protection and environmental protection, *in isolation* from their possible effects on trade. Those provisions therefore clearly fall outside the [CCP]".[144] Indeed, for these provisions the link with trade is more difficult to establish as these standards regulate environmental and social protection independently from bilateral trade or investment between the contracting parties. In other words, they apply even where no trade or investment activities exists between the countries.[145] However, in the eyes of the Court, there is a specific link between trade and those more generally applicable standards, given that:

> "[b]y the above provisions of Chapter 13 of the envisaged agreement, the European Union and the Republic of Singapore undertake, *essentially*, to ensure that trade between them takes place *in compliance* with the obligations that stem from the international agreements concerning social protection of workers and environmental protection to which they are party.[146] The Court added that [h]aving regard to the difficulty in distinguishing, for *the purpose of compliance with those commitments*, between products and services which are traded between the European

---

Agreements: Emerging Compliance Issues' [2020] Common Market Law Review 1031, 1044–1045.
142 Highlighted by Gracia Marín Durán, above note 141, 1044.
143 See Section 5.1.1.
144 See Opinion of AG Sharpston, above note 107, para 491. Emphasis in original.
145 Marín Durán, above note 141, 1045.
146 Opinion 2/15, above note 1, para 152. Emphasis added.

Union and that third State and those that are not, the need to ensure in an effective manner that those commitments are complied with in the course of such trade justifies them covering all the activities in the sectors concerned.[147]"

The Court's reasoning is noteworthy and has significant constitutional implications. By accepting that provisions setting out (trade independent) minimum standards for social and environmental standards do have a specific link with trade as they have direct and immediate effects on it, the test on the scope of the CCP has been applied in a highly flexible manner.[148] A link is assumed even if, in some cases, the compliance with these standards is not taking place in the context of trade and investment activities between the two parties. Gracia Marín Durán has criticised the Court in this respect for not distinguishing between "direct and immediate effects" and "mere implications for trade".[149] Minimum-level clauses, according to her, fall short of these direct and immediate effects lacking discernible effects on bilateral trade, rather they might have some implied, indirect effects that would better qualify as implications for trade and thereby fall outside the scope of the CCP. Therefore, the Court's approach can be criticised for misunderstanding the legal effects of the said environmental and social minimum standards for trade and investment. However, one should also state that these provisions do not create new labour and environmental standards beyond those that have already been agreed at the international level. Moreover, in several past cases on the delimitation of the CCP, the Court decided to make full use of its discretion to modify and to adapt the parameters under which it considers the outer limits of the CCP.[150] It seems that the Court was aware of its extensive interpretation, as it justified its approach of stretching the scope of the CCP by making reference to SD. In the name of coherence and integration the Court found it to be logical that SD-related commitments fully fall under the CCP. In the words of the Court:

"It would, moreover, not be *coherent* to hold that the provisions liberalising trade between the European Union and a third State fall within

---

147   Ibid, para 153. Emphasis added.
148   Kleimann, above note 135, 12.
149   Marín Durán, above note 141, 1046.
150   Ibid. "The parameters the Court has considered or emphasized in its past reviews cannot be said to have advanced significant clarity or predictability of their appropriate application on a case-by-case basis."

the common commercial policy and that those which are designed to ensure that the requirements of sustainable development are met when that liberalisation of trade takes place fall outside it. The *conduct of trade in accordance with the objective of sustainable development*—as has been stated in paragraph 147 of this opinion—forms an *integral* part of that policy."[151]

The Court, here, operationalises SD within international trade and sees no other logical way of doing so than to make SD an integral part of the competence itself.[152] It endorses an understanding that trade does not operate in a legal vacuum but has to be in compliance with other—non-economic—standards and moreover, that FTAS can be a tool to harness SD spill-overs in third countries. From a constitutional law perspective, the Court accorded considerable normative effects to general objectives and namely the SD objective. The Court even accepts that objectives impact on competences. This again stands in clear contrast to the reasoning of the Advocate General. For the latter, general objectives are not relevant for the determination of the scope of the CCP but rather "[t]he purpose of those provisions is to require the [EU] to contribute to certain objectives in its policies and activities".[153] For the Court, it seems that contributing to such objectives, or at least to contribute to SD, requires to integrate the objective into the scope of the policy's competence. The potential impacts for determining the scope of the CCP are potentially significant because the Court opened the door for arguments that other non-economic standards that establish certain minimum levels fall under the CCP. At the same time, Opinion 2/15 does not bind the EU for the appreciation of future trade agreements. Potentially, future TSD chapters of EU FTAS might be more substantial on the Parties' commitments, and thus the Court might need to enter into a discussion of potential further legal bases next to Article 207 TFEU.[154] As mentioned before, making SD part of the scope of the CCP,

---

151 Opinion 2/15, above note 1, paras 163. Emphasis added.
152 At the same time, the Court mentioned this limitation by saying that the CCP competence cannot be exercised in order to regulate the levels of social and environmental protection in the Parties' respective territory, see Opinion 2/15, above note 1, paras 164–166. TFEU, Art 207(6): "The exercise of the competences conferred by this Article in the field of the common commercial policy shall not affect the delimitation of competences between the Union and the Member States, and shall not lead to harmonisation of legislative or regulatory provisions of the Member States in so far as the Treaties exclude such harmonisation." Consider also, TFEU, Arts 3(1)(d) and (2) and 4(2)(b) and (e).
153 AG Sharpston, above note 107, para 495.
154 On this point also, Beaucillon, above note 141, 827.

allowed the Court to avoid to engage into a categorisation of the provisions in the TSD Chapter as being ancillary or incidental to the predominant trade and investment aims of the FTA.[155]

Finally, a second argument made by the Court also requires some reflexion. The Court made a curious statement in order to show another specific link with trade as it stated that the agreement could be suspended for breach of one of the provisions contained in the TSD Chapter.[156] In other words, the Court suggests that a material breach of the SD commitments could lead to a suspension of the provisions regulating trade and investment based on Article 60(1) of the Vienna Convention on the Law of Treaties since "[the TSD] Chapter plays an essential role in the envisaged agreement".[157] Moreover, the parties agreed to make the liberalisation of trade subject to the condition of compliance with their international obligations concerning social protection of workers and environmental protection.[158] The Court introduced a conditionality approach even though the agreement does not contain a specific suspension clause.[159] Therefore, the Court's reasoning is surprising, as the consequences of such conditionality are not clear. Clearly, the Court made an excessive interpretation of the customary law rule of *exceptio non adimpleti contractus*. From an SD perspective, one can note that the Court seeks to create an incentive for compliance with international social and environmental standards, especially because Chapter 13 on SD only is subject to a soft enforcement mechanism. At the same time, in practice the Court's finding will not bring about such a conditionality scenario since the TSD chapter of the FTA provides that any breach

---

155 The classical approach of the Court in order to determine whether non-economic objectives can fall under the CCP consists of asking whether such provisions are simply ancillary or incidental to the predominant trade objectives or whether they impose independent obligations to constitute a distinct objective requiring a separate legal basis. The Court applied to Chapter 13 the test of "specific link" and "direct and immediate effects" in order to determine whether the chapter falls under the CCP.

156 Opinion 2/15, above note 1, paras 161: "Finally, the link which the provisions of Chapter 13 of the envisaged agreement display with trade between the European Union and the Republic of Singapore is also specific in nature because a breach of the provisions concerning social protection of workers and environmental protection, set out in that chapter, authorises the other Party—in accordance with the rule of customary international law codified in Article 60(1) of the Convention on the law of treaties [...]—to terminate or suspend the liberalisation, provided for in the other provisions of the envisaged agreement, of that trade."

157 Ibid, paras 162.

158 Ibid, paras 166.

159 Traditionally, the EU uses conditionality clauses in combination with suspension clauses in order to establish compliance with human rights standards, see Section 5.3.2.

of its provisions can only be resolved through the chapter's specific dispute settlement mechanism.[160]

4.3 SD and the Re-Orientation of the Common Commercial Policy

The CCP proved to be suitable for integrating various policy objectives. It served as a vehicle to advance non-economic interest in trade relations with third countries.[161] Since the Lisbon reform, a new impetus has been given to the CCP allowing it to operate in a more "value-driven framework".[162] Article 207(1) TFEU states the CCP "shall be conducted in the context of the principles and objectives of the Union's external action".[163] The post-Lisbon CCP is subject to its specific objectives, such as trade liberalisation, and a set of multiple principles and objectives applicable to all EU external action.[164] The European Commission seeks to build on a value-based and "responsible" trade and investment policy based on the non-economic objectives contained in the Lisbon Treaty.[165]

Opinion 2/15 was a decisive decision for spelling out the significance of SD within the CCP. The Court referred to Article 207(1) TFEU on the CCP, which makes, in its second sentence, a direct link between the external objective of SD and the CCP providing that the CCP "shall be conducted in the context of the principles and objectives of the Union's external action."[166] Article 205 TFEU includes the same obligation, stating that "the Union's action on the international scene, pursuant to [Part Five of the TFEU], shall be guided by the principles, pursue the objectives and be conducted in accordance with the

---

160 On the dispute settlement mechanism of TSD chapters, see Section 5.2.2.
161 Dimopoulos A, 'The Effects of the Lisbon Treaty on the Principles and Objectives of the Common Commercial Policy' (2010) 15 European Foreign Affairs Review 153, 153; Kaddous, above note 65, 336; see also, Larik J, 'Much More Than Trade: The Common Commercial Policy in a Global Context', in: Evans MD and Koutrakos P (eds), *Beyond the Established Legal Orders: Policy Interconnections between the EU and the Rest of the World* (Hart 2011) 14–46; Wouters J et al (eds), *Global Governance through Trade: EU Policies and Approaches* (Edward Elgar Publishing 2015).
162 Krajewski, above note 77, 292. See also Kaddous, above note 76, 347–349.
163 TFEU, Art 207(1), second sentence.
164 Article 206 TFEU contains the specific trade policy objectives, whereas the general objectives of EU's external action are enshrined in Articles 3(5) and 21(1–2) TEU, and apply to the CCP by reference to Articles 205 and 207 TFEU.
165 Term used by the European Commission. See, European Commission, 'Trade for All' above note 2.
166 TFEU, Art 207(1) last sentence.

general provisions laid down in Chapter 1 of Title V of the [TEU]". As the Court points out, Chapter 1 of Title V of the TEU enshrines Article 21 TEU.[167] Finally, in Article 21(3) TEU, the first sentence provides that the EU is to "pursue the objectives set out in [Article 21(1) and (2) TEU] in the development and implementation of the different areas of the Union's external action [...]" and such external action makes reference to the CCP and again connects these provisions.[168] Given all these elements, the Court stated that: "the objective of [SD] henceforth *forms an integral part of the common commercial policy*."[169] This is a significant and far-reaching statement. On the one hand, the conclusion impacts the general orientation of the CCP, namely by influencing the trade liberalisation agenda of the EU. On the other hand, it highlights the normative impacts of objectives contained in Article 21 TEU.

4.3.1 *Managing the Interplay of Multiple Objectives within the CCP*

Having SD among the general objectives of EU external action and the specific objectives governing the CCP brings about the need to address the interactions between the various objectives. Multiple objectives might lead to tensions in the pursuit of them. What is the position of SD among the general objectives? Moreover, how does it impact on the specific CCP objectives? Should the critical objective of the CCP, which is to pursue trade and investment liberalisation, be of greater importance than the more abstract general objectives?

4.3.1.1 SD among Other General Objectives

Article 3(5) TEU generally states that "[i]n its relation with the wider world, the Union [...] shall contribute to the [SD] of the Earth". Article 21(2) TEU includes two aspects of SD. First, the EU shall aim to "foster the sustainable economic, social and environmental development of developing countries, with the primary aim of eradicating poverty".[170] Second, the EU shall aim to "help develop international measures to preserve and improve the quality of the environment and the sustainable management of global natural resources, in order to ensure [SD]".[171] The first aspect of SD is thus in cooperation with developing countries and the second aspect is linked to the protection of the environment. In a number of its trade and investment agreements, the EU describes SD as encompassing "economic development, social development

---

167 Opinion 2/15, above note 1, para 145.
168 Ibid, para 144.
169 Ibid, para 147. Emphasis added.
170 TEU, Art 21(2)(d).
171 TEU, Art 21(2)(f).

and environmental protection, all three being interdependent and mutually reinforcing".[172]

As discussed in the previous chapters, SD is under EU law as well as under international law a three-dimensional concept consisting of social, economic and environmental dimensions and thus it refers to a number of aspects and areas. At the international level, the range of areas relevant for SD became, in particular, apparent through the Agenda 2030's 17 SDGs.[173] Therefore, whilst SD is explicitly mentioned twice in Article 21 TEU, several of the other general objectives and goals overlap with the content of the SD and the SDGs. Consequently, the objective of SD absorbs some of the sub-categories of the EU's general objectives because they can be considered to form part of the SD agenda. The general objectives of Articles 3(5) and 21 TEU include the following objectives, explicitly next to SD: democracy, the rule of law, human rights and fundamental freedoms, human dignity, the principles of equality and solidarity, the principles of the United Nations Charter and international law, the EU's values and interests, its security and integrity, peace and conflict prevention, poverty eradication, the integration of all countries into the world economy, environmental protection and preservation of natural resources, natural disaster prevention, and lastly enhanced international cooperation and good governance.[174]

First, the social pillar of SD is within the EU's general objectives expressed through the principles of "equality and solidarity", "human rights" and "human dignity". They point to the central SD endeavour of social protection and decent work.[175] Also under the social pillar of SD, one can also find the rule of law amongst the EU's general objectives. The latter is another key component of the SD agenda.[176] Second, the environmental pillar of SD finds expression in the general objectives of preserving and improving the quality of the environment, as well as the sustainable management of natural resources. One

---

172 CETA, Art 22.1; EUJFTA, Art 16.1; EUMFTA, TSD chapter, Art 1(3)(a); EUSFTA, Art 12.1; EUVFTA, Art 13.1.
173 UN General Assembly, 'Transforming our world: the 2030 Agenda for Sustainable Development', [2015] A/RES/70/1 (hereafter Agenda 2030), pt 71: "We reiterate that this Agenda and the Sustainable Development Goals and targets, including the means of implementation, are universal, indivisible and interlinked".
174 TEU, Art 21(1–2).
175 Ibid, SDG 8: "Promote sustained, inclusive and sustainable economic growth, full and productive employment and decent work for all".
176 Ibid, SDG 16: "Promote peaceful and inclusive societies for sustainable development, provide access to justice for all and build effective, accountable and inclusive institutions at all levels".

can also add the assistance of "populations, countries and regions confronting natural and man-made disasters".[177] Third, the economic pillar of SD is clearly reflected in the EU's objective by encouraging "the integration of all countries into the world economy, including through the progressive abolition of restrictions on international trade" and the objective of "fair and free trade".[178] Lastly, the EU's objective for the promotion of "an international system based on stronger multilateral cooperation" also falls under the SD agenda and is, in particular, part of the global partnership for SD.[179]

It becomes apparent that SD absorbs a number of the general objectives of the EU's external action. One can even say that SD is the ultimate objective and thus, the meta-goal of the other more specific goals. For instance, the eradication of poverty ultimately seeks to establish SD. Likewise, the conservation of natural resources, in the end, pursues SD. This finding is critical for the CCP. As will be argued in the next section, the objective of trade and investment liberalisation should ultimately be for the benefit of SD. In other words, they are a sub-guiding objective for the CCP with the overarching goal of SD.

4.3.1.2 SD and the Specific CCP Objectives

The specific objectives of the CCP are set out in Article 206 TFEU:

> "By establishing a customs union in accordance with Articles 28 to 32, the [EU] shall contribute, in the common interest, to the *harmonious development of world trade*, the *progressive abolition of restrictions* on international trade and on foreign direct investment, and the *lowering of customs and other barriers*."[180]

The three aspects of the harmonious development of world trade, the abolition of restrictions as well as the lowering of customs and other barriers essentially constitute the objective of trade liberalisation.[181] Trade liberalisation has been

---

177 Ibid, SDG 15: "Protect, restore and promote sustainable use of terrestrial ecosystems, sustainably manage forests, combat desertification, and halt and reverse land degradation and halt biodiversity loss"; and SDG 13: "Take urgent action to combat climate change and its impacts".
178 With respect to "fair and free trade", the Court confirmed in Opinion 2/15 that SD absorbs this objective. See, Opinion 2/15, above note 1, para 146.
179 SDG 17: "Strengthen the means of implementation and revitalize the global partnership for sustainable development".
180 Emphasis added.
181 Krajewski M, 'Normative Grundlagen der EU-Außenwirtschaftsbeziehungen: Verbindlich, umsetzbar und angewandt?' (2016) EuR Heft 3, 241.

the key objective of the CCP since 1958.[182] With the Lisbon Treaty, the objective was even reinforced because the wording of the provision shifted from its original formulation of "aims to contribute" to "shall contribute".[183]

The liberalisation objective is not to achieve a complete liberalisation of trade and FDI conditions globally, which would be similar to the conditions in the EU internal market, nor does it oblige the EU to proceed with a unilateral liberalisation of trade and FDI conditions.[184] The references to "lowering" and "progressive abolition" indicate that the EU pursues, through its CCP, gradual trade and investment liberalisation.[185] In this sense, gradual and continuous development towards more liberalisation is the objective, suggesting that the level of liberalisation should at least be maintained and should not be restricted.[186] Moreover, the reference to the "harmonious development of world trade" as being part of the trade liberalisation objective is a central element for the CJEU to be taken into account. In 1987, the Court held that this objective presupposes that "commercial policy will be adjusted in order to take account of changes of outlook in international trade".[187]

Under the Lisbon Treaty, Article 205 TFEU subjects the CCP to the general objectives of EU external action. This means that the specific objective of the CCP, namely trade and investment liberalisation, has to coexist next to the general objectives.[188] Subjecting the CCP to other non-purely economic objectives may lead to tensions because market and growth increasing objectives can run counter social and environmental objectives. The reason is that such objectives suggest a restriction for trade and investment liberalisation than the promotion thereof. In principle, however, tensions cannot be solved through a sort of hierarchy as there is no hierarchy between objectives and nothing in the treaties indicates any prioritisation of one objective over another.[189] In practical terms, one can argue that the steering effects (*Steuerungswirkung*)

---

182 Vedder C, 'Linkage of the Common Commercial Policy to the General Objectives for the Union's External Action', in: Bungenberg M and Herrmann C (eds), *Common Commercial Policy after Lisbon* (Springer 2013) 117–118.
183 See also on this point, Dimopoulos, above note 161, 160.
184 This has been underlined by the Court from early on. See eg ECJ, Case 51/75 *EMI Records Limited v CBS United Kingdom Limited*, EU:C:1976:85, para 17.
185 Understood in this way, the objectives resemble those of the WTO. See preambles of the Marrakesh Agreement establishing the WTO and of the GATT (1947): "Substantial reduction of tariffs and other barriers to trade and to the elimination of discriminatory treatment in international commerce."
186 Dimopoulos, above note 161, 160–161; see also, Krajewski, above note 77, 295.
187 ECJ, Case 45/86 *Commission v Council*, EU:C:1987:163, para 19.
188 Krajewski, above note 181, 241.
189 See also Section 3.2.2.1.

of the specific objectives of the CCP might be more relevant than the general objectives because they are specifically concerned with trade and investment regulation.[190] At the same time, certain of the general objectives, such as the eradication of poverty, are also directly linked to trade and economic policies and can therefore guide decision-making.[191] The balancing or prioritising of the objectives is a matter of the discretion enjoyed by the EU institutions. However, which objective should be prioritised over another can and should not be determined in the abstract. It depends on a case-by-case proportionality assessment of context and circumstances of a trade and investment measures, and the partner country in question.

To what extent do these general objectives modify the very understanding of trade and investment liberalisation? The interaction of the specific and the general SD objective of the CCP seeks to achieve a more comprehensive trade policy. Therefore, trade and investment liberalisation should not be understood as an ultimate objective but as one sub-goal to achieve SD and even more broadly a state of welfare in the EU and in third countries. In fact, economic liberalisation has never been an end in itself, neither for EU commercial policy nor for the international trading system.[192] For instance, the General Agreement on Tariffs and Trade (GATT) of 1947 already indicated that trade liberalisation should contribute to such goals as the raising of the living standards and full employment.[193] Understood in this way, Articles 3(5) and 21 TEU add to the liberalisation objective a dimension linked to general public welfare.

Article 21(2) TEU contains one limb that has the potential to modify the specific commercial objective of liberalisation as it requires "the integration of all countries into the world economy, including through the progressive abolition of restrictions on international trade" to be taken into account.[194] Even more so, Article 3(5) TEU adds to the objective of *free* trade the commitment to

---

190 Krajewski, above note 181, 241.
191 Cremona M, 'Distinguished Essay: A Quiet Revolution—The Changing Nature of the EU's Common Commercial Policy' in: Bungenberg M et al (eds), *European Yearbook of International Economic Law 2017*, vol 8 (Springer International Publishing 2017) 10.
192 Krajewski, above note 77, 297.
193 GATT [1947], Preamble, recital 1. Today, the WTO Agreement contains SD as an objective in its own right. See also Quirico O, 'The Environmental Sustainability of the EU Investment Policy after Lisbon: Progressive International Developments', in: Levashova Y, Lambooy TE and Dekker IF (eds), *Bridging the Gap between International Investment Law and the Environment* (Eleven International Publishing 2016) 273.
194 See TEU, Art 21(2)(e).

fair trade.[195] In this particular respect, the general objectives are clearly targeting the very understanding of trade. It provides indications that international trade is not merely fair as long as it is in compliance with WTO law (*i.e.* not dumping or illegally subsidised for instance)[196] but rather that fair trade relates to regulating trade and investment in such a manner as to lead to an equitable allocation of economic advantages among the countries, and not least to take social and environmental concerns into account based on the framework of the general objectives. This means the CCP measures are to ensure trade and investment liberalisation in compliance with SD and requires it to be directed towards SD.[197] Under the reoriented CCP framework, it is not sufficient to pursue economic growth for its own sake.

4.3.2 Horizontal Coherence: The CCP and Other EU Policies

The multiple objectives applicable to the CCP can and should lead to more coherent approaches between the CCP and the other EU policies. The role of SD is interesting as the concept itself is beneficial to achieve policy coherence.[198] In the previous chapter, the argument has been made that the requirement for policy coherence under EU law is beneficial for SD. This section flips the argument and argues that SD is beneficial for coherence, especially horizontal coherence between the EU's key external policies.

Article 21(3) TEU adds to the general objectives, the requirement of coherence/consistency[199] across all EU external policies and between external and

---

195 TEU, Art 3(5): "[...] It shall contribute to peace, security, the sustainable development of the Earth, solidarity and mutual respect among peoples, *free and fair trade*, [...]". Emphasis added.

196 Cremona M, 'AXE 1: Les relations économiques extérieures de l'Union européenne au service du développement équitable et durable?' Table ronde présidé par Marise Cremona, in: Lamblin-Gourdin AS and Mondielli E (dir), *Le droit des relations extérieures de l'Union européenne après le Traité de Lisbonne* (Bruylant 2013) 186.

197 Ibid. See also, Vedder, above note 188, 182; and Opinion 2/15, above note 1, para 146; where the Court uses "free and fair trade" in the context of its SD reasoning.

198 SD itself is often considered to be beneficial in order to achieve policy coherence. See Gehne K, *Nachhaltige Entwicklung als Rechtsprinzip: Normativer Aussagegehalt, rechtstheoretische Einordnung, Funktionen im Recht* (Mohr Siebeck 2011), 261; Grosse Ruse-Khan H, 'A Real Partnership for Development? Sustainable Development as Treaty Objective in European Economic Partnership Agreements and Beyond' (2010) 13 Journal of International Economic Law 139. See also Section 7.2.1.

199 The terms are used interchangeably. For a discussion on the distinction, see Hillion C, 'Tous pour un, un pour tous! Coherence in the External Relations of the European Union', in: Cremona M (ed), *Developments in EU External Relations Law* (Oxford University Press 2009) 12–16.

internal policies (*i.e.* horizontal coherence).[200] The EU treaties entrust responsibility for ensuring coherence to the Council and the European Commission, assisted by the High Representative for Foreign Affairs and Security Policy.[201] The European Council, in addition, has the general mandate to "identify the strategic interests and objectives" of the EU including matters of the CCP.[202] Horizontal coherence, in essence, seeks to promote complementarity between norms and instruments.[203] Namely, the general objectives of EU external action affect all external policies according to the same set of objectives and thus have a structuring effect beneficial for coherence. Since they do not operate such structuring through a hierarchy, the preferred approach for EU institutions is to create synergies and complementarity between the different policies when exercising their competences.[204]

In general terms, the CCP, through the overall set of objectives should establish coherence with other key external policies of the EU, such as development cooperation, external environmental policy and the Common Foreign and Security Policy. In respect of policy coherence, the objective of SD is a supportive concept. Based on the objective of SD, the EU can adopt measures that are adopted in the framework of different external policies, but which all seek to achieve SD. For example, an international agreement on the preservation of natural resources as part of the EU's external environmental policy has the objective of SD.[205] The trade and investment agreements concluded under the CCP also have the objective of SD. In other words, different polices can be aligned through the presence of the same directing concept, which is SD. The more precise orientation of the CCP since the Lisbon Treaty towards a number of non-economic objectives related to SD requires that the EU promotes the development of poorer countries, high social and environmental standards and the respect for human rights. Therefore, coherence with the external

---

200   The focus here will be on horizontal coherence between the EU policies, not the vertical coherence, which describes the coherence between EU action and Member States' action.
201   TEU, Art 21(3).
202   TEU, Art 22.
203   Cremona M, 'Coherence and EU External Environmental Policy', in: Morgera E (ed), *The External Environmental Policy of the European Union: EU and International Law Perspectives* (Cambridge University Press 2012) 35.
204   Ibid, 38.
205   A number of MEAs concluded by the EU. Eg Convention on Biodiversity (CBD), Cartagena Biosafety Protocol, UNFCC Framework Convention on Climate Change, Paris Agreement on Climate Change, Aarhus Convention, Espoo Convention, UNCCD Convention to Combat Desertification in Africa.

actions of the CCP and development cooperation and environmental policy is key and measures taken by the EU must be consistent with other instruments of EU external action. This being so, the aim of policy coherence comes with specific substantive benchmarks for trade and investment agreements.

SD operating as an overarching objective is thus likely to enhance further the aim of horizontal policy coherence between the different external policies of the EU. In Opinion 2/15, the Court arguable went a step further and found that it would "not be *coherent* to hold that the provisions liberalising trade between the European Union and a third State fall within the common commercial policy and that those which are designed to ensure that the requirements of sustainable development are met when that liberalisation of trade takes place fall outside it."[206] Whilst the Court did not say that future MEAs and ILO Conventions are to be concluded under the CCP, it seems to suggest that the compliance with these instruments falls under the CCP.

Lastly, coherence in EU external action depends not only on the absence of legal contradiction between the different instruments. Coherence also stems from the cooperation between the different actors involved, especially between the Member States, on the one hand, and the EU's institutions on the other; as well as cooperation between the institutions themselves.[207] This aspect is vital as trade and investment agreements still are to be concluded as mixed agreements.[208] The principle of sincere cooperation is to ensure that each actor's competence is exercised with the purpose of contributing to the EU's external objectives, including SD and thereby to assert the "identity" of the EU as a global actor.[209]

4.3.3 *Turning the SD Objective into Investment Strategies*

The effects of objectives can be measured by the extent to which decision-makers are elaborating concrete policy approaches and legal implementation. Especially, SD requires context-based implementation and concretization.[210] For the CCP this means that the EU's institutions are to turn the SD objective in to concrete strategies for trade and investment agreements. In doing so they enjoy relatively wide discretion. In Opinion 2/15, the Court was silent on how to

---

206   Opinion 2/15, above note 1, paras 163. Emphasis added.
207   TEU, Art 13(2): "Each institution shall act within the limits of the powers conferred on it in the Treaties, and in conformity with the procedures, conditions and objectives set out in them. The institutions shall practice mutual sincere cooperation."
208   Below Section 4.4.2.
209   Hillion, above note 199, 35–36.
210   Sections 2.1.

integrate SD into the concrete measures falling under the CCP.²¹¹ The bottom-line that the Court underscored is that CCP measures cannot go against SD. At the same time, the Court also found that the EU has to "to *contribute*, in its relations with the wider world, to free and fair trade"²¹² it should ultimately be understood that the EU has to adopt measures under the CCP that are in compliance with SD and are also pro-active measures to achieve SD.²¹³

Despite the discretion, the objectives as set out in the EU treaties are to be implemented. For this, EU policy strategies are highly relevant as they are an expression of how the institutions intend to use their discretion. The set of general objectives provides for an improved and more coherent framework for foreign policy in general, including the CCP and EU investment law-making. The European Commission is given a central strategic mandate to shape the CCP. Right after the entry into force of the Lisbon Treaty, the Commission focused its first strategic paper on the idea that the trade and investment policy had its main purpose in the contribution to growth, job creation and competitiveness in Europe, whereas little attention has been given to the EU's general objectives.²¹⁴ The Commission even found that the CCP "has its own distinct economic logic and contribution to make to the external action of the EU".²¹⁵

Approaches shifted with the 2015 trade and investment strategy, which better brings trade and investment policy into the framework of the EU's general external action. Namely in its Communication "Trade for all—Towards a more responsible trade and investment policy".²¹⁶ In the words of the Commission:

> "One of the aims of the EU is to ensure that economic growth goes hand in hand with social justice, respect for human rights, high labour and environmental standards, health and safety protection. This applies to external as well as internal policies, and so also includes trade and

---

211 AG Bot likewise reiterates the discretion under the CCP. See Opinion of AG Bot (procedure Opinion 1/17), EU:C:2019:72, paras 32–33. See also, Asteriti A, 'Article 21 TEU and the EU's Common Commercial Policy: A Test of Coherence' in: Bungenberg M et al (eds), *European Yearbook of International Economic Law 2017*, vol 8 (Springer International Publishing 2017) 131.
212 Ibid, para 146.
213 Consider again, TEU, Article 21(2)(f) with the formulation of "help to develop international measures" with respect to SD has to be understood as requiring the EU to take pro-active actions, *i.e.* requiring actual promotion of SD through their international measures.
214 European Commission Communication, 'Trade, Growth and World Affairs: Trade Policy as a Core Component of the EU's 2020 Strategy', COM (2010) 612 final.
215 Ibid, 15.
216 European Commission, 'Trade for all', above note 2.

investment policy. The EU has been leading in integrating sustainable development objectives into trade policy and making trade an effective tool to promote sustainable development worldwide. The importance of the potential contribution of trade policy to sustainable development has recently been reaffirmed in the 2030 Agenda for Sustainable Development, including the SDGs, which will guide global action in the next 15 years".[217]

With the "Trade for all" strategy, the Commission seeks to contribute to Agenda 2030 and the related SDGs,[218] as further elaborated in a more detailed policy instrument.[219] For the Commission promoting SD goes hand in hand with ensuring that the EU's trade and investment policy is consistent with broader European values stating that EU treaties "demand that the EU promote its values, including the development of poorer countries, high social and environmental standards, and respect for human rights, around the world".[220] At the same time, the strong stance of the Commission on SD integration into CCP measures did not change the Commission's key concern, which concerns the competitiveness of European companies as being vital for the EU economy. SD or not, trade and investment liberalisation remains a fundamental strategy in the eyes of the Commission to ensure the access of EU companies to new markets in third countries supporting their economic growth.[221] This difficult articulation between the economic growth model and the SD objectives is the most important source of policy contradiction that can be identified in the law-making of the EU in concrete trade and investment agreements as analysed in the following chapters.

This being said, the "Trade for all" strategy is one of the key instruments allowing to understand how the Commission intends to use its discretion in

---

217   Ibid, 15. Emphasis omitted.
218   Ibid. See also European Commission, 'Report on the Implementation of the Trade Policy Strategy Trade for All Delivering a Progressive Trade Policy to Harness Globalisation', COM (2017) 491 final.
219   European Commission, 'Commission Staff Working Document, Key European Action supporting the 2030 Agenda and the Sustainable Development Goals', SWD (2016) 390 final, 29: "The EU is at the forefront of using its trade and investment policy to support inclusive growth and sustainable development in developing countries." Therein, the EU is one of its main supporters and has formulated several EU initiatives related to the achievement of Agenda 2030.
220   Ibid, 15.
221   Ibid, 4: "Approximately 90% of global economic growth in the next 10 to 15 years is expected to be generated outside Europe".

integrating SD into EU IIAS. The themes of the trade agenda on SD can be divided into two key components: first, SD integration in the narrow sense, meaning the integration of social and environmental commitments and elements in the law-making of EU IIAS; second, SD-related sub-topics, namely, the role of developing countries, corporate social responsibility (CSR), human rights protection, the fight against corruption and promoting good governance. The "Trade for all" strategy is complemented by a number of other communications and non-papers of the Commission that more specifically deal with the right to regulate in the public interests.[222]

1) Social and environmental integration:
   - SD "should be a core component" of EU IIAS and should be taken into account "in all relevant areas" (such as energy and raw materials or public procurement);
   - EU IIAS "should contain far-reaching commitments" on core labour rights, such as the fundamental conventions of the ILO, as well as on ensuring compliance with the ILO Decent Work Agenda.
   - "[C]ore labour standards (abolition of child labour and forced labour, non-discrimination at the workplace, freedom of association and collective bargaining)" shall be effectively implemented through EU IIAS;
   - EU IIAS should also contain "far-reaching commitments on environmental protection in relation to multilateral environment agreements";
   - EU IIAS shall increase the "priority given to the sustainable management and conservation of natural resources (biodiversity, soil and water, forests and timber, fisheries and wildlife) and to the fight against climate change";
   - EU IIAS shall, through aid and cooperation, help contracting partners to ensure high levels of labour rights protection and environmental protection;
   - Sustainability impact assessments shall be conducted on trade and investment agreements, including "an in-depth analysis of the possible effects of new agreements on [least developed countries]";
   - EU IIAS should enhance dialogues with stakeholders and civil society.

---

222   Eg, European Commission, 'Concept Paper—Investment in TTIP and beyond—the path for reform. Enhancing the right to regulate and moving from current ad hoc arbitration towards an Investment Court', available at <https://trade.ec.europa.eu/doclib/docs/2015/may/tradoc_153408.PDF>.

2) SD-related topics:
   – EU IIAs should support inclusive growth in developing countries. Job creation is among the more concrete objectives the Commission highlights in this respect. Moreover, the EU's stated objective is to enhance certain types of investment to promote SD, particularly for its relations with developing countries. The EU has explicitly stated that the private sector's funds shall be channelled into the SD of developing countries.[223] In general, the aim is to integrate into global value chains whilst benefitting thereof.
   – EU IIAs should strengthen responsible supply chains and CSR. According to the Commission's CSR definition, the concept means "the responsibility of enterprises for their impact on society".[224] Moreover, the Commission's understanding is that CSR covers at the very least, human rights, labour and employment practices, environmental issues and combating bribery and corruption.[225] According to the Commission, CSR also "offers a set of values on which to build a more cohesive society and on which to base the transition to a sustainable economic system".[226] In sum, the Commission seems to underline that CSR seeks to establish corporate behaviour that goes beyond what national law requires.
   – EU IIAs should promote and defend human rights. The Commission targets in this respect precisely, the abolition of worst violations of basic labour rights and the improvement of both, impact

---

223 The New European Consensus on Development 'Our World, Our Dignity, Our Future', Joint Statement by the Council and the representatives of the Governments of the Member States meeting within the Council, the European Parliament and the European Commission, [2017] (New European Consensus on Development), para 53: "The private sector can contribute to the implementation of the 2030 Agenda. The EU and its Member States, in close coordination with the European Investment Bank, will promote the mobilisation of private resources for development [...]. This includes sustainable agriculture, safe and clean energy, integrated water resource management, resilient infrastructure, health, sustainable tourism, green and circular economy, telecommunications and digital technology".

224 European Commission Communication, 'Corporate Social Responsibility', COM (2011) 681 final, 6, para 3.1.

225 Ibid. The previous definition of CSR was: "CSR is a concept whereby companies integrate social and environmental concerns in their business operations and in their interaction with their stakeholders on a voluntary basis"; see, European Commission Communication, 'Implementing the Partnership for Growth and Jobs: Making Europe a Pole of Excellence on Corporate Social Responsibility', COM (2006) 136 final.

226 European Commission, above note, 3, para. 1.2.

assessments of EU IIAs in the course of negotiation and *ex post* evaluations as regards their human rights impacts analysis.
- In EU IIAs, corruption should be addressed and the implementation in practice of the core anti-corruption conventions should be ensured and "ambitious" provisions should be targeted. Trade and investment agreements should be used to monitor domestic reforms in the fight against corruption.

2) The right to regulate[227]:
- References to SD and the right to regulate to achieve legitimate policy objectives are made in the preamble of IIAs to public health, safety, environment, public morals and the promotion and protection of cultural diversity. According to the Commission, the "reference in the preamble to the right to regulate already gives a very important interpretative guidance".
- An operational provision (specific Article) refers to the right of Governments to take measures to achieve legitimate public policy objectives based on the level of protection that they deem appropriate. In the eyes of the Commission, such provision "allows setting the right context in which investment protection standards are applied".
- Clarified and improved formulations of the investment protection standards, in order to leave less room for unwarranted interpretations and to prevent abuse:
  - Fair and equitable treatment: the scope of the standard is limited to a closed list of types of behaviour consistent with consolidated judicial views in the EU (like denial of justice, arbitrary conduct and breach of due process).
  - Indirect expropriation: the concept is to be explained in an annex which clarifies that for indirect expropriation to occur there must be a substantial taking away from the investor of the attributes of property (i.e. the right to use, enjoy and dispose of the investment). The annex seeks, in particular, excluding claims against legitimate public policy measures.
- The right for EU IIAs Contracting Parties "to adopt binding interpretations in order to control the interpretation of the agreement, and correct possible errors by the tribunals".

---

227 Key points of the European Commission, 'Concept Paper', above note 222.

4.4 EU International Investment Agreements

Since the Lisbon Treaty, the EU has external competences in the field of foreign investment that encompass post-establishment treatment of investors and investor-State dispute settlement. As a result, the EU is vested with external power to conclude IIAs with third countries covering all aspects of international investment law. The following discusses the internal decision-making procedure of the EU for the adoption of IIAs, the practice of concluding EU IIAs as mixed agreements, and lastly the scope and content of EU IIAs.

4.4.1 *The Decision-Making Procedure for the Conclusion of EU IIAs*

The conclusion of EU IIAs follows the general rules, enshrined in Article 218 TFEU applicable for adopting international agreements by the EU. With the Lisbon Treaty, the CCP is no longer subject to special decision-making rules but has been integrated into the ordinary legislative procedures.[228] In terms of institutional balance, the Lisbon Treaty modified the decision-making within the Council and increased the role and powers of the European Parliament for the adoption of trade and investment agreements.[229]

The EU treaties grant the European Commission the prerogative to initiate negotiations with a third country on matters of foreign investment.[230] Based on the Commission's political choice, it subsequently makes recommendations to the Council on the opening of negotiations. The latter, in return, has to approve the opening of the negotiations through the adoption of a decision. The official decision of the Council also constitutes the negotiating mandate detailing the area in which the Commission is authorised to negotiate. To this effect, the Commission is the main actor in carrying out the negotiations of EU IIAs. The Council remains, however, indirectly involved, as the Commission has to report back to a special committee of the Council regularly on the negotiation process.[231] Moreover, the European Parliament has obtained a role at all stages of negotiation *i.e.* the Parliament has a right to be fully informed on the negotiations based on Article 218(10) TFEU, which is corroborated for the CCP by the reporting obligation for the Commission under Article 207(3) TFEU.

---

228 See TFEU, Art 207(3) cross-reference to TFEU, Art 218.
229 Cremona M, 'Distinguished Essay: A Quiet Revolution—The Changing Nature of the EU's Common Commercial Policy' in: Bungenberg M et al (eds), *European Yearbook of International Economic Law 2017*, vol 8 (Springer International Publishing 2017) 26.
230 TFEU, Art 207(3).
231 TFEU, Art 207(3), sub-para 3. The special committee is called the "Trade Policy Committee". See also Krajewski, above note 77, 308.

Once the negotiations on an EU IIA are finalised, the agreement needs to be approved. In this respect, it is the Council that plays the main role, being in charge of the signature and adoption (*i.e.* ratification) of the agreement. In this vein, the Council first takes a decision authorising the signing of the agreement expressing the intention of the EU to be bound by the agreement. At this stage, the Council can, based on Article 218(5) TFEU, also decide to apply the agreement provisionally. As far as the Council's decision-making is concerned in view of adopting such a decision, Articles 207(4) and 218(8) TFEU foresee the qualified majority voting as being the basic voting rule for the Council. This general rule is subject to exceptions set out in Article 207(4) TFEU.

For three specific measures, unanimity is required. First, the unanimity requirement exists for agreements concerning trade in services, commercial aspects of intellectual property and foreign direct investment "where such agreements include provisions for which unanimity is required for the adoption of internal rules".[232] This requirement establishes a parallelism between the internal and external decision-making procedures of the Council. These exceptions highlight that EU Member States preferred to maintain a certain degree of control over international agreements in these fields, including FDI.[233] Unanimity in the Council for the adoption of IIAs is only required if respective internal legislation also needs to be adopted by unanimity. For instance, internal EU legislation on capital movements does not require unanimity but is subject to qualified majority voting in the Council.[234] Second, a further exception to the general rule of qualified majority voting in the Council is that unanimity is required for decisions in relation to the conclusion of agreements in the field of trade in culture and audio-visual services, where they might risk prejudicing the EU's cultural and linguistic diversity.[235] Third, unanimity is also required for EU measures in the field of trade in social, education and health services, where these risk seriously disturbing the national organisation of such services.[236]

Once the Council has issued its decision approving the signature of the agreement, the European Parliament must consent to the conclusion thereof. For trade and investment agreements, the special procedure under Article

---

232 TFEU, Art 207(4), sub-para 2.
233 Krajewski, above note 77, 306.
234 TFEU, Art 64(2). However, according to TEFU, Art 64(3) an exception to this rule can namely exist for "measures which constitute a step backwards in Union law as regards the liberalisation of the movement of capital to or from third countries".
235 TFEU, Art 207(4)(a).
236 TFEU, Art 207(4)(b).

218(6) TFEU involving the Parliament's consent is applicable.[237] This is a significant innovation of the Lisbon Treaty. The requirement to have the consent of the European Parliament on EU IIAs should strengthen their democratic legitimacy. Moreover, it enhances the Parliament's influence in the negotiating process as the Commission negotiating the agreement seeks also to shape the agreement's content according to the observations of the Parliament to obtain its final consent at the stage of concluding the agreement.[238] When the consent from the Parliament is obtained, the Council can adopt a decision to ratify the agreement. Here again, the voting requirements follow the principle of qualified majority except for those fields that also require unanimous voting at the stage of authorising the signature of the agreement.[239] Through its final approval, the Council ratifies the agreement.

4.4.2 *EU IIAs as Mixed Agreements*

The adoption of mixed agreements reflects a long-established practice in EU external relations when the EU cannot conclude an agreement alone for political or legal reasons. Mixed agreements are thus agreements signed by both the EU and its Member States, and both the EU and the Member States are, as a matter of international law, parties to that agreement. To conclude an international agreement as mixed agreement or EU-only agreement is in most cases based on political choices depending on a number of factors, including the political importance of the agreement.[240] However, mixity becomes a legal requirement for the EU if parts of the international agreement fall entirely outside its competences but within the Member States' exclusive competence.[241] The legal bases on which EU external measures rest are a central element to establish the involvement of the EU Member States for the conclusion of an international agreement.

---

237 There are five categories of agreements where consent from the European Parliament must be obtained, see TFEU, Art 218(6), sub-para 2, lit a: (i) association agreements; (ii) agreements on Union accession to the European Convention for the Protection of Human Rights and Fundamental Freedoms; (iii) agreements establishing a specific institutional framework by organising cooperation procedures; (iv) agreements with important budgetary implications for the Union; (v) agreements covering fields to which either the ordinary legislative procedure applies, or the special legislative procedure where consent by the European Parliament is required.
238 See on this point also, Krajewski, above note 77, 310.
239 TFEU, Art 207(4).
240 Kaddous, above note 61, 449; Cremona, above note 112, 250.
241 ECJ, Cases C-13/07 *Commission* v *Council*, EU:C:2009:190, Opinion of AG Kokott, para 121; Opinion of AG Sharpston, above note 107, para 78.

The conclusions of post-Lisbon IIAs, such as the CETA, highlighted that EU IIAs need to be adopted as mixed agreements. The European Commission has, prior to Opinion 2/15, suggested, as a sole legal basis for both agreements, Article 207 TFEU and, as such, they could have been adopted as EU-only agreements without the need for recourse to mixity. However, it soon became apparent that differences existed between the Commission and the Council on the nature of the EU's competence to conclude these agreements. In the case of the FTA with Singapore, the differences lead to Opinion 2/15.[242] After discussing the matter informally, the Commission decided to submit the CETA as a mixed agreement.[243]

In Opinion 2/15, the Court highlighted that the conclusion of post-Lisbon EU IIAs demands the involvement of the EU Member States. The Court deduced from the shared nature of competence on non-direct foreign investment that the FTA with Singapore "cannot be approved by the [EU] alone".[244] Whilst the Court was not stating that mixity was a legal obligation, the latter being here a political question because none of the areas of the said FTA fall entirely outside the scope of competences of the EU, it shows that the Court was aware of the opposition coming from the Member States to adopt it as an EU-only agreement.[245] This means that despite the exclusive competence over FDI, the EU Member States' participation cannot be excluded. As a consequence, post-Lisbon EU IIAs are in principle concluded as mixed agreements entailing considerable implications for their negotiation and conclusion because all EU Member States must first sign and subsequently ratify each agreement.[246] The need for coherence and coordination between the EU and its Member States is thus of central importance for adopting EU IIAs.[247] In light of the practical and political hurdles that come with mixity, the European Commission

---

242 Opinion 2/15, above note 1, para 11: "Since differences of opinion became apparent in consultations within the Trade Policy Committee on the nature of the European Union's competence to conclude the envisaged agreement, the Commission made the present request for an opinion."

243 In July 2016 (before Opinion 2/15 was rendered), the European Commission proposed to conclude CETA as a mixed agreement; see press release available at <http://europa.eu/rapid/press-release_IP-16-2371_en.htm>.

244 Opinion 2/15, above note 1, para 244. The Court did not make such a statement following its conclusion that the competence for ISDS was shared.

245 Cremona, above note 112, 251.

246 Dimopoulos, above note 9, 138.

247 Heliskoski J, *Mixed Agreements as a Technique for Organizing the International Relations of the European Community and Its Member States* (Kluwer Law International 2001) 78–86 and 95–100.

decided, in the aftermath of Opinion 2/15, to divide the initial FTAs reached with Singapore in 2014 and Vietnam in 2016, respectively into two separate instruments, namely a trade agreement and an investment protection agreement.[248] The rationale behind is to facilitate the entry into force of those parts of the initial agreement that are related to trade because the EU has exclusive external competence over international trade matters. Thus, for the EU's relations with Singapore and Vietnam two separate agreements exist, which are substantively, however, strongly interconnected and can therefore be considered as forming a whole.

4.4.3 Content and Scope of EU IIAs

Except for the ECT, the content and scope of pre-Lisbon IIAs were clearly distinguishable from traditional BITs of the EU Member States.[249] Pre-Lisbon EU IIAs are characterised by a focus on market integration and development principles, whereas the BITs of its Member States have a strong emphasis on investment protection and contain a direct enforcement mechanism through investor-State arbitration. With the competence shift of the Lisbon Treaty, the scope of EU IIAs became, compared to pre-Lisbon IIA practice, much broader, encompassing all aspects of foreign investment regulation. Unlike other major players in the international investment regime, the EU has not adopted a Model IIA to maintain certain negotiation flexibility.[250] Despite the absence of a model, the EU has developed, over the years, a unique approach combining its past practice, Member States' BIT experience and new innovative approaches.

---

248   Trade and Investment Agreements between the European Union and Singapore (authentic texts as of April 2018; not yet in Official Journal of the EU), ie EU-Singapore Free Trade Agreement (hereafter EUSFTA) and EU-Singapore Investment Protection Agreement (hereafter EUSIPA); Trade and Investment Agreements between the European Union and Vietnam (authentic text as of August 2018; not yet in Official Journal) ie EU-Vietnam Free Trade Agreement (hereafter EUVFTA) and EU-Vietnam Investment Protection Agreement (hereafter EUSIPA).

249   Dimopoulos A, 'Shifting the Emphasis from Investment Protection to Liberalization and Development: The EU as a New Global Factor in the Field of Foreign Investment' (2010) 11 The Journal of World Investment & Trade, 6–8.

250   The Commission stated from early on that it does not seek to elaborate an EU Model IIA finding that "a one-size-fits-all model for investment agreements with 3rd countries would necessarily be neither feasible nor desirable". See also Reinisch A, ' "Putting the Pieces Together … an EU Model BIT?" ' (2014) The Journal of World Investment & Trade 679; and Dickson-Smith KD, 'Does the European Union Have New Clothes?: Understanding the EU's New Investment Treaty Model' (2016) The Journal of World Investment & Trade 773.

The following suggests a distinction between two types of EU IIAs.[251] The first model groups those EU IIAs that have a limited set of provisions on investment (*i.e.* the "market integration model"). They are mainly found in pre-Lisbon IIAs but not necessarily so. Their main characteristic is investment liberalisation commitments by regulating the admission and establishment of investment. The second model groups the EU IIAs that also contain, next to investment liberalisation commitments, substantive standards of investment protection as well as a mechanism for the settlement of investor-State disputes (*i.e.* the "liberalisation and protection model").

4.4.3.1 The Market Integration Model

The EU has concluded IIAs based on the market integration model with the Western Balkan countries in so-called Stabilisation and Association Agreements; with countries from the Mediterranean area in Euro-Mediterranean Association Agreements;[252] as well as with former Soviet Union countries, typically in Partnership and Cooperation Agreements.[253] Furthermore, the EU has adopted such provisions in free trade agreements with individual economies, such as Chile, Korea and recently Japan.[254] Especially, the agreement with Japan of 2017 highlights that the market integration model is not necessarily the model of the pre-Lisbon era but still finds application today. Approaches based on market integration can also be found in economic partnership agreements with African Caribbean Pacific (ACP) countries and regional groups, such as with the CARIFORUM States.[255] Depending on the parties' political and economic priorities, these IIAs can vary in terms of coverage and scope of commitments. Nevertheless, all these agreements are characterised by the absence of investment protection standards, such as fair and

---

251 Multilateral IIAs to which the EU is a party are not dealt with in the present context. Namely the GATS [1994], the TRIMS Agreement [1994], and the Agreement on the European Economic Area, [1994] OJ L 1/572.

252 Eg EC-Algeria EMA, [2005] OJ L 265/2; EC-Egypt EMA, above note 34; EC-Morocco, [2000] OJ L 70/2; and EC-Tunisia EMA, [1998] OJ L 97/2.

253 Eg EC-Azerbaijan PCA, [1999] OJ L 246/3; EC-Georgia PCA, [1999] OJ L 205/3; EC-Kyrgyzstan PCA, [1999] OJ L 196/48; EC-Moldova PCA, [1998] OJ L 181/3; EC-Russia PCA, [1997] OJ L 327/3. See also the more recent agreements, EU-Armenia CPA, [2018] OJ L 23/4; EU-Kazakhstan PCA, [2016] OJ L 29/3.

254 See EC-Chile Association Agreement, [2002] OJ L 352/3; EUKFTA, above note 43; Economic Partnership Agreement between the European Union and Japan (EUJFTA), [2018] OJ L 330/3.

255 Partnership Agreement between the Members of the African, Caribbean and Pacific Group of States of the one part, and the European Community and its Member States, of the other part, signed in Cotonou, [2000], OJ L 317 (last revision of 2010).

equitable treatment, full protection and security or protection against expropriation.[256] Instead of investor-State dispute settlements, the market integration model first relies on consultations and negotiations between the parties and a subsequent possibility for traditional inter-State dispute resolution. The following four elements (investment liberalisation, non-discrimination, public policy, and cooperation) are relevant to understanding EU IIAs.[257]

First, EU IIAs have a strong focus on the admission of foreign investment, which includes the degree of liberalisation of capital movements and the conditions applicable to the establishment of foreign investors.[258] Since investment liberalisation has important political and economic impacts for the respective countries, the degree of opening-up their markets to foreign companies varies according to the specific objective pursued through the agreement. For instance, the agreements with the Western Balkan countries grant broad market access rights, given that the countries of this region might become Members of the EU in the long run.[259] Important market access rights are also present in the association agreements seeking to create intensive socio-economic relations, yet they also provide for a number of sector-specific restrictions concerning establishment rights.[260] Economic partnership agreements (EPAs) as well as free trade agreements (FTAs) follow more clearly the GATS model of liberalisation. As such, they provide for most favoured nation treatment of foreign investors' admission and contain the sectors for which establishment has been liberalised *i.e.* through a "positive-list approach". The liberalised sectors can go beyond the service sector, as has been the case, for instance, for the FTA with Korea.[261] Relating to the liberalisation of capital movements, a guarantee of free transfer of capital relating to an established investment activity figures in most EU IIAs, whereas a number of them also expand their coverage to other non-direct investments, namely portfolio investments.[262] Lastly, some

---

256   An early and isolated inclusion of a FET standard can be found in Lomé IV Convention, [1990] OJ L 229/3, Art 258(b).
257   In the following chapters of the present study, the EU approaches will be compared to those of other international actors. For the methodology for the present study see Section 1.4.
258   See also Dimopoulos, above note 9, 20 and 147.
259   Such as Albania, Montenegro, Serbia and Macedonia.
260   Eg EC-Jordan EMA, above note 34, Art 30 in combination with Annexes V and VI.
261   EUKFTA, Arts 7.9 et seq.
262   Such commitment adds a condition of reciprocity for the third country to the EU unilateral liberalisation of capital movements as set out in TFEU, Art 63(1): "[…] all restrictions on movement of capital […] between Member States and third countries shall be prohibited". See eg EU-Ukraine Association Agreement, [2014] OJ L 161/3, Art 145; EC-Israel EMA,

EU IIAS contain a specific provision entitled "Market Access", which generally prohibits the adoption or the maintenance of specific limitations imposed on foreign companies concerning access to the foreign market.[263]

Second, EU IIAS based on the market integration model of the EU make use of non-discrimination standards for the post-establishment treatment of investment. In most EU IIAS of this category, the post-establishment treatment of investment is linked to the provisions on establishment. Hence, the guarantee of non-discrimination once established in the host State is only applied to those investments in the sectors that have been liberalised. For instance, in the association agreement with Ukraine, national treatment and most favoured nation treatment apply to both the establishment and the post-establishment stage of direct investments.[264] A different approach can be found in the agreements with the Western Balkan countries. They foresee a guarantee of non-discrimination regarding the investment activity in the host State independent of whether its establishment likewise benefitted from the parties' specific commitments on establishment.[265] Lastly, the agreements with Central Asian States show that non-discriminatory treatment for the post-establishment phase can be subject to different exceptions than for the pre-establishment phase.[266]

Third, it is interesting to note that EU IIAS, without investment protection standards and investor-State dispute settlement, took into account public policy considerations seeking a balance between the interests of investors and those of the contracting parties. An illustrative example in this respect is the EPA with the CARIFORUM States,[267] which was concluded before the entry into force of the Lisbon Treaty. The EPA contains provisions on investor behaviour and provides that contracting parties shall not relax their environmental, health and labour standards in order to encourage foreign investment.[268]

[2000] OJ L 147/3, Art 31; EU-Montenegro Association Agreement, [2010] OJ L 108/3, Art 63(4); EUKFTA, above note 43, Art 8(2)(2); see also Dimopoulos, above note 9, 141.

263 See Strik, above note 15, 96. See eg, EU-CARIFORUM EPA, above note 43, Art 67(2).

264 Eg EU-Ukraine Association Agreement, Art 88.

265 Eg EC-Albania Association Agreement, OJ L 107/166, Art 50; EU-Montenegro Association Agreement, above note 156, Art 53; EU-Serbia Association Agreement, [2013] OJ L 278/16, Art 53; EC-Macedonia, [1997] OJ L 348/2, Art 48.

266 See EU-Kazakhstan PCA, Arts 45 (on MFN) and 46 (on NT). See also EC-Jordan EMA, above note 34, Art 30.

267 See Hoffmeister F and Ünüvar G, 'From BITs and Pieces towards European Investment Agreements', in: Bungenberg M, Reinisch A and Tietje C (eds), *EU and Investment Agreements: Open Questions and Remaining Challenges* (Nomos; Dike 2013) 62–63.

268 EC-CARIFORUM EPA, Arts 72–73. According to its Article 72, the parties are to take the necessary measures to ensure that the investors do not engage in corruption, that they act in accordance with core labour standards and do not operate in a manner that

Moreover, the said EPA, but also the agreements with Chile, and Korea, provide a general exception clause that allows the host States to adopt proportionate and non-discriminatory measures that are necessary to protect and secure public morals, public order, human, animal and plant life or health, exhaustible natural resources, national cultural treasures, and other public policy objectives.[269]

Fourth, EU IIAs based on the market integration model generally emphasise the importance of cooperative action for investment promotion.[270] The objective of the cooperation is to create "a favourable and stable environment for investment" by essentially focussing on the establishment of a clear and transparent administrative regime that allows easier and better access to information on foreign investment opportunities and regulation as well as the creation of a legal environment conducive to investment. In particular, the agreements concluded between the EU and developing countries highlight the EU's commitment to building up the institutional capacities required for effective investment promotion in these countries.[271]

4.4.3.2   The Investment Liberalisation and Protection Model

EU IIAs with substantive standards of investment protection combined with investor-State dispute settlement are a phenomenon of the post-Lisbon treaty practice, with the sole exception of the 1994 Energy Charter Treaty (ECT) to which both the EU and its Member States are contracting parties.[272] In the post-Lisbon era, the substantive investment protection standards are part of comprehensive FTAs, which either contain a specific chapter on investment,[273]

---

circumvents international environmental law. Similar commitments can also be found in the FTA with Korea; see EUKFTA, Arts 13(3–5).

[269] EC-Chile Association Agreement, Art 91; EC-CARIFORUM EPA, Art 224; EUKFTA, Art 2.15.

[270] Some of the EU IIAs solely establish a cooperative framework for investment promotion without any pre- and post-establishment rights. See for instance the EU-Pakistan Cooperation Agreement, [2004] OJ L 378/23.

[271] A fundamental pillar in this respect is the financial support offered by the EU and its Member States. The EPAs with the states of the South African Development Community (SADC) or with the CARIFORUM States refer to the European Development Fund (EDF) thereby providing an opportunity for those countries to use the instrument for their investment promotion. See EU-SADC EPA, [2016] OJ L 250/3, Art 12(3); and EU-CARIFORUM EPA, Art 7(3).

[272] The ECT is geared towards trade and investment in the energy sector. Its investment protection provisions follow the approaches taken in traditional BITs of EU Member States also including the possibility of ISDS. Energy Charter Treaty (ECT).

[273] The "new generation" of comprehensive EU FTAs adopted post-Lisbon CJEU, Opinion 2/15, above note 2, paras 17 (definition of the European Parliament) and 140: "in addition to the classical provisions on the reduction of customs duties and of non-tariff barriers to trade

or have an accompanying agreement on investment protection.[274] Among the EU IIAs of this category are the agreements with Canada, Mexico, Singapore, and Vietnam.[275]

Looking at their content, it becomes readily apparent that they do not constitute a shift away from the previously discussed market integration model but rather an extension thereof. In that sense, agreements falling under this category likewise have a strong emphasis on market access and investment liberalisation commitments.[276] Moreover, this type of agreement also seeks to provide a nuanced balance between investors' interests and those of the contracting parties, as such public purpose considerations are, in particular, fostered by the provisions on the host State's right to regulate. Yet, the substantive investment protection standards and investor-State dispute settlement clearly reach beyond the market integration model.

Post-Lisbon EU IIAs build upon the traditional investment standards, including post-establishment non-discrimination, fair and equitable treatment (FET), full protection and security, and protection against expropriation and the guarantee of free transfer of funds. Concerning the FET standard, the EU introduced a novelty. Under EU IIAs, FET provisions contain a defined and closed list of the measures that can constitute a breach of the standard, namely denial of justice, a fundamental breach of due process, manifest arbitrariness, targeted discrimination on manifestly wrongful grounds, or abusive treatment of investors.[277] Moreover, legitimate expectations are no longer a core element of the FET standard but appear to be rather supplementary issues that adjudicators can consider when assessing the main elements of FET. A further key

---

in goods and services, provisions on various matters related to trade, such as intellectual property protection, investment, public procurement, competition and sustainable development".

274   Such is the case for the trade and investment relations with Vietnam and Singapore.
275   Comprehensive Economic and Trade Agreement (CETA) between Canada, of the one part, and the European Union and its Member States, of the other part, [2017] OJ L 11/23 (hereafter CETA); Free Trade Agreement between the European Union and Mexico (authentic texts as of April 2018; not yet in Official Journal of the EU) (hereafter EUMFTA); Trade and Investment Agreements between the European Union and Singapore (authentic texts as of April 2018; not yet in Official Journal of the EU) (hereafter EUSFTA and EUSIPA; the EUSIPA contains investment protection provisions); Trade and Investment Agreements between the European Union and Vietnam (authentic text as of August 2018; not yet in Official Journal) (hereafter EUVFTA and EUVIPA; the EUVIPA contains investment protection provisions).
276   CETA, Arts 8.4–8.7; EUMFTA, Ch 'Investment', Arts 5–12; EUSFTA, Arts 8.8–8.12; EUVFTA, Arts 8.3–8.8.
277   See eg CETA, Art 8.10 (2)(a-e).

standard of international investment law is the protection against direct and indirect expropriation. EU IIAs aim to define the notion of indirect expropriation better.[278] Interpretative annexes clarify the situations in which indirect expropriation is given. These annexes also contain a regulatory exception stating that measures that are designed and applied to protect legitimate public welfare objectives do, under certain conditions, not constitute indirect expropriation.[279] The most significant innovation of EU IIA constitutes the shift from investor-State arbitration to a so-called Investment Court System (ICS). For each bilateral relation, EU IIAs establish such ICS consisting of a tribunal of first instance and an appellate mechanism.[280]

4.5 SD and the Autonomy of the EU Legal Order

SD is concerned with States' regulatory autonomy to enact domestic legislation in the pursuit of SD. The CJEU, in Opinion 1/17, used the concept of autonomy under EU law to include the choice of the level of protection. Opinion 1/17 of the Court on the compatibility of the CETA dispute settlement system is mainly concerned with procedural questions. Nevertheless, several points are of importance for the analysis at hand. First, in Opinion 1/17, the Court found that the principle of autonomy can be violated not only when an international agreement concluded by the EU contains an external tribunal that can invalidate an act of EU law (because that power only belongs to the CJEU). According to the reasoning in Opinion 1/17, autonomy is also breached if it affects the ability of EU institutions to adopt measures to protect the public interest namely in a situation in which an investment tribunal scrutinises such measures when applying investment protection standards, such as FET. The link between the level of protection of public interest and SD lies in the idea that States are to determine such level according to their concrete SD needs and ambitions, which include social, economic and environmental aspects.[281] There are differences and varying priorities of States in implementing the

---

278 CETA, Annex 8-A; EUMFTA, 'Annex on Expropriation'; EUSIPA, Annex 1; EUVIPA, Annex 4.
279 Ibid.
280 CETA, Arts 8.27 et seq; EUMFTA, Ch 'Resolution of Investment Disputes', Arts 11 et seq; EUSIPA, Art 3.1 et seq; EUVIPA, Arts 3.1 et seq.
281 Such measures can encompass a large bulk of policy areas. The CETA Joint Interpretative Instrument mentions the following, pt 1(d): "the protection and promotion of public health, social services, public education, safety, the environment, public morals, social or consumer protection, privacy and data protection and the promotion and protection of cultural diversity".

SDGS.[282] Each region, State and even sub-region might have different environmental and socio-economic constraints to which it needs to respond adequately and responsively to the cultural and political importance given by society in question. Second, the reasoning of the Court in Opinion 1/17, is relevant for the analysis at hand since the Court found that CETA contains enough safeguards not to undermine the EU's legislative choices of the level of public interest and thus respects the prerogatives of the EU legislator. The examination of the build-in safeguards in the concrete investment protections provisions under CETA and other EU IIAS is the core of Chapter 6 on investment protection standards. Therefore, this section focusses on the reasoning of the Court concerning the principle of autonomy. It considers the interlinkages between autonomy and the right to regulate SD matters and reflects upon the implications for the EU as a global actor.

4.5.1 *In Compliance with the Autonomy of the EU Legal Order: The Investment Court System (ICS)*

Opinion 1/17 on the mechanism for investor-State dispute resolution under CETA provided an opportunity for the Court to examine for the first time an EU IIA's compatibility with EU primary law.[283] One of the main questions put to the Court was: does the envisaged ISDS mechanism prevent the EU from operating in accordance with its unique constitutional framework as defined by the CJEU? In Opinion 1/17, the Court examined the ICS as to its compatibility with the autonomy principle in a twofold manner: First, the Court examined whether the ICS has or not jurisdiction to interpret and apply rules of EU law other than the provisions of CETA.[284] Second, it examined whether CETA tribunal awards might "have the effect of preventing the EU institutions from operating in accordance with the EU constitutional framework".[285]

4.5.1.1 The Principle

The principle of the autonomy of EU law has originally been developed by the CJEU to articulate the relationship between EU and national law of the Member States. From early on, the Court asserted that EU law became an autonomous source of law that is distinct form the legal orders of the Member

---

282 Agenda 2030, para 59: "We recognise that there are different approaches, visions, models and tools available to each country, in accordance with its national circumstances and priorities, to achieve sustainable development [...]".
283 See for the origins of Opinion 1/17, Section 4.1.2.
284 Opinion 1/17, above note 5, paras 120–136.
285 Opinion 1/17, above note 5, paras 137–161.

States.[286] Autonomy has served to justify the primacy and direct effect of EU law.[287] The primary function of autonomy is to guarantee the integrity of the EU legal order. Over time, autonomy has developed into a more comprehensive concept turning into a principle for self-assertation of the EU towards its Member States and its relations with third States under international law.[288] Put differently, the principle construes EU law as autonomous, not depending for its validity on national or international law.[289] The Court used autonomy to limit the effects deriving from international law by separating the international legal order from the EU legal order.[290] EU law must be autonomous from international law in the sense that no international agreement can "affect the allocation of powers fixed by the Treaties"[291] or "have the effect of prejudicing the constitutional principles of the [Treaties]".[292]

The CJEU sees itself as the guardian of the EU legal order. Article 19(1), second sentence TEU, vests the Court with the mandatory, binding and final jurisdiction on the interpretation and application of EU law. Thus, Article 19 TEU embodies the role and prerogatives of the Court as the EU institution assigned with the exclusive authority to provide an authentic interpretation of EU primary law rules and determine the validity and interpretation of EU secondary law rules. Based on its precedent, the Court has developed the idea of the self-contained and autonomous nature of EU law and its monopoly of interpretation thereof.[293] Christina Eckes finds that "one could conclude that the autonomy of EU law as a self-contained and self-referential normative system is implicitly reaffirmed in every decision that claims its legality and legitimacy by

---

286   ECJ, *Case 26/62 Van Gend en Loos* EU:C:1963:1, 3. See also, Case 106/77 *Amministrazione delle Finanze dello Stato v Simmenthal*, EU:C:1978:49.
287   ECJ, Case 6/64 *Flaminio Costa v ENEL*, EU:C:1964:66, 614.
288   As the CJEU has underlined on several occasions, "the autonomy of EU law with respect both to the law of the Member States and to international law is justified by the essential characteristics of the EU and its law, relating in particular to the constitutional structure of the EU and the very nature of that law". See ECJ, Opinion 2/13, above note 77, para 170; see also ECJ, Case C-284/16 *Slowakische Republik v Achmea BV*, EU:C:2018:158, para 33.
289   Eg Opinion 1/17, above note 5, para 109.
290   Ziegler KS, 'Closing Chapter: Piecing the Puzzle Together: Beyond Pluralism and Autonomy: Systemic Harmonization as a Paradigm for the Interaction of EU Law and International Law' (2016) 35 Yearbook of European Law 667, 683. The author finds that the Court has started to endorse a move to compartmentalise the EU's legal order (in the early 2010s).
291   ECJ, Joined Cases C-402/05 P and C-415/05 P *Kadi and Al Barakaat*, EU:C:2008:461, para 282.
292   Ibid, para 285.
293   See, *Costa v ENEL*, above note 287, 593–594.

resting on earlier interpretations of the law".[294] To this end, the Court regularly relies on a number of typical features of EU law ensuring its judicial autonomy, such as the system of preliminary reference provided for under Article 267 TFEU[295] and the prohibition for Member States to settle their disputes in other fora elsewhere than the CJEU as set out in Article 344 TFEU.

In principle, an international agreement can establish a court or tribunal to which the EU is subject.[296] For the CJEU, each decision on the EU's ability to do so triggers a test of whether the normative commitments may have the potential to undermine the Court-construed autonomy of the EU legal order.[297] In the past years, what could be observed is that the Court has been consolidating a relatively restrictive jurisprudence on the question of whether or not the EU can subject itself to an international dispute settlement mechanism.[298] In Opinion 1/91, the Court blocked the accession of the EU to the European Economic Area (EEA) Court finding that no external tribunal can decide upon the repartition of competence between the EU and its Member States.[299] It also warranted the EU to submit itself to the Unified Patent Court and the European Court of Human Rights (ECtHR).[300] In both opinions, the Court found that its exclusive task of reviewing EU acts would be undermined if the EU was subject to the jurisdiction of the respective dispute settlement mechanisms. Especially Opinion 2/13 suggested that the mere possibility of providing an interpretation of EU law suffices for autonomy to be breached.[301] In the context of international investment law and arbitration, the Court ruled in the *Achmea* judgment that the principle of autonomy prevents two Member States from setting up an investor-State dispute settlement mechanism through a BIT *inter se*.[302] Conversely, the Court found that CETA's ICS does not undermine the monopoly of final interpretation of the Court.

---

294   Eckes C, 'The Autonomy of the EU Legal Order' [2020] 4(1): 1 Europe and the World: A Law Review, 4.
295   On 267 TFEU, Opinions 1/09 and 2/13 had underscored the pivotal importance of judicial dialogue for ensuring the uniform interpretation of EU law "thereby serving to ensure its consistency, its full effect and its autonomy as well as, ultimately, the particular nature of [that] law" see Opinion 2/13, above note 77, paras 176 and 196–200.
296   *Achmea*, above note 288, para 57.
297   Eckes, above note 294, 5.
298   Exception as here the Court accepted the external mechanism: Eg ECJ, Opinion 1/00 *European Common Aviation Area*, EU:C:2002:231, para 24.
299   ECJ, Opinion 1/91, *First Opinion on the EEA Agreement*, EU:C:1991:490.
300   Opinion 2/13, above note 77, Opinion 1/09 above note 124.
301   Opinion 2/13, above note 77, para 208.
302   *Achmea*, above note 288, para 59.

4.5.1.2 The Court's Monopoly of Final Interpretation

Belgium's first concern relating to the compatibility of the ICS with the autonomy of the EU legal order was that the investment court could undermine the exclusive jurisdiction of the Court to render final interpretations on EU law. Belgium argued that CETA's applicable law provision does not warrant a situation in which a tribunal has to "undertake an assessment of the effect" of EU primary law.[303] According to the arguments of Belgium, Article 8.31(2) CETA, on applicable law cannot prevent such a situation. The provision, which became instrumental in the Court's reasoning, reads:

> "For greater certainty, in determining the consistency of a measure with this Agreement, the Tribunal may consider, as appropriate, the domestic law of a Party as *a matter of fact*. In doing so, the Tribunal *shall follow the prevailing interpretation* given to the domestic law by the courts or authorities of that Party and any meaning given to domestic law by the Tribunal *shall not be binding* upon the courts or the authorities of that Party."[304]

The question that the Court had to answer was whether the CETA ICS has the power to apply and interpret EU law. The Court examined the applicable law provision and held that it was sufficiently clear when it states that the CETA tribunal decides disputes exclusively on the basis of the CETA and international law.[305] It sets out that "the law of the Contracting State party to the dispute" must not be applicable. Thus, such tribunal will not have jurisdiction "to determine the legality of a measure, alleged to constitute a breach of [CETA], under the domestic law of a Party".[306] In other words, an ICS tribunal considers domestic law "as facts" and as construed by domestic courts and it would namely not consider domestic law as a proper source of law. Considering domestic law as facts and not as the applicable law is the common practice of international courts.[307] Investment tribunals apply the same line of reasoning. Their mandate is to review the conformity of domestic law (what can

---

303 Opinion 1/17, above note 5, para 49.
304 CETA, Art 8.31(2). Emphasis added.
305 Opinion 1/17, above note 5, paras 121–123.
306 Opinion 1/17, above note 5, para 121.
307 PCIJ, *Certain German Interests in Polish Upper Silesia*, Series A No 7, at 19. See also the WTO, Appellate Body, India-Patens (US), 1998, para 65: "Municipal law may serve evidence of facts and may provide evidence of State practice. However, municipal law may also constitute evidence of compliance or non-compliance with international obligations."

include measures of general application and even constitutional law) with the international investment law obligations. In doing so, they do not review the act according to the host State' national law but according to the IIA. For instance, the tribunal in *Saluka v. Czech Republic* found it not "necessary to determine the legality" of the measure under scrutiny, neither under Czech national law nor under EU law.[308] According to the *Saluka* tribunal "the only relevant question is whether the Czech Government's [measure] constituted unfair and inequitable treatment" of the investor.[309] In Opinion 1/17, the Court acknowledged that ICS tribunals will do an "examination of the effect of that measure" and that an "examination may, on occasion, require that domestic law of the respondent Party be taken into account."[310] Nonetheless, EU law will not be the applicable law in any of the future disputes under the CETA. The applicable law provision of CETA was thus instrumental in the Court's reasoning. In this respect, the CETA is different from the agreement establishing a Patent Court as examined in Opinion 1/09 and the ISDS mechanism in the BIT applicable in the *Achmea* case.[311] The Patent Court was rejected because it would have had the mandate "to interpret and apply [...] the future regulation of the Community patent and other instruments of European Union law".[312]

Furthermore, under CETA, EU law may not only be acknowledged as a fact but tribunals must take account of the case-law of the EU courts.[313] Hereto, Belgium raised the concern that it could be that the CJEU has not yet issued a final interpretation on a question of EU law, i.e. has not yet given a determinative interpretation to an act of EU law and an investment tribunal would necessarily be the first to provide an interpretation. The reasoning in Opinion 1/17 suggests that it is not required that the Court has pronounced first on the meaning to be given to an act of EU law before that act can be the subject

---

308 *Saluka Investments BV v The Czech Republic*, UNCITRAL, Partial Award, 17 March 2006, para 444.
309 Ibid.
310 Opinion 1/17, above note 5, para 131.
311 The Achmea decision originates in a request for a preliminary ruling by the Bundesgerichtshof in May 2016. In the German proceedings, the Slovak Republic challenged a 2012 arbitral award, which was rendered on the basis of a 1992 BIT between NL and Slovakia. The award was in favour of the Dutch investor (active in the sector of private health insurance); the Slovak Republic has constantly argued that the tribunal lacked jurisdiction as recourse to an investment tribunal was incompatible with EU law.
312 Opinion 1/17, above note 5, paras 123–124.
313 Ibid, paras 130–131.

matter of an investment dispute.[314] What matters instead is that the EU institutions are not bound by any "external" interpretation of EU law.

Since there was a heated debate surrounding the *Achmea* judgement, it is worth noting that the constitutional threats for the EU legal order stemming from CETA are different from those coming from intra-EU BITs. In the words of Advocate General Bot, "the premises which must guide the line of reasoning are different" in the two scenarios.[315] The ISDS mechanism was found to be incompatible in the *Achmea* case because EU law is among the applicable laws in an investment arbitration under that BIT and even more so because the CJEU has no means to control such application.[316] In *Achmea*, both, Articles 267 and 344 TFEU precluded provisions such as the applicable law provision of the BIT in question.[317] The Achmea case shows that autonomy *inter se* focuses on establishing external primacy of EU law. This limits the ability of Member States to cooperate at the international level outside the EU legal order.[318] In this sense, the principle of autonomy protects the full effectiveness of EU law, which implies the uniform interpretation of the law. If the Member States want to submit a dispute, the mechanism must be part of the EU jurisdictional system. Conversely, in Opinion 1/17, there was no need to answer the question whether Article 267 TFEU was infringed because the ICS "stands outside the EU judicial system" and because the agreement was not concluded between two or more Member States but by the EU itself involving the participation of a third State.[319]

Another difference between *extra* and *inter se* autonomy is that the principle of mutual trust fully applies in an intra-EU setting but not in a relationship with a non-EU State. Within, the EU legal system, the principle namely

---

314   Opinion 1/17, above note 5, para 131; Riffel C, 'The CETA Opinion of the European Court of Justice and Its Implications—Not That Selfish After All' (2019) 22 Journal of International Economic Law 503, 516–517. The author highlights that before Opinion 1/17 this question was not clear.
315   Opinion of AG Bot, above note 211, para 106.
316   *Achmea*, above note 288, paras 40–42.
317   Ibid, para 62.
318   Dimopoulos A, 'Achmea: The principle of autonomy and its implications for intra and extra-EU BITs', EJIL Talk (March 2018).
319   Opinion 1/17, para 113; at 114: "The courts envisaged by the CETA are indeed separate from the domestic courts of Canada, the Union and its Member States. The CETA Tribunal and Appellate Tribunal cannot, consequently, be considered to form part of the judicial system of either of the Parties." Consider in contrast, *Achmea*, para 58: "the possibility of submitting those disputes to a body which is not part of the judicial system of the EU is provided for by an agreement which was concluded not by the EU but by Member States" was problematic and in breach of autonomy (here namely Article 344 TFEU).

requires that all Member States comply with EU law, including the respect for the right to an effective remedy before an independent tribunal laid down in Article 47 of the EUCFR.[320] As for international agreements with third States, the principle of mutual trust is not applicable.[321]

The Court also had to examine whether the ICS Appellate Tribunal applies EU law. This question had to be treated separately since Article 8.31 CETA concerns the tribunal of first instance only. According to the Court, the intention of the CETA contracting parties was not to "confer on the Appellate Tribunal jurisdiction to interpret domestic law".[322] Here, the reasoning of the Court is curious as it suggests that the mere intention of the parties is sufficient to ensure that EU law is not applied and interpreted. Whilst it is possible to assume that the applicable law is the same for the tribunal of first instance and the appeal court, it is not clear why the Contracting Parties' intention could be sufficient. Finally, the Court added that the ICS has no jurisdiction to interpret EU law also because the CETA explicitly allows the EU (and not a tribunal under the ICS) to determine the appropriate respondent in a case at hand.[323]

Taking all these elements together, the Court came to the conclusion that the ICS has no jurisdiction to apply or interpret EU law and is thus in compliance with the autonomy of EU law. This conclusion might have come to the surprise of those that applied previous case law on autonomy to the ICS.[324] Such as Opinion 2/13, where the "very existence of [...] a possibility" of conflicts between the European Convention of Human Rights and EU primary law allowed the Court to find that autonomy was infringed since deciding upon such conflict is the sole competence of the CJEU.[325] Whereas, based on the strict separation between EU law and the IIA, in Opinion 1/17, the Court did not have to enter into a discussion on the risk or the possibility for EU law to be interpreted by ICS tribunal. In a clear extra-EU setting, the critical

---

320 Opinion 1/17, above note 5, para 128 and case law cited.
321 Ibid, para 129.
322 Ibid, para 133.
323 Ibid, para 132. See CETA, Art 8.21(3): "The European Union shall, after having made a determination, inform the investor as to whether the European Union or a Member State of the European Union shall be the respondent."
324 Eg Gatti M, 'Opinion 1/17 in Light of Achmea: Chronicle of an Opinion Foretold?' [2019] European Papers Vol. 4 (2019) No 1; <www.europeanpapers.eu> 109. The author argued that the Achmea test should apply (at 119) and highlighted that the ICS would not pass the said test (at 120).
325 Opinion 2/13, above note 77, paras 208. See also, Eeckhout P, 'Opinion 2/13 on EU Accession to the ECHR and Judicial Dialogue: Autonomy or Autarky' (2015) 38 Fordham International Law Journal 955, 966–967 and 974–979.

question is not the possibility of interpretation but whether arbitral awards result in *binding* interpretations of EU law that the EU institutions would have to follow.[326]

The strict separation between law and facts under the CETA as endorsed by the Court, cannot preclude instances where EU law has, at least, to be "taken into account" when assessing the compatibility of a measure with the investment protection standards under CETA. The reasons for the Court's conclusions lie in the heavily conceptual approach the Court is taking when assessing questions of autonomy. Christina Eckes speaks of an "absolute conceptual autonomy" as how the Court sees and upholds autonomy and thereby safeguards the autonomy of the EU legal order.[327] Put differently, the Court's conception of autonomy is absolute and not relative to the subject at hand and namely not factual.[328] For the CETA this means that in practice the divide between the international and the EU legal order might be blurred to a certain extent but that this does not change the Court's conceptual (and rather abstract) approach. This twist between conceptual and factual is highlighted in the consequences of the Court's reasoning. Following Opinion 1/17, the EU and its Member State are not bound by future ICS tribunals' interpretations on EU law matters. Factually, interpretations of ICS tribunals are, however, liable to entail concrete effects for the EU and its Member States when it contributes to finding a violation of CETA and awards damages. Situations are likely to occur where a measure must not be changed under EU law but if the EU or a Member State will not change the measure, they might face recurring claims and potential compensation payments.

4.5.2 *Safeguarding Regulatory Autonomy*

After determining that ICS tribunals have no jurisdiction to apply and interpret EU law, the Court examined the second concern raised by Belgium relating to the autonomy of the EU legal order. The argument has been made that when ICS tribunals have to assess the facts of a given investment dispute, this may include assessing EU primary law that is the basis on which the contested

---

[326] Angelos Dimopoulos argued that "when an agreement is concluded by the EU, a binding interpretation of EU law that would result in a violation of autonomy exists only when an international agreement concluded by the EU exhibits a special link to EU law". The CETA has no such special link whereas for the ECHR such was the case. See Dimopoulos, above note 318.

[327] The term "absolute conceptual autonomy" is used by Christina Eckes, see Eckes, above note 294, 3.

[328] Ibid.

measure was adopted thereby weighing the business interest of the foreign investor against the public interests relied upon by the EU as a defence to its measure.[329] Such a setting might prevent the EU institutions from operating in accordance with the EU constitutional framework and thus would violate the principle of autonomy.

The Court first acknowledged that the scope of jurisdiction of future ICS tribunals is relatively large. On the one hand, the definition of investment under CETA is broad and "permits the envisaged tribunals to hear a wide range of disputes".[330] On the other hand, the term measure is also broadly defined under CETA and can encompass measures of general application or measures that are implementing an act of general application.[331] In a second step, the Court makes a general statement setting out criteria when the principle of autonomy is breached:

> "[...] the jurisdiction of those tribunals would adversely affect the autonomy of the EU legal order if it were structured in such a way that those tribunals might, in the course of making findings on restrictions on the freedom to conduct business challenged within a claim, *call into question the level of protection of a public interest* that led to the introduction of such restrictions by the Union with respect to all operators who invest in the commercial or industrial sector at issue of the internal market, rather than *confine itself to determining whether the treatment of an investor* or a covered investment is vitiated by a defect mentioned in Section C or D of Chapter Eight of the CETA."[332]

> "It must be emphasised, in that regard, that EU legislation is adopted by the EU legislature following the *democratic process* defined in the EU and FEU Treaties, and that that legislation is deemed, by virtue of the principles of conferral of powers, subsidiarity and proportionality laid down in Article 5 TEU, to be both *appropriate* and *necessary* to achieve a legitimate objective of the Union. In accordance with Article 19 TEU, it is the *task of the Courts of the European Union to ensure review of the compatibility of the level of protection of public interests* established by such

---

329 Opinion 1/17, above note 5, para 137.
330 Ibid, para 139.
331 Ibid, para 143: "While it is thus stated in the CETA that the dispute must concern a measure that relates to the claimant or its covered investment, that agreement does not however preclude that measure from being one of general application or from implementing an act of general application."
332 Ibid, para 148. Emphasis added.

legislation with, inter alia, the EU and FEU Treaties, the Charter and the general principles of EU law."[333]

The Court made a statement that introduces novel institutional criteria on how to assess infringements with the autonomy of the EU legal order.[334] The principle of autonomy is breached if ICS tribunals are affecting the ability of the EU institutions to adopt measures to protect the public interests. The ability to legislate in the public interest is affected when an ICS tribunal does not confine itself to determine whether the treatment of an investor was contrary to the CETA protection standards but goes as far as to weigh the freedom to conduct business against the public interests set out in EU primary law and "calls into question the level of protection of a public interest".[335] Such weighing exercise would be of the same nature as those of the Court when it reviews the validity of EU secondary law. Yet it is the sole competence of the CJEU to assess whether a measure adopted by the EU intuitions is *necessary* and *appropriate* to achieve a legitimate objective of the EU. In other words, the proportionality analysis of a measure is the Court's competence, especially since such measures are adopted by the EU intuitions "following the democratic process" under EU law. Put differently, it is for the EU courts alone to review the compatibility of the level of protection of public interests established by EU legislation with EU primary law, including the proportionality principle set out in Article 5 TEU.

Belgium and some Member States, moreover, highlighted the fact that the ICS tribunals could order the EU or the Member States to pay damages, so that certain regulations would no longer be made by them. The Court to some extent agreed with this possibility that corresponds with regulatory chill in view of the wide scope of application of investment protection and even considered that an agreement which would oblige the EU to waive certain regulations in the general interest was contrary to EU law.[336] Therefore too, if the ICS tribunals would indeed weigh between the private and the public interest that would be a clear risk that the EU institutions might have to abandon a specific level of protection in order to avoid being repeatedly compelled

---

333   Ibid, above note, para 151. Emphasis added.
334   Previously, the Court's control relating to autonomy was mainly concerned with the allocation of competences and the control of EU law (including preliminary ruling). See Cremona M, 'The Opinion Procedure under Article 218(11) TFEU: Reflections in the Light of Opinion 1/17' [2020] Europe and the World: A law review, 6.
335   Opinion 1/17, above note 5, para 151.
336   Ibid, paras 149–150.

to pay damages to claimant investors, the principle of autonomy would be infringed. In a way, the Court confirmed the fundamental criticism of many on the effectiveness of international investment protection and investment arbitration, and the associated risk of regulatory chill at the domestic law level.[337]

Despite these considerable reservations on the ICS tribunal's competence, the Court subsequently found that CETA contained sufficient "safeguards" that would ensure in the future that no tribunal calls into question the level of public interest protection within the EU legal order. How could the Court come to this result? It considered a number of provisions of the CETA that address issues of the right to regulate in the public interest and regulatory autonomy. It started with quoting the CETA's general exceptions clause and found it sufficient to prove that the ICS tribunals have "no jurisdiction to declare incompatible with the CETA the level of protection" established by the EU.[338] Whilst the general exception clause, by referring to a number of public interests is apt to function as a safeguard, the clause does, under CETA, not apply to the key investment protection standards, namely FET but only to non-discrimination.[339] Yet FET and the protection against indirect expropriation pose most threats to the right to regulate.[340] A fact that was not mentioned by the Court. In addition, the Court found comfort in the provision on the right to regulate, which is the first provision of the CETA Section D on investment protection. By quoting the article, the Court found the reaffirmations of the right to regulate to be sufficient to ensure that future ICS tribunals would not call into question the level of protection set by the EU institutions. Here too, the Court's analysis is brief and omits to mention that the clause of Article 8.9(1) CETA is not an exception clause but merely a clause that reaffirms a right that at any rate belongs to sovereign States and the EU. Still using the same questionable methodology, the Court quoted passages of the Joint Interpretative Instrument to show the extent to which the right to regulate is further preserved. Finally, the Court mentions that the CETA negotiators have included the police power doctrine into the indirect expropriation provision and approved the FET provision in finding that FET is "specifically circumscribed".[341] In light of the considerable international debate on the right to regulate and how to best safeguard it through calibrating IIAs, the analysis of the Court looks extremely brief. It

---

337   On regulatory chill see, Section 2.5.3.1.
338   CETA, Art 28; Opinion 1/17, above note 5, paras 152–153.
339   CETA, Section C 'Non-discriminatory Treatment'. See Section 6.1.2.
340   See Section 2.5.1.
341   Opinion 1/17, above note 5, paras 157–159.

does not enter into key legal and policy questions of international investment governance.[342]

4.5.2.1 The Court's Assumption-Based Risk Assessment

Based on its general overview of the CETA provisions that seek to restate the Parties' right to regulate, the Court validated the ICS by trying to demonstrate that the EU institutions are not affected by it and that the European democracy will not be weakened. Many observers probably agree with the Court that the CETA provisions on the right to regulate and the better circumscription of the protection standards reduce the likelihood of excessive investment protection "attacks" on legitimate EU or Member State regulatory activities in the public interest. While the actual effectiveness can only be tested in subsequent cases, what can be said at this point is that they do not entirely exclude the possibility of control under international law based on the investment protection standards of the CETA.[343] By assuming that this would be the case, the Court based its analysis on what has been called a "pious hope".[344] Indeed, the assumptions made by the Court are striking and arguably wrong. They are based on a general, *ex ante* and abstract overview of certain key provisions without mentioning the remaining discretion of future ICS adjudicator when assessing a measure adopted by the EU.

The analyses of investment tribunals have included proportionality analyses of a measure in question (including its aptitude and necessity to achieve a legitimate objective).[345] At the same time, international tribunals rarely call into question the level of protection or find that an objective would not be legitimate. For instance, the tribunal in the *Bilcon v. Canada* found it relevant to explicitly state that there was not "the slightest issue with the level of protection for the environment" under Canadian domestic law.[346] The WTO Appealed

---

342   The debate has been considered in Section 2.5.
343   See on this point also, Holterhus TP, 'Das CETA-Gutachten Des EuGH: Neue Maßstäbe Allerorten...' VerfassungsBlog (May 2019).
344   Flavier H, 'L'avis 1/17 sur le CETA : De l'autonomie à l'hermétisme', Journal d'Actualité des Droits Européens No 19 (2019).
345   On proportionality, see Section 7.4.2.
346   Consider, *William Ralph Clayton, William Richard Clayton, Douglas Clayton, Daniel Clayton and Bilcon of Delaware Inc v Government of Canada*, PCA Case No 2009-04, Award on Jurisdiction and Liability of 17 March 2015, para 598: "In arriving at its conclusion in this case, the Tribunal is not suggesting that there is the slightest issue with the level of protection for the environment provided in the laws of Canada and Nova Scotia. Each is free under NAFTA to adopt laws that are as demanding as they choose in exercising their sovereign authority. Canada and Nova Scotia have both adopted high standards. There can be absolutely no issue with that under Chapter Eleven of NAFTA. The Tribunal's concern

Body is likewise extremely careful when assessing the Member States' choices regarding their level of public interest protection.³⁴⁷ The issue with regulatory autonomy is the intrusiveness of the methodology used (e.g. proportionality) and the possible sanctions in the form of compensation payments. According to the statement made by the CJEU itself, only the EU courts are competent to decide about the level of protection of public interest and evaluate the appropriateness and the necessity of a measure.³⁴⁸ Nothing in the built-in safeguards of CETA can prevent ICS tribunals from concluding that an EU public interest measure violated the guarantees under CETA having the consequence of compensation payments. In short, this means that the likelihood of successful claims against public interest measures is reduced, but there is no guarantee.

4.5.2.2 The Court's Instructions on How to Implement EU IIAS

The Court must have been aware that it cannot be sure *ex ante* on how future ICS use their margin of appreciation. Despite finding that the built-in safeguards are sufficient, it promoted future judicial restraint of adjudicators when applying the CETA provision on investment. Based on the investment protection standards, the general exception clause as well as the Joint Interpretative Instrument, the Court found that

> "[...] the *discretionary powers* of the CETA Tribunal and Appellate Tribunal *do not extend to permitting them to call into question the level of protection of public interest determined by the Union following a democratic process.*"³⁴⁹
>
> "[...] the Parties have taken care to ensure that *those tribunals have no jurisdiction to call into question the choices democratically made within a Party relating to, inter alia, the level of protection* of health and life of humans and animals, the preservation of food safety, protection of plants

---

is actually that the rigorous and comprehensive evaluation defined and prescribed by the laws of Canada was not in fact carried out."

347   See, WTO, Appellate Body, *European Communities—Measures Affecting Asbestos and Asbestos-Containing Products*, WT/DS135/AB/R, adopted 11 April 2001, paras 21, 165 and 168. At 168: "[...] we note that it is undisputed that WTO Members have the right to determine the level of protection of health that they consider appropriate in a given situation. France has determined, and the Panel accepted, that the chosen level of health protection by France is a "halt" to the spread of asbestos-related health risks. By prohibiting all forms of amphibole asbestos, and by severely restricting the use of chrysotile asbestos, the measure at issue is clearly designed and apt to achieve that level of health protection [...]."

348   Consider again, Opinion 1/17, above note 5, para 151.

349   Ibid, para 154. Emphasis added.

and environment, welfare at work, product safety, consumer protection, or equally fundamental rights."[350]

Opinion 1/17 suggests that public interest consideration, including the level of protection should be the *domaine réservé* of States and accordingly, adjudicators seized under the CETA should observe deference when reviewing regulatory choices of the Contracting Parties. The envisaged tribunals should not question the level of protection of any public interest reflected in measures limiting a Canadian investor's freedom to conduct business. The Court is providing guidance on the future implementation of the agreement. To some extent, the Court tries to determine how international law should be read, which is actually beyond the Court's own jurisdiction. In Opinion 1/17, the Court is going a step further as it usually does when assessing the compatibility of international agreements. Usually, the principle of autonomy constrains an international tribunal not to discuss questions of EU law. Here, the Court seeks to limit how ICS tribunals would apply *international law*. According to Marise Cremona, the Court expanded the notion of an "envisaged agreement" to include how the parties envisage its implementation, as expressed through political statements.[351] She underlined that the prior nature of Article 218(11) TFEU review renders some degree of looking forward inevitable, especially since, often, not every detail of the envisaged agreement will be known. However, the approach taken in Opinion 1/17 is a novelty. The reliance on assurances external to the agreement coupled with specific directions from the Court on the limits of an external tribunal's jurisdiction has the effect of reaching forward, beyond the Opinion procedure, trying to influence the future implementation of the agreement.[352] On the contrary, from a purely EU law perspective, the Court's finding quite clearly means that calling into question the level of protection of public interests would be incompatible with autonomy and unconstitutional. The latter can have quite concrete consequences, such as that an award that calls into question the level of protection of public interests might very well not be enforced within the EU.

4.5.3 *Implications for the EU as a Global Actor*
Despite the short and assumption-based analysis of the Court, its finding has implications for the EU as a global actor within international investment

---

350   Ibid, para 160. Emphasis added.
351   Cremona M, 'The Opinion Procedure under Article 218(11) TFEU: Reflections in the Light of Opinion 1/17' [2020] Europe and the World: A law review, 8–9.
352   Ibid.

governance. Whether they are beneficial to safeguard the right to regulate in the public interests, including SD, shall be addressed here. What can be said is that with Opinion 1/17, the Court engaged in consolidating the EU's investment policy. By finding that the ICS is in compliance with the EU legal order, it confirmed and thus enabled the European Commission in its approaches that are shaping the EU's policy and the EU as a global actor in the field.

A first key issue relates to the implications for the EU as a global actor from an international law perspective and the current transformation endeavours of the IIA regime. Given that the right to regulate and regulatory autonomy of host State is one of the key aspects of the reform, it seems that the Court took a pro-active move to safeguard the policy space of the EU legislator when adopting public interest measure and setting levels of protection. The Court's approach towards regulatory autonomy is *a priori* positive since it fosters the basic idea that States have the right to regulate, including to set the levels of protection, which they consider appropriate and necessary. The SDGs and SD implementation require regulation at the national level.[353] Generally, the domestic legislator is closest to the socio-economic needs of its society and environmental imperatives of its territory. Thus, proximity often provides a convincing argument for subsidiarity, i.e. domestic regulation, especially in the field of SD.[354] For the Court, subsidiarity is also required because weighing the different interests at stake—private business interests and broader societal interests—is more legitimately being done at the EU level through democratic processes. The Court fosters the objective to promote and safeguard the States' right to regulate and sought to prescribe how future adjudicators should exercise their discretion. The Court is not trying to pre-define how the different interests would need to be balanced in future cases but states that such balancing is the competence of the EU courts. Arguably, the Court's decision reveals a certain amount of distrust in investment tribunals as not sufficiently taking into account the regulatory choices of host States. At the same time, once direct access is given to foreign investors to claim against measures that potentially violate their protection guarantees, a certain degree of weighing of the interest at stake is inevitable. From an SD perspective, nothing militates in principle against investment tribunals to weigh and ensure that solutions are found where private and public interests are clashing. To the contrary, the global SD agenda considers international adjudicators as forming part of it

---

353 For the linkages between the right to regulate and SD, see Section 2.5.
354 There are, however, exceptions to this statement, namely where international regulation is more beneficial than isolated national action, such as in the field of climate change mitigation.

and being among the actors to implement SD. The legal development of SD depends on international courts and tribunals, including investment arbitration. Therefore, the degree of mistrust of the Court can be seen as an obstacle to the SD evolution and the concept's crystallisation within the international investment law. In order to protect the right to regulate of the EU institutions, the Court decided that it was more appropriate to reduce the discretion of future ICS tribunals. If it occurs nonetheless that an award "calls into question" the EU's choice of the level of protection of public interests, the EU or Member States might not execute the award. The prevailing investor that seeks enforcement might face obstacles to do so at least within the EU. Domestic courts of the EU could invoke that the ICS tribunals either exceeded their jurisdiction or that the ICS award contravenes the public policy of the EU by overstepping the limits formulated by the Court.[355] Such a scenario, undermines the effectiveness of the dispute settlement put in place by the EU and arguably weakens the EU as a global actor if in the end, the investment guarantees and dispute settlement mechanisms remain without effective implementation.

A second relevant question is whether Opinion 1/17 has implications for the EU's position in international investment governance. In the past, the principle of autonomy has served the Court to protect the independence of EU law from international law impacts and to establish the EU as an autonomous global actor.[356] With Opinion 1/17, the Court tries to do a balancing act between allowing the EU to submit itself to the ICS, whilst at the same insulating the EU's democracy and regulatory choices from the (potential) interference of investment tribunals.[357] The Court imposes itself as the guardian, not only of the EU's constitutional order but likewise of its democratic order.[358] Taking aspects of democracy into account in the field of external relations of the EU is *a priori* a positive development. One the one hand, the Court replies to the concerns expressed by the general public in Europe requiring more democratic control of comprehensive trade and investment agreements. On

---

355 Reinisch A, 'Will the EU's Proposal Concerning an Investment Court System for CETA and TTIP Lead to Enforceable Awards?—The Limits of Modifying the ICSID Convention and the Nature of Investment Arbitration' (2016) 19 (4) Journal of International Economic Law 761. August Reinisch suggests that for the purpose of ICS award enforcement, it is important that these awards are qualified awards under the New York Convention.
356 Eckes, above note 294, 3–4.
357 Opinion 1/17, Opinion of Advocate General Bot, above note 211, para 174: "[…] in such a way as to maintain the specific characteristics of EU law but also to ensure the European Union's involvement in the development of international law and of a rules-based international legal order".
358 Flavier, above note 344.

the other hand, the Court gives effect to the values and objectives enshrined in the EU treaties and which are to be taken into account in all EU external action according to Article 21 TEU.[359] Following the reasoning of Opinion 1/17, democratic choices within the EU include setting the level of protection of public interest by the EU institutions. It would certainly undermine the EU's credibility at the international scene, if the EU has set itself the task of promoting democracy as well as high levels of protection for SD matters and not include the same objectives concerning the internal effects of the agreements it concludes.

However, one should not overlook that Article 21 TEU also contains the objective to promote the development of international law.[360] This mention in the EU treaties should in principle foster the EU's openness towards international law. The weighing of the different objectives contained in Article 21 TEU is part of the discretion enjoyed by all EU institutions, including the CJEU. In Opinion 1/17, the Court gave particular weight to the concerns of regulatory autonomy and the EU's democratic order. The Court, therefore, could argue that a decision of an international tribunal compelling the EU to comply with international law would undermine its constitutional order when it calls into question the level of protection of public interest. Even though investment tribunals have in the past been reluctant to call such choices into question and more openness towards international law would not be as dramatic as suggested by the Court. Addressing risks on the EU's democratic order appears as an easing of those voices that consider ISDS as a threat to the levels of protection in Europe. The Court's approval of the ICS and the simultaneously evoked limitations of the discretionary powers of ICS adjudicators shows that the Court is enabling the policy agenda of the EU intuitions, mainly of the European Commission.

Indeed, the policy dimension of Opinion 1/17 should not be overlooked as a number of political factors were present when the Court had to decide upon the CETA's compliance with EU primary law. First, the investment policy was marked by Opinion 2/13, in which the Court confirmed the exclusive competence of the EU over FDI but ruled that indirect investment and ISDS are of shared competence. Therefore, EU IIAS are to be adopted as mixed agreements, which arguably weakens the effectiveness of the EU to conclude IIAs.[361] Second, during the proceedings of Opinion 1/17, there was a shared

---

359 TEU, Art 21.2(b): "consolidate and support democracy, the rule of law, human rights and the principles of international law".
360 Ibid. See also, TEU, Art 3(5).
361 See Sections 4.4.2.

position from the Council, the Commission and the majority of intervening Member States to see the ICS as compatible with EU law. Third, the public concerns against ISDS has been an additional factor and the judges certainly were aware that the outcome of the Opinion and its take on regulatory autonomy will be closely observed by the wider public. Fourth, finding the ICS incompatible with the EU treaties would have considerably weakened the EU as an actor in the ongoing negotiation on a multilateral investment court (MIC) at UNCITRAL. Especially since the EU is among the most active actors in the process and one of its main drivers. Finally, over the past years, ISDS has become a powerful system with important financial interests involved. The EU entered international investment governance when the *acquis* of investors' prerogatives was already well-established. The EU's position is namely different than it is in the human rights context under the ECHR.[362] As for ISDS, it seems that the EU has the limited choice of participating with the possibility to modernise the system.

Consequently, finding that the ICS was not compatible with EU primary law, would have had far-reaching consequences for the EU and its investment policy. The factors reveal the extent to which the Court's legal analysis was influenced by the political agenda of the European Commission (and most Member States), which is to have an ISDS mechanism and investment protection standards in new-generation trade and investment agreements that are to some extent modernised. At the same time, the Court had to formulate limits of the ICS concerning the regulatory autonomy of the EU and its capacity to regulate matters of public interest. Thus, the Court found that the modernisation of international investment law cannot undermine the EU constitutional framework. For future IIAs, the opinion reiterates that the EU must not conclude an investment protection agreement that falls short in safeguarding the right to regulate in SD matters, including the choice of the level of protection for public interests.[363]

4.6   Concluding Remarks

This chapter addressed numerous aspects of the EU's international investment policy, ranging from constitutional to institutional and substantive law

---

[362] In comparison, the EU's position in the Council of Europe and ECHR is different. The EU is the most dominant actor within the framework of the Council of Europe. All EU Member States are members of the Council of Europe.

[363] The Court quite closely follows the Commission, see Section 4.3.3.

aspects. It revealed the complex legal and political framework in which the EU has to shape and operationalise its investment policy. The analysis focussed on the implications of SD as a general objective that forms an integral part of the CCP. The key argument made is that from a constitutional law perspective, SD impacts the core of the traditional economic liberalisation orientation of the CCP arguing that SD should be the ultimate goal of the policy, and trade and investment liberalisation is a means to achieve it.

The EU is vested with the competence to conclude IIAs that include all aspects of international investment law, namely investment protection and a mechanism for direct investor-State dispute settlement as well as TSD chapters that contain certain non-economic aspects. EU IIAs are characterised by a strong focus on investment liberalisations commitments based on pre-Lisbon EU IIA practice. Whilst the competence shift enabled the EU to play a more vital role in international investment law than before the Lisbon Treaty, in practical terms, the EU is still facing legal and political obstacles due to the fact that important aspects of IIAs, such as non-direct investment and investor-State dispute settlement, are of shared competences between the EU and its Member States. For SD, however, the EU disposes of exclusive competence on trade-related SD matters, such as TSD chapters. Through Opinion 2/15, SD has gained in centrality within the CCP. The scope of the CCP with respect to non-economic aspects has been broadened. The Court's reasoning illustrates that the general objectives and especially SD, which apply to the CCP can broaden the examination of the "specific link" and the "effects" on trade criteria and thereby stretch the scope of the CCP. From an EU constitutional law perspective, the reasoning might be troublesome, the chapter has also argued that the Court's approach enables integrating SD within the CCP, by making it an "integral part" of it.

As a general objective of EU external action, SD is binding in nature. Its implementation is the task of the EU institutions. The particularity of Article 21 TEU is that it comes with a whole set of general objectives and in principle and all of them apply to the CCP. Hence, the question of how the different objectives interact with each other is inevitable. One conclusion that can be made is that SD absorbs many of the principle and objectives contained in Article 21 TEU and also Article 3(5) TEU. For instance, the objectives of "fair trade", the "eradication of poverty", the preservation and improvement of the quality of the environment and also aspects of good governance and the rule of law. The absorbing effects of SD lie in the broad nature and the very essence of SD to be a concept that connects three main pillars that are otherwise isolated from each other. Thereby, it contains sub-goals seeking to achieve social development, economic development and environmental sustainability. The current SDGs reflect very well the sub-goals of SD as a whole. Article 21 TEU as a general welfare promoting provision bears considerable overlaps with the SDGS. Thus, SD streamlines the set of general objectives applicable to the CCP. Broader social and environmental goals, concerns and interests must now be integrated whilst at the same time allowing economic interests to still come into play.

General objectives have another critical component. They apply to various EU (external) policies. For the CCP, this means that it has the same general objectives than, for instance, EU external environmental policy. In this respect, SD deploys in the EU legal order its trans-policy character. The benefits thereof are that specific legal principles that originate from one policy can migrate to another. For instance, this mean that principles such as precaution can find relevance and application in trade and investment agreements.[364] From this perspective also, SD is capable of fostering coherence between the CCP and other EU policies. For instance, Article 21 TEU requires to encourage "the integration of all countries into the world economy" and the eradication of poverty. Both objectives are *a priori* key goals of the EU's development cooperation that seeks to support developing countries. Considering the coherence that derives from the same SD objective, measures taken under the CCP should also integrate these objectives, or at the very least CCP measure should not undermine these goals. As a result, the exercise of the CCP competence has become more complex in light of the general objectives since more and broader issues have to be taken into account by policy-makers. At the same time, the applicability of the general objectives renders the CCP a more balanced and less isolated policy.

Opinion 2/15 reiterated the obligation for the EU institutions to integrate SD into EU trade and investment agreements. It has been demonstrated in Chapter 3 of the present book that Union objectives are binding but come with considerable discretion for the institutions on how to implement them. This is the same as far as SD within the CCP is concerned. Based on the integration requirement and as emphasised by the Court in Opinion 2/13, the EU institutions have to undertake social and environmental integration when adopting measures under the CCP. Whilst this is a discernible mandate, it does not foresee how the provisions of an EU IIA are to be drafted. Therefore, the European Commission has adopted key policy instruments to set out the post-Lisbon trade agenda that integrates several concrete ideas of SD integration. It includes TSD chapters that set out minimum levels of social and

---

[364] Consider Section 5.1.3.

environmental standards, commitments not to lower SD standards to attract foreign investment, and promote a high level of SD protection within the contracting parties. SD integration also concerns concrete topics that are highly relevant for SD, such as human rights, the fight against corruption and climate change mitigations. These approaches mirror many of the ideas discussed at the international law level and are currently being implemented by other States and regions. In the context of the SD-investment nexus, soft law instruments and policy documents are of great importance to define the contours and current understanding thereof.

Another central aspect of post-Lisbon investment law-making is to ensure that the right to regulate of the EU and its Member States is preserved in all its IIAs. Opinion 1/17 reiterated that an international agreement concluded by the EU would constitute an unacceptable impairment of the autonomy of the Union legal order if it establishes a judicial body that has the jurisdiction to control the choice of the level of protection of public interests decided within the EU in the democratic process. Yet in Opinion 1/17, the Court was satisfied that the CETA's built-in safeguards ensure the operation of the institutions in accordance with the EU constitutional framework. Unlike in previous case law on autonomy, the Court was not concerned with the application and interpretation of EU law but with its control based on international law standards.

In conclusion, the EU as an international actor in international investment governance, comes with a complex and comprehensive legal framework that shapes its way of action. The Court has so far not provided further guidance on how SD integration should be performed in IIAs. The EU institutions elaborate the trade and investment strategies and targets when negotiating IIAs with third countries. The next chapters analyse how the EU operates SD integration in its IIAs and whether the EU lives up to its legal and policy ambitions. The EU approaches are then also compared to those of other States and actors, revealing the extent to which the EU engages with the ongoing debate on how to transform international investment law and governance.

PART 2

Legal Effects of SD and the Emerging Transformation of International Investment Law and Governance

∴

CHAPTER 5

The Integration of Sustainable Development through Regulatory Linkages between Investment, Labour Standards and Environmental Protection under EU IIAS

The previous chapters have shown that an increasingly well-developed normative framework on SD and international investment law exists. It has been found that SD integration has different functions, namely that IIAs can be a suitable means to promote investments that are advancing SD, that IIAs should not undermine but support SD-advancing laws and regulations at the domestic level, and finally, that IIAs can enhance international cooperation on SD.[1] The EU is legally bound to integrate SD into its CCP and according to the European Commission, one of the goals of EU IIAs is "to maximise the potential of increased trade and investment to decent work and to environmental protection".[2] Hence, SD should impact how EU IIAs are drafted and how the EU shapes its investment policy and law-making. In the present chapter, the analysis now turns to the law-making of the EU and examines concrete IIAs provisions. The focus is on how the EU uses its SD objective and strategies to create regulatory linkages between investment, labour standards and environmental protection and how EU IIAs contribute to the international cooperation on SD.

The key approach of the EU consists of integrating a specific chapter on SD in comprehensive trade and investment agreements, mostly entitled "Trade and Sustainable Development". This EU practice, started in 2009 with the EU-South Korea FTA, which was the first EU IIA that contained a specific chapter on SD. The earlier EPA with the CARIFORUM States contained similar provisions than those subsequently incorporated in the TSD chapter of the FTA with Korea, but the agreement itself does not have a specific TSD chapter.[3] Today, the inclusion of TSD chapters constitute a critical part in the "value-based" trade and investment agenda of the European Commission.[4] The CJEU, in

---

1 See, Section 2.3.
2 European Commission Communication, 'Trade for All Towards a more responsible trade and investment policy', (hereafter: 'Trade for All'), COM (2015) 497 final, 17.
3 The EU-CARIFORUM EPA contains, however, a chapter on trade and environment.
4 European Commission, 'Trade for All', above note 2, 17.

Opinion 2/15 has stressed that the TSD chapter contained in the EU-Singapore FTA "plays an essential role" in the said agreement.[5] Overall, TSD chapters contain various commitments to cooperate, to exchange information and to take account of scientific information, as well as the obligation for the EU and its partner countries, to implement effectively the principles concerning the fundamental rights at work and the obligations deriving from the multilateral environmental agreements to which they are a party.

From an international investment governance perspective, TSD chapters are highly interesting as they are an example of explicit SD integration containing several clauses that have the purpose of creating trade/investment-SD regulatory linkages. Are the TSD chapters of the EU becoming the blueprint for the cooperation on trade and investment related SD promotion and cooperation? In order to situate the EU IIA practice, two benchmarks are used. The first benchmark derives from the international normative framework of SD. International legal principles, soft law and current developments concerning SD create legal obligations and expectations that the EU should not ignore. In the international comparison, it is especially the United States and Canada that have through the NAFTA treaty experience of combining investment with labour and environmental protection.[6] The second benchmark arises from the EU's constitutional framework. The focus here is whether the EU lives up to its own self-imposed obligations and expectations that are based on EU primary law.[7] It might be convenient to recall that the present book is not about the best ways to achieve SD through IIAs from a normative standpoint. Instead, it is interested in how investment governance is developing as regards SD integration.[8] For most of the explicit SD clauses, there are no conclusive answers

---

5 ECJ, Opinion 2/15 *Free Trade Agreement with Singapore*, EU:C:2017:376, para 162: "Indeed, [the SD] Chapter plays an essential role in the envisaged agreement".

6 US and Canadian treaty practice have for a long time created inter-linkages between trade/investment on the one hand, and labour and environmental protection, on the other hand. In the context of NAFTA, labour and environmental cooperation issues are dealt with in side-agreements that are attached to the FTA, see North American Agreement on Environmental Cooperation (NAAEC) and North American Agreement on Labor Cooperation (NAALC). See also, NAFTA, Art 1114. Subsequent US FTAs, such as the CPTPP, typically include one chapter on the environment, and one chapter on labour, See eg, US-Chile FTA; US-Oman FTA; US-Colombia FTA, US-Korea FTA; and CPTPP. See also USMCA, Ch 23 and 24. Canada, in contrast, maintained for some of its FTAs the approach of adopting side agreements on the environment and labour. See eg, Canada-Chile FTA; Canada-Colombia FTA; Canada-Jordan FTA; Canada-Panama FTA.

7 European Commission, 'Trade for all', above note 2, 15: "EU has been leading in integrating sustainable development objectives into trade policy and making trade an effective tool to promote sustainable development worldwide."

8 For the methodology of the present study, see Chapter 1.

on their effectiveness. This is due to the fact that they are novel and have not been sufficiently tested. To explain the underlying rationale of global actors for adopting or not adopting certain treaty approaches, occasionally, the analysis has to delve into the debate and the controversies at stake.

In this regard, Chapter 5 starts by looking at how the EU, through its IIAs, sets out a level-playing field for investment in the context of SD. It then analyses the institutional and procedural arrangements that seek to ensure the respect of the SD clauses and foresee the involvement of civil society in the monitoring of trade and investment agreements. The analysis also examines the additional and innovative fields of cooperation on linkages of SD and investment, such as climate change mitigation or the fight against corruption, and how and to what extent EU IIAs foster foreign investors' responsibilities. Lastly, the instrument of Sustainability Impact Assessments (SIAs) in the negotiation phase is discussed.

5.1 Establishing a Level Playing Field for Investment in the Context of SD

The EU has an overall objective to ensure a level playing field for investment in the context of SD in its IIAs. First, the agreements' aim in general, is to ensure that trade and investment contribute to SD. Second, they seek to avoid a "race to the bottom" through selectively weakening domestic labour or environmental protections. Third, EU IIAs aim to strengthen the multilateral governance and standards on labour (ILO) and the environment (MEAs) thereby avoiding a parallel set of bilateral rules on these issues. Lastly, EU IIAs seek to ensure the parties' commitment to a high level of protection. To these ends, a set of different provisions in EU IIAs are designed to ensure that international investment does not lead to a lowering of environmental and labour standards but, instead, to their promotion and elevation. The interaction between these provisions is not straightforward. The EU and its partners do not seek regulatory integration or harmonisation of their respective social and environmental laws and standards.[9] Yet each of the clauses limits or at least impacts on the contracting parties' right to regulate in environmental and labour matters.[10]

---

9 Eg EUSFTA, Art 12.1(4) in fine: "In light of the specific circumstances of each Party, it is not their intention to harmonise the labour and environment standards of the Parties".
10 Marín Durán G, 'Sustainable Development Chapters in EU Free Trade Agreements: Emerging Compliance Issues' [2020] Common Market Law Review 1031, 1036.

5.1.1 *Non-Lowering of Standards Clauses*

A first type of labour- and environment-related provisions contained in EU IIAs are those which aim to prevent unfair competitive advantages between the contracting parties. Such advantages can occur if low or lowered labour or environmental standards are used to keep or to attract investment.[11] "Non-lowering of standards" clauses aim to suppress the temptation of host States to lower their environmental and labour standards as an incentive to attract foreign investment. Such a prohibition on lower environmental and social standards will obviate a "race to the bottom" with respect to SD regulation.[12] The typical formulation of these provisions in EU IIAs, which are mostly entitled "Upholding Levels of Protection", is the following:

1. The Parties stress that weakening the levels of protection in environmental or labour areas is detrimental to the objectives of this Chapter and that it is inappropriate to encourage trade and investment by weakening the levels of protection afforded in domestic environmental or labour law.
2. A Party shall not waive or derogate from, or offer to waive or derogate from, its environmental or labour laws, in a manner affecting trade and investment between the Parties.
3. A Party shall not, through a sustained or recurring course of action or inaction, fail to effectively enforce its environmental and labour laws, as an encouragement for trade and investment.[13]

The "non-lowering standards clauses" are drafted in a mandatory language. Both, the EU and its partners are prohibited to "to weaken or reduce" environmental and labour protection standards as a means to encourage trade

---

11 Marín Durán G, 'The Role of the EU in Shaping the Trade and Environment Regulatory Nexus: Multilateral and Regional Approaches' in: Van Vooren B, Blockmans S and Wouters J (eds), *The EU's Role in Global Governance: The Legal Dimension* (Oxford University Press 2013) 226.

12 The underlying assumption in this regard is that, under free trade, firms will migrate to countries where environmental and labour regulations are less stringent because using cheaper production and processing methods will give them a competitive edge; see OECD, 'Environment and Regional Trade Agreements' (OECD Publishing 2007) 110–111.

13 Eg EUVFTA, Art 13.3. For a different formulation see CETA (on labour) Art 23.4:
    1. The Parties recognise that it is inappropriate to encourage trade or investment by weakening or reducing the levels of protection afforded in their labour law and standards.
    2. A Party shall not waive or otherwise derogate from, or offer to waive or otherwise derogate from, its labour law and standards, to encourage trade or the establishment, acquisition, expansion or retention of an investment in its territory.
    3. A Party shall not, through a sustained or recurring course of action or inaction, fail to effectively enforce its labour law and standards to encourage trade or investment.

and investment.[14] The clauses contain a threefold commitment: a general statement in which the parties recognise that lowering labour and environmental standards to encourage trade or investment is inappropriate (1);[15] an obligation not to waive, to derogate or to offer to waive labour and environmental standards (2);[16] and third the obligation not to fail to effectively enforce domestic labour and environmental laws (3).[17] The first commitment is a 'best-endeavour' formulation setting out the general understanding of the contracting parties on this issue and inviting them not to lower standards, as this would be "inappropriate".[18] The two following commitments are the central ones and are clearly written in a binding way. Additionally, and only with respect to labour standards, EU IIAs contain a statement in which the parties "recognise that the violation of fundamental principles and rights at work cannot be invoked or otherwise used as a legitimate comparative advantage and that labour standards should not be used for protectionist trade purposes".[19]

It is important to note that EU practice with respect to the non-lowering of standards clauses is not uniform. The main difference between the formulations of these provisions, having important practical implications, is that some of the clauses prohibit derogations if they are made "in order to encourage trade or investment".[20] Other clauses in EU IIAs prohibit derogations that are made "in a manner affecting trade and investment between the Parties".[21] In other words, some EU IIAs contain a subjective condition pointing to the motivation behind the derogation and some EU IIAs provide for a somewhat objective condition looking at the effects of the measure. However, a major difficulty remains that one has to prove not only that there has been a weakening of environmental and labour standards, but also that this has been done with the intention to encourage trade and/or investment; or that the derogation is affecting trade and investment between the parties.

---

14   CETA, Arts 23.4 and 24.5; EUKFTA, Art 13.7; EUSFTA, Art 12.1(3); EUVFTA, Art 13.3.
15   CETA, Arts 23.4(1) and 24.5(1); see also, EUVFTA, Art 13.3(1).
16   CETA, Arts 23.4(2) and 24.5(2); see also, EUSFTA, Art 12.12(1); EUVFTA, Art 13.3(2).
17   CETA, Arts 23.4(3) and 24.5(3); see also, EUSFTA, Art 12.12(2); EUVFTA, Art 13.3(3).
18   In the FTAs with Mexico and Mercosur, one can also find that parties "should" not weaken the levels of protection. See, EUMFTA, TSD chapter, Art 2(3); EUMERFTA, TSD chapter, Art 2(3).
19   EUMFTA, TSD chapter, Art 3(7); EUVFTA, Art 13.4(4). For a different formulation, see EUSFTA, Art 12.1(3).
20   Eg EUMFTA, TSD chapter, Art 2(3–5).
21   Eg EUSFTA, Art 12.12. Combinations even exist, see EUVFTA, Art 13.3(2–3); see also TTIP Proposal, TSD chapter, Art 17: "[…] in order to encourage, or in a manner affecting, trade or investment". The TTIP proposal is available at <http://trade.ec.europa.eu/doclib/docs/2015/september/tradoc_153807.pdf>.

In light of IIA practice, non-lowering of standards clauses are part of those provisions that became relatively common when treaty partners decided to integrate labour- and environment-related provisions into investment agreements.[22] Treaty practice varies with respect to the degree of bindingness of the provisions. A number of international actors, including Canada, prefer best-efforts formulations (only) stating that the parties recognise that the lowering of standards is inappropriate.[23] US treaty practice started with the non-binding formulation contained in NAFTA.[24] In subsequent agreements concluded by the United States, the clauses were then drafted in a binding way and specifically prohibited contracting parties from waiving or derogating from its national environmental and labour laws.[25] African instruments mainly contain binding non-lowering clauses stating that a relaxation of domestic environmental and labour legislation in order to attract investments is prohibited.[26] Surprisingly, the Morocco-Nigeria BIT only contains a best-efforts provision and only with respect to labour standards.[27] Overall, non-lowering of standards clauses became a tool for developed and developing countries likewise to address risks of "race to the bottom".

With respect to the subjective or objective qualifier as to when derogation is prohibited, it is also interesting to cast a glance on the approaches of other international actors. US IIAs generally provide that it is prohibited to waive, derogate, or fail to enforce labour and environmental protection "in a manner

---

22   Gordon K and Pohl J, 'Environmental Concerns in International Investment Agreements: A Survey', OECD Working Papers on International Investment (OECD Publishing 2011) 7. The origin of these clauses is the NAFTA, Art 1114.2.

23   2004 Canadian Model BIT, Art 11; See also Austrian Model BIT, Art 4; Japan-Iraq BIT, Art 22.

24   NAFTA, Art 1114.2: "The Parties recognize that it is inappropriate to encourage investment by relaxing domestic health, safety or environmental measures. Accordingly, a Party should not waive or otherwise derogate from, or offer to waive or otherwise derogate from, such measures as an encouragement for the establishment, acquisition, expansion or retention in its territory of an investment of an investor […]."

25   2012 US Model BIT, Arts 12 and 13. For the US approach with respect to FTAs, it is interesting to note that the non-lowering of standards clause is in the investment chapter under NAFTA, but has then moved in subsequent US FTAs into the chapter on environment/the chapter on labour referring to both, trade and investment. See also, Canadian Model BIT, Art 11 and Switzerland-Mexico BIT, Art 3.

26   PAIC, Art 37.1. The PAIC also sets out the obligation for African Union Member States not to relax their domestic labour legislation as an encouragement for the establishment, maintenance or expansion of an investment in its territory. See also SADC Model BIT, Art 22.2.

27   Morocco-Nigeria BIT, Art 15(3).

affecting trade or investment between the Parties".[28] The United States thus more clearly opts for the objective assessment looking on whether a distortion of investment between the parties has occurred.[29] Conversely, Canada links the non-lowering clauses to the States' intent, which explains why this approach found its way into CETA.[30] The same approach has also been adopted in African instruments. It is difficult to state whether an objective assessment is preferable to a subjective assessment, because both approaches bear practical difficulties: it is difficult to prove the intent of the State and it is also difficult to establish actual economic effects of legislative changes.[31] Relying on State intent has been criticised because derogations based on a different motivation but having investment-encouraging effects would remain permissible. The US approach has also been criticised for overly limiting the benefits of non-lowering of standards clauses, rendering countries' obligations to protect labour and environmental rights meaningless.[32] The effectiveness of non-lowering of standards clauses to a large extent depends on how they can be enforced. Therefore, the question on whether the EU's approach is more beneficial for SD integration needs to be tested at the enforcement stage. This issue is further discussed hereafter.[33]

From the EU's point of view, non-lowering of standards clauses are part of the EU's array of articles to integrate SD. Written in a binding way, these clauses should effectively avoid that contracting parties derogate from their domestic levels of protection.[34] It has been argued that the EU includes these

---

28 2012 US Model BIT, Arts 12 and 13. DR-CAFTA, Art 16.2.1(a) "A Party shall not fail to effectively enforce its labor laws, through a sustained or recurring course of action or inaction, in a *manner affecting trade* between the Parties, after the date of entry into force of this Agreement." Emphasis added.

29 The US formulation has been incorporated into CPTPP. See CPTPP, Art 19.5(1) regarding labour and Art 20.3(4) regarding the environment.

30 2004 Canadian Model BIT, Art 11: "[...] not waive or otherwise derogate from, or offer to waive or otherwise derogate from, such measures as an encouragement for the establishment, acquisition, expansion or retention in its territory of an investment of an investor".

31 Gött H and Holterhus TP, 'Mainstreaming Investment-Labour Linkage Through "Mega-Regional" Trade Agreements' in: Gött H (ed), *Labour Standards in International Economic Law* (Springer International Publishing 2018) 245–6.

32 Polanski S, 'Twenty Years of Progress at Risk—Labor and Environmental Protections in Trade Agreements', GEGI Policy Brief No 4, 10/2017.

33 Under EU IIAs, if a contracting party considers that the other contracting party has engaged in environmental or social dumping to attract foreign investment, it can start a consultative enforcement mechanism; see below Section 5.2.2.

34 Prislan V and Zandvliet R, 'Labor Provisions in International Investment Agreements: Prospects for Sustainable Development' Grotius Centre Working Paper 2013/003/IEL, 24.

clauses not predominantly for their SD purposes but rather for the purpose of fair competition among States by maintaining a certain level of protection.[35] However, even if these clauses' rationale are competitiveness considerations, the EU explicitly referred to this approach in its SD strategy and sees these clauses to have a positive impact on national environmental protection and respect of labour standards in the EU and globally.[36]

5.1.2   *Implementation of International Standards*

Next to the non-lowering of standards clauses, EU IIAS also contain provisions that seek to promote respect for international standards and rules on environmental protection and labour rights. Typically, the EU and its contracting partners "reaffirm their commitment to effectively implement" international standards.[37] These provisions seek, on the one hand, to maintain a minimum-level of commitments in social and environmental matters, and on the other hand, they seek to further the take-ups and effective implementation of existing international labour and environmental regime.[38] Namely, they do no seek to establish a parallel system of normative SD standards. As the CJEU stated in Opinion 2/15, this type of provision has the purpose to essentially ensure that trade and investment between the contracting parties "take place in compliance with the obligations that stem from the international agreements concerning social protection of workers and environmental protection to which they are party".[39] For the sake of clarity, it is convenient to distinguish here between the international commitments in the field of environmental protection and those on labour rights.

---

[35]   Marín Durán G, 'Innovations and Implications of the Trade and Sustainable Development Chapter in the EU–Korea Free Trade Agreement' in: Harrison J (ed), *The European Union and South Korea* (Edinburgh University Press 2013); Marín Durán G, 'The Role of the EU in Shaping the Trade and Environment Regulatory Nexus: Multilateral and Regional Approaches', in: Van Vooren B, Blockmans S and Wouters J (eds), *The EU's Role in Global Governance: The Legal Dimension* (Oxford University Press 2013) 236. The author considers the economic competitiveness considerations as the main rationale behind TSD chapters. See also, Gött and Holterhus, above note 31, 247.

[36]   See Section 4.3.3.

[37]   Eg EUVFTA, Art 13.4(2) (for labour) and Art 13.5(2) (for environment). A different formulation can be found in the FTA with Mexico, ie "shall effectively implement", see EUMFTA, TSD chapter, Art 4(2) (for environment).

[38]   Marín Durán, above note 10, 1038.

[39]   Opinion 2/15, above note 5, para 152.

5.1.2.1 International Labour Standards

A characteristic of EU IIA practice, concerning international labour standards is to enumerate the relevant commitments and instruments.[40] An instrument that is constantly mentioned is the ILO's 1998 Declaration on Fundamental Principles and Rights at Work and its Follow-up (hereafter: ILO Declaration).[41] This instrument is one of the most important ILO instruments as it sets out the four basic rights at work, which are restated in the EU IIAs.[42] In addition, EU IIAs mostly include a reaffirmation of the parties' commitment to implement the eight ILO Fundamental Conventions that the parties have ratified.[43] If a contracting party has not yet ratified all eight conventions an additional sentence requires them to "make continued and sustained efforts" towards the ratification of the remaining ones.[44] There is no formal obligation to ratify these conventions, but partners are strongly encouraged to do so.[45] For instance, during the negotiations of CETA, as Canada ratified the last two ILO Convention, something which the country had not yet done.[46] Finally, most of the EU IIAs restate the parties' obligations as a member of the ILO to further emphasise the partner countries' commitments to international labour protection.[47]

40　CETA, Arts 23.3; EUJFTA, Art 16.3; EUMFTA, TSD chapter, Art 3, EUSFTA, Art 12.3; EUVFTA, Art 13.4.

41　ILO, Declaration on Social Justice for a Fair Globalisation adopted by the International Labour Conference at its Ninety-seventh Session, Geneva, 10 June 2008.

42　EUVFTA, Art 13.4(2); EUSFTA, Art 12.3; EUJFTA, Art 16.3(2). The four basic principles are workers' freedom of association, the abolition of forced labour and of child labour as well as workplace-related discrimination.

43　The eight Fundamental ILO Conventions are: (1) Convention Concerning Forced or Compulsory Labour No 29 [1930]; (2) Equal Remuneration Convention No 100 [1951]; (3) Convention Concerning the Abolition of Forced Labour No 105 [1957]; (4) Freedom of Association and Protection of the Rights to Organise Convention No 87 [1948]; (5) Right to Organise and Collective Bargaining Convention No 98 [1949]; (6) Discrimination (Employment and Occupation) Convention No 111 [1958]; (8) Minimum Working Age Convention No 138 [1973]; (8) Worst Forms of Child Labour Convention No 182 [1999]. See also Section 2.2.2.2.

44　CETA, Art 23.3(4).

45　EUMFTA, TSD chapter, Art 3.4: "Each Party shall make continued and sustained efforts towards ratifying the fundamental ILO Conventions".

46　In the course of the CETA negotiation, Canada ratified two Fundamental ILO Conventions that it had not ratified before, ie the 1949 ILO Convention No 98 on the Right to Organise and Collective Bargaining Convention (in June 2017) and the 1973 ILO Convention No 138 on Minimum Age (in June 2016).

47　Such obligations comprise inter alia: financial obligations, reporting obligations, obligations to respect the ILO Declaration and the obligation to work for the implementation of the 2008 ILO Declaration on Social Justice for a Fair Globalisation, above note 31.

Even though it is part of the obligations of an ILO member to work for the realisation of the 2008 ILO Declaration on Social Justice for a Fair Globalisation, a number of EU IIAs also restate this instrument.[48] More specifically, Parties commit to promote standards in their domestic legislation that relate to acceptable minimum employment standards, non-discrimination in terms of conditions of work, and occupational safety and health.[49] A further ILO instrument that parties seek to promote under EU IIAs is the Decent Work Agenda.[50] This agenda links the work of ILO with the SDGs and has four key elements: employment creation, social protection, rights at work, and social dialogue. Lastly, requirements are also set out with regard to judicial proceedings for the enforcement of labour laws to be "fair, accessible and transparent".[51]

Referring to the core ILO instruments is a treaty technique that can also be found in other IIAs. Yet, none of the IIAs adopted by other international actors expressly mentions as many instruments as the EU does within its TSD chapters. For instance, the CPTPP only mentions the 2008 ILO Declaration.[52] The US approach, as it has developed since the NAFTA side agreement NAALC, is to focus on national laws.[53] National law-making should be guided by international standards and should (at least) incorporate the four basic principles of the ILO Declaration. Hence, a typical formulation that can be found in agreements concluded by the United States is that parties shall adopt and maintain international labour standards, as stated in the ILO Declaration and its Follow-up.[54] More along the lines of the EU approach is the Morocco-Nigeria BIT, in which the parties also reaffirm their obligations as members of the ILO, as well as their commitments under the ILO Declaration.[55]

The comparison of other treaty practice highlights that only EU IIAs contain a restatement of the commitments under all eight ILO Fundamental Conventions and their eventual ratification. One can question whether to add the ILO Fundamental Conventions is of practical relevance as they address the same set of labour standards than the 1998 ILO Declaration. However, the

---

48 CETA, Art 23.3(2); EUMFTA, TSD chapter, Art 3.8.
49 Ibid.
50 References to the Decent Work Agenda are aspirational; see EUMFTA, TSD chapter, Art 10.2(a); EUJFTA, Art 16.2; EUSFTA, Art 12.3(2).
51 Eg EUMFTA, TSD chapter, Art 3.9.
52 CPTPP, Art 19.3.
53 NAALC does not refer to any instrument of ILO or other international standards. Yet, it foresees general cooperation with ILO (see NAALC, Art 45); and lists core labour principles (see NAALC, annexe 1).
54 US-Korea FTA, Art 19.2.
55 Morocco-Nigeria BIT, Art 15.1.

ILO Declaration's commitments are not only less specific than those under the relevant Conventions; the Declaration, in contrast to the Conventions, is also not directly subject to the ILO supervisory mechanisms that can clarify the instruments' legal meaning.[56] Consequently, the EU's approach to restate and encourage the ratification of the eight ILO Conventions reveals that the EU goes a step further than many other States and global actors in this respect. The stated ambition of the EU is to have a reference to the core labour instruments. In this respect the EU lives up to its goals as the specific references enhance the clarity of the content of the labour standards.[57] Moreover, the EU seeks effective implementation of the standards.[58] At the same time, whilst the incorporation of ILO instruments is in principle a positive feature, most of the international labour law instruments listed in EU IIAs contain vague provisions. And the obligations to implement specific ILO instruments or other standards do not further prescribe the means and procedures to achieve these regulatory goals. Interestingly, the EU-Mercosur FTA includes a commitment for the parties to ensure that administrative and judicial proceedings are available and accessible to permit effective action to be taken against infringements of labour rights.[59] Finally, EU IIAs contain several commitments to long-term dialogue, cooperation and exchange between the contracting parties is foreseen, on a bilateral level as well as within the context of the ILO.[60]

5.1.2.2 Multilateral Environmental Agreements (MEAs)

The EU's approach with respect to multilateral environmental agreements (MEAs) is different from the one concerning international labour law. EU IIAs do not, in general, enumerate specific MEAs but make a general statement that "each Party shall effectively implement the MEAs, protocols and amendments to which it is a party".[61]

The question of which MEAs are relevant in this context therefore automatically comes up. The EU-Colombia/Peru FTA, which constitutes an exception

---

56   Ebert FC, 'The Comprehensive Economic and Trade Agreement (CETA): Are Existing Arrangements Sufficient to Prevent Adverse Effects on Labour Standards?' 2 (2017) International Journal of Comparative Labour Law and Industrial Relations 33, 304.
57   Ibid, 304–305.
58   European Commission, 'Trade for all', above note 2, 17.
59   EUMERFTA, TSD chapter, Art 4.11.
60   Eg EUMFTA, TSD chapter, Art 3.6; EUMERFTA, TSD chapter, Art 4.1.
61   CETA, Art 24.4(2); EUMFTA, TSD chapter, Art 4(2). The FTA with Mexico adds the importance of the international environmental governance, namely through the United Nations Environment Assembly (UNEA) and the United Nations Environment Programme (UNEP).

for EU IIA practice contains an exhaustive list referring to eight instruments that the parties considered relevant in this context, such as: the Montreal Protocol on Substances that Deplete the Ozone Layer, the Basel Convention on the Transboundary Movements of Hazardous Wastes and their Disposal, the Stockholm Convention on Persistent Organic Pollutants, the Convention on International Trade in Endangered Species of Wild Fauna and Flora (CITES), the Convention on Biological Diversity and its Cartagena Protocol, the Kyoto Protocol and the Rotterdam Convention on the Prior Informed Consent Procedure for Certain Hazardous Chemicals and Pesticides in International Trade.[62] Yet, most of the EU IIAs do not list MEAs. Presumably, the reason is that, compared to international labour law, the set of conventions and rules of international environmental law is far more diverse and dispersed. Therefore, EU IIAs are less explicit and refer in more general terms to international environmental law than when making reference to international labour standards. This allows for more flexibility as to which MEAs are relevant for the trade/investment-environment nexus. Recent trends show that this is the approach most international actors adopt. For instance, the CPTPP also contains a general reference to MEAs,[63] and a similar approach can also be found in the Morocco-Nigeria BIT and other IIAs.[64] Conversely, some US FTAs contain enumerations of specific MEAs, with variations cornering the chosen MEAs in each of the treaties.[65]

Moreover, EU IIAs mention an important principle governing the relationship between international trade and environmental law, which is the principle of mutual supportiveness.[66] This principle is interconnected with other principles that seek to mitigate potential legal conflicts, such as the principle of harmonisation, systemic integration as well as the presumption against

---

62 See EU-Colombia/Peru FTA, Arts 268 and 270.
63 CPTPP, Art 20.4.
64 Morocco-Nigeria BIT, Art 13.1; See eg Belgium/Luxembourg-Barbados BIT, Art 11(3); Belgium/Luxembourg-Ethiopia BIT, Art 5(3); Belgium/Luxembourg-Guatemala BIT, Art 13(3); Belgium/Luxembourg-Libya BIT, Art 5(3); Belgium/Luxembourg-Mauritius BIT, Art 5(3). See also Gordon and Pohl, above note 14.
65 US FTAs also provides for a closed, but very different list of MEAs (only including CITES and the Montreal Protocol from the above list in the EU-Colombia/Peru FTA) and other regional environmental agreements, see eg US-Korea FTA, annex 20-A; US-Panama FTA, annex 17.2(1).
66 This principle's emergence can be traced back to the debates on the interplay between trade and environmental obligations. See Boisson de Chazournes L and Mbengue MM, 'A "Footnote as a Principle"—Mutual Supportiveness in an Era of Fragmentation', in: Hestermeyer HP et al, *Coexistence, Cooperation and Solidarity—Liber Amicorum Rüdiger Wolfrum—Vol II* (Martinus Nijhoff Publishers 2011) 1615–1638.

conflicts.67 In this vein, under EU IIAs, contracting parties "stress the need to enhance the mutual supportiveness between trade and environmental policies, rules and measures".68

Compared to other international actors, one finds that US IIAs regularly refer to the principle of mutual supportiveness. Whereas, some of the US FTAs likewise contain best-efforts provisions and a general statement of principle.69 One also finds, in more recent US FTAs provisions that go beyond this.70 These provisions require the contracting parties "to seek to balance [their] obligations" under the FTA and under MEAs in the event of inconsistencies.71 These types of "balancing efforts" under recent US FTAs arguably better resemble the coordinating benefits that mutual supportiveness seeks to promote.72 As a consequence, the EU approach appears to be less precise. Besides US treaty practice, the principle of mutual supportiveness has not yet found widespread recognition in other IIAs, a circumstance that might lie within the trade origin of the principle. From an EU law and policy perspective, the synergies that EU IIAs are seeking to achieve by mentioning the principle of mutual supportiveness is a welcome feature. SD integration is to a certain extent ensured since the provision seeks to provide for synergies instead of conflicts between the different sets of international law, international economic law and international environmental law. However, the statement made in EU IIAs is quite minimalistic, and the provisions are formulated in a purely programmatic manner making it unclear whether it can truly serve as a tool for conflict resolution. EU IIAs do not provide more guidance as to the commitment to promote mutually supportive solutions even though such synergies between trade and foreign investment on the one hand and environmental protection, on the other hand, are at the heart of the concept of SD.73 At the very least, EU IIAs ensure that future adjudicators are invited to engage with the concept and find

---

67 Potestà M, 'From Mutual Supportiveness to Mutual Enforcement? The Contribution of US Preferential Trade and Investment Agreements to the Effectiveness of Environmental Norms', in: Hofmann R, Schill S and Tams CJ (eds), *Preferential Trade and Investment Agreements: From Recalibration to Reintegration* (Nomos 2013) 175.
68 CETA, Art 24.4(1).
69 DR-CAFTA, Art 17.12: "[...] the Parties shall continue to seek means to enhance the mutual supportiveness of multilateral environmental agreements to which they are party and trade agreements to which they are party".
70 Potestà, above note 67, 176.
71 Eg US FTAs with Peru, Art 18.13(4); Panama, Art 17.13(3); Colombia, Art 18.13(4); and Korea, Art 20.10(3).
72 Potestà, above note 67, 177.
73 Viñuales JE, *Foreign Investment and the Environment in International Law* (Cambridge University Press 2012) 27.

mutually supportive solutions through a reference to the principle of mutual supportiveness.[74]

5.1.3 *Promoting High Levels of Protection*

Under EU IIAs, the non-lowering of standards and the reaffirmation of international commitments are complemented by best-endeavour provisions that seek to ensure that the laws and policies of contracting parties "provide for and encourage high levels of domestic protection in the environmental and social areas".[75] Contracting parties, moreover, "shall continuously endeavour to improve those laws and polices".[76] While the wording of the provisions is hortatory, they seek to impact national law-making on SD matters and promote high levels of protection. The parties' commitment to fostering high protection levels is accompanied by the explicit recognition that each contracting party is free to set its SD priorities and establish its levels of protection.[77] This means that "high" is relative depending on national needs and priorities.

Provisions encouraging parties to adopt high levels of protection are not unique to EU IIAs. Already the NAFTA side-agreements NAAEC and NAALC contain such provisions, which provide that "each Party shall ensure that its laws and regulations provide for high levels of environmental [and labour] protection and shall strive to continue to improve".[78] North American treaty practice continued to include these statements.[79] For labour legislation only, the Morocco-Nigeria BIT also requires the parties to provide for high levels of protection, and add that such protection shall be "appropriate to [the] economic and social situation" of the party in question.[80] The Morocco-Nigeria BIT's provision, moreover, points to an interesting aspect, which is to take into account national particularities that might justify different levels of protection.[81] This stresses the circumstance that developing countries might be

---

74   See *S.D. Myers Inc v Government of Canada*, NAFTA, UNCITRAL, First Partial Award, 13 November 2000, para 247. The tribunal considered that the legal context of NAFTA, Art 1102 included the principle of mutual supportiveness.
75   EUVFTA, Art 13.2(2); see also EUJFTA, Art 16.2(1); EUSFTA Art 12.2(2). See also, CETA, Art 23.2; and Art 24.3.
76   EUVFTA, Art 13.2(2); see also EUJFTA, Art 16.2(1); EUSFTA Art 12.2(2).
77   The provisions on high levels of protection figure in the same article as the reaffirmation of the right to regulate. See CETA, Art 23.2; and Art 24.3, EUVFTA, Art 13.2(1)(b). Eg EUJFTA, Art 16.2(1); EUVFTA, Art 13.2; EUSFTA Art 12.2; EUMFTA, TSD chapter, Art 2.
78   NAAEC, Art 3; NAALC, Art 2 (both provisions are entitled "Levels of protection").
79   CPTPP, Art 20.3(3) (only for the environment).
80   Morocco-Nigeria BIT, Art 15.5.
81   Consider in this respect, Rio Declaration, Principle 11: "States shall enact effective environmental legislation. Environmental standards, management objectives and

cautious to adopt high levels of protection because the socio-economic costs of compliance might be too high or adequate controls and implementation would require additional financial and human resources. Overall, general commitments to high levels of protection are an increasing treaty practice but not yet a common theme contained in IIAs.[82]

From an EU law perspective, the question that comes up in this respect is whether the stated objective of a "high level" of social and environmental protection is beneficial for the right of the parties to regulate in these fields. Given that EU IIAs also recall that each State has the right to regulate and set the level of protection for SD measures, safeguards to a certain extent the regulatory space of the contracting parties.[83] Conversely, a State measure that seeks to increase the SD protection standards could therefore be seen to be consistent with the given IIA.[84] In Opinion 1/17, the CJEU clearly emphasised that the choice of the level of protection of public interest cannot be called into question by an international investment tribunal. Doing so would be contrary to the EU constitutional order.[85] Therefore, it is for the EU fundamental that its IIAs do not undermine EU institutions' ability in setting the level of protection they deem necessary and appropriate.

Finally, EU IIAs contain provisions relating to how new environmental and labour laws should be adopted at the national level. If a contracting party seeks to "adopt or modify" its SD laws and policies it has to be done "in a manner consistent with the internationally recognised standards, and the agreements to which a Party is party" in the field of environmental and labour protection.[86] EU IIAs thus seek to impact on national SD regulation in the sense that they require compliance with existing international labour and environmental regimes. The obligation to ensure "high levels" of environmental and labour protection should, therefore, be read in conjunction with the other provisions

---

priorities should reflect the environmental and developmental context to which they apply. Standards applied by some countries may be inappropriate and of unwarranted economic and social cost to other countries, in particular developing countries". See UN Conference on Environment and Development, 'Rio Declaration on Environment and Development and Agenda 21', [1992] Doc A/CONF.151/26Rev 1.

82 See further, Gordon K, Pohl J and Bouchard M, 'Investment Treaty Law, Sustainable Development and Responsible Business Conduct: A Fact-Finding Survey' (2014) OECD Working Papers on International Investment 2014/01.

83 Reid E, *Balancing Human Rights, Environmental Protection and International Trade: Lessons from the EU Experience* (Hart Pub 2015) 188–189.

84 See Sections 6.1.

85 ECJ, Opinion 1/17 *EU-Canada CET Agreement*, EU:C:2019:341, paras 148 and 151. See Section 4.5.

86 See EUVFTA, Art 13.2(1)(c).

of the TSD chapter, mostly those on the international standards, as they provide guidance.[87] In addition to that, EU IIAs also provide that when contracting parties prepare and implement measures aimed at the protection of human health and safety at work (labour legislation), natural resources or eco-systems (environmental legislation), that "each Party shall take into account existing relevant scientific and technical information and related international standards, guidelines or recommendations".[88] This commitment adds to the objective of high levels of protection, as national laws shall, to the best available way, be in compliance with the latest scientific insights. These provisions encompass the situation in which there is a lack of "full scientific certainty" and threats of serious or irreversible damage to the environment or to occupational safety and health exist.[89] In such cases, contracting parties acknowledge that cost-effective measures, based on the precautionary principle may be adopted.[90] EU IIAs thus add to the right to regulate that labour and environmental legislation can be based on the precautionary principle and shall be consistent with the IIA as a whole. The precautionary principle captures the idea that regulatory intervention may still be legitimate, even if the supporting evidence is incomplete or speculative and the economic costs of regulation are high.

Compared to the practice of other international actors, EU IIAs are yet the only ones to make reference to the principle of precaution. From an EU law perspective, the importance of precaution does not come a surprise. The principle is binding under the EU treaties and among the key principles of EU environmental policy.[91] The fact that EU IIAs add the principle of precaution to the right to regulate needs to be welcomed as the principle is central to SD in that it commits States to avoid economic activity which may cause significant harm to human health, natural resources or eco-systems, including in the face of scientific uncertainty.[92] At the same time, legislation having

---

[87] Marín Durán, above note 35, 131.
[88] CETA, Arts 23.3(3) and 24.9(2); EUMFTA, TSD chapter, Art 11.
[89] Ibid.
[90] See EUMFTA, TSD chapter, Art 11. CETA does not mention the precautionary principle expressively, it is, however, mentioned in the CETA, Joint Interpretative Instrument, para 1(d). See Joint Interpretative Instrument on the Comprehensive Economic and Trade Agreement (CETA) between Canada and the European Union and its Member States, [2017] OJ L 11/3.
[91] TFEU, Art 191(2).
[92] Cordonier Segger M-C and Khalfan A, *Sustainable Development Law Principles, Practices, and Prospects* (Oxford University Press 2004) 101. Consider also, the precautionary principle as fundamental for SD; Rio Declaration, Principle 15: "In order to protect the environment, the precautionary approach shall be widely applied by States according to their

protectionist purposes can arguably more easily disguised in precautionary measures. Therefore, measures based on the principle of precaution require up-to-date and independent scientific judgment and need to be transparent. Conscious of such risks, EU IIAs further provide that contracting parties after having adopted a measure based on the principle of precaution have to subject them to "periodic review in light of new scientific information".[93] The downside of the EU's approach is that the provision lacks to provide how such a review should unfold. It is uncertain whether this implies a review by experts of the State's administration or whether this should bring about the requirement for contracting parties to ensure appropriate review by a judicial body at the national level.[94] In sum, by referring to the precautionary principle, the EU integrated one of the critical environmental law principles under EU law. To better live up to its own ambitions, the EU could have drafted more precise provisions, thereby making precaution more effective in the context of SD regulation at the national level.

5.2 Institutional and Procedural Arrangements

EU IIAs establish special bodies and procedures to monitor the implementation of TSD chapters, which are distinct from the general institutional provisions in comprehensive FTAs. The enforcement of labour and environment provisions is characterised by soft compliance mechanisms, such as monitoring and consultations. This relatively weak enforcement mechanism is one of the main points of criticism of the EU approach. Criticism also exists as regards the effectiveness of civil society involvement. It has been argued that the processes to exchange with civil society have little impacts on national decision-making and on the decisions that are taken in the main treaty bodies of EU trade and investment agreements. As mentioned before, TSD chapters are yet a rare treaty practice in international investment governance. Canada and the United States are currently the only other global actors adopting similar approaches like the EU. However, the practice of all three reveals the practical difficulties of effective SD implementation.

---

capabilities. Where there are threats of serious or irreversible damage, lack of full scientific certainty shall not be used as a reason for postponing cost-effective measures to prevent environmental degradation".
93 Eg EUMFTA, TSD chapter, Art 11.
94 On the need for judicial review for measures based on the precautionary principle, see Cordonier Segger and Khalfan, above note 92, 101.

5.2.1 *Institutional Set-Up*

Under EU IIAs, different bodies are responsible for the monitoring and overseeing the implementation of the TSD chapters. Firstly, most of the comprehensive FTAs concluded by the EU establish specialised committees that deal with specific aspects of the agreement; this includes for each agreement a "Committee on Trade and Sustainable Development" (hereafter: Committee on TSD).[95] The Committees on TSD are inter-governmental bodies. They are composed of senior officials of each party and mostly involve trade experts, and labour and environmental experts.[96] Their main task is to oversee the implementation of the TSD chapter and to guide the contracting parties' further cooperation through, in particular, the realisation of the cooperative activities envisaged in the agreement. The Committees on TSD must meet as regularly as necessary.[97] After each meeting, they are to report to the "Trade Committee".[98] The latter is the main institutional body of a comprehensive FTA, having the power to adopt decisions that are binding upon the contracting parties.

Secondly, since the 2010 EU-Korea Free Trade Agreement, EU IIAs more actively engage with civil society through direct exchanges. To do so, so-called Domestic Advisory Groups (DAGs) are set up in the EU and in the partner country or countries. These DAGs are composed of members of independent civil society organisations and should represent in a balanced manner business organisations, trade unions and environmental and other organisations.[99] To become a member of a DAG within the EU, an organisation should be non-profit, EU-based, an expert in SD as well as duly registered in the civil society dialogue database of the European Commission.[100] The EU establishes a specific DAG for each IIA individually. These EU DAGs are assisted by the European Economic and Social Committee, which serves as their secretariat.

---

95 CETA, Art 26.2(1)(g) and Art 22.4(1); EUVFTA, Art 17.2(1)(e); EUMFTA, TSD chapter, Art 14; The EUSFTA does not have a specialised committee on TSD. Under the EU-Mercosur FTA, such committees are called Sub-Committee, see EUMERFTA, Art 14.
96 Marín Durán, note above 35, 136.
97 Eg EUSFTA, Art 12.15(3).
98 Eg EUVFTA, Art 17.1; also called Joint Committee, see CETA Art 26.1.
99 EU-Central America FTA, Art 294.4: "The Advisory Groups of the Parties shall comprise independent representative organizations, in a balanced representation of economic, social and environmental stakeholders including, among others, employers and workers organizations, business associations, non-governmental organizations and local public authorities".
100 European Commission, Registration for Civil Society Dialogue, available at <http://trade.ec.europa.eu/civilsoc/register.cfm>.

The primary function of the DAGs is to give advice on the implementation of the TSD chapter. Members of a given DAG are to meet several times a year to select and discuss the issues they wish to evaluate. DAGs can report to the specialised Committee on TSD and can thereby express concerns to the intergovernmental body.

Thirdly, another body set-up by the TSD chapters are joint meetings, that are sometimes designated as Civil Society Forums.[101] The function of joint meetings is to find ways through which civil society can best monitor the implementation of the TSD chapter and raise issues of concern in a direct exchange, as well as to build awareness within civil society on matters relevant to SD, such as environmental risk factors and labour standards.[102] Joint meetings gather once a year and express their views on the achievement of SD to the specialised Committee on TSD. However, their designations and their precise composition can vary from one EU IIA to another.[103] A joint meeting can be composed of the DAGs of each contracting party (DAG-to-DAG meeting), which can also involve non-DAG stakeholders.[104] Conversely, joint meetings can also be composed of the relevant DAGs on the one hand, and the intergovernmental body, on the other hand.[105] Within EU treaty practice, there is thus a difference between those meetings that involve government representatives and those that do not.

Compared to other international actors, the EU is a pioneer by including in its comprehensive FTAs, an institutional framework that allows for dialogue between and among civil society organisations. The United States and Canada have started to incorporate fora to engage with civil society in their treaty practice, as can be seen in the CPTPP.[106] However, the North American approach, and in particular the one of the United States, which started with NAALC, is not primarily concerned with dialogue and exchange, but rather on granting interested groups the right to directly file submissions regarding a Party's

---

101   CETA, Art 22.5; EUVFTA, Very important Art 13.15(5) not using this terminology.
102   See eg 'Joint Statement by the Chairs of the Korea DAG and the EU DAG', 6th meeting of the EU-Korea Civil Society Forum under the EU-Korea FTA, 11 April 2018; available at <https://www.eesc.europa.eu/en/agenda/our-events/events/6th-meeting-eu-korea-civil-society-forum-under-eu-korea-free-trade-agreement/documents>.
103   For more detail see, Orbie J, Martens D and Van den Putte L, 'Civil Society Meetings in European Union Trade Agreements: Features, Purposes, and Evaluation', CLEER Working Paper 2016/3, 13–15.
104   Eg EUVFTA, Art 13.15(5).
105   Eg CETA, Art 22.5 in conjunction with Arts 23.8(3) and 24.13.
106   CPTPP, Art 19.14 on "Public Engagement".

commitments or obligations arising under a labour chapter of US FTAs or the NAALC.¹⁰⁷

The European Commission regularly praises the involvement of civil society in EU IIAs. Yet, to live up to its ambitions, the EU's approaches are to be effective.¹⁰⁸ Indeed, the EU approach looks, on paper, well fitted for SD purposes. Nevertheless, their actual implementation and thus *de facto* realisation can be questioned. Much depends on the ways in which these meetings are held and then to what extent their reports have impacts on national decision-making and on decisions taken by the main body under an EU FTA, *i.e.* the Trade Committee.¹⁰⁹ So far no clear evidence exists on the benefits of these mechanisms.¹¹⁰ But even in theory, it is unfortunate that the Committees on TSD have no power of directly issuing recommendations to the contracting parties but have only been attributed with the competence to report back to the Trade Committee on the issues raised concerning the implementation of the TSD chapters. It is not clear, why other specialised committees under comprehensive EU FTAs can issue direct recommendations to the contracting parties, but not the Committees on TSD.¹¹¹ The benefits of recommending SD-relevant measures and adaptation *directly* to the contracting parties would avoid that SD matters are being re-discussed within the Trade Committee before—finally and if ever—become recommendations addressed to the contracting parties. Lastly, the EU is not coherent in its IIAs on the composition of the joint meetings as some agreements foresee the participation of government representatives,¹¹² whilst others do not.¹¹³ EU institutions should be more guided by the objective of coherence and effectiveness. The preferred option arguably then is to have government representatives within the joint meetings because civil society members can then directly express their concerns about

---

107 NAALC, Art 29.2; see also US bilateral FTAs with Jordan, Chile, Singapore, Australia, Morocco, Bahrain, and Oman. See, Oehri M, 'Civil Society Activism under US Free Trade Agreements: The Effects of Actorness on Decent Work' (2017) 5 Politics and Governance 40.
108 European Commission, 'Trade for All', above note 2, 15.
109 Orbie J, Van den Putte L and Martens D, 'Civil Society Meetings in EU Free Trade Agreements: The Purposes Unravelled' in: Gött H (ed), *Labour Standards in International Economic Law* (Springer International Publishing 2018) 140.
110 Ibid, 137.
111 Eg CETA, Art 6.14(4): "The Joint Customs Cooperation Committee may formulate resolutions, recommendations, or opinions and present draft decisions to the CETA Joint Committee that it considers necessary for the attainment of the common objectives and sound functioning of the mechanisms established in this Chapter [...]."
112 Eg CETA, Art 22.5 in conjunction with Arts 23.8(3) and 24.13.
113 Eg EUVFTA, Art 13.15(5).

the implementation of the TSD chapters. Otherwise, the communication line is less direct as their concerns are referred to the inter-governmental body through a written report.[114]

5.2.2 *Enforcement of the Commitments on Labour and the Environment*

The non-lowering of standards clauses and the minimum-level commitments with international SD standards depend upon effective enforcement mechanisms to ensure their respect. More concretely, enforcement is essential, on the one hand, to ensure a level playing field conducive to fair competition with a similar level of environmental and social protection, and on the other hand, to enhance the impact of the commitments on social and environmental protection, which is ultimately beneficial for SD. While the scope of TSD chapters has been considerably expanded since the first TSD chapter, the EU-Korea FTA, arguably enhancing the impact of SD, the EU maintained a "soft" enforcement mechanism, consisting of consultation and dialogue. Furthermore, the dispute settlement procedure under TSD chapters is explicitly excluded from the general State-to-State dispute settlement mechanism under EU FTAS.

5.2.2.1 A Two-Stage Framework for Dispute Resolution

TSD chapters in EU IIAs provide for consultative mechanisms composed of two stages: governmental consultations and the subsequent establishment of a Panel of Experts if consultations fail. Pursuant to this specific mechanism, contracting parties are first held to seek a mutually satisfactory resolution through consultations. The latter can involve the specialised Committee on TSD if one of the parties requests it.[115] Advice can be brought in from the DAGs or joint meetings; and depending on the subject matter it can also involve expert advice coming from international organisations, such as the ILO where matters about the compliance of the ILO Conventions are at stake.[116] If a solution is reached during the first stage of dispute settlement, the consultations' outcome will be made publicly available.[117]

If, however, no solution could be found at the stage of consultations, the interested party can request to convene a Panel of Experts.[118] Such expert

---

114 EUVFTA, Art 13.15(5).
115 Eg CETA Arts 23.9(4) and 24.14(4).
116 Eg mentioning ILO: CETA, Art 23.9(3); EUVFTA, Art 13.16(3); see also CETA Art 24.14(3).
117 Eg CETA Arts 23.9(5) and 24.14(5).
118 See eg Request for the establishment of a Panel of Experts by the European Union under the EUKFTA, available at <https://trade.ec.europa.eu/doclib/press/index.cfm?id=2044>.

panels are composed of three panellists and are selected jointly by the parties within ten working days.[119] Depending on the subject matter of the dispute, panellists must be experts in either international environmental or international labour law, and additionally, in international dispute resolution. They must be independent and not depend on any international organisation or government. Moreover, if the dispute relates to the application of a specific international agreement (e.g. ILO Conventions or MEA), panellists are held to seek information from the relevant bodies established by such agreement. The expert panel first issues an interim report with the possibility for the parties to comment. Lastly, a final report is issued and made publicly available.[120] In the case that a panel of experts concluded that one contracting party has not conformed with its commitments under a TSD chapter, there is no sanction that follows, instead the parties "shall engage in discussions and shall endeavour, within three months of the delivery of the final report, to identify an appropriate measure or, if appropriate, to decide upon a mutually satisfactory action plan".[121] In these discussions, the contracting parties "shall take into account the final report" of the panel of experts.[122] The specialised Committees on TSD will then monitor the subsequent implementation of the final report by the party that has not conformed to its SD obligations.[123] In the follow-up procedure, civil society through DAGs and joint meetings can submit observations to the specialised Committees on TSD thereby assisting in the monitoring process.[124]

---

119 If no agreement can be found as to who shall be the members of the panel, the selection procedure set out for the general State-State arbitration mechanism applies, see eg CETA, Art 29.3–7.

120 Eg CETA, Art 24.15(10): "The Panel of Experts shall issue to the Parties an interim report and a final report setting out the findings of fact, its determinations on the matter, including as to whether the responding Party has conformed with its obligations under this Chapter and the rationale behind any findings, determinations and recommendations that it makes […]".

121 Eg CETA Art 24.15(11). See also EUJFTA, Art 16.18(6); EUMFTA, TSD chapter, Art 17(9); EUSFTA, Art 12.17(9); EUVFTA, Art 13.17(9).

122 Ibid.

123 Eg CETA Art 24.15(11): "[…] The Committee on Trade and Sustainable Development shall monitor the follow-up to the final report and the recommendations of the Panel of Experts. The civil society organisations, through the consultative mechanisms referred to in Article 24.13.5, and the Civil Society Forum may submit observations to the Committee on Trade and Sustainable Development in this regard". See also, EUMERFTA, TSD chapter, Art 17.11.

124 Eg EUVFTA, Art 13.17(9).

5.2.2.2 Soft Enforcement and Sanction-Based Enforcement

The dispute settlement system under TSD chapters of EU IIAs does not foresee sanctions in the case of a violation of SD provisions. The dispute settlement mechanism reflects the EU's collaborative approach for the implementation and enforcement of TSD chapters.[125] However, criticism has been fierce concerning the effectiveness of the commitments on environmental protection and labour rights under EU IIAs.[126]

In an international comparison it is mainly the treaty practice of the United States and Canada that provides for similar labour and environmental provisions in their FTAs and that opted for enforcement mechanisms in this respect.[127] The substantive SD obligations include for the contracting parties to effectively enforce domestic labour and environmental laws, and prohibit them from lowering such standards. The main difference between the North American approaches and the one taken by the EU lies within the enforcement mechanism of these provisions as both the United States and Canada use, as a last resort, inter-State arbitration as an enforcement mechanism, which can lead to the withdrawal of trade concessions.[128] Looking more specifically at US FTAs, they start off similarly to EU IIAs as they first require the parties to engage in consultations if one party considers that the other party has failed to comply with its labour and environmental commitments.[129] If consultations fail, a special body established by the agreement and composed of representatives of the parties shall further attempt to resolve the dispute

---

125 Marín Durán, above note 5, 1042.
126 Zimmer R, 'Sozialklauseln im Freihandelsabkommen der Europäischen Union mit Kolumbien und Peru', Recht der Internationalen Wirtschaft 2011, 625–632; Marx A et al, *Dispute Settlement in the Trade and Sustainable Development Chapters of EU Trade Agreements* (Leuven Centre for Global Governance Studies 2017) 10; Bartels L, 'Human Rights and Sustainable Development Obligations in EU Free Trade Agreements' in: Wouters J et al (eds), *Global Governance through Trade: EU Policies and Approaches* (Edward Elgar Publishing 2015) 89; Bronckers M and Gruni G, 'Taking the Enforcement of Labour Standards in the EU's Free Trade Agreements Seriously' [2019] Common Market Law Review 1591; Ebert, above note 56, 307.
127 See below Section 5.2.2.
128 Beginning with the NAFTA side agreement on labour (NAALC) these commitments have been made subject to review by arbitral panels and have created the possibility that sanctions could be levied on a party that fails to live up to its commitments, see NAALC, Art 41. Eg also, US-Peru FTA, Art 21.16; Canada-Peru FTA, Art 2114 (both provisions are entitled "Non-Implementation—Suspension of Benefits"). See also, Potestà, above note 67, 182.
129 Eg US-Peru FTA, Arts 17.7(1) and 18.12(3); US-Colombia FTA, Arts 17.7(1) and 18.12(1–2); US-Panama, Arts 16.7(1) and 17.11(1–2); US-Korea, Arts 19.7(1) and 20.9(1).

through the typical diplomatic means of good offices, conciliation or mediation.[130] Unlike under EU IIAs, if these diplomatic means still do not lead to a mutually satisfactory solution, US FTAs allow the subject to be referred to the agreement's inter-State dispute settlement mechanism.[131] The remedies available for the violations of the environmental or labour clauses of US FTAs are the same as those foreseen for other violations of the agreement, *i.e.* trade sanctions against the non-complying party.[132]

To date, the US approach was tested only once in a case filed by the United States against Guatemala under the DR-CAFTA.[133] The United States claimed that the treatment of workers in Guatemala was in violation of their labour rights, including forming unions and engaging in collective bargaining.[134] According to the United States, those failures amounted to a breach of the DR-CAFTA because Guatemala failed "to effectively enforce its labour laws, through a sustained or recurring course of action or inaction, *in a manner affecting trade between the Parties*, after the date of entry into force of this Agreement".[135] The claim made by the United States focussed especially on the authorities' failure to enforce national court orders and a failure to conduct a proper investigation and impose penalties. After a process that lasted several years, the arbitral panel concluded in its final report that Guatemala did not fail to conform to its obligations under the DR-CAFTA. The panel made conclusive findings that Guatemala violated central labour rights, it also found that these violations were *not* affecting trade or investment between the Parties.[136]

---

130   Eg US-Peru FTA, Arts 17.7(6) and 18.12(4)-(5)(a); US-Colombia FTA, Arts 17.7(6) and 18.12(4)-(5)(a); US-Panama, Arts 16.7(6) and 17.11(4)-(5)(a); US-Korea, Arts 19.7(4) and 20.9(3).

131   Eg US-Peru FTA, Arts 17.7(6–7) and 18.12(6); US-Colombia FTA, Arts 17.7(6–7) and Art 18.12(6); US-Panama, Arts 16.7(6–7) and Art 17.11(6); US-Korea, Arts 19.7(4–5) and 20.9(6). However, a first generation of US FTAs only provided for the possibility to resort to consultations for issues falling under the chapter on the environment; see eg US-Chile FTA, Art 19(6); US-Singapore FTA, Art 18(7).

132   Eg US-Peru FTA, Arts 21.15 and 21.16: See for similar formulations, US-Colombia FTA, Art 21.15–16; US-Panama FTA, Art 20.14–152; US-Korea FTA, Art 22.12–13.

133   Office of the US Trade Representative, 'In the Matter of Guatemala—Issues Relating to the Obligations Under Article 16.2.1(a) of the CAFTA-DR', Summary; available at <https://ustr.gov/issue-areas/labor/bilateral-and-regional-trade-agreements/guatemala-submission-under-cafta-dr>.

134   For more background information on the case, see International Labour Rights Forum, 'Wrong Turn for Workers' Rights: The U.S.—Guatemala CAFTA Labor Arbitration Ruling—And What to Do About It', March 2018.

135   DR-CAFTA, Art 16.2(1)(a). Emphasis added.

136   Final Report of the Panel, 20 June 2017; available at <https://ustr.gov/issue-areas/labor/bilateral-and-regional-trade-agreements/guatemala-submission-under-cafta-dr>.

Therefore, the panel ultimately dismissed the claims. The outcome of the arbitration has been criticised as well as the restrictive language of the labour provisions containing the requirement of a nexus between the violations of labour rights on the one hand, and trade and investment, on the other hand.[137] In terms of dispute settlement, the example shows that following complaints of Guatemalan trade unions to US authorities, the United States started a stringent enforcement mechanism against one of its trade partners in order to seek the enforcement of labour rights.[138] The case remains an isolated example. Under no other US FTA, an arbitral panel has been initiated to solve labour or environmental matters.

Whether soft or sanction-based enforcement mechanisms are more beneficial for effective SD integration is a difficult question and there is not yet enough State practice and international debate on the issue. The EU for its parts is still in the process of finding the right approach. The European Parliament has questioned whether the soft and promotional approaches taken in recent EU IIAs are effective and appropriate.[139] As a consequence, the European Commission published a Non-Paper that evaluates the EU's soft compliance mechanism under TSD chapters.[140] The two options discussed were to either strengthen the existing mechanism or to move to a sanctions-based model. The Commission points out that no comprehensive empirical analysis exists that would allow for an assessment.[141] In addition, the Commission adds that the sanctions-based model "would not easily fit the EU's model" as such model traditionally favours soft compliance mechanisms.[142]

The EU has its policy reasons why it remains reluctant to include sanctions.[143] First, the EU approach seeks to strengthen the existing multilateral governance structure, rather than to create a parallel legal structure and

---

137   International Labour Rights Forum, above note 134.
138   Ibid; see also Polanski, above note 32.
139   European Parliament, Resolution on Human Rights and Social and Environmental Standards in International Trade Agreements, 25 Nov 2010, 2009/2219(INI), para 22(a); Resolution on Implementation of the 2010 Recommendations of Parliament on Social and Environmental Standards, Human Rights and Corporate Responsibility, 5 July 2016, 2015/2038(INI), paras 21–22.
140   The European Commission issued a non-paper in which it discusses the pros and cons of a sanction-based approach. See non-paper of the Commission services, 'Trade and Sustainable Development (TSD) chapters in EU Free Trade Agreements (FTAs),' July 2017.
141   Ibid. See also, Marín Durán, above note 10, 1055.
142   Commission services, 'Non-Paper', above note 140, 3.
143   Ibid. The following is based on the 2017 EU non-paper, above note 140.

dispute settlement on environment and labour issues.¹⁴⁴ For example, when a party is not complying with one of the ILO Conventions, it would be more beneficial to foster the enforcement mechanisms of the ILO than to establish a parallel dispute settlement under a comprehensive FTA.¹⁴⁵ Second, for the EU, the main benefit of TSD chapters is that through transparency, dialogue and consultations, mutually satisfactory solutions for SD can be found and that SD matters are brought effectively to the attention of the contracting partners. As a consequence, the enforcement plays a subordinated role. Third, the EU is concerned that sanctions contained in the TSD chapter could undermine the EU's bargaining powers to foster cooperation in the trade/investment-SD nexus. The EU considers that countries are more likely to engage in substantive commitments on SD if the monitoring and enforcement are soft and based on dialogue, cooperation and consultations.

Despite the absence of the mandatory nature of the expert panel's final report under EU IIAs, the impact of the initiation of such a procedure is by no means neutral.¹⁴⁶ A decisive feature of the proceedings is that the final report is made public, in this way, it can be an essential means of putting pressure on the contracting party that is in default of its obligations. Moreover, the possibility for a strong enforcement mechanism on paper is in practice not necessarily more effective to achieve SD objectives within the framework of a comprehensive FTA. There is no tangible proof that stronger enforceability better guarantees the respect and enforcement of labour rights and environmental protection, particularly if the stronger enforcement mechanism is scarcely used in practice as can be highlighted by the practice of the United States.¹⁴⁷ Lastly, as is the case for environmental protection in particular, a State's failure to comply with its SD commitments might not always be intentional. Therefore,

---

144 Opinion 2/15, above note 5, para 154. The Court has stressed that "[...] the scope of the obligations stemming from the international agreements to which the envisaged agreement refers is a matter covered by the interpretation, mediation and *dispute settlement mechanisms* that are in force for those international agreements [...]." Emphasis added.

145 On a discussion of the interaction between TSD chapters of EU FTAs and the ILO supervisory mechanism, see Marx et al, above note 126, 48–59.

146 Commission indépendante, 'Rapport au Premier ministre—L'impact de l'Accord Economique et Commercial Global entre l'Union européenne et le Canada (AECG/CETA) sur l'environnement, le climat et la santé', Sep 2017.

147 For more details, see Scherrer C et al, 'An Analysis of the Relative Effectiveness of Social and Environmental Norms in Free Trade Agreements' (European Parliament 2009), available at <www.europarl.europa.eu/activities/committees/studies.do?language=EN>. This study finds that the enforcement mechanisms in the US FTAs are not generally implemented in practice, but, rather, serve as a deterrent. See also Marín Durán, above note 74, 138.

"soft responsibility" mechanisms, such as consultation and monitoring with the aim to find mutually agreed a solution have their benefits.[148] Indeed, the type of procedure chosen by the EU for the TSD chapters resembles the soft compliance mechanisms established in many multilateral environmental agreements.[149] The aim is not to sanction the defaulting contracting party but to initiate a process of cooperation between the parties to enable the contracting party whose efforts to protect the environment are considered insufficient to consolidate its regulatory framework. In international environmental law, compliance mechanisms are especially beneficial because this mechanism allows it to be taken into account that a lack of compliance is not necessarily the result of wilful actions of the defaulting state party but of other factors, such as lack of information or lack of capacity.[150] In this vein, compliance mechanisms often encompass assistance and adaptation measures.[151]

The EU is meanwhile strengthening the enforcement mechanisms under TSD chapters. It launched a complaints system that allows interested parties to report breaches of SD commitments directly to the European Commission. Complaints are channelled through a centralised Single Entry Point system in DG Trade.[152] The Chief Tarde Enforcement Officer is managing the Single Entry Point. Moreover, under the EU-Korea FTA, a first panel report has been

---

148 For a proposal of how to improve the current system (for the example of labour), see Stoll P-T, Gött H and Abel P, 'A Model Labour Chapter for Future EU Trade Agreements' in: Gött H (ed), *Labour Standards in International Economic Law* (Springer International Publishing 2018) 410–419.

149 See for instance, Convention on International Trade in Endangered Species of Wild Fauna and Flora (CITES) [1973], Art VIII(7); Montreal Protocol on Substances that Deplete the Ozone Layer [1987], Arts 7 and 8; Protocol to the Convention on Long-Range Transboundary Air Pollution on Further Reduction of Sulphur Emissions [1994], Art 7; Kyoto Protocol to the United Nations Framework Convention on Climate Change [1997], Art 18; Cartagena Protocol on Biosafety to the Convention on Biological Diversity [2000], Art 34; Stockholm Convention on Persistent Organic Pollutants (POPs) [2001], Art 17; Vienna Convention for the Protection of the Ozone Layer [1985], Art 5.

150 Fitzmaurice M et al, 'Environmental Compliance Mechanisms', Oxford Bibliographies, available at <http://www.oxfordbibliographies.com/display/id/obo-9780199796953-0010>.

151 Ibid. Another option is to consider sanctions as a "last resort option" consisting of stringent enforcement through State-State arbitration in case that all consultative means fail. Following the example of the Kyoto Protocol, which provides for sanctions as a remedy of last resort. This includes that a contracting party can no longer be eligible to participate in the mechanisms under Arts 6, 12 and 17 of the Protocol. See eg Kyoto Enforcement Branch of the Compliance Committee, CC-2007-1/Greece/EB, Final Decision, 17 April 2008, para 18.

152 European Commission, Press Release, available at <https://ec.europa.eu/commission/presscorner/detail/en/ip_20_2134>.

issued.[153] The Panel concluded that Korea needs to adjust its labour laws and practices to comply with the principle of freedom of association. The country also needs to continue the process of ratifying the four fundamental ILO Conventions in order to comply with the agreement. The panel confirmed that the two commitments at issue are legally binding and have to be respected regardless of their effect on trade. In the follow-up, TDS Committee monitors the implementation of the panel report by Korea. The extent to which Korea will implement the panel report will provide further insights into the effectiveness of the EU's soft enforcement mechanism. Currently, the approaches taken by the EU go in the right direction. With the soft enforcement mechanism contained in EU trade and investment agreements, the EU contributes to finding solutions on how to ensure respect for SD commitments.

5.2.3 Transparency and Public Information

TSD chapters of EU IIAS contain commitments to transparency. The contracting parties "shall ensure" that measures of general application aimed at protecting the environment or labour conditions that could affect trade and investment between the parties are "developed, introduced and administered in a transparent manner".[154] In addition, contracting parties should duly notice and provide opportunities for interested persons to submit their views. A specific chapter on transparency further regulates the procedure of notification and submission of views by stakeholders.[155] In this respect, CETA has an additional provision on public information and awareness pursuant to which the parties shall encourage public debate in particular among and with non-state actors.[156] Such debates are to further the development and definition of policies that may lead to the adoption of environmental or labour laws. Moreover, parties are bound to promote public awareness of the labour and environmental laws that exist already at the national level and how interested groups can enforce them.[157]

The beneficiaries of transparency provisions are not only the other contracting party but also civil society organisations and economic operators,

---

153 Panel of Experts Proceeding Constituted under Article 13.15 of the EU-Korea Free Trade Agreement, Report of the Panel of Experts, 20 January 2021.
154 EUSFTA, Art 12.13. See also EUKFTA, Art 13.9 adding: "[...] and with appropriate and timely communication to and consultation of non-state actors including the private sector [...]".
155 CETA, Ch 27; EUJFTA, Ch 17; EUSFTA, Ch 13 EUVFTA, Ch 14 (all these chapters are entitled 'Transparency').
156 CETA, Arts 23.6 and 24.7.
157 CETA, Arts 23.6 and 24.7.

including foreign investors.[158] For partner countries and other stakeholders, transparency in general and in the context of SD contributes to a perception of fairness and enhances confidence in the governance and institutions of a State.[159] Concerning labour and environmental regulations, this seems particularly relevant as there can be an underlining fear of protectionist measures or *a contrario* of a watering down of protection standards. Transparency in decision-making related to SD allows civil society groups to play a consultative role and it can further encourage public debate and awareness. Transparency is a key issue in the EU's comprehensive FTAs. Commitments on transparency have been incorporated into TSD chapters and, in addition, another specific chapter on transparency sets out the details of its application and implementation. This approach can be welcomed as it, on the one hand, embeds transparency in the context of SD with the overall transparency objective of the treaty framework, and on the other hand, it underlines that transparency is a prerequisite for effective public participation and the involvement of the civil society.

Compared to other global actors, it is mainly the United States that incorporate commitments on transparency in their FTAs, however in general and not specifically on legislation on SD matters.[160] The CPTPP, for its part, make specific reference to transparency for environmental regulation in order to ensure effective public participation.[161] At the same time, a specific provision on transparency with respect to SD measures is so far unique EU treaty practice. From an EU policy perspective, one can note that transparency is among the key objectives of the European Commission's trade and investment strategy.[162] EU's IIAs are to support efforts of promoting international standards of transparency and good governance.

In international investment law, transparency is a raising issue that relates to investment facilitation and investor-State dispute prevention.[163] Under EU

---

158 The term civil society organisation includes representatives from general interests associations, trade unions, professional organisations, and business interests associations; see, Kohler-Koch B and Quittkat C, 'What Is Civil Society and Who Represents Civil Society in the EU?—Results of an Online Survey among Civil Society Experts' (2009) 28 Policy and Society 11, 13.
159 UNCTAD, *Transparency* (United Nations 2012) 1-2.
160 Specific chapters on transparency can be found in a number of FTAs concluded by the United States. Eg US-Australia FTA, Ch 20; US-Chile FTA, Ch 20; US-Korea FTA, Ch 21; US-Oman FTA, Ch18.
161 CPTPP, Art 20.7.
162 European Commission, 'Trade for All', above note 2, 6.
163 70 WTO Members stated in 2017 that an investment facilitation framework, would "improve the transparency and predictability of investment measures; streamline and

IIAs, foreign investors can indirectly participate in the consultations with civil society groups at the national and transnational level provided that they are members of a business organisation.[164] The participation of foreign investors *via* business organisations in discussing the implementation of the TSD chapter can, for instance, have the benefit of business being informed about the cooperative activities between the contracting parties on SD. As such economic operators can provide their expertise and are informed about the legislative changes on SD matters. In this way, the institutional set-up of TSD chapters could have a dispute preventive aspect because foreign investors are better informed about host States' policy changes and amendments to the legal framework. This preventive aspect can also play out in a different scenario. For example, foreign investors concerned that a contracting party to an EU IIA is disregarding its transparency commitments under the TSD chapter regarding its social or environmental legislation. Here again, if a business organisation, in the name of foreign investors, can raise concerns about the lack of transparency within a contracting party through these forums, the consultations can have a dispute preventive impact. Not least because the lack of transparency has, in past investor-State disputes, played a role in the assessment of an alleged breach by the host State of the fair and equitable treatment standard.[165]

As far as dispute prevention and facilitation is concerned, EU IIAs differ considerably with the Brazilian Cooperation and Investment Facilitation Agreements (CIFAs) that have a clear focus on both of these matters. CIFAs incorporate the long-term perspective that States need to cooperate and maintain a fluent and organised dialogue with investors to foster sustained investments. They establish entities such as "National Focal Points", also called

---

speed up administrative procedures and requirements; and enhance international cooperation, information sharing, the exchange of best practices, and relations with relevant stakeholders, including dispute prevention". See, Joint Ministerial Statement on Investment Facilitation for Development at the Eleventh Ministerial Conference held in Buenos Aires, Argentina, in December 2017, WT/MIN(17)/48.

164 Eg BusinessEurope is an association representing enterprises of all sizes in the EU. BusinessEurope is namely party of the EU DAG established under the EUKFTA.

165 *Tecnicas Medioambientales Tecmed, S.A. v United Mexican States*, ICSID Case No ARB (AF)/00/2, Award, 29 May 2003, para 154. This approach has been adopted in a number of subsequent awards, such as *MTD Equity Sdn. Bhd. & MTD Chile S.A. v Republic of Chile*, ICSID Case No ARB/01/7, Award, 25 May 2004, paras 114–115; *CMS Gas Transmission Company v The Argentine Republic*, ICSID Case No ARB/01/8, Award, 12 May 2005, paras 279–281; *Azurix Corp v The Argentine Republic*, ICSID Case No ARB/01/12, Award, 14 July 2006, paras 360–361, 372, 392, 408; *Metalclad Corporation v The United Mexican States*, ICSID Case No ARB(AF)/97/1, Award, 30 Aug 2000, paras 74–101. Yet, FET provisions of EU IIAs do not contain transparency as part of the elements falling under the said standard, see Section 6.1.1.

"Ombudsmen".[166] Under Brazilian IIAs, investors can submit requests, enquiries, suggestions and complaints to the National Focal Points.[167] The EU, in particular, the European Commission might further develop on investment facilitation in the near future and explore how the facilitation of investment can relate to and be supportive of SD.

5.2.4 Ex post *SD Review of IIA Implementation*

A further procedural arrangement under EU IIAs' TSD chapters consists of reviewing the impacts of trade and investment agreements concerning the actual social, economic and environmental impacts after entering into force.[168] The rationale behind *ex post* SD reviews is that contracting partners can react to negative impacts, and, if need be, amend the agreement.[169] EU IIAs generally provide that each party commits "to review, monitor and assess the impact of the implementation of" the agreement in question on SD as concerns its territory "in order to identify any need for action that may arise in connection" with the agreement.[170] *Ex post* SD reviews are overseen by the specialised Committees on TSD. It is noteworthy that the parties themselves are in charge to conduct the SD review once the agreement has entered into force. Conversely, independent consultants conduct *ex ante* SIAs, which are discussed hereafter.

---

166 For more details see, Xavier Junior EC, 'A Latin American View on the CETA Investment Chapter' in: Mbengue MM and Schacherer S (eds), *Foreign Investment Under the Comprehensive Economic and Trade Agreement (CETA)* (Springer International Publishing 2019) 332–333.
167 Eg Brazil-Ethiopia CIFA, Art 18(3) "The National Focal Point, among other responsibilities, shall:
   a) Endeavour to follow the recommendations of the Joint Committee and interact with the National Focal Point of the other Contracting Party, in accordance with this Agreement;
   b) Follow up in a timely manner on requests and enquiries of the other Contracting Party or of investors of the other Contracting Party with the competent authorities and inform the stakeholders on the results of its actions;
   c) Assess, in consultation with relevant government authorities, suggestions and complaints received from the other Contracting Party or investors of the other Contracting Party and recommend, as appropriate, actions to improve the investment environment;
   d) Seek to prevent differences in investment matters, in collaboration with government authorities and relevant private entities; [...]".
168 See European Commission, 'Handbook for Trade Sustainability Impact Assessment' (hereafter SIA Handbook), 2nd ed, 2016, 8.
169 Ebert, above note 56, 323.
170 Eg CETA, Art 22.3(3).

Looking at other global actors, it appears that *ex post* SD reviews provided for in IIAs remain a rare practice that has not yet found widespread acknowledgement. Canada, for instance, has started to review the impacts of its FTAs with third countries on matters of SD including human rights. An interesting example is the Canada-Colombia FTA, which is accompanied by a side agreement on human rights. The side agreement requires both parties to prepare annual reports on the human rights impact of the related FTA.[171] The reports that have been issued to date under the Canada-Colombia FTA have attracted significant criticism relating to *inter alia* the short and non-transparent consultation procedure. Civil society organisations, in particular, highlighted that the impact assessment had been conducted in a superficial manner, lacking analysis of key issues despite Colombia's desolate social and human rights record.[172] The Canadian experience is relevant for the EU as well, as it suggests that a transparent methodology with a solid procedural and institutional framework is fundamental otherwise such assessments will mainly serve to superficially legitimise controversial trade and investment agreements rather than dealing with actual and potential SD concerns caused by these agreements.

Within the EU, the *ex post* evaluations are prepared by Commission services in accordance with the related Commission guidelines and tools.[173] It seems problematic that the same entity that negotiated the agreement is also in charge of the impact assessment.[174] At least, the Commission cannot carry out these assessments without considering the views of interested stakeholders, making it clear that civil society plays a monitoring role in this respect and is indeed encouraged to provide advice.[175] Taking up again the Commission ambition of having effective SD integration, one needs to point out that the provisions of EU IIAs neither specify which type of methodology should be used for the reviews nor their frequency.[176] They only state that

---

171 Annual Report Pursuant to the Agreement concerning Annual Reports on Human Rights and Free Trade between Canada and the Republic of Colombia for the period 1 Jan 2015 to 31 Dec 2015; available at <https://www.canadainternational.gc.ca/colombia-colombie/bilateral_relations_bilaterales/rep-hrft-co_2015-dple-rapp.aspx?lang=eng>.
172 Ebert, above note 56, 323.
173 SIA Handbook, above note 168, 8.
174 The Guiding Principles for Human Rights Impact Assessments, as elaborated by the UN Special Rapporteur on the Right to Food, highlight the importance of the assessment being carried out by an actor "that is independent from the Executive which is negotiating, or has negotiated, the trade or investment agreement". See UN General Assembly, Human Rights Council, 'Report of the Special Rapporteur on the right to food—Olivier De Schutter', [2011] A/HRC/19/59/Add.5, para 4.3.
175 Eg EUMFTA, SD chapter, Art 18.
176 See on this point also, Commission indépendante, above note 146, 24.

the parties can "exchange information and experience with regard to methodologies and indicators for trade sustainability assessments".[177] However, the European Commission announced that *ex post* reviews would be conducted on an annual basis concerning "the implementation of the most significant FTAs".[178] Yet the guidance provided in the actual EU IIAS remains very limited on the nature and scope of the assessments. Therefore, and in order to live up to its own ambitions, the EU could further elaborate to define what the specific and binding evaluations and review mechanisms have to entail.[179]

5.3 Additional Fields of Cooperation on SD-Investment Linkages

The previous sections have discussed how the EU cooperates with its trade and investment partners on environmental protection and labour rights. The analysis now turns to the more specific cooperation fields that are also relevant for investment-SD linkages, such as climate change mitigation and renewable energies, human rights, development cooperation and anti-corruption. The EU included these elements in their investment relations with third countries. These fields, being important components of SD, thus add to the cooperative framework for social and environmental protection. Through these provisions, the contracting parties typically, first, reaffirm their commitments to work together, and second, agree to promote and facilitate investments in the specific field of action.[180]

---

177 EUVFTA, Art 13.14(1)(b).
178 European Commission Communication, 'Trade for All', above note 2, 10.
179 Emphasising this point, see Joint Interpretative Instrument on the Comprehensive Economic and Trade Agreement (CETA) between Canada and the European Union and its Member States, [2017] OJ L 11/3, para 10(a): "Commitments related to trade and sustainable development, trade and labour and trade and environment are subject to dedicated and binding assessment and review mechanisms. Canada and the European Union and its Member States are fully committed to make effective use of these mechanisms throughout the life of the agreement. Furthermore, they are committed to initiating an early review of these provisions, including with a view to the effective enforceability of CETA provisions on trade and labour and trade and the environment."
180 The EU has used the notions of promotion and facilitation in an interchangeable way. A distinction between the two notions is however regularly discussed; see eg Hees F and Barreto da Rocha Paranhos P, 'Investment Facilitation: Moving Beyond Investment Promotion', Columbia FDI Perspectives, No 228, 6/2018.

5.3.1 *Climate Change Mitigation and Renewable Energy Sources*

Addressing the issue of climate change requires a gradual transition to a low-carbon economy.[181] This transition in return requires, first and foremost, technology and financing making investments in this field indispensable.[182] The main idea is that IIAs should be used as complementary instruments to support responsible action on climate change by providing incentives to encourage investments that support mitigation goals, including targeted financial or technical supports for clean energy investment. In this respect, EU IIAs incorporate provisions that seek to foster investment promotion in the renewable energy sector.[183] Yet depending on the partner country, the provisions on climate change are different as regards their ambition.

In the FTA with Mexico, the parties address the issue of climate change and energy transition by recognising the "urgent threat" and the role of trade and investment in addressing it, as well as by stressing the importance of effectively implementing the current international framework.[184] In the FTA with Korea, the parties "recognise the need to cut emissions in order to stabilise greenhouse gas concentration at a level that would prevent dangerous anthropocentric interference with the climate system".[185] The interesting part of the EU approach is, however, the provisions on the promotion of investment aimed at pursuing a transition to a low-carbon economy, to climate-resilient development, as well as to green growth that is based on actions on climate change mitigation and adaptation, including eco-system renewable energies and energy-efficient solutions.[186] The FTAs with Singapore and Vietnam go a step further as they contain a specific chapter on investment in renewable

---

181 Corfee-Morlot J et al, 'Towards a Green Investment Policy Framework: The Case of Low-Carbon, Climate-Resilient Infrastructure' (2012) OECD Environment Working Papers 48, 12.

182 See Alschner W and Tuerk E, 'The Role of International Investment Agreements in Fostering Sustainable Development', in: Baetens F (ed), *Investment Law within International Law: Integrationist Perspectives* (Cambridge University Press 2013) 221.

183 It shall be noted here that the so-called renewable energy ISDS cases are of limited interest in the discussion here because this section is concerned with provisions of IIAs that seek to promote the energy transition to renewable energy sources. The focus here is namely, not on the right to regulate in the renewable energy sector at the national level. The right to regulate is dealt with in Chapter 6.

184 EUMFTA, TSD chapter, Art 5(1). See Framework Convention on Climate Change (UNFCCC), [1994] OJ L 33/13; and the Paris Agreement on Climate Change, [2015] OJ L 282/4, under the latter the Parties are namely held to communicate their Nationally Determined Contributions (NDCs).

185 EUKFTA, Art 24.1. See also UNFCCC, Art 2.

186 EUMFTA, TSD chapter, Art 5(2); EUVFTA, Art 13.6; EUKFTA, Art 24.1(a-g).

energy generation.¹⁸⁷ The issue is thus not treated within the TSD chapters. The stated objective of the chapters on renewable energies is however linked to SD and is in line with global efforts to reduce greenhouse gas emissions. In other words, the parties share the common objectives of "promoting, developing and increasing the generation of energy from renewable and sustainable sources, particularly through facilitating trade and investment".¹⁸⁸ The said chapters cover specific rules for the renewable energy sector on non-discriminatory treatment in general (licensing and authorisation procedures), on local content in particular and further on the use of international standards.¹⁸⁹ The EU-Mexico FTA also contains an SD-relevant chapter that exists next to the TSD chapter. It is specifically dedicated to "Energy and Raw Materials". The chapter contains provisions on the facilitation of "the development of common standards on energy efficiency and sustainable renewable energy".¹⁹⁰ The parties also seek to cooperate "to reduce or eliminate trade and investment distorting measures in third countries affecting energy and raw materials";¹⁹¹ and "to coordinate their positions in international fora where trade and investment issues related to energy and raw materials are discussed and [to] foster international programmes in the areas of energy efficiency, renewable energy and raw materials".¹⁹²

Compared to other international actors' treaty practice, EU IIAs are innovative in creating these specific linkages between investment and climate change mitigation through the promotion of renewable energies. Even though climate change is an urgent threat and foreign investment is needed to ensure the mandatory energy transition, references to these issues are still rare in IIAs. Recent treaties that are on other matters keen to integrate SD concerns, such as the Morocco-Nigeria BIT or the CPTPP, do not mention climate change at all. The PAIC contains a reference, which is addressed to investors and points to the importance of technology transfer in the sector and thus the support for developing countries in adopting mitigation and adaptation actions.¹⁹³ Hence,

---

187 The full title is "Non-Tariff Barriers to Trade and Investment in Renewable Energy Generation", see EUVFTA, Chapter 7 and EUSFTA, Chapter 7.
188 EUVFTA, Art 7.1; EUSFTA, Art 7.1.
189 Such standard-setting bodies are the International Organization for Standardization and the International Electrotechnical Commission, see EUVFTA, Art 7.5(2); EUSFTA, Art 7.5(1).
190 EUMFTA, Ch 'Energy and raw materials', Art 10.1(b).
191 EUMFTA, Ch 'Energy and raw materials', Art 11(a).
192 EUMFTA, 'Energy and raw materials', Art 11(b).
193 PAIC, Art 30.2: "Investors are encouraged to provide adequate financial resources, including for the transfer of technology, needed for implementing measures to assist the Member States that are particularly vulnerable to the adverse effects of climate change in meeting costs of adaptation to or mitigation of those adverse effects".

EU IIAS, in contrast to most other IIAS, create linkages between the climate change regime and IIAS. These linkages are particularly important because the current climate change regime does not sufficiently emphasise the need for foreign investment.[194] The Paris Agreement is silent on such linkages or on any economic tool to accentuate the transition to low-carbon economies. Under the Kyoto Protocol,[195] there was an international agreement that sought among other things, "to incentive private-sector investments across a range of climate friendly projects and activities" through the market-based flexible mechanisms.[196] Yet, the Kyoto Protocol is "clinically dead" as its amendment has not entered into force. Consequently, the attention could be more on IIAS, which can play a crucial role in scale-up and (re)direct investment to meet climate change mitigation and adaptation needs.[197]

From an EU perspective, climate change mitigation and the promotion of renewable energy sources stand high in the political agenda of the EU.[198] The New European Development Consensus states that the EU and its Member States "will implement the 2030 Agenda and the Paris Climate Change Agreement through coordinated and coherent action, and will maximise synergies".[199] In light of this statement, the EU approach in its IIAS does not seem to go far enough. Namely, the principle of policy coherence would require the EU to pursue the fight against climate change through its development cooperation but should likewise do so through the CCP. Moreover, policy coherence is lacking when one compares the EU IIAS amongst them. As mentioned before,

---

194 Güven B and Johnson L, 'International Investment Agreements: Impacts on Climate Change Policies in India, China, and beyond', Trade in the Balance: Reconciling Trade and Climate Policy, Report of the Working Group on Trade, Investment, and Climate Policy (Boston University 2016) 50.

195 Kyoto Protocol to the UNFCCC, [2004] OJ L 49/3; (entry into force: 16 Feb 2005; Kyoto's first period of commitment was 2008–2012).

196 Kyoto Protocol, Arts 6, 12 and 17. See Firger DM, 'The Potential of International Climate Change Law to Mobilise Low-Carbon Foreign Direct Investment', in: Dupuy PM and Viñuales JE (eds), *Harnessing Foreign Investment to Promote Environmental Protection: Incentives and Safeguards* (Cambridge University Press 2013) 177. See also Baetens F, 'The Kyoto Protocol in Investor-State Arbitration: Reconciling Climate Change and Investment Protection Objectives', in: Cordonier Segger MC, Gehring MW and Newcombe AP (eds), *Sustainable Development in World Investment Law* (Kluwer Law International 2011) 683–715.

197 Güven and Johnson, above note 194, 50.

198 See Joint Statement by the Council and the representatives of the governments of the Member States meeting within the Council, the European Parliament and the Commission, 'The New European Consensus on Development 'Our World, Our Dignity, Our Future'', 2017/C 210/01, paras 44–46.

199 Ibid, para 45.

the provisions addressing the challenges of climate change are not systemically included in all IIAs. Substantively, those EU IIAs that address climate change contain highly programmatic provisions, which leads to doubts concerning their effectiveness. The modernisation process of the ECT highlights that climate change mitigation through IIAs would require more substantial changes in treaty texts and should namely lead to the complete exclusion of investment protection of fossil fuels.[200] The EU IIAs' commitments should, therefore, constitute a starting point for more inter-State cooperation on the interlinkages of foreign investment and the fight against climate change. To be in line with the EU's policy agenda, such as the European Green Deal, climate change mitigation as well as the transition to renewable energies should be further developed and more comprehensively addressed through EU investment and trade agreements.

5.3.2 *Human Rights*

The interlinkages between investment and SD also concern the promotion and respect of human rights. Agenda 2030 states explicitly that it "is grounded in" the Universal Declaration of Human Rights and other international human rights treaties.[201] The EU traditionally also underlines that the respect for human rights constitutes an integral part of SD.[202] Certain labour rights discussed before acquired the status of human rights yet other than that the SD chapters contained in EU IIAs do not contain any explicit reference to human rights.[203] This EU practice seems even more surprising when considering that the EU has a relatively long treaty practice of including human rights clauses into its cooperation and trade agreements.[204]

With respect to the EU IIAs that are examined in the present book, one has to go beyond the actual IIAs and look into the broader treaty framework that exists between the EU and its investment partner countries. In fact, before concluding trade and investment agreements, the EU regularly first adopts a political framework agreement with certain third countries. These agreements

---

200 Statement of Members of the European Parliament on the modernisation of the ECT, 2 Nov 2020. See Section 2.4.1.
201 UN General Assembly, 'Transforming our world: the 2030 Agenda for Sustainable Development', [2015] A/RES/70/1 (hereafter Agenda 2030), para 10.
202 Cotonou Agreement, [2000] OJ L 317/3 (last modified 2010), Art 9.1.
203 See, above note 32. See also, Vandenberghe J, 'On Carrots and Sticks: The Social Dimension of EU Trade Policy' (2008) European Foreign Affairs Review 561, 565.
204 The first mention of human rights in an EU cooperation and trade agreement was the 1989 Lomé IV Agreement, see Art 5 thereof. For more details, see Bartels L, *The European Parliament's Role in Relation to Human Rights in Trade and Investment Agreements* (European Union 2014) 6.

are mostly called Partnership and Cooperation Agreements and apply in the context of the comprehensive FTAs through cross-referencing.[205] Under these cooperation agreements, the respect for human rights and democratic principles are made the basis for the agreement, i.e. an "essential element" of it. Consequently, essential element clauses are often not contained in the FTA but in the broader cooperative framework based on partnership agreements.[206] In addition, whether such clauses are included at all depends on the contracting partner country. For instance, the FTAs with Vietnam and Mexico are accompanied by cooperation agreements that contain a human rights clause.[207] Conversely, the FTAs with Canada and Japan are not subject to these clauses. The wording of human rights clauses can also vary being more or less explicit to the human rights instruments they refer to.[208] A typical formulation is that "[r]espect for democratic principles and fundamental human rights, proclaimed by the Universal Declaration of Human Rights, underpins the domestic and external policies of both Parties and *constitutes an essential element of this Agreement.*"[209]

A principal characteristic of such human rights clauses is that they allow one party unilaterally and immediately to suspend the agreement if the other party violates the principles contained in the essential element clause. This possibility is based on non-execution clauses which, in return, state that a party may take "appropriate measures" if the other party violates the essential elements clause.[210]

---

205   For the EU-Vietnam overall relations, see EUVFTA, Art 17.22(2), EUVIPA, Art 4.20(2), both provisions state: "This Agreement shall be part of the overall relations between the Union and its Member States, on one side, and Viet Nam, on the other side, as provided for in the Partnership and Cooperation Agreement and shall form part of the common institutional framework."

206   This is notwithstanding the fact that many FTAs concluded by the EU do contain such clauses, see eg EU-Colombia/Peru FTA, Art 1(1).

207   EU-Mexico Economic Partnership, Political Coordination and Cooperation Agreement [2000] OJ L 276/45, Art 1; EU-Vietnam Comprehensive Partnership and Cooperation Agreement [2016] OJ L 329/8, Art 1.

208   See for instance, the EU-Vietnam Cooperation Agreement, Art 1, which is an example of a very extensive provision.

209   Eg EU-Mexico Economic Partnership, Political Coordination and Cooperation Agreement, Art 1. Emphasis added. See also EU-Central America Association Agreement [2012] OJ L346/3, Art 1.

210   Again, taking the example of the EU-Vietnam relations, the enabling clauses are: EU-Vietnam Cooperation Agreement, Art 57; EUVFTA, Art 17.18(2) and EUVIPA, Art 4.16(2). Eg the formulation of EUVIPA, Art 4.16(2): "If either Party considers that the other Party has committed a material breach of the Partnership and Cooperation Agreement, it may take appropriate measures with respect to this Agreement in accordance with Article 57 of the Partnership and Cooperation Agreement."

Such measures can include the suspension of any obligation existing between the parties, including financial commitments or trade benefits. Non-execution clauses, in general, also state that priority must be given to measures that "least disrupt the functioning" of the treaty framework and that suspension would be a measure of last resort.[211] In practice, these clauses have been invoked on numerous occasions since 1995, most frequently in response to a *coup d'Etat*, but also for flawed electoral processes.[212] The clauses have, however, never been invoked to justify restrictive trade measures.[213]

In the context of an IIA, one can question whether one can suspend the application of the investment-related provisions as a reaction to a non-respect by a partner country of fundamental human rights, under the EU-Vietnam treaty framework for instance. Leaving political reasons besides not to do so, the EU could indeed trigger the clause.[214] Yet the EU would, most likely not suspend the application of the investment-related provisions. Sanctioning its contracting party through the suspension of those provisions would not make sense from an EU point of view because it is the EU's interest that these provisions continue to apply, the inclusion of which the EU has strongly supported and insisted on.[215] In the investment context, it appears that the suspension of investment liberalisation and protection based on a violation of an essential element provision are unsuitable;[216] even more so because foreign investment needs particular protection in countries where human rights records are low.

Considering the IIA practice of other international actors, it can first be noted that essential element clauses remain a specific feature of the EU's external action. Second, IIA practice of other countries and regions does not display a strong emphasis on the integration of human rights clauses. Only a few actors have started to mention human rights explicitly in the operative part of

---

211 EU-Vietnam Cooperation Agreement, Art 57.4. See also, Bartels, above note 204, 11. Lorand Bartels underlines that the language of enabling clauses used invites parties to act in light of the principle of proportionality.
212 Bartels L, 'Human Rights and Sustainable Development Obligations in EU Free Trade Agreements' (2013) 40 Legal Issues of Economic Integration, 297.
213 Ibid.
214 See the enabling clause in the EUVIPA (which contains the provisions on investment protection and liberalisation), ie Art 4.16(2).
215 Dimopoulos A, *EU Foreign Investment Law* (Oxford University Press 2011) 243.
216 See also Hoffmeister F, 'The Contribution of EU Trade Agreements to the Development of International Investment Law', in: Hindelang S and Krajewski M (eds), *Shifting Paradigms in International Investment Law: More Balanced, Less Isolated, Increasingly Diversified* (Oxford University Press 2016) 364–365.

the treaty.[217] This trend is to some extent unfortunate as several investment tribunals have, in past cases, had to tackle the question of whether and to what extent they may take human rights into account.[218] Many African instruments contain human rights obligations that are directly addressed to foreign investors.[219] And indeed, the most important textual inclusions of human rights in IIAs are currently under provisions on corporate social responsibility, a subject that will be further discussed hereafter.[220]

As regards human rights, the chosen approach by the EU institutions seems to be lacking in terms of integration and policy coherence. Based on its constitutional framework, human rights protection ranks high figuring among the values as well as the key objectives of the EU.[221] In addition hereto, the key strategy for EU's CCP requires that human rights are promoted and defended through trade and investment measures.[222] The commitment to integrate human rights provisions in its IIAs are limited to those human rights that constitute fundamental labour rights but EU IIAs do not seek to ensure a better

---

217   Morocco-Nigeria BIT, Art 15 entitled "Investment, Labour and Human Rights Protection". The content of the provision then shows that the provision is concerned with labour rights. As mentioned before, some fundamental labour rights are indeed human rights.

218   Eg *Urbaser SA and Consorcio de Aguas Bilbao Bizkaia, Bilbao Biskaia Ur Partzuergoa v The Argentine Republic*, ICSID Case No ARB/07/26, Award, 8 Dec 2016; *Suez, Sociedad General de Aguas de Barcelona SA and Vivendi Universal SA v Argentine Republic*, ICSID Case No ARB/03/19, Decision on Liability, 30 July 2010; *Hulley Enterprises Limited (Cyprus) v The Russian Federation*, UNCITRAL, PCA Case No AA 226, Final Award, 18 July 2014. For a more detailed analysis of the case law on investment and human rights, see Kriebaum U, 'Human Rights and International Investment Law' in: Radi Y (ed), *Research Handbook on Human Rights and Investment* (Edward Elgar Pub 2018), 13 et seq, see namely footnote 1 on the abundant literature on the subject. See also Kriebaum U, 'Foreign Investments & Human Rights—The Actors and Their Different Roles', in: Calamita NJ et al (eds), *Current Issues in Investment Treaty Law. Volume IV: The Future of ICSID and the Place of Investment Treaties in International Law* (British Institute of International and Comparative Law 2013) 45–59.

219   SADC Model BIT, Art 15; PAIC, Art 24; Indian Model BIT, Art 12, in particular 12.1(i) and (v).

220   See below Section 5.4. Eg Canada-Colombia FTA, Art 816 on corporate social responsibility provides that "[...] these principles address issues such as labour, the environment, human rights [...]"; see also Canada-Peru FTA, Art 810. Human rights violation by investors has indeed occurred in the past, a telling example in this respect is the *Ogoni* case in Nigeria. See African Commission on Human and People's Rights 155/96, *The Social and Economic Rights Action Center and the Center for Economic and Social Rights v Nigeria*, 13–29 Oct 2007.

221   See Section 3.2.1.

222   European Commission, 'Trade for All', above note 2, 15–16.

human rights protection (beyond labour issues) in the partner countries.[223] More specifically, the lack of explicitly referring to human rights in TSD chapters is surprising and incoherent with the EU's own understanding of SD as to include human rights.[224]

5.3.3 Development Cooperation

Development cooperation is a further field of cooperation, establishing a linkage between SD and investment under EU IIAs.[225] In the context of development cooperation purposes, the integration of SD into its IIAS suggests that the EU should also consider the special needs of developing countries. According to the EU, this means that investment in developing countries will be promoted and facilitated to boost sustainable economic growth and poverty reduction.[226] Indeed, aspects of development cooperation have long been integrated into the CCP.[227]

The FTA with Vietnam contains, next to the TSD chapter, a specific chapter on "Cooperation and Capacity Building".[228] In this chapter the parties "commit to deepen cooperation in areas of mutual interest taking into consideration the different levels of development" existing between the EU and Vietnam.[229] The cooperation and capacity building shall foster SD in all its dimensions, including sustainable growth and the reduction of poverty. By analysing the chapter more closely, it becomes apparent that the commitments are kept to a minimum. For instance, the means of cooperation are listed as only "the exchange of information, experience and best practices".[230] And only "where

---

223 For a recent and comprehensive study on the issue, see Kube V, *EU Human Rights, International Investment Law and Participation Operationalizing the EU Foreign Policy Objective to Global Human Rights Protection* (Springer International Publishing 2019).
224 At least, *ex ante* Sustainability Impact Assessments of the EU include human rights; see below Section 5.5.
225 Development cooperation (also development aid) seeks in general to support the economic, environmental, social, and political development of developing States. The EU has a specific external policy of "Development Cooperation", see TFEU, Art 208.
226 European Development Consensus, above note 194, para 52: "The EU and its Member States will promote and facilitate trade and investment in developing countries in support of [SD]." See Alschner and Tuerk, above note 178, 217: "Foreign investment (in particular FDI) can lead to the generation and the dissemination of knowledge and technology, support entrepreneurship, job creation and other spill-over effects".
227 ECJ, Opinion 1/78 *Commodity Agreement on Natural Rubber*, EU:C:1979:224, para 44 and 45; and ECJ, Case 45/86 *Tariff Preferences*, EU:C:1987:163, para 20.
228 EUVFTA, Ch 16.
229 EUVFTA, Art 16.1(2).
230 EUVFTA, Art 16.2(3).

appropriate" may it be considered to include technical assistance and capacity building.[231] The short length of the chapter on development contained in the FTA with Vietnam, can be explained by the existence of before mentioned broader cooperation agreement concluded with Vietnam prior to the FTA. The latter contains a further set of provisions that set out the content of cooperation including technical assistance, training and capacity building[232] as well as trade and investment promotion. Under the cooperation agreement, investment promotion namely includes the "promotion of technology transfer between enterprises, transparency of policies, laws and regulations, market information, [as well as] institutional development".[233]

Looking at other international actors, and in particular, agreements involving at least one developing country, shows that IIAs can go beyond the approaches of the EU. Most prominently is the Brazilian approach, which has amongst its main pillars the improvement of institutional governance related to the investment activity in the host State.[234] The PAIC as well as the BIT between Morocco and Nigeria stipulate the means of how host States should be assisted in their endeavours of investment promotion and facilitation.[235] Similar to the EU approach, the CPTPP contains a dedicated chapter on "Development". The said chapter explicitly refers to the SDGs and sets out that the contracting parties aim at "an open trade and investment environment that seeks to improve welfare, reduce poverty, raise living standards and create new employment opportunities in support of development".[236] Parties moreover acknowledge a number of SD-related concerns, such as sustainable economic growth, women employment, as well as education and science. The CPTPP mentions as potential means financing programmes, capacity building and the facilitation of public-private partnerships.[237] The CPTPP chapter on

---

231   Ibid.
232   EU-Vietnam Cooperation Agreement, Art 7.2(b).
233   EU-Vietnam Cooperation Agreement, Art 13.
234   Eg Brazil-Malawi CIFA, Annex 1, 'Agenda for further Investment Cooperation and Facilitation'. The agenda includes for instance that "[t]he Parties hereby undertake to promote technological, scientific and cultural cooperation through the implementation of actions, programs and projects for the exchange of knowledge and experience, in accordance with their mutual interests and development strategies. The Parties agree that the access and the eventual technology transfer will be carried out, whenever possible, without charge and aimed at contributing with effective trade of goods, services and related investment". See also Brazil-Angola CIFA; Brazil-Mozambique; Brazil-Ethiopia CIFA; Brazil-Suriname CFIA.
235   PAIC, Art 6; Morocco-Nigeria BIT, Art 25.
236   CPTPP, Art 23.1(1).
237   CPTPP, Art 23.6.

development is longer and more explicit than the equivalent chapter of the EU-Vietnam FTA. At the same time, the approach under the CPTPP also rests on soft law language. Financial assistance is only a possibility and depends on the discretion of the contracting parties to give it effect.

The fact that other EU IIAs do not contain development-related provisions shows that the EU has taken different approaches to cooperation in this field, seemingly dependent on the negotiating partner's level of development.[238] Hence, linkages are being made by taking into account the development needs of its contracting party. Nevertheless, the effectiveness of such provisions, in particular as regards the FTA with Vietnam can still be questioned. With regard to its post-Lisbon IIAs, the EU could have taken inspiration from the EPA with the CARIFORUM States, which contains firm commitments on the part of the EU for development aid, including next to technical assistance also financial assistance intending to help to improve their regulatory regimes and thereby to enhance their institutional capacity to attract and benefit from foreign investment.[239] It was a feature of pre-Lisbon EU IIAs practice to acknowledge for developing countries the importance of the creation of an environment favourable to foreign investment and supporting the stimulation of foreign investment initiatives.[240] The partnership as a whole between the EU and Vietnam thus involves development cooperation, more concrete cooperative measures could have been included in the IIA to better link trade and investment with the development needs of Vietnam. Pre-Lisbon IIAs show, linkages between SD and investment can also encompass a dimension of supportive non-economic measures, such as technical assistance and capacity building.[241]

5.3.4 *Anti-Corruption*
Another specific linkage that international investment governance is starting to make is the link between investment law and the fight against corruption. The fight against corruption is part of the global SD agenda.[242] The SDGs linked

---

238 FTAs with developed economies, such as Canada, Japan or Singapore do not contain this kind of commitments.
239 EU-CARIFORUM EPA, Art 7; see in particular Art 7(3): "EC financing is to be carried out according to the framework of rules and relevant procedures provided for the Cotonou Agreement in particular the programming procedure of the European Development Fund (EDF) [...]." See also EU-CARIFORUM EPA, Art 8(3).
240 Dimopoulos, above note 215, 240–241.
241 Ibid, 240–241. More generally on this point, see Marín Durán, note above 10, 227.
242 The 2002 Johannesburg World Summit on Sustainable Development offered opportunities for Governments to express their determination to attack corruption and to make people aware of the devastating effect that corruption has on development. See

the fight against corruption to a broader endeavour of good governance and fostering the rule of law.[243] The UN Convention against Corruption (UNCAC) states that corruption jeopardises SD as well as the rule of law.[244]

With the 2018 FTA, the EU and Mexico took an innovative step for the linkage between trade/investment and SD. The agreement provides for cooperation on anti-corruption measures in a specific chapter.[245] The chapter's objective is to combat active and passive bribery of public officials as well as in the private sector affecting trade and investment.[246] In this context, Mexico and the EU reaffirm their commitments under a number of specific provisions of the UNCAC.[247] The chapter also covers cooperation on preventive measures, on the criminalisation of corruption under domestic law and effective enforcement of national anti-corruption laws. The parties emphasise the need for international cooperation and information exchange as well as the close cooperation of all relevant international bodies working against corruption in the UN, the OECD, the G20, the Financial Action Task Force (FATF), the Council of Europe as well as the Organization of American States.[248] The enforcement of the specific chapter on anti-corruption can be compared with the enforcement procedure under the TSD chapter i.e. first consultation and in a second phase, expert panels, which ultimately means also with respect to corruption a cooperative mechanism has been chosen.[249] Again, any finding of corruption would not lead to sanctions, such as the suspension of trade and investment benefits granted under the FTA. Lastly, the parties state the role of the civil society, reaffirming their commitment under the UNCAC to take appropriate measures to promote the active participation of civil society and community-based organisations.[250]

References to anti-corruption in IIAs started to be introduced around a decade ago.[251] Some IIAs have short statements in which the parties ensure

---

World Summit on Sustainable Development, 'Johannesburg Declaration on Sustainable Development', [2002] A/CONF.199/20.

243 SDG 16: "Promotion of peaceful and inclusive societies for [SD], provide access to justice for all and build effective, accountable and inclusive institutions at all levels" and Target SDG 16.3 "Substantially reduce corruption and bribery in all their forms".

244 United Nations Convention against Corruption (UNCAC), [2008] OJ L 287/1, preamble, recital 3.

245 EUMFTA, Ch 'Anti-corruption'.

246 EUMFTA, Ch 'Anti-corruption', XX.3 and XX.4.

247 Mexico, the EU and all its Member States are parties to UNCAC.

248 EUMFTA, Ch 'Anti-corruption', XX.1(6).

249 Consider again Section 5.2.2.

250 EUMFTA, Ch 'Anti-corruption', Art XX.13; cross-referencing to UNCAC, Art 13(1).

251 OECD, 'International Investment Agreements: A survey of Environmental, Labour and Anti-corruption Issues' (OECD 2008).

to undertake measures to combat corruption regarding matters related to investment.[252] The United States and Canada have, in particular, developed a treaty practice to include more detailed provisions with a particular focus that contracting parties are required to adopt or maintain the necessary legislative or other measures to establish that corruption is a criminal offence under its law.[253] The CPTPP has a chapter dedicated to anti-corruption and transparency.[254] There is thus another parallel between the EU and the North American approach in terms of introducing specific chapters on anti-corruption cooperation. The behaviour of economic operators, including investors plays a vital role in the fight against corruption.[255] Therefore, the EU, as the United States and Canada, include promotional measures on responsible business conduct in this respect.[256] In contrast thereto, IIAs of developing countries started the trend to impose not only obligations on States to cooperate in the fight against corruption but started to introduce direct obligations on foreign investors not to engage in corruptive practices.[257]

From the EU perspective, the European Commission found that the fight against corruption is part of its trade and investment policy.[258] Addressing the issue within an IIA, such as the FTA with Mexico serves such policy purposes. The new provisions on anti-corruption measures and the reference to international standards both need to be welcome. The challenge remains the concrete effectiveness of the EU's approach, which might be undermined by the soft enforcement possibilities for the provisions concerning anti-corruption. Lastly, the EU approach does not consist of addressing direct obligations on

---

[252] Eg Japan-Lao's Democratic Republic BIT, Art 10: "Each Contracting Party shall ensure that measures and efforts are undertaken to prevent and combat corruption regarding matters covered by this Agreement in accordance with its laws and regulations". See also Morocco-Nigeria BIT (2016), Art 17.1.

[253] See the provision on Anti-Corruption in US FTAs figures in the chapter on Transparency: see Chapter 18 of the US-Oman FTA, Art 18.5 (on corruption); or Chapter 21 of the US-Korea FTA, Art 21.6 (on corruption). See also, Canada-Peru FTA, Art 1908.

[254] CPTPP, Ch 26.

[255] Typically, corruptive conduct is of shared responsibility between an investor and host State authorities. See eg the discussion in *Metal-Tech Ltd v The Republic of Uzbekistan*, ICSID Case No ARB/10/3, Award, 4 Oct 2013, para 389.

[256] Eg EUMFTA, Ch 'Anti-corruption', Arts XX.7 and XX.9; CPTPP, Arts 26.6(1) and 26.10.

[257] Eg Morocco-Nigeria BIT, Art 17.2-3. See also PAIC, Art 21; SADC Model BIT, Art 10.

[258] European Commission, 'Trade for All', above note 2, 19: "Corruption is a plague on economies and societies. It holds countries back from development, distorting public procurement, wasting scarce public funds, discouraging investment, hampering trade and creating unfair competition."

foreign investor as regards anti-corruption as is further discussed in the following section.

5.4 Fostering the Responsibility of Foreign Investors

Since the start of the SD agenda in 1992, the international community has been preoccupied with strengthening the participation of the private sector in order to achieve SD.[259] With the adoption of the Agenda 2030, the important role of the private sector in achieving SD has been reiterated.[260] The EU likewise stressed that corporate respect for labour and human rights, as well as environmental protection and the embedding thereof in corporate operations and value chains are indispensable for SD and the achievement of the SDGs.[261] IIAs do not systematically prescribe which behaviours investors should adopt. This said, reference to investors' behaviour combined with obligations is an increasing, yet relatively contentious development in international investment law.[262]

EU IIAs refer to CSR in a specific provision as well as in the preamble of the agreements. The CSR provisions in TSD chapters of a comprehensive FTA are rather short and general but make reference to several internationally recognised standards and guidelines. Indeed, with respect to CSR such international soft law instruments perform a complementary role to IIAs.[263] EU IIAs typically refer to several of the most important internationally recognised guidelines and principles. First, all post-Lisbon EU IIAs incorporate the OECD Guidelines for Multinational Enterprises[264] (hereafter: OECD Guidelines).[265] Second, some EU IIAs also make reference to the ten principles of the United

---

259 The 1992 Agenda 21 has insisted that international corporations "should recognize environmental management as among the highest corporate priorities and as key determinant to [SD]". See Agenda 21, above note 80, para 30.3. See also Johannesburg Declaration, above note 237, para 27: "Private sector [...] has a duty to contribute to the evolution of equitable and sustainable communities and societies".

260 Agenda 2030, above note 201.

261 Council of the European Union, 'Conclusions on Business and Human Rights', [2016] Doc 10254/16.

262 See Section 2.6.3.

263 Boisson de Chazournes L, 'Environmental Protection and Investment Arbitration: Yin and Yang?' Anuario Colombiano de Derecho Internacional (2017) 10, 401.

264 OECD, 'OECD Guidelines for Multinational Enterprises', annexed to 2000 OECD Declaration on International Investment and Multinational Enterprises, DAFFE/IME(2000)/20; (2001) 40 ILM 237 as amended.

265 Eg CETA, Art 22.3(2)(b).

Nations Global Compact Initiative[266] (hereafter: UN Global Compact).[267] Third, another international CSR instrument, which EU IIAs incorporate are the UN Guiding Principles on Business and Human Rights[268] (UNGPs).[269] TSD chapters of EU IIAs that refer to it thus indirectly promote human rights given that otherwise, TSD chapters do not contain references to human rights. Lastly, some EU IIAs also contain the Tripartite Declaration of Principles for Multinational Enterprises and Social Policy of ILO[270] (hereafter: ILO Tripartite Declaration).[271] The EU-Mexico FTA adds a further instrument, which is the OECD Due Diligence Guidance for Responsible Supply Chains.[272] The common strand of all these instruments is that they contain best practices and voluntary standards for foreign investors without any binding obligation on them *per se*. They are directly addressed to multinational enterprises but generally use a soft language, such "should" or "should take into account" commitments.

5.4.1 *Direct versus Indirect Investor Obligations*

IIAs can contain indirect investor obligations, which are obligations that require the contracting parties to adopt measures aimed at regulating and guiding the behaviour of multinational enterprises, including foreign investors.[273] In

---

266 UN Global Compact, 'United Nations Global Compact: The Ten Principles' [2004].
267 EUMFTA, TSD chapter, Art 9.2(b).
268 UN Human Rights Council, 'Guiding Principles on Business and Human Rights: Implementing the United Nations 'Protect, Respect and Remedy' Framework" [2011] A/HRC/17/31.
269 EUMFTA, TSD chapter, Art 9.2(b); EUVFTA, Art 13.10(2)(e).
270 ILO, 'Tripartite Declaration of Principles concerning Multinational Enterprises and Social Policy' [1977; last amended 2017].
271 EUMFTA, TSD chapter, Art 9.2(b); EUVFTA, Art 13.10(2)(e).
272 EUMFTA, TSD chapter, Art 9(3) (specific provision on "Trade and Responsible Management of Supply Chains"); and EUMERFTA, TSD chapter, Art 10.3; See also OECD, 'Due Diligence Guidance for Responsible Supply Chains of Minerals from Conflict-Affected and High-Risk Areas', (OECD Publishing 2016). This instrument provides a framework for detailed due diligence as a basis for responsible supply chain management of minerals, including tin, tantalum, tungsten and gold, as well as all other mineral resources. In May 2017, the European Union adopted Regulation No 2017/821, which seek to implement the suggestions of the OECD. See Regulation No 2017/821 of the European Parliament and of the Council of 17 May 2017 laying down supply chain due diligence obligations for Union importers of tin, tantalum and tungsten, their ores, and gold originating from conflict-affected and high-risk areas [2017] OJ L 130/1.
273 Nowrot K, 'Obligations of Investors', in: Bungenberg M and others (eds), *International Investment Law—A Handbook* (CH BECK; Hart; Nomos 2015) 1165, pt 18. See also, Mbengue MM, 'Les obligations des investisseurs étrangers' in: Société française pour le droit international (Colloque de Paris Vincennes—Saint-Denis), *L'entreprise multinationale et le droit international* (Pedone 2017) 295–337.

contrast hereto stand direct investor obligations, which are obligations directly addressed to foreign investors.[274] Direct obligations have not yet gained widespread recognition in investment treaty practice and one finds their inclusion mainly in IIAs and model treaties of developing countries.

5.4.1.1 CSR Commitments Addressed to States/the EU

EU IIAs contain specific CSR provisions, which mainly refer to best business practices related to CSR in general;[275] or to internationally recognised CSR guidelines and standards. These provisions are all addressed to the contracting parties and not to foreign investors directly. The EU hence uses indirect investor obligations in order to foster the responsibilities of foreign investors.[276]

The CSR provisions of EU IIAs vary, first regarding their formulation and second, their degree of bindingness for the contracting parties. The Singapore-EU FTA, for instance, contains a soft provision providing only that the contracting parties "*should* make special efforts to promote" voluntary CSR practices.[277] The CETA formulates that the parties "agree to strive to promote" economic activities that promote decent work and environmental protection including by "encouraging the development and use of voluntary best practices of [CSR] by enterprises".[278] A slightly more binding "shall" formulation can be found in the FTAs with Japan and Mexico, which provide that the parties "shall encourage" CSR;[279] or "shall promote" CSR and also "shall support" the dissemination and use of international guidelines.[280] Despite their variations, all of the provisions are best-endeavour commitments. The general statements on CSR are followed by at least one of the four main instruments mentioned here above.[281] The reference to international standards usually is not accompanied by other standards. Nevertheless, the EU-Vietnam FTA specifies that CSR promotion

---

274   Ibid, 1161, pt 11.
275   Eg EU-Colombia/Peru FTA, Art 271; and EU-Central America FTA, Art 288.
276   See also Nowrot, above note 273, 1165, pt 18.
277   EUSFTA, TSD chapter, Art 12.11(4).
278   CETA, Art 22.3(b): continues "such as those in the OECD Guidelines for Multinational Enterprises, to strengthen coherence between economic, social and environmental objectives"; and EUVFTA, Art 13.10(2)(e).
279   EUJFTA, Art 16.5(e). See also EUVFTA, Art 13.10(e): parties "agree to promote CSR".
280   EUMFTA, TSD chapter, Art 9(2)(a-b).
281   CETA only refers to the OECD Guidelines; EUJFTA and EUSFTA refer to the OECD Guidelines and the ILO Tripartite Declaration; the EUVFTA refers to the Guidelines of the OECD, ILO as well as the Global Compact; the EUMFTA refers to all three instruments and also adds the UN Guiding Principles on Business and Human Rights.

can include the "exchange of information and best practices, education and training activities and technical advice" between the contracting parties.[282]

Considering international investment governance in general, CSR commitments addressed to the contracting parties worded in best-endeavour obligations has become the mainstream approach.[283] For instance, under the CPTPP, the parties generally "reaffirm the importance" of encouraging CSR.[284] A very similar formulation can be found in the PACER Plus Agreement.[285] Canada in particular, like the EU, only includes hortatory CSR obligations addressed to the contracting parties mostly formulated as "should encourage" and seldom "shall encourage".[286] The EU and several other actors thus prefer commitments addressed to themselves, leaving them with discretion as to how CSR promotion unfolds at the national level. The minor differences in the wording of these provisions, *i.e.* their variations of "should" or "shall" commitments should not be overrated. A "shall" obligation to promote remains still relatively soft as the verbs "to promote" or "to encourage" are flexible including a variety of measures that a contracting party can take in order to satisfy such CSR obligation.

From an EU perspective, it is interesting to highlight the EU's approach taken in its EPA with the CARIFORUM as it shows that CSR provision addressed to States can be drafted in a much more precise way making the commitments clearer and arguably more effective.[287] Its Article 72, entitled "behaviour of investors", provides a detailed run-through of how CSR can be put into effect by spelling out certain standards addressed to investors, which shall be ensured by the contracting parties for instance through domestic legislation.[288] Through the formulation "shall" the contracting parties have the obligation to pursue CSR implementation precisely on the stated issues, which are related to four key aspects of investor behaviour: corruption and bribery (lit. a); compliance with core labour standards

---

[282] EUVFTA, Art 13.10(e).
[283] See also Gordon K, Pohl J and Bouchard M, 'Investment Treaty Law, Sustainable Development and Responsible Business Conduct: A Fact-Finding Survey' (2014) OECD Working Papers on International Investment 2014/01.
[284] CPTPP, Art 9.17.
[285] PACER Plus, Art 5(2); See also Chile-Hong Kong China SAR BIT, Art 16.
[286] See Canadian BITs with Guinea, Art 16; with Burkina Faso, Art 16; with Serbia, Art 16. An exception constitutes the BIT with Côte d'Ivoire as it contains a binding obligation: "shall encourage", see Art 15. Similar hereto are Canadian FTAs, eg Canada-Peru FTA, Art 810.
[287] EU-CARIFORUM EPA, Art 72. A similar provision can be found in the Indian Model BIT, Art 11.
[288] EU-CARIFORUM EPA, Art 72 ab initio.

as stipulated in the ILO Declaration on Fundamental Rights at Work (lit. b); not circumventing with international labour and environmental standards (lit. c); and finally the relationship between the investor and local communities (lit. d). From post-Lisbon EU IIA practice, it becomes apparent that the EU favours a general reference to the concept of CSR and the use of internationally recognised CSR instruments instead of explicitly mentioning the elements. The approach taken in the (pre-Lisbon) EPA with the CARIFORUM has not been followed even though the EU already had treaty practice in this respect seeking to foster corporate compliance with SD regulations and objectives.[289]

5.4.1.2 CSR Commitments Directly Addressed to Foreign Investors

Certain global actors, in particular, developing countries pursue an IIA treaty practice consisting of also including direct investor obligations.[290] Treaty practice can be distinguished between those CSR provisions for investors drafted in best-efforts obligations and those that are clearly binding obligations for investors. The former approach can mainly be found in Brazilian IIA practice, where investors "shall strive to achieve" a contribution to SD, or "shall endeavour to comply" with voluntary CSR principles and standards.[291] Such formulation can also be found in the Indian Model BIT, according to which, investors "shall endeavour to voluntarily incorporate internationally recognised standards".[292] Other countries have opted for even softer formulations towards investor obligation stating that investors "should make efforts" to responsible business conduct.[293]

Several African instruments contain provisions with clear and binding obligations. The PAIC for example contains a whole set of investor obligations, *i.e.* no less than six articles, which relate to corporate governance,[294] socio-political

---

289 Council of the European Union, 'Conclusions on Business and Human Rights', [2016] Doc 10254/16.
290 There are many reasons behind such approaches. One reason for developing countries is that their domestic legislation and enforcement mechanisms are often not sufficiently effective in order to ensure responsible business conduct in their territory. Moreover, several developing countries seek through the incorporation of direct investor obligations to mitigate the asymmetry of traditional IIAs, which only provided for rights of investors without stating their obligations. See Section 2.6.3.
291 Brazil-Suriname CIFA, Art 15.1–2; see also Brazil-Ethiopia CIFA, Art 14.1–2; Brazil-Malawi CIFA, Art 9.1–2.
292 Indian Model BIT, Art 12.
293 Eg Argentina-Qatar BIT, Art 12.
294 PAIC, Art 19.

obligations,[295] bribery,[296] CSR in general,[297] the use of natural resources,[298] human rights[299] and environmental impact assessments.[300] Similar approaches, although less extensive, can be found in the model BITs of Ghana and Botswana.[301] The BIT between Morocco and Nigeria is yet one of the rare examples of a concluded treaty that provides for a series of investor obligations: First, investors "shall" conduct environmental and social impact assessments of their investment prior to starting the activity.[302] Second, investors shall not bribe or engage in corruption.[303] And third, investors once established have to maintain environmental standards, uphold human rights and act in accordance with the ILO Declaration.[304]

In sum, the EU's approach concerning the fostering of investor responsibilities is to include CSR commitments that are addressed to the contracting parties and that are mostly written in a hortatory manner. The EU's approach is similar to those of other recent IIAs of capital-exporting countries, in particular, those of Canada and the United States. Yet, it should be noted that any reference to

---

295 PAIC, Art 20. The provision contains a non-exhaustive list of obligations referring to "(a) Respect for national sovereignty and observance of domestic laws, regulations and administrative practices; (b) Respect for socio-cultural values; (c) Non-interference with political affairs; (d) Non-interference in intergovernmental relations; and (e) Respect of labour rights".

296 PAIC, Art 21: "(1) Investors shall not offer, promise or give any unlawful or undue pecuniary or other advantage or present, whether directly or through intermediaries, to a public official of a Member State, or to a member of an official's family or business associate or other person in order that the official or other person act or refrain from acting in relation to the performance of official duties. (2) Investors shall also not aid or abet a conspiracy to commit or authorize acts of bribery".

297 PAIC, Art 22.

298 PAIC, Art 23: "(1) Investors shall not exploit or use local natural resources to the detriment of the rights and interests of the host State. (2) Investors shall respect rights of local populations, and avoid land grabbing practices vis-à-vis local communities".

299 PAIC, Art 24. The provision contains the following principles: (a) support and respect the protection of internationally recognised human rights; (b) ensure that they are not complicit in human rights abuses; (c) eliminate all forms of forced and compulsory labour, including the effective abolition of child labour; (d) eliminate discrimination in respect of employment and occupation; and (e) ensure equitable sharing of wealth incurred from investments.

300 SADC Model BIT, Art 13; ECOWAS Supplementary Act 12(1): "[I]nvestors and investments shall conduct an environmental and social impact assessment of the potential investment."

301 Ghana Model BIT, Art 12; Botswana Model BIT, Art 11.

302 Morocco-Nigeria BIT, Art 14.2–3. With respect to the environmental impact assessment, investors are held to apply the precautionary principle.

303 Ibid, Art 17.

304 Ibid, Art 18.

CSR is a recent phenomenon and that the large bulk of IIAs still in force do not contain any mention to CSR.[305] Explicit references to CSR as well as the incorporation of instruments should thus be welcomed and add to the SD integration within EU IIAs. Under EU IIAs, investors are made aware that all contracting parties, *i.e.* the host and the home State seek to ensure that investment activities abide by certain internationally recognised CSR standards. Given that an ever more widening number of countries are agreed on the CSR principles, the monitoring and focus on investor behaviour has been heightened in recent years.[306] The inclusion of the major internationally recognised standards by the EU fosters this general trend. At the current state of treaty practice, the differences in approach of, on the one hand, capital-exporting countries, and on the other hand, capital-importing countries is striking. So far, no concluded IIA with direct investor obligations has been adopted having at least one capital-exporting country as a contracting party. This shows that developed States are not interested in bestowing their companies with additional obligations when operating aboard and the EU is no exception in this respect. The European Commission should closely monitor whether actual positive spill-over effects occur due to the inclusion of voluntary standards in EU IIAs given that there exists already evidence that this approach has in the past not proven sufficient to ensure investment activities are conducted in compliance with SD.[307]

5.4.2 *Issues of Enforcing Investor Obligations*

IIAs dealing with direct obligations for investors have to foresee how the enforcement of such provisions operates as otherwise, they remain ineffective.[308] The treaties and model treaties that contain direct investor obligations consider the need to ensure effective enforcement mechanisms, albeit different approaches exist. A first approach is to state in the IIA the possibility to file a civil liability claim in the home State of the investor if the investor breached one or more of the obligations stated in the IIA. An example in this respect is the Morocco-Nigeria BIT, which states that "[i]nvestors shall be subject to civil actions for liability in the judicial process of their *home state* for the acts

---

305 Gordon, Pohl and Bouchard, above note 283.
306 Boisson de Chazournes, above note 263, 401.
307 Daniel C, Wilde-Ramsing J, Genovese K and Sandjojo V, *Remedy Remains Rare: An analysis of 15 years of NCP Cases and Their Contribution to Improve Access to Remedy for Victims of Corporate Misconduct* (OECD Watch 2015). See also, Daniel C et al (eds), *Glass half full? The State of Accountability in Development Finance* (Centre for Research on Multinational Corporations (SOMO) 2016). See also, Section 2.6.3.
308 Mbengue, above note 273, 335.

or decisions made in relation to the investment where such acts or decisions lead to significant damage, personal injuries or loss of life in the host state".[309] The underlying rationale of such liability clauses is that a home State bears duties relating to the accountability of its multinational corporations investing aboard.[310] In fact and irrespectively of the existence of an IIA, a number of jurisdictions have accepted in the past to deal with social and human rights violations of their companies that exercise business aboard.[311] At the same time, often enough victims affected by a foreign investment find it challenging to surpass the jurisdictional hurdles of home State proceedings.[312] US courts, for instance, regularly decline to hear cases on oversee disputes based on the *forum non conveniens* doctrine.[313] European national courts, on the other hand, are often reluctant to hear such cases albeit for different reasons than it is the case for US courts.[314] The main hurdle in European jurisdictions is the centrality of the nationality of the defendants. In other words, European courts will typically not impute the nationality of a parent company to its subsidiaries.[315] European companies evade liability by organizing and doing business through local subsidies established in the host State.[316] The expected benefit of the investor liability clause of the Morocco-Nigeria BIT is thus to clarify that the home State has to bring about the possibility within its national court system that jurisdiction can be found to hear claims based on alleged violations of investors' obligation. The SADC Model is even more explicit on this specific aspect as it states "[h]ome states shall ensure that their legal systems and rules allow for, or do not prevent or unduly restrict, the bringing of court actions on their merits before domestic courts relating to the civil liability of Investors and Investments for damages resulting from alleged acts, decisions

---

309 Morocco-Nigeria BIT, Art 20 (with the title "investor liability").
310 Levashova Y, 'The Accountability and Corporate Social Responsibility of Multinational Corporations for Transgressions in Host States through International Investment Law' (2018) 14 Utrecht Law Review 40, 46–47; see also Sornarajah M, *The International Law on Foreign Investment* (Cambridge University Press 2017) 144.
311 For an overview see, Schrempf-Stirling J and Wettstein F, 'Beyond Guilty Verdicts: Human Rights Litigation and Its Impact on Corporations' Human Rights Policies' (2017) 145 Journal of Business Ethics 545.
312 Steinitz M, *The Case for an International Court of Civil Justice* (Cambridge University Press 2019) 89–98.
313 Ibid, 84. The doctrine, which is mostly known in common law jurisdictions, constitutes a rule whereby a court acknowledges that another forum or court is more appropriate to hear the case in question and therefore sends the case to such a forum.
314 Excluding the United Kingdom, where the *forum non conveniens* doctrine can apply.
315 Steinitz, above note 312, 85.
316 Ibid.

or omissions made by Investors in relation to their Investments in the territory of the Host State."[317]

A second approach that can be found in treaty practice to render direct investor obligations effective consists of allowing respondent States in an investor-State dispute settlement proceeding to file a counterclaim relating to alleged breaches of investor obligations. Such possibility is namely foreseen in the Investment Agreement of COMESA stating that "[a] Member State against whom a claim is brought [...] may assert as a defense, counterclaim, right of set off or other similar claim, that the COMESA investor bringing the claim has not fulfilled its obligations under this Agreement [...]."[318] A very similar approach can be found in the SADC Model BIT[319] and the Pan-African Investment Code. The latter states, "[a] Member State may initiate a counterclaim against the investor before any competent body dealing with a dispute under this Code for damages or other relief resulting from an alleged breach of the Code."[320] The rationale of explicitly stating the possibility for a host State to submit a counterclaim is based on the fact that in practice, tribunals often enough deny jurisdiction on counterclaims due to the absence of a clear treaty provision expressly allowing for such claims by the State.[321] The inclusion of an express reference to counterclaims clarifies that investors consent to the tribunal's jurisdiction over these claims.

A third approach can be seen in conditioning the IIA protection and access to ISDS to the respect of the stated investor obligations. The Morocco-Nigeria BIT, for instance, links the direct investor obligation relating to corruption to the definition of the investment and thus the scope of the agreement. The BIT states that "[a] breach of [the Article on anti-corruption] by an investor or investment is deemed to constitute a breach of the domestic law of the Host State Party concerning the establishment and operation of an investment".[322] And according to the investment definition contained in the said BIT,

---

317 SADC Model BIT, Art 17(2).
318 COMESA Investment Agreement, Art 28(9).
319 SADC Model BIT, Art 19(2): "A Host State may initiate a counterclaim against the Investor before any tribunal established pursuant to this Agreement for damages or other relief resulting from an alleged breach of the Agreement."
320 PAIC, Art 43(2).
321 See *Spyridon Roussalis v Romania*, ICSID Case No ARB/06/1, Award, 7 December 2011, paras 859–877; and *Saluka Investments BV v The Czech Republic*, UNCITRAL, Decision on Jurisdiction over the Czech Republic's Counterclaim, 7 May 2004. It is noteworthy that the Convention on the Settlement of Investment Disputes Between States and Nationals of Other States (ICSID Convention) accepts counterclaims under certain conditions, see ICSID Convention, Art 46; and ICSID Arbitration Rules, Rule 40.
322 Morocco-Nigeria BIT, Art 17(4). See for a similar provision, SADC Model BIT, Art 10.3: "A breach of this article by an Investor or an Investment is deemed to constitute a breach of

investments have to made in accordance with the host State laws.[323] As such, where investments have been made through corruption, the investor will lose the protection offered under the Morocco-Nigeria BIT. Even though the EU does not favour an approach of direct investor obligations, it has incorporated such a "tit for tat" approach in its IIAs, which foresees that if the investment was made through fraudulent or corruptive investor behaviour, the investor loses the possibility to submit a claim to investor-State dispute settlement is only possible.[324] Thus, investors are deprived of the remedy of ISDS that would otherwise be available to them under EU IIAs. Both, the issue of "in accordance with host State laws"[325] as well as the issue of certain exclusions from the scope of investor-State dispute resolution[326] will be further discussed in the next chapter.

5.5 SD Integration during the Negotiation Phase of EU IIAs

Shaping SD integration for EU IIAs includes integrating social and environmental concerns in the making of trade and investment agreements. An important mechanism in this regard are Sustainability Impact Assessments (SIAs).[327] The main purpose of SIAs is to support negotiations by providing the European Commission with an *ex ante* analysis of the potential economic, social, human rights, and environmental impacts of envisaged agreements.[328] The EU has conducted SIAs on all important trade agreements since 1999.[329] The first SIA was adopted during the preparation phase of the World Trade Organization Millennium Round of negotiation. At the time, pressure was

---

the domestic law of the Host State Party concerning the establishment and operation of an investment".

323 Morocco-Nigeria BIT, Art 1(3).
324 Eg CETA, Art 8.18(3): "For greater certainty, an investor may not submit a claim under this Section if the investment was made through fraudulent misrepresentation, concealment, corruption or conduct amounting to an abuse process".
325 See Section 6.3.1.
326 See Section 6.4.2.
327 Kube V and Pedreschi L, 'The Social Dimension of the Common Commercial Policy', in: Cortese F and Ferri D (eds), *The EU Social Market Economy and the Law: Theoretical Perspectives and Practical Challenges for the EU* (Routledge 2018) 278.
328 The human rights impact assessment forms part of SIAs since 2015. See European Commission, 'Guidelines on the Analysis of Human Rights Impacts in Impact Assessments for Trade-related Policy Initiatives', available at <http://trade.ec.europa.eu/doclib/docs/2015/july/tradoc_153591.pdf>.
329 SIA Handbook, above note 168, 8.

coming from civil society groups that insisted on making trade policies more compatible with environmental and social aspects, ultimately leading the EU to adopt SIAs.[330] As of today, the EU has concluded more than 20 SIAs in support of its trade negotiations.[331] The fact that SIAs became common practice for the EU is remarkable since the EU has no legal obligation to adopt these mechanisms.[332] The practice is grounded in political and technical reasons. Politically, the adoption of SIAs symbolises the EU's commitment to align its international economic agreements with SD going beyond a focus on economic benefits. Technically, SIAs can serve as a tool to maximise the concrete benefits of trade liberalisation by also addressing environmental and social concerns.[333] Today, the EU underlines that SIAs lead to a more responsible trade and investment policy.[334] In other words, SIAs are key instruments for the EU making its commercial policy more responsive to environmental and societal concerns. The self-imposed guidelines constitute an ambitious overall framework for the *ex ante* assessment of trade and investment agreements.[335] At the same time, conducting impact assessments of major trade and investment agreements is not an EU specificity. The United States and Canada, in particular, also have a long practice of impact assessments of their economic agreements with third countries.[336] Their approaches differ, however, to the EU approach. One striking difference is that US and Canadian impact assessments are limited to environmental impacts thus excluding social and human rights impacts.[337]

---

330 For more details see Cordonier Segger M-C, Gehring M and Stephenson S, 'Sustainability Impact Assessments as Inputs and as Interpretative Aids in International Investment Law' (2017) 18 The Journal of World Investment & Trade 163, 168 et seq.

331 A list of all accomplished SIAs as well as the respectively related position paper of the European Commission can be found at <http://ec.europa.eu/trade/policy/policy-making/analysis/policy-evaluation/sustainability-impact-assessments/index_en.htm>.

332 Cordonier Segger, Gehring and Stephenson, above note 330, 169.

333 See also Marín Durán G and Morgera E, *Environmental Integration in the EU's External Relations: Beyond Multilateral Dimensions* (Hart Pub 2012) 235.

334 SIA Handbook, above note 168, 3.

335 See also, Kube and Pedreschi, above note 327, 279.

336 Starting with the first NAFTA Effects study carried out by the North American Commission for Environmental Cooperation; see Commission for Environmental Cooperation, *Potential NAFTA Effects: Claims and Arguments 1991–1994* (CEC 1996).

337 For more details on the comparison between the Canadian, EU and US approaches, see Reynaud P, 'Sustainable Development and Regional Trade Agreements: Toward Better Practices in Impact Assessments' 2013 8 McGill International Journal of Sustainable Development Law & Policy 2, 242. Reynaud came to the conclusion that the EU approach has a more rigorous methodology, and could, therefore, better identify impacts and opportunities.

5.5.1 The Procedure of Sustainability Impact Assessments

EU SIAs are independent studies that are prepared by consulting agencies which are contracted by the Commission. The Commission assures, however, the supervision of the consultant's activity through so called inter-service steering groups that involve all interested Commission services as well as the European External Action Service (EEAS).[338] The Commission has the responsibility to supervise the consultants yet the consultants bear the main responsibility for the content and outcome of the SIA. Conversely, US and Canadian impact assessments are conducted by government officials instead of consultancy agencies.[339] One can argue about which of the two approaches is more beneficial, efficient and more independent. An argument that the European Commission often advances is that having recourse to external consultants would imply greater technical expertise and greater independence.[340] Others also underline the benefits of external consultants by highlighting that they can bring additional research and policy expertise into the policy process.[341] A fundamental aspect seems to be how the consultants are chosen, in other words what is the level of transparency when it comes to awarding a consultancy contract. At the EU level, the process starts with a public tender and interested consultancy agencies are required to submit a proposal that includes the intended methodology and scope as well as a financial proposal.[342] A selection committee involving different Directorates-Generals of the Commission is subsequently in charge of selecting the external consultants.[343] Even though

---

338 SIA Handbook, above note 168, 11.
339 See US Government, Office of the United States Trade Representative, 'Guidelines for Implementation of Executive Order 13141: Environmental Review of Trade Agreements' (USTR 2000); Department of Foreign Affairs and International Trade Canada, 'Framework for Conducting Environmental Assessments of Trade Negotiations' (DFAIT 2001). See also, Government of Canada, 'The Cabinet Directive on the Environmental Assessment of Policy, Plan and Program Proposals' (Privy Council Office and Canadian Environmental Assessment Agency 2016).
340 SIA Handbook, above note 168, 6: "SIAs are carried out by external consultants in a neutral and unbiased manner, under strict rules on the absence of conflicts of interest". See also Reynaud, above note 337, 242.
341 Dias Simões F, 'External Consultants as Actors in European Trade and Investment Policymaking', in Amtenbrink F, Prévost D and Wessel RA (eds), *Netherlands Yearbook of International Law 2017*, vol 48 (TMC Asser Press 2018) 119.
342 Alf L, Assmann C, Bauer M, Weinkopf J, 'Towards a Transatlantic Dialog on Trade and the Environment: A Comparison of Approaches to Environmental Impact Assessments of Trade Agreements in the US and EU.' School of Advanced International Studies, Henry Luce Foundation, 2008 EcoLogic. <http://ecologic.eu/sites/files/event/2013/transatlantic-lunch-jan-08-final_report.pdf>.
343 Ibid.

the discretion is with the European Commission to choose the consultants that it considers most appropriate, there are procedural requirements that the Commission must respect and no Commission service can decide alone which applicant will be chosen. In order to further foster the consultant's independence, they are, based on the consultancy contract, required to exercise their task in an independent and unbiased manner.³⁴⁴

SIAs are launched soon after the Council of the European Union has formally authorised the Commission to enter into negotiations. This means in general not later than six months after the start of negotiations, to ensure that the analysis can usefully feed into the negotiating process.³⁴⁵ Once the consultants have been chosen, the SIAs procedure starts. The procedure consists of three main phases. The first phase generally consists of setting the analysis's methodological framework, which will be presented in an "inception report". In the second phase, the consultants prepare an "interim report" in which preliminary findings are reported. During both phases, there are consultations with civil society and stakeholders. In this respect, SIAs also have an informative purpose facilitating the outreach to stakeholders affected by the agreement under negotiation. During the SIA process consultations take place within the EU but also within partner countries. Lastly, a SIA process comes to an end by the adoption of a final report, which is published on the European Commission website.³⁴⁶ The European Commission reacts to the report by taking a position on the results of the SIA in the form of a "position paper". These documents identify to what extent the European Commission agrees with the consultants. Where needed they seek to explain the disagreement, add complementary analysis and flag lessons learnt from the assessment.³⁴⁷

5.5.2 *The Methodology of Sustainability Impact Assessments*

SIAs on trade and investment agreements combine public debate elements with an objective analysis.³⁴⁸ The outreach to stakeholders plays a significant

---

344 SIA Handbook, above note 168, 6.
345 This is indeed an important improvement as it occurred at the beginning of the SIA practice that SIAs were launched too late into the negotiating process with the result that their assessment had little impact on the treaty in question. For instance, the SIA on the EU-Chile Association Agreement was completed only after the conclusion of the negotiations in November 2002.
346 SIA Handbook, above note 168, 9–13.
347 See also Marín Durán and Morgera, above note 333, 236.
348 George C and Kirkpatrick C, 'Sustainability Impact Assessment of World Trade Negotiations: Current Practice and Lessons for Further Development' Working Paper Series, Paper No 2, Manchester, 2003, 7.

part. With respect to the public debate component, the study involves meetings with stakeholders, targeted roundtables, bilateral contacts with experts and online consultation. For the technical part of the SIA, consultants are held to identify SD impacts for the EU and its negotiating partners and to some extent also for third countries that could result from the envisaged trade and investment agreement. The provisions on trade and investment are scrutinised through a four-fold analysis including an economic analysis, a social analysis, a human rights analysis and an environmental analysis.[349] The approaches taken are of quantitative and qualitative nature depending on the availability of relevant statistics.[350] Sector-studies are also included in order to gain more in-depth results. Moreover, the used methodology under SIAs typically also includes to canvassing the compatibility of the envisaged trade and investment agreement with core international conventions, such as the human rights conventions of the United Nations, the conventions of the International Labour Organization, the European Convention on Human Rights, as well as relevant multilateral environmental agreements.[351]

In a discussion on international investment governance and IIAs, one needs to highlight that SIAs have been developed for trade agreements. Thus, they have a focus on trade aspects rather than on investment matters and provisions. This being said, the methodology that applies to assess trade provisions should not be the same as the one to apply investment provisions.[352] The reason lies

---

[349] Eg SIA on CETA, see 'A Trade SIA Relating to the Negotiation of a Comprehensive Economic and Trade Agreement (CETA) Between the EU and Canada', Final Report, June 2011, Trade 10/B3/B06, 14 and 26–27. The human rights assessment was not yet part of the SIA on CETA.

[350] The qualitative analysis typically follows that quantitative analysis (that is based on figures and statistics); See LSE Enterprise Ltd, 'Trade Sustainability Impact Assessment of the Comprehensive Trade and Investment Agreement between the European Union and Japan, Final Inception Report', March 2015, 21: "The second part of the analysis relies on a qualitative methodology. Using the quantitative data of the first section as a basis and making constant reference to it, this section qualitatively complements the analysis of the decent work impacts. In order to do so, the quantitative sources mentioned in section 3.3 will be complemented by an assessment of the likely/possible compliance with provisions in the prospective agreement having a major impact on the employment effects of the agreement, such as those dealing with non-tariff barriers. The principal sources will be the experience with existing FTAs of each partner, discussions with negotiators and stakeholders. Furthermore, the qualitative analysis expands on other social dialogue issues, core labour standards and the impact on human rights issues, while using the feedback obtained from the stakeholder consultation."

[351] SIA Handbook, above note 168, 20 and 23.

[352] Blobel D, Görlach B and Ingwersen W, 'Investment: The Context Matters', in Ekins P and Voituriez T (eds), *Trade, Globalization and Sustainability Impact Assessment: A Critical Look at Methods and Outcomes* (Earthscan 2009) 103.

in the fact that trade-flows can more readily be predicted based on the existence of a trade agreement, whereas investment flows cannot. The correlation between the existence of an IIA and any increase in foreign investments within a contracting party to the IIA in much less evident.[353] As already discussed at the outset of the present book, there is no conclusive evidence concerning the increase of investment flows thanks to the existence of an IIA.[354] Hence, the causal chain analysis that seeks to trace the SD impacts of a given trade measure must be adapted to the investment context.[355] Consequently, the assessments of the material impacts of the IIA, e.g. to what extent does an agreement lead to economic growth, have to be considered with the necessary caution. The EU-Chile SIA final report for instance acknowledged this fact in its assessment of the provision on investment liberalization in the service sector. The report found that "information on sustainability issues is generally not fully available and consistent with the possible partial expectations of economic data".[356] The analysis of SIAs relating to investment provisions can, however, based on a qualitative (rather than a quantitative) study consider potential regulatory impacts, such as by questioning to what extent an agreement has direct or indirect constraints for the domestic legislator in adopting environmental and social laws.[357] So far, this has not been fully implemented into the EU methodology.[358] The agreements are mainly assessed in light of the *international* legal framework as mentioned above, which implies a compatibility assessment of the IIA with international conventions that relate to SD matters. Therefore, the EU should further enhance the assessment of the regulatory impacts for domestic legislators in the SIA analysis.

5.5.3 *Sustainability Impact Assessment in Practice*

Past experience of SIAs allows assessing the extent to which these mechanisms have served the SD integration requirement.[359] To further gain an understanding of a SIA procedure and their impact on international investment governance, three concrete examples shall be further analysed.

---

353   Idid.
354   See Section 1.2.
355   Blobel, Görlach and Ingwersen, above note 352, 106.
356   Planistat, 'Sustainable Impact Assessment (SIA) of the trade aspects of negotiations for an Association Agreement between the European Communities and Chile (Specific agreement No 11) Final Report', October 2002, 41. See <https://trade.ec.europa.eu/doclib/docs/2005/february/tradoc_112362.pdf>.
357   Reynaud, above note 337, 213.
358   Blobel, Görlach and Ingwersen, above note 352, 108.
359   Marín Durán and Morgera, above note 333, 242.

5.5.3.1 The SIA Process Relating to the CETA

With respect to post-Lisbon comprehensive FTAs with substantive investment liberalisation and protection provisions, an insightful example is the SIA on the CETA.[360] The SIA final report considers that, overall, the investment chapter would have positive economic impacts. For Canada, it predicts an increase in investment flows, namely in the financial, energy and mining sectors. For the EU, it also predicts an increase of inward investment coming from Canada, however on a smaller scale than for European investments into Canada. The social impacts of the investment chapter are considered to be positive but might potentially also lead to negative impacts. Positive in this respect would be that jobs were likely to be created in Canada and the EU. A negative component might be that it leads to worker displacement and wage inequalities.[361] With respect to the environmental impacts of the investment chapter, the report points out that the increase in investment in the energy and mining sector might have negative impacts on the environment in both contracting parties but to a more considerable extent in Canada. At the same time, the report highlights the opportunity that some new investments might gravitate towards green technology.[362] With respect to the question of investor-State dispute settlement, the CETA SIA was clearly dismissive as to the economic, social and environmental benefits of this mechanism.[363] The report stated that the economic benefits would be unclear and the social and environmental impacts were judged to be rather negative since investor-State dispute settlement, according to this report, reduces the policy space, not in a significant manner but to such an extent that the final benefits of investor-State dispute settlement appear unclear.[364] Ultimately, they recommended not to introduce investor-State dispute settlement but to use only State-State enforcement mechanisms.

The European Commission issued a position paper on the CETA SIA.[365] The Commission states that it took note of the relatively mixed social and

---

360 Development Solutions, 'A Trade SIA Relating to the Negotiation of a Comprehensive Economic and Trade Agreement (CETA) Between the EU and Canada', Final Report, June 2011, Trade 10/B3/B06 (hereafter CETA SIA Final Report).
361 Ibid, 338.
362 Ibid, 339.
363 It should be noted that the CETA SIA was finalised before the modifications from ISDS through arbitration to the Investment Court System (ICS). Yet, the report was dismissive on the direct dispute settlement mechanism for investors against States rendering the commentary still relevant.
364 CETA, SIA Final Report, above note 357, 338.
365 Ie almost six years after the finalisation of the CETA SIA Final Report. The reason for the European Commission was to "take proper account of the changes made to the

environmental impacts of the investment-related provisions and underlines that it fully shares the consultants' point of view in this respect.[366] In its response, the Commission further underlined that the key objective of the CETA investment chapter was the protection of investors whilst at the same time guaranteeing the policy space of the EU, its Member States and partner countries.[367] According to the Commission, the specific safeguards introduced in the CETA investment chapter are sufficient to address the concerns of preserving policy space. It mainly pointed to the specific provision on the right to regulate, the newly drafted provision of the fair and equitable treatment standard and lastly the Investment Court System. As a result, the Commission's assessment of the risks of ISDS differs from that of the independent consultants expressed in the CETA SIA.[368]

5.5.3.2 The SIA Process Relating to the EU-Japan FTA

The negotiations with Japan started in March 2013, a few months later, the European Commission commissioned the London School of Economics (LSE) Enterprise, which is an independent consultancy company. The SIA process was completed in March 2016 before the EU and Japan concluded the FTA in July 2017.[369]

In their final report,[370] the consultants found in their economic analysis that the EU is still underperforming in exports (or goods and services) to Japan when compared to the United States, the FTA between the EU and Japan could improve this situation. At the same time, the main growth component of the FTA was not only exports, but also investments. There would be a relatively low rate of EU FDI in Japan. Hence, the FTA could improve the business environment according to the consultants. The social analysis section of the report concludes that economic gains are not created at the cost of

---

investment protection and investment dispute resolution parts of CETA, which were agreed in 2016." See European Commission, 'European Commission services' position paper on the trade sustainability impact assessment of a Comprehensive Economic & Trade Agreement between the EU and Canada', April 2017.

366 Ibid, 12.
367 Ibid, 13.
368 Ibid, 13.
369 See information on the European Commission's webpage <https://ec.europa.eu/trade/policy/policy-making/analysis/policy-evaluation/sustainability-impact-assessments/index_en.htm>.
370 The following is based on London School of Economics Ltd, 'Trade Sustainability Impact Assessment of the Free Trade Agreement between the European Union and Japan—Final Report' 2016; available at <https://trade.ec.europa.eu/doclib/docs/2016/may/tradoc_154522.pdf>.

social variables and interests. Instead, the analysis suggests that income will be distributed geographically to the benefit for those who traditionally do not gain from trade and investment liberalisation and there would be no negative impact on income inequality. Moreover, jobs were more likely to be created than eliminated. As regards, the human rights aspect, the consultants found that stakeholder consultations did not reveal any possible adverse effects on human rights from the EU-Japan FTA. Finally, as regards the environmental pillar, the consultants found no negative impact on greenhouse gases and CO_2 emissions from the FTA. On the contrary, the FTA would favour relatively less energy and emission intensive sectors, leading to a reallocation towards these cleaner sectors. Also, the FTA would increase innovation with improved resource-use efficiency and pollution prevention. The consultants also noted that a variety of environmental organisations representing civil society interests in the EU were consulted for the overall environmental analysis but that minimal feedback was received. A circumstance that indicates, according to the Commission that that the EU-Japan FTA negotiations are not a major concern for environmental stakeholders.[371]

5.5.3.3 The SIA Process Relating to the China-EU CAI

Another interesting example is the SIA on the EU-China Comprehensive Agreement on Investment Agreement (CAI) for which negotiations are ongoing at the time of writing. The China-EU CAI will be the first standalone investment agreement of the EU. Its negotiations were launched in November 2013.

Through the SIA,[372] the consultants confirmed the potential economic benefits of the agreement and also concluded that in overall there were positive social, environmental and human rights impacts on China and the EU. At the same time, the consultants proposed a number of policy measures in order to strengthen such outcomes. For instance, the consultants made suggestions in order to foster the parties' commitments to comply with international social and environmental standards.[373] In this respect, the environmental provisions of the CAI should ensure that international environmental standards are

---

371 European Commission Services' Position Paper on the Trade Sustainability Impact Assessment in Support of Negotiations of a Free Trade Agreement between the European Union and Japan, Feb 2017.
372 Ecorys Nederland, Oxford Intelligence, TNO, Reichwein China Consult, 'Sustainability Impact Assessment (SIA) in support of an Investment Agreement between the European Union and the People's Republic of China', Nov 2017; available at <https://trade.ec.europa.eu/doclib/docs/2018/may/tradoc_156862.pdf>.
373 Ibid.

effectively implemented at the national level. Moreover, the SIA final report takes a strong stand on enhancing corporate social responsibility and the implementation of the pilot programme on "Responsible Supply Chains in Asia", which is a programme co-funded by the EU.[374] The need for promoting CSR practices was in particular stressed through the stakeholder consultations that have been conducted by the consultants. In the same context of CSR, the SIA final report underlines the State's duty to protect and promote the rule of law. In its position paper, the Commission fully agrees with the recommendation and states its intent to include them in the final agreement with China.[375] Based on the latter document, the Commission officially endorses that CSR should be a key element for the final China-EU CAI.

5.5.4 Benefits and Limits of Sustainability Impact Assessments

SIAs are policy instruments and are namely no legal instrument. Their existence is to some extent the result of the political discretion of the EU institution seeking to integrate SD at the level of treaty negotiation. There is no subsequent (legal) requirement for the European Commission to take the results of a SIA process and recommendations of the final reports into account when negotiating a trade and investment agreement with a third country. The limits of SIAs concern the SIAs' impacts on the negotiation, implementation and interpretation of trade and investment agreements.

First, certain SIAs had an influence on the drafting outcomes of economic agreements concluded by the EU. A good example in this respect is the SIA on the EU-Korea FTA. The agreement was the first to include a specific chapter on SD. The SIA final report recommended that the TSD chapter should include substantive SD commitments on core labour standards and multilateral environmental agreements, as well as a set of cooperative actions in the area of social and environmental protection. In the related position paper, the European Commission endorsed these recommendations.[376] In its negotiations, the EU could consequently convince Korea to include such provisions in the TSD chapter of the FTA. This example shows that SIAs have played a role in the integration of SD into EU IIAs in the past by namely assisting the

---

374 See, ILO, EU and OECD, 'Responsible Supply Chains in Asia—Action Fact Sheet'; available at <http://mneguidelines.oecd.org/Responsible-Supply-Chains-in-Asia-Fact-Sheet.pdf>.

375 European Commission, 'Position Paper on the Sustainability Impact Assessment in support of negotiations of an Investment Agreement between the European Union and the People's Republic of China', May 2018, 10.

376 European Commission, 'Position Paper: Trade SIA of the FTA between the EU and the Republic of Korea', June 2010.

EU to shape the content of the TSD chapter. Based on the assessment for the FTA with Korea, the EU started to systematically include a specific chapter on SD matters, i.e. to create regulatory linkages between trade-labour and trade-environment. However, for other SIAs, the tangible impacts on the negotiating strategies or even the drafting of the agreement are far less evident. It might be a weakness of the whole SIA process that the European Commission is free to pick and choose between the points of a SIA final report that it considers important and those that it considers less important. The CETA SIA illustrates the limits of a SIA's influence over the Commission's policy choices. Here, a clear departure of the negotiations' actual outcome and the recommendations made by the consultants can be seen because the latter recommended not to include any investor-State dispute settlement. The final reports of the SIAs conducted in the context of other post-Lisbon IIAs, such as for the FTA with Japan, do not make apparent any substantial influence of the SIA final report on the content and drafting of the SD or investment-related provisions of the said agreement.[377] At the same time, the limited influence of SIAs on the negotiation is less problematic. Requiring that SIAs need to be followed would provide the contracted external consultants too much weight over highly delicate economic and political questions. The remaining discretion of the EU institutions concerning the SIA procedure is thus not as problematic as one might think. The possibility for the EU institutions to consider SIAs in a flexible manner is beneficial because, these assessments are characterised by a high level of uncertainty as they imply a complex exercise *per se* based on probabilities, which is, in addition, expected to be adaptive to another complex and unpredictable process that is trade and investment negotiations.[378] Therefore, SIAs are essential instruments to integrate SD influencing political discretion but they should not subordinate political discretion.

Second and with respect to the implementation of the agreement, one can argue that SIAs can, together with the position paper of the European Commission play a beneficial role in the monitoring and implementation of the agreement, such as for "institutionalised dialogues" and financial and technical assistance provided by the EU that are relevant for the SD of its

---

377 European Commission, 'Position Paper on the Trade Sustainability Impact Assessment in Support of Negotiations of a Free Trade Agreement Between the European Union and Japan', Feb 2017.

378 George C and Kirkpatrick C, 'Sustainability Impact Assessment of the World Trade Negotiations: Current Practice and Lessons for Further Development', New Directions in Impact Assessments for Development, Conference, University of Maastricht, Nov 2003, 23 et seq.

partner countries.³⁷⁹ Already the first SIAs made recommendations on how the agreement should be further implemented and monitored in order to better ensure SD compatible outcomes for the EU and its partner countries.³⁸⁰ For instance, the SIA final report on the EU-Chile Association Agreement found that through increased industrialisation, trade and investment arising from the EU-Chile Association Agreement, negative impacts on the environment in Chile could be enhanced finding that these impacts could not be outweighed by the benefits of promoting cleaner technologies in sectors such as forestry, mining or fisheries.³⁸¹ Consequently, the report made various propositions to the EU with respect to mitigation measures: the EU should support Chile to implement industry best practices and corporate social responsibility standards in the field of the environment. Also, technology transfer should be fostered, and the EU-Chile dialogue on these matters should be strengthened.³⁸² However, the follow-up is also based on the political will of the contracting parties. The Commission is free to decide not to follow the consultants' recommendation on the implementation of an agreement given that SIAs are non-binding instruments.

Third and with respect to the interpretation of the finalised treaty text, it has been argued that SIAs together with the position papers of the European Commission could, as a supplementary means of interpretation, be of benefit for the interpretation of EU IIAs.³⁸³ However, the present book considers that for the interpretation of a final EU IIA, its SIA and the position paper of the European Union are of very limited significance.³⁸⁴ According to Article 32 of the Vienna Convention on the Law of Treaties (VCLT), there are two categories of supplementary means: the so-called *travaux préparatoires* as well

---

379   See also Marín Durán and Morgera, above note 333, 249.
380   For one of the first SIA that was conducted, namely the SIA for the EU-Chile Association Agreement there was an issue of timing. It was launched two years after the negotiations on the agreement have started and finalised a few weeks after the agreement was concluded. Hence it could not be taken into account for the drafting of the agreement. See, PLANISTAT-Luxembourg and CESO-CI, 'Sustainability Impact Assessment of Trade Aspects of Negotiations for an Association Agreement between the EC and Chile, Final Report (revised)', Nov 2002 (Chile SIA Final Report).
381   Ibid, 111–112.
382   Ibid.
383   Cordonier Segger, Gehring and Stephenson, above note 330.
384   See for more details, see Schacherer S, 'The CETA Investment Chapter and Sustainable Development: Interpretative Issues' in: Mbengue MM and Schacherer S (eds), *Foreign Investment Under the Comprehensive Economic and Trade Agreement (CETA)* (Springer International Publishing 2019) 207–238.

as the circumstances of the conclusion of the treaty.[385] Firstly, SIAs as well as position papers can hardly be accepted as *travaux préparatoires* because the EU unilaterally adopts them. Consequently, they do not, in principle, express a common intention of the parties.[386] Second, SIAs and position papers could alternatively be considered as "circumstances of the conclusion of the treaty". In determining the circumstances of a treaty conclusion, adjudicators enjoy indeed greater flexibility.[387] Namely, unilateral acts can more easily be accepted to fall under this category.[388] However, in this respect, the crucial question seems to be more about the degree of relevance for the purpose of treaty interpretation of EU IIAs. Article 32 VCLT allows the recourse to supplementary means of interpretation in two situations. The first is to confirm the meaning that resulted from the interpretation under Article 31 VCLT. The second is to determine the meaning when the interpretation under Article 31 VCLT, either leaves the meaning ambiguous or obscure or leads to a result, which is manifestly absurd or unreasonable.[389] As will be discussed in Chapter 7, EU IIAs contain several *expressis verbis* references to SD. Through these textual

---

385 Aust A, *Modern Treaty Law and Practice* (2nd ed, Cambridge University Press 2007) 244 et seq; Le Bouthillier Y, 'Interpretation of Treaties, Art.32 1969 Vienna Convention', in: Corten O and Klein P (eds), *The Vienna Conventions on the Law of Treaties: A Commentary* (Oxford University Press 2011) 851 et seq; Dörr O, 'Article 32. Supplementary Means of Interpretation', in: Dörr O and Schmalenbach K (eds), *Vienna Convention on the Law of Treaties: A Commentary* (Springer 2012) 581 et seq; Villiger ME, *Commentary on the 1969 Vienna Convention on the Law of Treaties* (Martinus Nijhoff Publishers 2009) 442 et seq.

386 The ICJ accepted the Libyan minutes of the negotiations as travaux préparatoires in the *Territorial Dispute* case, see *Case Concerning the Territorial Dispute (Libyan Arab Jamahiriya/Chad)*, Judgment, Judgment ICJ Rep 1994, 6, paras 55–56. In contrast thereto, *Award in the Arbitration regarding the Iron Rhine ("Ijzeren Rijn") Railway between the Kingdom of Belgium and the Kingdom of the Netherlands*, Reports of International Arbitral Awards, Vol XXVII, Decision, 24 May 2005, 35–125, para 48.

387 Le Bouthillier, above note 385, 858, pt 39; Dörr, above note 385, 581, pt 27; See also, *Kiliç İnşaat İthalat İhracat Sanayi Ve Ticaret Anonim Şirketi v Turkmenistan*, ICSID Case No ARB/10/1, Award, 2 July 2013, para 9.13.

388 *European Communities (EC)—Customs Classification of Frozen Boneless Chicken Cuts*, Appellate Body Report, (2005) WT/DS286/AB/R, para 289.

389 It becomes readily apparent from Article 32 VCLT that it only applies subsequently to the interpretation exercise under Article 31 VCLT. Adjudicators are in principle not obliged to refer to supplementary means in both situations. If the interpretation under Article 31 VCLT leads to unsatisfactory results, the recourse to supplementary means becomes a "practical necessity", see Mbengue MM, 'Rules of Interpretation—Article 32 of the Vienna Convention on the Law of Treaties' (2016) 31 ICSID Review 388, 408; see also, Yasseen MK, *Interprétation des traités d'après la Convention de Vienne* (Martinus Nijhoff 1976) 83; and the Law of Treaties: A Commentary (Oxford University Press 2011) 851 et seq; Aust, above note 385, 245.

inclusions in the actual treaty text, there is a clear requirement to interpret the whole agreement in light of SD making recourse to the supplementary means of interpretation a possible but unnecessary exercise.[390]

5.6   Concluding Remarks

This chapter brought together the EU's main approaches of SD integration in investment and trade agreements. The provisions discussed throughout the chapter are those that can mainly be found in TSD chapters of EU IIAs. Such chapters are part of the EU's ambition to base its trade and investment policy on specific core values ensuring that economic growth "goes hand in hand" with social equity, respect for human rights, and high social and environmental standards.[391] With what can be called SD clauses, EU IIAs introduce a panoply of provisions and approaches, of which many are novel and yet unique in international investment governance. Other approaches have been tested by the treaty practice of other international actors, such as Canada and the United States. A set of aspects are to be highlighted before concluding on the EU as a global actor in developing new approaches for IIAs.

A first aspect relates to the overall function of TSD chapters seeking to impact the parties' conduct regarding environmental and labour protection standards. TSD chapters include three types of commitments concerning the parties' regulatory behaviour in SD matters. First, parties agree to comply and implement international standards to ensure that trade and investment between the EU and its partners take place in compliance with the obligations that stem from international agreements concerning the social protection of workers and environmental protection. In the same vein, the parties commit to cooperate in international fora responsible for social and environmental aspects and to promote the ratification of the fundamental ILO Conventions. Second, TSD chapters in EU IIAs set out a further obligation for the parties to "uphold levels of protection" concerning environmental and social protection. Third, TSD chapters provide for commitments to high levels of protection in the fields of social and environmental standards. Using these provisions, the EU seeks to combine SD promotion and its own economic competitiveness considerations within the TSD chapters.

---

390 The more relevant interpretative techniques for the interpretation of EU IIAs in light of SD, see Section 7.3.
391 European Commission, 'Trade for All', above note 2, 15.

Whilst harmonisation is excluded, international convergence of regulations is, according to the EU, needed not only to avoid the temptation to use environmental and social protection arguments to justify protectionism but also to prevent some countries from exploiting a comparative advantage as cheap production locations.[392]

Another critical aspect is that SD integration in EU IIAs requires sufficiently effective mechanisms for monitoring and enforcing compliance with the SD commitments. The institutional settings, as well as the resolution of disputes under TSD chapters, follow a special regime, which is different from other chapters contained in a comprehensive FTA of the EU. With respect to the implementation monitoring, TSD chapters provide that specialised committees composed of government representatives are in charge of overseeing their implementation and guiding further cooperative actions envisaged in the agreement. As discussed in the present chapter, specialised committees on SD can report to the mostly called "Trade Committees", which are the main bodies created under a comprehensive FTA, and which have, in general, the power to adopt binding decisions on the parties. Moreover, each contracting party has to set up national entities that allow for the consultation and discussion among civil society on matters related to the TSD chapter's implementation. These nationally established entities compromise independent civil society representatives and should be composed of business organisations, trade unions and environmental and/or social organisations. Their main task is to advise on the chapter's implementation. In addition, all civil society representatives of the contracting partners are to meet on an annual basis. The main purpose of such annual fora is to establish dialogues between stakeholders as well as for the EU and its partners to receive advice on the implementation and further cooperative action. The EU is among the rear global actors seeking the contact and exchange with civil society compared to other States and actors.

Concerning the enforcement of the TSD chapter, the approach of the EU is essentially cooperative and non-confrontational. If a dispute between the parties occurs under an TSD chapter, the parties are first held to seek a mutually satisfactory resolution of the matter through consultations. If consultations continue to remain fruitless, any party may request that a Panel of Experts be convened. For its assessment, a panel can consult the contracting parties, international organisations and civil society groups. At the end of the process, a panel renders a final report, whose implementation is subsequently

---

392 Marín Durán, above note 10, 131.

monitored by the specialised committee established under the TSD chapter. As highlighted in the present chapter, global actors are yet in the process of finding the suitable approaches to ensure the effective enforcement of SD clauses. Whilst the United States has opted for enforcement through fines or economic sanctions, the EU maintains a cooperative and consultative approach. The EU has been criticised for such soft enforcement mechanism. At the same time, the practical (and political) difficulties of the sanction-based model have been highlighted by US practice. Conversely, the EU's intention with a soft enforcement mechanism are that it can thereby arguably better convince contracting parties to create these linkages by including an TSD chapter. Moreover, the EU's goal is to foster the procedural links with other institutional mechanisms, such as of ILO or established under MEAs, so as to promote coordination among the various levels of decision-making.

Another aspect discussed in the present chapter is that TSD chapters under EU IIAs set out a variety of areas in which the parties agree to promote and facilitate trade and investment that are beneficial for SD. Next to cooperative commitments in the field of labour and environmental protection, EU IIAs introduce a number of specific topics that also fall under the umbrella of SD. For instance, the parties further state their commitment to cooperate in the fight against climate change, to promote low-carbon technologies and energy efficiency, as well as biodiversity conservation. Climate change mitigation and the promotion of investment in renewable energy sources is one of the areas in which the EU cooperates with its partners to establish linkages between investment and SD. In addition, EU IIAs also contain provisions on the cooperation concerning CSR, including on the effective implementation and follow-up of internationally agreed guidelines. All of these provisions are drafted as soft law incentives. Compared to other international actors, it has been shown that the EU does not provide for more stringent commitments regarding the SD responsibilities for foreign investors. EU IIAs, like those of other capital-exporting countries, only contain commitments on the contracting parties to promote CSR practices. The issue of direct investor obligations under IIAs is very contentious. International investment governance is increasingly divided on this issue as many developing countries chose to use IIAs to set out clear and binding investor obligations. For the EU, it seems that the efficiency of its policy should be scrutinized in the future also considering compliance and enforcement of investor obligations at the EU and the Member States' levels. Otherwise, the credibility of the SD promotion statements under trade and investment agreements is seriously undermined.

Finally, the EU's policy approach includes *ex ante* SD impact assessments, so-called SIAs. The EU has a relatively long practice to integrate SD at the moment of negotiating IIAs with third countries by the use of impact assessments of the envisaged treaties with respect to their actual SD impacts. SIAs are important political tools that serve the European Commission as guidelines in their negotiations. However, the Commission is not legally bound to follow the recommendations of the SIA consultants. The EU is yet among the very few global actors that adopt the approach of SIAs. Whilst the process should be continuously improved by the EU, the fact that SIAs are taking place contributes positively to the SD integration into EU investment law and policy-making.

In sum, the EU approach in regulating the SD-investment linkages, is not to regulate in detail on how theses linkages should more precisely materialise. Most of the SD clauses are drafted in a way as to delegate the responsibility to the national legislator, which is then in charge to legislate in light of SD. The primary role of SD clauses under EU IIAs is to actuate and to support national SD measures. These provisions also vest the parties to the agreement with the power to set their priorities and promote their own SD policy. It should, however, also be noted that EU IIAs in form of comprehensive FTAs do not give priority to concerns related to environmental or labour protection. By reaffirming international commitments in these areas, the contracting parties under EU IIAs say little as regards their impact on investment activities regulated by the same instrument. EU IIAs provide certain bottom lines and incentives thereby inviting States to engage in legislative action for the benefit of SD or to gather consensus in order to—jointly with the contracting parties—foster existing international mechanisms. Whilst the linkages created by EU IIAs underscore the value-based trade and investment agenda of the EU, post-Lisbon EU IIAs display limited ambition towards concretely tackling pressing SD issues, remaining vague and approximate, and leaving the effective implementation and enforcement of environmental protection and labour rights up to the political will of contracting parties.

CHAPTER 6

Sustainable Development Integration in the Realm of Investment Liberalisation and Protection under EU IIAS

One of the critical functions of SD integration within international investment law remains to ensure that investment protection standards do not infringe or override States' policy space. IIA provisions on investment liberalisation and protection should not be an obstacle for States to achieve their SD objectives at the national level. Therefrom follows that IIAs should balance between the investor rights and the regulatory space of States. The general debate on the right to regulate is inherently connected to the endeavour of SD integration in international investment law-making. A different and increasingly relevant function of SD integration in international investment law is that IIAs can be a suitable means to promote investments that are advancing the SDGs.

The EU, according to its statements, is keen to integrate SD in the provisions on investment liberalisation and protection, which is not least corroborated by the numerous statements on the need to foster the right to regulate.[1] These efforts materialise through greater precision of protection standards, clearly drafted exceptions, and—to a much lesser extent—through more restrictive formulations of the investment definition.[2] Under EU IIAs, a foreign investor can directly invoke the substantive protection standards against the host State or the EU.[3] Therefore, the right to regulate is directly at stake in an investment dispute before investment tribunals under the Investment Court System (ICS) of EU IIAs are in charge of undertaking the balance between the host States' right to regulate pursuant to SD and the investors' rights based on EU IIAs. The CJEU found in Opinion 1/17 that the CETA contains enough safeguards not to undermine the EU's legislative choices of the level of public interest and

---

1 Eg European Commission Communication, 'Trade for All—Towards a more responsible trade and investment policy', COM (2015) 497 final (hereafter: 'Trade for All'); European Commission, 'Concept Paper: Investment in TTIP and beyond—The Path for Reform Enhancing the Right to Regulate and Moving from Current ad hoc Arbitration towards and Investment Court' [2015] (hereafter: 'TTIP and beyond'). See also, Section 4.3.3.
2 The main EU IIAs analysed in this chapter are the CETA, EUSFTA and EUSIPA, EUMFTA, EUVFTA and EUVIPA. See Chapter 1, 4.
3 Provisions on investment liberalisation are, however, excluded from the scope of ISDS under EU IIAS.

thus respect the EU legislator's prerogatives.[4] In other words, the Court found that the build-in safeguards in the concrete investment protections provisions under CETA and other EU IIAs are enough in the sense that they do not undermine the EU legal order.[5] The Court namely found that the provisions on FET and indirect expropriation, both provisions are mostly at stake in regulatory disputes, would not call into question the democratic choices of the EU and its partner countries.[6]

The present chapter analyses EU IIAs' substantive investment protection standards and market access provisions applying the double benchmark of whether the EU is a rule-maker at the international law level and whether EU investment law-making lives up to the EU's objectives and policy statements. It should be noted that no conclusive normative statements are being made on how investment liberalisation and protection provisions ought to look like to ensure SD outcomes.[7] Instead, the analysis is concerned with the governance structure of international investment law and how the integration of SD shapes these structures.[8] It questions how the EU contribute to the ongoing debate on finding the right balance between SD public interests and the interests of private investors? Is the EU contributing to use IIAs as a tool to promote investment activities that are supportive of SD? In this perspective, the chapter starts with the principal investment protection standards and considers clauses to introduce more regulatory flexibility, such as specific provisions on the right to regulate and general exceptions clauses. The analysis then turns to the issue of investment liberalisation, and the definition of investment. Lastly, the present chapter discusses certain procedural aspects of investor-State dispute resolution under EU IIAs that are relevant in the context of SD.

---

4   ECJ, Opinion 1/17 *EU-Canada CET Agreement*, EU:C:2019:341.
5   The reasoning has been criticised before. See Section 4.5.2.
6   Opinion 1/17, para 160. For the same opinion on the three most relevant investment protection standards in the context of regulatory disputes, see Henckels C, 'Protecting Regulatory Autonomy through Greater Precision in Investment Treaties: The TPP, CETA, and TTIP' (2016) 19 Journal of International Economic Law 27.
7   See Section 2.5, where the central aspects of the reform have been discussed.
8   This excludes the consideration of "real life" benefits for SD in host States through investment protection standards. In this respect, one might think of good governance and the rule of law promotion through investment protection standards, see Sattorova M, *The Impact of Investment Treaty Law on Host States: Enabling Good Governance?* (Hart Publishing 2018); Reinisch A, 'The Rule of Law in International Investment Arbitration', in: Pazartzis P et al (eds), *Reconceptualising the Rule of Law in Global Governance, Resources, Investment and Trade* (Hart Pub 2016) 291–307; Bonnitcha J, *Substantive Protection under Investment Treaties: A Legal and Economic Analysis* (Cambridge University Press 2014) 139. For the methodology of the present book, see Chapter 1.

6.1 Re-Balancing Investment Protection with SD Interests under EU IIA

Since the entry into force of the Lisbon Treaty, the EU has the competence to include in its IIAs provisions on investment protection.[9] For its post-Lisbon IIAs, it needed to be determined whether the EU continues with IIA models of its Member States. Yet, precisely those traditional European BITs were considered not sufficiently balancing the contained protection standards with public SD interests. Since the large bulk of European BITs has been concluded, international investment law has considerably changed. The increasing number of ISDS cases has triggered many if not all global actors to incorporate innovations that strike a better balance between investor protection and the preservation of policy-making flexibility. EU-internal political pressure and the evolved international investment governance made it impossible for the EU to adhere to the IIA approaches of its Member States. New approaches were elaborated and have been included in post-Lisbon EU IIAs.

6.1.1 *Fair and Equitable Treatment*

A first key standard that needed an overhaul was the FET standard, which has been at the centre of criticism. FET is an inherently broad and open-ended standard and creates significant risks of being used to constrain States' regulatory sovereignty.[10] In the past, investors systematically invoked FET with considerable success. The lack of precision has occasionally led to extensive interpretations. It has thereby restricted States' regulatory space, which ultimately is a "threat" to the regulation at the domestic level on SD-relevant issues, including the level of social and environmental protection.[11] The concept of legitimate expectations has, in particular, the potential allowing investment tribunals to scrutinise regulatory changes and inconsistent administrative treatment of investors.[12] Even though tribunals have started to adopt a more cautious approach when legitimate expectations are at stake, without any guidance in the text of the IIA, a tribunal can still find a measure in breach

---

9   See Section 4.2.
10 UNCTAD, 'Investment Policy Framework for Sustainable Development (IPFSD)' (United Nations 2015) 94.
11 Kläger R, '"Fair and Equitable" Treatment and Sustainable Development' in: Cordonier Segger M-C, Gehring MW and Newcombe AP (eds), *Sustainable Development in World Investment Law* (Kluwer Law International 2011) 251.
12 Henckels C, 'Protecting Regulatory Autonomy through Greater Precision in Investment Treaties: The TPP, CETA, and TTIP', Journal of International Economic Law (2016) 37.

of legitimate expectations without sufficiently paying deference to the right to regulate. In short, the basic problem with FET is that it potentially applies to an unlimited number of situations in which investors may claim that their investment was treated unfairly and inequitably. This lack of predictability undermines regulatory space, can provoke regulatory chill and it thus problematic from an SD point of view. As a result, most countries seek to address the balance between investor protection and the right to regulate by limiting the scope of FET.

For the EU, greater precision was the main objective concerning the drafting of the FET standard. The aim is to better guide future adjudicators and ultimately to safeguard regulatory space. The EU developed a novel approach for the first time in the course of the CETA negotiations.[13] By now, all EU IIAS contain clauses that identifies State measure that fall under the prohibition in the FET obligation. EU IIAS set out an exhaustive list of the elements which constitute a breach of the standard:

1. Each Party shall accord in its territory to covered investments of the other Party and to investors with respect to their covered investments fair and equitable treatment and full protection and security in accordance with paragraphs 2 through 6.
2. A Party breaches the obligation of fair and equitable treatment referenced in paragraph 1 if a measure or series of measures constitutes:
    (a) denial of justice in criminal, civil or administrative proceedings;
    (b) fundamental breach of due process, including a fundamental breach of transparency, in judicial and administrative proceedings;
    (c) manifest arbitrariness;
    (d) targeted discrimination on manifestly wrongful grounds, such as gender, race or religious belief;
    (e) abusive treatment of investors, such as coercion, duress and harassment; or
    (f) a breach of any further elements of the fair and equitable treatment obligation adopted by the Parties in accordance with paragraph 3 of this Article.
    [...][14]

---

13   Dumberry P, 'Fair and Equitable Treatment', in: Mbengue MM and Schacherer S (eds), *Foreign Investment Under the Comprehensive Economic and Trade Agreement (CETA)* (Springer International Publishing 2019) 97.
14   Eg CETA, Art 8.10(1–2). Likewise, see EUMFTA, Ch 'Investment', Art 15(1–2); EUSIPA, Art 2.4(1–2); EUVIPA, Art 2.5(1–2).

The enumeration is closed. Future tribunals cannot add elements to the list. The "evolution" of the standard undertaken by investment tribunals is barred because only the contracting parties can add additional elements to the list, as is expressly stated in the FET provision.[15] Content-wise, the EU IIAs' list reflects and confirms a number of elements that investment treaty tribunals have previously elaborated.[16] State measures that are manifestly arbitrary, discriminatory or that are a gross denial of justice and due process have namely been established in arbitration cases under NAFTA. Through the enumeration, the EU also excluded certain elements that have been considered by arbitral case law to constitute an aspect of FET, such as legitimate expectations and the obligation to ensure stability or predictability of the domestic legal framework applicable to foreign investors.[17]

Under EU IIAs, the FET standard is breached when a measure or a series of measures of a contracting party constitutes a "fundamental breach of due process, including a fundamental breach of transparency, in judicial and administrative proceedings".[18] In investment treaty case law, the lack of fair procedure or serious procedural shortcomings has been considered a violation of the FET standard, with most of such cases related to the right to be heard in judicial or administrative proceedings.[19] EU IIAs in this respect codify case law, by using the qualifier "fundamental" as for the nature of the breach. The wording of the provision suggests that there must be a certain level of seriousness to be in

---

15 Eg EUVIPA, Art 2.5(3): "Treatment not listed in paragraph 2 may constitute a breach of fair and equitable treatment where the Parties have so agreed in accordance with the procedure provided for in Article 4.3. (Amendments)." See also CETA, Art 8.10(3); EUMFTA, Ch 'Investment', Art 15(7); EUSIPA, Art 2.4(4). See also Dumberry, above note 13, 121.

16 According to arbitral case law, elements of the FET are legitimate expectations, non-discrimination, proportionality, predictability, due process, transparency, stability, freedom from coercion and harassment as well as a general duty of due diligence. See, De Brabandere E, 'States' Reassertion of Control over International Investment Law (Re)Defining "Fair and Equitable Treatment and Indirect Expropriation"', in: Kulick A, *Reassertion of Control over the Investment Treaty Regime* (Cambridge University Press 2017) 288–300; see also Kläger, above note 11, 246–249; Dumberry, above note 13, 104; Patrick Dumberry, moreover highlighted that the EU's list reflects the case law on NAFTA, Art 1105.

17 *Occidental Exploration and Prod. Co. v Republic of Ecuador,* UNCITRAL, LCIA Case No UN3467, Final Award, 1 July 2004, para 182: "[...] The stability of the legal and business framework is thus an essential element of fair and equitable treatment". See also, *CMS Gas Transmission Company v Argentina,* ICSID Case No ARB/01/8, Award, 12 May 2005, para 274.

18 Eg CETA, Art 8.10(2)(b).

19 Dolzer R and Schreuer C, *Principles of International Investment Law* (Second edition, Oxford University Press 2012) 154.

breach of the obligation.[20] The qualifier "fundamental" refers to the seriousness of the breach.[21] Accordingly, the threshold that this element of the FET standard is infringed is high. The following sub-element of the FET list prohibiting manifest arbitrariness, in particular, has been central for regulatory disputes.[22] EU IIAs, add a qualifier stating that only "manifest" arbitrariness amounts to a breach of the FET standard. Here, the qualifier does not relate to the seriousness of the arbitrariness but to how easily one can perceive or recognise the arbitrariness.[23] Given that NAFTA tribunals mainly developed the expression of manifest arbitrariness, the EU codifies existing case law and provides for a high threshold.[24]

Legitimate expectations have not explicitly been included in the list of elements that constitute a breach of the FET standard under EU IIAs. However, in a subsequent paragraph to the list, the FET provisions of EU IIAs make reference to legitimate expectations. In this respect, a tribunal "may take into account" that a party made "a specific representation to an investor to induce a covered investment, that created a legitimate expectation, and upon which the investor relied in deciding to make or maintain the covered investment, but that the Party subsequently frustrated".[25] Legitimate expectations are thus not among the elements listed in an EU FET clause but appear to be a supplementary aspect that a tribunal can, but does not have to, take into account when assessing the main elements set out in the list of FET breaches. The EU approach breaks with previous case law that found that a breach of legitimate expectations amounts to a breach of the FET standard.[26] Thereby the

---

20 Henckels, note above 12, 36.
21 For a different opinion, see Kriebaum U, 'FET and Expropriation in the (Invisible) EU Model BIT' (2014) The Journal of World Investment & Trade 454, 474.
22 Eg *Mobil Investment Canada Inc and Murphy Oil Corporation v Canada*, Decision on Liability, 22 May 2012, paras 152–153; or *PSEG Global Inc v Turkey*, ICSID Case No ARB/02/5, Award, 19 Jan 2007, paras 239–240. See also Henckels C, *Proportionality and Deference in Investor-State Arbitration: Balancing Investment Protection and Regulatory Autonomy* (Cambridge University Press 2015) 120–121.
23 Kriebaum, above note 21, 474. According to the tribunal in *Glamis v United States*, FET "requires something greater than mere arbitrariness, something that is surprising, shocking or exhibits a manifest lack of reasoning". See *Glamis Gold Ltd v The United States of America*, NAFTA, UNCITRAL, Award, 8 June 2009, para 617.
24 Eg *Eli Lilly and Company v Canada*, Final Award, 16 March 2017, UNCITRAL Case No UNCT/14/2, paras 222–223; *Cargill Incorporated v United Mexican States*, ICSID Case No ARB(AF)/05/2, Award, 18 Sep 2009, para 296. See especially, Dumberry, above note 13, 110.
25 CETA, Art 8.10(4); EUMFTA, Ch 'Investment', Art 15.4, EUSIPA, Art 2.4(3); EUVIPA Art 2.5(4).
26 See, *Saluka Investments BV v Czech Republic*, Partial Award, UNCITRAL, 17 March 2006, para 302, where legitimate expectations were considered to be "the dominant element"

EU clarified that the frustration of legitimate expectations cannot be in itself a breach of FET and also sought to determine which circumstances might give rise to legitimate expectations. The references to *specific* representation and the fact that the investor *relied* on it to make or maintain the investment are important factual conditions.[27] As a result, expectations that are merely based on existing regulations or vague promises should not be protected under this provision.[28]

Looking at the IIA practice of other countries and regions, there is a clear trend in drafting the FET standard with greater precision.[29] Unqualified fair and equitable treatment standards have become seldom IIA practice. The typical approaches are to narrow down the concept of legitimate expectations and to specify what FET includes.[30] For instance, the CPTPP as well as the Indian Model BIT set out that a denial of justice breaches FET.[31] Moreover, the CPTPP, like EU IIAs, excludes legitimate expectations to be sufficient to constitute a breach of FET.[32] Morocco's model BIT delineates the scope of the FET as well. It lists specific outrageous treatments such as a denial of justice, fundamental breach of due process, discrimination on wrongful grounds, as well as abusive treatment of investors but omits the aspect of "arbitrariness".[33] Morocco thus drafted a more cautious provision in the sense that the term arbitrariness bears in itself some vagueness.

---

      of the standard of FET. See also, *Biwater Gauff Ltd v United Republic of Tanzania*, ICSID Case No ARB/05/22, Award, 24 July 2008, para 602; *Rumeli Telekom SA and Telsim Mobil Telekomikasyon Hizmetleri AS v Kazakhstan* ICSID Case No ARB/05/16, Award, 29 July 2008, para 609.

27   See for more details, Wongkaew T, *Protection of Legitimate Expectations in Investment Treaty Arbitration: A Theory of Detrimental Reliance* (Cambridge University Press 2019).

28   Henckels, note above 12, 38.

29   Schill S and Jacob M, 'Trends in International Investment Agreements, 2010–2011: The Increasing Complexity of International Investment Law' in: Sauvant KP (ed), *Yearbook on International Investment Law & Policy 2011–2012* (Oxford University Press 2013) 142.

30   See 2012 US Model BIT, Art 5.2. See also ASEAN Investment Agreement, Art 11.2; ASEAN-Australia-New Zealand FTA, Ch 11, Art 6.2(b); CPTPP, Art 9.6; Nigeria-Morocco BIT, Art 7.

31   Indian Model BIT, Art 3.1: "No Party shall subject investments made by investors of the other Party to measures which constitute a violation of customary international law through: (i) Denial of justice in any judicial or administrative proceedings; or (ii) fundamental breach of due process; or (iii) targeted discrimination on manifestly unjustified grounds, such as gender, race or religious belief; or (iv) manifestly abusive treatment, such as coercion, duress and harassment." CPTPP, Art 9 in combination with Annex 9-A. See also COMESA Investment Agreement, Art 14.

32   CPTPP, Art 9.6(4).

33   Morocco BIT, Art 6.

A few international actors consider the standard too vague and, ultimately, do not include it in their investment instruments. This is the case for the IIAs of Brazil and the model treaties, such as the PAIC and the SADC model.[34] Noteworthy is that the USMCA whilst maintaining FET excludes the standard from investor-State dispute settlement, which hence avoids all risks of unwarranted interpretation.[35] Others modify the standard to only relate to "Fair Administrative Treatment".[36] The EU approach does omit any reference to customary international law. A certain divide remains to exist in international investment governance on the references in the FET clause to the minimum standard of treatment under customary international law.[37] The North American technique has not necessarily led to non-expansive interpretations of the standard.[38] The CPTPP maintains the reference to the customary law status, even though it has been unclear what the customary minimum standard of treatment requires in cases of regulatory changes.[39] In sum, the EU, like other States and actors, has made an effort to limit the risks of extensive interpretation by seeking to make the FET standard clearer and more predictable. With its FET provision, the EU proposes an innovative approach to circumscribe the standard more precisely.

The approach also seems to be perfectly in line with the policy goals of the EU institutions. The latter found that the most suitable way to address the challenge of better protecting regulatory space is to draft and define investor protection standards with greater precision.[40] Right at the beginning of the EU investment policy, the European Parliament called on the European

---

34   Eg Brazil-Malawi CIFA; PAIC; and recommendation made by SADC, see SADC Model BIT, Commentary, 22.
35   The USMCA contains an FET clause, see Art 14.6 (Minimum Standard of Treatment) and Annex 14-A. However, the USMCA eliminates ISDS between the United States and Canada, and between Mexico and Canada; for the relation between Mexico and the United States, ISDS still exists but FET is excluded from its scope, see USMCA, Annex 14-D, Art 14.D.3.
36   SADC Model BIT, Art 5, Option 2; see also South Africa, 'Protection of Investment Act', Act No 22 [2015] Official Gazette, Vol 606 No 39514, Sec 6.
37   NAFTA, Art 1105; see also USMCA, Art 14.6.
38   The *Bilcon v Canada* decision shows that NAFTA tribunals are not immune from taking expansive approaches. See *William Ralph Clayton, William Richard Clayton, Douglas Clayton, Daniel Clayton and Bilcon of Delaware Inc v Government of Canada*, PCA Case No 2009-04, Award on Jurisdiction and Liability of 17 March 2015, Dissenting Opinion of Arbitrator McRae, para 2.
39   Kläger R, *'Fair and Equitable Treatment' in International Investment Law* (Cambridge University Press 2011) 53 et seq.
40   European Commission, 'Trade for All', above note 1, 15; and European Commission, 'TTIP and beyond', above note 1, 6.

Commission "to produce clear definitions of investor protection standards" to avoid adjudicators ruling out legitimate public welfare measures.[41] The FET clause contained in EU IIAs is drafted in a more detailed and more precise manner. The list provides more straightforward interpretative guidance for future adjudicators, and it limits the eventuality for expanding the scope of the standard. This being said, the clause still leaves adjudicators with margins of appreciation. For instance, tribunals are to determine what amounts to a "fundamental" breach. Moreover, EU IIAs do not prescribe the content of due process *i.e.* what it concretely requires from States. Hereto, future tribunals would again need to go back to previous case law to determine the scope of the standard. As far as arbitrariness in concerned, EU IIAs provide a higher threshold than certain past arbitral decisions that consider arbitrary conduct sufficient to establish a breach.[42] The introduction of the high threshold seems to make it hard to argue that the adoption of a non-discriminatory public welfare measure can be a breach of the FET standard under EU IIAs. However, the concept of "arbitrariness" is, in itself, relatively imprecise.[43] Some tribunals have found that arbitrariness was given where a State could offer no reasons for their measure;[44] some others found arbitrariness where a State failed to implement a regulation.[45] Besides, certain tribunals have found that bad faith was required for a measure to be arbitrary.[46] All these considerations should not be understood as a general mistrust towards adjudicators tending to broaden the FET provision. The point is to reveal that a certain amount of discretion has not been excluded under EU IIAs.[47] As far as the concept of legitimate expectations is concerned, the EU lives up to its ambition of having

---

41   European Parliament, 'Resolution of 6 April 2011 on the future European international investment policy', 2010/2203 (INI), para 24.
42   Dumberry, above note 13, 110. Ibid. As in particular, NAFTA case law shows, regulatory measures have only, in very few cases, been considered arbitrary. With the exceptions of *Cargill Incorporated v United Mexican States*, ICSID Case No ARB(AF)/05/2, Award, 18 Sep 2009; and *Bilcon v Canada*, above note 38.
43   Henckels, note above 12, 37.
44   Eg *Siemens AG v The Argentine Republic*, ICSID Case No ARB/02/8, Award, 17 Jan 2007, paras 318–319.
45   Eg *Gami Investments Inc v United Mexican States*, UNCITRAL, Award, 15 Nov 2004, paras 94, 104–105.
46   *Teco Guatemala Holding LLC v Guatemala*, ICSID Case No ARB/10/23, Award, 19 Dec 2013, paras 629–630. See also *Elettronica Sicula S.p.A. (ELSI)* (United States of America v Italy), Judgement, ICJ Rep 1989, 15, para 128.
47   Henckels, above note 12, 37. Caroline Henckels adds that there is, however, still scope for improvement, *i.e.* whether the representation has to be in writing or whether verbal arrangements are sufficient is not mentioned in EU FET provisions.

more predictable protection standards. The concept is not part of the aspects that fall under FET and the conditions on when legitimate expectations arise put a significant constraint on the adjudicators because the condition of actual representation further adds clarity.[48] Opinion 1/17 confirmed and approved the CETA approach to FET. The CJEU ruled that the FET clause was sufficient in safeguarding that democratic choices of the parties are not called into question.[49] However, as just argued, the risk of regulatory challenges has not been eliminated.

6.1.2 Indirect Expropriation

The protection against indirect expropriation is a further central investment protection standard and generally invoked in regulatory disputes.[50] Indirect expropriation has also been described as "regulatory taking" or regulatory expropriation.[51] The concerns with indirect expropriation from an SD perspective are twofold. First, they relate to the surrounding uncertainties of when an indirect expropriation occurred; second, when an alleged expropriatory State measure could benefit from the regulatory exception freeing it to pay compensation. The latter exception is known as the doctrine of police powers and permits States to regulate or take actions in the public interest without them being considered as an indirect expropriation.[52] Arbitral case law has so far not established a coherent definition of the notion of indirect expropriation, nor of the conditions when the police power doctrine applies.[53] The EU sought to define the notion of indirect expropriation better and better describe the

---

48   The EUSIPA contains further clarification concerning the character of representation. See EUSIPA, Art 2.4(3), Footnote 10: "For greater certainty, representations made so as to induce the investments include the representations made in order to convince the investor to continue with, not to liquidate or to make subsequent investments".

49   Consider again, Section 4.5.2.

50   The present analysis is limited to indirect expropriation. Expropriation, in general, includes both direct expropriations (involving the transfer of title to States) and indirect expropriations (measures that substantially deprive the investor of the investment or that result in the effective loss of the investor's enjoyment of or control over their property).

51   See also Paparinskis M, 'Regulatory Expropriation and Sustainable Development', in: Cordonier Segger M-C, Gehring MW and Newcombe AP (eds), *Sustainable Development in World Investment Law* (Kluwer Law International 2011) 299–327.

52   See OECD, '"Indirect Expropriation" and the "Right to Regulate" in International Investment Law' (2004) OECD Working Papers on International Investment 2004/04), 5. For an overview on the police powers doctrine, see *Philip Morris v Uruguay*, above note 22, paras 288 et seq.

53   Henckels, above note 12, 40. See also Kriebaum U, 'Regulatory Takings: Balancing the Interests of the Investor and the State' (2007) The Journal of World Investment & Trade, 717.

circumstances in which the regulatory exception applies. Both elements are set out in a specific annexe on expropriation under EU IIAs.[54]

6.1.2.1 Clarifying the Meaning of Indirect Expropriation

Under EU IIAs, "indirect expropriation occurs if a measure or series of measures of a Party has an effect equivalent to direct expropriation, in that it substantially deprives the investor of the fundamental attributes of property in its investment, including the right to use, enjoy and dispose of its investment, without formal transfer of title or outright seizure".[55] The annexes on expropriation then further clarify the situations in which an indirect expropriation occurs:

1. [...]
2. The determination of whether a measure or series of measures of a Party, in a specific fact situation, constitutes an indirect expropriation requires a case-by-case, fact-based inquiry that takes into consideration, among other factors:
   - (a) the economic impact of the measure or series of measures, although the sole fact that a measure or series of measures of a Party has an adverse effect on the economic value of an investment does not establish that an indirect expropriation has occurred;
   - (b) the duration of the measure or series of measures of a Party;
   - (c) the extent to which the measure or series of measures interferes with distinct, reasonable investment-backed expectations; and
   - (d) the character of the measure or series of measure, notably their object, context and intent.
3. [...][56]

This list provides a set of criteria that need to be taken into account.[57] More guidance is provided to future tribunals as it sets out a method for considering four factors. First, the economic impact of the measure is to be taken into account by, however, also clarifying that the sole fact of adverse effect on the economic value of the investment is not sufficient, thereby excluding the controversial "sole effects" doctrine, which several investment tribunals have

---

54 CETA, Annex 8-A; EUMFTA, 'Annex on Expropriation'; EUSIPA, Annex 1; EUVIPA, Annex 4.
55 CETA, Annex 8-A(1–2); EUMFTA, 'Annex on Expropriation' (4); EUVIPA, Annex 4(1–2); EUSIPA, Annex 1.
56 Eg CETA, Annex 8-A(3).
57 Originally, the criteria derived from a leading US case on regulatory takings, *Penn Central Transport v City of New York*, 438 US 104, 123–125 (1978).

established.[58] The doctrine had been criticised as it only relies on the effects of a measure to decide whether an indirect expropriation has occurred.[59] Put differently, an adverse effect on the "value" of the investment is not sufficient to conclude that expropriation has taken place. The second and third factors that are to be taken into account for the assessment of an indirect expropriation are the duration of the measure as well as the interference with the "distinct, reasonable investment-backed expectations".[60] Whilst, the duration of the measure constitutes a straightforward indication, the third factor of investor expectations is less clear and arguably reintroduces some degree of vagueness.[61] In the context of indirect expropriation, "investment-backed expectations" are not expectations in general and should not be compared to legitimate expectation under the FET standard.[62] It has been argued that the term should be understood as meaning "the fact that an investor decides to proceed to a specific investment as he is expecting some profit in return".[63] Certain investment tribunals have used this criterion in the past to determine whether an indirect expropriation occurred.[64] While it might be relevant in a limited number of cases, the criterion is rather problematic and its utility limited.[65] The negative effects on the expected profits should therefore be read in the context of the three other factors making it only a supplementary element to be considered.

---

58   Kriebaum, above note 53, 724 and stated case law.
59   De Brabandere, above note 16, 304. A tribunal that applied the sole effect doctrine without paying attention to the government's intent, see for instance *Telenor Mobile Communications AS v The Republic of Hungary*, ICSID Case No ARB/04/15, Award, 13 Sep 2006, para 70.
60   Eg EUMFTA, Ch 'Investment', 'Annex on Expropriation' (4)(iii).
61   Henckels, above note 12, 41.
62   De Nanteuil A, 'Expropriation' in: Mbengue MM and Schacherer S (eds), *Foreign Investment Under the Comprehensive Economic and Trade Agreement (CETA)* (Springer International Publishing 2019) 136.
63   Ibid.
64   *Eureko BV v Republic of Poland*, Partial Award, 19 Aug 2005, para 242; *Tecnicas Medioambiantales Tecmed SA v Mexico*, ICSID Case No ARB(AF)/00/2, 29 May 2003, para 122.
65   De Nanteuil, above note 62, 135 et seq; at 135: "[...] legitimate expectations have nothing to do with deprivation. First of all, deprivation is a matter of fact that is linked to the relationship between the owner and his property, whereas legitimate expectations are part of a general treatment. Secondly, as expropriation is not unlawful *per se*, any investor is supposed to be aware of the risk of an expropriation potentially occurring. In that sense, there can be no expectation that a deprivation will never take place—only an expectation that, if it does, it will be conducted according to the conditions set up by the applicable treaty. However, such a self-evident interpretation would render the legitimate expectations doctrine devoid of substance".

The fourth factor relates to the character of the State measure, including its object, context and intent.[66] The introduction of this factor highlights that the EU and its contracting partners seek to emphasise the measure's goal and objective for the assessment of whether or not an indirect expropriation occurred. The intent does not relate to the intent to expropriate but rather to the potential public interest intent of a given measure.[67]

By using specific annexes that further define what constitutes an indirect expropriation, the EU follows well-established US and Canadian IIA practice.[68] This is further amplified by the similarities between the clauses on indirect expropriation in the CPTPP and EU IIAs.[69] Other countries and regions also provide for more precision and better define indirect expropriation, yet not necessarily by using an annexe.[70] However, an exception hereto is Brazil as the country decided to ban the concept of indirect expropriation altogether from the scope of its CIFAs.[71] The EU IIA practice does, in this respect, not provide innovation but follows North American practice and contributes to the consolidation of this approach. From an EU law and policy perspective, the objective was to clarify what amounts to an indirect expropriation under EU IIAs.[72] The four factors mentioned in the provision provide clarity. At the same time, despite the prescriptions of what constitutes an indirect expropriation under EU IIAs, the provisions do not indicate how to weigh the various factors. This is, thus, an element of discretion for future adjudicators. Moreover, the listed factors are non-exhaustive ("among other factors"), which leaves room for adjudicators to add further elements.

6.1.2.2 Permitted Regulation

The annexes on expropriation of EU IIAs provide that State measures, which are "designed and applied to protect legitimate public welfare objectives" do not constitute an indirect expropriation thereby codifying the doctrine of police powers.[73] For a State measure to fall under the scope of the regulatory

---

66   CETA, Annex 8-A(2); EUSIPA, Annex 1; EUVIPA, Annex 4(2). The exception of EUMFTA, which does not refer to the intent, see EUMFTA, 'Annex on Expropriation' (4).
67   Kriebaum, above note 21, 465.
68   2004 Canadian Model BIT, Art 13 and Annex B.13; 2012 US Model BIT, Art 6 and Annex B.
69   CPTPP, Annex 9-B. See also USMCA, Annex 14-B.
70   Eg ASEAN Investment Agreement, Annex 2; ASEAN-China Investment Agreement, Annex 2; Not using an annex: see eg Morocco-Nigeria BIT, Art 8; Indian Model BIT, Art 5.
71   See eg Brazil-Malawi CIFA, Art 8.
72   European Commission, 'TTIP and beyond', above note 1, 2.
73   Eg CETA, Annex 8-A(3): "For greater certainty, except in the rare circumstance when the impact of a measure or series of measures is so severe in light of its purpose that it appears manifestly excessive, non-discriminatory measures of a Party that are designed

exception under EU IIAs, three conditions must be fulfilled. First, the measure must be non-discriminatory, second, it must pursue a legitimate public interest, and third, the measure must not appear manifestly excessive in light of its purpose. The policy areas mentioned in EU IIAs are public health, safety and the environment, but the list is indicative and could be further extended to refer to other public interests.[74]

The three prongs of the police power doctrine overlap with two conditions of a lawful expropriation. Namely, the conditions of non-discrimination and the public interest purpose of the measure are both also conditions for an expropriation's lawfulness. Therefore, none of the two conditions can serve to distinguish between the examination of a lawful expropriation (for which compensation is due) and the applicability of the police power. In other words, a State measure can be non-discriminatory and pursuing a public interest, and yet be qualified as an expropriation.[75] Therefore, it is the third condition—requiring that the measure must not appear manifestly excessive in light of its purpose—that serves to determine whether a measure falls within the police powers exception or not. A measure can appear manifestly excessive "in rare circumstances when the impact of the measure is so severe in light of its purpose".[76] The third condition requires a case-by-case assessment and suggests that a tribunal has to weigh the importance of the measure's objective against its impact on the investment.[77] Weighing between the legitimate welfare objective and the impact on the investment implies a proportionality test.[78] Under EU IIAs, there is no such general carve-out for regulatory welfare

---

and applied to protect legitimate public welfare objectives, such as health, safety and the environment, do not constitute indirect expropriations." See likewise EUMFTA, 'Annex on Expropriation' (3); EUSIPA, Annex 1; EUVIPA, Annex 4(3).

74 De Nanteuil, above note 62, 151. Eg the preservation of the domestic currency, see *Saluka v Czech Republic*, above note 61, paras 271–272; or laws against bribery, see *EDF (Services) Limited v Romania*, ICSID Case No ARB/05/13, Award, 8 Oct 2009, para 308.

75 *Azurix Corp v Argentina*, ICSID Case No ARB/01/12, Award, 14 July 2006, para 311: "The argument made by the *S.D. Myers* tribunal is somehow contradictory. According to it, the BIT would require that investments not be expropriated except for a public purpose and that there be compensation if such expropriation takes place and, at the same time, regulatory measures that may be tantamount to expropriation would not give rise to a claim for compensation if taken for a public purpose. The public purpose criterion as an additional criterion to the effect of the measures under consideration needs to be complemented [...]". See especially, De Nanteuil, above note 62, 150.

76 Eg CETA, Annex 8-A(3).

77 Henckels, above note 12, 43.

78 Interestingly, the TTIP proposal contained a different formulation: "if they are necessary and proportionate in light of the above-mentioned factors and are applied in such a way that they genuinely meet the public policy objectives for which they are designed". The

measures. The formulation breaks with the more "radical" police powers doctrine for which any public welfare measure, regardless of its effects on foreign property, falls outside the scope of an indirect expropriation and no compensation is required.[79]

Compared to other global actors, the way in which the EU codified the police powers doctrine is similar to the approach that has started with North American treaty practice.[80] A number of IIAs formulate the three same prongs to set out the scope of the regulatory exception.[81] However, a certain fraction in international investment governance can be identified since some States and regions opt for the so-called radical police powers doctrines and formulate more precise carve-out provisions under which public welfare measure do not constitute an indirect expropriation regardless of the impact on the investment.[82]

For the EU, the codification of the police powers doctrine seeks to safeguard the right to regulate by stating that certain measures, including potential SD measures, are excluded from the scope of indirect expropriation. The European Commission has affirmed that the greater precision concerning indirect expropriation should lead to "particularly excluding claims against legitimate public policy measures".[83] In Opinion 1/17, the CJEU has also examined the CETA's provision on indirect expropriation. The provision passed the test of the Court, and the Court found that "the discretionary powers of the CETA tribunal and Appellate Tribunal do not extend to permitting them to call into question the

---

proposal is available at <http://trade.ec.europa.eu/doclib/docs/2015/september/tradoc_153807.pdf>.

79 Kriebaum, above note 21, 465; see in particular *Methanex v United States*, UNCITRAL, Final Award, 3 Aug 2005, Part IV, Ch D, para 7.
80 2004 Canadian Model BIT, Art 13 and Annex B.13; 2012 US Model BIT, Art 6 and Annex B.
81 Next to Canadian and US IIAs, see also, Austria-Kyrgyzstan BIT, Art 7(4); China-Uzbekistan BIT, Art 6(3): "Except in exceptional circumstances, such as the measures adopted severely surpassing the necessity of maintaining corresponding reasonable public welfare, non-discriminatory regulatory measures adopted by one Contracting Party for the purpose of legitimate public welfare, such as public health, safety and environment, do not constitute indirect expropriation."
82 Eg Indian Model BIT, Art 5.5: "Non-discriminatory regulatory measures by a Party or measures or awards by judicial bodies of a Party that are designed and applied to protect legitimate public interest or public purpose objectives such as public health, safety and the environment shall not constitute expropriation under this Article." See also PAIC, Art 11.3: "A non-discriminatory measure of a Member State that is designed and applied to protect or enhance legitimate public welfare objectives, such as public health, safety and the environment, does not constitute an indirect expropriation under this Code."; Rwanda-Turkey BIT, Art 6(2); Cambodia-Turkey BIT, Art 5(2).
83 European Commission, 'TTIP and beyond', above note 1, 2.

level of protection of public interest".[84] Considering the police powers doctrine as formulated in EU IIAS, this finding should come with a caveat. The balancing exercise provided for under the EU IIAS' formulation of the police powers doctrine, is ultimately a value judgment and lies within a tribunal's discretion. The treaty text does not provide any further guidance how to scrutinise a government's justifications for its actions.[85] The wording as it stands under EU IIAS gives future adjudicators the discretion to choose between a scenario of indirect expropriation and police powers exception. All depends on the appreciation of whether a situation of "rare circumstances" is present.[86] Given that the first and second conditions cannot in themselves serve as distinguishing elements between an indirect expropriation and a police powers situation, the balancing exercise will be the decisive step in the analysis. In other words, the question of delimitation between the two lies fully within the discretion of future adjudicators. At the same time, the qualifier of "rare" circumstances invites future adjudicators to take a cautious approach when accepting that the police powers exception would not apply. Moreover, the measure must appear "manifestly" excessive for the investor and investment. In this respect, the formulation provides a high threshold for a breach by a State when adopting the measure.[87]

6.1.3 *A Specific Provision on the Right to Regulate*

EU IIAS specifically dedicate a provision on the right to regulate, which is mostly entitled "Investment and Regulatory Measures".[88] For instance, Article 8.9 CETA starts off with '[f]or the purpose of this Chapter' and continues with

> "[...] the Parties reaffirm their right to regulate within their territories to achieve legitimate policy objectives, such as the protection of public health, safety, the environment or public morals, social or consumer protection or the promotion and protection of cultural diversity".[89] The

---

84 Opinion 1/17, above note 4, para 156 to be read with para 157 (which is specific on expropriation).
85 Henckels, above note 12, 43.
86 De Nanteuil, above note 62, 152.
87 Henckels, above note 12, 43.
88 CETA, Art 8.9; EUJFTA, Art 16.2(1); EUMFTA, Ch 'Investment', Art 1; EUSIPA, Art 2.2; EUVIPA, Art 2.2.
89 Eg CETA, Art 8.9(1). In the specific context of CETA, the interpretative instrument further plays a fundamental role in reaffirming the parties' right to regulate; see Joint Interpretative Instrument on the Comprehensive Economic and Trade Agreement (CETA) between Canada and the European Union and its Member States, [2017] OJ L 11/3.

second paragraph adds that '*the mere fact that a Party regulates*, including through a modification of its laws, in a manner which negatively affects an investment or interferes with an investor's expectations [...] *does not amount to a breach of an obligation under this Section* [*i.e.* Section D on investment protection]'.[90]

6.1.3.1 Reaffirming the Right to Regulate

The main purpose of provisions on regulatory measures is the reaffirmation of the right to regulate in the public interest, especially in the listed policy areas. The indicative list covers the most typical public interest areas for which regulation is essential to achieve them, such as social and environmental standards. Defining what is of public interest mainly belongs to the State (or the EU where applicable). In the same vein, setting the level of protection in order to best achieve such public interest is a matter that is to be decided by domestic legislators. Due to their affirmative nature, the right to regulate provisions operate as mutual recognition of the right of domestic authorities to regulate matters that fall within their borders. They function as a reminder that the right to regulate constitutes a basic attribute of sovereignty under international law. Put differently, the right to regulate is not granted by EU IIAs or any other international treaty. The purpose of reaffirming the right to regulate lies within the provision's interaction with the provisions on investment protection standards. In this vein, the second paragraph of the right to regulate provisions under EU IIAs points to the balancing exercise between investors' interests and States' regulatory measures in the public interest. The provision creates a direct link to the investment standards, especially to FET and indirect expropriation.[91] However, the right to regulate provisions do not operate as a general exception clause excluding a Contracting Party's liability based on the investment protection standards.[92] They serve interpretative purposes and adjudicators are to take the provision

---

90   Emphasis added. See also EUSIPA, Art 2.2(2).

91   Titi, 'The Right to Regulate', in: Mbengue and Schacherer (eds), *Foreign Investment Under the Comprehensive Economic and Trade Agreement (CETA)* (2019) 171. See also, Henckels, 'Indirect Expropriation and the Right to Regulate: Revisiting Proportionality Analysis and the Standard of Review in Investor-State Arbitration' (2012) 15 Journal of International Economic Law, 223.

92   Exceptions are justifications that, under certain conditions, a State's responsibility is excluded when it would otherwise be engaged for the violation of an international obligation; see, Crawford, *Brownlie's Principles of Public International Law* (2012) 563.

into account when an investment protection standard clashes with a host State's regulatory measure.[93]

Looking at the IIAs practice of other global actors, this type of provisions increaes in IIA practice.[94] The affirmation of the contracting parties' right to regulate can be found in IIAs of developing and developed countries.[95] Certain States and regions adopted approaches that are more explicit on what the right to regulate entails. For example, the SADC Model BIT provides guidance on how a host State's right to regulate should be understood, namely as "embodied within a balance of the rights and obligations of Investors and Investments and Host States, as set out in this Agreement".[96] The provision then adds an actual exception clause, stating that "[f]or greater certainty, non-discriminatory measures taken by a State Party to comply with its international obligations under other treaties shall not constitute a breach of this Agreement".[97] Another approach can be highlighted by the Indian Model BIT, which carves out certain regulatory areas from the scope of the treaty.[98] In terms of stated policy areas, the Nigeria-Morocco BIT provision, contrary to EU IIAs, explicitly mentions (economic) development measures of States.[99] The EU's list rather reflects the "Western political debate" but omits the policy

---

[93] This is not to say that under traditional IIAs, arbitral tribunals did not take the public interests into account in past cases. See in particular, *Philip Morris Brands sàrl, Philip Morris Products sa and Abal Hermanos sa v Oriental Republic of Uruguay*, ICSID Case No ARB/10/7, Award, 8 July 2016.

[94] Eg Argentina-Qatar BIT, Art 10; Greece-UAE BIT, Art 12; Switzerland-Georgia BIT, Art 9; Montenegro-Turkey BIT, Art 4.

[95] See eg SADC Model BIT, Art 20; Indian Model BIT, Art 2.

[96] SADC Model BIT, Art 20(1–2)
    1. In accordance with customary international law and other general principles of international law, the Host State has the right to take regulatory or other measures to ensure that development in its territory is consistent with the goals and principles of sustainable development, and with other legitimate social and economic policy objectives.
    2. Except where the rights of a Host State are expressly stated as an exception to the obligations of this Agreement, a Host State's pursuit of its rights to regulate shall be understood as embodied within a balance of the rights and obligations of Investors and Investments and Host States, as set out in this Agreement.
For greater certainty, non-discriminatory measures taken by a State Party to comply with its international obligations under other treaties shall not constitute a breach of this Agreement.

[97] Ibid.

[98] Indian Model BIT, Art 2 (on Scope and General Provisions).

[99] Morocco-Nigeria BIT, Art 23.1; see also Art 23(2): "[...] a Host State's pursuit of its rights to regulate shall be understood as embodied within a balance of the rights and obligations of Investors and Investments and Host States, as set out in the Agreement."

action relating to the promoting economic development, which could, however, be of relevance for the EU's investment relations with a developing country.[100] At the same time, the enumeration is not exhaustive suggesting that other legitimate objectives could be added. Finally, EU IIAs' formulation can be distinguished from agreements following North-American approaches, which mostly use language saying that the right to regulate protects measures "otherwise consistent with" the treaty obligations.[101] The latter formulation does not recognise an inherent right but functions as an expression of the primacy of the agreement in the case of conflict.[102]

For the European Commission, the introduction of a specific provision on the right to regulate was among the key components in rendering EU IIAs more sensible to public interest regulations, and they are a consequence of public concerns within the EU on the potential negative impacts of trade and investment agreements on the level of protection.[103] EU IIAs make the inherent right to regulate of the contracting Parties the starting point of legal analysis of the Section on investment protection standards. In the words of the European Commission, a specific provision on the right to regulate "allows setting the right context in which investment protection standards are applied".[104] The inclusion of a specific provision on the right to regulate should namely assure that investors' economic interests are taken into account but that such interests need to be balanced with the sovereign right of States to regulate in the broader public interest. Even though these kinds of provisions do not operate

---

100   Mann H, 'The New Frontier: Economic Rights of Foreign Investors versus Government Policy Space for Economic Development' in: Lim CL (ed), *Alternative Visions of the International Law on Foreign Investment: Essays in Honour of Muthucumaraswamy Sornarajah* (Cambridge University Press 2016) 290–291.
101   CPTPP, Art 9.16: 'Nothing in this Chapter shall be construed to prevent a Party from adopting, maintaining or enforcing any measure otherwise consistent with this Chapter that it considers appropriate to ensure that investment activity in its territory is undertaken in a manner sensitive to environmental, health or other regulatory objectives.' Originating from NAFTA, Art 1114 (on 'Environmental Measures'). See also 2012 US Model BIT, Art 12(5): "Nothing in this Treaty shall be construed to prevent a Party from adopting, maintaining, or enforcing any measure otherwise consistent with this Treaty that it considers appropriate to ensure that investment activity in its territory is undertaken in a manner sensitive to environmental concerns."
102   See Johnson et al., 'Aligning International Investment Agreements with the Sustainable Development Goals', (2020) 58 Columbia Journal of Transnational Law, 58 (101). The authors prescribe the North-American approach as 'self-cancelling' language for the right to regulate.
103   European Commission, 'TTIP and beyond' above note 1, para 1.1. See also Opinion 1/17, above note 4, paras 154 and 156.
104   Ibid, para 1.3.

as exceptions or carve-outs for certain policy areas, they have interpretative impacts. Under an EU IIA, future adjudicators cannot *not* take the regulatory purpose into account when an investment protection standard clashes with a host State's measure.[105]

6.1.3.2 Regulations on State Subsidies

EU IIAs' provisions on the right to regulate also address the question of State subsidies.[106] The question of regulatory space and flexibility relating to State subsidies has become increasingly relevant. State subsidies are needed to stimulate the energy transition from fossil to renewable energies due to climate change and resource depletion. In this respect, States use feed-in tariffs (FIT) as a type of subsidy. Regulatory changes concerning FIT schemes have provoked a wave of claims by foreign investors active in the field of renewable energy because where governments decide to modify or revoke such incentives there can arguably occur an indirect expropriation or a FET violation.[107] Interestingly, the EU is not the only global actor that started to link State subsidies with the right to regulate and investment protection. The CPTPP contains a paragraph that states "[f]or greater certainty, the mere fact that a subsidy or grant has not been issued, renewed or maintained, or has been modified or reduced, by a Party, does not constitute a breach of [the FET standard], even if there is loss or damage to the covered investment as a result".[108] Compared to the CPTPP, EU IIAs are more explicit and not limited to the application of the FET standard. The EU's approach is in its comprehensiveness yet unprecedented.[109] A key

---

105 This is not to say that in past cases, under traditional IIAs, arbitral tribunals did not take the public interests into account. See in particular, *Philip Morris Brands sàRL, Philip Morris Products sA and Abal Hermanos sA v Oriental Republic of Uruguay*, ICSID Case No ARB/10/7, Award, 8 July 2016.
106 Typically, in the third and fourth paragraph of the provision on the right to regulate, see eg EUSIPA, Art 2.2(3–4).
107 As the Spain case show, the question of whether and under what circumstances, economic operators investing in this particular field can or cannot expect that such subsidies be granted without subsequent adaptation or modifications is hotly debated. The significant number of investor claims against Spain illustrates this issue. The claims are based on the change in regulation on subsidies relating to solar energy. For an overview of the cases, see Schacherer S, *International Investment Law and Sustainable Development: Key Cases from the 2010s* (IISD, 2018) 10 *et seq.*
108 CPTPP, Art 9.6(5).
109 Tietje C and Crow K, 'The Reform of Investment Protection Rules in CETA, TTIP, and Other Recent EU FTAs: Convincing?', in: Griller S, Obwexer W and Vranes E (eds), *Mega-Regional Trade Agreements: CETA, TTIP, and TiSA; New Orientations for EU External Economic Relations* (Oxford University Press 2017) 97.

feature of the EU approach is that a clear distinction is made between the general right to regulate subsidies and unlawful State subsidies.

Concerning the State's general right to regulate subsidies, EU IIAs provide that a host State's "decision not to issue, renew or maintain a subsidy [...] does not constitute a breach of the [investment protection] provisions".[110] The carve-out applies unless one of the situations mentioned exists. Under letter (a), the granted regulatory flexibility does not apply when the party in question has made a "specific commitment" to investors under national law or contract. Under letter (b), the carve-out does not apply when the decision not to issue, renew or maintain the subsidy was taken "in accordance with any terms or conditions attached to the issuance, renewal or maintenance of the subsidy". As several of the recent renewable energy cases highlight, the question of whether a specific commitment has been made to the investor is a central element in assessing the legality of regulatory changes in light of the foreign investors' FET claims. An critical issue in the renewable energy case is whether a specific commitment can be derived from a general legal framework.[111] Some tribunals found that the commitment was not specific but nonetheless concluded that the investor had legitimate expectations.[112] By emphasising the condition of a specific commitment to investors under national law or in a contract, the EU takes an interesting step in addressing subsidies, which guides future adjudicators when assessing domestic regulation on State subsidies. Firstly, legitimate expectations cannot constitute in themselves a breach of FET. Secondly, in the absence of a specific commitment in law, contract, or the terms of the subsidy grant, liability based on the investment protection standards is excluded.

---

110   Eg CETA, Art 8.9(3). See in this respect, CETA, Art 8.10(4): "When applying the above fair and equitable treatment obligation, the Tribunal may take into account whether a Party made a *specific representation* to an investor to induce a covered investment, that created a legitimate expectation, and upon which the investor relied in deciding to make or maintain the covered investment, but that the Party subsequently frustrated." Emphasis added.

111   Eg *Philip Morris Brands SÀRL, Philip Morris Products SA and Abal Hermanos SA v. Oriental Republic of Uruguay*, ICSID Case No ARB/10/7, Award, 8 July 2016, para 426: "legitimate expectations depend on specific undertakings and representations made by the host State to induce investors to make an investment. Provisions of general legislation applicable to a plurality of persons or of category of persons, do not create legitimate expectations that there will be no change in the law". *Crystallex International Corporation v Bolivarian Republic of Venezuela*, ICSID Case No ARB(AF)/11/2, Award, 4 April 2016, para 547.

112   Eg *Cube Infrastructure Fund SICAV and others v Kingdom of Spain*, ICSID Case No ARB/15/20, Decision on Jurisdiction, Liability and Partial Decision on Quantum, 19 February 2019, para 388: "The Tribunal does not consider it necessary that a specific commitment be made to each individual claimant in order for a legitimate expectation to arise." See Section, 2.5.1.

EU IIAS contain a second carve-out more specifically on unlawful subsidies under EU law or international law. As a result of the unlawfulness, a State cannot grant the subsidy anymore or has to recover it. The reason for the EU to introduce the issue of illegal State subsidies in the context of the right to regulate is rooted in the fact that the EU can decide for subsidies granted by its Member States to certain enterprises to be unlawful State aid under EU law.[113] Therefore, the carve-out of State liability is essential to safeguard the EU regime of State aid law, which basically functions as a subsidy control at the EU level.[114] The competent authority to decide whether a given State aid is compatible with the EU internal market is the European Commission.[115] If the Commission has taken an unfavourable decision concerning an aid that has already been paid out, it requires the Member State to recover the aid with interests from the beneficiary.[116] Right to regulate provisions under EU IIAS provide EU Member States with the necessary leeway to comply with EU law obligations on State aid. It prevents that a Member State's decision to discontinue the granting and potentially the recovery of a measure involving unlawful State aid amounts to a breach of the investment protection standards, namely so the FET clause. In particular, the *Micula* case has highlighted the tension between international investment law and EU State aid law.[117] The carve-outs

---

113   *Ioan Micula, Viorel Micula, S.C. European Food S.A, S.C. Starmill S.R.L. and S.C. Multipack S.R.L. v Romania*, ICSID Case No ARB/05/20, Final Award, 11 Dec 2013.

114   TFEU, Art 107: "[...] any aid granted by a Member State or through State resources in any form whatsoever which distorts or threatens to distort competition by favouring certain undertakings or the production of certain goods shall, in so far as it affects trade between Member States, be incompatible with the internal market."

115   TFEU, Art 108.

116   In such a scenario, the Commission opens a 'recovery case' to enforce the implementation of its decision. If the Member State does not comply with the decision in due time, the Commission may refer it to the CJEU. Recovery aims to remove the undue advantage granted to a company (or companies) and to restore the market to its state before the aforementioned aid was granted. For more details, see Hofmann CHC and Micheau C (eds), *State Aid Law of the European Union* (Oxford University Press 2016).

117   In a decision of 2015, the European Commission declared the payment of compensation under an ICSID award of € 82 million plus interest in favour of Mr Ioan Micula et al. to be illegal State aid. See, *Ioan Micula, Viorel Micula, S.C. European Food S.A, S.C. Starmill S.R.L. and S.C. Multipack S.R.L. v Romania*, ICSID Case No ARB/05/20, Final Award, 11 Dec 2013. The Commission ordered Romania not to make any payments under the award and to recover any payments already made. Mr Micula et al. initiated annulment proceedings against the decision of the Commission. See, GC, Cases T-624/15, T-694/15 and T-704/15, *European Food SA and Others v European Commission*, EU:T:2019:423. The General Court annulled the Commission's decision in full. It upheld the arguments that the Commission had no prerogative over the payments under the award because the investors' right to compensation arose out of events arising before Romania's accession to the EU.

for illegal subsidies under EU IIAs seek to prevent situations like the *Micula* case in the future, where an obligation to pay compensation under the ICSID Convention has the same economic effect as the unlawful aid, which had to be recovered.

Beyond these specific internal EU law safeguards, the carve-out provision under EU IIAs also applies to those subsidies that are unlawful by virtue of international law.[118] In the near future, the international community might adopt legally binding instruments on the prohibition or the reduction of certain State subsidies. This discussion is particularly relevant in the debate on climate change mitigation. To implement the 2015 Paris Agreement, binding rules on the removal of environmentally harmful fossil fuel subsidies could constitute a significant next development.[119] EU IIAs can in this respect provide an exception to investment protection when a CETA Party has to implement an international law obligation, which requires from it to discontinue a subsidy for reasons of climate change mitigation, typically fossil-fuels subsidies. Given all these reasons, the EU introduced innovative treaty language for the delicate link between the right to regulate and State subsidies. The approach introduces predictability for States as well as investors. The EU contributes to the international debate relating to the right to regulate provisions;[120] and introduces explicit provisions on State subsidies that are likely to become highly for future SD implementation at the national level.

6.1.4 *The Post-Establishment Obligation of Non-Discrimination*

EU IIAs, like the great majority of IIAs, guarantee investors and investments non-discriminatory treatment.[121] The standard includes national treatment, which requires non-discrimination between domestic and foreign investors as well as most favoured nation (MFN) treatment, which requires

---

118   For example, the WTO Agreement on Subsidies and Countervailing Measures (SCM) prohibits two categories of subsidies, namely export subsidies and local content subsidies. See, SCM, Art 3.

119   It is interesting to note that both the Asia-Pacific Economic Cooperation (APEC) and the G20 have established peer review processes to help members meet their commitments to phase out inefficient fossil fuel subsidies. See, International Institute for Sustainable Development (IISD) and Global Subsidies Initiative (GSI), 'Building on Momentum: Recommendation from the GSI Fossil Fuel Subsidy Reform at the G20', Policy Brief, June 2016, <https://www.iisd.org/sites/default/files/publications/building-on-momentum-recommendations-ffsr-g20.pdf>.

120   See also European Commission, 'TTIP and beyond', above note 1, 1.1.

121   Reinisch A, 'National Treatment', in: Bungenberg M et al (eds), *International Investment Law—A Handbook* (CH BECK; Hart; Nomos 2015) 847.

non-discrimination between different foreign investors. Compared to FET and indirect expropriation, the MFN and national treatment standard are relatively infrequently invoked by investors and even more so, claims based on these standards are as good as never successful.[122] However, cases such as *Occidental v. Ecuador I* and *Corn Products v. Mexico* impacted on how States perceive the risks of these standards.[123] When assessing a claim based on national treatment or MFN treatment, tribunals only seldomly consider the regulatory purpose of the legislation or administrative act at stake.[124] Past arbitral case law reveals that tribunals assessed likeness on a factual assessment of the extent to which a foreign investor is adversely affected by the measure in comparison to domestic investors omitting the regulatory purpose.[125]

Under EU IIAs the non-discrimination standard in the post-establishment phase can collide with the right to regulate since post-establishment situations, such as expansion, conduct, operation, management, maintenance, use, enjoyment as well as sale or disposal, are subject to investor-State dispute settlement under EU IIAs.[126] Moreover, the general exception clause in the EU

---

122 According to UNCTAD's database, the national treatment standard has been invoked in 130 cases out of 983 cases (13%); an actual breach of the national treatment standard was found in 9 cases out of 647 finalised cases (ie 1,4% success rate). As regards, the MFN treatment standard, it has been invoked in 102 cases out of 983 (10%) and an actual breach was found in only 3 cases out of 647 finalised cases (ie 0,5% success rate). See UNCTAD, Policy Hub <https://investmentpolicy.unctad.org/> (last update 31 Oct 2019).

123 *Occidental Exploration and Production Co v Ecuador*, Final Award, LCIA/UNCITRAL, Case No UN 3467, 1 July 2004. The Occidental tribunal adopted a significant broad approach to likeness. The tribunal found that the investor that is a foreign exporter of oil was in "like situations" to domestic exporters of other products including seafood and flowers. See, paras 167–168, 173 and 177; *Corn Products International Inc v Mexico*, Decision on Responsibility, ICSID Case No ARB(AF)/04/01, 15 Jan 2008. In this case, the tribunal adopted a large economic sector approach in order to ground its finding on "like circumstances". It held that the US investor using high-fructose corn syrup (HFSC) for the production of beverages was in the same economic sector than domestic producers (the comparator) that use cane sugar for their products. See, paras 124, 126 and 135.

124 The large bulk of investor claims on discrimination are based on the national treatment standard, but for cases where an MFN treatment clause is at stake, there should be no difference in approaching the question of the appropriate comparator.

125 Mitchell AD, Heaton D and Henckels C, *Non-Discrimination and the Role of Regulatory Purpose in International Trade and Investment Law* (Edward Elgar Publishing 2016) 65–66 and 135.

126 See eg CETA, Art 8.18(1) "[…] an investor of a Party may submit to the Tribunal constituted under this Section a claim that the other Party has breached an obligation under (a) Section C, with respect to the expansion, conduct, operation, management, maintenance, use, enjoyment and sale or disposal of its covered investment". The issue of non-discrimination in the pre-establishment phase will be dealt with under the section on investment liberalisation. See Section 6.2.1.

IIAs discussed in the next section applies to the non-discrimination standard. EU IIAs provide, with respect to national treatment and MFN treatment, that each party "shall accord to an investor of the other Party and ta covered investment, treatment no less favourable than the treatment it accords, in like situations" to either its own investors or to investors of a third country.[127] EU IIAs thus include the concept of likeness. Even though adding "like situations" seeks to invite future arbitrators to find the appropriate comparator, EU IIAs do not provide further guidance.

In comparison, the CPTPP provides further clarification in this respect and sets out factors that the tribunal should take into account. The treaty provision as such reads similar to the ones found in EU IIAs, but the CPTPP then adds in a footnote to the articles that the likeness is dependent on "the totality of the circumstances, including whether the relevant treatment distinguishes between investors or investments on the basis of legitimate public welfare objectives".[128] In an interpretative instrument to the agreement, the CPTPP partners issued further clarification on the non-discrimination provisions.[129] The instrument namely clarifies that only intentionally discriminatory measures would breach the standard, that the claimant must be in a competitive relationship with a domestic investor, that the tribunal must take the objective of the measure into account and, finally, that in order to avoid liability, the differentiated treatment must be plausible and reasonably connected to a legitimate public welfare objective.[130] This formulation is reminiscent of the NAFTA case *Pope & Talbot* that established that if a difference in treatment can be justified based on a rational policy objective, is not based on a preference favouring domestic investors over foreign investors and does not unduly undermine the investment liberalising objectives, the foreign and the domestic investors were not in like circumstances.[131]

---

127 CETA, Arts 8.6(1) and 8.7(1); EUMFTA, Ch 'Investment', Arts 7 and 8; EUSIPA, Art 2.3; EUVIPA, Arts 2.3 and 2.4.

128 CPTPP, Art 9.6, Footnote 14: "For greater certainty, whether treatment is accorded in 'like circumstances' under Article 9.4 (National Treatment) or Article 9.5 (Most-Favoured-Nation Treatment) depends on the totality of the circumstances, including whether the relevant treatment distinguishes between investors or investments on the basis of legitimate public welfare objectives".

129 CPTPP, 'Drafters' Note on Interpretation of "In Like Circumstances" Under Article 9.4 (National Treatment) and Article 9.5 (Most-Favoured-Nation Treatment)', available at <https://www.mfat.govt.nz/assets/Trans-Pacific-Partnership/Other-documents/Interpretation-of-In-Like-Circumstances.pdf>.

130 See also Henckels, above note 12, 45.

131 *Pope & Talbot v Canada*, UNCITRAL, Award on the Merits of Phase 2, 10 April 2001, para 78.

In the same vein, by seeking to provide better guidance for future tribunals when applying the non-discrimination standards, a number of African investment model treaties and IIAs, such as the COMESA Investment Agreement, adopt the approach of having a list of elements that should be taken into account when assessing the "like circumstances". The provisions first state that the assessment of likeness is a case-by-case assessment and requires that all the circumstances of an investment activity are to be taken into account.[132] Subsequently listed are then, in a non-exhaustive list, the elements of the investment circumstances, *i.e.*: (a) its effects on third persons and the local community; (b) its effects on the local, regional or national environment; including the cumulative effects of all investments within a jurisdiction on the environment; (c) the sector the investor is in; (d) the aim of the measure concerned, (e) the regulatory process generally applied in relation to the measure concern, and (f) other factors.[133] The PAIC sets out an even longer list, namely adding the size of the investment.[134] In terms of how the various factors should be weighed, the Morocco-Nigeria BIT specifies that none of the elements is more relevant than any other and that the elements are not limited to the mentioned elements.[135] Compared to the US approach, the *effects* of the investment in the host States are a particular feature of African instruments. The comparison thus corroborates the finding that EU IIAs do little to integrate SD concerns with respect to the non-discrimination obligation even though the inclusion of the regulatory purpose of the measure is relevant from an SD perspective.[136] Being grounded in SD promotion reasons, a measure's regulatory purpose might include valid reasons for differential treatment between a foreign and a domestic investor.[137]

From an EU law and policy perspective, it seems incoherent at first that the European Commission did little to integrate safeguards in the provision

---

132 See COMESA Investment Agreement, Art 17(2); Morocco-Nigeria BIT, Art 6.3; SADC Model BIT, Art 4.2.
133 Ibid.
134 PAIC, Arts 7.3 and 9.3: "(a) Its effects on third persons and the local community; (b) Its effects on the local, regional or national environment, the health of the populations, or on the global commons; (c) The sector in which the investor is active; (d) The aim of the measure in question; (e) The regulatory process generally applied in relation to a measure in question; (f) Company size, and (g) Other factors directly relating to the investment or investor in relation to the measure."
135 Morocco-Nigeria BIT, Art 6.3.
136 Consider Section 2.5.1.
137 VanDuzer JA, Simons P and Mayeda G, *Integrating Sustainable Development into International Investment Agreements: A Guide for Developing Countries* (Commonwealth Secretariat 2012) 124 (hereafter: Commonwealth Secretariat).

on non-discrimination. Especially when reconsidering the safeguards in the FET standard and the provision on indirect expropriation. Here, the EU has done little to counter-balance the investment protection standard of non-discrimination with the public SD interests. However, it should be noted that EU IIAS provide for limitations of the scope of non-discrimination clauses through general exceptions typically provided in a specific provision.[138] Besides, limitations are introduced through reservations and other exceptions included in a number of schedules annexed to the agreements.[139] In Opinion 1/17, the Court based its reasoning heavily on the existence of general exception clauses and found that the right to regulate in the public interest was preserved thanks to their existence.[140] To further comment on the post-establishment obligation of non-discrimination, it is relevant to analyse the general exception clause under EU IIAS.

6.1.5 General Exception Clauses for SD Regulatory Flexibility under EU IIAS

Contained in an IIA, general exceptions fulfil a similar function as the general exceptions under WTO law, namely under the GATT and the GATS.[141] They are designed to single out important public policy areas so that they are not jeopardised by being challenged for their inconsistency with the investment liberalisation and protection obligations in an IIA.[142] Typically, they address exceptions for measures falling under the protection of the environment and of human and animal health.[143] Therefore, general exceptions are a further way

---

138   It is important to note that the EUSIPA has the general exceptions directly with the national treatment standard (following the wording of GATS, Art XIV), see EUSIPA, Art 2.3(3).
139   Relating to reservations and exceptions, see CETA, Art 8.15; see also above Section 6.2.1. The issue of schedules is not further analysed in the present study, as their elaboration is part of national investment law and policy. For the EU, the Member States mostly deal with the establishment of the schedules individually.
140   Opinion 1/17, above note 4, paras 152–153.
141   See Wu M, 'The Scope and Limits of Trade's Influence in Shaping the Evolving International Investment Regime' in: Douglas Z, Pauwelyn J and Viñuales JE (eds), *The Foundations of International Investment Law: Bringing Theory into Practice* (Oxford University Press 2014) 196–199.
142   In essence, exceptions are justifications that, under certain conditions, a State's responsibility is excluded when it would otherwise be engaged for the violation of an international obligation. Crawford J, *Brownlie's Principles of Public International Law* (8th ed, Oxford University Press 2012) 563.
143   See also Newcombe A, 'General Exceptions in International Investment Agreements', in: Cordonier Segger M-C, Gehring MW and Newcombe AP (eds), *Sustainable Development in World Investment Law* (Kluwer Law International 2011) 355–361.

to introduce regulatory flexibility, preserving policy space in areas relevant to SD.[144] However, their utility and effectiveness, to provide greater or clearer policy space for States to enact SD legislation, needs yet to be tested in practice.[145]

General exception clauses in IIAs are still a relatively novel but increasing phenomenon.[146] They are more often included in FTAs with investment chapters than in standalone BITs. EU IIAs confirm this general trend and contain general exceptions in a specific chapter or section, which apply to the investment liberalisation provisions and partially to the investment protection provisions. Chapters or sections on "Exceptions" under EU IIAs often cover a much broader array of fields.[147] In the following, the focus is on the general exceptions dealing with "environmental measures necessary to protect human, animal or plant life or health" as they mainly deal with policy space concerned with SD.[148]

The general exception clauses contained in comprehensive EU FTAs apply to the investment chapter/agreement but are limited to the provisions related to the establishment of the investment and non-discriminatory treatment.[149] The single exception hereto is the FTA with Mexico as the whole investment chapter is subject to the general exceptions.[150] EU IIAs integrate WTO-style exception clauses tailored according to Article XX of the GATT and Article XIV of the GATS. First, the GATS formulation has found incorporation into several EU IIAs.[151] The *chapeau* to such provisions generally states that:

> "[s]ubject to the requirement that measures are not applied in a manner which would constitute a means of arbitrary or unjustifiable discrimination between the Parties where like conditions prevail, or a disguised

---

144 Commonwealth Secretariat, above note 137, 244.
145 See Section 2.5.2.
146 Mitchell AD, Munro J and Voon T, 'Importing WTO General Exceptions into International Investment Law', in: Sachs L, Johnson L and Coleman J, *Yearbook on International Investment Law & Policy 2017* (Oxford University Press 2019) 307.
147 Eg CETA, Ch 28.
148 It is the typical formulation taken from Article XX of GATT. This excludes the exceptions for prudential measures (eg CETA, Art 28.4–5); security exceptions (CETA, Art 28.6); exceptions for taxation (CETA, Art 28.7); exceptions for culture (CETA, Art 28.9); and exceptions for non-disclosure of confidential information (CETA, Art 28.8).
149 Eg CETA, Art 28.3(1–2); EUVIPA, Art 4.6; EUSIPA, Art 2.3(3).
150 EUMFTA, Ch 'General exceptions', Art XX(1) and (4).
151 CETA, Art 28.3(2); EUVIPA, Art 4.6. The EUSIPA is a particular case. It contains the GATS-tailored list directly in the NT provision; see EUSIPA, Art 2.3(3).

restriction on trade in services, nothing in this Agreement shall be construed to prevent the adoption or enforcement by a Party of measures necessary:"[152]

An exhaustive list of policy objectives then follows the *chapeau*. The ones relevant for SD are "to protect human, animal or plant life or health" and those "relating to the conservation of exhaustible natural resources if such measures are applied in conjunction with restrictions on domestic investors or on the domestic supply or consumption of services".[153]

Second, some of the general exception clauses under EU IIAs also integrate Article XX of GATT. For instance, the CETA provides:

> "For the purpose of [...] Sections B (Establishment of investment) and C (Non-discriminatory treatment) of Chapter Eight (Investment), *Article XX of the GATT 1994 is incorporated into and made part of this Agreement.* The Parties understand that the measures referred to in Article XX (b) of the GATT 1994 include environmental measures necessary to protect human, animal or plant life or health. The Parties understand that Article XX (g) of the GATT 1994 applies to measures for the conservation of living and non-living exhaustible natural resources."[154]

Compared to other international actors, the EU approach is in line with the increasing trend in IIA practice to incorporate WTO-style exception clauses.[155] Canada has started the trend with its Model BIT of 2004.[156] Subsequently, general exceptions have been included in a great number of Canadian BITs with third countries.[157] This is a treaty practice which was then followed by other countries, such as Turkey and Japan.[158] African investment instruments vary

---

152   Eg EUVIPA, Art 4.6.
153   See eg EUVIPA, Art 4.6(b) and (c).
154   CETA, Art 28.3(1). Emphasis added. See also EUMFTA, Ch 'General exceptions', Art XX(1).
155   De Mestral A and Vanhonnaeker L, 'Exception Clauses in Mega-Regionals (International Investment Protection and Trade Agreements)' in: Rensmann T (ed), *Mega-Regional Trade Agreements* (Springer International Publishing 2017) 83. See also Mitchell, Munro and Voon, above note 146, 307; Newcombe, above note 143, 358. Whilst NAFTA contains a GATT-Art XX-tailored exception clause, the latter is, however, not applicable to Chapter 11 on investment.
156   2004 Canadian Model BIT, Art 10.
157   Eg Canadian BITs with China, Art 33; Côte d'Ivoire, Art 17; Mongolia, Art 17; or Serbia, Art 18.
158   Eg Japan-Iran BIT, Art 13; Turkey-Rwanda BIT, Art 5.

in this respect.¹⁵⁹ If WTO-style exception clauses are incorporated, the most important difference in treaty practice is whether or not they apply to all obligations on investment liberalisation and protection or are limited to e.g. non-discrimination. Canadian BITs and those of Japan and Turkey do not select to which of the investment obligations the exceptions apply and thus applying to all substantive investment clauses. Conversely, under the CPTPP, the general exception clause does not apply to the investment chapter altogether.¹⁶⁰

For most of its IIAs, the EU approach consists of limiting the application of the general exceptions to the provisions related to the establishment of the investment and the obligations on national treatment and MFN treatment.¹⁶¹ The reason is that through greater clarification, the EU has already sought to safeguard the policy space under the provisions on expropriation and fair and equitable treatment. To exclude the general exceptions to apply, namely to FET and indirect expropriation avoids uncertainties of how they impact the policy space already reflected in those provisions.¹⁶² It constitutes a further element of seeking to safeguard policy space needed to implement public SD measures at the domestic level.¹⁶³ However, the effectiveness of general exception clauses depends their drafting. The more comprehensive the list of permissible objectives, the more flexibility is granted; and the more lenient the nexus requirement between the measure taken and the objectives, the more flexibility is granted.

6.1.5.1 Permissible Objectives

The WTO-style general exception clauses under EU IIAs apply to the specific lists of recognised legitimate policy objectives, such as "environmental measures"¹⁶⁴

---

159 PAIC, Art 14; COMESA Investment Agreement, Art 22; SADC Model BIT, Art 25. However, the Morocco-Nigeria BIT does not contain a general exception clause.
160 CPTPP, Art 29.1.
161 With the exception of the EUMFTA. See EUMFTA, Ch 'General exceptions', Art XX(1) and (4).
162 Mitchell, Munro and Voon, above note 146, 347. See Sections 6.1.1 and 6.1.2. On the debate see Section 2.5.2. Concerns have, in particular, been raised that general exceptions in IIAs can limit the policy space granted through the police powers doctrine in the case of an alleged indirect expropriation. Keene A, 'The Incorporation and Interpretation of WTO-Style Environmental Exceptions in International Investment Agreements' (2017) 18 The Journal of World Investment & Trade 62, 85; Lévesque C, 'The Inclusion of GATT Article XX Exceptions in IIAs: A Potentially Risky Policy', in: Echandi R and Sauvé P (eds), *Prospects in International Investment Law and Policy* (Cambridge University Press 2013) 365.
163 European Commission, 'Trade for all', above note 1, 5, and 'TTIP and beyond' above note 1.
164 CETA, Art 28.3(1) referring to GATT XX(b).

necessary to protect human, animal or plant life or health. In addition, EU IIAs further extend the list by the "conservation of non-living resources"[165] thereby taking WTO case law involving Article XX of the GATT into account.[166] Conversely, the EU IIAs' provisions do not add the Appellate Body's finding that the said provision of the GATT also covers clean air.[167] In the debate on SD integration, the GATT or GATS formulations have been criticised since they do not cover all relevant non-economic SD policy areas.[168] For instance, with regard to human rights, GATT Article XX covers them only indirectly, through the references to public morals (let. a), human life or health (let. b) and prison labour (let. e).[169]

However, the list cannot and should not include any area of government action. The CPTPP is an example of an agreement, which has attempted, contrary to EU IIAs, to be more explicit concerning the permissible objectives. It explicitly includes an exception for "Tobacco Control Measures" into the set of exceptions.[170] The contracting parties of the CPTPP thus sought to be clear which policy area needs to be counterbalanced against investment liberalisation and protection standards.[171] While the parties to the CPTPP made this choice specific, the approach has its limits because States would need to consider the policy areas for which they want to retain flexibility for the future at the moment of treaty negotiation. In this respect, it is relevant to recall the basic idea of general exceptions, which is that, through a list of general and relatively broad policy areas, a State can pursue a wide range of interests or

---

165 CETA, Art 28.3(1) referring to GATT XX(g).
166 *United States—Import Prohibition of Certain Shrimp and Shrimp Products*, Appellate Body Report, (1998) WT/DS58/AB/R, paras 127–131.
167 *United States—Standards for Reformulated and Conventional Gasoline*, Appellate Body Report and Panel Report, (1996) WT/DS2/9, para 6.21. The Panel allowed reducing air pollution to be considered protecting human, plant or animal life or health (as per GATT Article XX(b)).
168 Sabanogullari L, 'The Merits and Limitations of General Exception Clauses in Contemporary Investment Treaty Practice' (2015) IISD Investment Treaty News.
169 Bartels L, 'Article XX of GATT and the Problem of Extraterritorial Jurisdiction: The Case of Trade Measures for the Protection of Human Rights' (2002) Journal of World Trade 353, 354–356.
170 CPTPP, Art 29.5; Quite clearly a reaction to *Philip Morris v Australia*, PCA Case No 2012–12, Award on Jurisdiction and Admissibility, 17 Dec 2015; and *Australia—Certain Measures Concerning Trademarks and Other Plain Packaging Requirements Applicable to Tobacco Products and Packaging*, Panel Reports (2018) WT/DS435/R, WT/DS441/R WT/DS458/R, WT/DS467/R.
171 CPTPP, Art 29.5. This exception does apply to the whole investment chapter of the CPTPP.

values in comparison to other types of exceptions.[172] A balance in treaty drafting between overly specific provisions and enough determinacy remains a challenge for investment law-making.

The regulatory flexibility granted through the general exception clauses under EU IIAs also depends on how the stated objectives will be interpreted. Most of the permissible objectives in EU IIAs, such as human health, have an ordinary meaning making it relatively easy to determine whether a given State measure falls under this category.[173] Yet, the objective of "public morals" is less clear and provides future adjudicators with greater discretion in deciding which policy area falls under this category.[174] To determine the outer limits of the policy areas stated, future adjudicators can, for their interpretation, either rely on previous investment arbitral or WTO case law. However, investment arbitration cases that had to interpret general exceptions are yet seldom.[175] Conversely, the "security exception" clause contained in the US-Argentina BIT had to be assessed in a number of investment claims against Argentina. Several tribunals that had to interpret this exception clause in light of the Argentinian emergency measures suggested a narrow interpretation of what type of measure falls under the exception, thereby limiting Argentina's regulatory space.[176] It has been argued that WTO jurisprudence might be more beneficial in this respect as it generally accepts that exception should not be interpreted narrowly and, in the case of doubt, it has been accepted that the measure falls within the alleged category providing an interpretation in favour of States.[177] The point in this respect is that EU IIAs leave it up to future adjudicators how the outer limits of the stated permissible objectives will be interpreted.[178]

---

172 Gagliani G, 'The Interpretation of General Exceptions in International Trade and Investment Law: Is a Sustainable Development Interpretive Approach Possible?' (2015) 43 Denver Journal of International Law & Policy 559, 580.
173 Henckels, above note 12, 47–48.
174 Ibid.
175 See *Bear Creek Mining Corporation v Republic of Peru*, ICSID Case No ARB/14/2, Award, 30 Nov 2017, paras 473–474. Here the tribunal did not further elaborate on the scope of the policy areas listed in the applicable general exceptions clause. *Copper Mesa Mining Corporation v Republic of Ecuador*, PCA No 2012-2, Award, 15 March 2016. The tribunal did not apply the clauses, see paras 6.58–6.67.
176 See eg *Enron Corporation v Argentina*, ICSID Case No ARB/01/3, Award, 15 May 2007, para 331; *Sempra Energy International v Argentina*, ICSID Case No ARB/02/16, Award, 18 Sep 2007, para 373.
177 *EC Measures Concerning Meat and Meat Products* (*Hormones*), Appellate Body Report, (1998) WT/DS26/AB/R, WT/DS48/AB/R, para 104. See also Mitchell, Munro and Voon, above note 146, 343.
178 The same is true for the great majority of IIAs that include general exceptions.

6.1.5.2 The Nexus Requirement "necessary for"

Under EU IIAs, the general exception clauses apply to the investment protection standard of non-discriminatory treatment.[179] For the exceptions to apply, a nexus between the impugned measure and an objective stated in the general exception clause needs to be established. EU IIAs state in this respect that non-conforming measures must be "necessary for" one of the permissible objectives. How the concept of "necessity" will be interpreted is another factor determining the granted regulatory space for SD measures under EU IIAs.[180] In other words, EU IIAs leave it up to the tribunal to find an interpretation of the concept of necessity.[181] This bears the risk that the necessity requirement is interpreted strictly making it hard for host States to benefit from the general exception clause. Compared to other IIAs, one can find different formulations, next to "necessary for", also "relating to" and "designed and applied to". Both alternatives are nexus requirements that are easier to attend for host States than the test of necessity because they require a simpler, more neutral nexus between the objectives and the measures. In contrast, whether something is necessary, comes with a weighing exercise that future adjudicators have to make. Namely, African investment instruments require that a measure is only "relating to"[182] or "designed and applied to"[183] achieve one of the permissible objectives. Such nexus requirements are more lenient and the objective of safeguarding regulatory space has consistently pursued.

6.2 The Lack of SD Integration in the Regulation of Investment Liberalisation under EU IIAs

The EU has traditionally been very keen to open up its own market for foreign capital and investment and to stipulate liberalisation obligations and market access commitments in its economic agreements with third countries. Obligations on liberalisation and market access are central elements of EU IIAs, as highlighted already by the pre-Lisbon IIA practice of the EU.[184] In its

---

179　CETA, Art 28.3(1–2); EUVIPA, Art 4.6; EUSIPA, Art 2.3(3).
180　Investment arbitral cases show that tribunals have not elaborated a consistent approach to what the concept of necessity entails. See, Section 2.5.2.
181　Henckels, above note 12, 48.
182　PAIC, Art 14(1).
183　COMESA Investment Agreement, Art 22.1; SADC Model BIT, Art 25. See also, SADC Model BIT, Commentary, 46–47.
184　See Section 4.1.1. See also, Dimopoulos A, *EU Foreign Investment Law* (Oxford University Press 2011) 149–152.

post-Lisbon IIAs, the EU combines investment protection with investment liberalisation.[185] Traditional IIAs, such as the BITs of EU Member States protect investments once established in a party's territory without granting rights of establishment.[186] Still a majority of IIAs do not contain provisions on investment liberalisation.[187] There is, however, an increasing IIA practice to provide for such commitments.[188]

Even where provisions on investment liberalisation are included in an IIA, they are often not subject to investor-State dispute settlement, and thus there are as good as no arbitration cases that shed light on the impacts of such provisions on the host State's regulatory space. EU IIAs do generally not subject the provisions on investment liberalisation to investor-State dispute resolution.[189] Post-Lisbon EU IIAs contain three types of elements falling under the framework of investment liberalisation that will be further discussed: pre-establishment rights granted through the guarantee of non-discriminatory treatment as regards the establishment of the investment, specific market access provisions, and finally prohibitions of certain domestic performance requirements.

6.2.1 *Pre-Establishment Rights*

EU IIAs stipulate pre-establishment rights[190] by extending national treatment and most-favoured nation (MFN) treatment to the pre-establishment

---

185   CETA and the FTA with Mexico include the investment liberalisation provisions in the chapters on investment, whereas the FTAs with Vietnam and Singapore include them in a specific chapter of the FTA, see EUSFTA, Ch 8 on "Services, Establishment and Electronic Commerce"; and EUVFTA, Ch 8 on "Liberalisation of Investment, Trade in Services and Electronic Commerce".

186   One can find promotional clauses related to the admission in some BITs. See eg Czech-Republic-Netherlands BIT, Art 2: "Each Contracting Party shall in its territory promote investments by investors of the other Contracting Party and shall admit such investments in accordance with its provisions of law".

187   De Mestral A, 'Pre-Entry Obligations under International Law', in: Bungenberg M et al, *International Investment Law—A Handbook* (BECK; Hart; Nomos 2015) 696–698.

188   UNCTAD, 'International Investment Arrangements: Trends and Emerging Issues', in: *UNCATD Series on International Investment Policies for Development* (United Nations 2006) 25.

189   CETA, Art 8.18 *a contrario*. Investment liberalisation provisions are subject to State-State dispute settlement, CETA, Art 29.2, EUSFTA Art 14.2; EUVFTA, Art 15.2. An exception here is the EUMFTA, Ch "Resolution of investment disputes", Art 2(1).

190   Pre-establishment rights (also rights of establishment) are rights of investors from one state party to invest in the territory of the other state party. The right of establishment entails not only a right to carry out business transaction but, in particular, to set up a permanent business presence. The notion of a right of admission is narrower as it is the right of entry only. See Gómez-Palacio I and Muchlinski P, 'Admission and Establishment',

phase.[191] This creates a right of establishment for foreign investors by requiring from the other contracting party treatment that is no less favourable than that accorded to domestic investors and other foreign investors with respect to their businesses in the host State market.[192] Post-Lisbon EU IIAs do not grant absolute pre-establishment rights to foreign investors but limit the scope of such rights by expressly excluding specific sectors, either through negative lists or positive lists.[193] EU IIA practice is not harmonised in this respect. Some EU IIAs use a negative list, which means that all the sectors are subject to liberalisation commitments unless they are excluded in a list. These long and complex lists are generally part of annexes to the actual agreement. CETA adopts a negative list approach,[194] and the same approach can be found in the EU-Japan FTA.[195] For those EU IIAs adopting a positive-list approach, the parties have prepared a list of the sectors to which the liberalisation commitments will apply. The EU, for the agreements with Vietnam, Singapore and also Korea, has used the positive list approach.[196]

Whilst positive lists compared to negative lists have been considered to be less burdensome for States as regards their implementation,[197] both approaches can put the host State at risk of an improper commitment that may constrain future government measures, such as later changing its domestic law because domestic economic needs should so require to close a sector listed as open in the agreement.[198] Moreover, market liberalisation can bring about undue restrictions on the sovereign power to regulate for the benefit of their local companies.[199] From an SD perspective, mainly economic development policies and measures at the national level might be undermined when IIAs grant extensive rights of establishment.

In an international comparison, EU IIA practice reflects a general trend in IIAs for increased pre-establishment rights for foreign investors.[200] The EU

---

in: Muchlinski P et al (eds), *The Oxford Handbook on International Investment Law* (Oxford University Press 2008) 230.

191   CETA, Arts 8.6 (NT) and 8.7 (MFN); EUMFTA, Ch 'Investment', Arts 7 (NT) and 8 (MFN); EUSFTA, Art 8.11 (NT); EUVFTA, Arts 8.5 (NT) and 8.6 (MFN).
192   Commonwealth Secretariat, above note 137, 107.
193   Mann H, 'Investment Liberalization: Some Key Elements and Issues in Today's Negotiating Context' Issues in International Investment Law (IISD 2007).
194   See CETA, Art 8.15 (on 'Reservations and Exceptions') applying to Arts 8.6 and 8.7.
195   EUJFTA, Art 8.12.
196   EUSFTA Art 8.7; EUVFTA, Art 8.7; EUKFTA, Art 7.7.
197   See Section 2.4.2.
198   SADC Model BIT, Commentary, 15.
199   Dimopoulos, above note 184, 148.
200   See eg CPTPP, Arts 9.4 (NT) and 9.5 (MFN); ASEAN Investment Area, Art 7(1).

approach that consists of extending the national as well as the MFN treatment to the pre-establishment phase originates in the US and Canadian approaches that started with NAFTA.²⁰¹ Especially, Canada has included pre-establishment commitments is all of its recent BITs.²⁰² The contrast with investment instruments from developing countries is noticeable. A number of model IIAs of developing countries specifically exclude any commitment that would grant the investor pre-establishment rights.²⁰³ For instance, the Indian Model BIT states that "[...] nothing in this Treaty shall extend to any Pre-investment activity related to establishment, acquisition or expansion of any investment, or to any measure related to such Pre-investment activities [...]".²⁰⁴ Capital-importing countries are more reluctant to liberalise access to their markets because it could signify too much competitive pressure on domestic firms and even lead to crowding them out from domestic markets.²⁰⁵

The EU, as a capital-exporting region, is interested in assuring its companies with a free global market economy. By setting out obligations on the admission and establishment of investment, the EU seeks, on the one hand, to ensure, for its own companies, access to new markets in third States, and on the other hand, to increase the competitiveness within the EU market through the presence of foreign companies.²⁰⁶ The EU, in this respect, pursues, through its IIAs, similar interests to those of other capital-exporting countries aiming at most widely liberalised markets globally. Traditionally, the United States, Canada and Japan, likewise have pushed for investment liberalisation in their relations with third countries.²⁰⁷ Attempts to generally restrict investment liberalisation based on the objective to better safeguard States' rights to regulate are not evident in EU IIAs. Yet again, the granting of non-discriminatory treatment with concerning establishment is never absolute under EU IIAs but limited by schedules excluding (or not including)

---

201 See NAFTA, Arts 1102, 1103 and 1106.
202 Eg Canadian BITs with Burkina Faso, Cameroon, Côte d'Ivoire, Guinea, Mali, Mongolia, Kuwait, Senegal.
203 PAIC, Art 4.4; SADC recommends not to include pre-establishment commitments, see SADC Model BIT, Commentary, 16, Morocco-Nigeria BIT, Art 3.
204 Indian Model, Art 2.2.
205 Johnson L, 'FDI, International Investment and the Sustainable Development Goals', in: Krajewski M and Hoffmann RT (eds), *Research Handbook on Foreign Direct Investment* (Edward Elgar Pub 2019) 127–128.
206 European Commission, 'Trade for All', above note 1, 4.
207 UNCTAD, IPFSD, 81. However, investment governance seems to shift in this respect since the Trump administration in the United States. See, Bonnitcha J, 'Investment Wars: Contestation and Confusion in Debate About Investment Liberalization' (2019) 22 Journal of International Economic Law 629.

specific sectors, many of which are highly sensitive SD sectors. In particular, the EU does not liberalise, under its IIAs, sectors such as health, water supply, education or social services.[208]

6.2.2   *Prohibitions of Market Access Restrictions*

A typical feature of EU IIAS is to include a separate provision on "market access".[209] Commitments that fall under such market access provisions seek to allow each other's investors to access the domestic market by prohibiting the adoption or the maintenance of specific limitations. This includes that one contracting party may not impose on investors of the other party limitations based on the number of suppliers or service operations, the total value of transactions, foreign capital participation by quantity, or any specific requirements for the legal form to be used. Such provision of EU IIAS typically reads as follows:

> 1. A Party shall not adopt or maintain with respect to market access through establishment by an investor of the other Party, on the basis of its entire territory or on the basis of the territory of a national, provincial, territorial, regional or local level of government, a measure that:
> (a)   imposes limitations on:
>   i.   the number of enterprises that may carry out a specific economic activity whether in the form of numerical quotas, monopolies, exclusive suppliers or the requirement of an economic needs test;
>   ii   the total value of transactions or assets in the form of numerical quotas or the requirement of an economic needs test;
>   iii.   the total number of operations or the total quantity of output expressed in terms of designated numerical units in the form of quotas or the requirement of an economic needs test;
>   iv.   the participation of foreign capital in terms of maximum percentage limit on foreign shareholding or the total value of individual or aggregate foreign investment; or

---

208   See, CETA, Annexes I-III (Annex I, especially, 'Reservation for existing measures and liberalization commitments'); EUJFTA, Annex 8-B 'Schedules for chapter 8', EUVFTA, Annexes 8-A, 8-B and 8-C, EUSFTA, Annexes 8-A and 8-B; EUMFTA, 'Annexes on Services and Investment'.

209   CETA, Art 8.4; EUMFTA, Ch 'Investment', Art 6; EUKFTA, Art 7.5; EUSFTA, Art 8.10; EUVFTA, Art 8.4. These provisions are inspired by GATS, Art XVI. See also, EUCCAI, Section II, Art 2.

v. the total number of natural persons that may be employed in a particular sector or that an enterprise may employ and who are necessary for, and directly related to, the performance of economic activity in the form of numerical quotas or the requirement of an economic needs test; or

(b) restricts or requires specific types of legal entity or joint venture through which an enterprise may carry out an economic activity.[210]

Compared to other international actors, the EU's approach in having market access provision is a real EU specificity. Neither the United States nor Canada usually include these types of provision, neither do other capital-exporting countries or regions. To have set out commitments prohibiting certain limitations of market access underlines the extent to what the opening of third country markets for EU companies is of central importance for the EU.[211] As the EU stresses, access to third countries' markets enhances European companies' global competitiveness and enables them to survive and achieve greater profits.[212] As mentioned before, market access provisions are part of the EU's trade and investment agenda pre-dating the competence shift through the Lisbon treaty. One of the key objectives of the CCP has been and still is trade and investment liberalisation.[213] The new paradigm of better safeguarding the right to regulate for the purpose of SD has to coexist with investment liberalisation. Suppose one accepts that SD is the ultimate goal, and investment liberalisation should serve that goal. In that case, the question arises whether the EU counter-balances its economic interests with considerations of social or environmental protection because, as is the case for the granting of pre-establishment rights under IIAs, the provisions on market access can impede future policy orientation and measures in the host State pursuing SD objectives.

In this respect, so far only the CETA contains a clarification that seeks to provide more regulatory flexibility for domestic measures affecting market access rights of foreign investors.[214] Under CETA, State measures "seeking to ensure the conservation and protection of natural resources and the environment, including a limitation on the available number and scope of concessions

---

210   CETA, Art 8.4(1).
211   European Commission, 'TTIP and beyond', above note 1, para 1.1.
212   Ibid. See also Dimopoulos A, 'Shifting the Emphasis from Investment Protection to Liberalisation and Development: The EU as a New Global Factor in the Field of Foreign Investment' (2010) 11 The Journal of World Investment & Trade 1, 15–17.
213   Section 4.3.1.2.
214   CETA, Art 8.4(2).

granted, and the imposition of a moratorium or ban" are consistent with the contracting parties' obligation to grant market access.[215] The precision in the text provides the host State with greater regulatory flexibility in this specific area. Moreover, the policy coherence requirement would instruct the EU not only to include such clarification in the CETA but likewise in all its other IIAs.[216] In sum, the EU maintains its trade and investment objective to achieve the maximal guarantees for market access rights without possible exceptions to it even though such exceptions might be beneficial for SD. Based on the requirement of SD integration and policy coherence, this approach should be reconsidered by the EU institutions to align it better with the broader policy objectives of the CCP.

6.2.3 *Prohibitions of Performance Requirements*

A further type of provision falling under investment liberalisation commitments of EU IIAs concerns performance requirements. Their purpose is to set out prohibitions for host States to impose conditions on foreign investors to meet specific goals with respect to their business activity (i.e. performance requirements).[217] In other words, performance requirements should not frustrate the rights of establishment by allowing host States to impose certain legal obligations.[218]

Under most EU IIAs, parties "shall not impose" a set of listed performance requirements in connection with the "establishment, acquisition, expansion, conduct, operation and management" of an investment.[219] The listed performance requirements are mainly based on those found in the WTO Agreement on Trade Related Investment Measures (TRIMS). For instance, the requirement

---

215   CETA, Art 8.4(2)(d). Also interesting is CETA, Art 8.4(2)(a), which provides that "a measure concerning zoning or planning regulation affecting the development of use of land, or another analogous measure" is consistent with the obligation to grant market access.
216   EUMFTA, Ch 'Investment', Art 6; EUKFTA, Art 7.5; EUSFTA, Art 8.10; EUVFTA, Art 8.4.
217   There is no uniform definition of what are performance requirements. However, one can generally understand "a variety of regulatory measures imposed by host State governments on the *activity* of multinational enterprises (MNEs) within their territory", see Collins D, *Performance Requirements and Investment Incentives under International Economic Law* (Edward Elgar Publishing 2015) 9–10. For an illustrative list see Nikièma S, 'Performance Requirements in Investment Treaties' (2014) IISD Best Practice Series, 2–3.
218   Ibid. See also Gómez-Palacio and Muchlinski, above note 190, 231. See also, UNCTAD, *Foreign Direct Investment and Performance Requirements: New Evidence from Selected Countries* (United Nations 2003).
219   CETA, Art 8.5; EUJFTA, Art 8.11; EUVFTA, Art 8.8. There is no equivalent provision in the EUSFTA. Extensive performance requirement prohibitions have been included in the EUCCAI, see Section II, Art 3.

for foreign companies to purchase domestic goods or services is an element included in both EU IIAs and the TRIMS.[220] At the same time, EU IIAs go beyond trade-related prohibitions of performance requirements. These TRIMS-plus prohibited performance requirements include the prohibition that investment is, under domestic law, subject to a "transfer of technology, a production process or other proprietary knowledge to a natural person or enterprise" in the territory of the host State.[221]

The trend to include prohibitions on certain performance requirements comes from North American IIAs, in particular the NAFTA. The latter was the first to adopt a comprehensive approach using a list of seven performance requirements, which "no party may impose".[222] The NAFTA provision was drafted as a best-endeavour commitment. Other IIAs of the United States subsequently adopted such a soft law approach with respect to prohibitions on performance requirements.[223] As mentioned before, EU IIAs provide for clearly binding prohibitions on performance requirements ("a Party shall not") with the sole exception of the FTA with Mexico, for which the NAFTA experience of Mexico certainly played a role in Mexico preferring to draft the provision as a best-endeavour commitment.[224] The CPTPP, in return, provides, however, for a binding commitment.[225] Regarding their content, North American IIAs contain an almost similar list of performance requirements also going beyond the TRIMS agreement.

As is the case for market access provision, prohibitions of performance requirements can affect the host State's ability to adopt measures to obtain their socio-economic development objectives. Whilst the economic benefits of performance requirements are still controversial,[226] it is often argued that performance requirements are able to serve as a tool for economic development policies. For instance, the transfer of technologies or the employment of local workers can help materialise beneficial spill-over effects for the host State.[227] Especially, developing countries may consider performance requirements as a useful tool to pursue their SD objectives.[228] Therefore, certain IIAs

---

220 CETA, Art 8.5(1)(c); EUJFTA, Art 8.11(1)(c); EUVFTA, Art 8.8(1)(c). See also TRIMS, Annex 1(a).
221 CETA, Art 8.5(1)(f); EUJFTA, Art 8.11(1)(g); EUVFTA, Art 8.8(1)(f).
222 NAFTA, Art 1106. See also Collins, above note 219, 132–142.
223 2012 US Model BIT, Art 7; See Turkey-US BIT, Art 11(7); US-Uruguay BIT, Art 8. See also 2004 Canadian Model BIT, Art 7.
224 EUMFTA, Ch 'Investment', Art 9.
225 CPTPP, Art 9.9.
226 Nikièma, above note 217.
227 UNCTAD, above note 218, 99.
228 Nikièma, above note 217.

and model IIAs of developing countries have started to include provisions that operate contrary to the prohibition of performance requirements as a *reaffirmation* of the right of host States to impose certain performance requirements on foreign investors.[229] They set out measures that a host State has the right to enact in relation to a foreign investment activity. For instance, the PAIC states the parties' right to require, where appropriate, a transfer of technology from foreign investors to local enterprises.[230]

Guaranteeing the right to adopt performance requirements in an IIA goes in the opposite direction to the EU approach. This difference in shaping the regulation of conditioning establishment rights shows the somewhat opposing objectives of capital-exporting countries and certain capital-importing countries. For the EU, setting out binding prohibitions on performance requirements guarantees the free flow of investments allowing it to pursue its global market liberalisation agenda. Whilst the EU approach does seem to be less problematic in its relations with other developed economies such as Japan and Canada, one needs, however, to criticise the fact that in the agreement with Vietnam, one finds no adaptation in terms of treaty drafting for the development needs of that country. Hence, the EU did, in its investment relations with developing countries, not sufficiently counter-balance its economic interests of market access for its own companies with SD concerns of developing third countries. Taken together, the granting of pre-establishment rights, market access provisions and the prohibition of performance requirements, the EU lacked to integrate SD in its approaches to investment liberalisation.

6.3 The Notion of Investment: Limited SD Integration under EU IIAs

Depending on their concrete formulation, definitions can serve as a tool to better ensure that IIAs do not subsidise SD-negative investments and might serve to steer the inflow of SD-beneficial investments.[231] Protecting any kind

---

229 Eg SADC Model BIT, Art 21.2; and Commentary, 41. PAIC, Art 17.
230 Eg PAIC, Art 17.2: "Member States may introduce performance requirements to promote domestic investments and local content. Measures covered by this Paragraph include, inter alia: [...] (c) Measures to enhance productive capacity, increase employment, increase human resource capacity and training, research and development including of new technologies, technology transfer, innovation and other benefits of investment through the use of specified requirements on investors;"
231 Columbia Center on Sustainable Investment, 'Costs and Benefits of Investment Treaties—Practical Considerations for States', (2018) Policy Paper, 15. See, Van Aaken A and Lehmann TA, 'Sustainable Development and International Investment Law'

of investment does not secure SD outcomes, and on the contrary, might negatively affect SD in the host States. Chapter 2 of the present book has recalled the long and complex debate on whether and how the definition of investment could serve SD purposes.[232] Whilst there is a common trend to reduce the scope of the definition to more precisely state the condition for being a "covered" investment under IIAs the integration of SD conditions in the definition of investment remains a highly controversial issue in IIA practice. EU IIAs define investments as meaning "any kind of assets" owned or controlled directly or indirectly by an investor of one of the contracting parties.[233] A non-exhaustive list of assets and, occasionally, certain exclusions follow. The definition also prescribes the characteristics of an investment to include: "a certain duration, the commitment of capital or other resources, the expectation of gain or profit or the assumption of risk".[234] The EU thus opts for a typical assets-based investment definition combined with an open list of assets. As argued in the following, the EU suggests little in linking the definition of an investment under its IIAs with SD purposes.

6.3.1 Narrowing Down the Scope of the Definition

While the broad and open-ended asset-based definition has remained widespread in BITs focusing on investment protection, more recent agreements have used techniques for narrowing the definition's scope. In particular, some treaties started to use a closed-list definition instead of an open-ended one or explicitly exclude certain types of assets. In the SD-investment debate, the assumption that any kind of investment is beneficial for economic growth and development has been challenged. In the SD perspective, IIAs are to ensure sustainable investment in the host State better. Therefore, one idea is to exclude those types of investment that are unlikely to promote SD outcomes. If a State targets long-term capital commitment, one approach consists of the explicit exclusion of portfolio investment in the definition clause. The argument here is that portfolio investment's positive development implications are very low since this type of investment can include short-term and speculative

---

in: Echandi R and Sauvé P (eds), *Prospects in International Investment Law and Policy* (Cambridge University Press 2013) 334; Jezewski M, 'Development Considerations in Defining Investment', in: Cordonier Segger M-C, Gehring MW and Newcombe AP (eds), *Sustainable Development in World Investment Law* (Kluwer Law International 2011) 216; Sornarajah M, *Resistance and Change in the International Law on Foreign Investment* (Cambridge University Press 2015) 151 et seq.

232   See Section 2.4.1.
233   CETA, Art 8.1; EUMFTA, Ch 'Investment', Art XX.3; EUSIPA, Art 1.2(1); EUVIPA, Art 1.2(h).
234   Ibid.

investment, which generally does not generate positive effects on the host States' economy. Direct investment is, in comparison, more likely to affect host States' economies positively in terms of employment, technology transfer or infrastructure.[235]

As far as EU IIAs are concerned, the exclusion of certain types of investment is done in some but not all IIAs, and clearly, none of the EU IIAs excludes portfolio investments. The two IIAs that contains some exclusions within the definition of investment are the CETA and the FTA with Mexico. For instance, under CETA, whilst claims to money or performance under a contract can qualify as an investment, the agreement excludes three type of claims to money. First, claims to money that arose solely from commercial contracts; second, domestic financing of such commercial contracts; and third, claims to money deriving from judgements or awards.[236] Under the FTA with Mexico, the definition of investment does "not include an order or judgment entered in a judicial or administrative action. Any alteration of the form in which assets are invested or reinvested shall not affect their character as investments provided that the form taken by any investment or reinvestment maintains its compliance with the definition of investment."[237] These precisions are not originating from an objective of rendering the definition in a way responsive to the channelling investment towards SD. In other words, EU IIAs do not adopt such an approach of excluding or restraining the agreement's scope regarding non-direct investments. On the contrary, the definition is asset-based and very open to non-direct investment.[238]

The manner in which the investment definition under EU IIAs is drafted is also typical for North American IIAs and IIAs of other capital-exporting countries.[239] Recent IIA practice shows that many IIAs adopt the same approach maintaining broad asset-based definitions with limited exclusions.[240] A small

---

235 See Section 2.4.1.1.
236 CETA, Art 8.1: "For greater certainty, claims to money does not include; (a) claims to money that arise solely from commercial contracts for the sale of goods or services by a natural person or enterprise in the territory of a Party to a natural person or enterprise in the territory of the other Party. (b) the domestic financing of such contracts; or (c) any order, judgment, or arbitral award related to sub-subparagraph (a) or (b)."
237 EUMFTA, Ch 'Investment, Art XX.3.
238 The EUSIPA and EUVIPA do not provide for exclusions. The definitions of investment under the CETA and the EUMFTA are also very open constituting an open assed-based definition. See for a classification, SADC Model BIT, Commentary, 9–14.
239 2004 Canadian Model BIT, Art 1; 2012 US Model BIT, Art 1; CPTPP, Art 9.1; Japan-Uruguay BIT, Art 1; Japan-Ukraine BIT, Art 1; Switzerland-Guatemala BIT, Art 1; Switzerland-Trinidad and Tobago BIT, Art 1.
240 CPTPP, Art 9.1; Canada-Cameroon BIT, Art 1; United-States-Rwanda BIT, Art 1; Japan-Iran BIT, Art 1.1.

group of States has, however, started a practice to exclude portfolio investment specifically. Those novel approaches are mainly coming from developing countries. For instance, the Indian Model BIT states that "[f]or greater clarity, investment does not include the following assets of an enterprise: (i) portfolio investments of the enterprise or in another enterprise". In the same vein, the Morocco-Nigeria BIT provides that the term "'Investment' does not include: [...] b) Portfolio investments [...]."[241]

The same rationale of not protecting indirect investment but targeting lasting and direct capital commitments also inspires the approach of setting out an enterprise-based definition of investment, in clear contrast to the prevailing asset-based definition. An enterprise-based definition requires the establishment or acquisition of an enterprise, as classically associated with FDI.[242] Under those definitions, the enterprise may possess assets included among the covered assets of an FDI investor.[243] This narrower investment definition, i.e. the enterprise-based approach, has its origins in the GATS. Its Article 1 (on Scope and Definitions) stets out that the GATS, in relation to investments, only applies to a service supplied through a commercial presence, which is defined as a corporation or branch of a corporation that is owned or controlled by suppliers from WTO member States.[244] In current IIA practice and model treaties one yet seldom finds this approach. Examples of thereof are namely contained in the Morocco-Nigeria BIT,[245] the Brazil-Malawi investment agreement,[246] the PAIC,[247] and the Indian model BIT.[248] This highlights that those (few)

---

241 Indian Model BIT, Art 1.4; Morocco-Nigeria BIT, Art 1; see also, PAIC, Art 4.4; Rwanda-Turkey BIT, Art 1.2; SADC Model BIT, Art 2. For instance, the Morocco-Nigeria BIT provides in its Art 1: "[...] For greater certainty, Investment does not include: (a) Debts securities issued by governments or loans to a government; (b) Portfolio investments; (c) Any claims to money that do not involve interests set out in sub-paragraphs (a) and (g) above; (d) Letters of bank; and (e) Claims to money with maturities less than three years."
242 SADC Model Bilateral Investment Treaty Template with Commentary.
243 Ibid.
244 GATS, Art 1(2)(c). The GATS also applies to services supplied through non-investment modes (GATS, Art 1(2)(a, b and d).
245 Morocco-Nigeria BIT, Art 1: "Investment means an enterprise within the territory of one State established, acquired, expanded or operated, in good faith, by an investor of the other State [...] An enterprise will possess the following assets: [...]".
246 Brazil-Malawi CIFA, Art 2.
247 PAIC, Art 3.4: "an enterprise or a company, as defined under Paragraph 1, which is established, acquired or expanded by an investor, including through the constitution, maintenance or acquisition of shares, debentures or other ownership instruments of such an enterprise, provided that the enterprise or company is established or acquired in accordance with the laws of the host State".
248 Indian Model BIT, Art 1.4.

States that have opted for an enterprise-based definition sustain the investment definition by specifically excluding portfolio investment.[249]

How the notion of investment is to be defined has not been at the centre of concern of the EU institutions. The subject found little to no mention in the strategic policy papers of the European Commission.[250] The exclusion of certain types of investment from the definition of investment is a way to clarify and narrow down the scope of an IIA.[251] However, the treaty technique has not been implemented coherently in EU IIAS as only the CETA and the FTA with Mexico contain certain exclusions. The reasons why the EU uses broad definitions of investment are that EU's past experience has shown that "outward investment makes a positive and significant contribution to the competitiveness of European enterprises, notably in the form of higher productivity".[252] In other words, outward investments of any kind are beneficial for economic growth within the EU. The Commission acknowledged that "while the aggregate balance is positive, negative effects may, of course, arise on a sector-specific, geographical and/or individual basis."[253] Where and how such negative effects arise should be further analysed. Consequently, taking the SD objective of the CCP more seriously, the EU and the Commission could further evaluate certain adaptations or exclusions—these are upcoming issues in investment governance—that would allow to better engage with the steering possibilities of IIAs to promote sustainable investment or, at the least, seek to avoid negative effects on SD.

6.3.2 *Enumerating Certain Criteria*

An important question in the debate of SD integration is whether an investment must contribute to the economic development of the host State. The controversial issue used to be whether the contribution to the host State's

---

249 Indian Model BIT, Art 1.4; Morocco-Nigeria BIT, Art 1; see also, PAIC, Art 4.4; Rwanda-Turkey BIT, Art 1.2; SADC Model BIT, Art 2. For instance, the Morocco-Nigeria BIT provides in its Art 1: "[...] For greater certainty, Investment does not include: (a) Debts securities issued by governments or loans to a government; (b) Portfolio investments; (c) Any claims to money that do not involve interests set out in sub-paragraphs (a) and (g) above; (d) Letters of bank; and (e) Claims to money with maturities less than three years."
250 Consider, European Commission, 'TTIP and beyond', above note 1.
251 Cazala J, 'La réaffirmation de l'Etat en matière de définition des investissements et investisseurs protégés' in: El Ghadban T, Mazuy C-M and Senegacnik A (eds), *La protection des investissements étrangers: vers une réaffirmation de l'État?* = *The protection of foreign investments: a reaffirmation of the State?: Actes du colloque du 2 juin 2017* (2018) 49.
252 European Commission Communication, 'Towards a comprehensive European international investment policy', COM (2010) 343 final, 3.
253 Ibid.

development is a jurisdictional condition under Article 25 of the ICSID Convention. The well-known *Salini* test establishes a set of four criteria: a contribution of money or assets, a certain duration, an element of risk and a contribution to the economic development of the host State.[254] By introducing the host State's development into the characteristics of an investment, a test of relationship between the investment activity and the impacts for the host State's economy has been created.[255] In Chapter 2, it has been discussed that the criterion on the contribution to the host State's development was received very differently by past tribunals. As a consequence, arbitral case law has developed three different approaches.[256] The first approach is to see the criteria as *flexible* indicating the typical characteristics of an investment.[257] In this understanding, the contribution to the host State's development becomes a possible element to be looked at but not a jurisdictional condition. In contrast, the second approach considers each of the four criteria as fixed meaning that they must be fulfilled to find the existence of an investment and thus the contribution to the host State's development becomes a jurisdictional condition. The third approach also considers the criteria as fixed but explicitly excludes the fourth *Salini* criterion.

The investment definition of EU IIAs contains the enumeration of certain characteristics that an investment should have to be considered a covered investment. These characteristics include the commitment of capital or other resources, the expectation of gain or profit, the assumption of risk, and a certain duration.[258] As the *Salini* test established four criteria, EU IIAs do not mention the full test and namely omit the most controversial criterion, which is that the contribution to the host State's development is indicative of an investment.[259] Under EU IIAs, the characteristics of an investment include "a certain duration and other characteristics such as the commitment of capital or other resources, the expectation of gain or profit, *or* the assumption of risk".[260] The

---

254 *Salini Costruttori v Morocco,* above note 244. The test arose from arbitrations that have looked at what qualifies an investment under the ICSID Convention.
255 SADC Model BIT, Commentary, 13.
256 Gaillard E, 'Identify or Define? Reflection on the Evolution of the Concept of Investment in ICSID Practice' in Binder C et al (eds), *International Investment Law for the 21st Century: Essays in Honour of Christoph Schreuer* (Oxford University Press 2009) 406 et seq.
257 Schreuer C et al (eds), *The ICSID Convention: A Commentary* (2nd ed, Cambridge University Press 2009) 128, at 153; 133, at pt 171; 133, at 172.
258 CETA, Art 8.1; EUMFTA, Ch 'Investment', Art XX.3; EUSIPA, Art 1.2(1); EUVIPA, Art 1.2(h).
259 Ibid, para 52.
260 Eg CETA, Art 8.1. Emphasis added; see also EUMFTA, Ch 'Investment', Art XX.3; EUSIPA, Art 1.2(1); EUVIPA, Art 1.2(h).

terms "such as" and especially the "or" used in the listing of the characteristics let understand that the enumeration of an investment's typical characteristics is flexible.²⁶¹ EU IIAs thereby follow those arbitral cases that favour the understanding of flexible criteria.²⁶²

Based on the divergences in arbitral case law, States opted for different approaches in their IIAs. The US Model BIT was the first instrument to codify the *Salini* test.²⁶³ It did so by excluding the contribution to the host State's economic development and by enumerating the other characteristics in a flexible manner.²⁶⁴ This approach has found widespread acceptance.²⁶⁵

The fixed criteria approach found, however, also proponents in IIA practice. A growing number of IIAs and model treaties, mostly of developing countries, refer explicitly to the contribution to the host State's economic development as one of the characteristics of an investment and making it a condition for treaty protection. This is the case for instance for the Indian Model BIT stating that "'investment" means an enterprise constituted, organized and operated in good faith [...], taken together with the assets of the enterprise, has the characteristics of an investment such as the commitment of capital or other resources, certain duration, the expectation of gain or profit, the assumption of risk *and* a significance for the development of the Party in whose territory the investment is made".²⁶⁶ The PAIC, as well as the SADC Model BIT, are even more explicit in making the contribution to the host State's development a

---

261   Eg Japan-Iran BIT, Art 1.1; Japan-Ukraine BIT, Art 1.1.
262   See in particular, *Ambiente Ufficio v Argentina*, ICSID Case No ARB/08/9, Decision on Jurisdiction and Admissibility, 8 Feb 2013, para 481: "Following Professor Schreuer's approach, the criteria assembled in the *Salini* test, while not constituting mandatory prerequisites for the jurisdiction of the Centre in the meaning of Art. 25 of the ICSID Convention, may still prove useful, provided that they are treated as guidelines and that they are applied in conjunction and in a flexible manner. In particular, they may help to identify, and exclude, extreme phenomena that must remain outside of even a broad reading of the term "investment" in Art. 25 of the ICSID Convention. Nonetheless, the basic character, and rationale, of the "non-definition" of investment allow Art. 25(1) of the ICSID Convention to cover a wide range of economic operations and assets, susceptible to include non-standard and atypical investments and capable of adapting to the evolving nature of economic activity."
263   2012 US Model BIT, Art 1.
264   2012 US Model BIT, Art 1: "'investment" means every asset that an investor owns or controls, directly or indirectly, that has the characteristics of an investment, including such characteristics as the commitment of capital or other resources, the expectation of gain or profit, or the assumption of risk. [...]".
265   Subsequent US IIAs, including the CPTPP and USMCA contain the same approach, eg CPTPP, Art 9.1.
266   Indian Model BIT, Art 1.4. (Emphasis added).

necessary condition to be fulfilled. Under both instruments, the investment "must have the following characteristics", which then also include "a significant contribution to the host State's economic development" in the case of PAIC,[267] and "significance for the Host State's development" in the case of the SADC Model BIT.[268] In the same vein, with, however, a slightly different formulation, the Morocco-Nigeria BIT links its contained enterprise-based definition with the requirement that such enterprise contributes to the SD of the host State.[269] The contribution to the SD of the host State is under the latter treaty a necessary condition. The particularity of the Morocco-Nigeria BIT is that here treaty drafters decided to use SD instead of "development" or "economic development". Lastly, it is relevant to highlight that the fixed criteria approach can also imply that the fourth *Salini* criterion is intentionally left out. This approach has been adopted in the recent Dutch Model BIT, which enumerates the three first criteria of *Salini* and links them with an "and" instead of an "or".[270] The Dutch Model clarifies that the criterion of host State's development is not to be taken into account.

Comparing the EU approach to other international actors, it becomes clear that the controversy that has occurred in arbitral case law is also evidenced through the different approaches in recent IIAs. Countries have different visions on how to link the definition of investment with development concerns. In the controversial setting, the EU found a middle ground in enumerating the typical characteristics of an investment in a flexible manner. By keeping the enumeration flexible even though not mentioning the host Stat's development, it is not completely excluded that future adjudicators take the contribution to the host State's development into account.[271] More from an EU

---

267 PAIC, Art 4.4.
268 SADC Model BIT, Art 2 (under options 2 and 3).
269 Morocco-Nigeria BIT, Art 1: "'Investment" Investment means an enterprise within the territory of one State established, acquired, expanded or operated, in good faith, by an investor of the other State in accordance with law of the Party in whose territory the investment is made taken together with the asset of the enterprise which contribute sustainable development of that Party and has the characteristics of an investment involving a commitment of capital or other similar resources, pending profit, risk-taking and certain duration. [...]"
270 Dutch Model BIT (2018), Art 1(a): "'investment" means every kind of asset that has the characteristics of an investment, which includes a certain duration, the commitment of capital or other resources, the expectation of gain or profit, and the assumption of risk. [...]"
271 For the same conclusion, see Bischoff JA and Wühler M, 'The Notion of Investment' in Mbengue MM and Schacherer S (eds), *Foreign Investment Under the Comprehensive Economic and Trade Agreement (CETA)* (Springer International Publishing 2019) 25.

policy angle, it has been stated several times that predictability is an objective of the European Commission. Therefore, making these criteria, and namely the development criterion a jurisdictional condition would arguably undermine this objective. The reason is that there is uncertainty when it comes to determining whether an investment actually made a contribution to the host State's development.[272] At the same time, the fourth criterion of development or even SD could have been mentioned. Such reference would better align the investment definition with the overall objective of the IIA, which is to contribute to SD.[273]

6.3.3 *In Accordance with Host State Law*

Subjecting the definitions of an investment to the laws and regulations of the host State is a further element in aligning IIAs with SD. Whilst the precise wording can differ, such requirement is designed to limit the agreement's protection to investments that are complying with domestic laws. Therefore, this type of provision has the potential for States to set domestic SD conditions that an investment has to respect to be a covered investment under a given IIA.[274] The definition of "covered investment" under EU IIAs sets out the requirement that investments are made "in accordance with the laws and regulations" of the host State.[275] If the investment was not made in accordance with the applicable law of the host State, a tribunal would consider that there was no covered investment making the treaty not applicable.[276] The EU approach bears benefits for SD since national legislation applicable to the establishment of foreign investment can include conditions and procedures pursuing SD objectives. Moreover, to make the application of the requirement more accessible, EU IIAs clarified the scope of dispute settlement, explicitly excluding protection for investments not made in compliance with domestic laws, thereby the legality requirement becomes an issue of jurisdiction of future tribunals under the ICS.[277] Indeed, the condition of an investment made "in accordance with host State's law" is frequently invoked in investment arbitration. And some tribunals have established a threshold of "serious illegality" whilst others have

---

272 See Section 2.4.1.2.
273 See Section 7.1.
274 See Section 2.4.1.3.
275 CETA, Art 8.1(b); EUMFTA, Ch 'Investment', Art XX.3; EUSIPA, Art 1.2(1); EUVIPA, Art 1.2(q).
276 Ibid.
277 See below Section 6.4.2. EU IIAs exclude access to ISDS for investments that have been made illegally or bad faith conduct.

not.²⁷⁸ The formulation of EU IIAs does not mitigate the uncertainties based on the different interpretations of the clause by arbitral tribunals. It is unclear whether EU IIAs require this high threshold or whether minor violations are sufficient.

In international investment governance, legality requirements have become a widespread and non-controversial treaty practice. More than half of IIAs today set out the requirement that investments are to be made "in accordance with the laws and regulations" of the host State.²⁷⁹ The practice is being continued in the majority of recently concluded IIAs²⁸⁰ as well as model IIAs.²⁸¹ The EU is hence taking part in further consolidating this treaty practice. A much less common practice is investment definitions that go further than including the requirement that the investment is made in accordance with host State laws, and tie the definition to a registration and approval requirement.²⁸² If an IIA contains a requirement that an investment is made in accordance with the laws and regulations of the host State, the failure of an investor to obtain the necessary approval for a particular investment would mean that an investment tribunal would have no jurisdiction. These so-called "admission clauses" limit the treaty scope to investments that have been admitted or approved by the host State in accordance with its domestic process.²⁸³

For example, the Philippines' Foreign Investment Act provides that a non-Philippine national can invest or do business in the Philippines in any sector

---

278 *Tokios Tokelės v Ukraine*, ICSID Case No ARB/02/18, Decision on Jurisdiction, 29 April 2004, para 86. See also *Alpha Projektholding GmbH v Ukraine*, ICSID Case No ARB/07/16, Award, 8 Nov 2010, para 297.

279 UNCTAD Policy Hub, IIA Mapping. See eg 2008 German Model BIT, Art 1.2; Argentina-Israel BIT, Art 1.1; France-Bahrain BIT, Art 1.1; Cameroon-Egypt BIT, Art 1.1; Japan-Ukraine, Art 1.1. It should be noted, however, that the legality requirement can also be contained in other provisions of an IIA, such as a provision on admission, eg Argentina-Netherlands BIT, Art 2.

280 Morocco-Nigeria BIT, Art 1; Argentina-Qatar BIT, Art 1.2.

281 Indian Model BIT, Art 1.4; SADC Model BIT, Art 2; PAIC, Art 4.4.

282 Bernasconi-Osterwalder N and Malik M, 'Registration and Approval Requirements in Investment Treaties' IISD Best Practice Series, Dec 2012. It is important to note that this type of requirement must not necessarily be included in the investment definition and can also be included in another provision of the IIAs concerned with the scope of the treaty, such as one dealing with the admission of investment. See Section 2.4.1.4.

283 As mentioned before, certain IIAs provide for the compliance of the investment with host States law, in provision that are dedicated to the admission of an investment (and not in the investment definition).

without the need for prior approval, except sectors in which foreign investment is restricted or prohibited under the "Negative List".[284] For those sectors that are listed, foreign investors need approval. In this way, host States can control the entry of foreign investment in certain sectors that can be critical to advance sustainable development policies.[285] Screening mechanisms can also encompass more specific tools, such as ESIAs that are required before an investment approval is given, and/or specific tests of social and economic benefits for the host State. The Namibia Investment Act is a telling example in this respect. The Act conditions the approval to several SD relevant aspects, including technology transfer, employment creation, the investment's contribution to economic and social policy programmes as well as the environmental impact of the investment activity.[286]

---

284 Foreign Investment Act of the Philippines (1991), Section 8 (especially List B). See also, Bonnitcha J, 'Investment Laws of ASEAN Countries: A comparative review' (IISD 2017) 17; available at <https://www.iisd.org/sites/default/files/publications/investment-laws-asean-countries.pdf>.

285 This is notwithstanding the fact that States can and should also consider closing certain sectors completely from foreign investment. See World Bank Group 'Investment Law Reform: A Handbook for Development Practitioners' (2010), 28–30; available at <https://openknowledge.worldbank.org/handle/10986/25206>.

286 Investment Act of Namibia (2016), Section 4 ('Powers and functions of Minister') provides in this respect:
   2) The Minister may approve the investment proposal after having considered and satisfied himself or herself that:
   a. the conditions set out in section 14 have been met; and
   b. a substantial number of the following requirements, as each case may require, are fulfilled or likely to be fulfilled in a specified period:
      i   the joint venture with Namibians;
      ii   the employment creation for Namibians;
      iii the contribution of the investment to the advancement of persons who have been socially, economically or educationally disadvantaged by past discriminatory laws and practices;
      iv   the contribution of the investment to the implementation of programmes and policies aimed at redressing social and economic imbalances in Namibia, including gender-based imbalances;
      v   the transfer of technology and technological skills;
      vi   the development of managerial skills;
      vii the promotion of research, development and innovation;
      viii the value addition to the natural resources and manufacturing sector and procurement of goods and services;
      ix   the environmental impact and contribution to environmental benefits; and
      x   other matters relating to the improvement of the economy and development benefits in the public interest as the Minister may prescribe.

National processes to approve the entry of investment to the domestic market are an increasingly important topic for international investment governance. The number of States that undertake screening procedures of foreign investment seeking to enter domestic markets is growing.[287] Some of the screening procedure have the objective to ensure that foreign investment entering the host States contributes to SD. The EU has introduced new legislation on foreign investment screening.[288] While the EU instrument is not explicitly concerned with SD, some of the reasons why the EU seeks and urges its Member States to more carefully screen and control foreign investment touch upon issues of the SDGs, such as employment security within the EU.[289]

The inclusion of registration and approval requirements is less common in IIA practice than the legality requirement. One finds such approaches mainly in IIAs of Southeast Asian countries. For instance, the Comprehensive Investment Agreement of the Association of Southeast Asian Nations (ASEAN) provides that a "covered investment means, with respect to a Member State, an investment in its territory of an investor of any other Member State in existence as of the date of entry into force of this Agreement or established, acquired or expanded thereafter, and has been admitted according to its laws, regulations, and national policies, and where applicable, *specifically approved in writing by the competent authority of a Member State*."[290] So far, EU IIAs do not address the relationship between investment screening measures and international investment law. The latter should, however, further be assessed. In particular, the question of whether the pre-establishment rights granted by EU IIAs could be used by foreign investors to challenge allegedly discriminatory or abusive use of the screening procedures. In addition, in the future, the EU institutions could further analyse whether screening criteria could also include SD relevant aspects that would allow defining what is socially desirable and environmentally acceptable as foreign investment activity within the EU market.

---

287 See, Sauvant KP and Mann H, 'Towards an Indicative List of FDI Sustainability Characteristics', October 2017, available at <http://e15initiative.org/publications/towards-an-indicative-list-of-fdi-sustainability-characteristics/>.

288 Regulation (EU) 2019/452 of the European Parliament and of the Council of 19 March 2019 establishing a framework for the screening of foreign direct investments into the Union.

289 Ibid. In addition, see Regulation of the European Parliament and of the Council on the establishment of a framework to facilitate sustainable investment, (EU) 2020/852final. This regulation provides a comprehensive sustainability taxonomy in order to promote sustainable finance and applies to the financial sector.

290 See, ASEAN Comprehensive Investment Agreement, Art 4(a) "Definitions". Emphasis added.

6.4 Procedural Aspects of Investor-State Dispute Resolution Relevant for SD

ISDS through arbitration has been criticised for a number of years.[291] The international discussions and debates on reform range from abandoning ISDS altogether to the establishment of a multilateral investment court.[292] In this general context, the EU is among the frontrunners as it has sought systemically to reform the ISDS mechanism in its IIAS. Under EU IIAS, investor-State disputes are to be resolved by an investment court system (ICS), which is intended to make the dispute settlement more court-like.[293] This institutionalisation aims to address the shortcomings of ISDS through arbitration better and enhance the legitimacy of the system.[294] SD is regularly considered to provide useful guidance for the reform of ISDS.[295] However, it doubtful that from the SD concept conclusions could be made that would favour a permanent investment tribunal over an *ad hoc* one. In other words, whether investor-State disputes are resolved by arbitration or by a permanent international court does, in theory, not impact on SD-friendly or SD-detrimental outcomes of disputes. The most fundamental concerns of SD lie within the substantive provisions of international investment law.[296]

---

291 For a relatively early account on the matter, see Waibel M et al (eds), *The Backlashes against Investment Arbitration—Perceptions and Realities* (Kluwer Law International 2010).

292 Bungenberg M and Reinisch A, *From Bilateral Arbitral Tribunals and Investment Courts to a Multilateral Investment Court* (Springer 2018).

293 For more details on the ICS see, Schacherer S, 'TPP, CETA and TTIP Between Innovation and Consolidation—Resolving Investor–State Disputes under Mega-Regionals', (2016) Journal of International Dispute Settlement, 628–653.

294 ECJ, Opinion of AG Bot (procedure Opinion 1/17 *Compatibility of the Investment Court System (ICS)*), EU:C:2019:72, para 17.

295 UNCTAD, IPFSD, 101 and 145–155. Schill SW, 'Reforming Investor–State Dispute Settlement: A (Comparative and International) Constitutional Law Framework' (2017) 20 Journal of International Economic Law 649, 660–661. Stephan Schill states that ISDS should not be an obstacle to SD, "but a tool for host states to achieve their development objectives".

296 See Section 2.5.3. As discussed in that section, SD would require much more systemic changes. For instance, as the SDGs are prone to "inclusive" solutions, it can be argued that certain interested persons or communities should also have standing before investment tribunals. It should not be overseen that civil society and local communities often lack efficient remedies if harm through an international investment occurs; whether ISDS is the proper forum for remediating these issues is beyond the present book's scope. See eg Steinitz M, *The Case for an International Court of Civil Justice* (Cambridge University Press 2019).

For EU IIAs, this means that the relevant point of SD integration is how investment tribunals under the ICS will interpret the investment protection standards.[297] Conversely, SD is relevant concerning specific procedural aspects of ISDS. The central SD principle of public awareness and public participation comes into play in this respect.[298] Important, thus, are issues such as the transparency of the proceedings, so that interested people and civil society groups are informed about the disputes taking place as well as allowing them to make their point of view heard by the tribunal through mechanisms of third party participation such as *amicus curiae* submission.[299] The last section of this chapter seeks, against this backdrop, to discuss issues around transparency and concludes with some exclusions from the scope of ISDS introduced by EU IIAs.

6.4.1 Transparency and amicus curiae *Participation*

Both transparency and *amicus curiae* participation are relevant in the discussion on SD because third parties need to be informed about investment disputes that potentially affect their interests or living conditions. Moreover, if the requirements are met, they should also be able to submit their written observations. The lack of transparency of the proceedings has been among the first criticisms raised against investment arbitration.[300] The NAFTA Free Trade Commission had taken the first steps towards clarifying that there was no general duty of confidentiality in investment arbitration under NAFTA.[301] The amendment of the ICSID Arbitration Rules was a further important step towards more transparency in investment arbitration.[302] Afterwards, the US and Canada incorporated provisions on transparency into their model BITs.[303] From then on, transparency provisions have been included in almost all IIAs.[304] The current most progressive global action towards more transparency include the UNCITRAL

---

297   Tribunals under the ICS are not competent to solve disputes based on TSD chapters. See Section 5.2.2.
298   Public participation is one of the fundamental aspects of SD, see Section 2.2.2.3.
299   Bernasconi-Osterwalder N, 'Transparency and Amicus Curiae in ICSID Arbitrations' in: Cordonier Segger M-C, Gehring MW and Newcombe AP (eds), *Sustainable Development in World Investment Law* (Kluwer Law International 2011) 189.
300   Malintoppi L and Limbasan N, 'Living in Glass Houses? The Debate on Transparency in International Investment Arbitration', (2015) 2 BCDR International Arbitration Review, 31.
301   NAFTA Free Trade Commission, 'Notes of Interpretation of Certain Chapter 11 Provisions', 31 July 2001, available at <http://www.sice.oas.org/tpd/nafta/Commission/CH11understanding_e.asp>.
302   ICSID Arbitration Rules (2006), Rule 37(2).
303   Malintoppi and Limbasan, above note 300, 38–40.
304   UNCTAD, 'Transparency' in: *UNCTAD Series on Issues in International Investment Agreements II*, (United Nations 2012) 37.

Rules on Transparency in Treaty-based Investor-State Arbitration as well as the related United Nations Convention on Transparency in Treaty-based Investor-State Arbitration, referred to as the Mauritius Convention.[305]

EU IIAs subject proceedings before the ICS to a detailed set of transparency rules, with some of them expressly referring to the UNCITRAL Transparency Rules.[306] The set of rules have three main aspects. First, EU IIAs provide rules to make available to the public any document related to the proceedings, including the notice of intent, request for arbitration or consolidation, the agreement to mediate, all pleadings, memorials and briefs submitted to the tribunal, as well as transcripts, minutes, orders, decisions and awards.[307] The CETA and the FTA with Mexico also add exhibits to the documents that can be requested from the tribunal.[308] EU IIAs contain a small derogation from the UNCITRAL Transparency Rules, about who has to publish the relevant documents prior to the constitution of the tribunal, which is not the registry but the respondent State.[309] Second, under EU IIAs, hearings are generally to be public.[310] Interestingly, EU IIAs go, in this respect, a step further than the UNCITRAL Transparency Rules since the disputing parties cannot be opposed to having *all* of the hearings in public.[311] If in one or several of the hearings confidential information of one of the parties is at stake, a tribunal under an EU IIA can make appropriate arrangements to protect the information. The requirement thus seems to allow the hearings to be punctually held in private but cannot extend to the whole of the proceedings.

Third, EU IIAs generally allow for *amicus curiae* briefs after consultation with the disputing parties.[312] The criteria of when to accept an amicus brief

---

305 The United Nations Convention on Transparency in Treaty-based Investor-State Arbitration was adopted on 10 Dec 2014 and opened for signature on 17 March 2015. See also United Nations Convention on Transparency in Treaty-based Investor-State Arbitration ("Mauritius Convention"), UN General Assembly, [2014] Res A/69/116.

306 EUMFTA, Ch 'Investment', Art 19; Art EUSIPA, Arts 3.16 and 3.17 in combination with Annex 8. Expressly opting in the UNCITRAL Transparency Rules: CETA, Art 8.36(1); EUVIPA, Art 3.46.

307 CETA, Art 8.36(2); EUMFTA, Ch 'Resolution of Investment Disputes', Art 19(3–4); EUSIPA, Annex 8, Art 1(1); EUVIPA, Art 3.46(2).

308 CETA, Art 8.36(3); EUMFTA, Ch 'Resolution of Investment Disputes', Art 19(6).

309 Eg CETA, Art 8.36(4); EUVIPA, Art 3.46(4); see also, UNCITRAL Transparency Rules, Art 2.

310 CETA, Art 8.36(5); EUMFTA, Ch 'Resolution of Investment Disputes', Art 19(2); EUSIPA, Annex 8, Art 2.

311 See UNCITRAL Transparency Rules, Art 6 in particular para 3 thereof. The EUVIPA, however, follows the UNICTRAL Rules in this respect, see EUVIPA, Art 3.46.

312 CETA, Art 8.36(1); EUMFTA, Ch 'Resolution of Investment Disputes', Art 24; EUSIPA, Art 3.17; EUVIPA, Art 3.46(2).

under EU IIAs are similar to those contained in the ICSID Arbitration Rules. The Rules provide that the tribunal, after consulting with the parties, may allow a non-disputing party to file a written submission within the scope of the dispute.[313] Likewise, a tribunal under the ICS takes into account a number of elements in deciding the relevance of an *amicus curiae* brief. Such elements are whether the third person has a significant interest in the proceedings and whether the third person's submission would assist the tribunal in the determination of a matter of fact or law within the scope of the dispute.

Compared to other international actors, on can acknowledge that with respect to issues of transparency a relatively harmonised IIA practice exists showing that transparency is not among the controversial issues of current international investment law-making. The CPTPP, based on the US approach, also has clear and stringent commitments to transparency, even though it does not explicitly incorporate the UNCITRAL Transparency Rules. Model treaties and IIAs of developing countries are, in essence, not different, all providing for transparency obligations.[314] EU IIAs thus perfectly reflect the global trend for full transparency. EU IIAs, with regard to certain aspects of transparency, go even beyond current transparency standards.[315] Based on its policy strategies, EU IIAs are to include provisions on "full, mandatory transparency of the arbitration process".[316]

Moreover, *amicus curiae* interventions are a useful means to ensure that the interests of people that are affected by the dispute to express their point of view.[317] The growing international consent with respect to allowing for *amicus curiae* briefs underlines that this has become a firmly accepted element of investor-State disputes also reflected in EU IIAs.[318] However, allowing them does not ultimately mean that they are accepted in a given procedure as more recent cases show.[319] Tribunals dispose of discretion not to grant the possibility of a written submission. It is interesting to highlight that EU institutions are considering that EU IIAs might, in the future, provide for a rule that confers a right to intervene to third parties with a direct and existing interest in

---

313   ICSID Arbitration Rules, Rule 37(2). See also UNCITRAL Transparency Rules, Art 4.
314   Indian Model BIT, Art 22; Morocco-Nigeria BIT, Art 10.
315   Malintoppi and Limbasan, above note 300, 42.
316   European Commission, 'TTIP and beyond', above note 1, 2.
317   Commonwealth Secretariat, above note 137, 428.
318   Zachariasiewicz M, 'Amicus Curiae in International Investment Arbitration: Can It Enhance the Transparency of Investment Dispute Resolution?' (2012) 29 Journal of Int'l Arbitration 2, 221.
319   See eg *Bear Creek Mining Corporation v Republic of Peru*, above note 175.

the outcome of a dispute.³²⁰ This would mean less discretion for the tribunal under the ICS to accept or not submissions of interested third parties. The discretion would then only relate to the assessment of whether given third parties have a "direct and existing interest in the outcome of a dispute".³²¹ Enhancing third parties' rights is a policy option that should be further analysed by the EU since the intervention of non-disputing parties allows taking into account the perspectives of other stakeholders.

6.4.2 *Exclusions from the Scope of Investor-State Dispute Resolution*

Lastly, EU IIAs contain certain exclusions from the scope of ISDS, thereby they address SD concerns, such as the fight against corruption.³²² Namely, EU IIAs exclude access to ISDS for investments that "[have] been made through fraudulent misrepresentation, concealment, corruption, or conduct amounting to an abuse of process".³²³ This type of provision is thus clearly concerned with corruption in the context of foreign investments.³²⁴ The benefit of the provision is that it deprives an investor of the remedy to directly enforce its rights against a host State or the EU. As has been discussed before, EU IIAs otherwise only provide for best-endeavour provision addressed to the contracting parties seeking to foster corporate social responsibility.³²⁵ Therefore, the said exclusion is a means to integrate the rationale of SD as corrupted investments cannot benefit from IIA protection.

Depriving investors of their right to have access to ISDS in the case of corruption or other fraudulent behaviour connected to their investment is, to date, seldom IIA practice.³²⁶ Therefore, the EU is introducing here a treaty technique that could inspire future IIA practice. From an EU policy perspective,

---

320   European Commission, 'TTIP and beyond', above note 1, para 11.3, para 3: "In addition to the possibility for the Tribunal to accept amicus curiae briefs, the EU proposal should confer a right to intervene to third parties with a direct and existing interest in the outcome of a dispute".
321   Ibid.
322   UNCTAD, IPFSD, 103.
323   Eg CETA, Art 8.18(3): "For greater certainty, an investor may not submit a claim under this Section if the investment has been made through fraudulent misrepresentation, concealment, corruption, or conduct amounting to an abuse of process." See also, EUMFTA, Ch 'Resolution of Investment Disputes', Art 2(3); EUVIPA, Art 3.27(2). The EUSIPA is an exception hereto, as it does not contain such a provision.
324   The fight against corruption is an essential aspect of the SD agenda. See above Section 5.3.4.
325   See above Section 5.4.2.
326   See, 2018 Dutch Model BIT, Art 16(2): "The Tribunal shall decline jurisdiction if the investment has been made through fraudulent misrepresentation, concealment, corruption, or similar bad faith conduct amounting to an abuse of process".

the fight against corruption stands very high in the political agenda of the EU institutions. In terms of efficiency, it has been criticised to bring in issues of corruption at the level of jurisdiction. The reason put forward was that the question of legality should, for certain violations of host State laws, including corruption, not be dealt with at the level of jurisdiction because that implies an "all or nothing" solution allowing States to avoid liability even though States or State representatives are often involved in acts of corruption.[327] However, excluding illegal investments from the benefits of ISDS remains one of the tools to integrate SD. The use of it is further highlighted by the treaty practice of many countries, including developing countries.[328] EU IIAs also exclude investments that were "made through fraudulent misrepresentation".[329] The provisions also cover situations of *treaty-shopping*. Given all these aspects, the exclusions seem to underscore the pursuance of the SD objective within EU IIAs.

6.5 Concluding Remarks

When the EU started to build its investment policy in 2009, the international investment regime was at the beginning of the period that is now called the era of re-orientation of international investment law. It meant from the start of the EU's investment policy that continuing in the same lines as EU Member States BITs was no option. New approaches that better safeguard the parties' right to regulate in the public interest needed to be adopted. In the past decade, the EU was able to suggest a number of new approaches in how to draft investment protection standards and managed to introduce more clarity as regards the main protection standards. Considering the effects of the SD objective within the CCP, these are positive developments.

FET as the key standard at stake in regulatory disputes as received an overhaul under EU IIAs. The content of FET is more explicitly described through an exhaustive list, which enumerates the kinds of State behaviours that breach

---

327 Van Aaken and Lehmann, above note 231, 335–336.
328 Many IIAs deal with corruption and other illegal investments through specific provisions on corruption. See SADC, Art 10 on 'Common Obligations against Corruption', see Art 10.3: "A breach of this article by an Investor or an Investment is deemed to constitute a breach of the domestic law of the Host State Party concerning the establishment and operation of an investment"; see also Morocco-Nigeria, Art 17.
329 Eg CETA, Art 8.18(3). See also EUMFTA, Ch 'Resolution of Investment Disputes', Art 2(3); EUVIPA, Art 3.27(2).

the standard. Moreover, EU IIAs narrow down the scope of protection of legitimate expectations by stating that a breach of the investor's legitimate expectation cannot in itself constitute a breach of the FET standard. With its FET provision, the EU singled out its own model. As regards indirect expropriation, the EU is following North American approaches. As such, the notion of indirect expropriation is further prescribed in an annexe to the treaty. The police power doctrine that allows for a regulatory exception has also been codified. Future adjudicators are better guided to draw the line between the existence of an indirect expropriation and the applicability of the exception. EU IIAs contain comprehensive provisions on the contracting parties' right to regulate. Whilst these provisions cannot exclude State's liability for a breach of the investment protection standards, they are setting the frame in which the latter has to be assessed.

Conversely, the treaty standard of non-discrimination in the post-establishment phase does not contain elements to increase regulatory flexibility. A reason hereto is that general exception clauses of EU IIAs apply to non-discrimination and thereby introduce safeguards. The general exceptions clauses under EU IIAs refer such to protect human, animal or plant life or health as well as the conservation of non-living resources as permissible objectives and require that the State measure taken was "necessary" in order to achieve one of the permissible objectives. Whilst differences in the scope and the formulation of general exception clauses exist, they are an increasing trend in international investment governance integrating SD into IIAs. As far as the substantive investment protection standards are concerned, one can conclude that the EU takes part in all reform approaches, occasionally suggesting new approaches. Moreover, the EU lives up to its policy statements, which focused on rendering investment standards more precise and introducing more flexibility clauses.

EU IIAs fall short on the issue of SD integration within investment liberalisation. The EU, in this respect, does not seem to counter-balance its economic interests of gaining more and more market access for its companies with the development needs of its partners. To what extent, however, developing countries are reluctant to open up their markets has been evidenced by their IIA practice, which predominantly seeks to exclude the granting of pre-establishment rights and, contrary to EU IIAs, reaffirms the host States' rights to enact performance requirements. Like other capital-exporting countries and regions, the EU has not made any attempt to link the definition of an investment with the development of the host State. Indeed, the gap in this respect between developed and developing countries is more and more consolidated. In terms of policy coherence, the EU did not integrate the rationale of SD in the provisions on investment liberalization. This reveals that the objective of trade and investment liberalisation of Article 206 TFEU has received greater attention than the SD objective. The strong commitments on pre-establishment rights, market access, and performance requirements under EU IIAs can have detrimental effects on the right to regulate of EU partner countries and the EU itself. Regulatory flexibility for economic reasons, such as the extinction of local firms due to the presence of foreign investment is no longer only a concern of developing countries but has reached the EU economy as well. This development is not least evidenced by the establishment of an EU investment screening mechanism. Therefore, a more coherent way of integrating SD, in terms of both, investment protection and liberalisation would, not least, benefit the EU itself in the long run.

The definition of investment is used in a minimal manner to channel *sustainable* investment. EU IIAs contain an extensive asset-based definition on investment, which allows for various types of investment to be eligible for the liberalisation and protection benefits granted under an IIA. The EU does not shape SD integration by adding SD as a criterion to the investment definition under its IIAs. Yet, to be a covered investment under an EU IIA, the investment must be made in accordance with host State laws, thereby limiting investment liberalisation and protection only to those investments that were at the moment of establishment in compliance with domestic law including social and environmental standards. EU IIAs leave it up to domestic law to define the validity of the investment and ultimately whether it is eligible for the benefits of investment liberalisation and protection. It is common treaty practice, in particular, for capital-exporting countries to favour broad and open definitions covering the widest range of the business activities of their companies. The argument for limiting investment liberalisation and protection to those investments that are beneficial for the SD of the host States comes mostly from developing countries. Their IIAs and model treaties link the investment definition with the criterion of "economic development" of the host State. These States seek to capture positive spill-over effects of investment activities in their territory. While the normative value remains subject to debate, international investment governance is divided when it comes to including the fourth *Salini* criterion. The EU, so far, seems to ignore that the definition of investment can be used to channel the type of investment that are more likely contribute to SD within the EU and abroad. In the future, these approaches should be reconsidered as to better align EU IIAs with the SD objective under the CCP.

By redrafting traditional IIA standards, the EU was keen to develop new approaches that all seek to safeguard the regulatory space for the EU and its partner countries, which is ultimately highly important for national measures that pursue SD objectives. The EU is thereby living up to its policy goals and participating in the global endeavour to render investment protection standards more precise and more predictable by withdrawing some of the discretion from adjudicators interpreting the standards. With Opinion 1/17, the CJEU approved the European Commission's approaches. The Court's reasoning leaves the reader with the impression that the regulatory space for setting the level of public interests would always be safeguarded. However, the present chapter has revealed the instances where EU IIAs delegate to adjudicators discretion in deciding on the often-delicate balancing act between investor interests and SD relevant measures. The remaining discretion for adjudicators makes clear that future adjudicators have their role to play in integrating SD when EU IIAs are being applied and interpreted. The next chapter analyses how SD should be taken into account when applying the substantive investment treaty provisions of EU IIAs.

CHAPTER 7

Sustainable Development Integration in the Interpretation of EU IIAS

Shaping SD integration for EU IIAS ultimately means that SD has to be taken into account at the moment of treaty interpretation. The interpretative purposes of SD within international law, in general, enjoy widespread acceptance.[1] Integrative judicial reasoning has been one of the main drivers of SD integration and the concretisation of SD in international law depends on it. International investment tribunals are, in this respect, playing a central role as they increasingly contribute to the concretisation of SD within international investment law.

SD has been integrated in EU IIAS running as a basic concept through the content of EU IIAS. Such SD integration in the treaty text will have implications for interpreting the IIA's substantive investment standards. Under EU IIAS, a foreign investor can directly invoke the substantive protection standards against the host State or the EU.[2] Therefore, future investment tribunals under the Investment Court System (ICS) of EU IIAS are mandated to further integrate SD. In applying the substantive standards, they are in charge of undertaking the balance between the investors' rights and the host States' right to regulate pursuing SD objectives. In this vein, adjudicators under EU IIAS play a central role in integrating SD in the sense of weighing the various—economic, social and environmental—interests at stake in future cases.

This last chapter analyses the extent to which EU IIAS favour an interpretation of its substantive standards in light of SD. *Expressis verbis* SD integration in the IIA text is analysed, such as the references to SD in preambles and specific objective provisions as well as chapters on "Sustainable Development and Trade" (hereafter: TSD chapters). The analysis then considers how TSD

---

1   Barral V, *Le développement durable en droit international: essai sur les incidences juridiques d'une norme évolutive* (Bruylant 2016) 247–339; Gehne K, *Nachhaltige Entwicklung als Rechtsprinzip: normativer Aussagegehalt, rechtstheoretische Einordnung, Funktionen im Recht* (Mohr Siebeck 2011) 293–296; International Law Association (ILA), 'International Law on Sustainable Development', Toronto Conference [2006], 4.2. Specifically, on international investment law, see eg Brown C, 'Bringing Sustainable Development Issues before Investment Treaty Tribunals', in: Cordonier Segger M-C, Gehring MW and Newcombe AP (eds), *Sustainable Development in World Investment Law* (Kluwer Law International 2011) 185–188.
2   See Section 6.1.

chapters interact with investment chapters. Lastly, general interpretative techniques and methods for the balancing of competing interests are discussed.

7.1 SD as the Objective of EU IIAS

SD is part of EU IIAS' treaty text and SD has been referred to on multiple occasions. Certain elements of EU IIAS, such as SD references within the agreements' preambles, are uncontroversial and have received widespread acceptance among most countries and regions. Other practices under EU IIAS, such as the inclusion of specific chapters on SD, suggest a more innovative approach. Both instances of SD integration, *i.e.* preambles and TSD chapters embedding the whole treaty in the global SD agenda, make SD a general and transversal objective of EU IIAS.

7.1.1 *Preambles and Objectives Provisions*

For most international agreements, the major textual inclusions of SD are found in preambles.[3] In this respect, economic agreements are no exception. Prominent examples include the preamble of the WTO Agreement,[4] as well as the preamble of the NAFTA.[5] The EU for its part has, as well, included a reference to SD in multiples preambles of its economic agreements with third countries.[6] For example, the 2002 EU-Chile FTA states "the need to promote

---

3   Barral, above note 1, 125–126.
4   Marrakesh Agreement establishing the WTO, preamble, recital 1:
    "Recognizing that their relations in the field of trade and economic endeavour should be conducted with a view to raising standards of living, ensuring full employment and a large and steadily growing volume of real income and effective demand, and expanding the production of and trade in goods and services, while allowing for the optimal use of the world's resources *in accordance with the objective of sustainable development,* seeking both to protect and preserve the environment and to enhance the means for doing so in a manner consistent with their respective needs and concerns at different levels of economic development." Emphasis added.
5   See, NAFTA, preamble, recital 13: the NAFTA parties have "resolved to promote sustainable development". See also *William Ralph Clayton, William Richard Clayton, Douglas Clayton, Daniel Clayton and Bilcon of Delaware Inc v Government of Canada (Bilcon v Canada),* UNCITRAL, PCA Case No 2009-04, Award on Jurisdiction and Liability, 17 March 2015, para 569. See also USMCA, preamble, recital 13.
6   Dimopoulos A, 'EC Free Trade Agreements: An Alternative Model for Addressing Human Rights in Foreign Investment Regulation and Dispute Settlement?' in: Dupuy PM, Petersmann EU and Francioni F (eds), *Human Rights in International Investment Law and Arbitration* (Oxford University Press 2009) 579.

economic and social progress for their peoples, taking into account the principle of [SD] and environmental protection requirements".⁷ Or the EU-CARIFORUM EPA, which states "the need to promote economic and social progress for [the] people in a manner consistent with [SD] by respecting basic labour rights in line with the commitments they have undertaken within the International Labour Organisation and by protecting the environment in line with the 2002 Johannesburg Declaration".⁸

Looking at post-Lisbon EU IIAs containing substantive investment protection standards, it becomes apparent that they all make reference to SD in their preambles.⁹ The CETA preamble, for instance, states the parties' commitment "to promote [SD] and the development of international trade in such a way as to contribute to [SD] in its economic, social and environmental dimensions".¹⁰ An SD reference in the preamble, confirms that the EU and the partner country understand the IIA as expressing synergies between international trade including investment and SD as it seeks to promote them in order "to contribute to [SD]". In this sense, international trade becomes a means to contribute to SD in its three pillars. Some of the EU IIAs, such as CETA, do not specifically mention the nexus between investment and SD in their preambles. Nevertheless, it is important to recall that "trade" needs to be understood broadly in this context as also to encompass investment as part of international trade policy in general and in particular so for the EU and its CCP.¹¹ The EU-Singapore FTA has a more appropriate formulation in its preamble stating the parties' determination "to strengthen their economic, trade, and investment relations in accordance with the objective of [SD], in its economic, social and environmental dimensions, and to promote trade and investment in a manner mindful of high levels of environmental and labour protection and relevant internationally recognised standards and agreements to which they are Parties".¹²

The inclusion of SD in preambles of investment agreements has received wide acceptance.¹³ From 2006 onwards, many adopted IIAs include SD in their

---

7   EU-Chile Association Agreement, preamble recital 4.
8   EU-CARIFORUM EPA, preamble recital 6.
9   Namely, CETA, EUJFTA, EUMFTA, EUSFTA, EUVFTA.
10 CETA, preamble, recital 4. See also EUVFTA, preamble, recital 4.
11 See Section 4.3. For the converging factors between trade and investment, see Kurtz J, *The WTO and International Investment Law: Converging Systems* (Cambridge University Press 2016) 10–20.
12 EUSFTA, preamble, recital 4.
13 Nowrot K, 'How to Include Environmental Protection, Human Rights and Sustainability in International Investment Law?' (2014) 15 The Journal of World Investment & Trade 612, 630. Gordon K, Pohl J and Bouchard M, 'Investment Treaty Law, Sustainable Development

preambles showing a general consensus that SD is one of the main goals to be achieved through IIAs.[14] Under the Morocco-Nigeria BIT the parties recognise "the important contribution investment can make to the [SD] of the state parties, including the reduction of poverty, increase of productive capacity, economic growth, the transfer of technology, and the furtherance of human rights and human development".[15] Several Canadian BITs, for their parts, also state SD to be the purpose of the agreement.[16] The Canada-Burkina Faso BIT elaborates more on the concept of SD. It considers that "investment is a form of [SD] that meets present needs without compromising the ability of future generations to meet their own needs and that it is critical for the future development of national and global economies as well as for the pursuit of national and global objectives for [SD]".[17] Numerous other examples could also be drawn on to demonstrate the frequency of SD references in IIAs. In this context, the EU's approach to incorporating SD into the preamble perfectly fits into the current IIA practice.

Whilst, the majority of IIAs as the ones of the EU understand SD in its three-pillar structure,[18] the US approach shows differences. The formulation found in preambles of agreements concluded by the United States mostly understand SD only with respect to the economic and environmental pillar as it links SD to the mutual supportiveness between trade and environmental policies and practices.[19] This approach has also been chosen for the Comprehensive and Progressive Trans-Pacific Partnership (CPTPP) Agreement, which includes a two-pillar SD reference in its preamble.[20] Considering, however, the evolution

and Responsible Business Conduct: A Fact-Finding Survey' (2014) OECD Working Papers on International Investment 2014/01, 10–12.

14 Early exceptions are three BITs concluded by the Netherlands: in 1994 with Bangladesh, in 1994 with Latvia and in 1999 with Costa Rica. According to UNCTAD, currently, 76 out of 2575 mapped treaties contain a reference to SD in their preambles all of which are rather recent treaties. Put into context, however, this only represents 2.9% of the examined treaties. For the calculation, the number of mapped treaties (2575) has been used. The current number of signed IIAs is 3'322; see UNCTAD, *World Investment Report 2018: Investment and the New Industrial Policies* (United Nations 2018) 89.
15 Morocco-Nigeria BIT, preamble, recital 2.
16 See eg Canada-Côte d'Ivoire BIT, Canada-Cameroon BIT, Canada-Guinea BIT.
17 Eg Canada-Burkina Faso, preamble recital 2.
18 Morocco-Nigeria BIT, preamble, recital 4.
19 Eg US-Uruguay FTA, preamble, recital 10; US-Colombia FTA, preamble, recital 13. However, an exception hereto is the US-Korea FTA, preamble, recital 7.
20 Comprehensive and Progressive Agreement for Trans-Pacific Partnership (CPTPP), preamble recital 12: "Promote high levels of environmental protection, including through effective enforcement of environmental laws, and further the aims of [SD], including through mutually supportive trade and environmental policies and practices".

of the concept of SD, the EU's approach is more accurate since the main characteristic of the concept is its three-pillar structure namely including the social dimension of SD.²¹

Moreover, preambular references to SD in post-Lisbon EU IIAs are often combined with references to other aspects and principles that are relevant for SD, such as human rights, the right to regulate or the concept of corporate social responsibility.²² EU IIAs thus underline the different policy areas and objectives that are linked to SD. Prominent elements of EU IIAs are the expressed desire to "promote economic growth and stability, to create new employment opportunities and improve the general welfare",²³ as well as the reaffirmation of the right to "adopt and enforce measures necessary to pursue legitimate policy objectives such as social, environmental, security, public health and safety, promotion and protection of cultural diversity".²⁴ Similar approaches can be found in the IIAs of other international actors highlighting that multiple purpose preamble are a further current trend.²⁵ For instance, the preamble to the COMESA Investment Agreement reaffirms the importance of "sustainable economic growth".²⁶ The preamble of the ASEAN Investment Agreement acknowledges the different levels of development of their members and the need for "special and differential treatment".²⁷

Lastly, some countries and regions include a specific article in the operative part of the agreement that states the objective of the IIA.²⁸ This type of provision can provide added weight to the objectives stated in the preamble. In doing so, the parties reinforce the purpose of the IIA and better set the direction for future interpretation.²⁹ Stating the agreement's objectives in terms of

---

21 The social pillar has been explicitly strengthened during the Johannesburg Summit on Sustainable Development in 2002. See World Summit on Sustainable Development, 'Johannesburg Declaration on Sustainable Development', [2002] A/CONF.199/20; see also Section 2.1.1.
22 Namely CETA, EUJFTA, EUMFTA, EUSFTA, EUVFTA.
23 Eg EUVFTA, preamble, recital 5.
24 See eg EUSFTA, preamble recital 7.
25 Reinisch A, 'The Interpretation of International Investment Agreements', in: Bungenberg M, Griebel J, Hobe S, Reinisch A (eds), *International Investment Law—A Handbook* (CH BECK Hart Nomos 2015) 400–401.
26 COMESA Investment Agreement, preamble, recital 1.
27 ASEAN Investment Agreement, preamble, recital 2. See for a similar approach Panama-Taiwan FTA, preamble, recital 5.
28 For instance, the model BITs of the United States, Canada, India do not contain such a provision.
29 See SADC Model BIT, Art 1 and Commentary, 8. See also Yasseen MK, *Interprétation des traités d'après la Convention de Vienne* (Martinus Nijhoff 1976) 57.

SD in a separate and specific provision constitutes, in particular, EU practice for economic agreement with developing countries. As such, the EPAs concluded in the framework of the Cotonou Agreement contain specific provisions on the objectives and principles guiding the application and interpretation of those agreements. Namely, the parties "reaffirm that the objective of [SD] is to be applied and integrated at every level of their economic partnership [...]".[30] However, some model investment agreements are more explicit in pointing out the objective of SD in a specific provision, such as the SADC Model BIT as well as the Pan-African Investment Code (PAIC).[31] Both instruments, also state the objective to increase and encourage investments but add that the latter should "support the [SD] of each Party".[32]

To find a provision stating the objective of SD in a post-Lisbon EU IIA, one needs to look into the chapters dedicated to SD, which start off with a provision on "Context and Objectives".[33] Through these provisions, the parties "reaffirm their commitment to developing and promoting international trade and their bilateral trade and economic relationship in such a way as to contribute to [SD]".[34] TSD chapters are crosscutting chapters for the purpose of comprehensive EU FTAs and thus the objective statements contained therein play a role for the whole agreement, including investment regulation.

7.1.2 Embedding EU IIAs in the Global SD Agenda

TSD chapters begin with references to the fundamental documents of the global SD agenda, such as the 1992 Rio Declaration and its Agenda 21, the 2002 Johannesburg Declaration, the 2008 ILO Declaration on Social Justice for a Fair Globalisation, as well as the Agenda 2030.[35] The EU thus places the TSD

---

30 Eg EU-CARIFORUM EPA, Art 3. See also EU-SADC EPA, Art 7 having the same formulation. Consider also, Cotonou Agreement, Arts 1–3.
31 SADC Model BIT, Art 1; PAIC, Art 1. See also IISD Model BIT, Art 1, with the sole objective of SD.
32 Eg SADC Model BIT, Art 1.
33 CETA, Art 22.1; EUJFTA, Art 16.1; EUMFTA, TSD chapter, Art 1; EUSFTA, Art 12.1; EUVFTA, Art 13.1.
34 Eg EUSFTA, Art 12.1(1) *in fine*.
35 The full list includes: Rio Declaration on Environment and Development of 1992, Agenda 21 on Environment and Development of 1992, the Johannesburg Declaration on Sustainable Development of 2002 and the Plan of Implementation of the World Summit on Sustainable Development of 2002, the Ministerial Declaration of the United Nations Economic and Social Council on Creating an environment at the national and international levels conducive to generating full and productive employment and decent work for all, and its impact on sustainable development of 2006, and the ILO Declaration on Social Justice for a Fair Globalisation of 2008.

chapter in its broader international context. This shows that TSD chapters are not an attempt by the EU to export its own environmental and labour norms and standards upon its partners.[36] To the contrary, the EU, together with its respective partners, reiterate at the outset of the TSD chapter, their joint SD endeavours at the international level.

The first article of the TSD chapters in EU IIAs also serves for setting the parties' understanding of SD in the context of trade and investment. To this end, the parties reaffirm their commitment to developing international trade "in a way as to contribute to [SD]" and seek "to strengthen their trade relations and cooperation" for SD promotion.[37] The EU and its partners also underline "the benefit of considering trade-related labour and environmental issues as part of the global approach to trade and [SD]".[38] Lastly, the parties reiterate that in their bilateral relationship, trade/investment and SD shall be mutually reinforcing.[39] In the FTA with Mexico, the parties more specifically express their goal to "enhance [SD] integration" in their trade and investment relationship.[40] From these statements, one needs to conclude that SD is the central guiding principle setting the framework of the design of the trade and investment relations of the EU and its partners. As a consequence, SD as an objective of the whole FTA and the provisions of the TSD chapters impact the other chapters of a comprehensive FTA of the EU.

7.2 The Relationship between Provisions on Investment and TSD Chapters

TSD chapters are a central feature of SD integration for EU IIAs. Hence, it is important to discuss the relationship between TSD chapters and the provisions on investment liberalisation and protection.[41] Three elements seem

---

36 Marín Durán G, 'Innovations and Implications of the Trade and Sustainable Development Chapter in the EU–Korea Free Trade Agreement' in: Harrison J (ed), *The European Union and South Korea* (Edinburgh University Press 2013) 131.
37 CETA, Art 22.1(1), EUSFTA, Art 12.1(2); EUVFTA, Art 13.1(2). With slightly different formulations, see EUJFTA, Art 16.1(1).
38 CETA, Art 22.1(2); EUKFTA, Art 13.1(2); EUSFTA, Art 12.1(2); EUVFTA, Art 13.1(4).
39 Eg EUSFTA, Art 12.1(2): "The Parties recognise that economic development, social development and environmental protection are interdependent and mutually reinforcing components of sustainable development." See likewise, CETA, Art 22.1(1); EUKFTA, Art 13.1(2); EUVFTA, Art 13.1(3).
40 EUMFTA, TSD chapter, Art 1.1.
41 EU treaty practice is not harmonised in this respect. Investment liberalisation and protection provisions can be part of a specific investment chapter, such as under the CETA and

particularly relevant to highlight, namely the aspect of mutual reinforcement between the two sets of provisions and coherence, the crosscutting issue of the right to regulate as well as the mutual exclusion with respect to the dispute settlement mechanisms. At the outset, it should be underlined that the EU's investment chapters/Investment Protection Agreements (IPAs) do not contain a provision that would provide further guidance as to how the contracting parties understand the interaction between the different chapters/instruments of a given comprehensive trade agreement. The CETA investment chapter only manages the interaction with the chapter on financial services.[42] EU treaty practice in this respect differs from those of the United States and Canada.[43] For instance, the Dominican Republic-Central America Free Trade Agreement (DR-CAFTA) provides in its investment chapter that "[i]n the event of any inconsistency between this Chapter and another Chapter, the other Chapter shall prevail to the extent of the inconsistency".[44] For EU FTAs the question remains open which chapter/instrument would prevail in case of inconsistency. Whether there is an inconsistency to begin with between the provisions on labour and environment on the one hand, and those on investment, on the other hand, is, first of all, a matter of interpretation. As for EU FTAs, by reading their TSD chapters, it appears more logical to perceive the intent of the EU and its partners in light of a general presumption against inconsistencies.[45] In other words, under EU IIAs, TSD chapters and investment chapters/IPAs are to be read in a harmonious way.

7.2.1 Mutual Reinforcement and Coherence

For EU IIAs, one can argue that the TSD chapters and the investment chapters/IPAs are to be read in a mutually reinforcing manner as both seek to contribute to the "systemic objective" of SD.[46] The overarching purpose of the inclusion of TSD chapters has to be understood as to ensure that trade and investments expand and develop in a way as to contribute to the objective of SD. Moreover,

---

the EUMFTA; or they can be part of a specific IPA, such is the case for the EUSFTA and the EUVFTA. See Section 6.2.

42 CETA, Art 8.3.
43 NAFTA, Art 1112(1); US-Colombia FTA, Art 10.2(1); US-Korea FTA, Art 11.2(1); Canada-Colombia FTA, Art 802; Canada-Panama FTA, Art 9.03.
44 DR-CAFTA, Art 10.2(1).
45 Report of the Study Group of the International Law Commission finalised by Martti Koskenniemi, Fragmentation of International Law: Difficulties arising from the Diversification and Expansion of International Law, UN Doc A/CN.4/L.682 (hereafter: ILC Report), paras 37 et seq.
46 Ibid, para 412, referring to "systemic" objective.

under TSD chapters, the EU and its investment partners define SD in its three-pillar structure and state, "that economic development, social development and environmental protection are *interdependent* and *mutually reinforcing* components of [SD]".[47] Thus, contracting parties agree that SD can serve as a means to reconcile competing interests, namely economic development, social development, and environmental protection.[48] The conflictual nature of the latter elements can, as such, be mitigated through the technique of "mutual supportiveness", or in the terminology of EU IIAs, "mutual reinforcement" between the different pillars and between the different areas of law.[49]

Initially, mutual supportiveness was developed for the trade-environment nexus.[50] The concept seeks to strengthen coherence, balance and interaction between the two.[51] Mutual supportiveness "is linked to a principle of normative cohesion or normative interconnection between different regimes".[52] Understood in this way, mutual supportiveness or reinforcement suggest more than a harmonious reading of the TSD chapters and the investment chapters/IPAs because the concept of harmonisation implicitly accepts that normative conflicts may arise if the presumption against conflict is rebutted while mutual supportiveness "plays down that sense of conflict" not to say excludes in the idea of conflict.[53] Consequently, EU IIAs should be read and implemented in that sense of mutual reinforcement. The normative cohesion created through TSD chapters between international investment law and international labour law and environmental protection, additionally responds to one of the obligations set out in the EU treaties, which is to ensure consistency and policy coherence between the different areas of its external action.[54]

---

47 Emphasis added. See, CETA, Art 22.1(1); EUKFTA, Art 13.1(2); EUSFTA, Art 12.1(2); EUVFTA, Art 13.1(3).
48 Generally, on the reconciling purposes of SD see Barral V, 'Sustainable Development in International Law: Nature and Operation of an Evolutive Legal Norm' (2012) 23 European Journal of International Law 377, 395–396. See also Section 2.2.
49 ILC Report, above note 45, para 412.
50 Pavoni R, 'Mutual Supportiveness as a Principle of Interpretation and Law-Making: A Watershed for the "WTO-and-Competing-Regimes" Debate?', 2010 European Journal of International Law 21:649–679.
51 Boisson de Chazournes L and Mbengue MM, 'A "Footnote as a Principle"—Mutual Supportiveness in an Era of Fragmentation', in: Hestermeyer HP et al (eds), *Coexistence, Cooperation and Solidarity—Liber Amicorum Rüdiger Wolfrum*—Vol II (Martinus Nijhoff Publishers 2011) 1619.
52 Ibid, 1617.
53 ILC Report, above note 45, para 412.
54 TEU, Art 21(3). See Section 4.3.2.

7.2.2 The Right to Regulate—A Crosscutting Issue

EU TSD chapters and investment chapters/IPAs seek to safeguard the States' right to regulate for the public interest. The crosscutting concern is that trade and investment relations between the EU and its partners should not undermine the pursuit of social and environmental policies and legislation.[55] Concerning TSD chapters, a reference to the right to regulate has always been part of the provisions contained therein. The EU-Korea FTA, for instance, provides that the parties to the agreement recognise "the right of each Party to establish its own levels of environmental and labour protection, and to adopt or modify accordingly its relevant laws and policies".[56] Moreover, parties are encouraged to adopt "high levels of environmental and labour protection", which should be "consistent with the internationally recognised standards or agreements".[57]

Investment chapters/IPAs also contain an apparent reference to the parties' right to regulate. For instance, the EU-Mexico FTA provides "[t]he Parties affirm the right to regulate within their territories to achieve legitimate policy objectives, such as the protection of public health, social services, public education, safety, environment or public morals, social or consumer protection, privacy and data protection, the promotion and protection of cultural diversity, or competition".[58] Other investment chapters/IPAs of EU IIAs also contain a specific provision on the right to regulate combined with a non-exhaustive enumeration of public policy objectives.[59] In contrast to the right to regulate as set out under the TSD chapters, the provisions on the right to regulate in the investment chapters are drafted more broadly encompassing regulatory areas that go beyond social standards and environmental protection.

Right to regulate affirmations have, in the context of investment protection, a very specific rationale. These statements have been included in order to better safeguard regulatory space for legitimate public welfare objective in the case of an investor claim alleging a breach of its investment guarantees due to the enactment of the measure.[60] Due to their minimalistic wording, they add nothing as to how to weigh the stated objectives in relation to investors' rights.

---

55 European Commission, Concept Paper: Investment in TTIP and beyond—The Path for Reform Enhancing the Right to Regulate and Moving from Current Ad Hoc Arbitration towards and Investment Court, [2015].
56 EUKFTA, Art 13.3. See also CETA, Arts 23.2 and 24.3; EUSFTA, Art 12.2; EUVFTA, Art 13.2.
57 Ibid.
58 EUMFTA, Ch "Investment", Art 1.
59 CETA, Art 8.9; EUSIPA, Art 2.2; EUVIPA, Art, 2.2.
60 See Section 2.5.

In fact, the pivotal issue in cases concerning the right to regulate of States has not been that legitimate regulatory objectives were not sufficiently recognised but to strike an adequate balance between the regulatory purposes and investment protection.[61] These clauses still leave it up to the adjudicators interpreting the treaty to strike the balance. At the same time, adjudicators are invited to take nuanced approaches in doing so. The parties' affirmation on the right to regulate contained in the TSD chapters serves, in the same vein, to foster the regulatory space of the national legislator but further underlines that the parties' do not seek to engage into regulatory integration for matters of social or environmental protection despite the fact that such regulation must to be in accordance with international minimum standards. As such the parties are namely free to decide upon the levels of environmental and social protection. Despite these slightly different rationales for the inclusion of provisions on the right to regulate, EU IIAs make a strong emphasis on the right to regulate, and particularly so for measures pursuing SD.

7.2.3 Mutual Exclusion Concerning Dispute Settlement

The relationship with respect to the dispute settlement mechanisms foreseen respectively in TSD chapters and investment chapters/IPAs is characterised by mutual exclusion of each other. In other words, there is no relationship or linkage between the enforcement mechanisms for the provisions specifically on SD and those related to investment liberalisation and protection. Each set of provisions is subject to a specific dispute settlement mechanism. For investment disputes, the stringent mechanism of investor-State dispute settlement has been put in place under EU IIAs allowing investors to sue a State party or the EU directly. In stark contrast to this, is the dispute settlement for SD matters, which is characterised by a "soft" mechanism, with cooperative and consultative rather than adjudicatory elements.[62]

Under EU IIAs, TSD chapters typically provide that "[f]or any matter arising under this chapter where there is disagreement, the Parties shall only have recourse to the procedures established under" the TSD chapter.[63] Consequently, disputes on SD matters are to be resolved through consultation between the contracting parties and, if such consultations are fruitless, an expert panel will

---

61   See Section 6.1. Gött H and Holterhus TP, 'Mainstreaming Investment-Labour Linkage Through "Mega-Regional" Trade Agreements' in: Gött H (ed), *Labour Standards in International Economic Law* (Springer International Publishing 2018) 243–244.
62   Ibid, 261.
63   Eg EUVFTA, Art 13.16(1). Emphasis added. See also CETA, Arts 23.11(1) and 24.16(1); EUMFTA, TSD chapter, Art 15; EUSFTA, Art 12.16(1).

be established that has the authority to adopt a report containing recommendations for the defaulting State. The parties are to implement this report, and there are no sanctions foreseen in the case of non-implementation thereof.[64] EU IIAs also exclude the TSD chapter from the scope of the agreement's general inter-State dispute settlement mechanism.[65] As far as the investment chapter is concerned, the scope of the investor-State dispute settlement is also clearly defined and limited to specific sections of the investment chapters/IPAs, *i.e.* the investment protection standards.[66] For instance, the EU-Singapore IPA provides that investor-State dispute settlement "shall apply to a dispute between a claimant of one Party and the other Party concerning treatment alleged to breach the provisions of Chapter Two (Investment Protection)".[67] The CETA, states an express exclusion: "[a] Tribunal constituted under this Section shall not decide claims that fall outside of the scope of this Article".[68] In addition and different than for the TSD chapter, investment chapters/IPAs are subject to the general inter-State dispute settlement.[69] As a result, as far as dispute settlement is concerned, no linkage has been made between the TSD chapters and the provisions regulating foreign investment; on the contrary, the two mechanisms mutually exclude each other. Given the strong enforcement mechanism for the investment chapters/IPAs and the soft enforcement mechanism for the TSD chapters, it seems *a priori*, more likely that the further implementation of the linkages between matters of SD and investment will occur in the factual assessment of a given case in investor-State dispute settlement procedures.[70] Links between the two chapters are, at the least, implicit if one considers, for instance, that the monitoring bodies of the TSD chapters

---

64   See Section 5.2.2.
65   Eg EUSFTA, Art 12.16(1) in fine: "Chapter Fourteen (Dispute Settlement) and Chapter Fifteen (Mediation Mechanism) do not apply to this Chapter".
66   Eg CETA, Art 8.18(1): "Without prejudice to the rights and obligations of the Parties under Chapter Twenty-Nine (Dispute Settlement), an investor of a Party may submit to the Tribunal constituted under this Section a claim that the other Party has breached an obligation under: (a) Section C, with respect to the expansion, conduct, operation, management, maintenance, use, enjoyment and sale or disposal of its covered investment, or (b) Section D, where the investor claims to have suffered loss or damage as a result of the alleged breach.
67   EUSIPA, Art 3.1(1).
68   CETA, Art 8.18(5).
69   CETA, Ch 29; EUMFTA, Ch 'Dispute Settlement'; EUSIPA, Art 3.25 et seq; EUVIPA, Art 3.1 et seq. The inter-State dispute settlement mechanism under these agreements applies with respect to any difference concerning the interpretation and application of the provisions of the given agreement.
70   Gött and Holterhus, above note 61, 262.

can influence subsequent treaty amendments or interpretative declarations adopted by the overarching treaty body.[71]

7.3 General Interpretative Techniques

SD is *expressis verbis* mentioned in the preambles and in TSD chapters that are included in EU IIAs. The preambles, as well as the TSD chapters, underline that SD is the purpose and also a contextual element for interpretation. Making SD an objective of IIAs has the purpose of complementing investment promotion and protection objectives with broader public policy objectives and can lead to more balanced interpretations and foster coherence between different policy objectives and different bodies of law.[72]

7.3.1 *Object and Purpose*

Interpretation in light of the object and purpose of the treaty is provided in Article 31 VCLT. The object and purpose describe the *ratio legis* of the treaty,[73] and are most often expressed in the preamble of a treaty.[74] EU IIAs are no exception in this respect. The preambles of EU IIAs constitute a set of multiple objectives, covering areas such as economic growth, trade liberalisation, investment protection, international security, democracy, human rights, and culture as well as SD including social and environmental protection.[75] Even though these agreements are predominantly economic instruments, the objectives contained in their preamble are not predominantly of economic concern. A consequence of this is that adjudicators under EU IIAs have to consider all the aspects of the preamble and have to apply a balanced approach to investment protection on the one side and other societal values on the other side.

---

71   In CETA, the monitoring body of the labour provisions may submit recommendations to the CETA Joint Committee.
72   UNCTAD, 'Investment Policy Framework for Sustainable Development (IPFSD)' (United Nation 2015) 92.
73   Yasseen, above note 31, 55.
74   *Siemens A.G. v The Argentine Republic*, ICSID Case No ARB/02/8, Decision on Jurisdiction, 3 Aug 2004, para 81: "The Tribunal shall be guided by the purpose of the Treaty as expressed in its title and preamble [...]"; *Aguas del Tunari v Bolivia*, ICSID Case No ARB/02/3, Decision on Jurisdiction, 21 Oct 2005, para 216; *Société Générale v Dominican Republic*, UNCITRAL, LCIA Case No UN 7927 Decision on Jurisdiction, 19 Sep 2008, para 32; See also Gazzini T, *Interpretation of International Investment Treaties* (Hart Pub 2016) 157 et seq.
75   CETA, preamble, recitals 1–12.

The reference to SD in the preamble of EU IIAS, in particular, suggests a balance and reconciliation between the three pillars of economic and social development and environmental protection. For instance, the tribunal in *Bilcon v. Canada*[76] found that the idea of promoting both economic development and environmental integrity is integrated into the Preamble's endorsement of the principle of SD.[77] This led the tribunal to acknowledge that environmental regulation will "inevitably be of great relevance for many kinds of major investments in modern times" and that under NAFTA "economic development and environmental integrity can not only be reconciled but can be mutually reinforcing".[78] In the case *Adel A. Hamadi Al Tamimi v. Oman*, the Tribunal used the reference to SD contained in the US-Oman FTA not in order to balance investment protection and environmental protection but in order to foster its finding on the high importance of environmental protection and conservation under the US-Oman FTA.[79]

In the EU IIA form of comprehensive FTAS, the object and purpose can, apart from the preamble, also be found in specific objective provisions. For the set of investment protection standards, a specific objective is "to enhance the investment relations between the Parties".[80] At the same time, SD operates in EU IIAS as a transversal and crosscutting objective, as it is stated in the objective provision of the TSD chapters.[81] The aim of increased investment flows has to go hand in hand with SD promotion. Consequently, it is also relevant for the investment protection standards.[82] Therefore, the latter statements foster the interpretation in light of SD based on the object and purpose of EU IIAS.

---

76 *Bilcon v Canada,* above note 5.
77 Ibid, para 596.
78 Ibid, para 597.
79 *Adel A. Hamadi Al Tamimi v Sultanate of Oman,* ICSID Case No ARB/11/33, Award, 3 Nov 2015, para 389, footnote 777. The Preamble to the US–Oman FTA includes as one of the Treaty's objectives the desire to "strengthen the development and enforcement of environmental laws and policies, promote [SD], and implement this Agreement in a manner consistent with the objectives of environmental protection and conservation".
80 Eg EUVIPA, Art 1.1.
81 CETA, Art 22.1; EUJFTA, Art 16.1; EUMFTA, TSD chapter, Art 1, EUSFTA, Art 12.1; EUVFTA, Art 13.1. See also EUVIPA, preamble recital 6: "REAFFIRMING their commitments to the principles of sustainable development in the Free Trade Agreement".
82 See also CETA, Joint Interpretative Instrument [2017] OJ L 11/3, para 1(b) and (d). The instrument emphasises that CETA embodies the parties' commitment to "free and fair trade in a vibrant and forward-looking society" and state that it is in particular not the objective of CETA to undermine the States' right to regulate in the interests of SD concerns (such public health, social services, environment and cultural diversity).

7.3.2 Contextual Interpretation

SD references in EU IIAS play a role in contextual interpretation. Article 31 VCLT provides for the contextual interpretation of a treaty or in the words of the Convention an interpretation of the "terms in their context".[83] According to Article 31(2) VCLT, the context is the treaty text in its totality including annexes and the preamble, as well as certain accords and instruments.[84] As the investment protection provisions of EU IIAS are part of a comprehensive treaty framework, this constitutes an essential difference to traditional BITs. The rules on investment are thus not isolated but interact and relate to a whole treaty framework. For EU IIAS this means that the instances that were presented above: the preamble and TSD chapters are clearly part of the context of these agreements.[85] TSD chapters have thus a considerable impact on the interpretation of substantive investment protection standards. The fact that TSD chapters form part of the context is generally also stated directly in the TSD chapters. For instance, the CETA states:

> Accordingly, the Parties agree that the rights and obligations under Chapters Twenty-Three (Trade and Labour) and Twenty-Four (Trade and Environment) are to be considered in the *context* of this Agreement.[86]

What does this mean for future adjudicators under EU IIAS? In the case law of investment tribunals, one does not yet find many examples of disputes under broader treaty frameworks as the large bulk of disputes have been decided based on BITs. Yet as the numbers of comprehensive FTAs with investment chapters are rising[87] so are the disputes based on these agreements. A good example is the case *Adel A. Hamadi Al Tamimi v. Oman*.[88] The dispute fell under the Oman–United States FTA. The investor's claims for expropriation, breach

---

83 Contextual interpretation has a long tradition; see *Case on the Diversion of Water from the Meuse* (Netherlands v Belgium), Judgment, 28 June 1937, PCIJ Rep Series A/B No 70, 21. "The Treaty brought into existence a certain régime which results from all of its provisions in conjunction. It forms a complete whole, the different provisions of which cannot be dissociated from the others and considered apart by themselves".
84 Yasseen, above note 29, 33.
85 For the specific case of CETA, the joint interpretative instrument also forms part of the context thereof as it qualifies as "[a]ny agreement relating to the treaty which was made between all parties in connection with the conclusion of the treaty" pursuant to VCLT, Art 31(2)(a).
86 CETA, Art 22.2 in fine. Emphasis added. See also EUMFTA, TSD Chapter, Art 1.1.
87 UNCTAD, *World Investment Report 2017: Investment and the Digital Economy*, Figure III.1.1 Trends in IIAs signed 1980–2016, 111.
88 *Adel A Hamadi Al Tamimi v Sultanate of Oman*, above note 79.

of the minimum standard of treatment and breach of national treatment arose out of Oman's alleged interference in the operation of his mining companies. According to Oman, the investor was in non-compliance with the environmental requirements necessary for mining activities. In the tribunal's assessment of whether Oman was in breach of the minimum standard of treatment, it took into account the chapter on the environment contained in the US-Oman FTA by stating that the said chapter "although it does not fall directly within the Tribunal's jurisdiction, provides further *relevant context*" in which the provisions of the chapter on investment must be interpreted.[89] In its analysis, the tribunal found that when it comes to determining any breach of the minimum standard of treatment "the Tribunal must be guided *by the forceful defence of environmental regulation and protection provided in the express language of the Treaty*".[90] The tribunal ultimately concluded that Oman did not breach the standard as it cannot be breached through any mere misapplication of a State's law or regulation,. It added that this would be so particularly "in a context such as the US-Oman FTA, where the impugned conduct concerns the good-faith application or enforcement of a State's laws or regulations relating to the protection of its environment".[91]

Similar contextual arguments have been made in cases under the investment chapter of the Dominican Republic-Central America Free Trade Agreement (DR-CAFTA). An illustrative example is the case *Aven and others v. Costa Rica*.[92] The dispute concerns the revocation of an environmental permit for the investor's hotel, beach club and villa construction project to protect wetlands and a protected forest. Costa Rica argued that the DR-CAFTA Chapter 17 on the Environment has implications on the interpretation of Chapter 10 on Investment.[93] In the tribunal's analysis, the relationship between the two chapters was indeed central. The tribunal, namely, discussed how to reconcile the investor's rights and the State's right to apply and enforce environmental regulations. In order to address that relationship, the tribunal applied Article 31(2) VCLT. The tribunal began by noting that the investment chapter of the DR-CAFTA contained a provision that parties are not prevented "from

---

89 Ibid, para 388. Emphasis added.
90 Ibid, para 389. Emphasis added.
91 Ibid, para 390.
92 *David R. Aven, Samuel D. Aven, Carolyn J. Park, Eric A. Park, Jeffrey S. Shioleno, Giacomo A. Buscemi, David A. Janney and Roger Raguso v The Republic of Costa Rica*, ICSID Case No UNCT/15/3, Award, 18 Sep 2018.
93 Ibid, Rejoinder Memorial of Costa Rica, 28 Oct 2016, para 42: "[…] Chapter 10 is not a stand-alone chapter, but rather is part of a broader trade agreement, which provides an express and deliberately agreed policy space in relation to the environment in Chapter 17 […]."

adopting, maintaining, or enforcing any measure otherwise consistent with [the investment chapter] that it considers appropriate to ensure that investment activity in its territory is undertaken in a manner sensitive to environmental concerns".[94] The tribunal first found that this provision would "essentially subordinate" the investor protections to the right of Costa Rica to ensure that the investments are carried out "in a manner sensitive to environmental concerns".[95] Nevertheless, the tribunal added that this subordination was not "absolute" by stressing that a State's implementation and enforcement of environmental measures would still need to be fair, non-discriminatory, and in compliance with due process.[96] Moreover, the tribunal found that "[i]t is not a question of 'not-applying' those [investment protection] provisions [...], but rather *giving preference* to the standards of environmental protection that were stated to be of interest to the Treaty Parties at the time it was signed".[97] While one can question what the tribunal precisely meant by giving preference and simultaneously denying an absolute subordination of environmental protection standards, what should retain attention here is the fact that the tribunal considered, based on Article 31.2 VCLT, the investment protection standards by duly taking into account the parties' intention and interests to implement and enforce environmental measures.

Another example is the case *Berkowitz and others v. Costa Rica*.[98] The claims, in this case, arose out of an alleged expropriation of the investor's right to establish an ecological park. Costa Rica denied the permit for environmental reasons. Here again, *inter alia* invoked Chapter 17 of the DR-CAFTA on "Environment" to sustain the argument that contracting parties to the DR-CAFTA enjoy "a certain level of discretion" in implementing their environmental laws.[99] In its Interim Award, the tribunal did not address these arguments made by Costa Rica. There are more pending investment cases under FTAs concerning SD aspects where such argumentation will most likely be used.[100]

---

94   DR-CAFTA, Art 10.11. This provision is identically worded to NAFTA, Art 1114. NAFTA tribunals have not construed Art 1114 for having much impact. Whilst acknowledging the States' environmental concerns they confirmed the force of the investment protection standards, see *Metalclad Corporation v Mexico*, ICSID Case No ARB(AF)/97/1, Award, 30 Aug 2000, para 98.
95   *Aven v Costa Rica*, above note 92, para 412.
96   Ibid.
97   Ibid. Emphasis added.
98   *Aaron C Berkowitz, Brett E Berkowitz, Trevor B Berkowitz and others v The Republic of Costa Rica*, ICSID Case No UNCT/13/2, Interim Award, 25 Oct 2016.
99   Ibid, para 108.
100 See for instance, under the Colombia-US FTA: *Cosigo Resources and others v Colombia*, UNCITRAL, pending (initiated 2016); under the Canada-Colombia FTA: *Eco Oro Minerals*

It needs to be seen how the respective tribunals will address these arguments. For EU IIAs in the form of comprehensive FTAs there is no doubt that the investment chapters/IPAs need to be read together with the SD chapters.[101] The contextual interpretation would in particular play a role when the implementation and enforcement of social and environmental measures are alleged to be inconsistent with the investment protection guarantees.

7.3.3 Evolutionary Interpretation

The VCLT is silent on the question of evolutionary interpretation.[102] There is a certain *lacuna* on how temporal considerations should operate in determining the meaning of treaty provisions.[103] Should adjudicators understand a treaty contemporaneously at the date of its conclusion, or should a treaty be understood as evolving over time and set into the time and circumstances when deciding a dispute?[104] By including the concept of SD into a treaty, the parties' agree to some extent "to open the treaty" to an evolutionary interpretation.[105] A case that certainly underlines this argument is the *Shrimp-Turtle* case decided by the WTO Appellate Body.[106] Under the old GATT, in Article XX(g) the term "exhaustible natural resources" used to be understood as not implying living resources, thus sea turtles were *a priori* excluded. The Appellate Body, however, gave the term an evolutionary understanding. It acknowledged the objective of SD in the WTO Agreement and thus found that *"it must add colour, texture and shading* to [the] interpretation of the agreements annexed to the WTO Agreement", in this case, the GATT.[107] The generic term "natural resources" was found not to be "static" but rather "by definition

---

Corp. v Republic of Colombia, ICSID Case No ARB/16/41, pending (initiated 2016); under the Central America-Panama FTA: *Álvarez y Marín Corporación and others v Panama*, ICSID Case No ARB/15/14, pending (initiated 2015).

101 Hoffmeister F, 'The Contribution of EU Trade Agreements to the Development of International Investment Law', in: Krajewski M and Hindenlang S (eds), *Shifting Paradigms in International Investment Law—More Balanced, Less Isolated, Increasingly Diversified*, (Oxford University Press 2016) 361.

102 Dupuy PM, 'Evolutionary Interpretation', in: Cannizzaro E (ed), *The Law of Treaties Beyond the Vienna Convention* (Oxford University Press 2011) 127.

103 Ibid, 127.

104 Pauwelyn J and Elsig M, 'The Politics of Treaty Interpretation' in: Dunoff JL and Pollack MA (eds), *Interdisciplinary Perspectives on International Law and International Relations: The State of the Art* (Cambridge University Press 2013) 453.

105 Barral, above note 1, 394–395.

106 *United States—Import Prohibition of Certain Shrimp and Shrimp Products*, Appellate Body Report, (1998) WT/DS58/AB/R.

107 Ibid, para 153. Emphasis added.

evolutionary".[108] Consequently, current international environmental law and modern scientific knowledge lead to the conclusion that exhaustible natural resources also include living species such as sea turtles.

The interesting question is thus whether the references to SD in EU IIAS can be considered as an invitation for future adjudicators to engage in evolutionary interpretations, namely when generic terms are to be interpreted. Giving the inherent evolutionary character of SD and its associated needs and concerns, it appears to be that an evolutionary reading of EU IIAS will be useful in the future in order to update terms and standards in light of contemporary understandings of them.[109] Questions on the socio-economic development of societies change, and interpretations should take this into account, in particular as such imperatives might not necessarily correspond with those at the time of conclusion of the IIA. This logic holds even more accurate when questions of environmental protection, including climate change mitigation, are at stake because scientific knowledge is continuously growing, this means that adjudicators should take account of the potential new norms and knowledge when interpreting an IIA as has also been reiterated by the International Court of Justice (ICJ) in the case of *Gabčíkovo-Nagymaros*.[110] In other words, what is to be considered "sustainable" will evolve over time according to physical, social and economic evolution as well as scientific progress.[111] In addition, EU IIAS not only have SD as a central objective and contextual element but also include provisions that make a specific recognition of the need to exchange scientific information and a reaffirmation of the precautionary principle.[112]

---

108   Ibid, para 130.
109   *Dispute regarding Navigational and Related Rights* (Costa Rica/Nicaragua), Judgment, ICJ Rep 2009, 213. The term "commerce" contained in a treaty of 1858 was interpreted in the light of the understanding of commerce in 2009. See also *Legal Consequences for States of the Continued Presence of South Africa in Namibia, notwithstanding Security Council Resolution 276(1970)*, Advisory Opinion, ICJ Rep 1971, 16, para 53. See also Barral, above note 1, 439; Pauwelyn and Elsig, above note 104, 454.
110   *Case Concerning the Gabčíkovo-Nagymaros Project* (Hungary/Slovakia), Judgment, ICJ Rep 1997, 7, para 140: "[...] Owing to new scientific insights and to a growing awareness of the risks for mankind—for present and future generations—of pursuit of such interventions at an unconsidered and unabated pace, new norms and standards have been developed, set forth in a great number of instruments during the last two decades. Such new norms have to be taken into consideration, and such new standards given proper weight, not only when States contemplate new activities but also when continuing with activities begun in the past. [...]"
111   Ibid. See also Barral, above note 1, 394–395.
112   CETA, Art 23.3(3) last sentence, and Art 24.8(2) together with CETA Joint Interpretative Instrument, para 1(d); EUMFTA, TSD chapter, Art 11; EUSFTA, Art 12.5; EUVFTA, Art 13.11. See Section 5.1.3.2.

Hence, an evolutionary interpretation based on new scientific knowledge seems to be accepted by the parties of EU IIAs. In sum, future adjudicators under EU IIAs can and also should consider evolutionary interpretation where it appears necessary.

7.4 Methods for the Balancing between Competing Interests

The interpretative techniques discussed so far in connection with EU IIAs, allow for the integration of SD during the interpretation process, thus bringing about a balancing exercise between the economic interests of foreign investors and other non-economic interests. There are further methods and techniques for the balancing of competing interests. Not all of them are specific to the concept of SD but are relevant for effective SD integration. These methods encompass the principle of integration, proportionality analyses, as well as the use of a deferential standard of review.

7.4.1 *Integration*

The principle of integration is fundamental for SD and the principal means for its achievement.[113] The VCLT itself contains an interpretation technique related to integration, namely systemic integration.[114] Article 31.3(c) of the VCLT and the principle of integration in the context of SD both serve as interpretative method.[115] For the sake of clarity, the principle of integration as an interpretative tool shall be presented first, followed by the specific technique of systemic integration under the VCLT.

First, for adjudicators, the principle of integration can be a useful method to ground a balancing exercise between considerations that are in tension. Indeed, at the very heart of the concept of SD lies the balancing of economic, social and environmental concerns. Hence, SD is suggested as a tool to resolve possible conflicts between the various interests of social justice, economic

---

113 See Section 2.2.1; see also, UN Conference on Environment and Development, 'Rio Declaration on Environment and Development and Agenda 21', [1992] Doc A/CONF.151/26Rev 1 (hereafter Rio Declaration), Principle 4: "In order to achieve SD, environmental protection shall constitute an integral part of the development process and cannot be considered in isolation from it."

114 For more details see, McLachlan C, 'The Principle of Systemic Integration and Article 31(3)(c) of the Vienna Convention' (2005) 54 International and Comparative Law Quarterly 279.

115 International Law Association (ILA), 'Toronto Conference 2006: International Law on Sustainable Development', pts 4.1 and 4.2.

growth and environmental protection. Adjudicators under EU IIAs that have to deal with a conflict between a State's interest for environmental protection and the economic interests of an investor may reconcile the conflict by making reference to SD as set out in the IIA itself. The principle of integration in the context of SD has already served several international courts and tribunals in their reasoning. In the *Gabčíkovo-Nagymaros* case, the ICJ sets out that the new standards of environmental protection "have to be taken into consideration" in other words they have to be integrated when States contemplate new economic activities but also when continuing with activities begun in the past.[116] This balancing approach through integration was then directly linked to the concept of SD.[117] In the *Iron Rhine* arbitration, a dispute between Belgium and the Netherlands on a railway, the tribunal first found that there were "emerging principles" of international law relating to the protection of the environment. In its reasoning, the tribunal relied on the principle of integration of the Rio Declaration;[118] and consequently found that Belgium's economic interests and the environmental concerns of the Netherlands had to be reconciled.[119] The tribunal further concluded that each of the parties' interest was legitimate meaning that Belgium had a right to reactivate the railway line, but appropriate environmental measures had to be adopted. According to the tribunal, each disputing party thus had legitimate interests, which require reconciliation. As a result, the Tribunal held that the associated financial costs of the environmental measures had to be carefully balanced between them.[120]

Turning to investment arbitration, tribunals have started to consider the integrative purposes of SD as can be seen in cases such as *Bilcon v. Canada*, *S.D. Myers v. Canada* or *Adel A. Hamadi Al Tamimi v. Oman*.[121] Yet, despite the considerations of the balancing effects of SD, it can still be discussed whether the approaches taken in these cases led to fully integrative and thus mutually

---

116   *Gabčíkovo-Nagymaros Project*, above note 110, para 140.
117   Ibid, para 140: "The need to reconcile economic development with protection of the environment is aptly expressed in the concept of sustainable development".
118   *Award in the Arbitration regarding the Iron Rhine ("Ijzeren Rijn") Railway between the Kingdom of Belgium and the Kingdom of the Netherlands*, Decision, 24 May 2005, Reports of International Arbitral Awards XXVII, para 59: "[...] these emerging principles now integrate environmental protection into the development process. Environmental law and the law on development stand not as alternatives but as mutually reinforcing, integral concepts [...]".
119   Ibid, para 221.
120   Ibid, para 220.
121   *Bilcon v Canada*, above note 5; *S.D. Myers Inc. v Government of Canada*, NAFTA, UNCITRAL, First Partial Award, 13 Nov 2000; or *Adel A. Hamadi Al Tamimi v Oman*, above note 79.

supportive solutions between the conflicting interests at stake. It rather seems that the tribunals' final solutions were "either/or"-solutions meaning either for the benefit of the economic interests or for the benefit of the environmental concerns.[122] As for future tribunals under EU IIAs, the argument made here is not to suggest that SD integration requires any specific outcome yet the concept of SD should serve as a balancing factor and at best to achieve mutually supportive solutions. In other words, SD integration into the interpretative process requires that, in the exercise of the adjudicator's discretion, balancing and weighing between economic and non-economic interest takes place and the idea of achieving mutually supportive solutions is taken seriously.

Second, and more specifically on systemic integration, Article 31.3(c) VCLT states that "any relevant rules of international law applicable in the relations between the parties" shall be taken into account. The purpose of systemic integration is to place and understand the treaty in question within its "normative environment more widely".[123] In this respect, custom and general principles, as well as other international conventions, can be relevant.[124] Systemic integration is among the interpretation techniques of international investment tribunals even though most of them do generally not explicitly refer to Article 31.3(c) VCLT.[125] For the interpretation of IIA provisions, investment tribunals mainly rely on customary international law.[126] But they occasionally also take into account other international treaties and conventions for the interpretation of investment provisions.[127] In the *Suez v. Argentina*[128] case, *amici*

---

122   See Boisson de Chazournes and Mbengue, above note 51, 1621: On *S.D. Myers v Canada*, above note 121, the authors considered it not to be a mutual reinforcing approach as priority was ultimately only given to trade concerns. In *Adel A. Hamadi Al Tamimi v Oman*, above note 79, the tribunal decided solely in favour of environmental concerns. In *Bilcon v Canada*, above note 5, the tribunal avoided to see an actual conflict of the economic interest and the environmental policy of Canada, it stated that there was no conflict but that the issue was that Canadian environmental norms were not properly applied.

123   ILC Report, above note 45, para 415.

124   McLachlan, above note 114, 310 et seq.

125   Rosentreter D, *Article 31(3)(c) of the Vienna Convention on the Law of Treaties and the Principle of Systemic Integration in International Investment Law and Arbitration* (Nomos 2015) 457. Such omission by tribunals is however immaterial; see, Report of the Study Group of the ILC, para. 468. Consider also *AAPL v Sri Lanka*, ICSID Case No ARB/87/3, Final Award, 27 June 1990, para 21.

126   Reinisch, above note 25, 388–393.

127   Rosentreter, above note 125, 333–348. See for instance *Parkerings-Compagniet AS v Republic of Lithuania*, ICSID Case No ARB/05/8, Award, 11 Sep 2007.

128   *Suez, Sociedad General de Aguas de Barcelona, S.A. and Vivendi Universal, S.A. v Argentine Republic* (*Suez v Argentina*), ICSID Case No ARB/03/19, Decision on Liability, 30 July 2010.

curiae urged the tribunal to adopt a systemic integration approach.[129] In their view and by using the language of the WTO Appellate Body, human rights law "can add color and texture to the standards of treatment included in BITs".[130] However, the tribunal in Suez did not integrate human rights law considerations into its analysis of the BIT standards. Rather, it considered the two legal regimes as separate but not conflicting.[131] Thus, for that tribunal, there was no need to consider Argentina's human rights obligations in the context of the BIT claim. That a tribunal can very well take human rights instruments into account for its interpretation is well-illustrated by the later case of *Urbaser v. Argentina*.[132]

Systemic integration can and should play a role for EU IIAs, as other international obligations of the contracting parties can be relevant in a given case. In addition, their TSD chapters contain explicit references to a number of key international instruments in the fields of environmental and labour protection. Hence, integrating such international rules and standards into the interpretation process of investment provisions under EU IIAs is, in particular, convincing and mandated.[133] Systemic integration can also encompass soft law instruments, such as the Rio Declaration and other documents related to the global SD agenda, namely instruments on corporate social responsibility.[134] Moreover, despite the fact that the Rio Declaration is a soft law instrument some of its principles are today part of customary international law and can be relevant in an investment dispute.[135] Relevant principles of the Rio Declaration that can be relevant in an investor-States dispute are in particular

---

129   Ibid, Amicus Curiae Submission, 4 April 2007.
130   Ibid, para 15. See *Import Prohibition of Certain Shrimp and Shrimp Products*, above note 108, para 153.
131   *Suez v Argentina*, above note 128, para 262.
132   *Urbaser SA and Consorcio de Aguas Bilbao Bizkaia, Bilbao Biskaia Ur Partzuergoa v The Argentine Republic*, ICSID Case No ARB/07/26, Award, 8 Dec 2016, para 1200: "The BIT cannot be interpreted and applied in a vacuum. The Tribunal must certainly be mindful of the BIT's special purpose as a Treaty promoting foreign investments, but it cannot do so without taking the relevant rules of international law into account. The BIT has to be construed in harmony with other rules of international law of which it forms part [...]".
133   See in general on this argument, Newcombe A, 'Sustainable Development and Investment Treaty Law' (2007) 8 The Journal of World Investment & Trade 357, 405.
134   See Sections 2.1 and 2.6.3.
135   For instance, the tribunal in *S.D. Myers v Canada* explicitly mentioned the Rio Declaration because it is referred to in the NAAEC preamble and considered it in their interpretation of the national treatment clause. Thus, the Rio Declaration can have a direct impact on the interpretation of investment protection standards. See *S.D. Myers v Canada*, above note 135, paras 255–256.

the obligation to conduct environmental impact assessments[136] and the principle of prevention.[137] The extent of the impacts on the interpretation is part of the adjudicator's discretion.[138] The point here is that EU IIAs favour systemic integration for the application and interpretation of the investment protection standards.

7.4.2 *Proportionality Analysis*

A next method that could be used in the interpretation of EU IIAs is a proportionality analysis. This method is regularly used to balance competing interests by international and domestic courts and is generally understood to comprise a three-fold test: an analysis of the suitability of the measure to achieve the objective; a determination of the necessity of the measure in light of available alternatives, and lastly a balancing test that evaluates the importance of achieving the objective vis-à-vis the importance of avoiding the harm to the protected right or interest caused by the measure (*i.e.* proportionality *stricto sensu*).[139] In regulatory disputes, courts and tribunals generally use the proportionality analysis to determine whether an interference with a right or interest is justifiable, or whether the executive branch has gone beyond the bounds of its discretion.[140] The principle of proportionality has been considered the most suitable and most effective instrument to achieve equilibrium of the public and the individual interests.[141] Investment tribunals have, in cases that concern measures taken by the host State to protect public interests, used proportionality when applying the concept of indirect expropriation or when interpreting the standard of fair and equitable treatment.[142] Early tribunals applied

---

136   *Case Concerning Pulp Mills on The River Uruguay* (Argentina/Uruguay), Judgment, ICJ Rep 2010, 14, paras 204–205.
137   *Gabčíkovo-Nagymaros*, above note 110, para 53.
138   For instance, in *Allard v Barbados*, where the tribunal decided that in the given case the BIT standards is not affected by other international obligations of Barbados; see *Peter A. Allard v The Government of Barbados*, PCA Case No 2012-06, para 244: "[...] The fact that Barbados is party to the *Convention on Biological Diversity* and the *Ramsar Convention* does not change the [full protection and security] standard under the BIT, although considerations of a host State's international obligations may well be relevant in the application of the standard to particular circumstances."
139   Henckels C, *Proportionality and Deference in Investor-State Arbitration: Balancing Investment Protection and Regulatory Autonomy* (Cambridge University Press 2015) 24.
140   Ibid, 23.
141   Kulick A, *Global Public Interest in International Investment Law* (Cambridge University Press 2012) 168 et seq.
142   Kingsbury B and Schill SW, 'Public Law Concepts to Balance Investors' Rights with State Regulatory Actions in the Public Interest—the Concept of Proportionality', in: Schill S

the principle of proportionality in a rather unclear and sometimes implicit manner.[143] In more recent cases, proportionality has played an increasingly important role and is applied in a more elaborate manner.[144] For EU IIAs, proportionality analysis can serve as an instructive tool for adjudicators when confronted with regulatory disputes concerning public welfare measures pursuing SD. The benefits of proportionality lie within the clarity and structure of the balancing exercise.

At the same time, vesting arbitrators the powers of a full proportionality balancing between public and private interests raises concerns of legitimacy, in particular concerning the intrusiveness of the review of the public decision.[145] Indeed, the three prongs of proportionality (suitability, necessity and proportionality *stricto sensu*) constitute an ascending series in terms of the intrusiveness of the review of a public decision.[146] In particular, "suitability" and "necessity" are different from "proportionality *stricto sensu*" because the two former take as given the objectives that the public authority is pursuing, such as environmental protection, including for instance the specific levels of protection.[147] When it comes to the third step, the proportionality analysis in the strict sense, adjudicators intrude into the very choices of the public measure, as they balance between the costs and benefits of the decisions taken by the public authorities by questioning whether the adverse economic impact, for foreign investors, is disproportionate vis-à-vis the environmental benefits.

SD, as defined under EU IIAs, requires the integration of economic growth, environmental protection and social development; it does not prioritise one aspect over the other. With respect to the exercise of proportionality *stricto sensu* EU IIAs do not provide for any guidance in terms of how cost-benefits should be assessed. At the same time, SD as one of the key objectives of EU IIAs arguably warrants against adjudicators intruding too much on host State's

---

(ed), *International Investment Law and Comparative Public Law* (Oxford University Press 2010) 89–102.

143 Eg *Técnicas Medioambientales Tecmed SA v United Mexican States*, ICSID Case No ARB (AF)/00/02, Award, 29 May 2003, para. 122; *LG&E Capital v Argentina*, ICSID Case No ARB/02/1, Decision on Liability, 3 Oct 2006, para 195.

144 Henckels, above note 139, 194.

145 Alvarez JE, ' "Beware: Boundary Crossings"—A Critical Appraisal of Public Law Approaches to International Investment Law' (2016) 17 The Journal of World Investment & Trade 171. See also Kurtz, above note 60, 202.

146 Ortino F, 'Investment Treaties, Sustainable Development and Reasonableness Review: A Case Against Strict Proportionality Balancing' (2017) 30 Leiden Journal of International Law 71, 88.

147 Ibid.

regulatory autonomy and on their ability to make often difficult policy determinations. The actual outcome of regulatory SD measures will depend on the relevance given by the domestic decision-maker to the various economic, social or environmental needs. This argumentation converges to some extent with the findings of the CJEU in Opinion 1/17.[148] The Court clearly stated that ICS tribunals have "no jurisdiction to call into question the choices democratically made within a Party relating to, inter alia, the level of protection" of SD matters.[149] The statement of the Court means that, at least under EU law, the proportionality analysis (*stricto sensu*) is unconstitutional as it violates the autonomy of the EU legal order. Therefore, future adjudicators under EU IIAS should only very cautiously undertake the third step of the proportionality (*stricto sensu*) analysis. Instead, adjudicators should pay due deference as to the underlying values and interest, or in other words to the choices made by public authorities.[150]

7.4.3 *Standard of Review and Deference*

Lastly, the standard of review and deference shall be discussed in the context of SD integration in EU IIAS. Both are important elements in investment disputes relating to regulatory measures of host States adopted in light of SD.[151] The standard of review refers to the degree of scrutiny that an adjudicator adopts when it reviews a decision or measure of a primary decision-maker. When reviewing host State measures, investment tribunals can adopt different standards of review. At the one extreme, one would find a tribunal that shows total reliance on the decision of the host State; and on the other extreme; one would find a tribunal that looks at the legal and factual issues *de novo*.[152] This being said, the standard of review can be

---

148 Section 4.5.
149 ECJ, Opinion 1/17 *EU-Canada CET Agreement,* EU:C:2019:341, para 160.
150 There is, however, at least one exception to this finding, which is that the treaty standard itself mandates a (full) proportionality analysis. In the case of indirect expropriation, EU IIAs set out the type of review. See eg CETA, Annex 8-A(3): "For greater certainty, except in rare circumstances when the impact of a measure or series of measures is so severe in light of its purpose that it appears manifestly excessive, non-discriminatory measure of a Party that are designed and applied to protect legitimate public welfare objectives, such as health, safety and the environment do not constitute an indirect expropriation."
151 Henckels C, 'Balancing Investment Protection and Sustainable Development in Investor-State Arbitration: The Role of Deference' in: Bjorklund A (ed), *Yearbook of International Investment Law and Policy 2012–2013* (Oxford University Press 2014) 305.
152 Schill SW and Djanic V, 'International Investment Law and Community Interests', Society of International Economic Law (SIEL), Working Paper No 2016/01, 19.

very deferential or very strict. The standard of review refers to the intensity with which the method of review, for instance, the proportionality analysis is applied. Adjudicators in investor-State disputes are regularly confronted with the question of the appropriate standards of review.[153] However, IIAs do not, in general, provide for further guidance to tribunals specifying the applicable standard of review. EU IIAs are no exception in this respect, also omitting any guidance.

There are "legitimacy" reasons as well as practical reasons for why a given tribunal does or does not adopt a deferential approach. Firstly, a State has a regulatory autonomy and its decision-making is in principle, proximate to its society and is embedded in a specific national context. Public authorities (of a State or of the EU) are thus better situated to assess the specific societal needs. Moreover, at least in democracies, regulations benefit from democratic legitimacy. As such the domestic legislator is in a better position to decide certain trade-offs than investment tribunals.[154] Secondly, practical reasons might also require deference. This is mainly because the primary decision-maker has more expertise or institutional competence with respect to the issue at stake than the investment tribunal. For instance, measures to combat climate change often involve important scientific research and expertise, which the tribunal may not possess. As far as EU IIAs are concerned, the objective of SD, the repeated references to the parties' right to regulate as well as the findings of the Court in Opinion 1/17, all favour the understanding that future adjudicators should accord public authorities deference with respect to their public interest decisions.[155] Consequently, the parties' policy space for effectively safeguarding non-economic interests would be respected.[156]

---

153 Henckels, above note 139, 23. See also Henckels C, 'Balancing Investment Protection and the Public Interest: The Role of the Standard of Review and the Importance of Deference in Investor-State Arbitration' (2013) 4 Journal of International Dispute Settlement 197.

154 Schill SW, 'Deference in Investment Treaty Arbitration: Re-Conceptualizing the Standard of Review' (2012) 3 Journal of International Dispute Settlement 577, 600–602.

155 Opinion 1/17, above note 149, para 154. In the same line of reason (in the context of renewable energy subsidies), see *Greentech Energy Systems v The Italian Republic*, SCC Arbitration V 2015/095, Dissenting Opinion of Giorgio Sacerdoti, 5 Dec 2018, para 50 et seq.

156 Schill and Djanic, above note 152, 20. The authors point out that "exercising deference should not result in tribunals surrendering their adjudicative function by yielding uncritically to decisions made at the domestic level".

7.5 Concluding Remarks

There is little doubt that EU IIAs favour SD to be taken into account at the moment of interpreting the IIAs when assessing potential breaches of the investment protection standards. SD has become a key objective of the EU's trade and investment policy and SD likewise is the overarching and transversal objective of its trade and investment agreements. The main points of *expressis verbis* inclusions in the EU IIAs are the preambles and TSD chapters. The latter restate the SD objective and embed the agreement in the global SD agenda. Their existence recalls what has been argued in the previous chapters of this book that the regulation of trade and investment is not an end in itself but a means to promote SD within the EU and globally.[157]

Particular importance is attached to the right to regulate since both, TSD chapters and investment chapters/IPAs emphasis the policy space of contracting parties to enact domestic regulation on key SD policy areas. At the same time, the interrelationship between TSD chapters and provisions on investment is not straightforward. First, there is no linkage between the enforcement mechanisms for the provisions specifically on SD and those related to investment liberalisation and protection. Each set of provisions is subject to a specific dispute settlement mechanism. Second, EU IIAs do generally not regulate how the substantive provisions in the TSD chapter interact with provisions on investment protection and liberalisation. It has, in this respect been argued that TSD chapters and investment chapters/IPAs should be read in a mutually reinforcing manner. The reason is, on the hand that SD itself suggests the mutual supportiveness of its interconnected pillars and, on the other hand, TSD chapters of EU IIAs explicitly refer to the concept of mutual reinforcement. Also called mutual supportiveness, the concept seeks to strengthen coherence, balance and interaction between the two different legal regimes. As a result, TSD chapters and investment chapters/IPAs are to be read harmoniously. The normative cohesion created through TSD chapters between international investment law and international labour law and environmental protection highlights that the EU as a global actor responds to one of the obligations set out in the EU treaties, which is to ensure consistency and policy coherence between the different areas of its external action.

The present chapter was also concerned with how SD integration at the moment of treaty interpretation and application may unfold more concretely. It has been shown that interpretation of EU IIAs pursuant to SD is possible

---

157 See Section 4.3.

based on different interpretative techniques, such as object and purpose interpretation, evolutionary interpretation and contextual interpretation. Especially, the contextual interpretation of investment chapters of comprehensive FTAs has become a recurrent phenomenon in arbitral cases. The rules on investment are no longer isolated but interact and relate to a whole treaty framework. TSD chapters have thus a considerable impact on the interpretation of substantive investment protection standards.

Finally, specific methods that structure the balancing of competing interests have been looked at. An SD-inherent method relates to the principle of integration. As has been argued throughout the present book, integration is a key means to achieve SD through law-making. By the same token, integration as an interpretative method requires that, in the exercise of the adjudicator's discretion, balancing and weighing between economic and non-economic interest takes place and the idea of achieving mutually supportive solutions should be taken seriously. The mutual supportiveness is, moreover linked to an interpretation of systemic integration. A number of SD instruments (binding treaties or soft law) can in this way be referred to when applying investment protection standards under EU IIAs. A next and basic method to balance competing interests is the proportionality analysis. It provides a method for adjudicators who are confronted with cases where State measures regulating SD objectives interfere with foreign investment activities. At the same time, the proportionality analysis should not be applied too stringently because, in that case, investment tribunals would intrude too much on host States' regulatory autonomy by determining sensitive domestic policy choices. Rather, deference should be paid. As far as EU IIAs are concerned, the objective of SD, the repeated references to the parties' right to regulate as well as the findings of the Court in Opinion 1/17, all favour the understanding that future adjudicators should accord public authorities deference with respect to their public interest decisions.

Given all these elements, it seems that through its textual inclusion, SD is increasingly challenging perceptions on the right balance between investors' interests and those of States to regulate in the public interests. Certainly, the extent to which SD pushes for a reconsideration of the weight one attributes to the interests at stake will remain a topic of the upcoming years. With the strengthened global SD agenda, States' public interests, including the achievement of the SDGs, have gained weight when counterbalanced with private investor rights.

CHAPTER 8

Conclusion

International investment law is in the process of renewal. While some might call it transformation, others would rather speak of reform or adjustment. Certainly, however, international investment law has to find answers to the social and environmental challenges of the 21st century. The concept of SD serves as an expression of most of these challenges to international investment law-making and offers, at the same time, new and innovative solutions to the more systemic problems of the IIA regime. A majority of countries use the concept as a guiding principle to moving away from traditional postcolonial investment treaty models of the late 1950s. Newer approaches are emerging that are more holistic and that rebalance rights and obligations of different stakeholders. At the same time, risks exist that historical patterns are reproduced in response to these attempts neutralising the effect of SD-guided developments and maintaining the one-sided focus on investor protection.

The present book was an attempt to capture the many dynamics of international investment governance that are provoked by the new paradigm of SD. It focused on a new yet critical actor, the EU. The intention of the analysis was not to provide a further account of how international investment law ought to look like in order to better ensure SD outcomes in host countries and globally. Such normative debates are fundamental, but their claims only have as much effect as the power structure of a governance system allows them to have. Therefore, SD integration in international investment law in the 21st century depends on the visions that global actors have on how to balance investor interests, market access and competitiveness with broader societal needs and ecological imperatives, as well as their vision of the role of the regulatory State in ensuring sustainable investment activities. The case of the EU shows to a particular extent the dichotomy that can exist between idealistic aspirations based on value-driven policy and the real-life economic constraints that the EU is facing. With a shrinking EU market, access to foreign markets is vital for European companies and ultimately to sustain economic growth within the EU. With the aim to provide governance answers, this book examined what SD requires from the EU and other States and international actors. It depicted the EU's constitutional framework that shapes its investment law-making and revealed the EU institutions' SD strategies. Its results show where approaches of the EU investment law-making are innovative and clearly aligned with the

SD paradigm, where the EU adhered to mainstream approaches and where SD integration has so far been ignored.

8.1   On the EU as a Global Actor

The CCP is the EU's powerhouse that enables it to be a key actor in international trade and investment. The attribution of exclusive competence over FDI has allowed the EU to develop its own investment law- and policy-making since the entry into force of the Lisbon Treaty. In particular, post-Lisbon, the EU was able to conclude IIAs that cover the entire spectrum of international investment regulation. The EU treaties mandate the EU institutions to pursue a number of general objectives, including SD when exercising the conferred competences over foreign investment. Moreover, according to its statements, the EU seeks to use its investment law-making to advance non-economic objectives. With the "Trade for all" strategy, the Commission seeks to contribute to Agenda 2030 and the related SDGs.[1] For the Commission promoting SD goes hand in hand with ensuring that the EU's trade and investment policy is consistent with broader European values stating that EU treaties "demand that the EU promote its values, including the development of poorer countries, high social and environmental standards, and respect for human rights, around the world".[2] The strong stance of the Commission on SD integration into CCP measures did not change the Commission's key concern, which is the competitiveness of European companies as being vital for the EU economy. The challenging articulation between the economic growth model and the SD objectives is the most important source of policy contradiction that can be identified in the law-making of the EU in concrete trade and investment agreements. The present book has revealed that SD integration in EU investment law-making has had mixed outcomes. Compared, in particular, to the approaches of developing countries, SD integration of EU IIAs does not go as far as the IIAs and model agreements of the former. At the same time, the EU contributes to building a new type of IIA and adds potential tools to ensure that SD can operationalise within international investment law. A characteristic of EU IIAs is that SD integration is mostly concerned with building inter-relationships between international economic law, on the one hand, and international social and environmental standards, on the other. Moreover, of

---

1 European Commission Communication, 'Trade for all Towards a more responsible trade and investment policy', COM (2015) 497 final.
2 Ibid, 15.

central interest for the EU is to preserve policy space to adopt public welfare measures at the domestic level. The following briefly revisits the key aspects.

EU IIAs include specific chapters on SD. These chapters contain several SD relevant elements. Their main purpose is to impact the parties' conduct regarding environmental and labour protection standards. In this sense, they provide incentives for the contracting parties to improve their national environmental and social regulations applicable to investment activities within their territory, and to foster international cooperation on these issues. The three elements of commitments under TSD chapters in EU IIAs can also be found in recent IIAs of other global actors. Namely, the reaffirmation of international environmental and social standards, non-lowing of standards clauses and commitments on fostering cooperation on the SD-investment nexus can be found in IIAs of Canada, the United States, Asian IIAs as well as African IIAs and model treaties. For the non-lowering clauses, treaty practice can vary concerning the degree of the bindingness of the provisions. A number of international actors prefer best-effort formulations stating that the parties recognise that the lowering of standards is inappropriate. Current US treaty practice drafts these provisions in a binding way. African instruments, likewise, mainly contain binding non-lowering clauses.

Debates are ongoing on how to ensure compliance with the commitments under TSD chapters and different actors are proposing different solutions. Under EU IIAs, the enforcement of the TSD chapter is essentially cooperative and non-confrontational. If a dispute between the parties occurs relating to the provisions contained in the TSD chapter, the parties are first held to seek a mutually satisfactory resolution of the matter through consultations. If consultations continue to remain fruitless, any party may request that a Panel of Experts be convened. At the end of the process, a panel renders a final report, whose implementation is monitored but failures of non-implementation are not sanctioned. US IIAs and some African IIAs both allow the enforcement of these provisions through State-State arbitration. However, the experiences of the US have shown the practical (and political) difficulties of the sanction-based model. This being said, the EU should continue to endeavour the legal possibilities for an effective enforcement mechanism.

EU IIAs provide for the promotion of voluntary CSR practices but do not include any further concrete obligations. Direct investor obligations under IIAs are highly contentious, and the EU, like other capital-exporting countries, does not provide for any direct investor obligations. In contrast, hereto are the IIA practices of several developing countries, which have chosen to use IIAs for setting out binding investor obligations. The latter group of countries seek to rebalance investment protection standards with obligations for investors. In

CONCLUSION   389

more general terms, international investment governance is currently characterised by increasing investors' accountability and soft law instruments, such as the OECD Guidelines. EU IIAs deal with the issue of investor accountability and responsibility in a very succinct manner. Whilst the use of direct investor obligation is one aspect, EU IIAs also do not provide more explicit commitments addressed to the contracting parties to ensure CSR of their companies domestically.

A general characteristic of the TSD chapters in EU IIAs is the emphasis on incentivising its partners to adopt measures, either national or international, to improve the regulation of foreign investment in light of SD. The aim is not to regulate in detail on how this should be achieved. EU IIAs provide certain bottom lines and invite partner countries to engage in legislative action for the benefit of SD or to gather consensus to foster existing international mechanisms jointly with the contracting parties.

As regards the findings on SD integration in the realm of investment protection, it became apparent that the central concern of the EU is the need to safeguard regulatory space under its IIAs. In this sense, all post-Lisbon EU IIAs contain a specific provision that reaffirms the contracting parties' right to regulate. Furthermore, the EU sought to redraft a number of traditional investment protection standards. Most noteworthy in this respect is the FET standard to which the EU has a specific approach that sets out an exhaustive list of the breaches that constitute a violation of the standard. Other countries, such as the United States and India, also opt for establishing lists, but the EU approach is more comprehensive. Certain countries and regions, such as Africa and Brazil, prefer to ban the standard all together form their IIAs. The EU has also sought to better define the concept of indirect expropriation and followed hereto North American approaches. To ensure more regulatory flexibility for domestic SD measures, EU IIAs include general exceptions, which is a novel yet increasing practice in international investment governance. Indeed, concerning the investment protection standards, the EU was keen to develop new approaches that seek to better safeguard the regulatory space for the EU and its partner countries, which is ultimately highly important for national measures that pursue SD objectives. Other international actors adopted similar approaches in this respect. The EU is thus fully participating in the endeavour to render the protection standards clearer and better predictable.

In contrast hereto are the EU's approaches to investment liberalisation. Little has been done to integrate SD integration in the provisions on investment liberalisation. The EU approach is characterised by prohibitions of performance requirements and other domestic conditions that might limit the market access of European companies. International investment governance starts to be fragmented in this respect. More and more developing countries are reluctant to provide access and establishment rights to their markets as is evidenced by their IIA practice. Some of their recent instruments explicitly exclude the granting of pre-establishment rights and, contrary to EU IIAS, reaffirms the host States' rights to enact measures that they consider beneficial for their economic development, such as performance requirements. Hence, when it comes to investment liberalisation, the EU does not seem to counterbalance its economic interests in gaining more and more market access for its companies with its partners' development needs. The paradigm of SD does not seem to be fully accommodated within the EU's CCP. Admittedly, this would constitute a real reorientation since traditionally the CCP embraces liberalisation and open global markets in order to achieve economic growth. Nevertheless, both policy coherence and SD integration requirements should guide the EU institutions to reconsider its investment liberalisation approaches in light of SD.

Moreover, the EU has integrated, like other international actors, limitations into the definition of investment. Yet, like other capital-exporting countries and regions, such as the United States, Canada and Japan, the EU has not attempted to link the definition of an investment with the development of the host State. Linking the investment definition with the development of the host State is another highly controversial aspect within international investment governance. The division in this respect between visions of developed and developing countries is becoming more and more consolidated. EU IIAS prescribe that covered investments should be made in accordance with host State laws, which has become a mainstream treaty practice. Otherwise, the investment definition even though it could be a tool to channel investment activities that beneficial for SD, has not been among the provisions for which SD has played a role under EU IIAS.

Through Sustainability Impact Assessments (SIAS), the EU seeks to integrate SD during the negotiation phase of EU IIAS. SIAS assess potential future consequences of the IIAS on social and economic development, human rights and environmental protection for the contracting parties. Whilst the EU has no legal obligation to conduct SIAS, it does so on all its trade and investment agreements. In a global comparison, so far only Canada and the United States have developed similar practices. However, these two countries do not conduct SIAS that are as comprehensive in scope as those of the EU because they are mostly limited to the environmental impacts of trade and investment agreements under negotiation. In other words, EU practice in this respect appears to be innovative, if not standard-setting in international investment governance.

Lastly, SD integration should take place at the level of interpreting EU IIAS. The investment standards, such as FET or the protection against indirect expropriation, as well as the set of general exceptions, have to be interpreted and assessed in the future. These provisions are to be analysed in the light of SD given that the concept runs through the whole treaty framework of EU IIAS. In line with widespread global IIA practice, post-Lisbon EU IIAS contain SD references in their preambles. The existence and content of TSD chapters further allow future adjudicators to engage in contextual interpretation when assessing investment provisions. TSD chapters enhance systemic integration as they combine international investment law with other fields of international law relevant for SD, such as international labour law and international environmental law. Consequently, EU IIAS ensure that their investment provisions are interpreted in the light of SD.

8.2 On the EU's Discretion to Integrate SD

Based on the analysis of post-Lisbon EU IIAS, what conclusion can be drawn for the normative impact of SD as a Union objective and overarching guiding principle of EU investment law-making? Whilst Union objectives are binding and require all EU institutions to pursue them. They are no strict rules which can be either respected or violated. For the EU's investment law-making, it is thus difficult to conclude that the EU did not respect or even violated EU primary law based on the content of its post-Lisbon EU IIAS.[3] These characteristics of Union objectives are upheld by the CJEU, which traditionally declined to invalidate EU measures in the light of Union objectives. On the contrary, the Court emphasises the "scope of manoeuvre" for the EU institutions in conducting their policies and, in particular, when negotiating international economic agreements. As a result, the EU institutions have an obligation to integrate SD into their post-Lisbon investment law-making, but the extent of integration is subject to their discretion.

The existence of discretion does not mean its exercise would be purely political, going beyond the scope of legal arguments and law. Legal systems, law-making and law application, have to "accept" discretion as part of the system when it is impossible to consider before a particular situation arises what sacrifice or compromise of interests or values should be made.[4] The

---

3   TEU, Arts 3(5) and 21, in combination with TFEU, Arts 206–207.
4   Hart HLA, 'Direction' [written in 1956] (2013) Harvard Law Review 127, 663.

fact that a legal system, here the EU constitutional order, provides authorities with discretion means that the attributed "scope of manoeuvre" must be exercised against a legal framework, including a number of principles that operate as benchmarks. Under EU law, Union objectives should, first of all, be conceived as "optimisation requirements" in the sense that they require their realisation "to the greatest extent possible given the legal and factual possibilities".[5]

The normative SD framework seeks to guide decision-makers to fix certain misalignments between the scope and impact of economic forces and actors and the integration of environmental and social protection. The EU institutions decide how balancing the three SD pillars is most appropriately done for their society. The discretion must, however, be exerted against the normative SD framework. The analysis of this book tried to sketch out this framework under international law as well as under EU law, as well as its concretisation in international investment law and the EU's CCP.

SD integration not only forms part of the SD normative framework but has become the key method and main means of achieving SD within the international law context and for EU policy and law-making. From the start of the global SD agenda, the principle of integration has been fundamental for the operationalisation of SD. According to Principle 4 of the Rio Declaration "[i]n order to achieve [SD], environmental protection shall constitute an integral part of the development process and cannot be considered in isolation from it". Regarding international investment law the integration of SD is one of the topics most vividly discussed, debated and further developed by stakeholders. The paradigm shifts in international investment law and governance show to what extent SD can translate into concrete treaty drafting. The requirement of (social and environmental) integration, Articles 9 and 11 TFEU, is also firmly embedded within the EU legal order and relevant for all internal and external EU policies, including the CCP. In the words of the Court, "in defining and implementing its policies and activities, the Union shall take into account requirements linked to [...] the guarantee of adequate social protection" and also "environmental protection requirements must be integrated into the definition and implementation of the Union's policies and activities, in particular with a view to promoting [SD]".[6]

---

5 Alexy R, *A Theory of Constitutional Rights* (Oxford University Press 2002) 47. See also, Larik J, 'Good Global Governance through Trade: Constitutional Moorings', in: Wouters J et al (eds), *Global Governance through Trade: EU Policies and Approaches* (Edward Elgar Publishing 2015) 59.
6 ECJ, Opinion 2/15, *Free Trade Agreement with Singapore*, EU:C:2017:376, para 146.

A further benchmark of how the EU institution should exercise discretion to operationalise SD with its investment law-making is the principle of coherence. Policy coherence is a well-established requirement under EU law but it also finds expression in the international SD framework. Coherence is conceptually connected to mutual supportiveness, reconciliation and thus to the SD balance. This means that substantial synergies between investment, on the one hand, and social and environmental protection, on the other, should be enhanced through law-making. This further means that decision-makers are to strive for coherence between the different EU policies. For the CCP this can signify that an IIA should not run counter the object and purpose of an international agreement that has been concluded under the EU's development cooperation. Concretely this would mean that if the EU has concluded a development cooperation agreement with developing country with the objective of poverty reduction and human rights promotion, an IIA with the same country should likewise take into account the development needs of that partner country. Lastly, policy coherence demands from decision-makers to integrate SD coherently in all aspects of international investment law. As an example of incoherence in this respect, one can mention again the integration of SD within the investment protection under EU IIAs on the one hand, and the absence thereof within investment liberalisation, on the other hand.

Beyond these two key principles, the SD normative framework is composed of a number of substantive legal principles, under both international and EU law. The list of principles is not a mere set of policy aspirations but concrete, mostly binding legal principles. These are the key principles of international and EU environmental law, international and EU human and social rights, and equity principles, such as solidarity, social inclusion, and poverty reduction. The EU institutions should, when integrating SD, be guided by these principles connected to SD.

In sum, exercising its discretion in light of the legal framework on SD, enshrined in the EU treaties and international law, is, for the EU, thus not about violating precise rules but about ensuring that its investment law-making lives up to the expectations and aspirations created and developed under international and EU law. Finally, discretion should be understood as an enabling tool. The reason is that SD needs significantly differ from one investment partner county to another and SD needs also change over time. There is, thus, an underlying need for the EU, depending on its partner country and current needs, to adapt and ultimately exercise its discretion differently. The discretion that has been entrusted to the EU institutions should allow further adaptation of EU IIAs according to current and future SD challenges.

8.3 Outlook: IIAs and Other Instruments

The IIAs of the EU and other international actors show, through the adoption of new IIAs, that it is possible to shift away from traditional BITs and that IIAs can be designed and drafted by integrating the rationale of SD. Despite this general trend, the present book's analysis has also revealed that there is still much debate on how to ensure SD integration within IIAs. Different global actors are finding different approaches and legal tools to frame how such integration should look. In particular, capital-importing and capital-exporting countries/regions seem to perceive the appropriateness of IIAs to integrate SD differently. Developing countries seek to use their IIAs to internationalise the environmental and social regulation of investment activities as well as to establish international obligations directly applicable to foreign companies. In contrast, the IIAs of developed countries/regions, such as the EU, focus on softer approaches to ensuring that investment is regulated in an SD-friendly manner. Their IIAs contain provisions that do not impose direct obligations, but rather incentivise States party to the IIA to modify their national regulation. In other words, for the IIAs of the latter, national law has to play the central role in ensuring sustainable investment activity. In essence, both developing and developed countries/regions, lastly, seek the same outcome, which is to better ensure that foreign investment is environmentally friendly and that real spill-over effects for social and economic development take place.

While the global discourse and scholarly debate on SD have been mostly focussed on the connection between IIAs and regulatory space for legitimate public interest measures pursuing SD, the real challenge of the upcoming years is to shape how IIAs can and should operate as a tool to ensure long-term sustainable investments and not least to harness investment for the SDGs. The new approaches of the EU can, in this respect, serve as a starting point to initiating and increasing cooperation on the SD-investment nexus. At the same time, IIAs as a legal instrument for this endeavour must be further critically assessed. The focus should not be overly on IIAs but international investment regulation needs to be considered and designed within a broader regulatory framework. This ultimately implies the need to look at other legal instruments, next to IIAs, stemming from national and international law. Doing so is not least relevant for the EU and its action and policies related to the regulation of foreign investment. Four sets of legal regimes and instruments are central for the regulation of international investment and which are to play an increased role in ensuring sustainable investments.

Firstly and most obviously, national law plays a fundamental role in setting out the concrete mechanisms and SD obligations under which an investment activity has to operate. In particular, for sectors that have a substantial impact on the ecological and social environment, such as the extractive industry, large-scale infrastructure projects or the provision of public services (*e.g.* water distribution, sewage or public transportation), national law must ensure that social and environmental standards are respected. In this respect, the rule of law and an administration which is functioning well are prerequisites. At the national level also, national investment policies and strategies should fully integrate SD and be geared towards the realisation of the SDGs. Screening mechanisms can also play a role in this respect given that national concerns with regard to the liberalisation of critical infrastructure can be taken care of by such mechanisms. It is interesting to note that the EU has taken the initiative in establishing an EU-wide screening mechanism. The proposed mechanism is, so far, only concerned with those investments that may affect "security or public order" in the EU.[7] Nonetheless, national screening mechanisms can serve as a tool for States to ensure that foreign investment activities contribute to SD.

Second, the role of investment contracts for the achievement of sustainable investment has to be increased. The reason is that investment contracts are crucial for defining the terms of an investment project. Hence, they are the direct instrument by which to include obligations on foreign companies and their responsibilities in terms of SD objectives, such as poverty reduction, education as well as environmental protection. For the EU, picking up on the issue of investment contracts could imply that the EU starts initiatives on non-binding guidelines for responsible investment contracts seeking to achieve the commitment of European companies to include such guidelines in future investment contracts. One of the central issues that these guidelines should entail is the transparency of investment contracts. The reason is that these contracts affect public interests. Appropriate disclosure of the contracts would allow the investor and the State to communicate transparently with those affected.[8] Transparency of the contract's terms is vital as it allows public involvement. Transparency should, in particular, lead civil society, parliaments and the media to scrutinise these contracts by also requiring their approval for investment projects that have important social and environmental impacts.

Third, next to international investment law and IIAs, other regimes of international law, such as international environmental law and international labour

---

7 See Sections 2.4.1.3 and 6.3.1.
8 Cotula L, *Investment Contracts and Sustainable Development: How to Make Contracts for Fairer and More Sustainable Natural Resource Investments* (International Institute for Environment and Development 2010) 85 et seq.

law, should increase mechanisms to harness investments for the SDGs. The climate change regime is an illustrative example in this regard. Specifically, it was the Kyoto Protocol, which sought, among other objectives, to direct investment towards low-carbon energy technologies and other forms of emission reduction. However, the Kyoto Protocol is no longer applicable, and its amendment has never entered into force. The Paris Agreement on Climate Change is silent on such linkages or on any economic tool to accentuate the transition to climate-friendly economies. Innovation should thus also come from international climate change law to change the patterns of investment activities. The same logic applies for other treaty regimes of international environmental law, such as the protection of biological diversity,[9] or the international regulation of freshwater. Moreover, the extent to which international agreements have beneficial SD impacts on the regulation of investment can be highlighted by conventions, such as the United Nations Convention against Corruption or agreements, such as the Espoo Convention on Environmental Impact Assessments in a transboundary context, as well as the Aarhus Convention dealing with public participation and access of justice in environmental matters. However, these treaty regimes should be strengthened. As the EU confirms in its IIAs, the increased cooperation in environmental and social matters at the international level is an endeavour that should be further pursued in the future to better ensure sustainable investment activities.[10]

Finally, the role of soft law for SD-friendly international investment regulation needs to be stressed. Regulatory linkages between SD and investment governance raise many controversial issues, as discussed throughout the present book. For instance, it seems, in the near term, unlikely that international consensus will be found on how to foster the responsibility and accountability of multinational companies under international law. One way to convince all stakeholders, namely States and multinational companies, to agree to specific standards is by using soft law instruments. The numerous guidelines dealing with corporate social responsibility highlight the extent to which recourse is being made to soft law instruments. Indeed, whenever it is difficult to gather global consensus on a given issue, soft law becomes highly relevant in order to find a maximum of consensus at the international level and can lead in terms

---

9   See Rukundo O and Carbrera J, 'Investment Promotion and the Protection in the UNCBD: An Emerging Access and Benefit Sharing Regime' in: Cordonier Segger M-C, Gehring MW and Newcombe AP (eds), *Sustainable Development in World Investment Law* (Kluwer Law International 2011) 722–743.
10 See Section 5.1.2.

of setting out a roadmap for collective action.[11] Soft law has, with respect to the achievement of SD, an important facilitating function, which is not to constrain States but to enable them to take action given that most aspects of SD can ultimately only be achieved through collective action. Soft law instruments, as a more informal and more flexible way of producing normative effects in the international system and should thus continue to play an important role in international investment governance on SD.

11   Abi-Saab G, 'Eloge du « droit assourdi ». Quelques reflexions sur le role de la *soft law* en droit international contemporain', in: *Nouveaux itinéraires en droit. Hommage à François Rigaux* (Bruylant 1993) 67.

Bibliography

Abi-Saab G, 'Eloge du « droit assourdi ». Quelques réflexions sur le rôle de la *soft law* en droit international contemporain', in: *Nouveaux itinéraires en droit. Hommage à François Rigaux* (Bruylant 1993).

Alexy R, *A Theory of Constitutional Rights* (Oxford University Press 2002).

Alf L, Assmann C, Bauer M, Weinkopf J, 'Towards a Transatlantic Dialog on Trade and the Environment: A Comparison of Approaches to Environmental Impact Assessments of Trade Agreements in the US and EU. School of Advanced International Studies, Henry Luce Foundation, 2008 EcoLogic.

Alfaro L, 'Gains from Foreign Direct Investment: Macro and Micro Approaches World Bank's ABCDE Conference' (2016) The World Bank Economic Review.

Alschner W and Tuerk E, 'The Role of International Investment Agreements in Fostering Sustainable Development', in: Baetens F (ed), *Investment Law within International Law: Integrationist Perspectives* (Cambridge University Press 2013) 217.

Alvarez JE, *The Public International Law Regime Governing International Investment* (AP All-Pocket 2011).

Alvarez JE, '"Beware: Boundary Crossings"—A Critical Appraisal of Public Law Approaches to International Investment Law' (2016) 17 The Journal of World Investment & Trade 171.

Amato G, Baquero Cruz J and European University Institute (eds), *Genèse et destinée de la Constitution Européenne: commentaire du Traité établissant une Constitution pour l'Europe à la lumière des travaux préparatoires et perspectives d'avenir = Genesis and Destiny of the European Constitution* (Bruylant 2007).

Amselek P, *Méthode Phénoménologique et Théorie Du Droit* (LGDJ 1964).

Anderson KM, *Social Policy in the European Union* (Palgrave Macmillan 2015).

Ankersmit L, 'Opinion 2/15: Adding Come Spice to the Trade & Environment Debate' European Law Blog, June 2017.

Aseeva A, '(Un)Sustainable Development(s) in International Economic Law: A Quest for Sustainability' (2018) 10 Sustainability 4022.

Asteriti A, 'Article 21 TEU and the EU's Common Commercial Policy: A Test of Coherence' in: Bungenberg M et al (eds), *European Yearbook of International Economic Law 2017*, vol 8 (Springer International Publishing 2017) 111.

Aust A, *Modern Treaty Law and Practice* (Third edition, Cambridge University Press 2013).

Baars et al, 'The Role of Law in Global Value Chains: A Research Manifesto' (2016) 4 London Review of International Law 57.

Baetens F (ed), *Investment Law within International Law: Integrationist Perspectives* (Cambridge University Press 2013).

Baetens F (ed), 'The Kyoto Protocol in Investor-State Arbitration: Reconciling Climate Change and Investment Protection Objectives', in: Cordonier Segger M-C, Gehring MW and Newcombe AP (eds), *Sustainable Development in World Investment Law* (Kluwer Law International 2011) 681.

Barnard C and Peers S, *European Union Law* (Second edition, Oxford University Press 2017).

Barnard C and Scott J (eds), *The Law of the Single European Market: Unpacking the Premises* (Hart Pub 2002).

Barral V, 'Sustainable Development in International Law: Nature and Operation of an Evolutive Legal Norm' (2012) 23 European Journal of International Law 377.

Barral V, *Le développement durable en droit international: essai sur les incidences juridiques d'une norme évolutive* (Bruylant 2016).

Barral V and Dupuy P-M, 'Principle 4: Sustainable Development through Integration', in: Viñuales JE (ed), *The Rio Declaration on Environment and Development: A Commentary* (Oxford University Press 2015) 157.

Barral V and Dupuy P-M, 'Sustainable Development and Integration' in: Aguila Y and Viñuales JE (eds), *A Global Pact for the Environment—Legal Foundations*, (C-EENRG Report 2019-1) 44.

Barrett S, *Environment and Statecraft: The Strategy of Environmental Treaty-Making* (Oxford University Press 2005).

Bartels L, 'Article XX of GATT and the Problem of Extraterritorial Jurisdiction The Case of Trade Measures for the Protection of Human Rights' (2002) Journal of World Trade 353.

Bartels L, 'The Trade and Development Policy of the European Union' (2007) 18 European Journal of International Law 715.

Bartels L, 'Human Rights and Sustainable Development Obligations in EU Free Trade Agreements' (2013) 40 Legal Issues of Economic Integration 297.

Bartels L, *The European Parliament's Role in Relation to Human Rights in Trade and Investment Agreements* (EP Publications Office 2014).

Basedow R, 'A Legal History of the EU's International Investment Policy' (2016) 17 The Journal of World Investment & Trade 743.

Baumgartner J, *Treaty Shopping in International Investment Law* (Oxford University Press 2016).

Beaucillon C, 'Opinion 2/15: Sustainable is the New Trade. Rethinking Coherence for the New Common Commercial Policy' (European Papers (www.europeanpapers.eu) 2017).

Behn D and Langford M, 'Trumping the Environment? An Empirical Perspective on the Legitimacy of Investment Treaty Arbitration' [2017] The Journal of World Investment & Trade 14.

Berge T and Alschner W, 'Reforming Investment Treaties: Does Treaty Design Matter?', IISD Investment Treaty News, Oct 2018.

Bernasconi-Osterwalder N, 'Transparency and Amicus Curiae in ICSID Arbitrations', in: Cordonier Segger M-C, Gehring MW and N ewcombe AP (eds), *Sustainable Development in World Investment Law* (Kluwer Law International 2011) 189.

Bernasconi-Osterwalder N and Malik M, 'Registration and Approval Requirements in Investment Treaties' IISD Best Practice Series, Dec 2012.

Bernasconi-Osterwalder N and Brauch MD, 'Redesigning the Energy Charter Treaty to Advance the Low-Carbon Transition' TDM 1 (2019).

Bernasconi-Osterwalder N, Cosbey A, Johnson L and Vis-Dunbar D, *Investment Treaties and Why They Matter to Sustainable Development: Questions and Answers* (IISD 2012).

Besson S and d'Aspremont J (eds), *The Oxford Handbook on the Sources of International Law* (Oxford University Press 2017).

Bhumika M, 'International Investment Agreements and Industrialization: Realizing the Right to Development and the Sustainable Development Goals', Human Rights Council [2018] A/HRC/WG.2/19/CRP.5.

Biaggini G, Diggelmann O and Kaufmann C (eds), *Polis Und Kosmopolis: Festschrift Für Daniel Thürer* (Dike; Nomos 2015).

Binder C et al, *International Investment Law for the 21st Century* (Oxford University Press 2009).

Biondi A, Eeckhout P and Ripley S (eds), *EU Law after Lisbon* (Oxford University Press 2012).

Bischoff JA, 'Just a Little Bit of "Mixity"? The EU's Role in the Field of International Investment Protection Law' (2011) Common Market Law Review 1527.

Bischoff JA and Wühler M, 'The Notion of Investment' in: Mbengue MM and Schacherer S (eds), *Foreign Investment under the Comprehensive Economic and Trade Agreement (CETA)*, vol 15 (Springer International Publishing 2019) 19.

Bjorklund AK (ed), *Yearbook on International Investment Law and Policy 2012-2013* (Oxford University Press 2014).

Blanke H-J and Mangiameli S, 'Article 21 [The Principles and Objectives of the Union's External Action]' in: Blanke HJ and Mangiameli S (eds), *The Treaty on European Union (TEU)* (Springer 2013) 833.

Blanquet M, *La prise de décision dans le système de l'Union européenne* (Bruylant 2011).

Blobel D, Görlach B and Ingwersen W, 'Investment: The Context Matters', in: Ekins P and Voituriez T (eds), *Trade, Globalization and Sustainability Impact Assessment: A Critical Look at Methods and Outcomes* (Earthscan 2009).

Bodansky D, Brunnée J and Hey E (eds), *The Oxford Handbook of International Environmental Law* (Oxford University Press 2007).

Boisson de Chazournes L, 'Environmental Protection and Investment Arbitration: Yin and Yang?' 10 Anuario Colombiano de Derecho Internacional 385.

Boisson de Chazournes L and Mbengue MM, 'A "Footnote as a Principle". Mutual Supportiveness and Its Relevance in an Era of Fragmentation' in: Seibert-Fohr A et al (eds), *Coexistence, Cooperation and Solidarity (second vol)* (Brill 2011) 1615.

Boisson de Chazournes L and Mbengue MM, 'The Principles of Precaution and Sustainability' in: Cottier T and Nadakavukaren Schefer K (eds), *Elgar Encyclopedia of International Economic Law* (Edward Elgar Publishing 2017) 612.

Bonnitcha J, *Substantive Protection under Investment Treaties: A Legal and Economic Analysis* (Cambridge University Press 2014).

Bonnitcha J, 'Investment Wars: Contestation and Confusion in Debate About Investment Liberalization' (2019) 22 Journal of International Economic Law 629.

Bonnitcha J, Poulsen LNS and Waibel M, *The Political Economy of the Investment Treaty Regime* (Oxford University Press 2017).

Bosselmann K, *The Principle of Sustainability: Transforming Law and Governance* (Second edition, Routledge 2016).

Bosse-Platière I, *L'article 3 du Traité UE: recherche sur une exigence de cohérence de l'action extérieure de l'Union européenne* (Bruylant 2009).

Boute A, 'The Potential Contribution of International Investment Protection Law to Combat Climate Change' (2009) 27 Journal of Energy & Natural Resources Law 333.

Boyle AE and Freestone D (eds), *International Law and Sustainable Development: Past Achievements and Future Challenges* (Oxford University Press 1999).

Bronckers M and Gruni G, 'Taking the Enforcement of Labour Standards in the EU's Free Trade Agreements Seriously' [2019] Common Market Law Review 1591.

Brown C, 'Bringing Sustainable Development Issues before Investment Treaty Tribunals' in: Cordonier Segger M-C, Gehring MW and Newcombe AP (eds), *Sustainable Development in World Investment Law* (Kluwer Law International 2011) 171.

Brown C and Miles K (eds), *Evolution in Investment Treaty Law and Arbitration* (Cambridge University Press 2011).

Brown GW, McLean I and McMillan A (eds), *The Concise Oxford Dictionary of Politics and International Relations* (Fourth edition, Oxford University Press 2018).

Brown Weiss E, 'Climate Change, Intergenerational Equity, and International Law' The Vermont Journal of International Law (2008) 615.

Bugge HC, Voigt C and Norges F (eds), *Sustainable Development in International and National Law: What Did the Brundtland Report Do to Legal Thinking and Legal Development, and Where Can We Go from Here?* (Europa Law Publishing 2008).

Bungenberg M, 'The Division of Competences Between the EU and Its Member States in the Area of Investment Politics' in: Bungenberg M, Griebel J and Hindelang S (eds), *International Investment Law and EU Law* (Springer 2011).

Bungenberg M et al, (eds), *International Investment Law—A Handbook* (CH BECK; Hart; Nomos 2015).

Bungenberg M and Herrmann C (eds), *Common Commercial Policy after Lisbon* (Springer 2013).

Bungenberg M and Reinisch A, *From Bilateral Arbitral Tribunals and Investment Courts to a Multilateral Investment Court* (Springer 2018).

Bungenberg M, Reinisch A and Tietje C (eds), *EU and Investment Agreements: Open Questions and Remaining Challenges* (Nomos; Dike 2013).

Bürgi Bonanomi E, *Sustainable Development in International Law Making and Trade: International Food Governance and Trade in Agriculture* (Edward Elgar Publishing 2015).

Burgstaller M, 'European Law and Investment Treaties' (2009) Journal of International Arbitration 181.

Calamita NJ, 'The Making of Europe's International Investment Policy: Uncertain First Steps' (2012) Legal Issues of Economic Integration 301.

Calamita NJ (ed), *Current Issues in Investment Treaty Law. Volume IV: The Future of ICSID and the Place of Investment Treaties in International Law* (British Institute of International and Comparative Law 2013).

Calliess C, 'Kollektive Ziele und Prinzipien im Verfassungsrecht der EU— Bestandsaufnahme, Wirkungen und Perspektiven', in: Hiebaum C, Koller P and Internationale Vereinigung für Rechts- und Sozialphilosophie (eds), *Politische Ziele und juristische Argumentation: Symposium der Internationalen Vereinigung für Rechts- und Sozialphilosophie, 11. bis 12. Oktober 2002 in Graz* (Steiner 2003) 85.

Calliess C, Blanke H-J and Kluth W (eds), *EUV/AEUV: das Verfassungsrecht der Europäischen Union mit Europäischer Grundrechtecharta; Kommentar* (4. Aufl, BECK 2011).

Campbell AIL, 'The Limits of the Powers of International Organisations' (1983) 32 International and Comparative Law Quarterly 523.

Cannizzaro E (ed), *The Law of Treaties beyond the Vienna Convention* (Oxford University Press 2011).

Carlevaris A, 'The Conformity of Investments with the Law of the Host State and the Jurisdiction of International Tribunals' [2008] The Journal of World Investment & Trade 35.

Cazala J, 'La réaffirmation de l'Etat en matière de définition des investissements et investisseurs protégés', in: El Ghadban T, Mazuy C-M and Senegacnik A (eds), *La protection des investissements étrangers: vers une réaffirmation de l'État ? = The protection of foreign investments : a reaffirmation of the State ? : actes du colloque du 2 juin 2017* (2018) 37.

Ceyssens J, 'Towards a Common Foreign Investment Policy?—Foreign Investment in the European Constitution' (2005) 32 Legal Issues of Economic Integration 259.

Chi M, *Integrating Sustainable Development in International Investment Law: Normative Incompatibility, System Integration and Governance Implications* (Routledge 2018).

Claussen K, 'Reimagining Trade-Plus Compliance: The Labor Story' (2020) 23 Journal of International Economic Law 25.

Colen L and Guariso A, 'What Type of Foreign Investment Is Attracted by Bilateral Investment Treaties?' LICOS—Discussion Paper Series 346/2014.

Colen L, Maertens M and Swinnen J, 'Foreign Direct Investment as an Engine for Economic Growth and Human Development' in: De Schutter O, Swinnen JFM and Wouters J (eds), *Foreign Direct Investment and Human Development: The Law and Economics of International Investment Agreements* (Routledge 2013) 70.

Collins D, *Performance Requirements and Investment Incentives under International Economic Law* (Edward Elgar Publishing 2015).

Collins L, 'Environmental Rights for the Future? Intergenerational Equity in the EU' (2007) 16 Review of European Community & International Environmental Law 321.

Columbia Center on Sustainable Investment, 'Costs and Benefits of Investment Treaties—Practical Considerations for States' (2018) Policy Paper, available at <http://ccsi.columbia.edu/files/2018/04/Cost-and-Benefits-of-Investment-Treaties-Practical-Considerations-for-States-ENG-mr.pdf>.

Commission indépendante, 'Rapport au Premier Ministre—L'impact de l'Accord Economique et Commercial Global entre l'Union européenne et le Canada (AECG/CETA) sur l'environnement, le climat et la santé', available at <https://www.gouvernement.fr/sites/default/files/document/document/2017/09/rapport_de_la_commission_devaluation_du_ceta_-_08.09.2017.pdf>.

Cordonier Segger M-C, Gehring MW and Stephenson S, 'Sustainability Impact Assessments as Inputs and as Interpretative Aids in International Investment Law' (2017) 18 The Journal of World Investment & Trade 163.

Cordonier Segger M-C, Gehring MW and Newcombe AP (eds), *Sustainable Development in World Investment Law* (Kluwer Law International 2011).

Cordonier Segger M-C and Khalfan A, *Sustainable Development Law Principles, Practices, and Prospects* (Oxford University Press 2004).

Corfee-Morlot J et al, 'Towards a Green Investment Policy Framework: The Case of Low-Carbon, Climate-Resilient Infrastructure' (2012) OECD Environment Working Papers 48.

Corten O and Klein P (eds), *The Vienna Conventions on the Law of Treaties: A Commentary* (Oxford University Press 2011).

Cortese F and Ferri D (eds), *The EU Social Market Economy and the Law: Theoretical Perspectives and Practical Challenges for the EU* (Routledge 2018).

Cotula L, *Investment Contracts and Sustainable Development: How to Make Contracts for Fairer and More Sustainable Natural Resource Investments* (International Institute for Environment and Development 2010).

Crawford J, *Brownlie's Principles of Public International Law* (Eighth edition, Oxford University Press 2012).

Cremona M (ed), *Developments in EU External Relations Law* (Oxford University Press 2008).

Cremona M, 'Values in EU Foreign Policy', in: Evans MD and Koutrakos P (eds), *Beyond the Established Legal Orders: Policy Interconnections between the EU and the Rest of the World* (Hart Pub 2011) 275.

Cremona M, 'AXE 1: Les relations économiques extérieures de l'Union européenne au service du développement équitable et durable?' Table ronde presidé par Marise Cremona' in: Lamblin-Gourdin A-S (ed), *Le droit des relations extérieures de l'Union européenne après le Traité de Lisbonne* (Bruylant 2013) 186.

Cremona M, 'Structural Principles and Their Role in EU External Relations Law' (2016) 69 Current Legal Problems 35.

Cremona M, 'Distinguished Essay: A Quiet Revolution—The Changing Nature of the EU's Common Commercial Policy' in: Bungenberg M et al (eds), *European Yearbook of International Economic Law 2017*, vol 8 (Springer International Publishing 2017) 3.

Cremona M, 'Shaping EU Trade Policy Post-Lisbon: Opinion 2/15 of 16 May 2017' (2018) 14 European Constitutional Law Review 231.

Cremona M, 'Coherence and EU External Environmental Policy', in: Morgera E (ed), *The External Environmental Policy of the European Union: EU and International Law Perspectives* (Cambridge University Press 2012) 33.

Cremona M, 'The Union as a Global Actor: Roles, Models and Identity' 41 Common Market Law Review 553.

Cremona M, 'The Opinion Procedure under Article 218(11) TFEU: Reflections in the Light of Opinion 1/17' [2020] Europe and the World: A law review <https://scienceopen.com/document?vid=08a7f1a9-ed57-4631-bbea-33dd05d024c6>.

Cremona M and Witte B de (eds), *EU Foreign Relations Law: Constitutional Fundamentals* (Hart Pub 2008).

Crockett A, 'Stabilisation Clauses and Sustainable Development: Drafting for the Future', in: Brown C and Miles K (eds), *Evolution in Investment Treaty Law and Arbitration* (Cambridge University Press 2011) 516.

Daniel C et al, *Remedy Remains Rare: An Analysis of 15 Years of NCP Cases and Their Contribution to Improve Access to Remedy for Victims of Corporate Misconduct* (OECD Watch 2015).

Daniel C et al, *Glass Half Full? The State of Accountability in Development Finance* (2016) Centre for Research on Multinational Corporations (SOMO).

Davis KE and Trebilcock MJ, 'The Relationship between Law and Development: Optimists versus Skeptics' (2008) 56 American Journal of Comparative Law 895.

De Brabandere E, 'States' Reassertion of Control over International Investment Law (Re)Defining 'Fair and Equitable Treatment and Indirect Expropriation', in: Kulick A, *Reassertion of Control over the Investment Treaty Regime* (Cambridge University Press 2017) 285.

De Búrca G, 'EU External Relations: The Governance Mode of Foreign Policy', in: Van Vooren B, Blockmans S and Wouters J (eds), *The EU's Role in Global Governance: The Legal Dimension* (Oxford University Press 2013) 39.

De Búrca G, 'Europe's raison d'être', in: Kochenov D and Amtenbrink F, *The European Union's Shaping of the International Legal Order* (Cambridge University Press 2014) 21.

De Luca A, 'New Developments on the Scope of the EU Common Commercial Policy under the Lisbon Treaty, Investment Liberalization vs. Investment Protection?', in: Sauvant, K (ed), Yearbook on International Investment Law & Policy 2010/2011 (Oxford University Press 2012) 165.

De Mello LR, 'Foreign Direct Investment in Developing Countries and Growth: A Selective Survey' (1997) 34 Journal of Development Studies 1.

De Mestral A, 'Pre-Entry Obligations under International Law', in: Bungenberg M et al, (eds), *International Investment Law—A Handbook* (CH BECK; Hart; Nomos 2015) 685.

De Mestral A and Vanhonnaeker L, 'Exception Clauses in Mega-Regionals (International Investment Protection and Trade Agreements)' in: Rensmann T (ed), *Mega-Regional Trade Agreements* (Springer International Publishing 2017) 75.

De Nanteuil A, 'Expropriation' in Makane Moïse Mbengue and Stefanie Schacherer (eds), *Foreign Investment Under the Comprehensive Economic and Trade Agreement (CETA)*, vol 15 (Springer International Publishing 2019) 127.

De Sadeleer N, *EU Environmental Law and the Internal Market* (Oxford University Press 2014).

De Schutter O, Swinnen JFM and Wouters J (eds), *Foreign Direct Investment and Human Development: The Law and Economics of International Investment Agreements* (Routledge 2013).

De Witte B, 'Too Much Constitutional Law in the European Union's Foreign Relations?', in: Cremona M and Witte B de (eds), *EU Foreign Relations Law: Constitutional Fundamentals* (Hart Pub 2008) 3.

Dernbach J, 'Achieving Sustainable Development: The Centrality and Multiple Facets of Integrated Decisionmaking' (2003) 10 Indiana Journal of Global Legal Studies 247.

Dhondt N, *Integration of Environmental Protection into other EC Policies: Legal Theory and Practice* (Europa Law Publ 2003).

Dias Simões F, 'External Consultants as Actors in European Trade and Investment Policymaking', in Amtenbrink F, Prévost D and Wessel RA (eds), *Netherlands Yearbook of International Law 2017*, vol 48 (TMC Asser Press 2018) 109.

Dickson-Smith KD, 'Does the European Union Have New Clothes?: Understanding the EU's New Investment Treaty Model' (2016) The Journal of World Investment & Trade 773.

Dietz T, Dotzauer M and Cohen ES, 'The Legitimacy Crisis of Investor-State Arbitration and the New EU Investment Court System' (2019) 26 Review of International Political Economy 749.

Dimopoulos A, 'EC Free Trade Agreements: An Alternative Model for Addressing Human Rights in Foreign Investment Regulation and Dispute Settlement?' in: Dupuy PM, Petersmann E-U and Francioni F (eds), *Human Rights in International Investment Law and Arbitration* (Oxford University Press 2009) 565.

Dimopoulos A, 'Shifting the Emphasis from Investment Protection to Liberalization and Development: The EU as a New Global Factor in the Field of Foreign Investment' (2010) 11 The Journal of World Investment & Trade vii.

Dimopoulos A, 'The Effects of the Lisbon Treaty on the Principles and Objectives of the Common Commercial Policy' (2010) 15 European Foreign Affairs Review 153.

Dimopoulos A, *EU Foreign Investment Law* (Oxford University Press 2011).

Dimopoulos A, 'The Involvement of the EU in Investor-State Dispute Settlement: A Question of Responsibilities' (2014) Common Market Law Review 1671.

Dimopoulos A, 'Integrating Environmental Law Principles and Objectives in EU Investment Policy: Challenges and Opportunities', in: Levashova Y, Lambooy TE and Dekker IF (eds), *Bridging the Gap between International Investment Law and the Environment* (Eleven International Publishing 2016) 247.

Dimopoulos A, 'Achmea: The Principle of Autonomy and Its Implications for Intra and Extra-EU BITs' EJIL Talk (27.03.2018).

Dolzer R and Schreuer C, *Principles of International Investment Law* (Second edition, Oxford University Press 2012).

Dolzer R and Stevens M, *Bilateral Investment Treaties* (M Nijhoff 1995).

Dörr O and Schmalenbach K (eds), *Vienna Convention on the Law of Treaties: A Commentary* (Springer 2012).

Douglas Z, Pauwelyn J and Viñuales JE (eds), *The Foundations of International Investment Law: Bringing Theory into Practice* (Oxford University Press 2014).

Drescher W, 'Ziele und Zuständigkeiten', in: Marchetti A and Demesmay C (eds), *Der Vertrag von Lissabon: Analyse und Bewertung* (Nomos 2010) 59.

Driffield N and Hughes D, 'Foreign and Domestic Investment: Regional Development or Crowding Out?' (2003) 37 Regional Studies.

Dumberry P, 'Fair and Equitable Treatment' in: Mbengue MM and Schacherer S (eds), *Foreign Investment Under the Comprehensive Economic and Trade Agreement (CETA)*, vol 15 (Springer International Publishing 2019) 95.

Dumberry P, *Fair and Equitable Treatment: Its Interaction with the Minimum Standard and Its Customary Status* (Brill 2018).

Dunoff JL and Pollack MA (eds), *Interdisciplinary Perspectives on International Law and International Relations: The State of the Art* (Cambridge University Press 2013).

Dupuy P-M, *L'unité de l'ordre juridique international. Cours général de droit international public*, vol 297 (Martinus Nijhoff 2002).

Dupuy P-M, 'Evolutionary Interpretation' in: Cannizzaro E (ed), *The Law of Treaties beyond the Vienna Convention* (Oxford University Press 2011) 123.

Dupuy P-M, Francioni F and Petersmann E-U (eds), *Human Rights in International Investment Law and Arbitration* (Oxford University Press 2009).

Dupuy P-M and Viñuales JE (eds), *Harnessing Foreign Investment to Promote Environmental Protection: Incentives and Safeguards* (Cambridge University Press 2013).

Ebert FC, 'The Comprehensive Economic and Trade Agreement (CETA): Are Existing Arrangements Sufficient to Prevent Adverse Effects on Labour Standards?' (2017) International Journal of Comparative Labour Law and Industrial Relations 295.

Echandi R and Sauvé P (eds), *Prospects in International Investment Law and Policy: World Trade Forum* (Cambridge University Press 2013).

Eckes C, 'The Autonomy of the EU Legal Order' [2020] 4(1): 1. Europe and the World: A law review [19].

Eeckhout P, *EU External Relations Law* (Second edition, Oxford University Press 2011).

Eeckhout P, 'A Normative Basis for EU External Relations? Protecting Internal Values Beyond the Single Market' in: Krajewski M (ed), *Services of General Interest Beyond the Single Market* (TMC Asser Press 2015) 219.

Eeckhout P, 'Opinion 2/13 on EU Accession to the ECHR and Judicial Dialogue: Autonomy or Autarky' (2015) 38 Fordham International Law Journal 955.

Eeckhout P and Ortino F, 'Towards an EU Policy on Foreign Direct Investment', in: Biondi A, Eeckhout P and Ripley S (eds), *EU Law after Lisbon* (Oxford University Press 2012) 312.

Ekins P and Voituriez T (eds), *Trade, Globalization and Sustainability Impact Assessment: A Critical Look at Methods and Outcomes* (Earthscan 2009).

El Ghadban T, Mazuy C-M and Senegacnik A (eds), *La protection des investissements étrangers: vers une réaffirmation de l'État ? = The protection of foreign investments : a reaffirmation of the State ? : actes du colloque du 2 juin 2017* (2018).

Eliantonio M and Stefan O, 'Soft Law Before the European Courts: Discovering a "Common Pattern"?' (2018) 37 Yearbook of European Law 457.

European Commission and Directorate-General for Trade, *Handbook for Trade Sustainability Impact Assessment: Second Edition* (Publications Office 2016).

Evans MD and Koutrakos P (eds), *Beyond the Established Legal Orders: Policy Interconnections between the EU and the Rest of the World* (Hart Pub 2011).

Firger D, 'The Potential of International Climate Change Law to Mobilise Low-Carbon Foreign Direct Investment', *Harnessing Foreign Investment to Promote Environmental Protection: Incentives and Safeguards* (Cambridge University Press 2013).

Fitzmaurice M et al, 'Environmental Compliance Mechanisms' Online dictionary, available at <http://www.oxfordbibliographies.com/display/id/obo-9780199796953-0010>.

Flavier H, 'L'avis 1/17 Sur Le CETA : De l'autonomie à l'hermétisme' Journal d'Actualité des Droits Européens No 19 (2019).

Frey C, 'The Role of Mega-Regionals in the Decarbonization of the Economy' in: Rensmann T (ed), *Mega-Regional Trade Agreements* (Springer International Publishing 2017) 275.

Gaillard E, 'Identify or Define? Reflection on the Evolution of the Concept of Investment in ICSID Practice', in Binder C and et al (eds), *International Investment Law for the 21st Century: Essays in Honour of Christoph Schreuer* (Oxford University Press, 2009) 403.

Gagliani G, 'The Interpretation of General Exceptions in International Trade and Investment Law: Is a Sustainable Development Interpretive Approach Possible?' (2015) 43 Denver Journal of International Law & Policy 559.

Gammage C, *North-South Regional Trade Agreements as Legal Regimes: A Critical Assessment of the EU-SADC Economic Partnership Agreement* (Edward Elgar Publishing 2017).

García-Bolívar O, 'Economic Development at the Core of the International Investment Regime' in: Brown C and Miles K (eds), *Evolution in Investment Treaty Law and Arbitration* (Cambridge University Press 2011) 586.

Gatti M, 'Opinion 1/17 in Light of Achmea: Chronicle of an Opinion Foretold?' [2019] European Papers Vol. 4 (2019) No 1, 109.

Gazzini T, 'Bilateral Investment Treaties and Sustainable Development' [2014] The Journal of World Investment & Trade 929.

Gazzini T, *Interpretation of International Investment Treaties* (Hart Pub 2016).

Gehne K, *Nachhaltige Entwicklung als Rechtsprinzip: normativer Aussagegehalt, rechtstheoretische Einordnung, Funktionen im Recht* (Mohr Siebeck 2011).

George C and Kirkpatrick C, 'Sustainability Impact Assessment of World Trade Negotiations: Current Practice and Lessons for Further Development' Working Paper Series, Paper No 2, Manchester, 2003.

George C, (eds), *Impact Assessment and Sustainable Development: European Practice and Experience* (Edward Elgar 2007).

Gilles A, *La définition de l'investissement international* (Larcier 2012).

Gillespie A, *The Long Road to Sustainability: The Past, Present, and Future of International Environmental Law and Policy* (Oxford University Press 2017).

Globerman S, 'Investing Abroad and Investing at Home: Complements or Substitutes?' (2012) 20 Multinational Business Review 217.

Gómez-Palacio I and Muchlinski P, 'Admission and Establishment' in: Muchlinski P, Ortino F and Schreuer C, *Oxford Handbook of International Investment Law* (Oxford University Press 2008) 227.

Gordon K and Pohl J, 'Environmental Concerns in International Investment Agreements: A Survey' (2011) OECD Working Papers on International Investment 2011/01.

Gordon K, Pohl J and Bouchard M, 'Investment Treaty Law, Sustainable Development and Responsible Business Conduct: A Fact-Finding Survey' (2014) OECD Working Papers on International Investment 2014/01.

Gött H and Holterhus TP, 'Mainstreaming Investment-Labour Linkage Through "Mega-Regional" Trade Agreements' in: Gött H (ed), *Labour Standards in International Economic Law* (Springer International Publishing 2018) 233.

Grabitz E, Hilf M and Nettesheim M, *Das Recht der Europäischen Union: Band I: EUV/AEUV, Rechtsstand: Juli 2010* (41. Aufl, Beck CH 2010).

Griller S, Obwexer W and Vranes E (eds), *Mega-Regional Trade Agreements: CETA, TTIP, and TiSA ; New Orientations for EU External Economic Relations* (Oxford University Press 2017).

Grosse Ruse-Khan H, 'A Real Partnership for Development? Sustainable Development as Treaty Objective in European Economic Partnership Agreements and Beyond' (2010) 13 Journal of International Economic Law 139.

Govaere I and Garben S (eds), *The Interface between EU and International Law: Contemporary Reflections* (Hart 2019).

Harding T and Javorcik BS, 'Investment Promotion and FDI Inflows: Quality Matters' (2013) 59 CESifo Economic Studies 337.

Harrison J et al, 'Governing Labour Standards through Free Trade Agreements: Limits of the European Union's Trade and Sustainable Development Chapters: Governing Labour Standards through FTAs' (2018) JCMS: Journal of Common Market Studies.

Hees F and Barreto da Rocha Paranhos, 'Investment Facilitation: Moving Beyond Investment Promotion' Columbia FDI Perspectives, No 228, 6/2018.

Heliskoski J, *Mixed Agreements as a Technique for Organizing the International Relations of the European Community and Its Member States* (Kluwer Law International 2001).

Henckels C, 'Balancing Investment Protection and the Public Interest: The Role of the Standard of Review and the Importance of Deference in Investor-State Arbitration' (2013) 4 Journal of International Dispute Settlement 197.

Henckels C, *Proportionality and Deference in Investor-State Arbitration: Balancing Investment Protection and Regulatory Autonomy* (Cambridge University Press 2015).

Henckels C, 'Protecting Regulatory Autonomy through Greater Precision in Investment Treaties: The TPP, CETA, and TTIP' (2016) 19 Journal of International Economic Law 27.

Henckels C, 'Balancing Investment Protection and Sustainable Development in Investor-State Arbitration: The Role of Deference' in: in: Bjorklund A (ed), *Yearbook of International Investment Law and Policy 2012-2013* (Oxford University Press 2014) 305.

Hepburn J, 'In Accordance with Which Host State Laws? Restoring the "Defence" of Investor Illegality in Investment Arbitration' (2014) 5 Journal of International Dispute Settlement 531.

Hepburn J and Kuuya V, 'Corporate Social Responsibility and Investment Treaties', in: Cordonier Segger M-C, Gehring MW and Newcombe AP (eds), *Sustainable Development in World Investment Law* (Kluwer Law International 2011) 585.

Herrmann CW, 'Common Commercial Policy After Nice: Sisyphus Would Have Done a Better Job' (2002) 39 Common Market Law Review 7.

Hiebaum C, Koller P and Internationale Vereinigung für Rechts- und Sozialphilosophie (eds), *Politische Ziele und juristische Argumentation: Symposium der Internationalen Vereinigung für Rechts- und Sozialphilosophie, 11. bis 12. Oktober 2002 in Graz* (Steiner 2003).

Hillion C, 'Tous Pour Un, Un Pour Tous! Coherence in the External Relations of the European Union' in: Cremona M (ed), *Developments in EU External Relations Law* (Oxford University Press 2008) 10.

Hillion C and Koutrakos P (eds), *Mixed Agreements Revisited: The EU and Its Member States in the World* (Hart Pub 2010).

Hindelang S, *The Free Movement of Capital and Foreign Direct Investment: The Scope of Protection in EU Law* (Oxford University Press 2009).

Hindelang S and Krajewski M (eds), *Shifting Paradigms in International Investment Law: More Balanced, Less Isolated, Increasingly Diversified* (Oxford University Press 2016).

Hinojosa-Martínez LM, 'The Scope of the EU Treaty-Making Power on Foreign Investment: Between Wishful Thinking and Pragmatism' (2016) 17 The Journal of World Investment & Trade 86.

Hoffmeister F, 'The Contribution of EU Trade Agreements to the Development of International Investment Law' in: Hindelang S and Krajewski M (eds), *Shifting Paradigms in International Investment Law: More Balanced, Less Isolated, Increasingly Diversified* (Oxford University Press 2016) 357.

Hoffmeister F and Ünüvar G, 'From BITs and Pieces towards European Investment Agreements', in: Bungenberg M, Reinisch A and Tietje C (eds), *EU and Investment Agreements: Open Questions and Remaining Challenges* (Nomos; Dike 2013) 57.

Hofmann HC, 'General Principles of EU Law and EU Administrative Law', in: in: Barnard C and Peers S, *European Union Law* (Second edition, Oxford University Press 2017) 198.

Hofmann R, Schill S and Tams CJ (eds), *Preferential Trade and Investment Agreements: From Recalibration to Reintegration* (Nomos 2013).

Hofmann R and Tams CJ (eds), *International Investment Law and General International Law: From Clinical Isolation to Systemic Integration?* (Nomos 2011).

International Finance Corporation, *Climate Investment Opportunities in Emerging Markets* (World Bank, 2016).

Holterhus TP, 'Das CETA-Gutachten Des EuGH: Neue Maßstäbe Allerorten...' VerfBlog, 2019/5/03, <https://intr2dok.vifa-recht.de/receive/mir_mods_00005821>.

International Labour Rights Forum, 'Wrong Turn for Workers' Rights: The U.S.—Guatemala CAFTA Labor Arbitration Ruling—and What To Do About It', available at <https://laborrights.org/sites/default/files/publications/Wrong%20Turn%20for%20Workers%20Rights%20-%20March%202018.pdf>.

International Law Association (ILA), 'Toronto Conference 2006: International Law on Sustainable Development', available at <http://www.ila-hq.org/index.php/publications/order-reports> (last accessed 31 Jan 2019).

International Law Commission (ILC), 'Fragmentation of International Law: Difficulties Arising from the Diversification and Expansion of International Law. Report of the Study Group of the International Law Commission. Finalised by Martti Koskenniemi' (2006) UN Doc a/CN.4/L.682.

Jans JH and Vedder HH, *European Environmental Law: After Lisbon* (Fourth edition, Europa Law Publ 2012).

Jezewski M, 'Development Considerations in Defining Investment', in: Cordonier Segger M-C, Gehring M W and Newcombe AP (eds), *Sustainable Development in World Investment Law* (Kluwer Law International 2011) 211.

Johannsen SLE, 'Die Kompetenz Der Europäischen Union Für Ausländische Direktinvestitionen Nach Dem Vertrag von Lissabon' (2009) Beiträge zum Transnationalen Wirtschaftsrecht 46.

Johnson L, 'FDI, International Investment and the Sustainable Development Goals', in: Krajewski M and Hoffmann RT (eds), *Research Handbook on Foreign Direct Investment* (Edward Elgar Pub 2019) 126.

Jordan A and Adelle C (eds), *Environmental Policy in the EU: Actors, Institutions and Processes* (Third edition, Routledge 2013).

Kaddous C, *Le droit des relations extérieures dans la jurisprudence de la Cour de justice des Communautés européennes* (Helbing & Lichtenhahn; Bruylant 1998).

Kaddous C, 'Une confrontation des perspectives: La stratégie de l'Europe 2020 et la relance du marché intérieur' in: Moreiro González CJ (ed), *EU2020: the Lisbon Process revisited = EU2020 = le Processus de Lisbonne revisité* (Difusión Jurídica 2012) 15.

Kaddous C, 'Reflections on the Changes in the European Union's Common Commercial Policy', in: Biaggini G, Diggelmann O and Kaufmann C (eds), *Polis Und Kosmopolis: Festschrift Für Daniel Thürer* (Dike; Nomos 2015) 335.

Kaddous C, 'De quelques défis liés à la conclusion des accords mixtes', in: *Liber amicorum Antonio Tizzano: de la Cour CECA à la Cour de l'Union: le long parcours de la justice européenne* (G Giappichelli 2018) 448.

Kaddous C and Piçarra N, 'Topic 3: The External Dimension of EU Policies. An Update on the Roles of the EU institutions and Member States. An Assessment of the

Current Challenges on Trade, Investment Protection and the Area of Freedom, Security and Justice', XXVIII FIDE Congress, Estoril 23-26 May 2018, Final Report.

Kahl W (ed), *Nachhaltigkeit als Verbundbegriff* (Mohr Siebeck 2008).

Kahl W (ed), *Nachhaltigkeit durch Organisation und Verfahren* (Mohr Siebeck 2016).

Kahn P and Wälde T (eds), *Les aspects nouveaux du droit des investissements internationaux = New Aspects of International Investment Law* (Nijhoff 2007).

Kaltenborn M, Krajewski M and Kuhn H (eds), *Sustainable Development Goals and Human Rights* (Springer 2020).

Karl J, 'The Competence for Foreign Direct Investment, New Powers for the European Union?' (2004) Journal of World Investment and Trade 413.

Keene A, 'The Incorporation and Interpretation of WTO-Style Environmental Exceptions in International Investment Agreements' (2017) 18 The Journal of World Investment & Trade 62.

Kingsbury B and Schill SW, 'Public Law Concepts to Balance Investors' Rights with State Regulatory Actions in the Public Interest—the Concept of Proportionality' in: Schill SW, *International Investment Law and Comparative Public Law* (Oxford University Press 2010) 75.

Kiss A-C and Doumbe-Bille S, 'Conférence des Nations Unies sur l'environnement et le développement (Rio de Janeiro juin 1992)' (1992) 38 Annuaire français de droit international 823.

Kistenkas FH, 'Sustainable Development: New Thoughts, New Policy, New Law?' in Mauerhofer V (ed), *Legal Aspects of Sustainable Development* (Springer International Publishing 2016) 535.

Kläger R, *'Fair and Equitable Treatment' in International Investment Law* (Cambridge University Press 2011).

Kläger R, ' "Fair and Equitable" Treatment and Sustainable Development', in: Cordonier Segger M-C, Gehring MW and Newcombe AP (eds), *Sustainable Development in World Investment Law* (Kluwer Law International 2011) 237.

Klamert M, *The Principle of Loyalty in EU Law* (Oxford University Press 2014).

Kleimann D, 'Reading Opinion 2/15: Standards of Analysis, the Court's Discretion, and the Legal View of the Advocate General' EUI RSCAS 2017/23.

Kochenov D and Amtenbrink F, *The European Union's Shaping of the International Legal Order* (Cambridge University Press 2014).

Kohler-Koch B and Quittkat C, 'What Is Civil Society and Who Represents Civil Society in the EU?—Results of an Online Survey among Civil Society Experts' (2009) 28 Policy and Society 11.

Koutrakos P, *EU International Relations Law* (Second edition, Hart Pub 2015).

Kovar J, 'A Short Guide to the Rio Declaration' (1993) 4 Colorado Journal of International Environmental Law and Policy 119.

Krajewski M, 'External Trade Law and the Constitution Treaty; Towards a Federal and More Democratic Common Commercial Policy'; (2005) 42 Common Market Law Review 91.

Krajewski M, 'The Reform of the Common Commercial Policy' in: Biondi A, Eeckhout P and Ripley S (eds), *EU Law after Lisbon* (Oxford University Press 2012) 292.

Krajewski M, 'Normative Grundlagen Der EU- Außenwirtschaftsbeziehungen: Verbindlich, Umsetzbar Und Angewandt?' (2016) Heft 3 EuR.

Krajewski M and Hoffmann RT (eds), *Research Handbook on Foreign Direct Investment* (Edward Elgar Publishing 2019).

Krämer L, 'Sustainable Development in the EC', in: Bugge HC, Voigt C and Norges F (eds), *Sustainable Development in International and National Law: What Did the Brundtland Report Do to Legal Thinking and Legal Development, and Where Can We Go from Here?* (Europa Law Publishing 2008) 377.

Kriebaum U, 'Regulatory Takings: Balancing the Interests of the Investor and the State' (2007) The Journal of World Investment & Trade 717.

Kriebaum U, 'FET and Expropriation in the (Invisible) EU Model BIT' (2014) The Journal of World Investment & Trade 454.

Kriebaum U, 'Foreign Investments & Human Rights—The Actors and Their Different Roles', in: *Current Issues in Investment Treaty Law. Volume IV: The Future of ICSID and the Place of Investment Treaties in International Law* (British Institute of International and Comparative Law 2013) 45.

Kriebaum U, 'Human Rights and International Investment Law' in: Radi Y (ed), *Research Handbook on Human Rights and Investment* (Edward Elgar Pub 2018) 13.

Kube V and Pedreschi L, 'The Social Dimension of the Common Commercial Policy', in: Cortese F and Ferri D (eds), *The EU Social Market Economy and the Law: Theoretical Perspectives and Practical Challenges for the EU* (Routledge 2018) 272.

Kube V, *EU Human Rights, International Investment Law and Participation Operationalizing the EU Foreign Policy Objective to Global Human Rights Protection* (Springer International Publishing 2019).

Kulick A, *Global Public Interest in International Investment Law* (Cambridge University Press 2012).

Kulick A (ed), *Reassertion of Control over the Investment Treaty Regime* (Cambridge University Press 2017).

Kurtz J, *The WTO and International Investment Law: Converging Systems* (Cambridge University Press 2016).

Lafferty W and Hovden E, 'Environmental Policy Integration: Towards an Analytical Framework' (2003) 12 Environmental Politics 1.

Lamblin-Gourdin A-S (ed), *Le droit des relations extérieures de l'Union européenne après le Traité de Lisbonne* (Bruylant 2013).

Langlet D and Mahmoudi S, *EU Environmental Law and Policy* (Oxford University Press 2016).

Larik J, 'From Speciality to a Constitutional Sense of Purpose: On the Changing Role of the Objectives of the European Union' (2014) 63 International and Comparative Law Quarterly 935.

Larik J, *Foreign Policy Objectives in European Constitutional Law* (Oxford University Press 2016).

Larik J, 'Good Global Governance through Trade: Constitutional Moorings', in: Wouters J et al (eds), *Global Governance through Trade: EU Policies and Approaches* (Edward Elgar Publishing 2015) 43.

Larik J, 'Much More Than Trade: The Common Commercial Policy in a Global Context', in: Evans MD and Koutrakos P (eds), *Beyond the Established Legal Orders: Policy Interconnections between the EU and the Rest of the World* (Hart Pub 2011) 13.

Lee M, *EU Environmental Law, Governance and Decision-Making* (Second edition, Hart Pub 2014).

Legum B and Petculescu I, 'GATT Article XX and International Investment Law' in: Echandi R and Pierre Sauvé P (eds), *Prospects in International Investment Law and Policy* (Cambridge University Press 2013) 340.

Leino P, 'The Journey Towards All That Is Good and Beautiful: Human Rights and "Common Values" as Guiding Principles of EU Foreign Relations Law', in: Cremona M and Witte B de (eds), *EU Foreign Relations Law: Constitutional Fundamentals* (Hart Pub 2008) 259.

Levashova Y, Lambooy TE and Dekker IF (eds), *Bridging the Gap between International Investment Law and the Environment* (Eleven International Publishing 2016).

Levashova Y, 'The Accountability and Corporate Social Responsibility of Multinational Corporations for Transgressions in Host States through International Investment Law' (2018) 14 Utrecht Law Review 40.

Levashova Y, *The Right of States to Regulate in International Investment Law: The Search for Balance between Public Interest and Fair and Equitable Treatment* (Kluwer Law International BV 2019).

Lévesque C, 'The Inclusion of GATT Article XX Exceptions in IIAs: A Potentially Risky Policy' in: Echandi R and Sauvé P (eds), *Prospects in International Investment Law and Policy* (Cambridge University Press 2013) 363.

Lim CL (ed), *Alternative Visions of the International Law on Foreign Investment: Essays in Honour of Muthucumaraswamy Sornarajah* (Cambridge University Press 2016).

Mahnoush H, Arsanjani W and Reisman M, 'Interpreting Treaties for the Benefit of Third Parties: The "Salvors' Doctrine" and the Use of Legislative History in Investment Treaties' (2010) 104 The American Journal of International Law 597.

Malintoppi L and Limbasan N, 'Living in Glass Houses? The Debate on Transparency in International Investment Arbitration' (2015) 2 BCDR International Arbitration Review.

Mann H, 'Investment Liberalization: Some Key Elements and Issues in Today's Negotiating Context' Issues in International Investment Law (IISD 2007).

Mann H, 'The New Frontier: Economic Rights of Foreign Investors versus Government Policy Space for Economic Development', in: Lim CL (ed), *Alternative Visions of the International Law on Foreign Investment: Essays in Honour of Muthucumaraswamy Sornarajah* (Cambridge University Press 2016) 289.

Manners I, 'Normative Power Europe: A Contradiction in Terms?' (2002) 40 JCMS: Journal of Common Market Studies 235.

Marín Durán G, 'The Role of the EU in Shaping the Trade and Environment Regulatory Nexus: Multilateral and Regional Approaches', in: Van Vooren B, Blockmans S and Wouters J (eds), *The EU's Role in Global Governance: The Legal Dimension* (Oxford University Press 2013) 224.

Marín Durán G, 'Innovations and Implications of the Trade and Sustainable Development Chapter in the EU–Korea Free Trade Agreement' in: Harrison J (ed), *The European Union and South Korea* (Edinburgh University Press 2013).

Marín Durán G, 'Sustainable Development Chapters in EU Free Trade Agreements: Emerging Compliance Issues' [2020] Common Market Law Review 1031.

Marín Durán G and Morgera E, *Environmental Integration in the EU's External Relations: Beyond Multilateral Dimensions* (Hart Pub 2012).

Martini C, 'Avoiding the Planned Obsolesce of Modern International Investment Agreements: Can General Exception Mechanisms Be Improved, and How?' 59 B.C. L. Rev. 2877 (2018), <https://lawdigitalcommons.bc.edu/bclr/vol59/iss8/13>.

Mary H-D, 'Do Bilateral Investment Treaties Attract Foreign Direct Investment? Only a Bit—and They Could Bite' Policy Research Working Paper No 3121.

Marx A et al, *Dispute Settlement in the Trade and Sustainable Development Chapters of EU Trade Agreements* (Leuven Centre for Global Governance Studies 2017).

Mbengue MM, 'Rules of Interpretation—Article 32 of the Vienna Convention on the Law of Treaties' (2016) 31 ICSID Review 388.

Mbengue MM, 'Les Obligations Des Investisseurs Étrangers', Société française pour le droit international (Colloque de Paris Vincennes—Saint-Denis), *L'entreprise multinationale et le droit international* (Pedone 2017) 295.

Mbengue MM, 'Preamble', in: Wolfrum R (eds), *The Max Planck Encyclopedia of Public International Law* (Online Edition; Oxford University Press 2012).

McGillivray D and Holder J, 'Locating EC Environmental Law' (2001) 20 Yearbook of European Law 139.

McLachlan C, 'The Principle of Systemic Integration and Article 31(3)(c) of the Vienna Convention' (2005) 54 International and Comparative Law Quarterly 279.

Meadows DH and et al (eds), *The Limits to Growth: A Report for the Club of Rome's Project on the Predicament of Mankind* (Universe Books 1972).

Mégret J, 'La spécificité du droit communautaire', Revue internationale de droit comparé (1967) 19–3, 565–577.

Meunier S and Nicolaïdis K, 'The European Union as a Conflicted Trade Power' (2006) 13 Journal of European Public Policy 906.

Michel V (ed), *Le Droit, Les Institutions et Les Politiques de l'Union Européenne Face à l'impératif de Cohérence: Actes Du Colloque Des 10 et 11 Mai 2007, Université Robert Schuman, Centre d'études Internationales et Européennes, Université de Strasbourg* (Presses universitaires de Strasbourg 2009).

Michel V, 'Les objectifs à caractère transversal', in: Neframi E (ed), *Objectifs et compétences dans l'Union européenne* (Bruylant 2013) 203.

Miles K, *The Origins of International Investment Law—Empire, Environment and the Safeguarding of Capital* (Cambridge University Press 2013).

Mitchell A, Munro J and Voon, Tania, 'Importing WTO General Exceptions Into International Investment Law', in: Sachs L, Johnson L and Coleman J, *Yearbook on International Investment Law & Policy 2017* (Oxford University Press 2019) 305.

Mitchell AD, Heaton DOF and Henckels C, *Non-Discrimination and the Role of Regulatory Purpose in International Trade and Investment Law* (Edward Elgar Publishing 2016).

Moloo R and Khachaturian A, 'The Compliance with the Law Requirement in International Investment Law' (2011) 34(6) Fordham International Law Journal 1473.

Monebhurrun N, 'The (Mis)Use of Development in International Investment Law: Understanding the Jurist's Limits to Work with Development Issues' (2017) 10 Law and Development Review.

Morgera E (ed), *The External Environmental Policy of the European Union: EU and International Law Perspecstives* (Cambridge University Press 2012).

Morgera E, 'Environmental Law', in: Barnard C and Peers S, *European Union Law* (Second edition, Oxford University Press 2017) 657.

Morgera E and Marín Durán G, 'Article 37', in: Peers S et al (eds), *The EU Charter of Fundamental Rights a Commentary* (CH BECK; Hart; Nomos 2014) 983.

Neframi E, *Les accords mixtes de la Communauté européenne: aspects communautaires et internationaux* (Bruylant 2007).

Neframi E (ed), *Objectifs et compétences dans l'Union européenne* (Bruylant 2013).

Neframi E, 'Le rapport entre objectifs et compétences : se la structuration et de l'identité de l'Union européenne', in: Neframi E (ed), *Objectifs et compétences dans l'Union européenne* (Bruylant 2013) 5.

Newcombe A, 'The Boundaries of Regulatory Expropriation in International Law', (2005) 20 ICSID Review 1.

Newcombe A, 'Sustainable Development and Investment Treaty Law' (2007) 8 The Journal of World Investment & Trade 357.

Newcombe A, 'General Exceptions in International Investment Agreements', in: Cordonier Segger M-C, Gehring MW and Newcombe AP (eds), *Sustainable Development in World Investment Law* (Kluwer Law International 2011) 351.

Nikièma S, 'The Definition of Investor' *IISD Best Practices Series* (2012).

Nikièma S, 'Performance Requirements in Investment Treaties' *IISD Best Practices Series* (2014).

Nikièma S, 'Indirect Expropriation' *IISD Best Practices Series* (2012).

Nowak C, 'Legal Arrangements for the Promotion and Protection of Foreign Investments Within the Framework of the EU Association Policy and European Neighbourhood Policy' in: Bungenberg et al (eds), *International Investment Law and EU Law* (Springer 2011) 105.

Nowrot K, 'How to Include Environmental Protection, Human Rights and Sustainability in International Investment Law?' (2014) 15 The Journal of World Investment & Trade 612.

Nowrot K, 'Obligations of Investors', in: Bungenberg M et al, (eds), *International Investment Law—A Handbook* (CH BECK; Hart; Nomos 2015) 1154.

OECD (ed), *Foreign Direct Investment for Development—Maximising Benefits, Minimizing Costs* (OECD 2002).

OECD, '"Indirect Expropriation" and the "Right to Regulate" in International Investment Law' (2004) OECD Working Papers on International Investment 2004/04.

OECD, 'Fair and Equitable Treatment Standard in International Investment Law', vol 2004/03 (2004) OECD Working Papers on International Investment 2004/03.

OECD (ed), *Environment and Regional Trade Agreements* (OECD 2007).

OECD (ed), *International Investment Law: Understanding Concepts and Tracking Innovations* (OECD 2008).

OECD, (ed) International Investment Agreements: A Survey of Environmental, Labour and Anti-Corruption Issues (OECD 2008).

OECD, (ed), *OECD Due Diligence Guidance for Responsible Supply Chains of Minerals from Conflict-Affected and High-Risk Areas* (Second edition, OECD 2013).

OECD, Green Growth and Sustainable Development Forum 2013: How to unlock investment in support of green growth? Issue Note 1 (OECD 2013), available at <https://www.oecd.org/greengrowth/gg-sd-2013.htm>.

OECD (ed) *Policy Framework for Investment: 2015 Edition* (OECD 2015).

Oehri M, 'Civil Society Activism under US Free Trade Agreements: The Effects of Actorness on Decent Work' (2017) 5 Politics and Governance 40.

Olney WW, 'A Race to the Bottom? Employment Protection and Foreign Direct Investment' (2013) 91 Journal of International Economics 191.

Orbie J, Martens D and Van den Putte L, 'Civil Society Meetings in European Union Trade Agreements: Features, Purposes, and Evaluation' CLEER Working Paper 2016/3.

Orbie J, Van den Putte L and Martens D, 'Civil Society Meetings in EU Free Trade Agreements: The Purposes Unravelled' in: Gött H (ed), *Labour Standards in International Economic Law* (Springer International Publishing 2018) 135.

Ortino F, 'Refining the Content and Role of Investment "Rules" and "Standards": A New Approach to International Investment Treaty Making' (2013) 28 ICSID Review 152.

Ortino F, 'Investment Treaties, Sustainable Development and Reasonableness Review: A Case Against Strict Proportionality Balancing' (2017) 30 Leiden Journal of International Law 71.

Ost F and de Kerchove M, *De la pyramide au réseau ? Pour une théorie dialectique du droit* (Publications des Facultés universitaires Saint-Louis 2002).

Pallemaerts M, 'Developing More Sustainability?', *Environmental Policy in the EU: Actors, Institutions and Processes* (Earthscan New York).

Pallemaerts M, 'The EU and Sustainable Development: An Ambiguous Relationship', in: Pallemaerts M and Azmanova A (eds), *The European Union and Sustainable Development: Internal and External Dimensions* (VUB Press 2006) 19.

Paparinskis M, 'Regulatory Expropriation and Sustainable Development', in: Cordonier Segger M-C, Gehring MW and Newcombe AP (eds), *Sustainable Development in World Investment Law* (Kluwer Law International 2011) 295.

Pauwelyn J and Elsig M, 'The Politics of Treaty Interpretation' in: Dunoff JL and Pollack MA (eds), *Interdisciplinary Perspectives on International Law and International Relations* (Cambridge University Press 2012) 445.

Pavoni R, 'Mutual Supportiveness as a Principle of Interpretation and Law-Making: A Watershed for the "WTO-and-Competing-Regimes" Debate?' (2010) 21 European Journal of International Law 649.

Pazienza P, *The Relationship between FDI and the Natural Environment: Facts, Evidence and Prospects* (Springer 2014).

Peers S et al (eds), *The EU Charter of Fundamental Rights a Commentary* (CH BECK; Hart; Nomos 2014).

Peters A, *Elemente Einer Theorie Der Verfassung Europas* (Duncker & Humblot 2001).

Polanski S, 'Twenty Years of Progress at Risk—Labor and Environmental Protections in Trade Agreements' GEGI Policy Brief No 4.

Potestà M, 'From Mutual Supportiveness to Mutual Enforcement? The Contribution of US Preferential Trade and Investment Agreements to the Effectiveness of Environmental Norms', in: Hofmann R, Schill S and Tams CJ (eds), *Preferential Trade and Investment Agreements: From Recalibration to Reintegration* (Nomos 2013) 167.

Prislan V and Zandvliet R, 'Labor Provisions in International Investment Agreements: Prospects for Sustainable Development' Grotius Centre Working Paper 2013/003/IEL.

Quirico O, 'The Environmental Sustainability of the EU Investment Policy after Lisbon: Progressive International Developments' in: in: Levashova Y, Lambooy TE and Dekker IF (eds), *Bridging the Gap between International Investment Law and the Environment* (Eleven International Publishing 2016) 273.

Radi Y (ed), *Research Handbook on Human Rights and Investment* (Edward Elgar Publishing 2018).

Redgwell C, 'Sources of International Environmental Law', in: Besson S and d'Aspremont J (eds), *The Oxford Handbook on the Sources of International Law* (Oxford University Press 2017) 939.

Reid E, *Balancing Human Rights, Environmental Protection and International Trade: Lessons from the EU Experience* (Hart Pub 2015).

Reinisch A, 'Investment Protection and Dispute Settlement in Preferential Trade Agreements: A Challenge to BITs?' (2009) 24 ICSID Review 416.

Reinisch A, 'The Division of Powers Between the EU and Its Member States "After Lisbon"' in: Bungenberg M et al (eds), *International Investment Law and EU Law* (Springer 2011) 43.

Reinisch A, 'EU on the Investment Path, Quo Vadis Europe—The Future of EU BITs and Other Investment Agreements' (2013) Santa Clara Journal of International Law 111.

Reinisch A, 'The Future Shape of EU Investment Agreements' (2013) 28 ICSID Review 179.

Reinisch A, '"Putting the Pieces Together ... an EU Model BIT?"' (2014) The Journal of World Investment & Trade 679.

Reinisch A, 'National Treatment', in: Bungenberg M et al, (eds), *International Investment Law—A Handbook* (CH BECK; Hart; Nomos 2015) 846.

Reinisch A, 'The Interpretation of International Investment Agreements' Bungenberg M et al, (eds), *International Investment Law—A Handbook* (CH BECK; Hart; Nomos 2015) 372.

Reinisch A, 'The Rule of Law in International Investment Arbitration', in: Pazartzis P et al (eds), *Reconceptualising the Rule of Law in Global Governance, Resources, Investment and Trade* (Hart Publishing 2016) 291.

Reinisch A, 'Will the EU's Proposal Concerning an Investment Court System for CETA and TTIP Lead to Enforceable Awards?—The Limits of Modifying the ICSID Convention and the Nature of Investment Arbitration' (2016) 19 Journal of International Economic Law 761.

Reinisch A, 'Jurisdiction and Admissibility in International Investment Law' (2017) 16 The Law & Practice of International Courts and Tribunals 21.

Reynaud P, 'Sustainable Development and Regional Trade Agreements: Toward Better Practices in Impact Assessments' 2013 8 McGill International Journal of Sustainable Development Law & Policy 213.

Riffel C, 'The CETA Opinion of the European Court of Justice and Its Implications—Not That Selfish After All' (2019) 22 Journal of International Economic Law 503.

Rosentreter D, *Article 31(3)(c) of the Vienna Convention on the Law of Treaties and the Principle of Systemic Integration in International Investment Law and Arbitration* (Nomos 2015).

Ross-Robertson A, 'Is the Environment Squeezed out of Sustainable Development?' (2000) Public Law 249.

Ruffert M, 'Art. 3 (Ex-Art. 2 EUV) [Ziele Der EU]', in: Calliess C, Blanke H-J and Kluth W (eds), *EUV/AEUV: das Verfassungsrecht der Europäischen Union mit Europäischer Grundrechtecharta ; Kommentar* (4. Aufl, BECK 2011) 41.

Rukundo O and Carbrera J, 'Investment Promotion and the Protection in the UNCBD: An Emerging Access and Benefit Sharing Regime', in: Cordonier Segger M-C, Gehring MW and Newcombe AP (eds), *Sustainable Development in World Investment Law* (Kluwer Law International 2011) 717.

Sabanogullari L, 'The Merits and Limitations of General Exception Clauses in Contemporary Investment Treaty Practice' *IISD Investment Treaty News* (2015).

Sacerdoti G et al (eds), *General Interests of Host States in International Investment Law* (Cambridge University Press 2014).

Sacerdoti G, 'The Admission and Treatment of Foreign Investment under Recent Bilateral and Regional Treaties' (2000) 105 Journal of World Investment 1.

Sachs J, *The Age of Sustainable Development* (Columbia University Press 2015).

Sachs L, Johnson L and Coleman J, *Yearbook on International Investment Law & Policy 2017* (Oxford University Press 2019).

Salacuse JW and Sullivan NP, 'Do BITs Really Work?: An Evaluation of Bilateral Investment Treaties and Their Grand Bargain', in: in: Sauvant KP and Sachs LE (eds), *The Effect of Treaties on Foreign Direct Investment* (Oxford University Press 2009) 109.

Sands P, 'International Law in the Field of Sustainable Development' (1994) 64 British Yearbook of International Law 303.

Sands P, *Principles of International Environmental Law* (Fourth edition, Cambridge University Press 2018).

Sattorova M, *The Impact of Investment Treaty Law on Host States: Enabling Good Governance?* (Hart Publishing 2018).

Sauvant KP (ed), *Yearbook on International Investment Law & Policy 2011-2012.* (Oxford University Press 2013).

Sauvant KP et al, 'Trends in FDI, Home Country Measures and Competitive Neutrality', *Yearbook on International Investment Law and Policy 2012-2013* (Oxford University Press 2014) 3.

Sauvant KP and Sachs LE (eds), *The Effect of Treaties on Foreign Direct Investment* (Oxford University Press 2009).

Schacherer S, 'TPP, CETA and TTIP Between Innovation and Consolidation—Resolving Investor–State Disputes under Mega-Regionals', (2016) Journal of International Dispute Settlement 628.

Schacherer S, 'The CETA Investment Chapter and Sustainable Development: Interpretative Issues' in: Mbengue MM and Schacherer S (eds), *Foreign Investment Under the Comprehensive Economic and Trade Agreement (CETA)*, vol 15 (Springer International Publishing 2019) 207.

Schermers HG and Blokker N, *International Institutional Law: Unity within Diversity* (Fifth edition, Martinus Nijhoff Publishers 2011).

Scherrer C et al, *An Analysis of the Relative Effectiveness of Social and Environmental Norms in Free Trade Agreements, for the European Parliament*, Policy Department External Trade (EP Publications Office 2019).

Scheyvens R, Banks G and Hughes E, 'The Private Sector and the SDGs: The Need to Move Beyond "Business as Usual" The Private Sector and the SDGs: Moving Beyond "Business-as-Usual"' (2016) 24 Sustainable Development 371.

Schill SW (ed), *International Investment Law and Comparative Public Law* (Oxford University Press 2010).

Schill SW, 'Deference in Investment Treaty Arbitration: Re-Conceptualizing the Standard of Review' (2012) 3 Journal of International Dispute Settlement 577.

Schill SW, 'Reforming Investor–State Dispute Settlement: A (Comparative and International) Constitutional Law Framework' (2017) 20 Journal of International Economic Law 649.

Schill SW, 'Authority, Legitimacy, and Fragmentation in the (Envisaged) Dispute Settlement Disciplines in Mega-Regionals', in: in: Griller S, Obwexer W and Vranes E (eds), *Mega-Regional Trade Agreements: CETA, TTIP, and TiSA ; New Orientations for EU External Economic Relations* (Oxford University Press 2017).

Schill SW and Jacob M, 'Trends in International Investment Agreements, 2010-2011: The Increasing Complexity of International Investment Law', in: Sauvant KP (ed), *Yearbook on International Investment Law & Policy 2011-2012.* (Oxford University Press 2013) 141.

Schill SW, Tams CJ and Hofmann R (eds), *International Investment Law and Development: Bridging the Gap* (Edward Elgar Publishing 2015).

Schill SW and Djanic V, 'International Investment Law and Community Interests' Society of International Economic Law (SIEL), Working Paper No 2016/01.

Schneiderman D, 'Legitimacy and Reflexivity in International Investment Arbitration: A New Self-Restraint?' (2011) 2 Journal of International Dispute Settlement 471.

Schokkaert J, *La pratique conventionnelle en matière de protection juridique des investissements internationaux: droit comparé, droit interne, conventions européennes* (Bruylant 2006).

Schrempf-Stirling J and Wettstein F, 'Beyond Guilty Verdicts: Human Rights Litigation and Its Impact on Corporations' Human Rights Policies' (2017) 145 Journal of Business Ethics 545.

Schreuer C et al (eds), *The ICSID Convention: A Commentary* (2nd ed, Cambridge University Press 2009).

Schrijver N, *The Evolution of Sustainable Development in International Law: Inception, Meaning and Status* (Martinus Nijhoff 2008).

Schrijver N and Weiss F (eds), *International Law and Sustainable Development: Principles and Practice* (Martinus Nijhoff Publishers 2004).

Shan W, 'Towards a Common European Community Policy on Investment Issues' (2001) 2 Journal of World Investment & Trade 603.

Shihata IFI, *MIGA and Foreign Investment: Origins, Operations, Policies and Basic Documents of the Multilateral Investment Guarantee Agency* (Martinus Nijhoff Publishers 1988).

Sinclair IM, *The Vienna Convention on the Law of Treaties* (Manchester Univ Press 1973).

Sommermann KP, *Staatsziele und Staatszielbestimmungen* (Mohr Siebeck 1997).

Sommermann KP, 'Article 3 TEU' in: Blanke HJ and Mangiameli S (eds), *The Treaty on European Union (TEU)* (Springer 2013) 179.

Sornarajah M, *Resistance and Change in the International Law on Foreign Investment* (Cambridge University Press 2015).

Sornarajah M, *The International Law on Foreign Investment* (Fourth edition, Cambridge University Press 2017).

Southern African Development Community, *SADC Model Bilateral Investment Treaty Template with Commentary* (2012).

Steinitz M, *The Case for an International Court of Civil Justice* (Cambridge University Press 2019).

Stoll P-T, Gött H and Abel P, 'A Model Labour Chapter for Future EU Trade Agreements' in: Gött H (ed), *Labour Standards in International Economic Law* (Springer International Publishing 2018) 381.

Storgaard LH, 'EU Law Autonomy versus European Fundamental Rights Protection—On *Opinion 2/13* on EU Accession to the ECHR' (2015) 15 Human Rights Law Review 485.

Strik P, *Shaping the Single European Market in the Field of Foreign Direct Investment* (Hart Pub 2014).

Talus K, *Introduction to EU Energy Law* (Oxford University Press 2016).

Terhechte JP, 'Art. 3 EUV', in: Grabitz E, Hilf M and Nettesheim M (dir), *Das Recht der Europäischen Union: Band I: EUV/AEUV, Rechtsstand: Juli 2010* (41 Aufl, Beck, CH 2010, mit Ergängzungen bis 2017) 9.

Terpan F, 'Soft Law in the European Union—The Changing Nature of EU Law: Soft Law in the European Union' (2015) 21 European Law Journal 68.

Thieffry P, *Droit de l'environnement de l'Union européenne* (2e éd, Bruylant 2011).

Tienhaara K, 'Regulatory Chill and the Threat of Arbitration: A View from Political Science', in: Brown C and Miles K (eds), *Evolution in Investment Treaty Law and Arbitration* (Cambridge University Press 2011) 606.

Tietje C and Crow K, 'The Reform of Investment Protection Rules in CETA, TTIP, and Other Recent EU FTAs: Convincing?' in: Griller S, Obwexer W and Vranes E (eds),

Mega-Regional Trade Agreements: CETA, TTIP, and TiSA ; New Orientations for EU External Economic Relations (Oxford University Press 2017) 87.

Titi C, *The Right to Regulate in International Investment Law* (Nomos 2014).

Titi C, 'The Right to Regulate' in: Mbengue MM and Schacherer S (eds), *Foreign Investment Under the Comprehensive Economic and Trade Agreement (CETA)*, vol 15 (Springer International Publishing 2019) 159.

UN General Assembly, 'Report of the World Commission on Environment and Development', 11 Dec 1987, UN-Doc. A/RES/42/187.

UNCTAD (ed), *Admission and Establishment* (United Nations 1999).

UNCTAD (ed), *Foreign Direct Investment and Performance Requirements: New Evidence from Selected Countries* (United Nations 2003).

UNCTAD (ed), *International Investment Arrangements: Trends and Emerging Issues* (United Nations 2006).

UNCTAD (ed), *The Role of International Investment Agreements in Attracting Foreign Direct Investment to Developing Countries* (United Nations 2009).

UNCTAD (ed), *World Investment Report 2011: Non-Equity Modes of International Production and Development* (United Nations 2011).

UNCTAD (ed), *Transparency* (United Nations 2012).

UNCTAD (ed), *Investing in the SDGs: An Action Plan* (United Nations 2014).

UNCTAD (ed), *Investment and the Digital Economy* (United Nations 2017).

UNCTAD (ed), *Investment and New Industrial Policies* (United Nations 2018).

United Nations (ed), *Principles for Responsible Contracts: Integrating the Management of Human Rights Risks into State-Investor Contract Negotiations: Guidance for Negotiators* (United Nations, Office of the High Commissioner for Human Rights 2015).

Van Aaken A, 'Smart Flexibility Clauses in International Investment Treaties and Sustainable Development' [2014] The Journal of World Investment & Trade 827.

Van Aaken A and Lehmann TA, 'Sustainable Development and International Investment Law' in: Echandi R and Sauvé P (eds), *Prospects in International Investment Law and Policy* (Cambridge University Press 2013) 317.

Van Harten G and Scott DN, 'Investment Treaties and the Internal Vetting of Regulatory Proposals: A Case Study from Canada' [2015] SSRN Electronic Journal <http://www.ssrn.com/abstract=2700238>.

Van Vooren B, *EU External Relations Law and the European Neighbourhood Policy: A Paradigm for Coherence* (Routledge 2012).

Van Vooren B, Blockmans S and Wouters J (eds), *The EU's Role in Global Governance: The Legal Dimension* (Oxford University Press 2013).

Vandenberghe J, 'On Carrots and Sticks: The Social Dimension of EU Trade Policy' (2008) European Foreign Affairs Review 561.

VanDuzer J, Simons P and Mayeda G, 'Integrating Sustainable Development into International Investment Agreements: A Guide for Developing Countries (Commonwealth Secretariat 2012).

Vedder C, 'Linkage of the Common Commercial Policy to the General Objectives for the Union's External Action', in: Bungenberg M and Herrmann C (eds), *Common Commercial Policy after Lisbon* (Springer 2013) 115.

Villiger ME, *Commentary on the 1969 Vienna Convention on the Law of Treaties* (Martinus Nijhoff Publishers 2009).

Viñuales JE, *Foreign Investment and the Environment in International Law* (Cambridge University Press 2012).

Viñuales JE, 'Re-Orienting the Sustainable Development Snake' (2013) SSRN Electronic Journal <http://www.ssrn.com/abstract=2200083> (last accessed 31 Jan 201).

Viñuales JE, 'The Rise and Fall of Sustainable Development' (2013) RECIEL (Review of European, Comparative and International Environmental Law).

Viñuales JE (ed), *The Rio Declaration on Environment and Development: A Commentary* (Oxford University Press 2015).

Viñuales JE, 'Investor Diligence in Investment Arbitration: Sources and Arguments' (2017) 2 ICSID Review 346.

Voiculescu A, 'Human Rights, Corporate Social Responsibility and the Shaping of the European Union's Linkage Strategy: "A Peaceful Revolution"?' in: Takács T, Ott A and Dimopoulos A (eds), *Linking Trade and Non-Commercial Interests: the EU as a global role model? CLEER* (CLEER Working Papers 2013/4).

Von Bogdandy A, 'Founding Principles of EU Law: A Theoretical and Doctrinal Sketch' (2010) 16 European Law Journal 95.

Voss J, 'The Protection and Promotion of European Private Investment in Developing Countries; An Approach towards a Concept for a European Policy on Foreign Investment; A German Contribution' (1981) 18 Common Market Law Review 363.

Waibel M and et al, *The Backlashes against Investment Arbitration—Perceptions and Realities* (Kluwer Law International 2010).

Waleson J, 'Corporate Social Responsibility in EU Comprehensive Free Trade Agreements: Towards Sustainable Trade and Investment" 42 Legal Issues of Economic Integration 143.

Weiler J, *The Constitution of Europe: 'Do the New Clothes Have an Emperor?' And Other Essays on European Integration* (Cambridge University Press 1999).

Weiss F and Steiner S, 'The Investment Regime under Article 207 TFEU: A Legal Conundrum, the Scope of "foreign Direct Investment" and the Future of Intra-EU BITs', in: Baetens F (ed), *Investment Law within International Law: Integrationist Perspectives* (Cambridge University Press 2013) 355.

Wessel RA, 'The Meso Level: Means of Interaction between EU and International Law: Flipping the Question: The Reception of EU Law in the International Legal Order' (2016) 35 Yearbook of European Law 533.

Wiers J, *Trade and Environment in the EC and the WTO: A Legal Analysis* (Europa Law Pub 2002).

Wolfrum R (eds), *The Max Planck Encyclopedia of Public International Law* (Oxford University Press 2012).

Wongkaew T, *Protection of Legitimate Expectations in Investment Treaty Arbitration: A Theory of Detrimental Reliance* (Cambridge University Press 2018).

Wouters J et al (eds), *Global Governance through Trade: EU Policies and Approaches* (Edward Elgar Publishing 2015).

Wu M, 'The Scope and Limits of Trade's Influence in Shaping the Evolving International Investment Regime', in: Douglas Z, Pauwelyn J and Viñuales JE (eds), *The Foundations of International Investment Law: Bringing Theory into Practice* (Oxford University Press 2014) 169.

Xavier Junior EC, 'A Latin American View on the CETA Investment Chapter' in: Mbengue MM and Schacherer S (eds), *Foreign Investment Under the Comprehensive Economic and Trade Agreement (CETA)*, vol 15 (Springer International Publishing 2019) 303.

Yasseen MK, *Interprétation des traités d'après la Convention de Vienne*, vol 151 (Martinus Nijhoff 1976).

Zachariasiewicz M, 'Amicus Curiae in International Investment Arbitration: Can It Enhance the Transparency of Investment Dispute Resolution?' (2012) Journal of Int'l Arbitration 29.

Ziegler KS, 'Closing Chapter: Piecing the Puzzle Together: Beyond Pluralism and Autonomy: Systemic Harmonization as a Paradigm for the Interaction of EU Law and International Law' (2016) 35 Yearbook of European Law 667.

Zimmer R, 'Sozialklauseln im Freihandelsabkommen der Europäischen Union mit Kolumbien und Peru' (2011) Recht der Internationalen Wirtschaft 625.

Table of Cases

Court of Justice of the European Union

Case 8/57 *Groupement des hauts fourneaux et aciéries belges,* EU:C:1958:9.
Case 26/62 *NV Algemene Transporten Expeditie Onderneming van Gend & Loos v Netherlands Inland Revenue Administration,* EU:C:1963:1.
Case 26/62 *Van Gend en Loos,* EU:C:1963:1.
Case 6/64 *Flaminio Costa v ENEL,* EU:C:1964:66.
Case 1/69 *Italy v Commission,* EU:C:1974:71.
Case 11/70 *Internationale Handelsgesellschaft mbH v Einfuhr- und Vorratsstelle für Getreide und Futtermittel,* EU:C:1970:114.
Case 22/70 *Commission v Council* (AETR), EU:C:1971:32.
Case 6/72 *Europemballage Corporation and Continental Can Company Inc. v Commission,* EU:C:1973:2.
Joined Cases 6 and 7/73 *Istituto Chemioterapico Italiano S.p.A. and Commercial Solvents Corporation v Commission,* EU:C:1974:18.
Case 8/73 *Hauptzollamt Bremerhaven v Massey-Ferguson,* EU:C:1973:90.
Opinion 1/75 *Local Cost Standard,* EU:C:1975:145.
Case 43/75 *Gabrielle Defrenne v Sabena,* EU:C:1976:56.
Case 51/75 *EMI Records Limited v CBS United Kingdom Limited,* EU:C:1976:85.
Opinion 1/76 *Draft Agreement establishing a European laying-up fund for inland waterway vessels,* EU:C:1977:63.
Case 33/76 *Rewe-Zentralfinanz EG v Landwirtschaftskammer für das Saarland,* EU:C:1976:188.
Case 41/76 *Donckerwolcke and Others v Procureur de la République,* EU:C:1976:182
Case 106/77 *Amministrazione delle Finanze dello Stato v Simmenthal,* EU:C:1978:49
Opinion 1/78 *Commodity Agreement on Natural Rubber,* EU:C:1979:224.
Case 139/79 *Maizena GmbH v Council of the European Communities,* EU:C:1980:250.
Case 15/81 *Gaston Schul Douane Expediteur BV v Inspecteur der Invoerrechten en Accijnzen, Roosendaal,* EU:C:1982:135.
Case 104/81 *Hauptzollamt Mainz v C.A. Kupferberg & Cie KG a.A.* EU:C:1982:362.
Case 240/83 *Procureur de la République v ADBHU,* EU:C:1985:59.
Case C-147/84 *Finsider v Commission,* EU:C:1985:358.
Case 179/84 *Bozzetti v Invernizzi,* EU:C:1985:306.
Case 12/86 *Demirel v Stadt Schwäbisch Gmünd,* EU:C:1987:400.
Case 45/86 *Tariff Preferences,* EU:C:1987:163.

Case 265/87 *Hermann Schräder HS Kraftfutter GmbH & Co KG v Hauptzollamt Gronau*, EU:C:1989:303.
Case 62/88 *Greece v Council (Chernobyl case)*, EU:C:1990:15329.
Case C-331/88 *The Queen v Minister of Agriculture, Fisheries and Food and Secretary of State for Health, ex parte: Fedesa and others*, EU:C:1990:391.
Case C-300/89 *Commission v Council (Titanium Dioxide)*, EU:C:1991:244.
Opinion 1/91 *European Economic Area (EEA) agreement*, EU:C:1991:490.
Opinion 2/91 *ILO Convention*, EU:C:1993:106.
Case C-106/91 *Ramrath v Ministre de la Justice*, EU:C:1992:230.
Opinion 2/92 *Third Revised Decision of the OECD on national treatment*, EU:C:1995:83.
Case T-572/93 *Odigitria v Council and Comission*, EU:T:1995:131.
Opinion 1/94 *Agreement establishing the World Trade Organization*, EU:C:1994:384.
Case C-84/94 *United Kingdom v Council* EU:C:1996:431.
Case C-268/94 *Portugal v Council*, EU:C:1996:461.
Case C-142/95 *P Associazione degli Agricoltori della provincia di Rovigo v Commission*, EU:C:1996:493.
Case C-284/95 *Safety High-Tech v S & T Srl*, EU:C:1998:352.
Case C-341/95, *Gianni Bettati v Safety High Tech*, EU:C:1998:353.
Case C-162/96 *A. Racke GmbH & Co. v Hauptzollamt Mainz*, EU:C:1998:293.
Case C-180/96, *United Kingdom of Great Britain and Northern Ireland v Commission of the European Communities*, EU:C:1998:192.
Case C-120/97 *Upjohn v The Licensing Authority*, EU:C:1999:14.
Case C-36/98 *Spain v Council*, EU:C:2001:64.
Case C-371/98 *R v Secretary of State for Environment Transport and the Regions, ex p First Corporate Shipping*, EU:C:2000:600.
Case C-467/98 *Commission v Denmark* (Open Skies), EU:C:2002:62.
Opinion 2/00 *Cartagena Protocol*, EU:C:2001:664.
Case C336/00 *Republik Österreich v Martin Huber*, EU:C:2002:509.
Case C-281/01 *Commission v Council (Energy Star)*, EU:C:2002:761.
Opinion 1/03 *New Lugano Convention*, EU:C:2006:8.
Case C94/03 *Commission v Council (Rotterdam Convention)*, EU:C:2006:2.
Joined Cases C-282/04 and C-283/04 *Commission v Netherlands*, EU:C:2006:208.
Case C-446/04 *Test Claimants in the FII Group Litigation v Commissioners of Inland Revenue*, EU:C:2006:774.
Case C-91/05 *Commission v Council*, EU:C:2008:288.
Joined Cases C-402/05 P and C-415/05 P *Kadi and Al Barakaat*, EU:C:2008:461.
Case C-438/05 *International Transport Workers' Federation and Finnish Seamen's Union v Viking Line ABP and OÜ Viking Line Eesti*, EU:C:2007:772.

Case C-181/06 *Deutsche Lufthansa* AG v ANA—*Aeroportos de Portugal* SA, EU:C:2007:412.
Cases C-13/07 *Commission v Council*, EU:C:2009:190.
Case C-326/07 *Commission v Italy*, EU:C:2009:193.
Opinion 1/08 *Agreements modifying the Schedules of Specific Commitments under the* GATS, EU:C:2009:739.
Opinion 1/09 *Patents Court*, EU:C:2011:123.
Case C-81/09 *Idryma Typou v Ypourgos Typou*, EU:C:2010:622.
Case C-212/09 *Commission v Portugal*, EU:C:2011:717.
Case C-43/10 *Nomarchiaki Aftodioikisi Aitoloakarnanias and Others*, EU:C:2012:560.
Case C-130/10 *Parliament v Council*, EU:C:2012:472.
Case C-366/10 *Air Transport Association of America and others v. Secretary of State for Energy and Climate Change*, EU:C:2011:864.
Joined Cases C-584/10 P, C-593/10 P *Commission, UK and Council v Kadi* (Kadi II), EU:C:2013:518.
Case C-414/11 *Daiichi Sankyo Co. Ltd and Sanofi-Aventis Deutschland GmbH v* DEMO *Anonimos Viomikhaniki kai Emporiki Etairia Farmakon*, EU:C:2013:520.
Joined Cases C-105/12 to C-107/12 *Nederlanden v Essent* NV *and Others*, EU:C:2013:677.
Case C-137/12 *Commission v Council*, EU:C:2013:675.
Case C-176/12 *Association de Médiation Sociale*, EU:C:2014:2.
Case C-377/12 *Commission v Council (Philippines)*, EU:C:2014:1903.
Case T-512/12 *Front Polisario v Council*, EU:T:2015:953.
Opinion 1/13 *Accession of third States to the Hague Convention*, EU:C:2014:2303.
Opinion 2/13 *Accession of the European Union to the European Convention for the Protection of Human Rights and Fundamental Freedoms*, EU:C:2014:2454.
Case C-263/14 *Parliament v Council*, EU:C:2016:435.
Case C-464/14 SECIL, EU:C:2016:896.
Case C-600/14 *Germany v Council*, EU:C:2017:935.
Opinion 2/15 *Free Trade Agreement with Singapore*, EU:C:2017:376.
Opinion of AG Sharpston (Opinion procedure 2/15), EU:C:2016:992,
Opinion 3/15 *Marrakesh Treaty*, EU:C:2017:114.
C-201/15 AGET *Iraklis*, EU:C:2016:972.
Case C-272/15 *Swiss International Air Lines*, EU:C:2016:993.
GC, Cases T-624/15, T-694/15 and T-704/15, *European Food* SA *and Others v European Commission*, EU:T:2019:423.
Case C-284/16 *Slowakische Republik v Achmea BV*, EU:C:2018:158.
Opinion 1/17 *Compatibility of the Investment Court System* (ICS), EU:C:2018:478.

Permanent Court of International Justice

Jurisdiction of the European Commission of the Danube, Advisory Opinion, 8 Dec 1927, PCIJ Rep Series B No 14.

Case on the Diversion of Water from the Meuse (Netherlands v Belgium), Judgment, 28 June 1937, PCIJ Rep Series A/B No 70.

International Court of Justice

Certain Expenses of the United Nations, Advisory Opinion, ICJ Rep 1962, 151.

Legal Consequences for States of the Continued Presence of South Africa in Namibia, notwithstanding Security Council Resolution 276(1970), Advisory Opinion, ICJ Rep 1971, 16.

Elettronica Sicula S.p.A. (ELSI) (United States of America v Italy), Judgement, ICJ Rep 1989, 15.

Case Concerning the Territorial Dispute (Libyan Arab Jamahiriya/Chad), Judgment ICJ Rep 1994, 6.

Legality of the Use by a State of Nuclear Weapons in Armed Conflicts, Advisory Opinion), ICJ Rep 1996, 66.

Case Concerning the Gabcíkovo-Nagymaros Project (Hungary/Slovakia), ICJ Rep 1997, 7.

Case Concerning the Gabcíkovo-Nagymaros Project (Hungary/Slovakia), Separate Opinion of Vice-president Weeramantry, ICJ Rep 1997, 88.

Dispute regarding Navigational and Related Rights (Costa Rica/Nicaragua), Judgment, ICJ Rep 2009, 213.

Case Concerning Pulp Mills on The River Uruguay (Argentina v Uruguay), Judgment, ICJ Rep 2010, 14.

Whaling in the Antarctic (Australia v Japan: New Zealand Intervening), Judgment, ICJ Rep 2014, 226.

Investor-State Arbitration (Alphabetical)

Aaron C Berkowitz, Brett E Berkowitz, Trevor B Berkowitz and others v The Republic of Costa Rica, ICSID Case No UNCT/13/2, Interim Award, 25 Oct 2016.

Adel A. Hamadi Al Tamimi v Sultanate of Oman, ICSID Case No ARB/11/33, Award, 3 Nov 2015.

Ambiente Ufficio v Argentina, ICSID Case No ARB/08/9, Decision on Jurisdiction and Admissibility, 8 Feb 2013.

TABLE OF CASES

Antin Infrastructure Services Luxembourg S.à.r.l & Antin Energia Termosolar B.V v The Kingdom of Spain, ICSID Case No ARB/13/31, Award, 15 June 2018.

Aguas del Tunari v Republic of Bolivia, ICSID Case No ARB/02/3, Decision on Jurisdiction, 21 Oct 2005.

Alpha Projektholding GmbH v Ukraine, ICSID Case No ARB/07/16, Award, 8 Nov 2010.

Álvarez y Marín Corporación and others v Panama, ICSID Case No ARB/15/14, pending.

Limited Liability Company AMTO v Ukraine, SCC Case No 080/2005, Award, 26 March 2008.

Asian Agricultural Products Ltd (AAPL) v Sri Lanka, ICSID ARB/87/3, Final Award, 27 June 1990.

Azurix Corp. v Argentina, ICSID Case No ARB/01/12, Award, 14 July 2006.

Bayindir Insaat Turizm Ticaret Ve Sanayi AS v Islamic Republic of Pakistan, ICSID Case No ARB/03/29, Decision on Jurisdiction, 14 Nov 2005.

Bear Creek Mining Corporation v Republic of Peru, ICSID Case No ARB/14/2, Award, 30 Nov 2017.

Biwater Gauff Ltd v United Republic of Tanzania, ICSID Case No ARB/05/22, Award, 24 July 2008.

Blusun S.A., Jean-Pierre Lecorcier and Michael Stein v Italian Republic, ICSID Case No ARB/14/3, Award, 21 Jan 2016.

Burlington Resources Inc. and ors v Republic of Ecuador and Empresa Estatal Petroleos del Ecuador (PetroEcuador), ICSID Case No ARB/08/5, Decision on Liability, 14 Dec 2012.

Burlington Resources Inc. and ors v Republic of Ecuador and Empresa Estatal Petroleos del Ecuador (PetroEcuador), ICSID Case No ARB/08/5, Interim Decision on Environmental Counterclaim, 11 Aug 2015.

Cargill Incorporated v United Mexican States, ICSID Case No ARB(AF)/05/2, Award, 18 Sep 2009.

Charanne B.V. and Construction Investments S.A.R.L. v The Kingdom of Spain, SCC, No 062/2012, Award, 27 Dec 2016.

Chemtura Corporation v Government of Canada, UNCITRAL, Award, 2 Aug 2010.

CME Czech Republic BV v Czech Republic, UNCITRAL, Partial Award, 13 Sep 2001.

CMS Gas Transmission Company v The Argentine Republic, ICSID Case No ARB/01/8, Award, 12 May 2005.

Compania del Desarrollo de Santa Elena v Republic of Costa Rica, ICSID Case No ARB/96/1, Final Award, 17 Feb 2000.

Cosigo Resources and others v Colombia, UNCITRAL, pending.

Cortec Mining Kenya Limited, Cortec (Pty) Limited and Stirling Capital Limited v. Republic of Kenya, ICSID Case No ARB/15/29, Award, 22 Oct 2018.

Crystallex International Corporation v Bolivarian Republic of Venezuela, ICSID Case No ARB(AF)/11/2, Award, 4 April 2016.

David R. Aven, Samuel D. Aven, Carolyn J. Park, Eric A. Park, Jeffrey S. Shioleno, Giacomo A. Buscemi, David A. Janney and Roger Raguso v The Republic of Costa Rica, ICSID Case No UNCT/15/3, Award, 18 Sep 2018.

Desert Line Projects LLC v The Republic of Yemen, Award, ICSID Case No ARB/05/17, 6 Feb 2008.

Eco Oro Minerals Corp. v Republic of Colombia, ICSID Case No ARB/16/41, pending.

EDF (Services) Limited v Romania, ICSID Case No ARB/05/13, Award, 8 Oct 2009.

Eiser Infrastructure Limited and Energia Solar Luxembourg S.à r.l. v The Kingdom of Spain, ICSID Case No ARB/13/36, Award, 4 May 2017.

Eli Lilly and Company v Canada, Final Award, 16 March 2017, UNCITRAL Case No UNCT/14/2.

El Paso Energy International Company v The Argentine Republic, ICSID Case No ARB/03/15, Award, 31 Oct 2011.

Enron Corporation v Argentina, ICSID Case No ARB/01/3, Award, 15 May 2007.

Eureko BV v Republic of Poland, Partial Award, 19 Aug 2005.

Eureko BV v Republic of Slovakia, PCA Case No 2008–13, Award on Jurisdiction, Arbitrability and Suspension, 26 Oct 2010.

Fedax NV v The Republic of Venezuela, ICSID Case No ARB/96/3, Decision of the Tribunal on Objections to Jurisdiction, 11 July 1997.

Fraport v Philippines, ICSID Case No ARB/03/25, Award I, 16 Aug 2007.

Greentech Energy Systems v The Italian Republic, SCC Arbitration V 2015/095, Award, 23 Dec 2018.

Ioan Micula, Viorel Micula, S.C. European Food S.A, S.C. Starmill S.R.L. and S.C. Multipack S.R.L. v Romania, ICSID Case No ARB/05/20, Final Award, 11 Dec 2013.

Isolux Infrastructure Netherlands B.V. v The Kingdom of Spain, SCC, Award, 11 July 2016.

Pantechniki SA Contractors and Engineers v Albania, ICSID Case No ARB/07/21, Award, 28 July 2009.

Phoenix Action Ltd v The Czech Republic, ICSID Case No ARB/06/5, Award, 15 April 2009.

Gami Investments Inc v United Mexican States, UNCITRAL, Award, 15 Nov 2004.

Glamis Gold Ltd v The United States of America, NAFTA, UNCITRAL, Award, 8 June 2009.

Gold Reserve Inc. v Bolivarian Republic of Venezuela, ICSID Case No ARB(AF)/09/1, Award, 22 Sep 2014.

Grand River Enterprises and ors v United States of America, NAFTA, UNCITRAL, Decision on Objections to Jurisdiction, 20 July 2006.
Hulley Enterprises Limited (Cyprus) v The Russian Federation, UNCITRAL, PCA Case No AA 226, Final Award, 18 July 2014.
Kiliç İnşaat İthalat İhracat Sanayi Ve Ticaret Anonim Şirketi v Turkmenistan, ICSID Case No ARB/10/1, Award, 2 July 2013.
KT Asia Investment Group BV v Republic of Kazakhstan, ICSID Case No ARB/09/8, Award, 17 Oct 2013.
LESI v People's Democratic Republic of Algeria, ICSID ARB/03/8, Award, 10 Jan 2005.
LG&E Energy Corp v Argentine Republic, ICSID Case No ARB/02/1, Decision on Liability, 3 Oct 2006.
Malaysian Historical Salvors Sdn, Bhd v Malaysia, ICSID Case No ARB/05/10, Award on Jurisdiction, 17 May 2007.
Malaysian Historical Salvors Sdn, Bhd v Malaysia, ICSID Case No ARB/05/10, Decision of the Application for Annulment, 16 April 2009.
Marion Unglaube and Reinhard Unglaube v Republic of Costa Rica, ICSID Case No ARB/08/1 and ICSID Case No ARB/09/20, Award, 16 May 2012.
Masdar Solar & Wind Cooperatief UA v The Kingdom of Spain, ICSID Case No ARB/14/01, Award, 16 May 2018.
Mesa Power Group, LLC v Canada, Award, 24 March 2016, UNCITRAL PCA Case No 2012–17.
Metalclad Corporation v Mexico, ICSID Case No ARB(AF)/97/1, Award, 30 Aug 2000.
Metal-Tech Ltd v The Republic of Uzbekistan, ICSID Case No ARB/10/3, Award, 4 Oct 2013.
Methanex v United States, UNCITRAL, Final Award, 3 Aug 2005.
Mobil Investment Canada Inc and Murphy Oil Corporation v Canada, Decision on Liability, 22 May 2012.
MTD Equity Sdn Bhd and MTD Chile S.A. v Republic of Chile, ICSID Case No ARB/01/7, Award, 25 May 2004.
Noble Energy v Ecuador, ICSID Case No ARB/05/12, Decision on Jurisdiction, 5 March 2008.
Novenergia v The Kingdom of Spain, SCC Case No 063/2015, Award, 15 Feb 2017.
Pac Rim Cayman LLC v Republic of El Salvador, ICSID Case No ARB/09/12, Award, 14 Oct 2016.
Patrick Mitchell v Democratic Republic of the Congo, ICSID Case No ARB/99/7, Decision on the Application for Annulment of the Award, 1 Nov 2006.
Philip Morris v Australia, PCA Case No 2012-12, Award on Jurisdiction and Admissibility, 17 Dec 2015.

Philip Morris Brands SÀRL, *Philip Morris Products* SA *and Abal Hermanos* SA *v Oriental Republic of Uruguay*, ICSID Case No ARB/10/7, Award, 8 July 2016.

Piero Foresti, Laura de Carli & Others v The Republic of South Africa, ICSID Case No ARB(AF)/07/01, Award, 4 Aug 2010.

PSEG Global Inc v Turkey, ICSID Case No ARB/02/5, Award, 19 Jan 2007.

Mondev International Ltd v United States of America, ICSID Case No ARB(AF)/99/2, Award, 11 Oct 2002.

Occidental Exploration and Prod. Co. v Republic of Ecuador (Occidental I), UNCITRAL, LCIA Case No UN3467, Final Award, 1 July 2004.

Parkerings-Compagniet AS *v Republic of Lithuania*, ICSID Case No ARB/05/8, Award, 11 Sep 2007.

Peter A. Allard v The Government of Barbados, PCA Case No 2012-06, Award, 27 June 2016.

Plama Consortium Limited v Bulgaria, ICSID Case No ARB/03/24, Decision on Jurisdiction, 8 Feb 2005.

Plama Consortium Limited v Bulgaria, ICSID Case No ARB/03/24, Award, 27 August 2008.

Pope & Talbot v Canada, UNCITRAL, Award on the Merits of Phase 2, 10 April 2001.

R. S. Lauder v Czech Republic, UNCITRAL, Award, 3 Sep 2001.

Rumeli Telekom SA *and Telsim Mobil Telekomikasyon Hizmetleri* AS *v Kazakhstan* ICSID Case No ARB/05/16, Award, 29 July 2008.

Rusoro Mining Ltd. v Bolivarian Republic of Venezuela, ICSID Case No ARB(AF)/12/5), Award, 22 Aug 2016.

Saba Fakes v Republic of Turkey, ICSID Case No ARB/07/20, Award, 14 July 2010.

Saipem SpA v The People's Republic of Bangladesh, ICSID Case No ARB/05/7, Decision on Jurisdiction, 21 March 2007.

Saipem SpA v The People's Republic of Bangladesh, ICSID Case No ARB/05/07, Award, 30 June 2009.

Salini Costruttori SpA and Italstrade SpA v Morocco, ICSID Case No ARB/00/4, Decision on Jurisdiction, 23 July 2001.

Saluka Investments BV *v The Czech Republic*, UNCITRAL, Decision on Jurisdiction over the Czech Republic's Counterclaim, 7 May 2004.

Saluka Investments BV *v The Czech Republic*, UNCITRAL, Partial Award, 17 March 2006.

Sanum Investments Limited v Lao People's Democratic Republic, UNCITRAL, PCA Case No 2013-13, Award on Jurisdiction, 13 Dec 2013.

SAUR *International* SA *v Argentina*, ICSID Case No ARB/04/4, Decision on Jurisdiction and Liability, 6 June 2012.

SAUR *International v Argentina*, ICSID Case No ARB/04/4, Award, 22 May 2014.

S.D. Myers Inc. v Government of Canada, NAFTA, UNCITRAL, First Partial Award, 13 Nov 2000.

Sempra Energy International v Argentina, ICSID Case No ARB/02/16, Award, 18 Sep 2007.

SGS Société Générale de Surveillance SA v Republic of the Philippines, ICSID Case No ARB/02/6, Decision on Objection to Jurisdiction, 29 Jan 2004.

Siemens A.G. v The Argentine Republic, ICSID Case No ARB/02/8, Decision on Jurisdiction, 3 Aug 2004.

Siemens AG v The Argentine Republic, ICSID Case No ARB/02/8, Award, 17 Jan 2007.

Société Générale v Dominican Republic, UNCITRAL, LCIA Case No UN 7927 Decision on Jurisdiction, 19 Sep 2008.

Spyridon Roussalis v Romania, ICSID Case No ARB/06/1, Award, 7 Dec 2011.

Suez, Sociedad General de Aguas de Barcelona SA and Vivendi Universal SA v Argentine Republic, ICSID Case No ARB/03/19, Decision on Liability, 30 July 2010.

Técnicas Medioambientales Tecmed SA v United Mexican States, ICSID Case No ARB (AF)/00/02, Award of 29 May 2003.

Teco Guatemala Holding LLC v Guatemala, ICSID Case No ARB/10/23, Award, 19 Dec 2013.

Telenor Mobile Communications AS v The Republic of Hungary, ICSID Case No ARB/04/15, Award, 13 Sep 2006.

Tokios Tokelės v Ukraine, ICSID Case No ARB/02/18, Decision on Jurisdiction, 29 April 2004.

Total SA v Argentine Republic, ICSID Case No ARB/04/01, Decision on Liability, 27 Dec 2010.

Tethyan Copper Company Pty Limited v Islamic Republic of Pakistan, ICSID Case No ARB/12/1, Award, 12 July 2019.

Tza Yap Shum v Republic of Peru, ICSID Case No ARB/07/6, Award, 7 July 2011.

Urbaser SA and Consorcio de Aguas Bilbao Bizkaia, Bilbao Biskaia Ur Partzuergoa v The Argentine Republic, ICSID Case No ARB/07/26, Award, 8 Dec 2016.

Victor Pey Casado v Chile, ICSID Case No ARB/98/2, Award, 8 May 2008.

Waste Management Inc v Mexico, ICSID Case No ARB(AF)/00/3, Final Award, 30 April 2004.

William Ralph Clayton, William Richard Clayton, Douglas Clayton, Daniel Clayton and Bilcon of Delaware Inc. v Government of Canada (Bilcon v Canada), PCA Case No 2009-04, Award on Jurisdiction and Liability, 17 March 2015.

World Duty Free Company Limited v Kenya, ICSID Case No ARB/00/7, Award, 4 Oct 2006.

Yaung Chi Oo Trading Pte Ltd v Government of the Union of Myanmar, ASEAN ID, Case No ARB/01/1, Award, 31 March 2003.

State-State Arbitration

Award in the Arbitration regarding the Iron Rhine ("Ijzeren Rijn") Railway between the Kingdom of Belgium and the Kingdom of the Netherlands, Reports of International Arbitral Awards, Vol XXVII, Decision, 24 May 2005.

In The Matter Of The Indus Waters Kishenganga Arbitration (Pakistan v India), Permanent Court of Arbitration, Partial Award, 18 Feb 2013.

World Trade Organization

United States—Standards for Reformulated and Conventional Gasoline, Appellate Body Report and Panel Report, (1996) WT/DS2/9.

United States—Import Prohibition of Certain Shrimp and Shrimp Products, Appellate Body Report, (1998) WT/DS58/AB/R.

EC Measures Concerning Meat and Meat Products (Hormones), Appellate Body Report, (1998) WT/DS26/AB/R, WT/DS48/AB/R.

EC—Measures Affecting Asbestos and Products Containing Asbestos, Panel Report, (2000) WT/DS135/R.

European Communities (EC)—Customs Classification of Frozen Boneless Chicken Cuts, Appellate Body Report, (2005) WT/DS286/AB/R.

China—Measures Related to the Exportation of Rare Earths, Tungsten, and Molybdenum, Panel Report, (2014) WT/DS431/R.

Australia—Certain Measures Concerning Trademarks and Other Plain Packaging Requirements Applicable to Tobacco Products and Packaging, Panel Reports (2018) WT/DS435/R, WT/DS441/R WT/DS458/R, WT/DS467/R.

Other Jurisdictions

Penn Central Transport v City of New York, 438 US 104, 123–125, 1978.

African Commission on Human and People's Rights 155/96, *The Social and Economic Rights Action Center and the Center for Economic and Social Rights v Nigeria*, 13–29 Oct 2007.

Kyoto Enforcement Branch of the Compliance Committee, CC-2007-1/Greece/EB, Final Decision, 17 April 2008.

Table of Treaties, Legislation and Other Documents

International Treaties

Bilateral Treaties Concluded by the EU

Agreement amending the fourth ACP-EC Convention of Lomé IV, [1990] OJ L 229/3.

Agreement on partnership and cooperation establishing a partnership between the European Communities and their Member States, of one part, and the Russian Federation, of the other part, [1997] OJ L 327/3.

Cooperation Agreement between the European Community and the former Yugoslav Republic of Macedonia, [1997] OJ L 348/2.

Partnership and Cooperation Agreement between the European Communities and their Member States and the Republic of Moldova, [1998] OJ L 181/3.

Euro-Mediterranean Agreement establishing an association between the European Communities and their Member States, of the one part, and the Republic of Tunisia, of the other part, [1998] OJ L 97/2.

Partnership and Cooperation Agreement between the European Communities and their Member States, of the one part, and Georgia, of the other part, [1999] OJ L 205/3.

Partnership and Cooperation Agreement between the European Communities and their Member States, of the one part, and the Republic of Azerbaijan, of the other part, [1999] OJ L 246/3.

Partnership and Cooperation Agreement establishing a partnership between the European Communities and their Member States, of the one part, and the Kyrgyz Republic, of the other part, [1999] OJ L 196/48.

Euro-Mediterranean Agreement establishing an association between the European Communities and their Member States, of the one part, and the Kingdom of Morocco, of the other part, [2000] OJ L 70/2.

Euro-Mediterranean Agreement establishing an association between the European Communities and their Member States, of the one part, and the State of Israel, of the other part, [2000] OJ L 147/3.

EU-Mexico Economic Partnership, Political Coordination and Cooperation Agreement [2000] OJ L 276/45.

Partnership agreement between the members of the African, Caribbean and Pacific Group of States of the one part, and the European Community and its Member States, of the other part ("Cotonou Agreement"), [2000] OJ L 317/3.

Agreement establishing an association between the European Community and its Member States, of the one part, and the Republic of Chile, of the other part, [2002] OJ L 352/3.

Euro-Mediterranean Agreement establishing an association between the European Communities and their Member States, of the one part, and the Hashemite Kingdom of Jordan, of the other part, [2002] OJ L 129/3.

Euro-Mediterranean Agreement establishing an Association between the European Communities and their Member States, of the one part, and the Arab Republic of Egypt, of the other part, [2004] OJ L 345/115.

Cooperation Agreement between the European Community and the Islamic Republic of Pakistan on partnership and development fields, [2004] OJ L 378/23.

Euro-Mediterranean Agreement establishing an Association between the European Community and its Member States, of the one part, and the People's Democratic Republic of Algeria, of the other part, [2005] OJ L 265/2.

Euro-Mediterranean Agreement establishing an Association between the European Community and its Member States, of the one part, and the Republic of Lebanon, of the other part, [2006] OJ L 143/2.

Economic Partnership Agreement between the CARIFORUM States, of the one part, and the European Community and its Member States, of the other part, [2008] OJ L 289/3.

Stabilisation and Association Agreement between the European Communities and their Member States, of the one part, and the Republic of Albania, of the other part, [2009] OJ L 107/166.

Stabilisation and Association Agreement between the European Communities and their Member States, of the one part, and the Republic of Montenegro, of the other part, [2010] OJ L 108/3.

Free trade agreement between the European Union and its Member States, of the one part, and the Republic of Korea, of the other part, [2011] OJ L 127/6. (EUKFTA)

Trade agreement between the European Union and its Member States, of the one part, and Colombia and Peru, of the other part, [2012] OJ L 354/3.

Agreement establishing an Association between the European Union and its Member States, on the one hand, and Central America on the other, [2012] OJ L 346/3.

Framework Agreement between the European Union and its Member States, on the one part, and the Republic of Korea, on the other part, [2013] OJ L 20/2.

Stabilisation and Association Agreement between the European Communities and their Member States of the one part, and the Republic of Serbia, of the other part, [2013] OJ L 278/16.

Agreement between the European Union and the Republic of the Seychelles on access for fishing vessels flying the flag of the Seychelles to waters and marine biological resources of Mayotte, under the jurisdiction of the European Union, [2014] OJ L 167/4.

Association Agreement between the European Union and its Member States, of the one part, and Ukraine, of the other part, [2014] OJ L 161/3.

Economic Partnership Agreement between the European Union and its Member States, of the one part, and the SADC States, of the other part, [2016] OJ L 250/3.

Comprehensive and enhanced Partnership Agreement between the European Union and the European Atomic Energy Community and their Member States, of the one part, and the Republic of Armenia, of the other part, [2018] OJ L 23/4.

Framework Agreement on Comprehensive Partnership and Cooperation between the European Union and its Member States, of the one part, and the Socialist Republic of Viet Nam, of the other part, [2016] OJ L 329/8.

Enhanced Partnership and Cooperation Agreement between the European Union and its Member States, of the one part, and the Republic of Kazakhstan, of the other part, [2016] OJ L 29/3.

Comprehensive Economic and Trade Agreement (CETA) between Canada, of the one part, and the European Union and its Member States, of the other part, [2017] OJ L 11/23.

Joint Interpretative Instrument on the Comprehensive Economic and Trade Agreement (CETA) between Canada and the European Union and its Member States, [2017] OJ L 11/3.

Economic Partnership Agreement between the European Union and Japan, [2018] OJ L 330/3; (EUJFTA).

Free Trade Agreement between the European Union and Singapore, [2019] OJ L 294; (EUSFTA).

Investment Protection Agreement between the European Union and Singapore, (authentic text as of April 2018; not yet in the Official Journal of the EU), available at http://trade.ec.europa.eu/doclib/press/index.cfm?id=961; (EUSIPA).

Free Trade Agreement between the European Union and Mexico (authentic text as of April 2018; not yet in the Official Journal of the EU), available at http://trade.ec.europa.eu/doclib/press/index.cfm?id=1833; (EUMFTA).

Free Trade Agreement between the European Union and Vietnam, [2019] OJ L 186; (EUVFTA).

Investment Protection Agreement between the European Union and Vietnam, (authentic text as of August 2018; not yet in the Official Journal), available at http://trade.ec.europa.eu/doclib/press/index.cfm?id=1437; (EUVIPA).

Free Trade Agreement between the European Union and MERCOSUR, (text as of July 2019; not yet in the Official Journal), available at https://trade.ec.europa.eu/doclib/press/index.cfm?id=2048; (EUMERFTA).

Comprehensive Agreement on Investment (CAI) between the European Union and China, (text as of January 2021; not yet in the Official Journal), available at https://trade.ec.europa.eu/doclib/press/index.cfm?id=2115; (EUCCAI).

Trade and Investment Agreements (Non-EU)

1959 Germany-Pakistan BIT, Date of signature: 25/11/1959, Date of entry into force: 28/04/1962.

1965 Belgium-Luxembourg Economic Union-Morocco BIT, Date of signature: 28/04/1965; Date of entry into force: 18/10/1967; Date of termination: 29/05/2002.

1979 Netherlands-Senegal BIT, Date of signature: 03/08/1979; Date of entry into force: 05/05/1981.

1985 United States-Turkey BIT, Date of signature: 03/12/1985; Date of entry into force: 18/05/1990.

1991 Czech-Republic-Netherlands BIT, Date of signature: 29/04/1991; Date of entry into force: 01/10/1992.

1992 North American Free Trade Agreement (NAFTA), Date of signature: 17/12/1992; Date of entry into force: 01/01/1994.

1994 Netherlands-Bangladesh BIT, Date of signature: 01/11/1994; Date of entry into force: 01/06/1996.

1994 Netherlands-Latvia BIT, Date of signature: 14/03/1994; Date of entry into force: 01/04/1995.

1995 Argentina-Israel BIT, Date of signature: 23/07/1995; Date of entry into force: 10/04/1997.

1996 Canada-Chile Free Trade Agreement, Date of signature: 05/12/1996; Date of entry into force: 05/07/1997.

1997 Austria-Chile BIT, Date of signature: 08/09/1997; Date of entry into force: 22/10/2000.

1999 Netherlands-Costa Rica BIT, Date of signature: 21/05/1999; Date of entry into force: 01/07/2001.

2000 Cameroon-Egypt BIT, Date of signature: 24/10/2000.

2000 United States-Jordan FTA, Date of signature: 24/10/2000; Date of entry into force: 17/12/2001.

2002 Switzerland-Guatemala BIT, Date of signature: 09/09/2002; Date of entry into force: 03/05/2005.

2003 Panama-Taiwan FTA, Date of signature: 21/08/2003; Date of entry into force: 01/01/2004.

2003 United States-Chile Free Trade Agreement, Date of signature: 06/06/2003; Date of entry into force: 01/01/2004.

2003 United States-Singapore FTA, Date of signature: 06/05/2003; Date of entry into force: 01/01/2004.

2004 Dominican Republic-Central America Free Trade Agreement (DR-CAFTA), Date of signature: 05/08/2004; Date of entry into force: 24/02/2012.

2004 France-Bahrain BIT, Date of signature: 24/02/2004; Date of entry into force: 03/10/2005.

2004 Belgium/Luxembourg-Libya BIT, Date of signature: 15/02/2004; Date of entry into force: 08/12/2007.

2004 United States-Australia FTA, Date of signature: 18/05/2004; Date of entry into force: 01/01/2005.

2004 United States-Bahrain FTA, Date of signature: 14/09/2004 Date of entry into force: 11/01/2006.

2004 United States-Morocco FTA, Date of signature: 15/06/2004; Date of entry into force: 01/01/2006.

2005 Belgium/Luxembourg-Guatemala BIT, Date of signature: 14/04/2005; Date of entry into force: 01/09/2007.

2005 Belgium/Luxembourg-Mauritius BIT, Date of signature: 30/11/2005; Date of entry into force: 16/01/2010.

2005 Comprehensive Economic Cooperation Agreement (CECA) between the Republic of India and the Republic of Singapore, Date of signature: Date of signature: 29/06/2005; Date of entry into force: 01/08/2005.

2005 United States-Uruguay BIT, Date of signature: 04/11/2005; Date of entry into force: 31/10/2006.

2006 United States-Oman Free Trade Agreement, Date of signature: 19/01/2006; Date of entry into force: 01/01/2009.

2006 United States-Uruguay Free Trade Agreement, Date of signature: 18/01/2006; Date of entry into force: 01/11/2006.

2006 United States–Colombia Free Trade Agreement, Date of signature: 22/11/2006; Date of entry into force: 15/05/2012.

2006 United States-Peru FTA, Date of signature: 12/04/2006; Date of entry into force: 01/02/2009.

2007 Investment Agreement for the COMESA Common Investment Area, Date of signature: 23/05/2007.

2007 United States-Panama FTA, Date of signature: 28/06/2007; Date of entry into force: 31/10/2012.

2008 Canada-Colombia Free Trade Agreement, Date of signature: 21/11/2008; Date of entry into force: 15/08/2011.

2008 Canada-Peru FTA, Date of signature: 29/05/2008; Date of entry into force: 01/08/2009.

2008 China-New Zealand Free Trade Agreement, Date of signature: 07/04/2008; Date of entry into force: 01/10/2008.

2008 Japan-Lao's Democratic Republic BIT, Date of signature:16/01/2008; Date of entry into force: 03/08/2008.

2008 United States-Rwanda BIT, Date of signature: 19/02/2008; Date of entry into force: 01/01/2012.

2009 ASEAN Comprehensive Investment Agreement, Date of signature: 26/02/2009; Date of entry into force: 24/02/2012.

2009 Agreement Establishing the ASEAN-Australia-New Zealand Free Trade Area, Date of signature: 27/02/2009; Date of entry into force: 10/01/2010.

2009 Belgium/Luxembourg-Barbados BIT, Date of signature: 29/05/2009.

2009 Canada-Jordan Free Trade Agreement, Date of signature: 28/06/2009; Date of entry into force: 01/10/2012.

2009 ASEAN-China Investment Agreement, Date of signature: 15/08/2009; Date of entry into force: 01/01/2010.

2009 Switzerland-China BIT, Date of signature: 27/01/2009; Date of entry into force: 13/04/2010.

2010 Canada-Panama Free Trade Agreement, Date of signature: 14/05/2010; Date of entry into force: 01/04/2013.

2010 Switzerland-Trinidad and Tobago BIT, Date of signature: 26/10/2010; Date of entry into force: 04/07/2012.

2011 United States-Korea Free Trade Agreement, Date of signature: 21/10/2011; Date of entry into force: 15/03/2012.

2011 Japan–Colombia BIT, Date of signature: 12/09/2011; Date of entry into force: 11/09/2015.

2012 Montenegro-Turkey BIT, Date of signature: 14/03/2012.

2012 Canada-China BIT, Date of signature: 09/09/2012; Date of entry into force: 01/10/2014.

2012 Japan-Iraq BIT, Date of signature: 07/06/2012; Date of entry into force: 25/02/2014.

2014 Canada—Côte d'Ivoire BIT, Date of signature: 30/11/2014; Date of entry into force: 14/12/2015.

2014 Greece-United Arab Emirates BIT, Date of signature: 06/05/2014; Date of entry into force: 06/03/2016.

2014 Switzerland-Georgia BIT, Date of signature: 03/06/2014; Date of entry into force: 17/04/2015.

2014 Canada-Cameroon BIT, Date of signature: 03/03/2014; Date of entry into force: 16/12/2016.

- 2014 Canada-Serbia BIT, Date of signature: 01/09/2014; Date of entry into force: 27/04/2015.
- 2015 Canada-Guinea BIT, Date of signature: 27/05/2015; Date of entry into force: 27/03/2017.
- 2015 Canada-Burkina Faso BIT, Date of signature: 20/04/2015; Date of entry into force: 11/10/2017.
- 2015 Brazil-Malawi Cooperation and Investment Facilitation Agreement (CIFA), Date of signature: 25/06/2015.
- 2015 Brazil-Angola Cooperation and Investment Facilitation Agreement (CIFA), Date of signature: 01/04/2015; Date of entry into force: 28/07/2017.
- 2015 Brazil-Mozambique Cooperation and Investment Facilitation Agreement (CIFA), Date of signature: 30/03/2015.
- 2015 Japan-Ukraine BIT, Date of signature: 05/02/2015; Date of entry into force: 26/11/2015.
- 2015 Japan-Uruguay BIT, Date of signature: 26/01/2015; Date of entry into force: 14/04/2017.
- 2016 Morocco-Nigeria BIT, Date of signature: 03/12/2016.
- 2016 Argentina-Qatar BIT, Date of signature: 06/11/2016.
- 2016 Rwanda-Turkey BIT, Date of signature: 03/11/2016.
- 2016 Chile-Hong Kong China SAR BIT, Date of signature: 18/11/2016.
- 2016 Japan-Iran BIT, Date of signature: 05/02/2016 ; Date of entry into force: 26/04/2017.
- 2016 Canada-Mongolia BIT, Date of signature: 08/09/2016; Date of entry into force: 24/02/2017.
- 2017 Pacific Agreement on Closer Economic Relations (PACER) Plus, Date of signature: 14/06/2017.
- 2018 Comprehensive and Progressive Agreement for Trans-Pacific Partnership (CPTPP), Date of signature: 08/03/2018; Date of entry into force: 30/12/2018.
- 2018 Agreement between the United States of America, the United Mexican States, and Canada (USMCA), Date of signature 30/11/2018.
- 2018 Brazil-Suriname Cooperation and Investment Facilitation Agreement (CIFA), Date of signature: 02/05/2018.
- 2018 Brazil-Ethiopia Cooperation and Investment Facilitation Agreement (CIFA), Date of signature: 11/04/2018.

Other International Agreements

- 1930 Convention Concerning Forced or Compulsory Labour, ILO Convention No 29. https://www.ilo.org/dyn/normlex/en/f?p=1000:12000:::NO:::.

1948 Freedom of Association and Protection of the Rights to Organise Convention, ILO Convention No 87. https://www.ilo.org/dyn/normlex/en/f?p=1000:12000:::NO:::.

1949 Right to Organise and Collective Bargaining Convention, ILO Convention No 98. https://www.ilo.org/dyn/normlex/en/f?p=1000:12000:::NO:::.

1951 Equal Remuneration Convention, ILO Convention No 100. https://www.ilo.org/dyn/normlex/en/f?p=1000:12000:::NO:::.

1957 Convention Concerning the Abolition of Forced Labour No 105. https://www.ilo.org/dyn/normlex/en/f?p=1000:12000:::NO:::.

1958 Discrimination (Employment and Occupation) Convention. ILO Convention No 111. https://www.ilo.org/dyn/normlex/en/f?p=1000:12000:::NO:::.

1965 Convention on the Settlement of Investment Disputes between States and Nationals of Other States (ICSID Convention). https://icsid.worldbank.org/en/Documents/resources/2006CRR_English-final.pdf.

1973 Convention on International Trade in Endangered Species of Wild Fauna and Flora (CITES), [2015] OJ L 75/3.

1973 Minimum Working Age Convention, ILO Convention No 138. https://www.ilo.org/dyn/normlex/en/f?p=1000:12000:::NO:::.

1975 Convention for the Protection of the Marine Environment and the Coastal Region of the Mediterranean, [1977] OJ L 240 (Barcelona Convention).

1981 African Charter on Human and Peoples' Rights. http://www.humanrights.se/wp-content/uploads/2012/01/African-Charter-on-Human-and-Peoples-Rights.pdf.

1985 Vienna Convention for the Protection of the Ozone Layer, [1988] OJ L 297/8

1987 Montreal Protocol on Substances that Deplete the Ozone Layer, [1991] OJ L 377/28.

1988 Additional Protocol To The American Convention on Human Rights in the Area of Economic, Social and Cultural Rights Protocol of San Salvador; http://www.oas.org/juridico/english/treaties/a-52.html.

1991 Convention on Environmental Impact Assessment in a Transboundary Context (Espoo Convention), [1992] OJ C 104/7.

1992 Framework Convention on Climate Change (UNFCCC), [1994] OJ L 33/13.

1992 Convention on Biological Diversity [1993] OJ L 309/3.

1992 North American Agreement on Environmental Cooperation (NAAEC), Date of signature: 17/12/1992; Date of entry into force: 01/01/1994. http://www.worldtradelaw.net/nafta/naaec.pdf.download.

1992 North American Agreement on Labor Cooperation (NAALC), Date of signature: 17/12/1992; Date of entry into force: 01/01/1994. https://www.dol.gov/ilab/reports/pdf/naalc.htm.

1994 Agreement establishing the World Trade Organization (WTO), [1994] OJ L 336/3.
1994 Energy Charter Treaty, [1998] OJ L 69/26.
1994 Protocol to the Convention on Long-Range Transboundary Air Pollution on Further Reduction of Sulphur Emissions, [1998] OJ L 326/34.
1997 Kyoto Protocol to the United Nations Framework Convention on Climate Change, [2004] OJ L 49/3.
1998 Convention on Access to Information, Public Participation in Decision-Making and Access to Justice in Environmental Matters (Aarhus Convention), [1998] OJ C 340/145.
1999 Worst Forms of Child Labour Convention, ILO Convention No 182. https://www.ilo.org/dyn/normlex/en/f?p=1000:12000:::NO:::.
2000 Cartagena Protocol on Biosafety to the Convention on Biological Diversity, [2002] OJ L 201/48.
2001 Stockholm Convention on Persistent Organic Pollutants (POPs), [2006] OJ L 209/3.
2003 UN Convention against Corruption, [2008] OJ L 287/1.
2010 Nagoya Protocol on Access to Genetic Resources and the Fair and Equitable Sharing of Benefits Arising from their Utilization to the Convention on Biological Diversity, [2014] OJ L 150/234.
2014 United Nations Convention on Transparency in Treaty-based Investor-State Arbitration (Mauritius Convention). https://treaties.un.org/doc/Treaties/2014/12/20141210 11-52 AM/CH_XXII_3.pdf
2015 Paris Agreement on Climate Change, [2015] OJ L 282/4.
2018 Regional Agreement on Access to Information, Public Participation and Justice in Environmental Matters in Latin America and the Caribbean (Escazú Convention). https://repositorio.cepal.org/bitstream/handle/11362/43583/1/S1800428_en.pdf.

Model Investment Agreements

Canada, 'Canadian Bilateral Investment Treaty Model', 2004, available at http://www.italaw.com/documents/Canadian2004-FIPA-model-en.pdf.
International Institute for Sustainable Development (IISD), 'IISD Model International Agreementon Investment for SustainableDevelopment', April 2005, available at https://www.iisd.org/pdf/2005/investment_model_int_agreement.pdf.
Austria, 'Austrian Model Bilateral Investment Treaty', 2008, available at https://investmentpolicyhub.unctad.org/Download/TreatyFile/4770.
Germany, 'German Model Bilateral Investment Treaty', 2008, available at

https://investmentpolicyhub.unctad.org/Download/TreatyFile/2865.

Ghana, 'BIT Model' 2008, available at https://investmentpolicyhub.unctad.org/Download/TreatyFile/2866.

SADC, 'SADC Model Bilateral Investment Treaty Template with Commentary', July 2012, available at https://www.iisd.org/itn/wp-content/uploads/2012/10/SADC-Model-BIT-Template-Final.pdf.

United States, 'U.S. Bilateral Investment Treaty Model', 2012, available at https://ustr.gov/sites/default/files/BIT%20text%20for%20ACIEP%20Meeting.pdf.

India, 'Model Text for the Indian Bilateral Investment Treaty', 2015, available at https://investmentpolicy.unctad.org/international-investment-agreements/treaty-files/3560/download

African Union, 'Pan-African Investment Code', 2016, available at https://repository.uneca.org/handle/10855/23009.

The Netherlands, 'Netherlands Model Investment Agreement', 2018, available at https://investmentpolicyhub.unctad.org/Download/TreatyFile/5695.

Morocco, 'Morocco Model BIT', 2019, available at https://investmentpolicy.unctad.org/international-investment-agreements/treaty-files/5895/download.

EU Regulations, Directives and Decisions

Directive 88/361 of the Council of 24 June 1988 for the implementation of Article 67 of the Treaty, [1988] OJ L 178/5.

Regulation No 443/92 of the Council of 25 Feb 1992 on financial and technical assistance to, and economic cooperation with, the developing countries in Asia and Latin America, [1992] OJ L 52/1.

Directive 92/43 of the Council of 21 May 1992 on the conservation of natural habitats and of wild fauna and flora [1992] OJ L 206 (Habitats Directive).

Decision 94/800 of the Council of 22 December 1994 concerning the conclusion on behalf of the European Community, as regards matters within its competence, of the agreements reached in the Uruguay Round multilateral negotiations (1986–1994), [1994] OJ L 336/1.

Decision 98/181 of the ECSC, Euratom, Council and Commission of 23 Sep 1997 on the conclusion, by the European Communities, of the Energy Charter Treaty and the Energy Charter Protocol on energy efficiency and related environmental aspects, [1997] OJ L 69/1.

Directive 2000/60 of 23 Oct 2000 establishing a framework for Community action in the field of water policy, [2000] OJ L 327/1.

Regulation No 2493/2000 of the European Parliament and of the Council of 7 November 2000 on measures to promote the full integration of the environmental dimension in the development process of developing countries, [2000] OJ L 288/1 (*no longer in force, end of validity date: 31/12/2006*).

Regulation No 2494/2000 of the European Parliament and of the Council of 7 November 2000 on measures to promote the conservation and sustainable management of tropical forests and other forests in developing countries, [2000] OJ L 288/6, (*no longer in force*).

Regulation No 980/2005 of the Council of 27 June 2005 applying a scheme of generalised tariff preferences, [2005] OJ L 169/1.

Regulation No 2371/2002 of the Council of 20 December 2002 on the conservation and sustainable exploitation of fisheries resources under the Common Fisheries Policy, [2002] OJ L 358/59.

Regulation No 1081/2006 of the European Parliament and of the Council of 5 July 2006 on the European Social Fund, [2006] OJ L 210/18.

Regulation No 1083/2006 of the Council of 11 July 2006 laying down general provisions on the European Regional Development Fund, the European Social Fund and the Cohesion Fund, [2006] OJ L 210/25.

Regulation No 1084/2006 of the Council of 11 July 2006 establishing a Cohesion Fund, [2006] OJ L 210/79, (*no longer in force*).

Directive 2009/28 of the European Parliament and of the Council of 23 April 2009 on the promotion of the use of energy from renewable sources and amending and subsequently repealing Directives 2001/77 and 2003/30, [2009] OJ L 140/16.

Regulation No 1219/2012 of the European Parliament and the Council, on establishing transitional arrangements for bilateral investment agreements between Member States and third countries, [2012] OJ L 351/40.

Regulation No 1300/2013 of the European Parliament and of the Council of 17 December 2013 on the Cohesion Fund and repealing Council Regulation No 1084/2006, [2013] OJ L 347/281.

Regulation No 1303/2013 of the European Parliament and of the Council of 17 December 2013 laying down common provisions on the European Regional Development Fund, the European Social Fund, the Cohesion Fund, the European Agricultural Fund for Rural Development and the European Maritime and Fisheries Fund and laying down general provisions on the European Regional Development Fund, the European Social Fund, the Cohesion Fund and the European Maritime and Fisheries Fund and repealing Council Regulation No 1083/2006, [2013] OJ L 347/320.

Decision No 1386/2013 of the European Parliament and the Council, [2013] OJ L 354/171.

Regulation No 912/2014 of the European Parliament and of the Council of 23 July 2014, establishing a framework for managing financial responsibility linked to investor-to-state dispute settlement tribunals established by international agreements to which the European Union is party, [2014] OJ L 257/121.

Regulation No 2019/452 of the European Parliament and of the Council of 19 March 2019 establishing a framework for the screening of foreign direct investments into the Union, [2019] OJ L 79/1.

Regulation No 2020/852 of the European Parliament and of the Council on the establishment of a framework to facilitate sustainable investment, [2020] OJ L 198/13.

Policy Documents and Soft Law Instruments

European Union

Commission of the European Communities, 'First Communication of the Commission about the Community's policy on the environment', SEC(71)2616 final.

Commission of the European Communities, 'Statement from the Paris Summit', Bulletin of the European Communities, [1972] No 10.

Commission of the European Communities, Report from the Commission to the Council, Investment Protection and Promotion Clauses in Agreements between the Community and Various Categories of Developing Countries: Achievements to Date and Guidelines for Future Action, COM(80) 24 final.

European Council, Presidency Conclusions (Rhodes), 'Declaration on the Environment', [1988] SN 4443/1/88.

European Council, Presidency Conclusions (Dublin), 'The Environmental Imperative', [1990] SN 60/1/90.

European Commission Communication, 'A Sustainable Europe for a better World—A European Union Strategy for Sustainable Development', COM (2001) 264 final.

European Council, Presidency Conclusions (Göteborg), [2001] SN 200/1/01 REV 1.

European Commission Communication, 'Towards a world partnership for sustainable development', COM (2002) 82 final.

European Council, Review Sustainable Development Strategy, [2006] Doc 10917/06.

Council of the European Union, 'Minimum Platform on Investment', [2006] Doc 15375/06.

European Commission Communication, 'Global Europe: Competing in the World', COM (2006) 567 final.

European Commission Communication, 'Implementing the Partnership for Growth and Jobs: Making Europe a Pole of Excellence on Corporate Social Responsibility', COM (2006) 136 final.

European Council, Review Sustainable Development Strategy, [2009] Doc 16818/09.

European Commission Communication, 'Europe 2020—A strategy for smart, sustainable and inclusive growth', COM (2010) 2020 final.

European Commission Communication, 'Trade, Growth and World Affairs: Trade Policy as a Core Component of the EU's 2020 Strategy', COM (2010) 612 final.

European Commission Communication, 'Towards a comprehensive European international investment policy', COM (2010) 343 final.

Council of the European Union, 'Council Conclusions on a comprehensive European international investment policy', [2010] Doc 3041.

Council of the European Union, 'Council Conclusions', 3041st Foreign Affairs Council Meeting, [2010].

European Parliament, 'Resolution of 6 April 2011 on the future European international investment policy', 2010/2203 (INI).

European Parliament, 'Resolution of 25 Nov 2010 on Human Rights and Social and Environmental Standards in International Trade Agreements', 2009/2219(INI).

European Commission, Communication, 'Rio+20: towards the green economy and better governance', COM (2011) 363 final.

European Commission Communication, 'Corporate Social Responsibility', COM (2011) 681 final.

European Parliament resolution of 6 April 2011 on the future European international investment policy 2010/2203(INI), [2012] OJ C 296E.

European Commission Communication, 'A policy framework for climate and energy in the period from 2020 to 2030', COM (2014) 15 final.

European Commission, 'Concept Paper: Investment in TTIP and beyond—The Path for Reform Enhancing the Right to Regulate and Moving from Current ad hoc Arbitration towards and Investment Court', [2015] available at http://trade.ec.europa.eu/doclib/docs/2015/may/tradoc_153408.PDF.

European Commission Communication, 'Closing the loop—An EU action plan for the Circular Economy', COM (2015) 614 final.

European Commission Communication, 'Trade for All Towards a more responsible trade and investment policy', COM (2015) 497 final.

European Commission, Communication from the Commission to the European Parliament, the Council, the European Economic and Social Committee and the Committee of the Regions, 'Next steps for a sustainable European future—European action for sustainability', COM (2016) 739 final.

European Commission, Commission Staff Working Document, 'Key European Action supporting the 2030 Agenda and the Sustainable Development Goals', SWD (2016) 390 final.

European External Action Service, 'Shared Vision, Common Action: A Stronger Europe, A Global Strategy for the European Union's Foreign and Security Policy' [2016].

The New European Consensus on Development 'Our World, Our Dignity, Our Future', Joint Statement by the Council and the representatives of the Governments of the Member States meeting within the Council, the European Parliament and the European Commission, [2017] (New European Consensus on Development).

European Parliament, 'Resolution of 6 July 2017 on EU action for sustainability', 2017/2009(INI).

European Parliament legislative resolution of 15 February 2017 on the draft Council decision on the conclusion of the Comprehensive Economic and Trade Agreement (CETA) between Canada, of the one part, and the European Union and its Member States, of the other part, 10975/2016—C8-0438/2016—2016/0205(NLE).

Council of the European Union, 'Conclusions on Business and Human Rights', [2016] Doc 10254/16.

European Commission, 'Commission Staff Working Document, Key European Action supporting the 2030 Agenda and the Sustainable Development Goals', SWD (2016) 390 final.

European Parliament, 'Resolution of 5 July 2016 on Implementation of the 2010 Recommendations of Parliament on Social and Environmental Standards, Human Rights and Corporate Responsibility', 2015/2038(INI).

European Commission, 'Report on the Implementation of the Trade Policy Strategy Trade for All Delivering a Progressive Trade Policy to Harness Globalisation', COM (2017) 491 final.

European Commission non-paper of the Commission services, 'Trade and Sustainable Development (TSD) chapters in EU Free Trade Agreements (FTAS)' [2017].

Resolutions, Declarations and Others

UN General Assembly, 'Charter of Economic Rights and Duties of States', [1974] A/RES/29/3281

ILO, 'Tripartite Declaration of Principles concerning Multinational Enterprises and Social Policy' [1977] (last revision 2017).

UN General Assembly, 'The International Development Strategy for the Third United Nations Development Decade', [1980] A/RES/35/56.

International Union for Conservation of Nature and Natural Resources, 'World Conservation Strategy: Living Resources for Sustainable Development' (IUCN 1980).

United Nations Conference on the Human Environment (Stockholm Conference) [1972] adopting the Declaration of the United Nations Conference on the Human Environment (Stockholm Declaration) [1973] A/CONF.48/14/REV.1.

European Social Charter (ETS No 35), adopted in 1961, the Revised European Social Charter (ETS No 163) [1996], available at https://rm.coe.int/168007cf93.

UN General Assembly, 'Programme for the Further Implementation of Agenda 21', [1997] A/RES/S-19/2.

Community Charter of Fundamental Social Rights of Workers [1989], available at https://www.eesc.europa.eu/resources/docs/community-charter--en.pdf.

UN General Assembly, 'Report of the World Commission on Environment and Development', [1987] A/RES/42/187 (Brundtland Report).

UN Conference on Environment and Development, 'Rio Declaration on Environment and Development and Agenda 21', [1992] Doc A/CONF.151/26Rev 1 ("Rio Declaration").

ILO Declaration on Fundamental Principles and Rights at Work and its Follow-up, adopted by the International Labour Conference at its Eighty-sixth Session, [1998] (last revision 2010).

UN General Assembly, 'United Nations Millennium Declaration', [2000] A/RES/55/2.

OECD, 'OECD Guidelines for Multinational Enterprises', annexed to 2000 OECD Declaration on International Investment and Multinational Enterprises, DAFFE/IME(2000)/20; (2001) 40 ILM 237 as amended.

World Summit on Sustainable Development, 'Johannesburg Declaration on Sustainable Development', [2002] A/CONF.199/20.

World Summit on Sustainable Development, 'Plan of Implementation of the World Summit on Sustainable Development', [2002] A/CONF.199/20.

UN Global Compact, 'United Nations Global Compact: The Ten Principles' [2004]. available at https://www.unglobalcompact.org/.

ILO, 'Declaration on Social Justice for a Fair Globalisation', adopted by the International Labour Conference at its Ninety-seventh Session, [2008].

UN General Assembly, 'Implementation of Agenda 21, the Programme for the Further Implementation of Agenda 21 and the outcomes of the World Summit on Sustainable Development', [2010] A/RES/64/236.

UN Human Rights Council, 'Guiding Principles on Business and Human Rights: Implementing the United Nations 'Protect, Respect and Remedy' Framework" [2011] A/HRC/17/31.

UN General Assembly, 'The Future We Want', Outcome Document adopted at Rio+20', [2012] A/RES/66/28.

UNCTAD, Investment Policy Framework for Sustainable Development 2015 (IPFSD) (United Nations 2015).

UN General Assembly, 'Transforming our world: the 2030 Agenda for Sustainable Development', [2015] A/RES/70/1 ("Agenda 2030").

G20, 'Guiding Principles for Global Investment Policymaking', [2016]; available at http://www.oecd.org/daf/inv/investment-policy/G20-Guiding-Principles-for-Global-Investment-Policymaking.pdf.

OECD, 'Better Policies for 2030—An OECD Action Plan on the Sustainable Development Goals', [2016]; available at http://www.oecd.org/dac/Better%20Policies%20for%202030.pdf.

ILO, 'Decent work for sustainable development: Ensuring no one is left behind', [2017] GB.329/HL/1.

Joint Ministerial Statement on Investment Facilitation for Development at the Eleventh Ministerial Conference held in Buenos Aires, Argentina, in December 2017, WT/MIN(17)/48.

Index

Aarhus Convention   36, 396
Achmea judgement   206–207
Adel A. Hamadi Al Tamimi v. Oman   371, 377
Agreement on Trade-Related Investment Measures (TRIMS)   61
Air Transport Association of America   123
amicus curiae   350–351
Association agreements, EU   153
Asymmetrical nature of ISDS   80
Aven and others v. Costa Rica   372
Azurix v. Argentina   71

Barral, Virginie   137
Bear Creek v. Peru   74
Bilcon v. Canada   213, 370, 377
Bot, Yves   207
Brazilian CIFAs   254, 308
Brundtland Report   21, 32, 103

Canada-Colombia FTA   256
Capital-exporting countries   59, 275–276, 333, 336, 338, 354–355, 388, 390, 394
Civil Society Forums   243
Claussen, Kathleen   86
Club of Rome   21
COMESA Investment Agreement   321, 361
Competitiveness   7, 61, 103–104, 140, 143, 186–187, 232, 292, 331, 333, 340, 386–387
Comprehensive Investment Agreement of the Association of Southeast Asian Nations   347
Convention on Drought and Desertification   25
Copper Mesa v. Ecuador   56, 74
Corn Products v. Mexico   319
Cotonou Agreement   145, 362
CPTPP   266, 273, 302–303, 308, 315, 320, 325–326, 335, 351, 360
Cremona, Marise   215

Declaration on Fundamental Rights at Work, ILO   274
Declaration on Social Justice for a Fair Globalisation, ILO   234
Desert Line v. Yemen   57

Development of infant industries   60
Domestic Advisory Groups (DAGs)   242–243, 245–246
Dutch Model BIT   343

Eckes, Christina   203
Energy Charter Treaty   xvi, 153, 199
Energy transition   87, 258–259, 315
Environment Action Programme (EAP)   103
Environmental impact assessment (EIA)   33, 144
Espoo Convention   396
EU Charter of Fundamental Rights   107
EU-CARIFORUM EPA   198, 225, 273, 359
Euro-Mediterranean Association Agreements   196
European Charter for Social Rights   133
European Convention of Human Rights   208
European Green Deal   261
European integration   104, 113, 125
Exclusive jurisdiction, CJEU   205

Fair Administrative Treatment   303
Fair and free trade   180
Fedax v. Venezuela   49
Fight against corruption   352
Financial Action Task Force   268
Financial assistance   267
Financing gaps for SD   44
forum non conveniens   277

Gabčíkovo-Nagymaros case   29–31
GATS   73, 75, 151, 197, 323, 326, 339
GATT   73, 75, 182, 322–323, 326, 374
Global Pact for the Environment   27
Green economy   23, 111, 140
Guiding Principles for Global Investment Policymaking, G20   43

International Convention for the Regulation of Whaling   32
International Labour Organization (ILO)
  Fundamental Conventions   185, 235, 245, 252
  Tripartite Declaration of Principles for Multinational Enterprises and Social Policy   92, 271

Investment certificate 57
Investment contract 93, 395–396
Investment Policy Framework for Sustainable Development, UNCTAD 43
Investment screening
 mechanisms 58–60, 97, 346, 355, 395
 procedures 347
Iron Rhine arbitration 29, 31, 377
IUCN Draft International Covenant on Environment and Development 26

Johannesburg Declaration 359, 362
Johnson, Lise 90
Joint Interpretative Instrument, CETA 159

Legitimate expectations 298, 300–301, 304, 307, 316, 354
Levels of protection
 democratic process 211, 216, 222
 high levels of protection 84, 188, 218, 238–239, 359, 366
 weakening domestic protection 227–228
Local communities 81–82, 90, 93

Malaysian Historical Salvors v. Malaysia 50
Margin of appreciation 123, 137, 214
Marín Durán, Gracia 174
Metalclad v. Mexico 71
Methanex v. United States 71
Micula case 318
Morocco-Nigeria BIT 230, 234, 236, 238, 259, 276–279, 321, 339, 343, 360
multilateral investment court (MIC) 219
Mutual supportiveness 27, 236–238, 365, 384–385, 393

New European Development Consensus 260
Normative power, EU 5

Objectives
 justiciability 124, 132
 legitimate objectives 211, 314
 public policy objectives 73, 190, 199, 366, 369
 steering effects 181
Occidental v. Ecuador I 319
OECD Due Diligence Guidance for Responsible Supply Chains 271

OECD Guidelines for Multinational Enterprises 91, 157, 270
Opinion 1/91 204
Opinion 1/94 151–152
Opinion 2/00 125
Opinion 2/13 204
Opinion 2/92 151

PACER Plus Agreement 273
PAIC 266, 274, 303, 321, 336, 339, 342, 362
Paris Agreement 25, 144, 260, 318, 396
Partnership and Cooperation Agreements 262
Pey Casado v. Chile 51
Philip Morris v. Uruguay 88
Polluter-pays principle 26
Pollution heaven 84
Poverty eradication 145, 178–180, 182
Poverty reduction 265, 393, 395
Precautionary principle 118, 221, 240–241
Principle of attribution 112–114
Principle of common but differentiated responsibilities 33
Proportionality
 EU 114, 123, 210–211
 method of review 380, 382
Pulp Mills case 29–30

Regulation No 1219/2012 157
Regulatory chill 78–79, 211
Right to a healthy environment 35
Rio Declaration 21–22, 104, 106, 108, 139, 362, 377, 379
Rule of law 36, 55, 119, 179, 220, 268, 395

Saba Fakes v. Turkey 51
Salini test 49–51, 53, 341–343
Saluka v. Czech Republic 206
Schreuer, Christoph 53
SD outcomes 83, 94, 96, 290, 297, 337
Sharpston, Eleanor 170
Shrimp-Turtle case 374
Sincere cooperation 121, 185
Single European Act 103, 105
Social dumping 85
Soft compliance mechanisms 241, 249
Soft law 38–39, 91, 109, 136–137
Spill-over effects 10, 13, 276, 355, 394
State aid, EU 317

INDEX

Stockholm Conference   20, 102
Strategy Europe 2020   141
Sustainable Development Strategy, EU   109

Technical assistance   266–267, 289, 446
Three-pillar structure   39
Tobacco Control Measures   326
Trade for all strategy   187, 387
Transfer of technology   335–336, 360
Treaty of Amsterdam   105–106
Treaty of Maastricht   104
Treaty-shopping   353

UN Convention against Corruption   92, 268
UN Guiding Principles on Business and Human Rights   92, 271
UNCITRAL Transparency Rules   350
UNCITRAL Working Group III   78, 82
United Nations Global Compact Initiative   271

Universal Declaration of Human Rights   34, 92, 261–262
Urbaser v. Argentina   90, 379
USMCA   303

Values   264, 327, 369, 382, 387
van Aaken, Anne   68
Vienna Convention on the Law of Treaties   176, 290, 369

Welfare   7, 19, 34–35, 41, 68–69, 72, 76–77, 95, 129, 145n237, 182, 201, 215, 221, 266, 304, 308–310, 320, 361, 366, 381, 382, 388
WHO Framework Convention on Tobacco Control   88
World Conservation Strategy   21

Yaung Chi Oo v. Myanmar   57

Zero hunger   24

Printed in the United States
by Baker & Taylor Publisher Services